Windows Vista™ Ultimate Bible

Joel Durham, Jr. and Derek Torres

BICENTENNIAL 1807 WILEY 2007 BICENTENNIAL

Wiley Publishing, Inc.

Windows Vista™ Ultimate Bible

Published by
Wiley Publishing, Inc.
10475 Crosspoint Boulevard
Indianapolis, IN 46256
www.wiley.com

Published simultaneously in Canada

ISBN: 978-0-470-09713-7

Manufactured in the United States of America

10 9 8 7 6 5 4 3 2 1

Library of Congress Control Number: 2006939600

This book is big enough for two, so I dedicate it to Shawn Carstens and Robin Durham: Sisters, friends, and dear ones. — JD

To Rudy and Donna Torres, and to Céline and our sons, Pablo and Victor-Emmanuel. — DT

About the Authors

Joel Durham, Jr.

I hate writing about myself in the third person for these author blurbs, so I'm going to put a stop to it right now. I'm Joel Durham Jr., and I'm one of your hosts for this adventure. I've been a computer and video game nerd all my life, and I've been writing professionally about computers, games, operating systems, consoles, and all that kind of stuff since 1997 — when Matt Firme gave me my big break by hiring me as *PC Gamer's* first Technical Editor. After a year in that blissful atmosphere I left that job, mainly to escape the San Francisco Bay area (having to get an interest-only ARM mortgage for a $750,000 2-bedroom house on a lot the size of a sheet of standard copier paper, and somehow survive on an editor's salary).

I moved back to upstate New York to be near family. Since then, I've been freelance writing for such markets as GameSpy, Gamecenter (I spent time as the Senior Technical Editor there before CNET closed the site down), 1UP, *Computer Gaming World*, ExtremeTech, *PC Magazine, Computer Source*, and a bunch more. I live with my wife (who defies logic by being too gorgeous to be interested in a geek like me, and yet she is), and the two smartest, cutest children in the world.

Derek Torres

I, too, hate writing about myself in the third person; knowing that Joel hated this odd phenomenon as much as I do was the real reason that I chose to write a few chapters for this book. Technical writer by trade, I've been into computers for a very long time and getting paid to do it since 1998 or so. My career as a tech writer took off in Paris, France, around the turn of the century where I worked for several software shops.

fter returning to the U.S. a few years ago, I decided to focus more on writing for software and iall business issues. Some of the people nice enough to publish my work include Microsoft (*Work entials* and the *Vista Expert Zone*), *Redmond Channel Partner* magazine, and STC's *Intercom* maga- I also write a column for the Information in Focus Web site and regularly present at technical nunication conferences in the U.S. and in Europe. Additionally, I've had the privilege of writ- co-writing several books on Windows operating systems.

Credits

Product Development Supervisor
Courtney Allen

Project Editor
Katharine Dvorak

Technical Editor
Loyd Case

Copy Editor
Paula Lowell

Editorial Manager
Robyn Siesky

Business Manager
Amy Knies

Vice President and Executive Group Publisher
Richard Swadley

Vice President and Executive Publisher
Bob Ipsen

Vice President and Publisher
Barry Pruett

Project Coordinator
Erin Smith

Graphics and Production Specialists
Denny Hager
Joyce Haughey
Jennifer Mayberry
Barbara Moore
Heather Pope
Amanda Spagnuolo
Ronald Terry

Quality Control Technician
John Greenough
Christine Pingleton

Proofreading
Christine Sabooni

Indexing
Techbooks

Wiley Bicentennial Logo
Richard J. Pacifico

Contents at a Glance

Contents

Part III: Support, Stability, and Security 231

Preface

There's another *Windows Vista Bible* out there. It's important to note that *Ultimate* in this book's title doesn't mean that this book, *Windows Vista Ultimate Bible*, is better than that other book. This book is focused differently. It's focused on the Ultimate edition of Vista.

While that other *Bible* is about Windows Vista, this one's about the Ultimate edition, written for the kind of people who would spend the extra money to get the most comprehensive, feature-packed operating system Microsoft has ever created. Gamers. Multimedia enthusiasts. People who do more with their PCs than write elaborate formulae for their spreadsheet programs.

Windows Vista Ultimate Bible is for people who look to their computers for entertainment. If you have ten times the number of photographs on your computer's hard drive than you do document files, you're in the right place. If you can't believe you ever lived without digital music and your trusty MP3 player, keep reading. If you're planning on purchasing Windows Vista — or have already purchased it — because you don't want to miss the new gaming experience that DirectX 10 is sure to bring, there's a pile of pages in this book just for you.

Windows Vista has been in development for more than five years. Formerly codenamed Longhorn, it went through development gyrations for what seemed like ages. As the time drew closer to its release, news of its feature set came more and more rapidly. First every month, then every week, and then every day, you could read about this feature being added and that one being removed. In fact, as I was writing this book, based on the first widely released beta version of the operating system, features were still coming and going. One day I would plan a chapter on Feature X, then it would be replaced by Feature Y, and the book would have to change with it.

The final set of Windows Vista features is an outstanding one. It's full of security features that should make Vista far safer than earlier versions of Windows. Vista is packed with new functionality and upgrades of all the included programs, from games to multimedia utilities. With each pre-release build Microsoft unveiled, the operating system became faster and more stable; Release Candidate 2 (which is the last one I got to work with before publication) is a rock.

The *Windows Vista Ultimate Bible* tells you how to keep it that way. While focused primarily on gaming and multimedia, the book also includes everything you need to know to get started using Windows Vista and all about its various departures from earlier Windows brews. It's all here for you.

The Best Ways to Use This Book

The *Windows Vista Ultimate Bible* chronicles your entire experience with Windows Vista's Ultimate edition; it takes you by the hand and walks you through every important step in getting it set up, secured, and stabilized. It introduces the new interface, the new features, all the things that make Windows Vista what it is. It tells you where to get multimedia and what to do with it, and how to get the most out of it. It talks games and gaming in depth, complete with performance tips.

Beyond a simple tutorial, this book can also serve as a reference tome. Need to know how to share your media files with your Xbox 360? It's in here. Want to learn about User Account Control? You can find it inside. Also included are step-by-step tutorials, guides, and plenty of information on almost all the applications and applets that Windows Vista installs for you.

You don't have to read the book in order. You can flip around as you please; it was written in a modular style, so if you think you already know everything you need to know about the Aero interface, the parental controls, and the new organization folders, skip that stuff and head to the section on music or the one on games. I did, however, try to design the book with a logical sense of progression from a foundation of basics on learning and securing your operating system, to having fun with it, so you can also wade in gradually by reading in order. What I'm trying to say is how you use this book is up to you.

Part I details getting Windows Vista onto your computer and learning all about its conventions and stunning new look. Part II explores the interface in depth and tells you how to customize it to tailor the look of your desktop to your whims. Part III is an important section on keeping Vista stable and secure, and finding out how to get help when you need it. Part IV tells you about networking, including sharing a home network connection, and Vista's Internet applications. Part V gets to the good stuff: It features a rundown on all the gaming and multimedia enhancements that make Vista so much better than prior Windows versions — and competitors. Part VI is your multimedia guide; Part VII is all about gaming; and Part VIII teaches you how to tweak the heck out of the operating system.

Read the *Windows Vista Ultimate Bible* in order, or jump around and pick up the exact knowledge you're looking for. It's designed for both.

What Are Those Icons For?

Throughout the book you'll encounter various icons that break up the text a bit, making the *Windows Vista Ultimate Bible* more readable. These bite-sized chunks of information may often be exactly what you were looking for, so be sure not to skip over them!

This icon appears when there's an interesting — and sometimes alternative — way to do something discussed nearby. It may be a useful trick or a faster way to accomplish a task.

NOTE Here you'll find tidbits of information that are related to the text they're situated near. The Note icon signifies that you're about to learn something interesting or useful, an aside that you won't want to miss.

CAUTION Be careful! Sometimes, if you make a wrong move at the wrong time, something unfortunate may occur. This important icon tries to get your attention to warn you about such a situation.

CROSS-REF This icon indicates where in the book you can find more information about a particular subject.

ON the WEB Look for this icon to appear when more information on a particular topic may be found on the Web, or for the URL of a Web site mentioned in the text.

How This Book Is Organized

The *Windows Vista Ultimate Bible* is organized to make it easy for you to find exactly what you're looking for at a glance. Each part contains chapters that logically go together, so you can flip through the book, or go straight to the table of contents or the index, and find what you need. It's also laid out in order for the Windows Vista beginner — and the Windows *anything* beginner, for that matter — to learn what you need to know to get started, and then to move on to more complex tasks.

Part I: Getting Started with Windows Vista Ultimate

Not sure where to begin? Then Part I is for you. It introduces you to Windows Vista and runs you through the very basics, including how to install the operating system, how to navigate through its file and menu systems, and where to change basic settings, as well as introduces the many programs that come with Windows Vista. If you don't know Windows conventions at all, or if you just want to learn how to get going with your new copy of Windows Vista Ultimate, turn to Part I.

Part II: The Windows Vista Interface

Going into far more detail about the new look, feel, and organizational foundation of Windows Vista, Part II introduces the shocking Aero desktop and all of its many features, such as Flip 3D and window transparencies. Windows XP veterans will appreciate a thorough comparison to that old standard. Of course, if you don't like Aero, you can choose from a number of other interfaces and styles.

Part III: Support, Stability, and Security

What do you do if something goes wrong? Microsoft stands behind its products and offers support in a number of ways. Part III begins with how you can go about getting assistance for your Vista conundrums, and then goes on to showing you how to avoid at least some of them. Windows Vista has long been touted as a major upgrade to the Windows family's stability and security, even since it was called Longhorn. Be sure to follow the guidelines to keep intruders out of your file system and to keep Vista from bogging down or crashing.

Part IV: Networking and the Internet

Microsoft more or less assumes that you have some sort of Internet connectivity, preferably an always-on broadband connection. Part IV shows you how to network multiple computers and share such an Internet connection among them using inexpensive equipment sold at every computer store (and many department stores). Then you'll learn about Windows Vista's Internet prowess, including its version of Microsoft's new Internet Explorer browser, the new mail reader called Windows Mail, and other fun online features.

Part V: Gaming and Multimedia Enhancements

Part V serves as an introduction to all the ways that Microsoft has made Windows Vista a friendlier operating system for the colorful, graphical, and aurally exciting pastimes of multimedia and gaming. From DirectX 10 to Windows Media Center, this part shows you what's new in Windows Vista for the kind of computer enthusiasts who consider the PC an entertainment device.

Part VI: Music, Movies, Video, and Audio

Vista gives you plenty of ways to startle your eyes and tickle your ears. This comprehensive part visits both video and audio, with guides to digital music and movie viewing. This part is for the MP3 generation: It tells you how to rip your CDs and acquire digital music online, and how to sync them up with your favorite MP3 player. Similarly, you can also learn where to find movie files, how to watch DVDs, and how to get the most out of your video experience. Programs like Windows Media Player 11 are covered in depth.

Part VII: Gaming on Windows Vista Ultimate

Nothing beats a quality first-person shooter or an intense round or two with a real-time strategy game, and this chapter is all about the new national pastime: videogames. Learn about the new gaming features, discover how to install games and where to look for them, get the inside scoop on the Games folder, which keeps all your titles in one handy place for you to organize as you please, and so on. How does Windows Vista work with the Xbox 360? What do you do if you try to run a pre-Vista game and it won't load up? Learn these things and more in Part VII.

Part VIII: Under the Hood: Tweaking Windows Vista

Finally, you can get your hands dirty by acting like a digital grease monkey and molding Windows Vista to your preferences. Every operating system since DOS has needed some extra hands-on help getting games to run at their very best, or just to achieve the most powerful computing experience.

Windows Vista might make a few assumptions as to what you want to do with it and load more overhead than you need; slim it down into a mean and trim beast of an OS using the information in Part VIII.

Appendix

Maintenance...it's the grunt-work that all computer power-users must deal with. Sometimes you'll have to upgrade your computer on the whole; other times you might realize that the hard drive is ridiculously fragmented. If you're not sure what to do, or what fragmentation is, check out the appendix, which tells you how to keep your Windows Vista installation in tip-top condition.

Joel Durham, Jr.

It would be a cliché to say that there are too many people to thank than I can fit in this space, so I won't say it. Instead, I'll just say that I would like to acknowledge some kind people who made this book possible, and I'm probably forgetting some, and to them I am sorry.

Thanks to Tom Heine for the opportunity; Courtney Allen for more generosity, patience, and concern than any one person should be able to wield; Lynn Haller, my agent and champion; Katharine Dvorak, my awesome (and very calming) editor; Loyd Case, who made sure my mistakes didn't become yours. Thanks to my family near and far for much-needed moral support (Emily Durham, Andrew Durham, Jeanne Durham, Janice Durham, Joel Durham Sr., Elizabeth Bianchi, my fabulous sisters mentioned in the dedication, Frank Boos, Betty Boos, and too many others). Thanks also go to a batch of company reps who generously bestowed me with parts and information: Phil O'Shaughnessy (Creative Labs), Michael L. Hall (Seagate), Susie Hughs (Lewis PR), Brian Mikol (Antec), Damon Muzny (AMD), Bruce Dugan (Rockstar Games), and, of course, the incomparable, indispensable Michael Wolf (Microsoft). Also, special thanks to Derek Torres for a fantastic barrage of words that truly saved my neck.

Derek Torres

I would like to thank Joel for having me on board for this project. He's been a pleasure to work with and I'm grateful to have had the chance to work with him. I would also like to thank our great team at Wiley, especially Katharine Dvorak and Courtney Allen. On a more personal level, I would like to thank my wife and sons for being so forgiving; writing a book can be very time-consuming and often requires more hours than one would like to spend. I want to also thank my family, especially my parents, and friends for their support in my writing career, even if they don't always understand why I enjoy it so much. Special thanks go to Pascale-Anne Brault for encouraging me to explore my love of writing. Thanks to Lynn for continually finding me great projects to work on.

Introduction

Windows has mojo. The venerable operating system made its mark on the computer industry more than two decades ago, and it hasn't looked back.

Back in the mid 1980s, the graphical user interface (GUI) was a rarity in the computer world. Most computers ran some form of DOS, a command-line interpreter. To navigate a computer's filing system, to run programs, and to organize files, users had to know DOS commands. Worse, DOS didn't offer multitasking (running multiple processes at once), so you had to exit your spreadsheet program to jump into your word processor and vice versa.

The earliest Windows operating systems, Windows 1.01 (circa 1985) and 2.0 (released in 1987), offered a limited version of multitasking. Windows 1.0 is barely recognizable as a Windows operating system; the program windows couldn't overlap, and the graphics were, of course, primitive.

It really wasn't until Windows 3.1 was released in 1992 that Windows truly lit the world on fire. Full of functionality, it was often dismissed as a "shell" for DOS (as it actually ran on top of DOS; you had to type WIN at the command prompt to run it). Windows was, however, a true operating system with its own file types, fonts, device drivers, and multitasking ability. Windows 3.1 and the subsequent, networking-friendly Windows for Workgroups 3.11 introduced powerful memory optimizations that could take advantage of vast banks of RAM (my first PC, an upgrade from my Commodore 64, had *four megabytes* of RAM installed!).

The rest, as the saying goes, is history. Windows went 32-bit in 1995 with Windows 95 (although it still contained a serious dose of 16-bit code for backward-compatibility). A 32-bit–only series called Windows NT was developed in parallel to the Windows consumer operating systems, and the two lines finally merged with Windows XP.

Where, however, did the GUI come from? Many curious people have come to believe that Microsoft stole the idea from Apple, but, in fact, it didn't originate there, either. Although it popularized GUI in 1983 with the Apple Lisa computer system, the Xerox Palo Alto Research Center (PARC) is the true origin of the computer screen as a "desktop." The Xerox Alto was the first computer to actually feature a desktop-style GUI, and Xerox went commercial with the idea in 1981 with the 8010 Star Information System.

Filtered through Apple's efforts, the GUI influenced Microsoft enough to base an operating system on it. Why Windows became the operating system of choice worldwide instead of the Macintosh OS is a topic of many discussions, online and off. The prevailing theory is that it was due to the fact that Apple developed a closed system with strictly compatible regulated hardware manufacturing whereas any manufacturer could build "IBM-compatible" PC parts. (They were called that because they were compatible with hardware and programs for the IBM PC, a popular Intel-based personal computer. Interestingly, IBM no longer makes personal computers.)

Regardless of how it got to be so big, Microsoft truly does dominate the world's computer market. Windows Vista is the latest in its long line of GUI-based operating systems, and it's safe to say that it's the most advanced and user-friendly operating system on the market today. Windows Vista Ultimate, the flagship edition, is comprised of every feature found in every other SKU of the Vista family; it's the one that has it all.

Now, it's time to learn about it.

Part I

Getting Started with Windows Vista Ultimate

Here we go! Windows Vista might look somewhat familiar to users of earlier Microsoft operating systems, but believe me, it's different. Almost every aspect has been tweaked, from data file organization to folder navigation. The Start Menu is upgraded, the desktop is different, and so on.

The chapters in Part I introduce the new operating system and help you install Windows Vista Ultimate, whether you're dropping it onto a freshly formatted hard drive or upgrading from Windows XP. They go on to teach you how to navigate through Windows Vista's new interface and make basic settings adjustments.

IN THIS PART

Chapter 1

Introducing the New Windows Operating System

IN THIS CHAPTER

- Exploring the Windows Vista interface
- Exploring safety and security improvements
- Looking at Windows Vista's multimedia and gaming enhancements
- Introducing Windows Ultimate Extras

It's been a long time coming. Microsoft hasn't released a new consumer operating system since Windows XP came out in October, 2001. Now, nearly six years later, Windows has once again been polished, modernized, and buffed to a glossy sheen for a newer consumer era. Windows Vista is here.

Windows XP was a big deal for the Windows family. Although Microsoft continued to release consumer operating systems built upon the Windows 95 kernel (including Windows 98, Windows 98 Second Edition, and Windows Me), it targeted only businesses and power users with its NT kernel offerings such as Windows NT and Windows 2000.

There was a difference. For backward compatibility to the days of MS-DOS and Windows 3.1 computing, Microsoft stuck with the 9x kernel for consumers. That kernel was an intricate meshwork of 16-bit (DOS) and 32-bit (NT) code that never truly abandoned the DOS conventions and never fully took advantage of the pure 32-bit power. The NT kernel, however, was built to be a 32-bit monster from the start, without the ambition to run 16-bit Windows 3.1 software or the thousands of games released for DOS.

In 2001, Windows XP brought the parallel lines of Windows business and consumer operating systems together at last. With its Compatibility Modes, it was able to run some DOS and Windows 3.1 software, but because the computing world had started its move to 32-bit in 1995, there wasn't as much demand for backward compatibility. Windows XP proved to be far more stable than any of the 9x flavors (especially the justifiably hated Windows Me), and it was multimedia-friendly and an excellent platform for gaming.

And aren't multimedia and gaming what computers are all about?

Although Microsoft has made a point of including strong game and multimedia support with all of its post-Windows 3.1 operating systems through the ever-evolving DirectX multimedia libraries, the company didn't fully and completely embrace the idea of full home multimedia until it released the Windows XP–based Windows Media Center Edition in 2003. And now, with Windows Vista, Microsoft is going after virtually every possible computer user in the world, from people in emerging markets (for example, third-world nations) to spoiled consumers, from timid technophobes to business power users. And, most important, Microsoft has now turned its all-seeing eye to dedicated gamers and multimedia enthusiasts.

The company released a number of different Windows Vista editions, each aimed at a different market segment. Windows Vista Starter, which is only available in emerging markets, is a bare-bones operating system for the simplest computers. Vista Home Basic is a notch above Starter, intended for homes with a single computer and users who don't need a bevy of fancy features—the kind of people who just want to check their e-mail and do some Web surfing and leave well enough alone. Home Premium is a more full-bodied consumer edition, with a stronger focus on multimedia and usability. It's one of several editions to feature the new desktop interface, Aero. A pair of Vista products aimed at various-sized companies includes the Business and Enterprise editions, with features that cater to networked businesspeople.

Then there's Ultimate. Windows Vista Ultimate is the edition for the true enthusiast, the person who spends hundreds of dollars on single upgrades just to run the latest games. Ultimate edition caters to people who can't imagine viewing home video without editing it through a PC first. This edition is the one for people who consider the PC not an appliance or a convenience or a luxury, but an essential cornerstone of existence, right up there with food, clothing, and shelter.

So, what's new in Windows Vista? A better question might be, "What's *not* new in this startling new operating system?" From the first glance, you can see that Windows Vista is obviously quite different from Windows XP. The interface is similar, but prettier. Windows Explorer is familiar, but so much more functional. Things are in different places. The browser is brand new. Everything is better organized. What's up with the icons giving you a glimpse into the files they represent? Even the old, standard games that haven't changed a bit since Windows 3.1 look improved. (Is that really Minesweeper?)

There's more. Behind the scenes, Windows Vista is a vastly improved operating system. It's more secure. It's less prone to critical failures and file corruption. It does things better, faster, more efficiently. Sometimes, it's as if your computer can read your mind.

As you progress through this book, you get to tear into all the aforementioned topics and more in exquisite detail. This chapter introduces you to Windows Vista and some of its startling new features.

The Vista Interface

The Windows Vista user interface represents a sweeping change from anything you may have ever seen before. This change is the most significant one in the Windows user experience since Microsoft went from Windows 3.x to Windows 95. The graphic user interface (GUI) is built upon the principles of the Windows GUI from Windows 95 to XP, but it's significantly different: The Start Menu has been overhauled; windows have nifty, transparent borders; and everything looks fresh and new. The look falls under Windows Aero, the new desktop interface, but the enhancements don't stop with visuals — the shell and search features are massively enhanced, and the new Sidebar is a handy addition.

Windows Aero

Windows Aero is the new Windows Vista user interface, and it's brilliant (Figure 1.1). Via the power of your computer's 3D graphics card, onscreen windows feature transparencies so you can see through their borders. Windows are animated in a more lively manner than in previous versions (Rather than pop or fade into view, they warp and expand, almost as if they're made of rubber.) The new screen font, Segue UI, is smoother and easier on the eyes.

CROSS-REF For more information on navigating the new Areo interface, see Chapter 3. For information about how to customize the interface, see Chapter 5.

NOTE You do have other options for your Windows Vista user interface. The theme is customizable, and you can also select a classic, Windows 9x-style interface from the Themes settings in the Control Panel. (Choose Start ➪ Control Panel and then click the Themes tab.)

FIGURE 1.1

The Windows Vista user interface, Aero, features a striking new look.

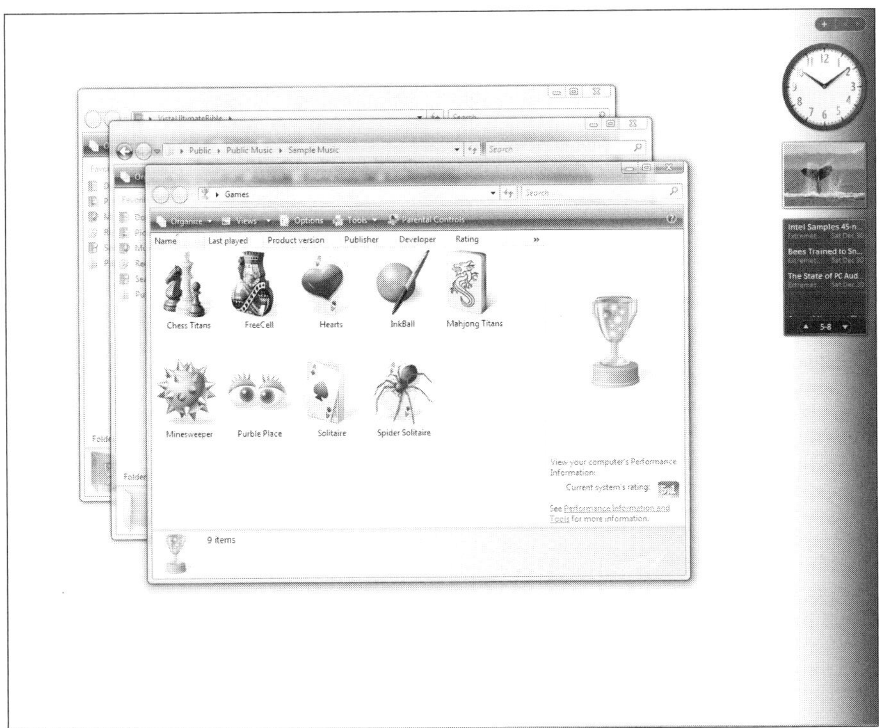

Aero's enhancements go beyond visuals, however. Microsoft drafted a new set of standards to complement its new look. Streamlined wizards help you accomplish your tasks. A tonal change in dialog boxes is supposed to make their message easier to understand and more friendly. Aero is fully enhanced by changes in the Windows shell.

The shell, which is the user interface beyond the visual appearance, is beefier and more user-friendly than in any operating system in history. It packs a number of changes from Windows XP:

- **Interactive paths:** When you navigate through the file system using the new Windows Explorer, the path in the navigation bar is interactive. You can click on any of the folders within the path to navigate directly to that folder. For example, if you navigate to C:\Users\<*your user name*>\Videos\, you can click the Users folder in the path to jump right into that folder.
- **Instant searches:** Each Windows Explorer window, by default, has a search text field in the upper-right corner. You can enter a search string there to search the current location, or you can search the entire computer by clicking Search in the Start Menu (which has its own Search text box). The Windows Search feature is heavily enhanced and searches the computer almost instantly.
- **Saved search folders:** After you perform a search, you can actually save it as its own virtual folder, as shown in Figure 1.2. By default, it saves the feature in C:\Users\<*your user name*>\Searches. From this location, you can "open" your Search folder at any time and it will update itself automatically.

FIGURE 1.2

Saving a search

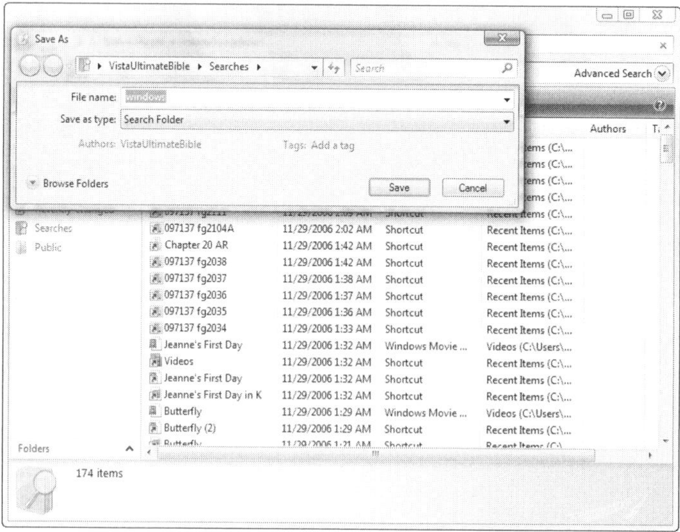

- **Live icons:** When you navigate to a folder that has a number of items in it, some of the icons will actually transform into thumbnails. This feature is not new, but this part is: The thumbnails actually show what's in the file as a preview. Many file types that Windows recognizes, such as photos, videos, Word documents, and Adobe Portable Document Format (PDF) files generate such previews.
- **The Games folder:** Windows Vista takes great pains to cater to gamers, and the Games folder is the shell's way of welcoming gamers to the new operating system. Windows Vista-aware games will automatically install their shortcuts to the Games folder, and the folder provides a centralized location for organizing games, setting parental restrictions, enabling compatibility modes for legacy games, and more.

CROSS-REF For a discussion of the Games folder, see Chapter 21.

- **Network Center:** Networking is easier than ever, and the shell makes navigating networks far more straightforward than it ever was before. The Network Center, shown in Figure 1.3, shows all of your networks and allows you to navigate through them, change sharing settings, set Internet options, and more.

CROSS-REF See Chapter 12 for information on networking.

FIGURE 1.3

The Network Center

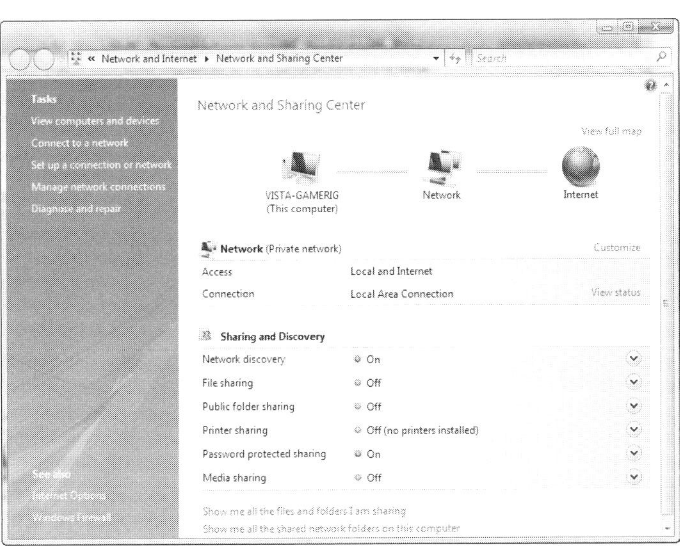

- **Contextual menu bars:** Each window contains a menu bar, but it doesn't look like the menu bars in Windows XP. Depending on the nature of the window, each menu bar presents different options. Each generally starts with Organize, then Views, but after that the options depend on what's in the folder. The Games window includes a Parental Controls option; many windows contain a Burn option so you can burn their contents to optical media. The Pictures window has a Slide Show option. Intelligent menu bars help you get the most out of your files instantly.

The Windows Sidebar

Off to the right on the Windows desktop sits the Sidebar (Figure 1.4). This convenience tool shows, by default, a small slideshow of stuff from the Pictures folder, an analog clock face with the current system time displayed, and an RSS feed organizer. Those little devices on the Sidebar are called gadgets, and you can customize them. You can add or remove a great deal of gadgets that come with Windows Vista, including a calculator, a currency converter, a notepad, puzzles, the Recycle Bin, a stick ticker, and more.

FIGURE 1.4

The Windows Sidebar is on the right. Also shown is the Sidebar customization window.

CROSS-REF See Chapter 8 for information about customizing the Windows Sidebar.

Furthermore, you can download dozens of Sidebar gadgets from the Internet. Microsoft provides a number of gadgets on its server for your convenience. At the time of this writing, you could choose from a number of games, a calendar, and a Seattle-area traffic meter!

Improved Safety and Security

Windows Vista takes security seriously. Redesigned from the ground up to prevent the myriad of exploits that have plagued earlier versions, Vista is easily Microsoft's most secure operating system. That's not to say no one will ever crack the security and threaten it, but it's far more prepared for the eventuality than earlier versions of Windows.

For information about all of Vista's improved safety and security controls, see the chapters in Part III of this book.

User Account Control

For example, Vista comes with a *User Account Control* (UAC), which is a powerful feature that only lets programs make major changes in the operating system if a user with Administrative privileges allows it. All users, including administrators, run in a secure mode. When a process tries to do something that requires administrative privileges, requested or not, it prompts the user for authorization. This can theoretically prevent rogue programs, such as malicious stuff from the Internet, from compromising Windows Vista.

Windows Firewall and Windows Defender

Speaking of the Internet, Windows Firewall is more powerful than ever, and Windows Defender (Microsoft's antispyware program), an optional download for Windows XP, is included and turned on by default in Windows Vista.

Parental Controls

Parental Controls allow administrators to restrict other users' access to certain media. Using Parental Controls, administrators can block access to objectionable Web content; they can prevent games from being played based on Entertainment Software Rating Board (ESRB) ratings; they can enact time controls to define when certain accounts may be accessed; and much more.

Better Applications

Windows Vista includes a number of new and beefed-up applications. Some are familiar: Windows Mail looks a lot like Outlook Express, only it's laced with new features. Others are brand new, like the built-in support for RSS Web feeds. Some of the applications included are as follows:

- **Windows Calendar:** This new calendar application, shown in Figure 1.5, lets you schedule meetings and other events, and presents reminders when a scheduled event comes along.

FIGURE 1.5

Windows Calendar

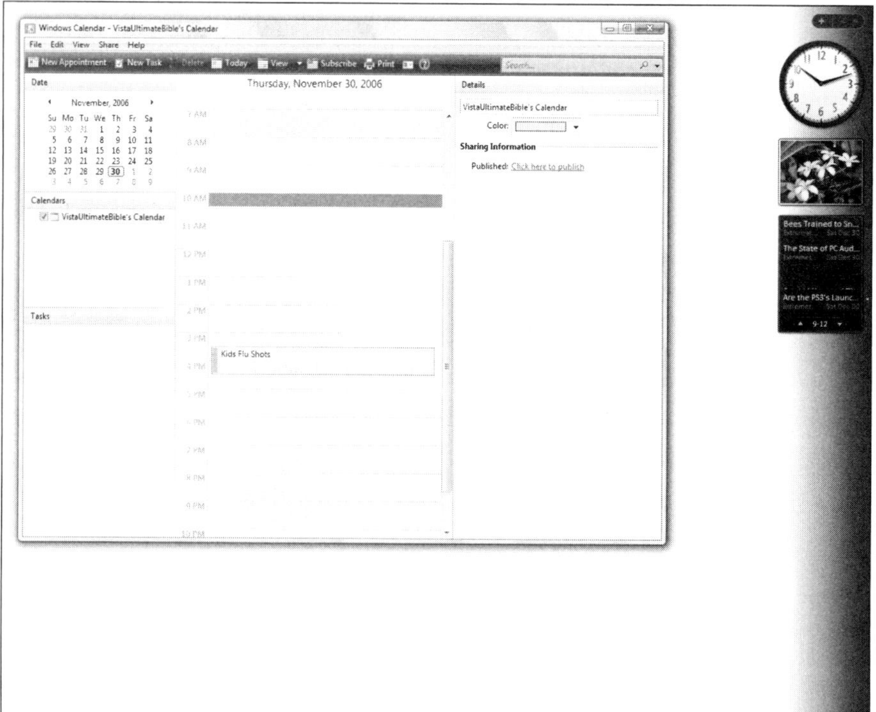

- **Media Player 11:** A new version of Windows Media Player, this application organizes your media files in a new and friendlier fashion. It also includes the MTV URGE music store.

CROSS-REF Media Player 11 is covered in depth in Chapter 17.

- **Media Center:** Alas, there will be no Windows Vista Media Center edition. Instead, Media Center is included with many of the Vista editions, including Ultimate. Media Center, shown in Figure 1.6, provides all the media-centric functionality of Windows Media Center and more.

FIGURE 1.6

Windows Media Center

CROSS-REF Detailed information about Windows Media Center can be found in Chapter 16.

- **Internet Explorer 7+:** A totally redesigned browser, IE7+ features tabbed browsing, a new Favorites Center, an integrated Search function, and a whole bunch of other new features.
- **Movie Maker:** An updated version of the video editing application found in Windows XP, Windows Movie Maker now supports high-definition video and DVD output.

This list is just a sampling of the applications included with Windows Vista. Others include Windows Contacts, Windows DVD Maker, Windows Backup, and more.

Multimedia and Gaming Enhancements

Windows Vista Ultimate is designed for multimedia and gaming, and it boasts a host of new features to make audio, video, and interactive experiences better than ever before. Besides the Games folder, mentioned earlier, it incorporates a bunch of other nifty upgrades.

Windows audio stack

For example, the Windows audio stack has been completely rewritten to get the most out of even the best sound cards on the market, providing an aural experience superior to that in previous versions. With 32-bit floating point accuracy and ultra-low latency, sound is accurate and, at last, as good as the audio equipment attached to your PC. Those $500 surround multimedia speakers have never sounded better! Also, check out the new audio controls that allow you to assign audio levels to each application, rather than a simple, system-wide audio control.

Multimedia organization

Multimedia organization is outstanding. In addition to the Games folder, which allows you to launch games from one centralized location, the Windows Pictures folder, shown in Figure 1.7, allows you to activate slide shows with the click of a button, and the Music folder lets you play all the tunes in the current folder from the Menu Bar, or burn them to a CD or DVD.

FIGURE 1.7

The Windows Pictures folder

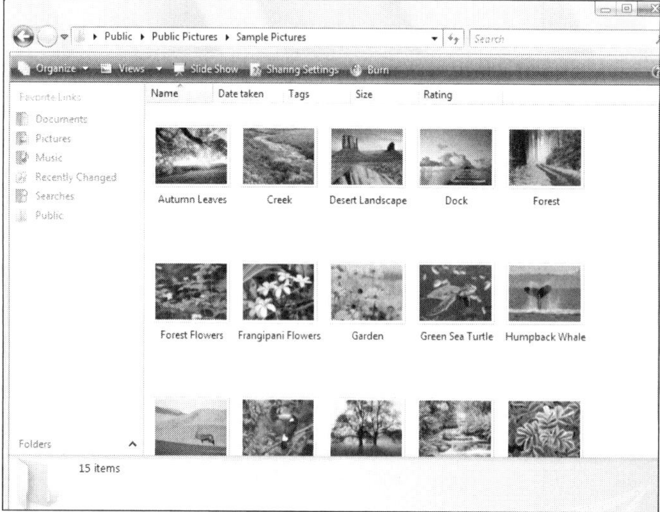

New games

Speaking of games, Vista Ultimate includes a number of new Windows games. Besides the old standards — Minesweeper, Solitaire, and Hearts (all of which have received a facelift) — you'll find Inkball, Majong Titans, and Chess Titans, which is shown in Figure 1.8, among others.

FIGURE 1.8

Chess Titans is one of the new games included with Vista Ultimate.

CROSS-REF To read more about the new games included with Vista Ultimate, see Chapter 6.

DirectX 10

Gaming is better than ever with DirectX 10 (the latest version of the gaming and multimedia capabilities in Windows). Featuring ultra-high-speed DLLs (dynamic link libraries) and a new graphics subsystem that, according to Microsoft, can display graphics eight times faster than DirectX 9.0c, DirectX 10 packs unified vertex and pixel shaders and more. Because DirectX 10 isn't backward compatible with older DirectX versions, Vista also includes DirectX 9L to run legacy games.

CROSS-REF For more in-depth information about the new DirectX 10, see Chapters 14 and 15.

Performance Rating and Tools

The Performance Rating and Tools control panel, shown in Figure 1.9, allows you to assess the system's performance and get a rating of each of the major subsystems, which are combined for an overall system rating.

FIGURE 1.9

The Windows Performance and Rating Tools control panel enables you to assess your system's performance.

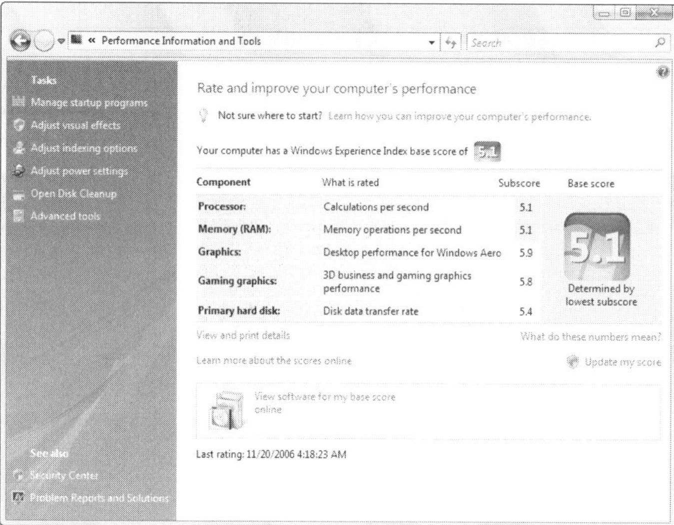

Windows Ultimate Extras

Windows Ultimate is unique in that it not only features *all* the features of the other Windows editions, but also includes downloadable Windows Ultimate Extras. Available through Windows Update, they are slated to include some pretty incredible software. Microsoft bills them as cutting-edge utilities and applications.

Flip 3D

Flip 3D is a cool way to breeze through the open applications on the Windows desktop. Plain-old Flip is the new name for the Alt+Tab combination that shows your open applications and lets you choose from among them. Now, however, you can also use the Windows key with Tab to present a 3D view of your open applications, as shown in Figure 1.10. The applications also show what's going on inside them. This Aero feature is both nifty and handy.

FIGURE 1.10

Flip 3D arranges your open applications in 3D.

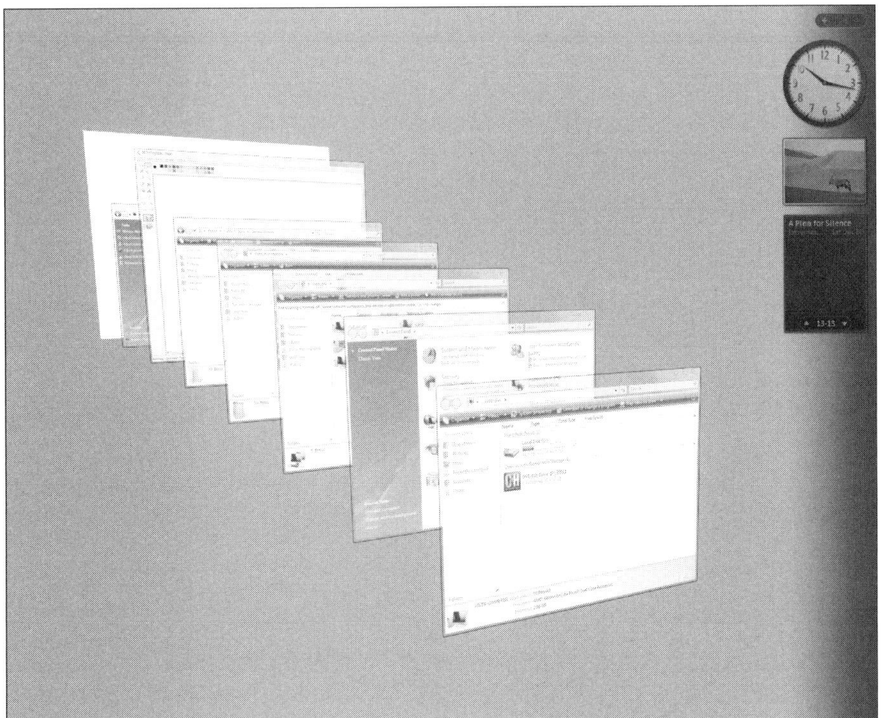

Summary

Windows Vista Ultimate is the first operating system to live up to its name. It truly is the ultimate in desktop operating systems. This book guides you through the new features with a strong focus on multimedia and gaming, as well as shows you how to install Windows Vista fresh or upgrade your legacy Windows installation; how to network multiple computers in a home environment; how to get the most out of your movies, photographs and music; and how to leverage the new gaming features to your advantage; and that's just the beginning.

Chapter 2

Installing Windows Vista Ultimate

IN THIS CHAPTER

Checking the system requirements

Installing Windows Vista on a newly formatted hard drive

Upgrading to Windows Vista

Completing the installation

Acquiring, installing, and maintaining device drivers

The greatest journey starts with a single step, and all that. Well, your Windows Vista Ultimate experience won't start without your installing the operating system.

Installation is the part where a program called an installer takes all the important files that came on the Windows Vista DVD and places them on the computer's hard drive. This process can take a while; Windows Vista Ultimate requires a minimum of 15GB of free hard drive space. Not all of that space gets used up by files, but nevertheless Vista is huge compared with previous Windows releases.

Before you start installing, you have to assess whether your computer is truly Vista-ready. Microsoft has published two sets of guidelines regarding a given computer's ability to run Vista: one for Vista Capable PCs, which is basically the bare minimum system that can run the core assets of the operating system; and one called Vista Premium Ready, and it represents the requirements for running Vista with some degree of eye candy (in the form of the Aero interface).

How realistic are the requirements? I installed various prerelease versions of Windows Vista Ultimate on a variety of PCs to gauge its performance; it certainly does vary. You can read more on that later in this chapter.

Installing may involve upgrading. You can install Vista either by wiping the hard drive clean and starting from scratch (which is really the best way to go about it) or by upgrading a previous version of Windows. The Vista installer will helpfully tell you which of your programs won't work with the new operating system.

After the computer is done copying files and getting its necessary information from you, the honorable user, you still won't be finished installing Windows Vista. You have to deal with device driver installation as well. *Device drivers* are little programs that mediate communication between your operating system and the computer's hardware. Because Windows Vista uses an entirely new driver model, drivers for previous versions of Windows probably won't work with it.

This chapter takes you through all the steps needed to do so, beginning with assessing system requirements, as well as the process of performing a new installation of Windows versus performing an upgrade. This chapter also tells you more than you ever wanted to know about device drivers.

Now it's time to take that first step to start a great journey. Grab your Vista DVD and rev up your hard drive.

The Installation Process: An Overview

What, exactly, are you getting yourself involved in?

If you're an old, war-torn installer of computer operating systems, you won't have much of a problem with Windows Vista. If you've never installed an OS before in your life, you also won't have much of a problem with Vista. The installation process makes for the most streamlined operating system installation you probably have experienced to date.

Windows Vista's graphical installation interface does almost everything for you. It requests a minimal amount of information and prompting, unlike previous versions of Windows that were much more hands-on. Vista's installer does its thing quietly, and although that gives you *less* control over optimization from the start, you can change almost every aspect of the OS after the installation has concluded.

CROSS-REF For more information about tweaking your Vista preferences, see the chapters in Parts I and VIII.

Preparing for the installation

Before you install Windows Vista Ultimate, you have to tackle a few tasks to pave the way for a smooth installation. First of all, make sure you have the computer to handle it. Upgrade any hardware *before* you install Windows Vista. (You're strictly limited in the number of times you can reinstall it without having to purchase a new copy.)

If you're upgrading your previous Windows OS to Vista, streamline the computer and test the hard drive first — and, of course, back up all of your important data before you get started. Installing Vista to a freshly formatted hard drive is easier and requires less prep time.

While upgrading an older version of Vista to Windows is less problematic than in past versions of Windows, the most trouble-free installation occurs if you perform a complete wipe of your existing hard drive. This option means you *really* need to back up your data. Also back up your licenses, uninstall all applications that require activation, and back up your Internet data.

Performing the installation

Depending on how you plan to install Vista, you must either boot the DVD-ROM it comes on or run the installer from within your previous version of Windows.

During the installation, Vista occasionally asks for information from you, such as who you are, what time zone you live in, and how you want your network set up (if you have a network). For the most part, however, the installation is "quiet," meaning it does what it needs to do with little input from you.

Finishing the installation

When the installation is through, you'll have a little checklist of things to do before you're truly done installing Windows Vista. You need Internet access at some point to activate the software. You have to install the latest device drivers for all of your computer's hardware. You might want to take a tour of Windows Vista. You definitely should install an antivirus program to round out Vista's security (it already has a firewall and an antispyware application built-in).

Then, at last, you'll be ready to explore the new OS. It's Microsoft's best effort by far, so get ready to enjoy it.

Official Hardware Requirements Versus Reality

If you're wondering whether your computer is up to the challenge of running Windows Vista, you're not alone. For an operating system, Windows Vista requires a monster of a system for you to truly be able to take advantage of its gorgeous visuals.

Microsoft published a pair of system requirements on its Get Ready Web site (`www.microsoft.com/windowsvista/getready`), which are listed in Tables 2.1 and 2.2.

TABLE 2.1

Windows Vista Capable PC Requirements

Item	Requirement
Processor	A modern processor* that runs at 800MHz or faster
Memory	512MB
Graphics hardware	DirectX 9 compatible

*By "modern processor," Microsoft probably means something in the Intel Pentium 4/AMD Athlon class or later.

Please note that these specifications are strictly for being able to run Vista in a stripped down, simplified graphical interface. Look at Table 2.2 for Microsoft's requirements for a more robust Vista experience.

TABLE 2.2

Windows Vista Premium Ready PC Requirements

Item	Requirement
Processor	1 GHz 32-bit or 64-bit
Memory	1GB or more
Graphics hardware	Support for DirectX 9 graphics with a WDDM driver, 128MB of graphics memory (minimum), support for Pixel Shader 2.0; 32 bits per pixel color
Storage	40GB hard drive with 15GB free; DVD-ROM drive
Other	Audio output; Internet access

NOTE The processor requirement listed in Table 2.2 indicates the actual operating frequency of the CPU, as opposed to its numbering or branding. For example, AMD Athlon CPUs are often numbered (Athlon 1200+) but they don't actually run at that speed. (For example, the Athlon 1800+ runs at 1530 MHz.)

Don't worry about the bit width of the CPU; any AMD, Intel, or VIA processor in the 1 GHz or faster range is, at minimum, a 32-bit processor.

The hardware requirement specifications listed on Microsoft's Web site are, at the very least, optimistic. Let's break them down:

- **Processor:** Vista might function with an 800 MHz CPU, but it won't function well. The slowest CPU I ran it on was a 1.5 GHz Pentium 4 and it crawled, even with a cavernous array of memory. Furthermore, things you might want to do on a Vista operating system that are processor-intensive, such as encoding video files and resizing photographs, will benefit from a much faster CPU. I suggest doubling the Premium Ready PC requirement: Don't run Vista on anything less than a 2 GHz CPU.
- **Memory:** The more, the merrier. I can't imagine running Vista in any form on 512MB of RAM. When I opened a bunch of applications, it slowed down to an unacceptable level with 1GB on a Pentium 4 Extreme Edition 3.40 GHz-based computer. It smoothed right out when I doubled the memory to 2GB. I consider 2GB to be the minimum memory requirement for decent performance when you open several programs at once.
- **Graphics hardware:** Vista runs fine on any DirectX 9-compliant card — unless you want to run it with Aero enabled. Take that 128MB memory requirement seriously. I don't have

a DirectX 9 graphics card with less than 256MB of onboard memory, and Aero ran fine with it on the aforementioned P4EE 3.40GHz machine, with 2MB of system memory.

- **Storage:** The idea of running Vista on a 40GB hard drive is laughable. As always, you want as much hard disk space as possible, as you'll inevitably install games and applications along with your operating system. Now that 320GB drives are less than $100 if you shop around, you have no reason to skimp on hard drive space. Also, a DVD-ROM drive is merely adequate; you should have a DVD burner for creating media and backing up files.

Therefore, my recommendations for a Windows Vista system with all the graphical goodness the OS can muster are as follows:

- 2 GHz processor
- 2GB of system memory
- 256MB DirectX 9 graphics card
- 250GB or larger hard drive
- DVD+/-RW drive

Also, I recommend having a killer sound card and a broadband Internet connection.

NOTE These recommendations are for the operating system alone and don't include the programs that you plan to run on it. Be sure to check the system requirements of any and all software you install on your system, and take the "minimum" requirements with a big grain of salt. Minimum requirements rarely take performance into account; they indicate what will *run* a program, but not what will make it run *well*.

Installing Vista on a Newly Formatted Hard Drive

Now it's time to roll up your sleeves and install this baby. This section shows you how to install a fresh copy of Windows Vista on a new hard drive.

NOTE Unlike most previous versions of Windows, Vista's installer can detect serial ATA (SATA) drives without your needing to install drivers from a floppy disk. It detected several of my drives, including the Seagate Barracuda SATA-2 drive I used for this walkthrough, without a hitch.

CAUTION The following steps are for installing Windows Vista on a new drive, or a drive recently wiped completely clean. If you're wiping out a drive for a clean installation of Vista, be sure to back up any important data first. (Backing up is covered later in this chapter.)

Booting the DVD

To get started, boot the Windows Vista DVD-ROM by turning on the computer and placing the Vista DVD in the drive. You may have to alter the BIOS through the Setup program to boot the DVD.

The BIOS, or Basic Input/Output System, is the chip containing the software that tells your computer where to look for an operating system, among other things.

All BIOS setup programs are different, so consult the instruction manual that came with your PC or its motherboard for instructions on how to make the optical drive first in the boot order. The option may be in a screen that looks similar to the one shown in Figure 2.1.

When you boot the system, you'll likely see a prompt asking you to press a key if you want to boot from the optical drive. Press a key when prompted.

FIGURE 2.1

This is where I set this motherboard to boot the DVD before the hard drive.

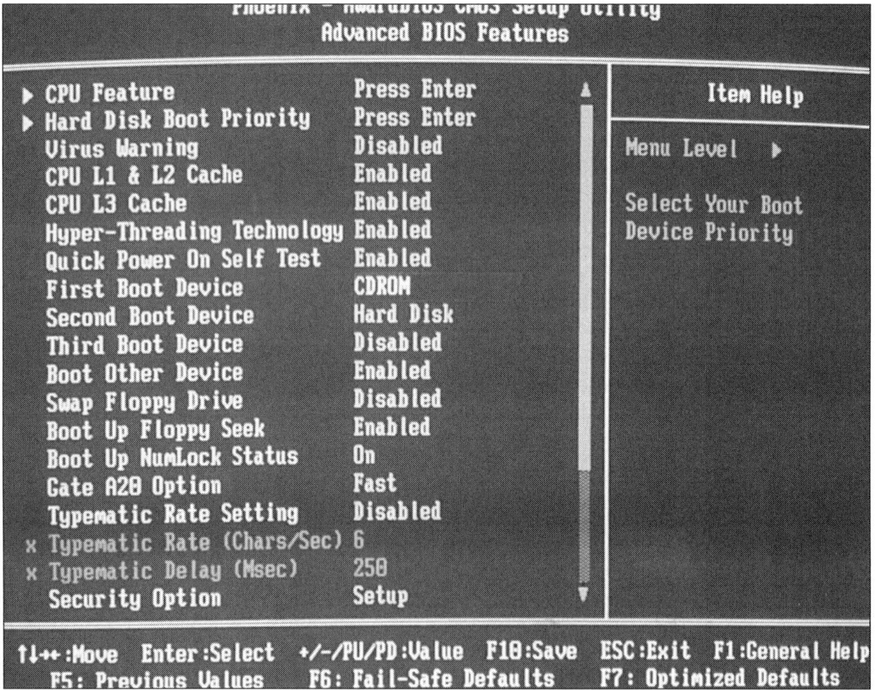

Giving the installer some information

After you boot the DVD, the Windows Vista installer launches. It loads a bunch of files as you sit and wait, and then it presents you with its first data-gathering screen (Figure 2.2), which asks for localization data. Enter the information and click Next.

The next prompt that appears, shown in Figure 2.3, offers you a couple of links — one to repair a computer (which shouldn't be necessary at this point) and the other to learn what you need to know about installing Windows. Click Install Now to proceed.

In the screen that appears, carefully type in your 25-character alphanumeric sequence product key (Figure 2.4). Don't worry about adding dashes, as the Vista installer does that for you. You can also elect, via a check box, whether to allow Windows to activate itself automatically after installation.

FIGURE 2.2

Vista wants to know where you live.

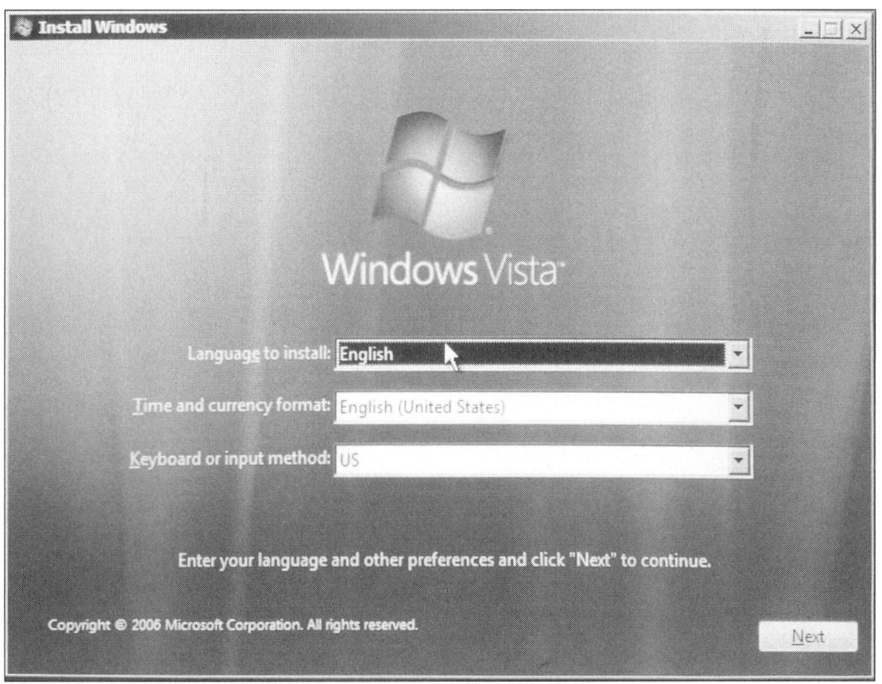

FIGURE 2.3

The Install Now button is ready for action.

The end-user license agreement (EULA) appears next. Read it thoroughly, because it contains information about how you are allowed to use Windows Vista. If you agree to its terms, click the check box, and then click Next.

FIGURE 2.4

Type in the product key.

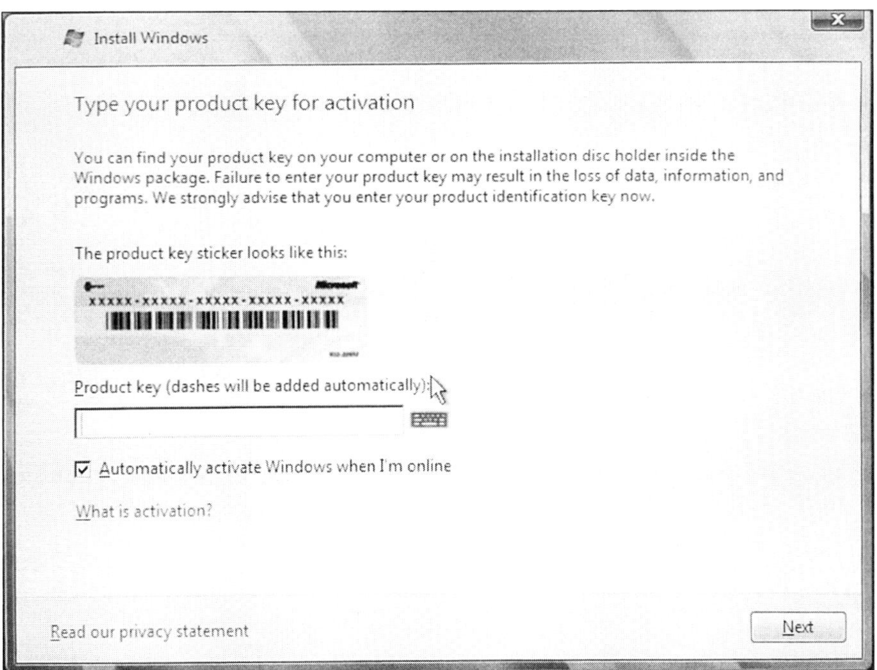

Now it's time to take care of hard drive matters. The next screen that appears (Figure 2.5) allows you to choose between an upgrade or a fresh installation — but notice that the upgrade installation option is not available. You have to run the Setup program through your previous version of Windows to perform an upgrade. Click Custom.

FIGURE 2.5

Click Custom, as there's nothing else to do.

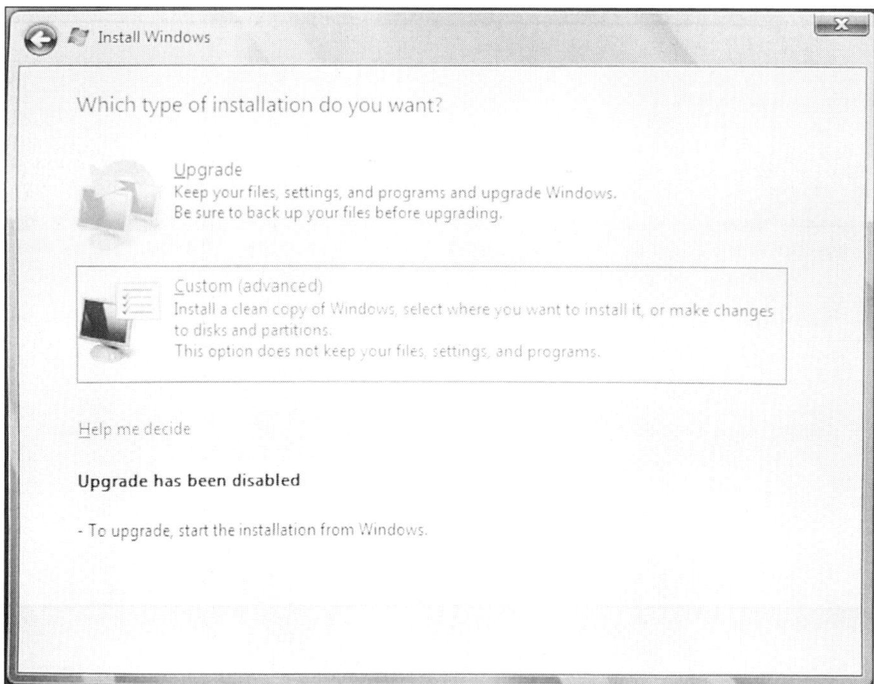

The drive configuration screen appears, as shown in Figure 2.6. Note that if a partition already exists on a drive that you're in the process of wiping clean, it will appear in this area. If you're wiping the drive clean, you might want to remove the partition or partitions by highlighting it/them and clicking Delete. Then, reallocate the disk space by clicking New. The easiest way to reallocate the space is to create one large partition (Figure 2.7), which Windows Vista can handle just fine. Advanced users can create multiple partitions, to which Windows Vista will assign drive letters.

FIGURE 2.6

This screen shows any partitions or unallocated space on your drive.

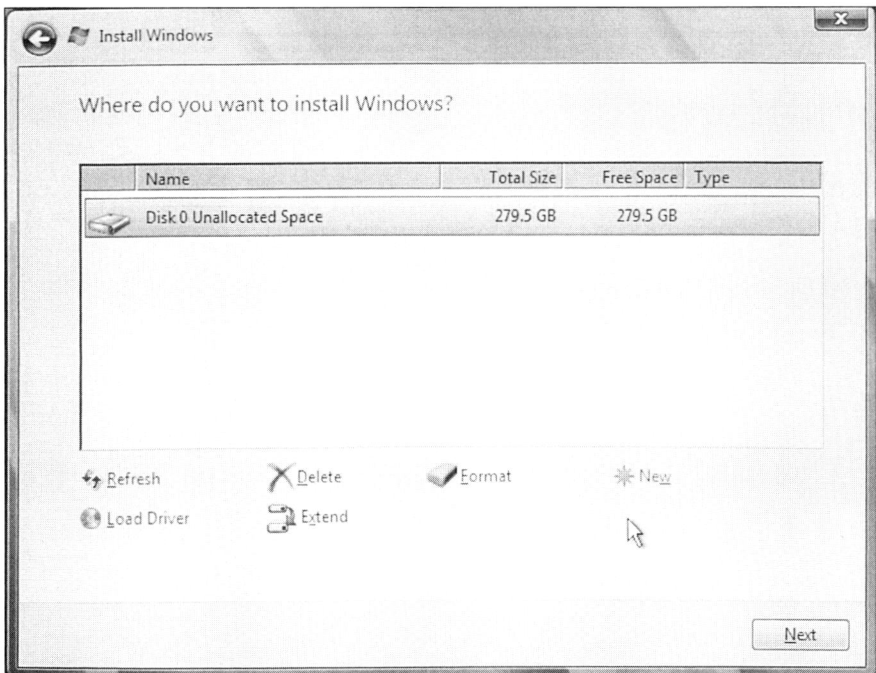

The next step is to format your partition or partitions. Click the Format button, and then click past the warning that all data on your drive will be permanently lost if you proceed with the format.

NOTE **You're not given a choice of which file system to use when you format the drive. Windows Vista automatically chooses NTFS for you. It won't run on a FAT system, which was used by DOS and some previous versions of Windows.**

When the format is complete, click Next. The file transfer begins.

FIGURE 2.7

Create a partition and click Apply.

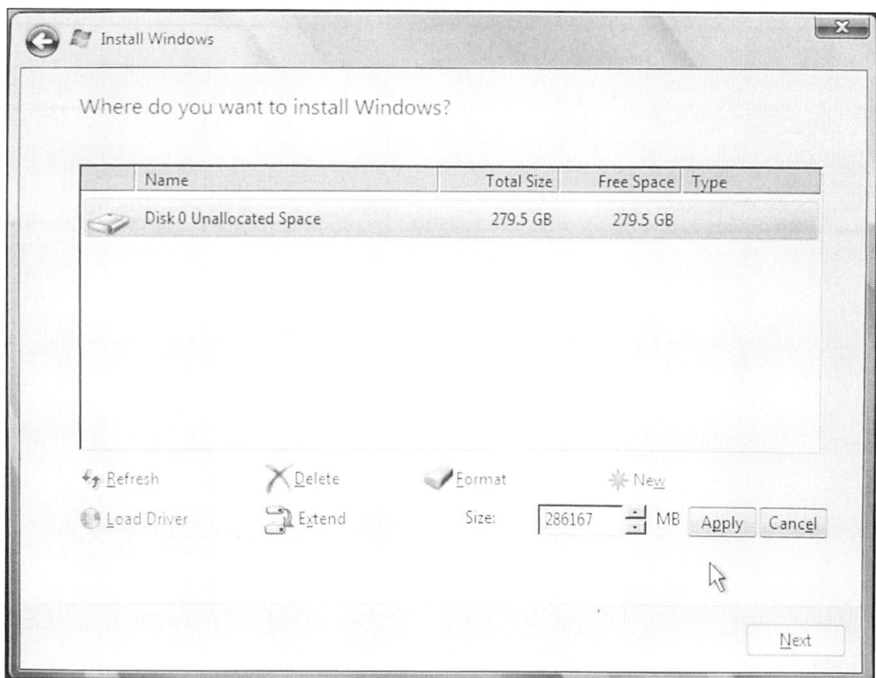

Letting the installer do its job

Now, the installer copies files to the hard drive, decompresses them, and performs other vital tasks. It's important that you do not interrupt it; don't shut down or reboot the computer.

The installer shows its progress as it goes, with each task displaying a percentage of completion, as shown in Figure 2.8. Sit back, grab something to drink, and relax for a while.

NOTE The time it takes for Windows Vista to complete its installation depends mightily upon the performance of the system on which it's being installed. A powerful system with lots of memory might finish up the installation in a half hour or so, while older or less lofty systems can have you waiting two hours or more.

CAUTION The Windows Vista installer will reboot the computer, possibly more than once. Don't boot the DVD! Once the installer reboots the machine, it's ready to run off the hard drive, so when you see the "Press any key..." prompt to boot the DVD, don't touch that keyboard!

FIGURE 2.8

The installer displays its progress through several steps.

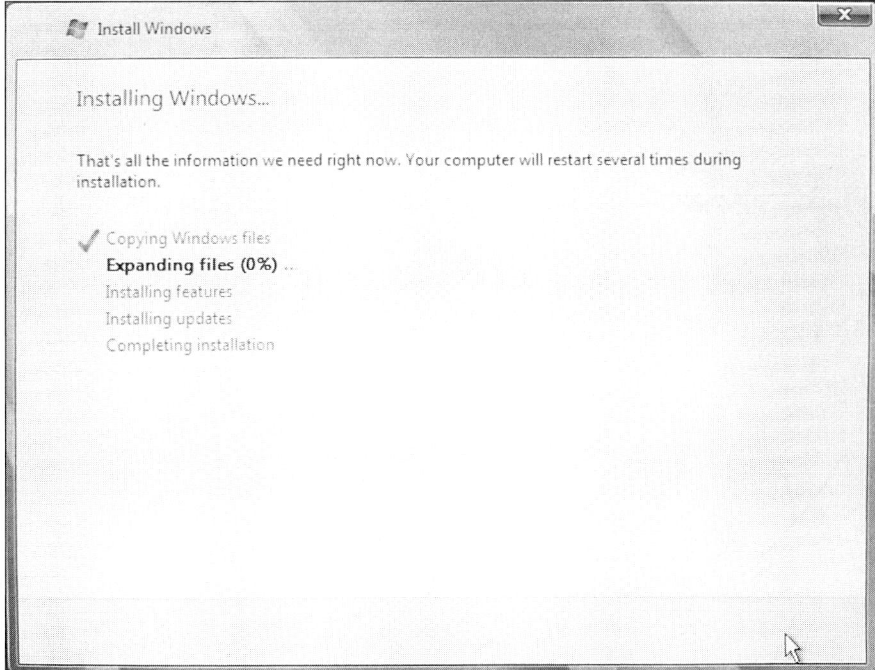

Providing more information

After the installer reboots one or more times, it begins asking you more questions. The first thing it wants to know is a user name, as shown in Figure 2.9.

FIGURE 2.9

Type in a user name and a password here.

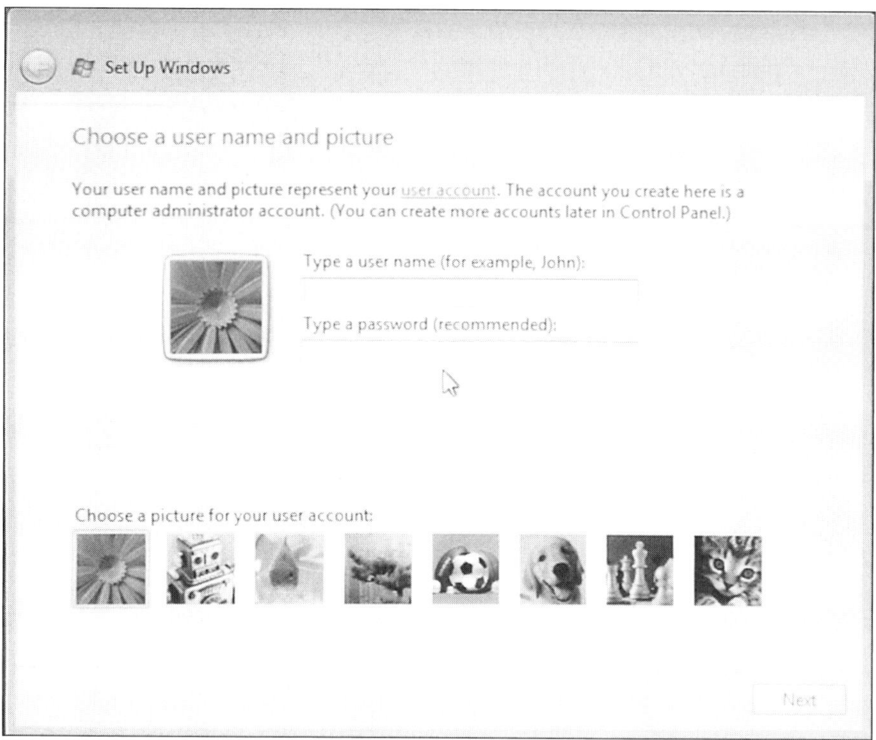

Type in a name and then a password. Click Next when you're done. (Be sure your user name and passwords are memorable — you will be asked for them later.) A screen requesting a computer name (what the computer will be called on the network) appears, as shown in Figure 2.10. You also have a chance to pick a background for your Windows Vista desktop. You can always customize it later.

FIGURE 2.10

Pick a PC name and a desktop background.

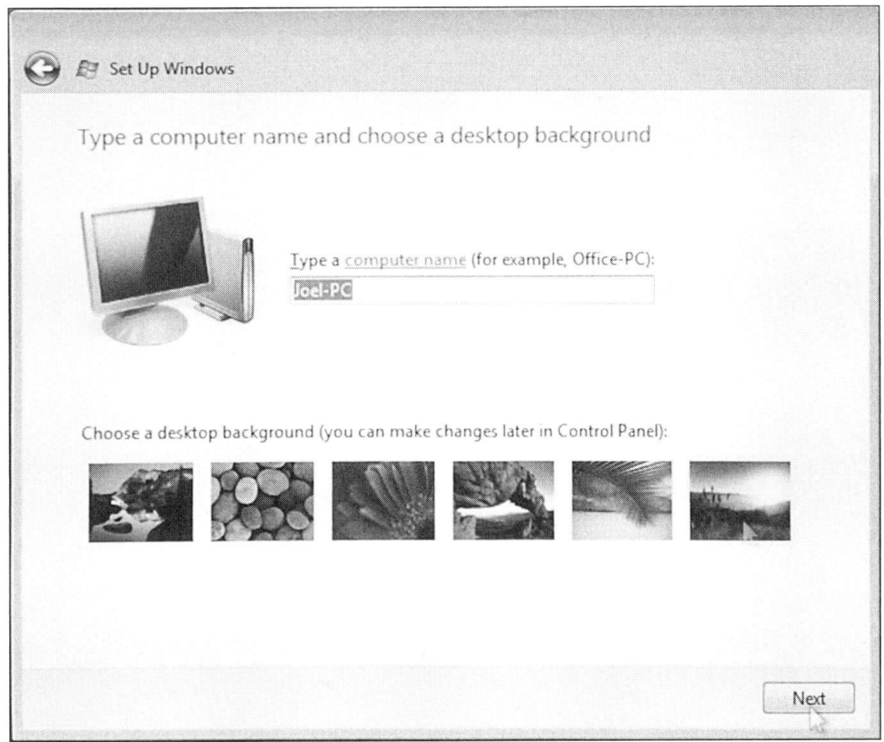

Windows still isn't done with its questions. Now it wants to know how you want its security settings configured (Figure 2.11). You're given three choices:

- Use recommended settings
- Install important updates only
- Ask me later

For peak security, choose the recommended settings.

FIGURE 2.11

Decide on your security requirements.

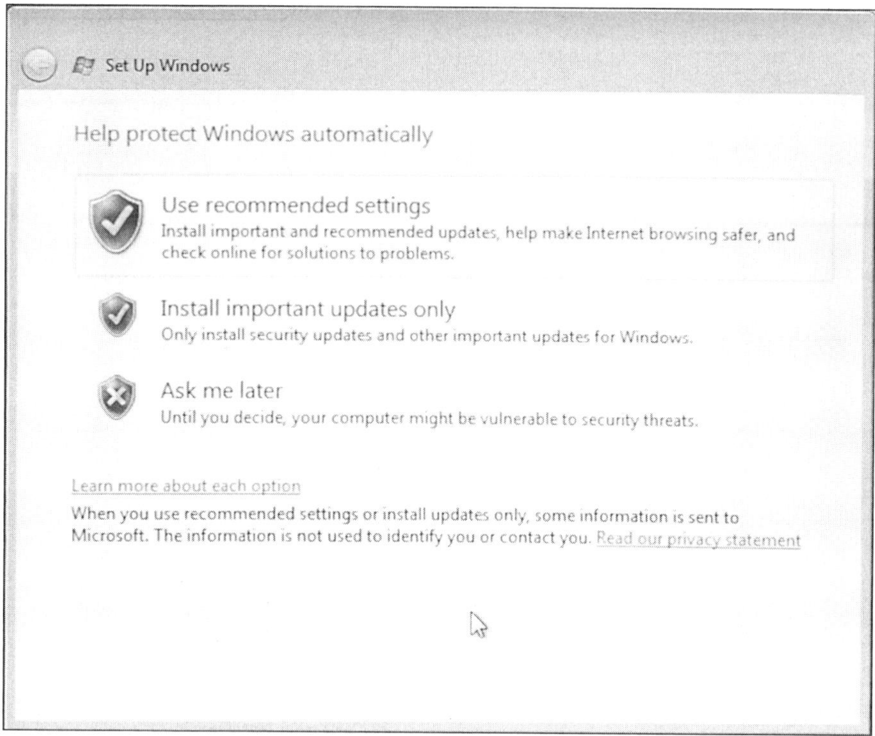

You're almost done! Now, Windows needs to know your time zone, and the current date and time (Figure 2.12). It defaults to the U.S. Pacific time zone (west coast bias). Set up the time as it is where you are.

FIGURE 2.12

Tell Vista about your time zone.

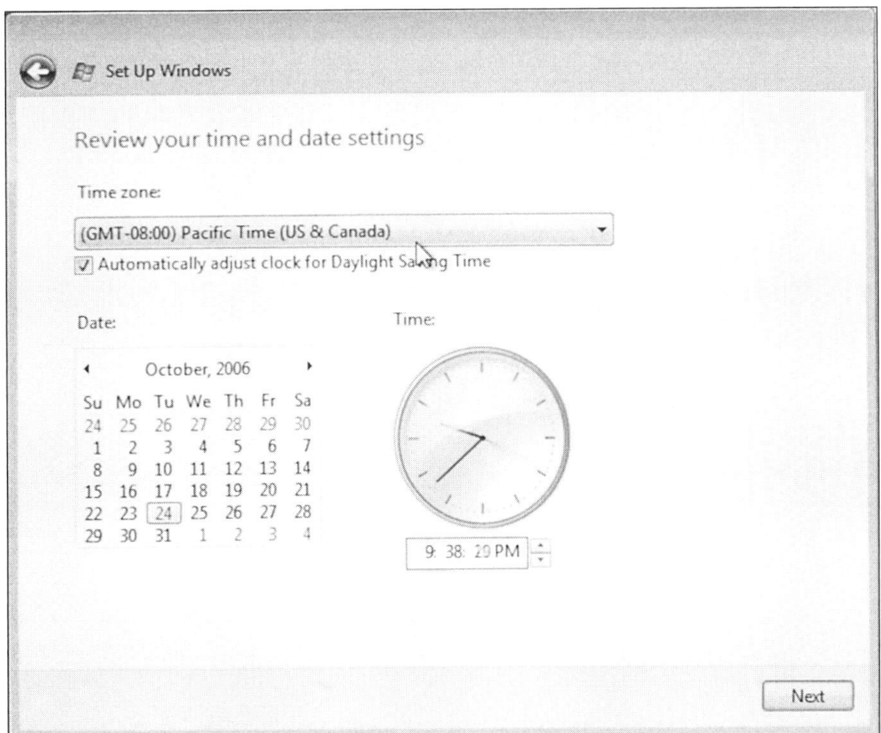

The final setup prompt, shown in Figure 2.13, asks where your computer is: at home, work, or in a public location. It asks this question to configure file sharing and to determine whether it can legally share your media files. Windows Vista takes digital copyrights very seriously. Choose the correct location of your computer.

FIGURE 2.13

Tell Vista where you're using your computer.

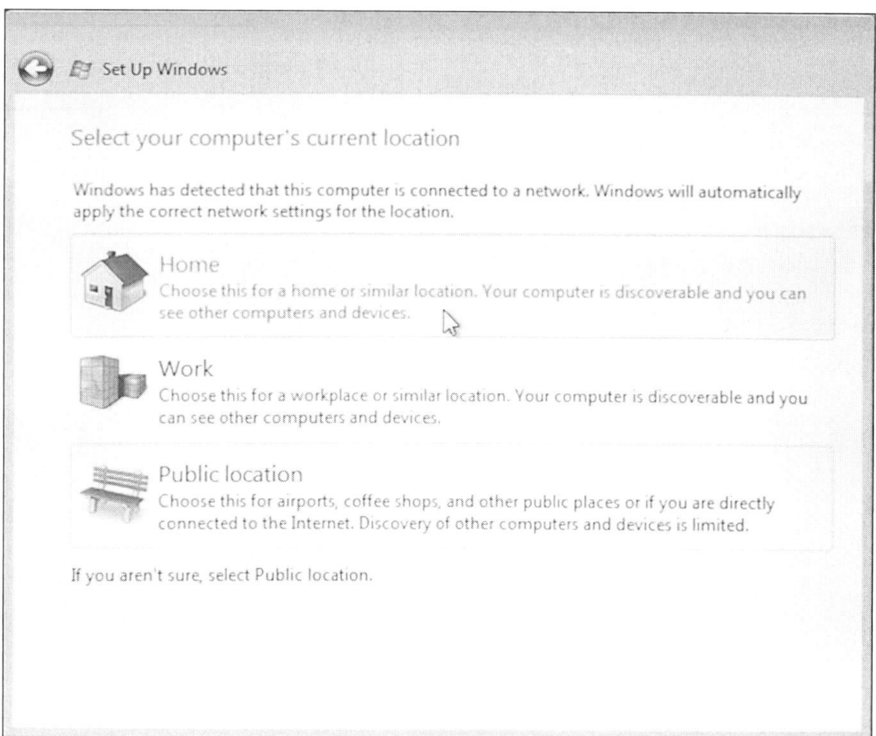

Vista then thanks you and tests the computer's performance (Figure 2.14), the results of which you can see in certain areas of the operating system.

FIGURE 2.14

This is where I set this motherboard to boot the DVD before the hard drive.

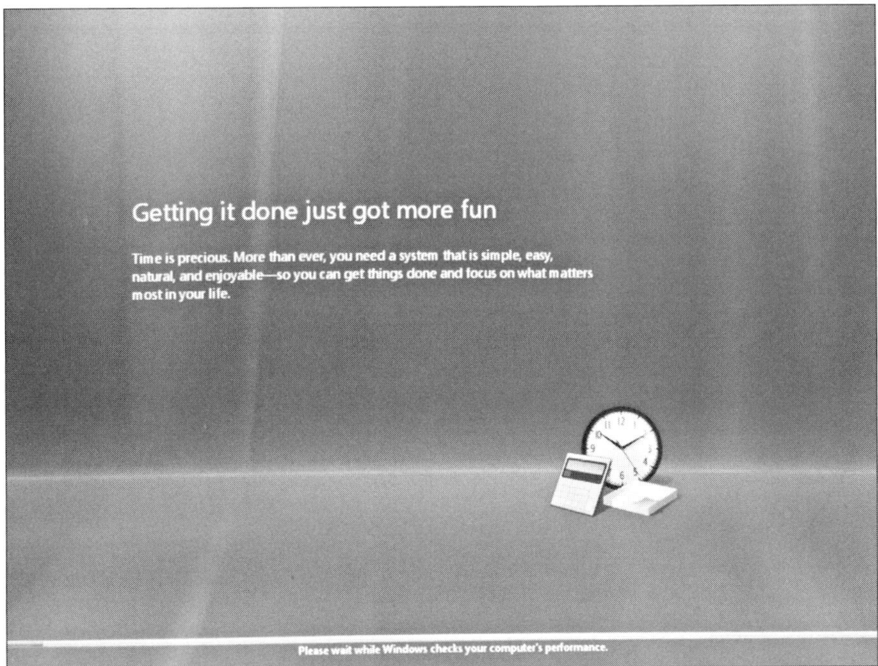

When Vista finally finishes the performance test, a login prompt appears. Type in the user name and password you set up earlier in the process; the Windows Vista desktop (Figure 2.15) appears for the first time.

Your installation is complete.

FIGURE 2.15

Your first glimpse of Vista

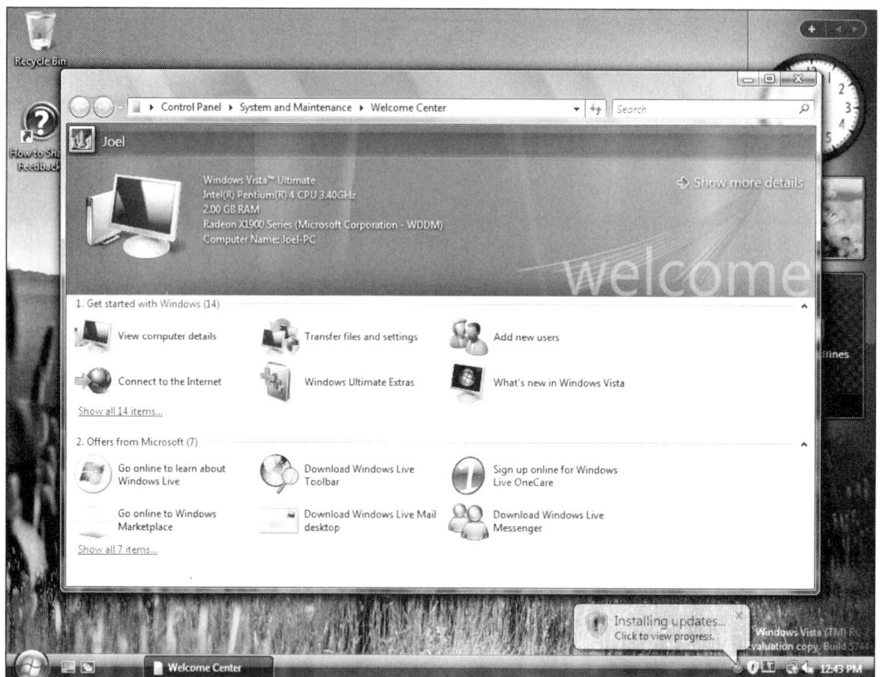

NOTE If, for some reason, the installation gets interrupted (due to a power failure or an accidental shutdown or reboot), what should you do? If the installation blows up before the first time Windows rebooted, start the installation process over from the beginning. If Windows managed to reboot before the installation was interrupted, start the computer and *don't* boot the DVD-ROM. Windows Vista should be able to pick up where it left off without retracing too many of its steps.

Upgrading from a Previous Version of Windows

If you are upgrading from an older version of Windows to Windows Vista, the actual installation is very similar to performing an installation on a clean hard drive. The major differences between the procedures involve preparing your computer for the upgrade.

Before you start a Windows Vista installation, I recommend that you take a few steps to ensure a smooth and trouble-free procedure. The most important step, of course, is to back up your files.

Backing up your files

This step is absolutely not optional. If you do not back up your data files, you may lose them forever.

Which files should you back up? The simple answer is *anything you can't re-create*. That means you don't have to back up programs themselves (you can always reinstall them), or anything you can easily download or otherwise acquire. What you should back up are anything and everything you've created with your computer, or with a device that you connected to your computer and uploaded the files.

- Back up all of your documents, spreadsheets, presentations, and all of your creative works.
- Back up your game saves unless you want to start the game over from the beginning.
- Back up your photographs.
- Back up your e-mail, your address book, and everything associated with it.

NOTE If you use Microsoft Outlook, there's no easy way to back that stuff up; I suggest using OutBack Plus 6, an inexpensive program available at `http://ajsystems.com/obp.html`.

- Back up your Web bookmarks and cookies by using the Export function in your browser.
- Back up music files, movie files, and anything else you've purchased online that you can't easily re-download.

If you're not sure about something, back it up. Go through your file system thoroughly and back up everything you need. Use a backup program, or copy all this stuff to removable media (such as DVD- or DVD+RW discs). Keep your backups safe while you perform the installation.

CAUTION I can't emphasize this enough: BACK UP YOUR STUFF. If you lose it, you will regret not backing it up. Your data are the reason you use the computer in the first place, so be sure to back up everything you've created with your computer.

Uninstalling or deactivating applications

Some applications, including several antivirus utilities, some Adobe applications, and a handful of others, require product activation. You should uninstall these applications, or at least deactivate them, before you proceed. If you don't and you try to reinstall or reactivate them after the Vista upgrade, the publisher might assume you're installing a single-user license to a second computer and prevent activation.

Follow the instructions provided by the software publisher to ensure a smooth transition. Look at the publisher's Web site for information on reactivation after a major upgrade, or a transfer to a different PC. Check the tech support sections, and contact the publisher if need be. You don't want to upgrade Windows only to discover that your mission critical applications no longer work — or that you're no longer allowed to use them!

Streamlining the file system

If you have lots of old stuff clogging up your Windows file system, now is the time to exorcise it. Uninstall any programs you never plan on using again, and delete any data files you no longer care about. Get rid of annoyances like empty folders. Getting rid of everything you don't need will make the installation faster.

When you're done, run Disk Cleanup if your version of Windows has it. In Windows XP, for example, click Start, then choose All Programs ⇨ Accessories ⇨ System Tools and click Disk Cleanup. Eliminate any temp files and other unnecessary garbage with this handy utility.

Be sure to empty the Recycle Bin!

TIP Defragmenting the hard drive is also a good practice. In XP, click Start, then navigate to All Programs ⇨ Accessories ⇨ System Tools and click Disk Defragmenter. Even if the application says that you don't need to defrag the drive, do it. Doing so results in less fragmentation during the Windows Vista installation.

Checking the hard drive with ScanDisk or CHKDSK

Be sure the hard drive doesn't have any problems before you install Vista. Windows 9x versions have Scandisk, which you should run to check the drive. Windows XP users must use a utility called CHKDSK, which they can invoke by typing in some commands at a command prompt.

To run CHKDSK from Windows XP, follow these steps:

1. **Click Start ⇨ Run.**
2. **Type** CMD **into the text box and press the Enter key.** A command prompt appears.
3. **Type the following command into the command prompt, exactly as shown:** CHKDSK /F.

   CHKDSK is a disk-checking utility for NT-kernel operating systems such as Windows Vista. The "/F" switch tells CHKDSK to fix any problems it encounters, if it can.
4. **Press Enter.** The command prompt box that appears informs you that you have to reboot to check the drive. It also asks whether you want to run CHKDSK on the next reboot.
5. **Press the Y key to indicate "yes."**
6. **Reboot the PC and allow CHKDSK to check the hard drive.** If it encounters any problems, it repairs anything it can automatically. If it finds problems it cannot repair, consider replacing the drive before you install Windows Vista.

Downloading Vista modem or network interface drivers

You can grab drivers for everything after you get Vista installed and online, but you may need drivers for your LAN or modem devices. If you have a cable, DSL, fiber, or T1 Internet connection, check online for Vista drivers for your computer's LAN device. If you're using dial-up, check for modem drivers.

To check for drivers, go to the manufacturer's Web site. If the LAN device is built into the motherboard, go to the motherboard maker's Web site for driver updates. Download them, and then place them on removable media (for example, burn them to an optical disc). If no Vista drivers are present, check with the manufacturer's tech support operators (via online chat, e-mail, or a phone call) to see whether you need Vista drivers, or whether Vista has built-in drivers for the device.

CAUTION If you fail to perform this crucial step and Windows Vista doesn't have its own drivers for your network device or modem, you might not be able to get online. If you can't get online, you can't upgrade Vista's other drivers, nor can you activate it online or update it with critical and optional updates.

Performing the upgrade

When the drive is streamlined and its integrity verified, and you've determined whether your computer needs Vista drivers for its network device, you can start the Windows Vista upgrade process. Place the Windows Vista DVD-ROM into the DVD drive and watch for the autorun window (Figure 2.16) to appear.

FIGURE 2.16

Vista's autorun window in Windows XP

Click the Install now button to start the installation process. The Windows Vista installer takes over from this point on.

It immediately starts asking for your assistance. Allow it to download updates for the installation on the first screen, shown in Figure 2.17.

It then asks for your Windows Vista product key (Figure 2.18). Type it in carefully. Don't type any dashes, as the Vista installer fills them in for you automatically.

FIGURE 2.17

Do download updates for installation, unless you're not online.

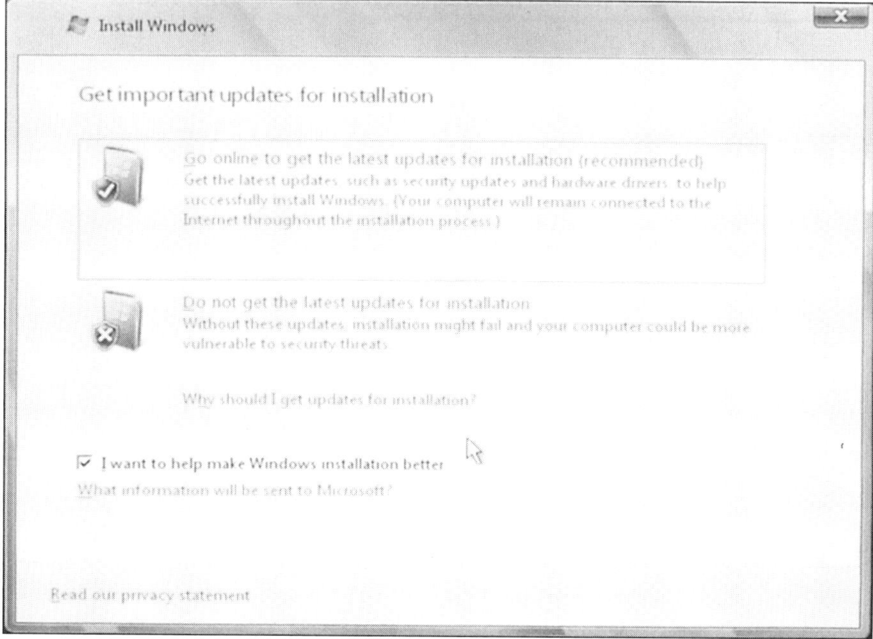

FIGURE 2.18

Enter your product key and click Next.

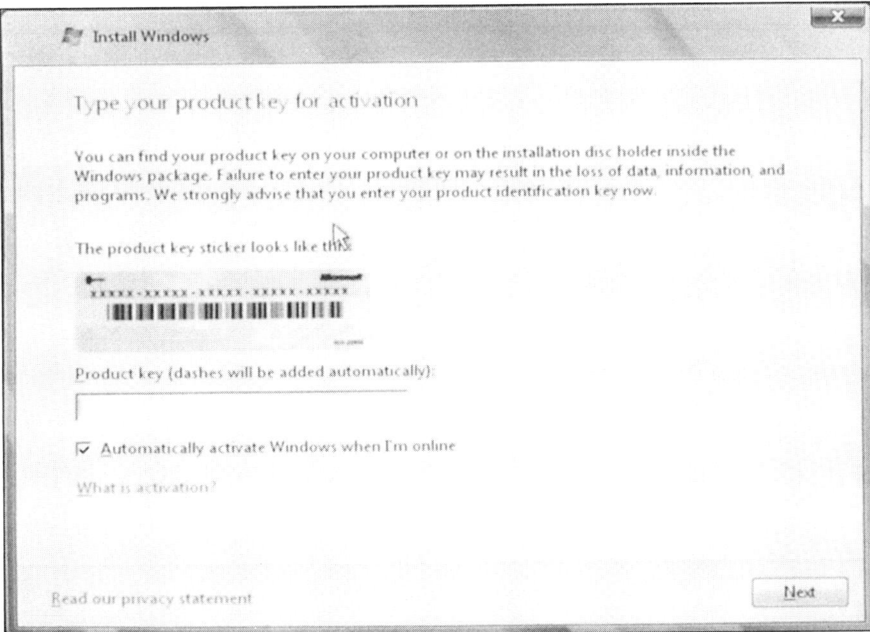

The EULA is next. Read it very carefully before you proceed with the installation. The EULA contains the terms and conditions under which you're allowed to use your copy of Windows Vista. Click the check box to accept the terms and then click Next.

The installation process continues by asking which type of installation you want to proceed with: an upgrade or a custom installation (Figure 2.19). Click Upgrade.

FIGURE 2.19

Click Upgrade to proceed.

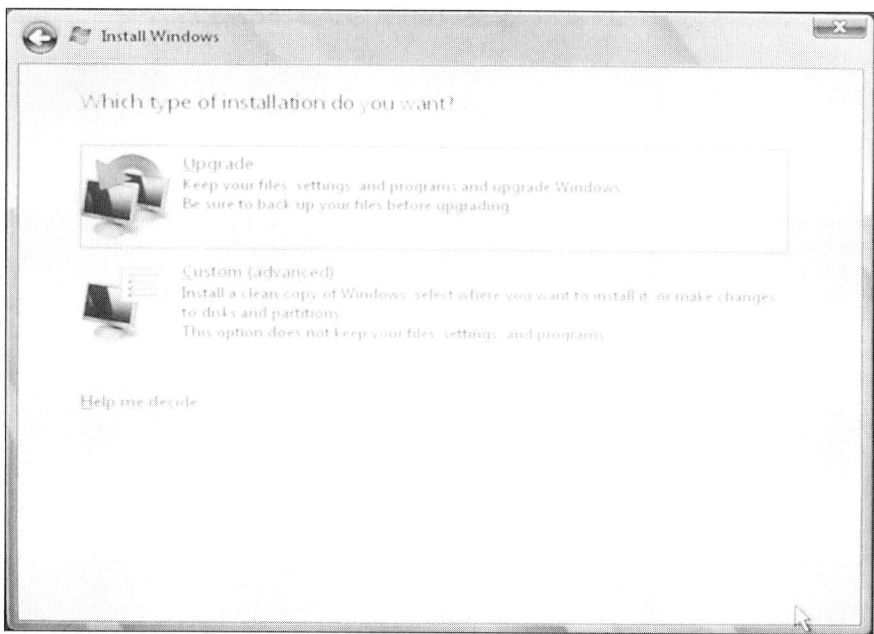

Next, Windows Vista's installer might show you a compatibility report, as shown in Figure 2.20. It might inform you that some of your programs or device drivers aren't compatible with Windows Vista. Observe it, and jot down the information if you want to (although it will also be saved to your desktop). You'll have to hunt the Web for updates after the upgrade is complete.

FIGURE 2.20

Vista will save the compatibility report to your desktop.

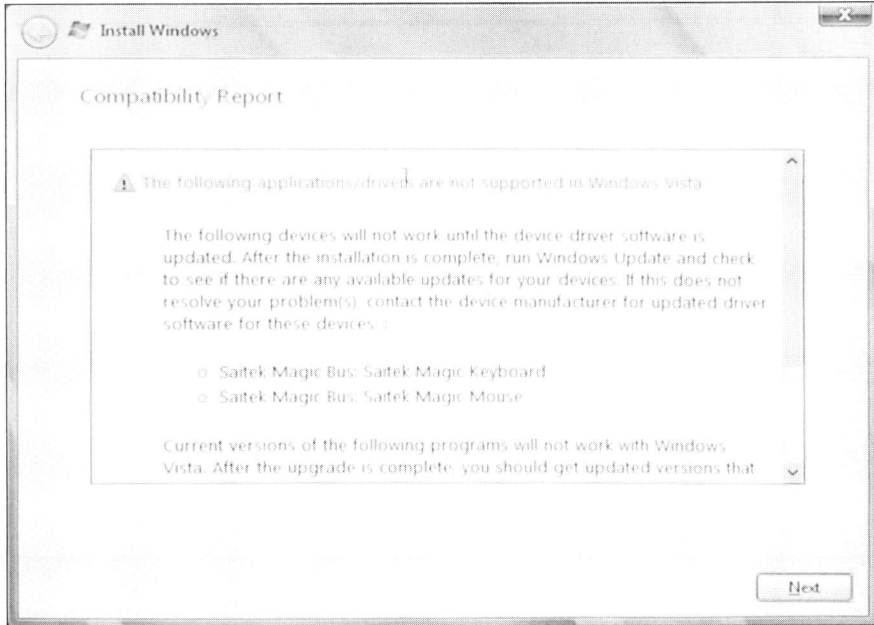

Sit back and wait a while. As shown in Figure 2.21, the installer now performs five steps, showing you its progress as it meanders through each one.

FIGURE 2.21

The Vista installer takes a while to copy files and perform other tasks.

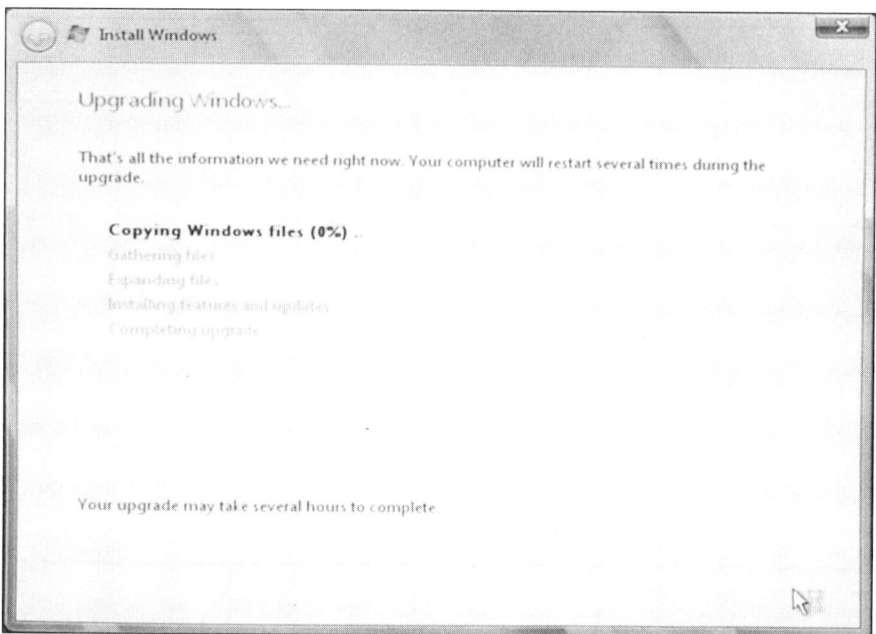

Note that an upgrade can take much longer than a fresh installation. I did both, several times, and the upgrades invariably took more than an hour whereas the fresh installations generally took about 45 minutes or so.

When Windows Vista's installer finally gets caught up, a security options screen appears, like the one shown in Figure 2.22. It offers you three choices:

- Use recommended settings
- Install important updates only
- Ask me later

Use the recommended settings for the most secure system; you can always alter them later.

FIGURE 2.22

Security settings made simple

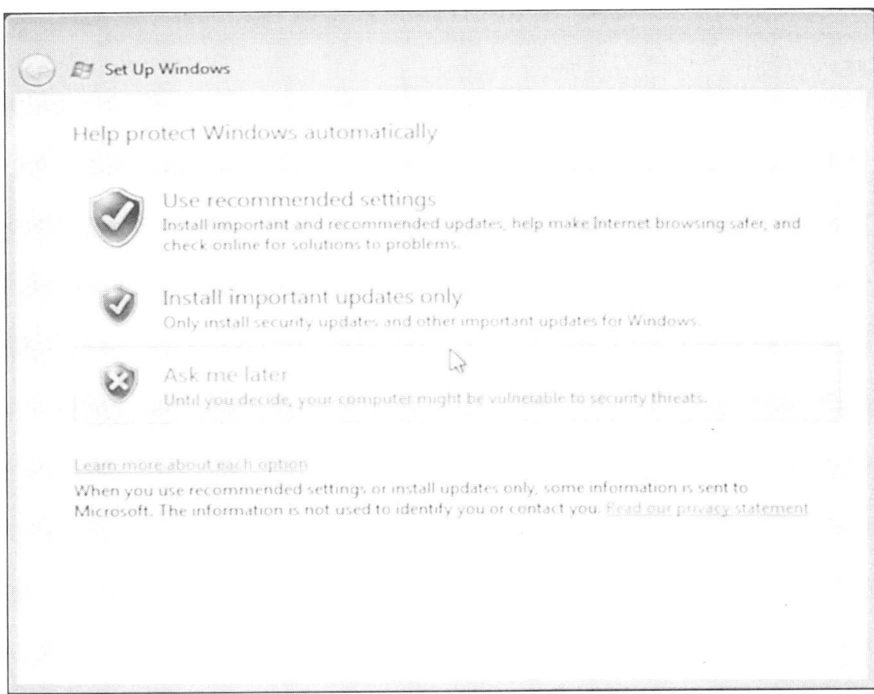

Next up is the time zone screen (Figure 2.23). Tell Windows Vista what time zone you live in and what day and time it is right now, and click Next.

Finally, Windows Vista wants know where your computer is for both security and network sharing purposes (Figure 2.24). Click the appropriate option, whether you're at home, at work, or on the road.

FIGURE 2.23

This screen wants to know what time it is.

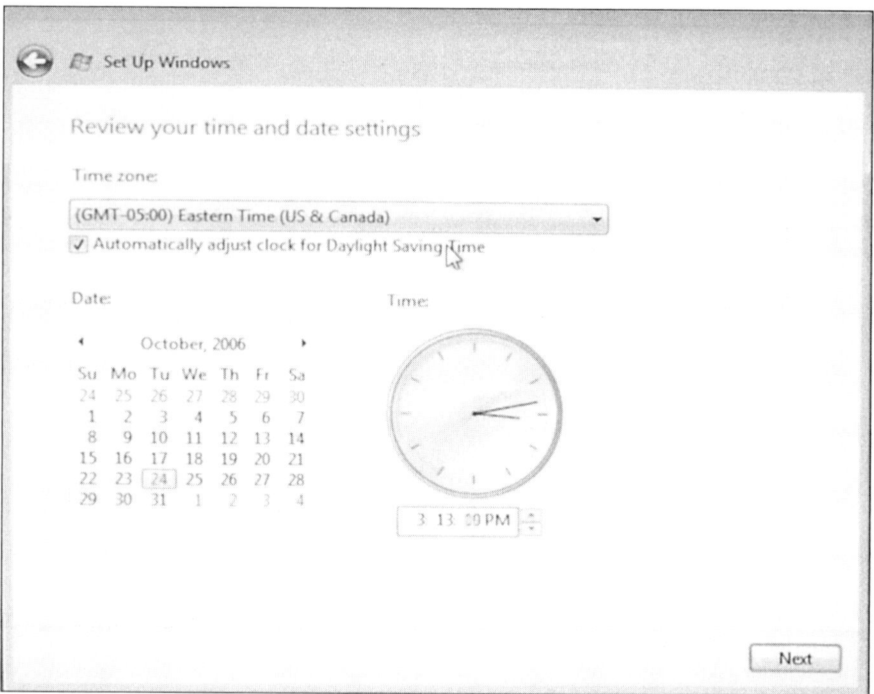

After you click past a Thank You screen, Windows Vista starts.

NOTE You may notice quite a delay between your clicking past the last screen and the Windows Vista desktop appearing. The hard drive will probably churn away for several minutes. Let it do its thing; it's working as fast as it can.

FIGURE 2.24

The Vista installer will take a while to copy files and perform other tasks.

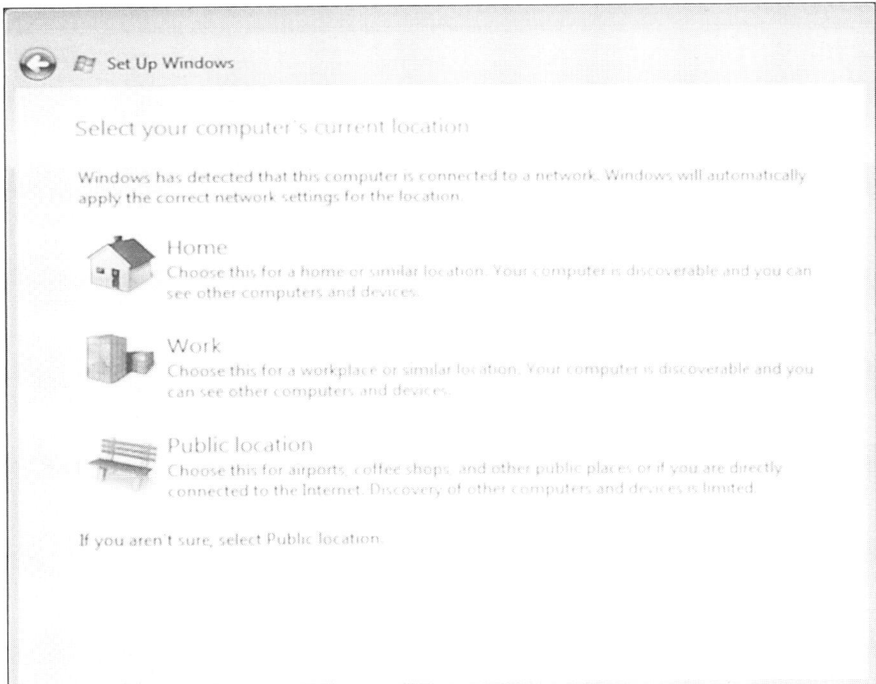

You may notice that some compatibility error messages appear as the desktop comes up. This means that you'll have to upgrade or remove any programs that aren't compatible with Windows Vista. If the upgrade encounters compatibility problems, a compatibility report, in the form of an HTML file, will appear on your desktop somewhere. Double-click it to open and view it. The compatibility report I received for my upgrade is shown in Figure 2.25.

FIGURE 2.25

Inevitably, some programs won't be compatible with Windows Vista.

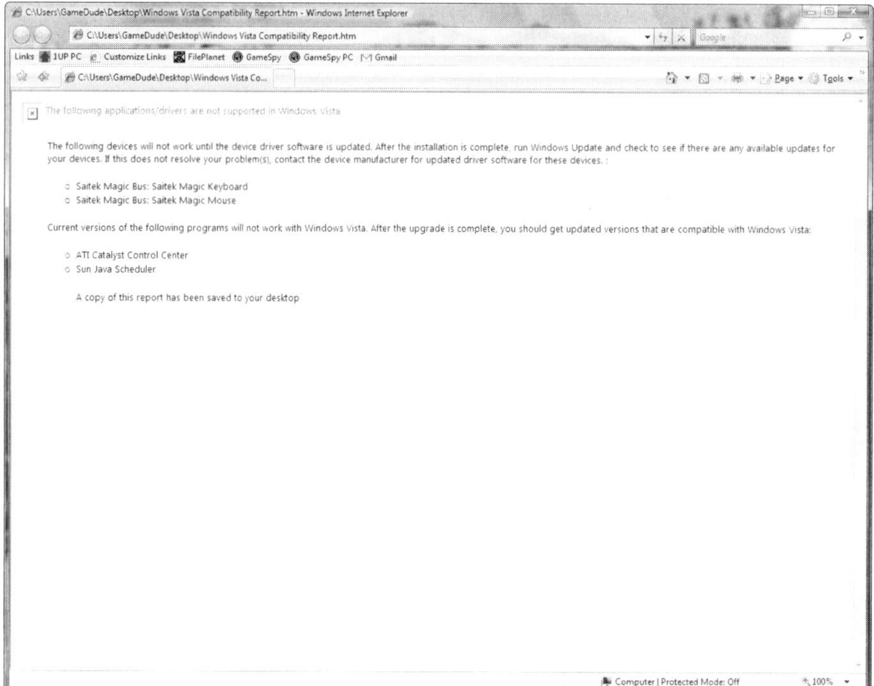

Performing the Finishing Touches

With the Windows Vista installation complete, you now have a variety of tasks to perform before you're really ready to use it. The first task to do is ensure that your computer has Internet access; if it doesn't, you won't be able to perform the next steps, which are to activate and update Windows Vista.

After you've updated the operating system, you must then update the device drivers for the important components in your system, including the graphics card, the audio device, and possibly the motherboard chipset. Other drivers that may be lurking around in need of updating are your system's LAN device drivers, its modem drivers, its printer drivers, drivers for various peripherals like keyboards and joysticks, and so on.

Establishing Net access

Windows Vista is very good at feeling out preexisting home networks. If your computer is connected to a LAN or a wireless LAN, and Windows Vista has the proper drivers for the computer's network interface, the operating system will probably find the network. Furthermore, if a shared or direct Internet connection exists, Vista will most likely find its way online without your help.

If it doesn't, you probably need to install drivers for your computer's network interface. If you upgraded from Windows XP or another version of Windows, you should have paid heed to my advice and downloaded the proper drivers before you installed Vista. Install them now.

After you install the driver, Vista will, again, probably find its way to your network. If it doesn't, you need to set up a network.

See Chapter 12 for instructions on setting up your home network.

If you're using a dial-up connection, Vista will either detect your modem and install its own drivers, or you'll need to install modem drivers yourself. Because Internet service providers differ in how they allow dial-in customers to use their services, you need to contact your ISP for instructions on dialing in from Windows Vista.

Updating and activating Windows Vista

If during the installation you chose to have Windows activate automatically, Windows will go ahead and activate itself three days after you log in for the first time. If you didn't opt for automatic activation, you can activate Windows Vista manually.

Activation is mandatory; if you don't activate Windows within a certain time period, it will lose most of its functionality.

To activate Windows Vista manually, follow these steps:

1. **Click the Start button (the round button in the bottom-left corner of the screen).**
2. **Click Control Panel.** The Control panel opens, as shown in Figure 2.26.

FIGURE 2.26

Windows Vista's Control Panel

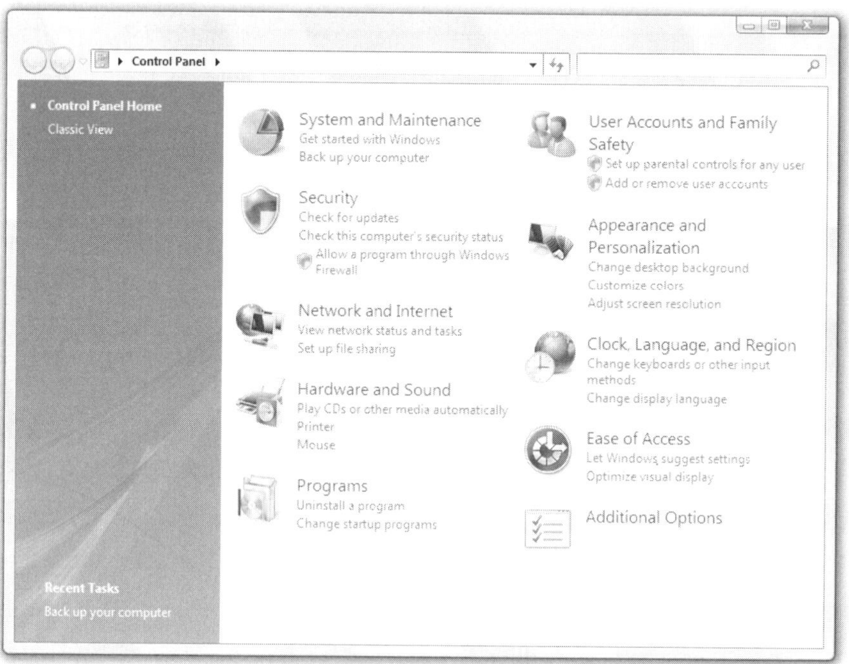

3. **In the Control Panel, click System and Maintenance.** The System and Maintenance window opens, as shown in Figure 2.27.

FIGURE 2.27

The System and Maintenance window

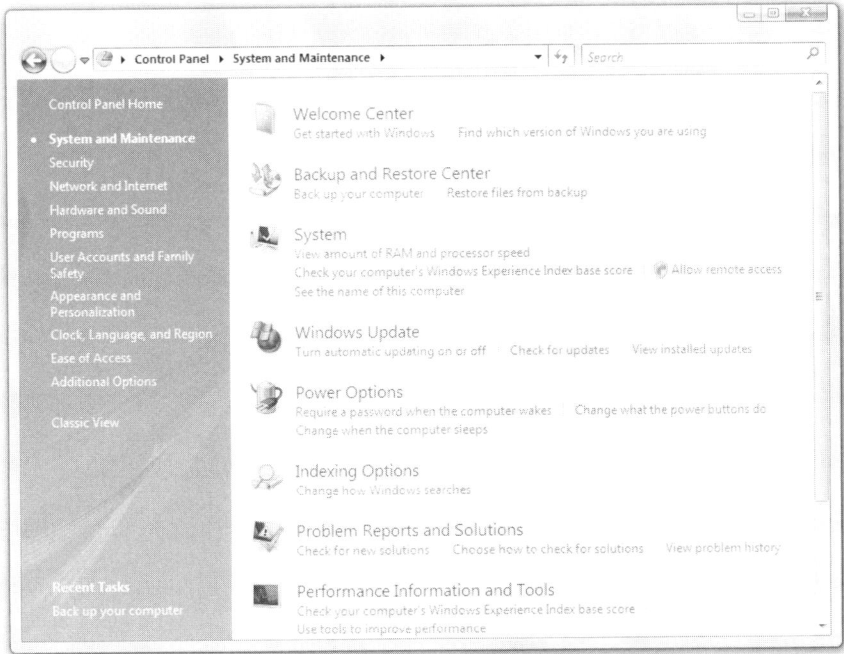

4. **Click System and scroll down to the bottom of the window.** This is where Windows tells you how much longer you have to activate Vista (Figure 2.28).
5. **Click Activate Windows Now.** A new window appears, as shown in Figure 2.29.

FIGURE 2.28

The System panel with the activation link at the bottom

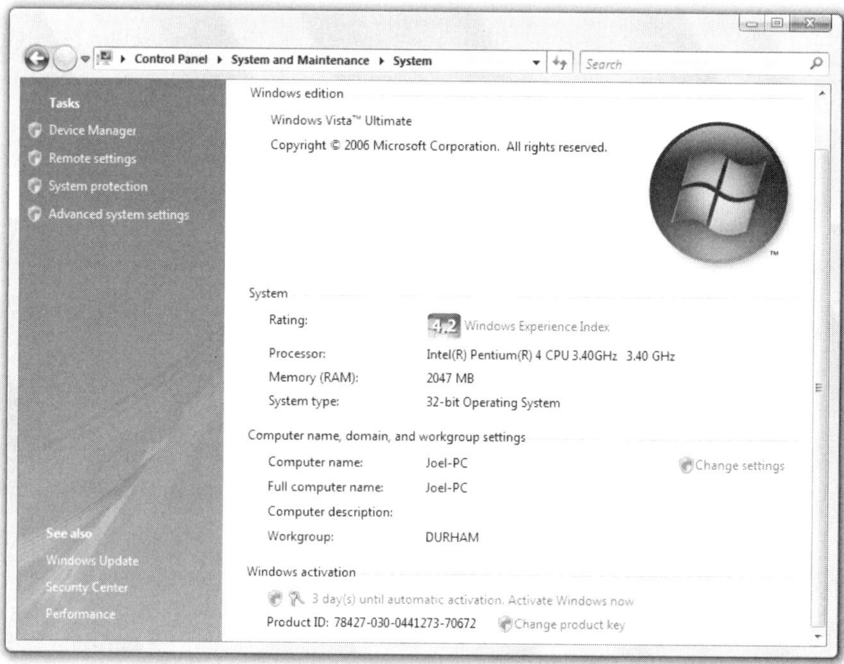

FIGURE 2.29

Getting ready to activate Windows

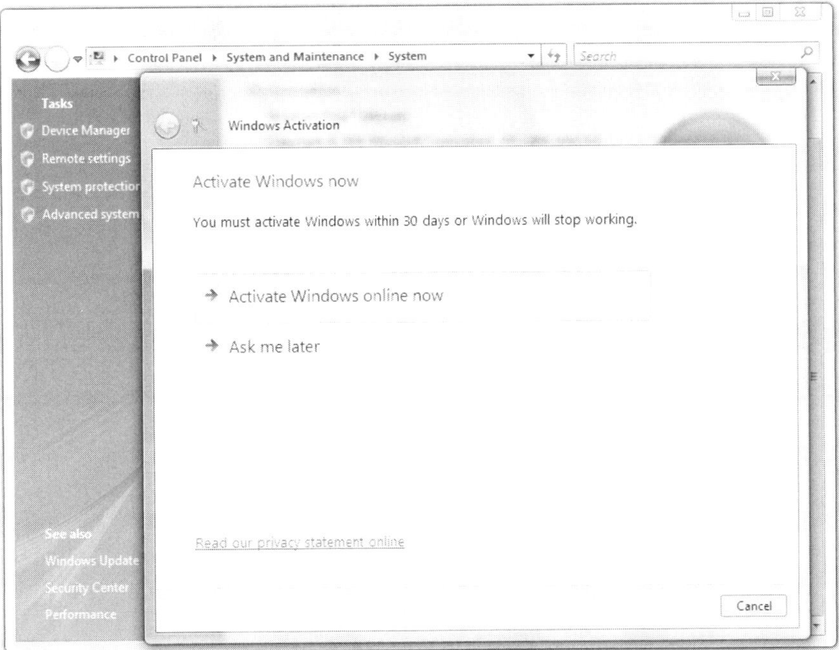

6. **Click Activate Windows Online Now.** Windows displays a progress bar (Figure 2.30). When activation is complete, an Activation Was Successful window appears, as shown in Figure 2.31. If the activation fails, the window may present you with a toll-free number to call to activate the operating system.

FIGURE 2.30

Activating Windows

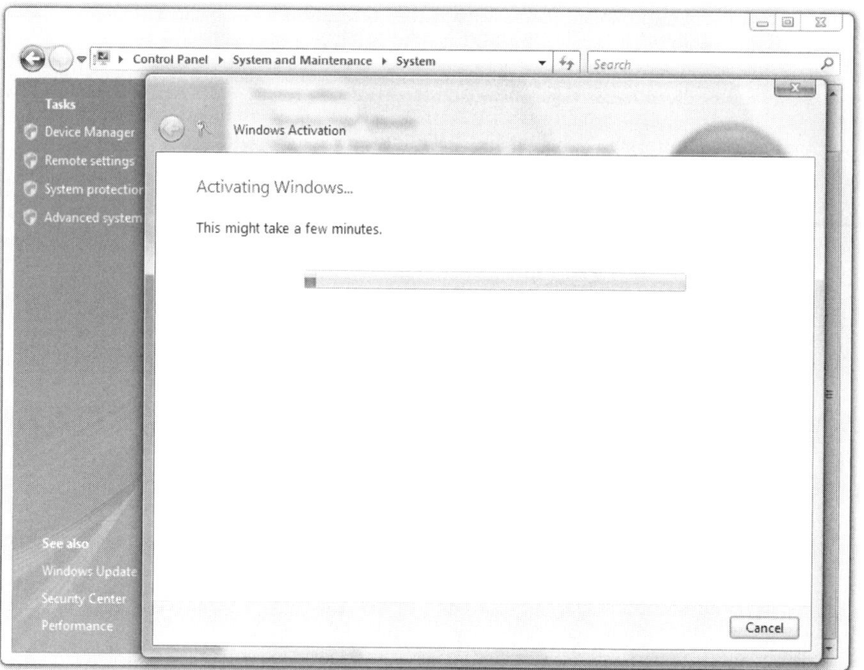

FIGURE 2.31

Finished with activation

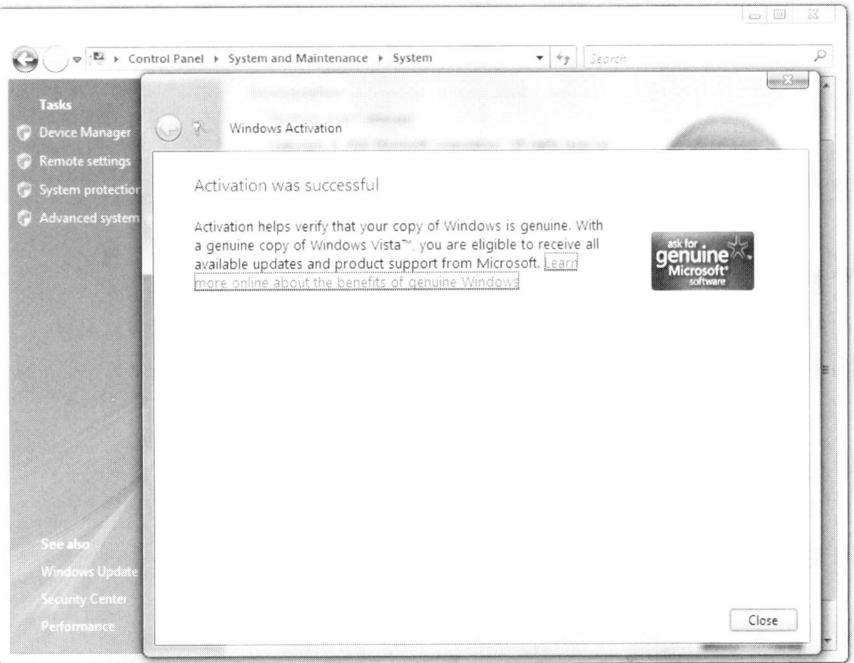

Windows might prompt you to install updates shortly after it realizes it's online. Regardless, be sure that all the critical updates are installed by checking them manually. Follow these steps:

1. **Click Start ➪ All Programs.**
2. **Click Windows Update.** The screen shown in Figure 2.32 appears.

3. **Click Check for Updates, a link in the upper-left side of the window.** Windows checks for updates (Figure 2.33).
4. **If Windows finds updates, it prompts you for permission to install them.** Always install critical updates, as they often contain security fixes and other important patches.

FIGURE 2.32

Windows Update

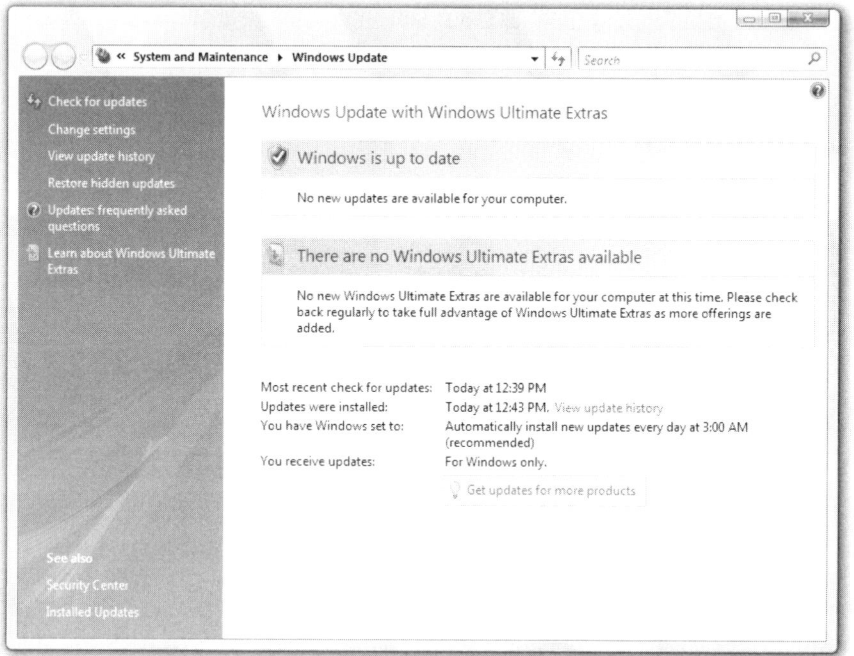

FIGURE 2.33

Checking for updates

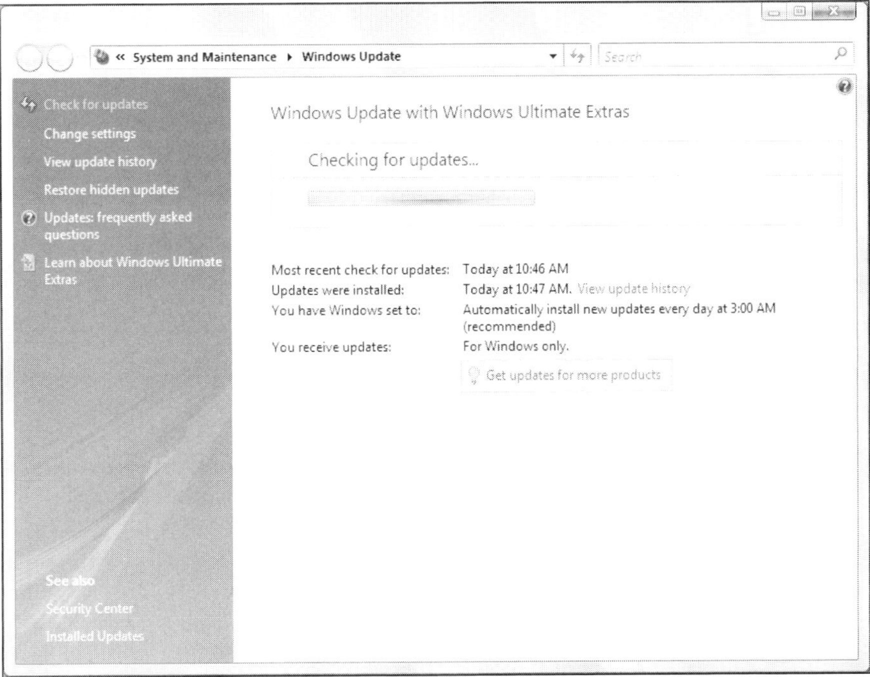

Updating your device drivers

Your next task is to update your system's device drivers. Some, but not all, of your system's components use drivers that are frequently updated, especially the graphics card, the audio device, and the motherboard chipset.

You need to visit the Web pages of each of the manufacturers' devices that your computer contains. Make a list and check it twice, and include the graphics, audio, and motherboard components, as well as networking, modem, keyboard, printer, mouse, joystick, gamepad, and anything else that might require a driver. Then, update the drivers methodically.

Use Internet Explorer (see Chapter 13) to navigate to the Web pages of those manufacturers, like ATI' s Web site shown in Figure 2.34.

Navigate to the support or download section of the Web site, and hunt for Windows Vista drivers for your product. Make sure you get the drivers right for your operating system's bit width! The x86 drivers are for the Windows Vista 32-bit versions, whereas x64 drivers are for Windows Vista's 64-bit platforms. Verify that you're downloading the proper driver and save it to your computer's hard drive.

The vast majority of drivers come with executable setup files that make the driver upgrade incredibly simple. ATI's graphics card drivers, for example, install very easily.

FIGURE 2.34

ATI's (really, AMD's) Web site contains driver updates for its products.

To install them, I launch the .EXE file that I downloaded. When I run the file it offers several prompts for me to follow, then it upgrades the drivers to the latest version.

Let's run through an example of a driver upgrade, this time for a SoundBlaster X-Fi audio card:

1. **You need a driver, so open Internet Explorer and visit** `www.soundblaster.com`, **whose home page is shown in Figure 2.35.**

FIGURE 2.35

The Creative Labs' SoundBlaster Web site

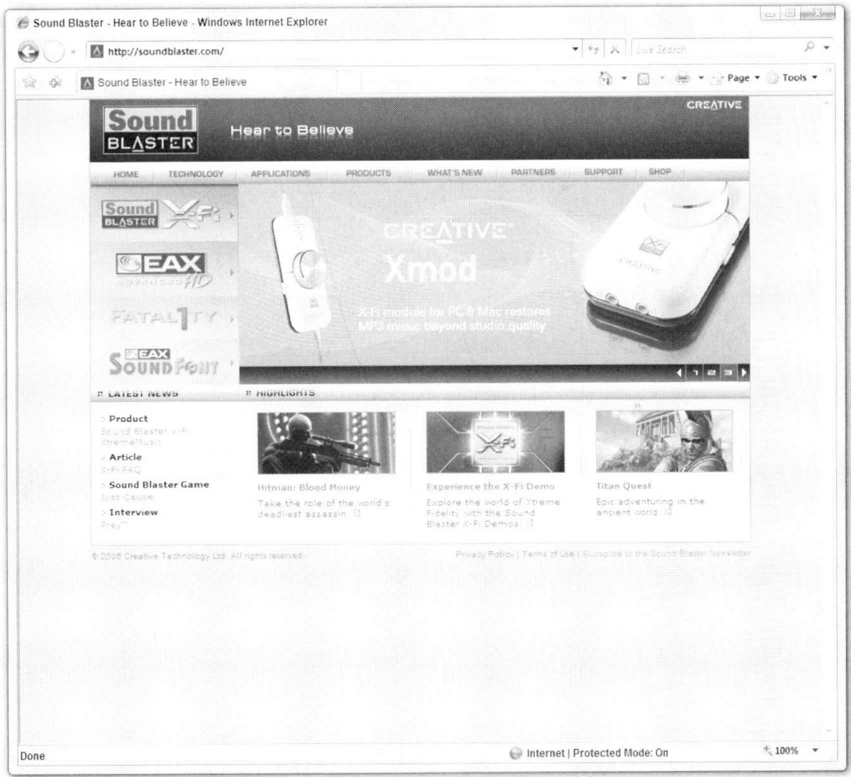

2. **Click the Support button.** The page shown in Figure 2.36 opens.

FIGURE 2.36

Creative Labs' support page

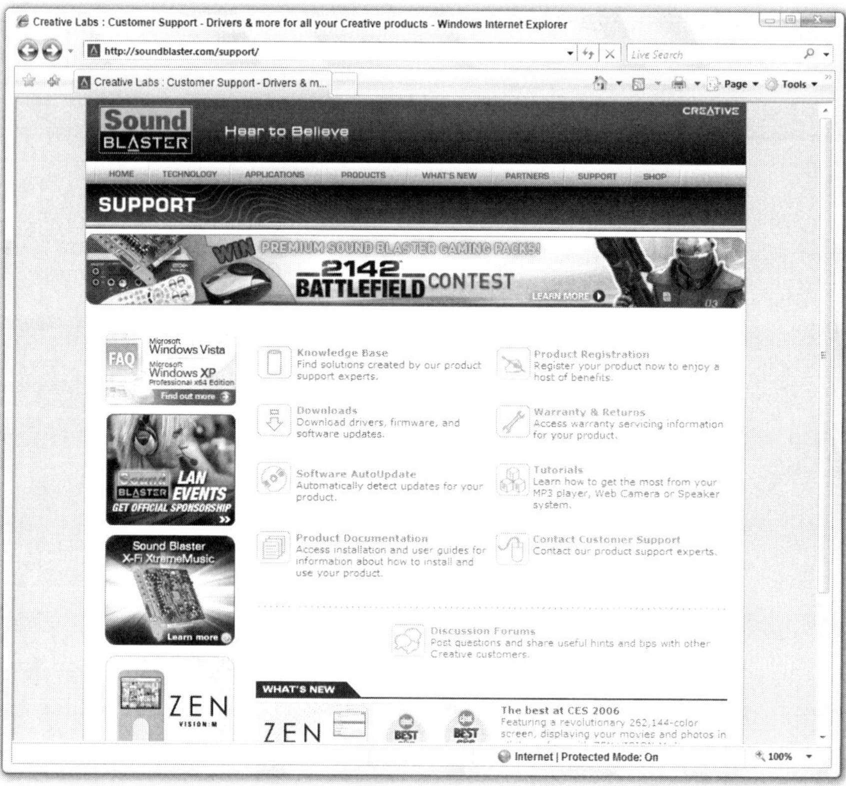

3. **Select your region on the next page, and then your product on the next (Figure 2.37), and click the Go! button to download the new driver.** Internet Explorer asks where you want to download it, the default destination being the Downloads folder. When the download completes, a screen that looks like Figure 2.38 appears.

FIGURE 2.37

Provide information for your driver download.

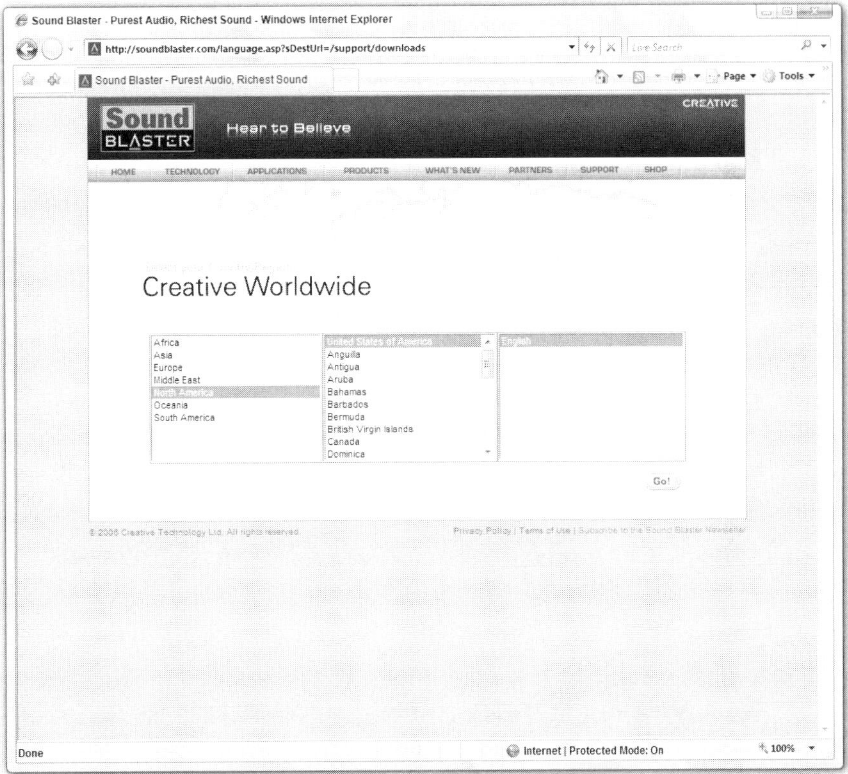

FIGURE 2.38

You can launch the driver upgrade now.

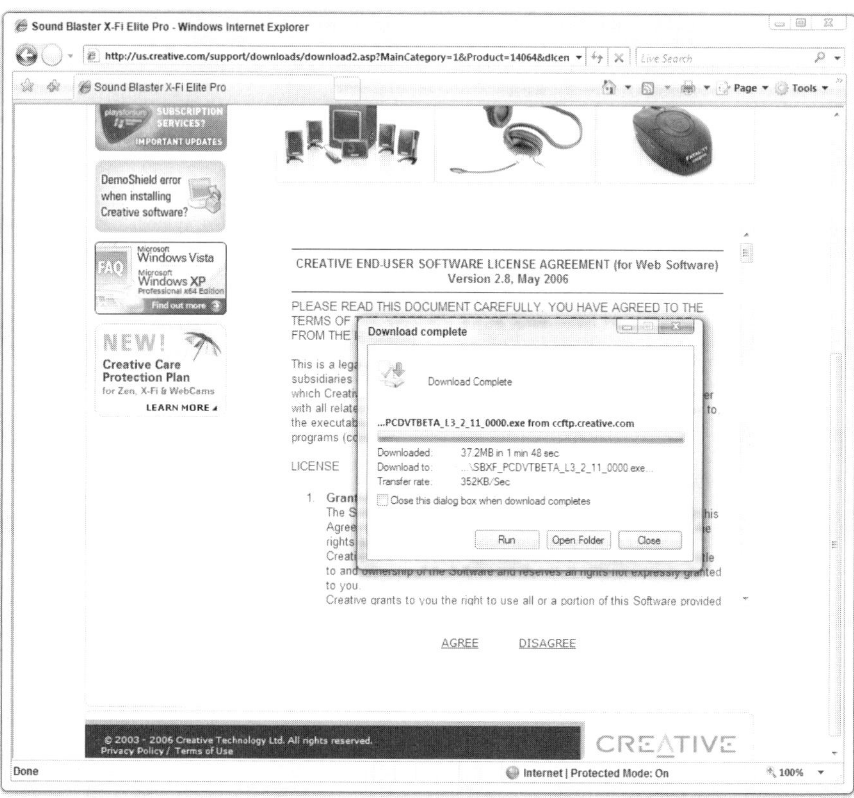

4. To open the file, either click Open on the download dialog box, or launch the file through the file system by navigating to the Downloads folder (or whatever folder you downloaded it to).

CROSS-REF See Chapter 3 for details on navigating through Windows Vista Ultimate.

NOTE You should close all of your open programs before you start the driver update. Many driver installations actually prompt you to shut down open programs, as does the Creative Labs updater.

5. **After it launches, the driver extracts files and prompts you to close any open programs, which you should do.** Then, a security warning might appear, asking whether you want to install the driver, as shown in Figure 2.39.

   Other security warnings might appear as well. Because you know you're purposely installing a device driver and any applications that come with it, don't worry about the warnings.

6. **Click Install to allow the installation to proceed.** When the installation is complete, in this case, Vista offers to restart the computer, as shown in Figure 2.40. Many driver installations require a reboot before they're truly finished.

7. **Go ahead and reboot the computer, as long as you don't have open files that may not have been saved.**

FIGURE 2.39

Windows won't install the driver without your permission.

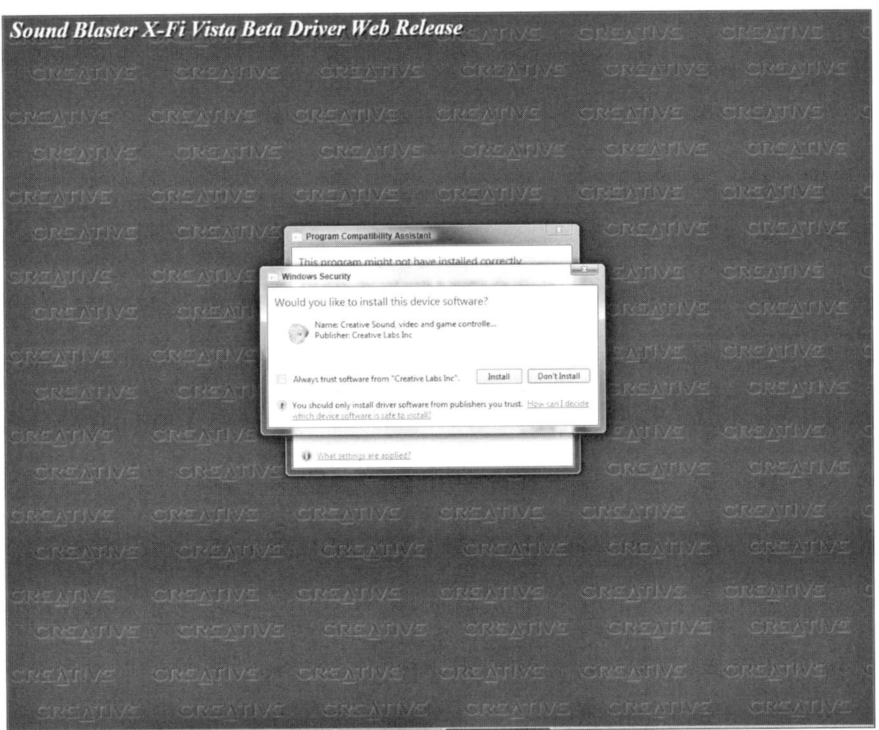

FIGURE 2.40

It's time to reboot.

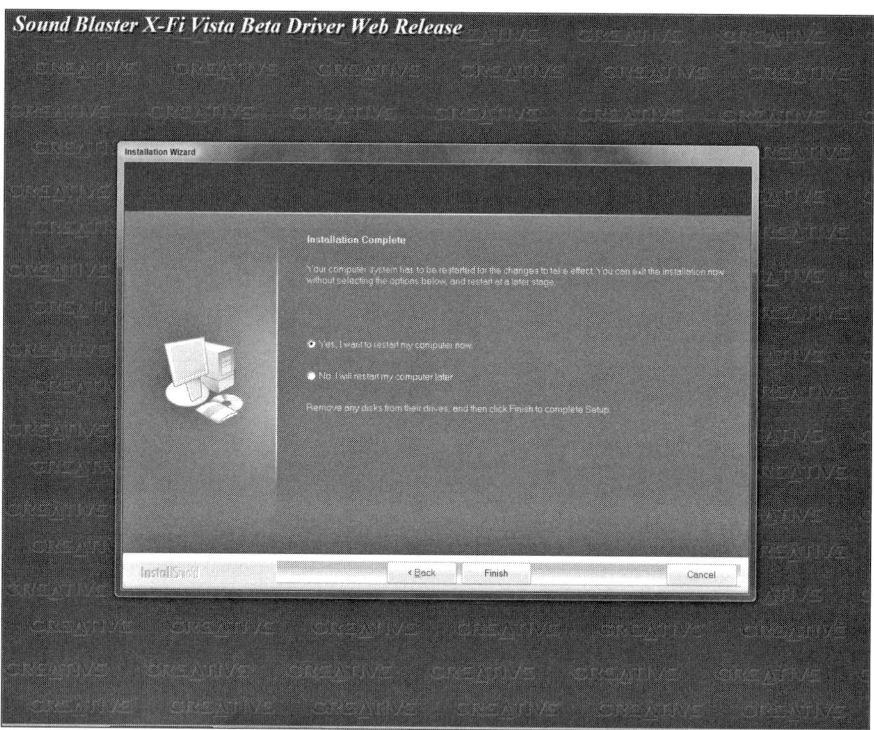

Update the drivers for all the hardware that needs drivers. Some components that *don't* need special drivers are hard drives, floppy drives, and optical drives. Windows often has proper drivers preloaded for certain motherboards, networking equipment, modems, and other components—but check the manufacturer's Web sites (or the Web site of your computer's manufacturer) to be sure there aren't any updates.

NOTE You need to keep your system's drivers up to date on an ongoing basis. That means you need to check the hardware manufacturers' Web sites regularly for new drivers for your system's hardware.

Graphics card drivers are updated especially frequently. The major players in the performance graphics market, Nvidia and AMD/ATI, have entire teams of dedicated programmers working on drivers all the time. New drivers can deliver increases in both performance and stability.

Make it a habit to check for new drivers for your system's hardware at least once each month, and check for graphics hardware drivers once a week or so. Keeping drivers up to date is a must.

Getting Started

Windows Vista presents you with a screen full of things to do right after installation. This window is called the Welcome Center and it looks like the window shown in Figure 2.41.

The Welcome Center appears each time Windows starts until you uncheck the box at the bottom instructing it to do so. You can always launch the Welcome Center through the Start Menu.

The Welcome Center contains a number of links. The first category, Get Started with Windows, is expandable; just click on the words *Show All 14 Items*. A window similar to the one shown in Figure 2.42 appears.

FIGURE 2.41

Windows Vista's Welcome Center

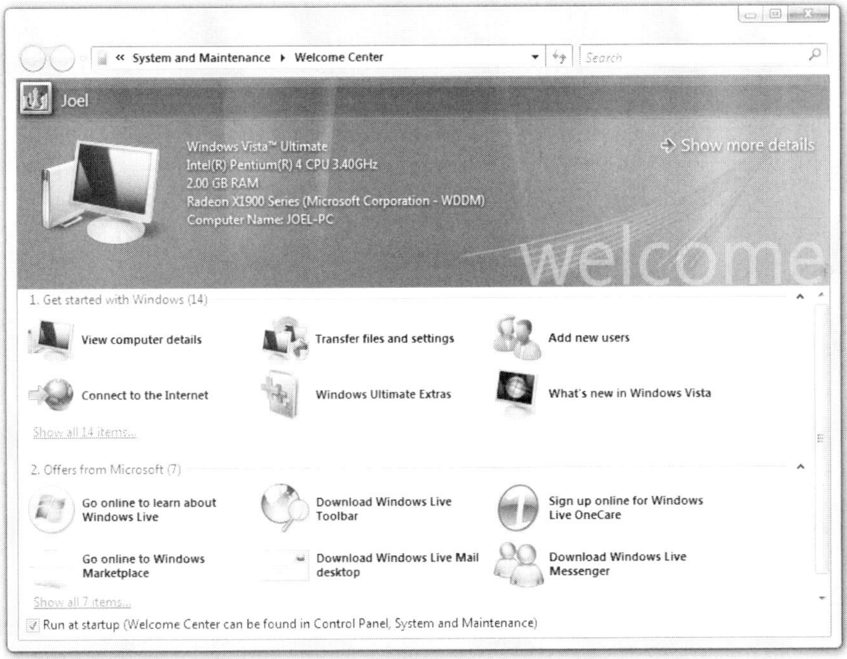

FIGURE 2.42

Things to do to get started with Windows Vista

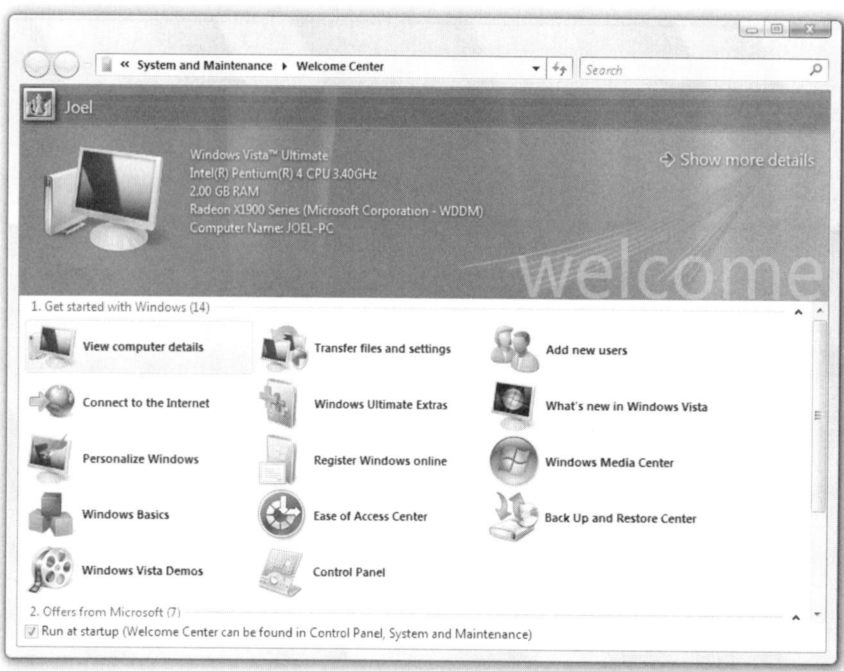

Check out the options that help you get started. You can get a look at Windows basics, check out demos in the form of media clips, personalize Windows, establish an Internet connection, and much more.

When you click on an item in the Welcome Center, the top area of the Welcome Center window provides a link to further explore the pertinent option. Items shown in the Welcome Center include:

- **View computer details:** Click this option to check out some of the specifications of the computer upon which you've just installed Windows Vista.
- **Transfer files and settings:** You can use Windows Easy Transfer to transfer files and settings from a different computer running Windows XP or Vista.
- **Add new users:** Use this option to add more user accounts to your computer. Each person can have his or her own user account with his or her own personal folders and settings.
- **Connect to the Internet:** This option helps you gain Internet access from the computer upon which you've just installed Vista.

- **Windows Ultimate Extras:** Check out programs, utilities, and other goodies that Microsoft offers for download exclusively to Windows Vista Ultimate users.
- **What's new in Windows Vista:** Click this option to see what Windows Vista has to offer that isn't available in previous versions of Windows operating systems.
- **Personalize Windows:** Click here to explore ways to make Windows Vista your own, such as changing the desktop background, the screen saver, fonts, sounds, and more.
- **Register Windows online:** This invokes the utterly optional Windows Vista Registration through Internet Explorer 7+.
- **Windows Media Center:** If your computer is serving as a media center PC (if it's connected to a television, for instance, or if it's part of an entertainment center) you should check out this option.
- **Windows Basics:** If you're brand new to a graphical user interface such as Windows, this option will instruct you from the ground up, including mastering the mouse and dealing with the file system.
- **Ease of Access Center:** Full of options for the disabled, this feature offers different ways to make it easier to see, hear, and deliver input to the computer.
- **Back Up and Restore Center:** It's a good habit to back up your important files on a regular basis. Click here to find out more about Windows Vista's backup and restore options.
- **Windows Vista Demos:** Not sure how to use the computer? Would video-based guidelines help? Click here.
- **Control Panel:** Click here to explore the Control Panel, which is where you can adjust hundreds of options regarding how you use your computer. Control Panel is the central location for all of Windows Vista's various settings.
- **Offers from Microsoft:** Microsoft provides a number of shortcuts to venture online and learn about various products and services the company offers to Windows Vista users.

Summary

Installing Windows Vista is quite simple, really. It does almost all the installation for you, only asking you for information that it absolutely cannot figure out on its own. It's the most hands-off installation routine available. Although this means that less customization upon installation is available than there was in earlier versions of Windows, that's okay because Windows Vista is amazingly customizable after the installation.

You have to take steps to prepare for an installation, especially if you're upgrading from an earlier version of Windows. The chapter demonstrates an upgrade from Windows XP that went smoothly; not all operating system installations do. *Back up your files* before you upgrade your copy of Windows or, better yet, install it on a fresh hard drive.

Even after all the files are copied and decompressed, you have more to do before you can really dig into the new operating system. You should activate it and update it right away, as critical updates often patch security flaws — at least, they did in prior versions of Windows. You should also update your system's device drivers, and then be sure to keep them up to date.

When the installation is complete, it's activated, and the drivers are in, Windows Vista is ready for prime time. Check out the Welcome Center to get started with essential tasks and education regarding the new operating system.

Chapter 3

Navigating Windows Vista Ultimate

IN THIS CHAPTER

Finding your stuff

Navigating the new shell

Searching in Windows Vista

When the Windows operating system made the leap from 3.x to 95, the transition was jarring. Users experienced a period of unfamiliarity, with the comfort of easily knowing where to find all their programs and utilities temporarily swept away. The awkward phase was worth it, though, because once users grew used to the Windows 95 system, with its Start Menu and right-click context menus, they found the new interface to be easier, more graceful, and less cluttered.

Such will probably be the case with Windows Vista. Having implemented sweeping changes to the shell, Microsoft has again turned the familiar upside-down, but once you get the hang of it you'll likely grow to love it.

The branching and mutating Start Menu is gone, replaced by a cleaner and more organized interface. The ubiquitous toolbar menus (File, Edit, View, and so on) are also missing from the navigation windows and replaced by a contextual toolbar whose menu buttons change depending on the function of the folder. Pictures, music, videos, and even games are better organized into their respective folders. The interface for navigating networks is centralized and streamlined. The window navigation interface meshes traditional icons with links, interactive path elements, and browser-like forward and back buttons. Sharing various items, both with other accounts on a single PC and with other computers across a network, is easier and more secure than ever.

The Windows search function is as fast as the best Internet search engine's Web search. When you search Windows Vista, the results appear instantly.

So where is everything and how do you do the simple tasks you're so used to doing? Read on.

Finding Your Stuff

Windows Vista organizes its programs and data in a similar fashion to Windows XP; it only looks different. For example, all the accessory programs (Calculator, Paint, Notepad, WordPad, and so on) are available; you just launch them a bit differently. When you right-click the empty desktop you might not see your graphic card's display properties as you would in Windows XP, but it's easy enough to get to. Let's look at this new shell and find the most important things.

The new Start Menu

Windows 95 changed the Windows operating system from a scattered mess of program groups to a stately and organized desktop interface. Everything you do in Windows begins with the Start Menu (with the exception of programs you launch through desktop icons, if you use them). The Start Menu for Vista will look unfamiliar at first; for Vista, Microsoft has redesigned the Start Menu most dramatically.

NOTE If you can't stand the new Start Menu and you pine for the classic, you can have it. Just click the Start button, find an empty area on the new Start Menu, and right-click. Click Properties. Then, click Classic Start Menu and click OK. You'll be back in business with nothing new to learn.

Take a look at the new Start Menu in Figure 3.1. You invoke it by clicking the round button with the Windows logo on the bottom left of the screen. You'll see several familiarities if you're a Windows XP veteran, but they feature a different look:

- The bulk of the window shows the most recently used programs.
- At the top left are links to your default browser and e-mail programs.
- Down the right side are links to special folders and other places.
- At the bottom left is a Search box, which allows you to quickly search the Internet or your computer.
- At the bottom right are options to put the computer to sleep and to lock the current user account, as well as an arrow button for more shutdown and logoff options.

Click All Programs to see a glaring change from old Windows conventions (Figure 3.2). Rather than ballooning into a larger menu, the Start Menu changes to reveal a list of its contents, with immediate links to commonly used programs. Applets and applications such as Windows Calendar, Windows Movie Maker, and Windows Photo Gallery are but a single click away. Below their entries are the traditional program groups, but once again, clicking on any of them does not cause the Start Menu to branch. Rather, it reveals their subfolders in the same window, as shown in Figure 3.3.

FIGURE 3.1

The new Start Menu's opening window

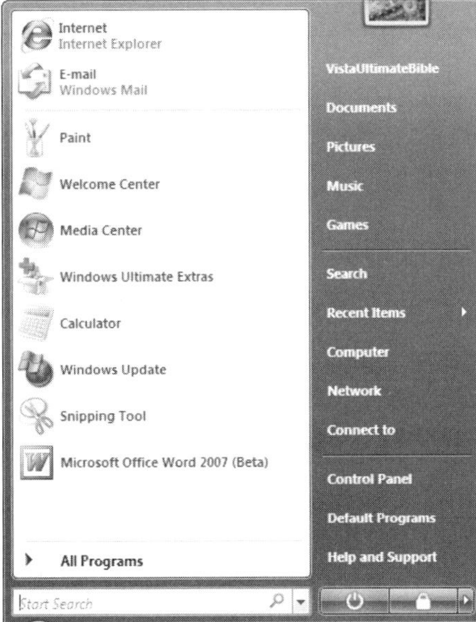

FIGURE 3.2

The All Programs button reveals common programs and program groups.

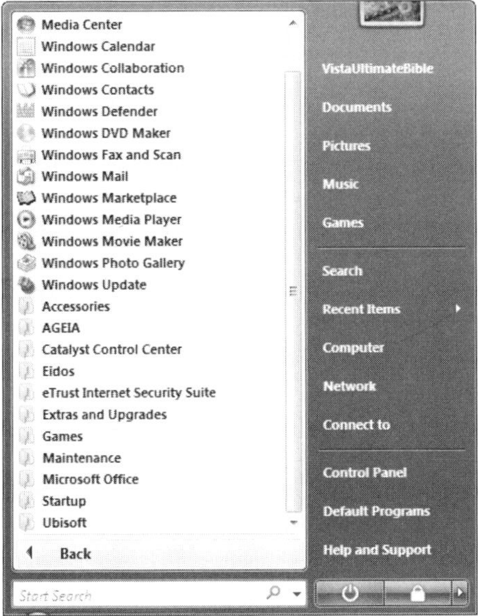

FIGURE 3.3

To reveal the contents of a program group, click it once. Here, I've clicked Accessories.

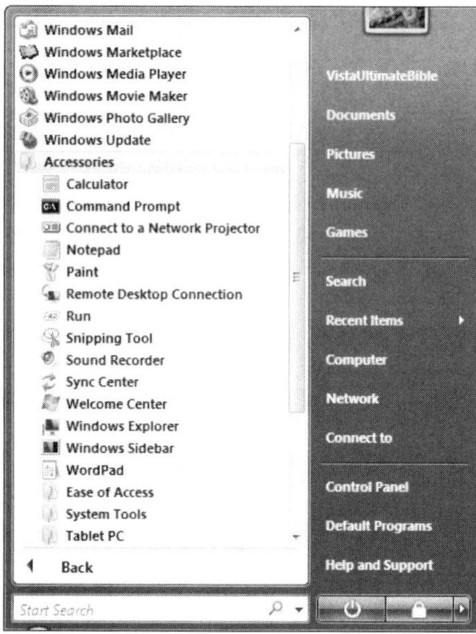

This Start Menu has a slider bar on the right. You can scroll through the Start Menu contents by sliding it up and down or by rolling your mouse wheel.

The Start Menu items on the right stay visible. They include the following:

- **Your user folder, named after your account name:** Mine is *VistaUltimateBible*. Clicking here opens a navigation window that shows the contents of a folder created especially for the current user account.
- **Documents:** This folder is the equivalent of the Windows XP My Documents folder. Click here to open a folder for anything you've saved in your Documents folder.
- **Pictures:** This link reveals a special folder for your image files, equivalent to the Windows XP My Pictures folder.
- **Music:** This link reveals a special folder for your audio files, equivalent to the Windows XP My Music folder.
- **Games:** This link invokes the Games folder, a central location for shortcuts to launch all the games you've installed in your computer.
- **Search:** Use this link to launch the Search interface.
- **Recent Items:** Hover over this entry to view documents, pictures, and other items you've recently opened. Right-click the link for more options, such as clearing its contents.

- **Computer:** Click this item to view the contents of your computer, similar to the My Computer interface from prior versions of Windows.
- **Network:** This link leads to an interface for navigating any networks your computer might be part of, similar to the Network Neighborhood window from Windows operating systems of yore.
- **Control Panel:** Click here to reveal the Control Panel, the central location for customizing Windows Vista and many of your computer's hardware devices.
- **Default Programs:** You can use this option to change the default programs associated with various file types, and the default programs used for various tasks like e-mail and Internet surfing.
- **Help and Support:** If you're looking for assistance with Windows Vista, this link is the place to get it.

See Chapter 9 for more details on getting help in Windows Vista.

Finally, you can click the picture attached to the upper right of the Start Menu to invoke the User Accounts dialog box. Here, you can make changes to your user account and manage other accounts if you have administrative privileges.

Your personal folders

The first five items in on the upper-right part of the Start Menu all call up the personal folders set aside specifically for your documents, pictures, music, and games. The top item, named after your account name, opens a folder for exploring special space assigned to you when your user account was created.

Click your user account name in the Start Menu to reveal a window like the one shown in Figure 3.4. You'll notice a number of subfolders already stored in your folder.

The Contacts subfolder is actually a mesh between a folder and an applet. If you open it by double-clicking it, you'll see an interface for storing information about people you know.

CROSS-REF See Chapter 13 for more information about the Contacts subfolder.

The Documents folder is intended for you to store data that you create with various programs and applications, such as Microsoft Office.

TIP You can open the Documents folder quickly by choosing Start ➪ Documents.

The Favorites folder contains your Internet Explorer favorites. The Music, Videos, and Pictures folders are intended for you to store your audio, video, and image files, respectively.

FIGURE 3.4

Your space: This area was set aside for you when your user account was created.

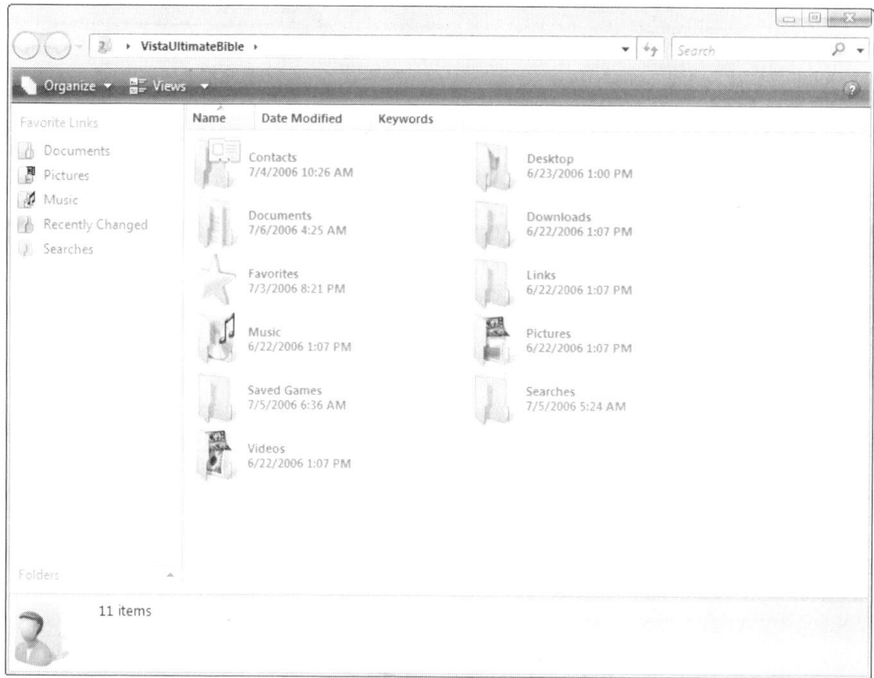

TIP You can open the Music and Pictures folders quickly by clicking the Start button and then clicking the appropriate link.

A Saved Games folder exists for saved game files. Hopefully, game developers will use it as the default location for game saves, but we'll have to wait and see.

Other folders include Desktop, which stores your various desktop icons, Download, which is a great place to save stuff you pull off the Web, and Searches, which stores your saved search files, discussed later in this chapter.

Some of the folders have special functions. The Pictures, Music, and Movies folders have special buttons in their toolbars for things like slideshows and playing music. You find out more about contextual toolbars shortly.

Navigating Through Windows

If you think the Start Menu looks odd, take a look at the windows. Invoke a window — for example, the Documents window (Start ➪ Documents). Mine is shown in Figure 3.5. Mildly familiar yet strikingly different, it holds a wealth of new functionality.

Links and icons

You'll notice several new things about ordinary navigation windows like these, besides the new Windows Aero look and feel. For one thing, the icons are significantly different, and more informative. To the left of the icon area is a column entitled Favorite Links. It shows a number of other folders to which you can navigate instantly with a single click.

Below that is the word *Folders*. Click it and a Windows Explorer–style map of the file system appears, as shown in Figure 3.6. You can navigate through it by single-clicking any of the folders shown; if a folder contains subfolders, a small arrow appears next to it. Click the arrow to expand the folder's contents.

FIGURE 3.5

The Documents window

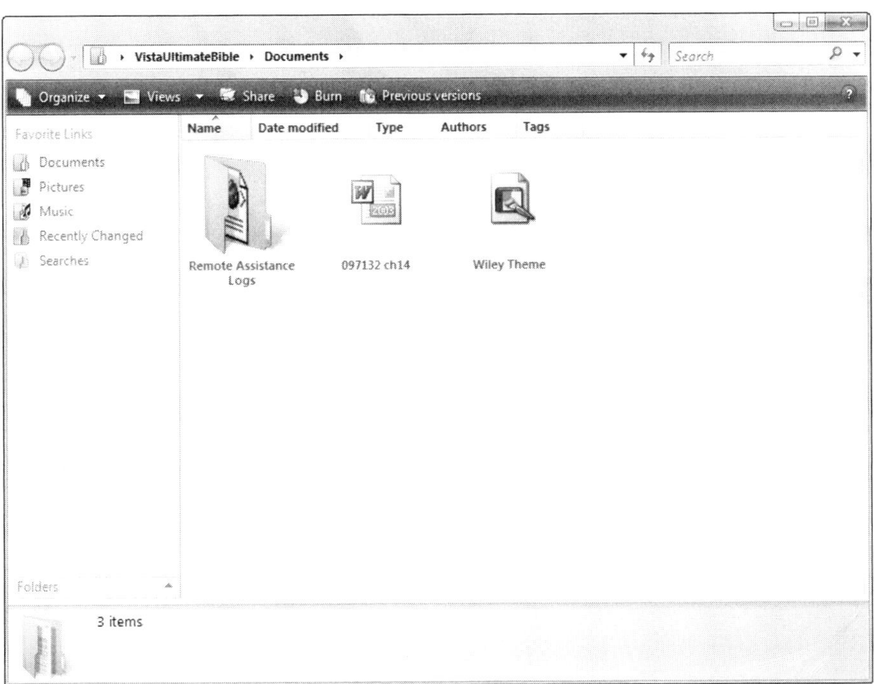

FIGURE 3.6

The Folders view lets you navigate quickly through the file system.

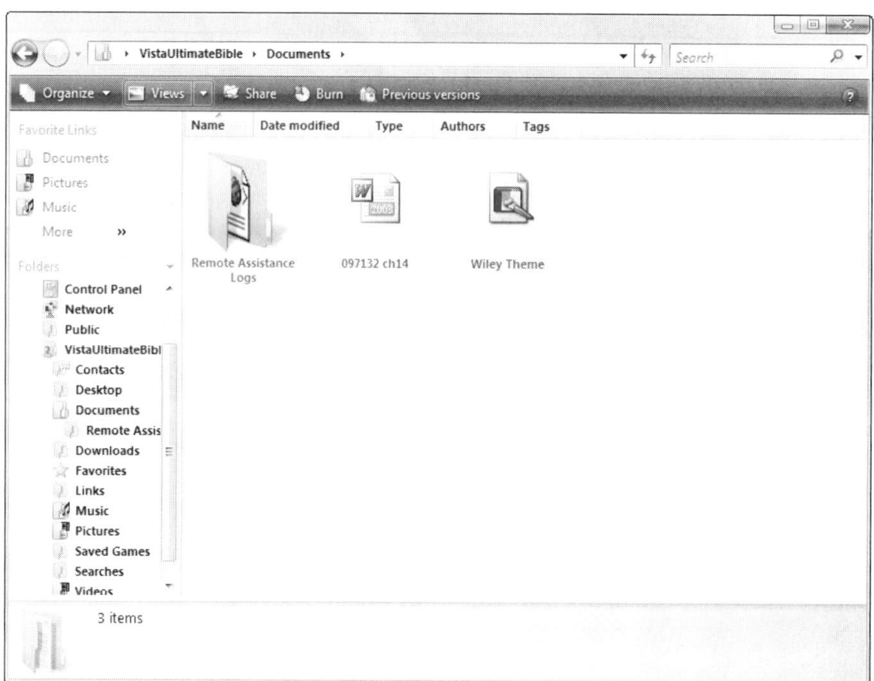

TIP You can add folders from this view to the Favorite Links area simply by dragging the folder from the Folders panel into the Favorite Links panel.

Contextual toolbars

Remember those drop-down menus from earlier versions of Windows, entitled File, Edit, View, and so on? They're gone. They've been replaced by buttons on a toolbar, which changes according to the function of the folder in which you're navigating.

Generally, you'll see an Organize button, a Views button, a Share button, and possibly others. The Organize button lets you create new folders; cut, copy, paste, undo, and redo; select everything in the folder; delete files; rename files; and more. One option in the Organize menu is called Layout, and it allows you to switch to the classic menu bar. It also lets you add a reading pane and a search pane to the folder.

The reading pane is interesting. If you click a file that Windows recognizes and for which it can generate a preview, the reading pane will function much like a preview pane in an e-mail program. For example, when you single-click a document file icon, a window something like the window shown in Figure 3.7 appears.

The lower area of the new folders view contains data about the currently selected file or subfolder. It can show all sorts of things, including the size of the file, the last time it was modified, more. Clicking Edit, which appears on the bottom right when some files are selected, invokes the file properties, exactly as if you right-click the file's icon and click Properties.

The contextual toolbars contain other options depending on what the folder is for. Open the Pictures folder (Start ➪ Pictures). Note in Figure 3.8 how the toolbar now contains an option called Slide Show. This launches a configurable slide show of the pictures in the current folder. Similarly, if you invoke the Music folder, a button called Play All appears, which you use to launch Media Player 11 and play all the songs in the folder.

FIGURE 3.7

A folder with the reading pane open

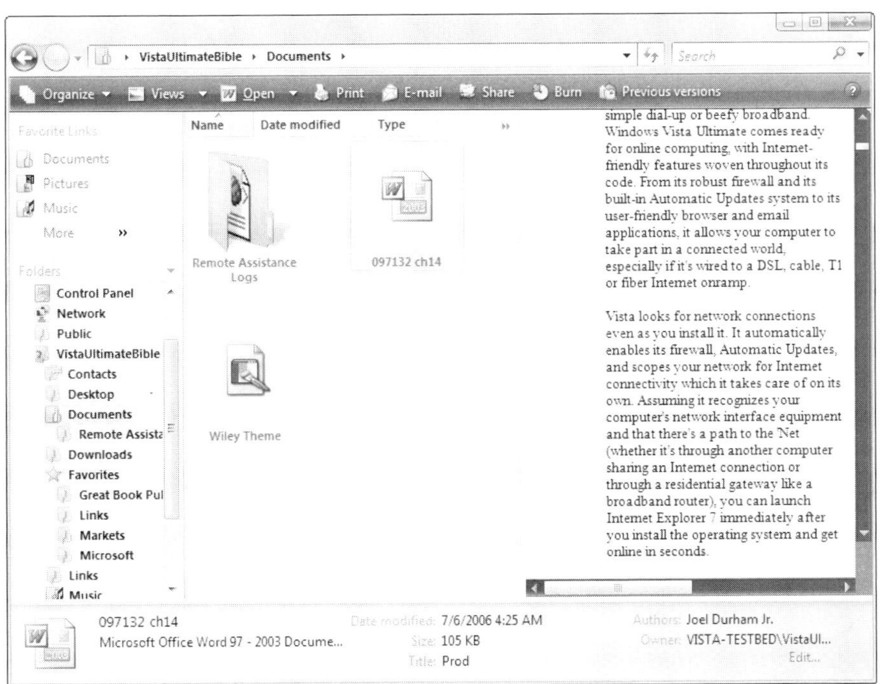

FIGURE 3.8

The Pictures folder toolbar contains a Slide Show button.

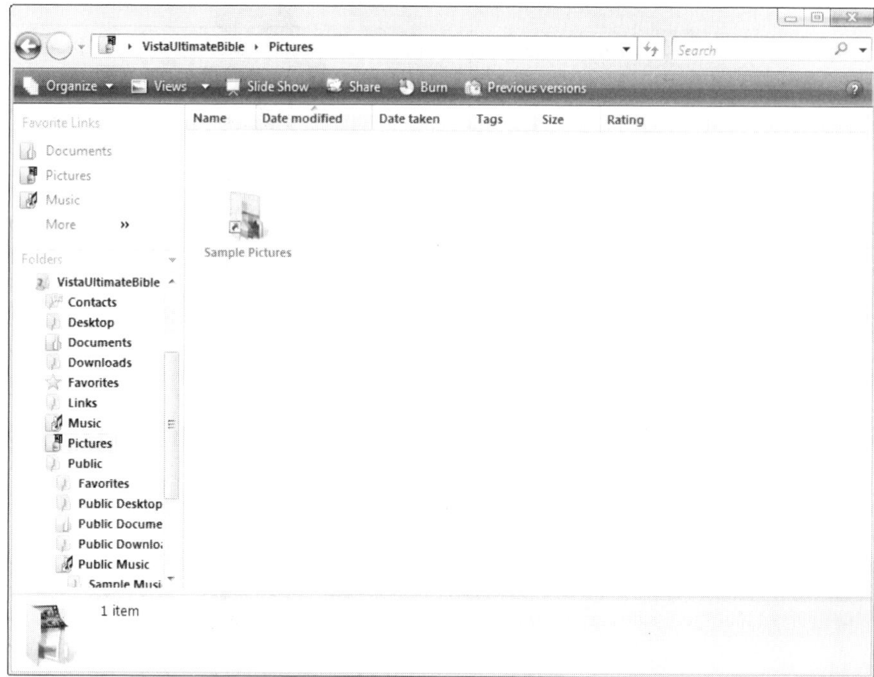

Most folder toolbars contain a Burn option, which prompts you to insert a writable disc into the optical drive tray; it then allows you to burn your files to a writable CD or DVD. A Share button allows you to set sharing options for both the network and for other user accounts on the same computer. The Previous versions button (shown pressed in Figure 3.9) searches for older versions of files in the current folder and, if it finds any, allows you to attempt to revert to prior versions. This feature is very handy for absent-minded authors who sometimes replace document files without preserving the old versions.

NOTE You'll encounter other special buttons in folder toolbars. Most are self-explanatory, but if you're not sure what one does, click the little question mark all the way over to the right to invoke the Help file for Windows folders.

FIGURE 3.9

The Previous versions window (part of the Properties window) looks for older versions of files.

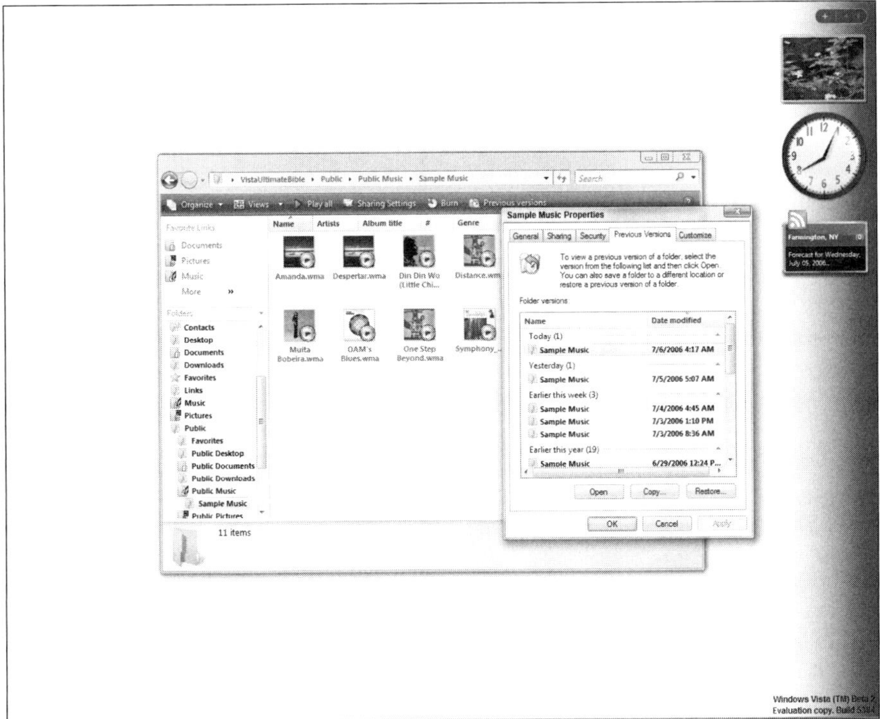

Share options

When you highlight a file or files within a folder, a Search button appears on the contextual toolbar. When you click it, you are offered different ways to set the file's sharing options.

A list showing every user account which is allowed to view the file appears. One of the user accounts will probably be the file's *owner*, the person who gets final say in who gets to do what with the file. You can add other accounts via a text box, and then change their permission levels through a drop-down box. Other users on the same computer can be *co-owners* of the file (which means they're allowed to alter it in any way) or they can have *read* permissions (meaning they can view it, but not change or delete it).

Breadcrumbs in the Path

By default, Windows displays the file system path at the top of each folder. The difference is that the path is now interactive. Whereas once it was displayed as a text string (for example, "C:\Program Files\Microsoft\"), Vista displays paths so that each item in the path is a live link. For example, if you look at the Pictures folder shown earlier in this chapter in Figure 3.8, you'll notice the path starts with my username (VistaUltimateBible) followed by a tiny arrow, and then the word *Pictures*. I can navigate to the VistaUltimateBible folder simply by clicking it in the path.

This concept has been referred to as "breadcrumbs," meaning that as you navigate through folders, you can find your way back to any folder in the path as easily as Hansel and Gretel could have as they traveled through the enchanted forest, dropping breadcrumbs to mark their path. Better still, in Windows Vista, birds won't come along and eat your crumbs!

If a file is already shared when you click the Share button, you can change its permissions or stop sharing the file altogether.

CROSS-REF Network sharing is a different matter altogether. For information about network sharing, check out Chapter 12.

CAUTION Be cautious in sharing your files, especially if you offer co-ownership permissions. If someone else decides to alter or delete it, the changes may be permanent. In most cases, I've found it more logical to offer the person who needs access to a file a copy of the file. That's not *always* practical: for instance, if you're preparing a report for a meeting and several people need to add to or edit it, you'll need to share the file. If, however, the kids want to check out digital photos and there's a chance they might wipe them out or use Windows Paint to draw moustaches on them, just drop a copy of the file into their appropriate personal folder.

Sharing has its benefits, but it also has pratfalls. If you share media files directly, for instance, rather than through Media Player 11's sharing dialog box (see Chapter 18), and that person tries to play the files, he or she might not have the appropriate digital rights.

NOTE Digital rights management (DRM), which online media stores inflict upon files they allow you to purchase and download, dictate which computers are allowed to enjoy the files.

One last thought on sharing: you should always, always, *always* have a backup of any files that you share on some sort of removable media or external drive. In fact, you should back up all of your important data files, regardless of whether you share them. Chapter 10 teaches you how to back up your files. Do it!

Where has My Computer gone?

A cornerstone of the classic Windows navigation scheme was the My Computer folder. Invoking it would show all the drives in the computer as well as some attached devices.

It's still there in Windows Vista, only it's simply called Computer. You can invoke the Computer folder, shown in Figure 3.10, by choosing Start ➪ Computer.

You can navigate through the file system by double-clicking icons, starting with the drive you want to explore. For example, double-click the C: drive to see all the folders within, and double-click on folders to see their subfolders and file contents.

NOTE The toolbar in the Computer window has two special buttons: the Change or remove a program button (which invokes an interface similar to the Windows XP Add/Remove Programs interface) and the Change a setting button, which invokes Control Panel.

FIGURE 3.10

Your computer is no longer called My Computer.

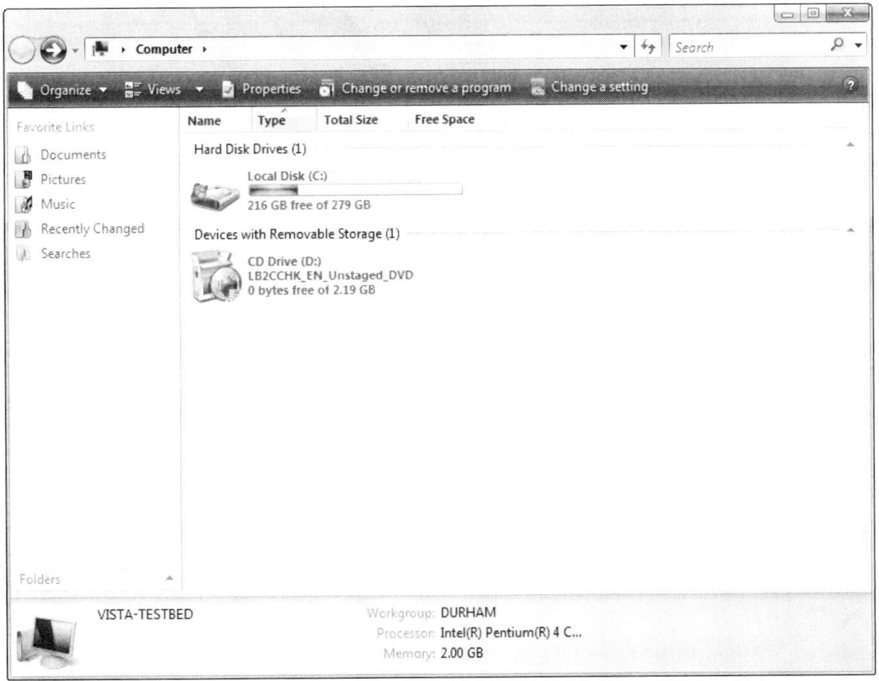

The Computer window shows a bit of data about installed hard drives, such as the total space of the drive and the remaining free space. You can get more information about the drive by right-clicking it and then clicking Properties.

CROSS-REF See Chapter 10 for more information about disk maintenance.

The Network interface

Click the Start button and click Network to invoke a window that functions similarly to My Network Places found in Windows XP. (See Figure 3.11.) If you're connected to a local area network, you can navigate it through this window as you would navigate any file system. You can also click the Network Center button to invoke a new interface for checking out the network and diagnosing problems.

CROSS-REF See Chapter 12 for more information about networking.

FIGURE 3.11

It's not called My Network Places or Network Neighborhood, but it's still the network explorer.

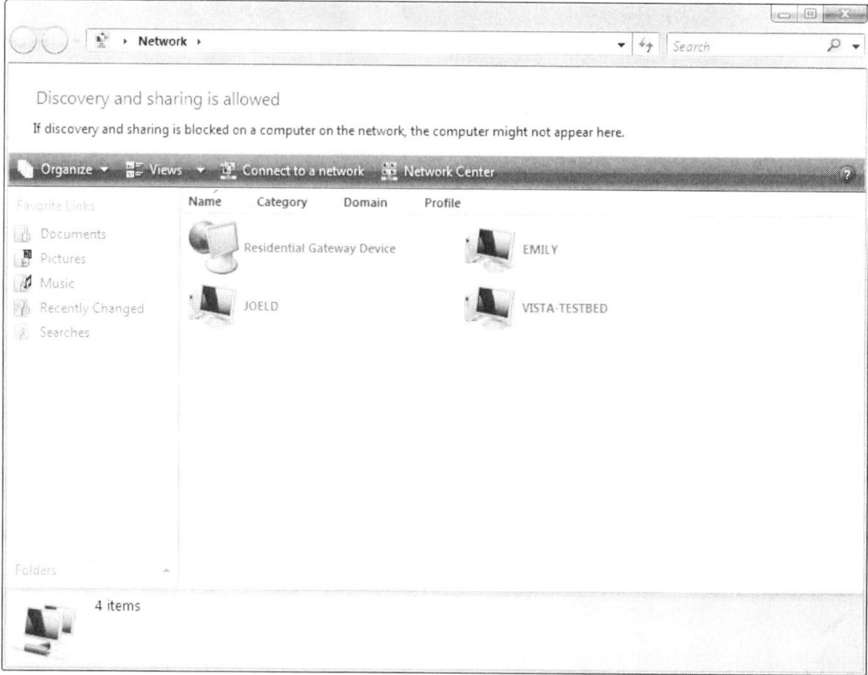

Searching in Windows Vista

Windows Vista is the first version of Windows to take searching seriously. Possibly prompted by the success of Google's Desktop Search, Vista's search function is everywhere: on toolbars, on the Start Menu, and in its own special dialog box.

Vista keeps an index of all the files and folders on the computer. When first installed, it starts building an index and, once built, monitors changes to files and folders and keeps itself updated at all times. The background indexing purportedly doesn't affect computer performance.

The Search is a universal function in Windows Vista. Any program can use it; for example, when you search from Microsoft Office 2007's Open dialog box, it uses the Windows search engine.

The toolbar Search box

Open any window in Vista's new Windows Explorer (for example, the Computer window shown earlier in Figure 3.10), and you'll see a search box on the right, next to the interactive path. You can type a search string into that box, and Windows will search the folder in which you're currently navigating and its subfolders. If you press Alt+Enter after you type in the string, Windows will search its index and provide the results instantly. See Figure 3.12.

FIGURE 3.12

Searches, such as this one for the Ghost Recon Advanced Warfighter game, are amazingly fast.

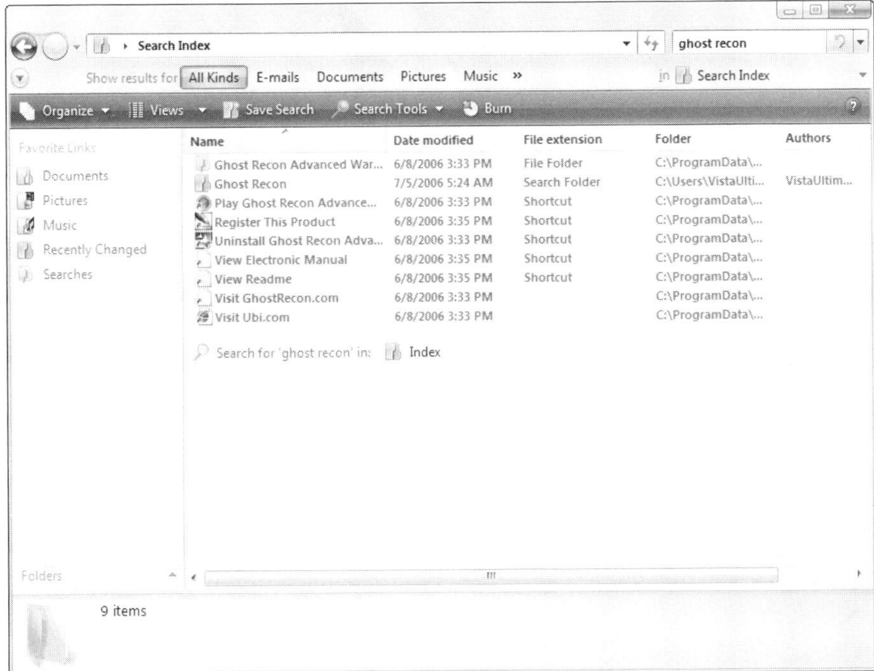

NOTE Most of the time, searching the index is preferable to allowing windows to sift through the file system. If, however, you're searching a network drive, an attached, removable storage device, or some other volume that's not indexed, you'll have to sit through the slower search method.

NOTE The Search box on the Start Menu functions in the same way, with one exception. When you begin a search, you can click on one of two options at the bottom of the screen: Search the Internet or Search the Computer to launch the Search interface.

The Search window

Click the Start button and then click Search to launch the dedicated Search interface shown in Figure 3.13. From there, you can type a search into the Search Box to instantly search the index, or you can customize your search in several ways.

FIGURE 3.13

The dedicated Search interface

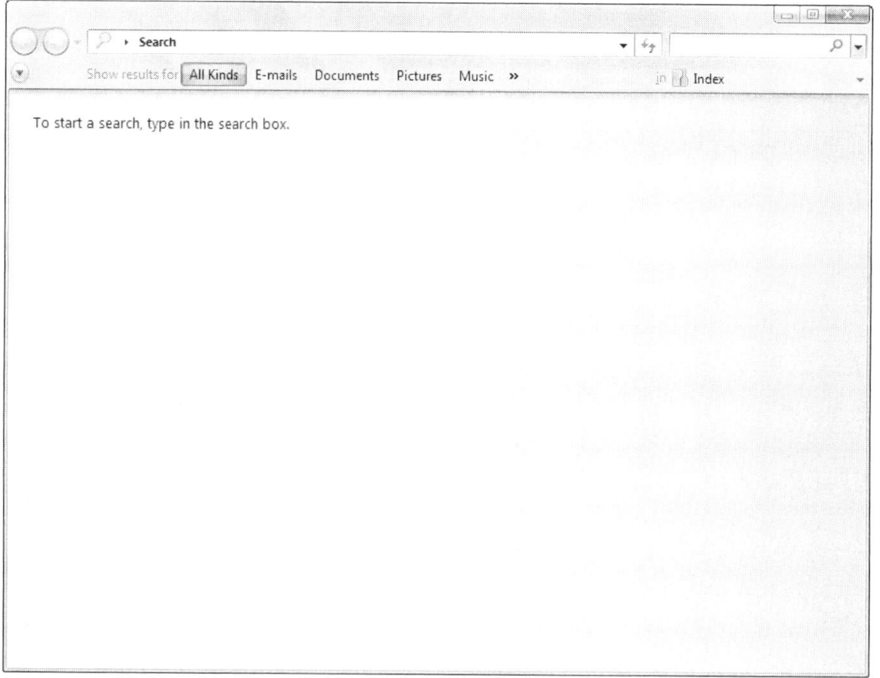

First, you can choose to bypass the index and search various locations, but this type of search is much slower. Click beneath the Search box on the Index button to set where you want to search.

If you click the down arrow in the Search box, you can elect to search the Internet or the index, and set various search options. Click Search Options to invoke the Folder Options window's Search tab shown in Figure 3.14.

FIGURE 3.14

The Search tab in the Folder Options dialog box

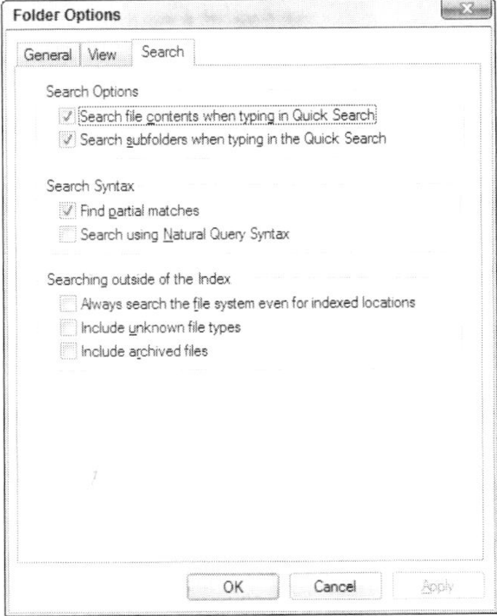

The Search tab lets you set how you want to search your computer. The check box options include the following:

- **Search file contents when typing in Quick Search:** This option tells Windows to search for your search string within files that contain text when performing a search.
- **Search subfolders when typing in the Quick Search:** If you want to exclude subfolders and limit your search to the files in the current folder only, uncheck this box.
- **Find partial matches:** With this box checked, Search will find words that contain the letters in your query. Unchecked, it will look for entire words that match the letters in your query.
- **Search using Natural Query Syntax:** This option allows you to use operators like AND and NOT to specify words to include or exclude in your search.

- **Always search the file system even for indexed locations:** If you want your searches to go really slowly, check this box. Note that it *doesn't* disable the background indexing.
- **Include unknown file types:** This option forces Search to include file types that Windows doesn't recognize.
- **Include archived files:** This option forces Search to include files that have been archived.

You can specify exactly what you want Search to look for via the buttons on the toolbar following the words *Show results for*. Using those buttons and the pull-down menu next to them, you can specify that you would like your results to be image files, documents, music files, contacts, RSS feeds, links, movies, and much more. The default is All Kinds, which searches everything in the index or file system.

NOTE You can save searches in Windows Vista. This powerful feature allows you to create a virtual folder which, by default, is saved in your \<*yourusername*>\Searches\ folder. After you perform a search, click Save Search on the toolbar to invoke the dialog box shown in Figure 3.15. Give the search a name and click Save. From then on, if you navigate to your Searches folder it will appear in the list under that name; double-click it to see updated results for that search.

FIGURE 3.15

Saving a Search as a new folder

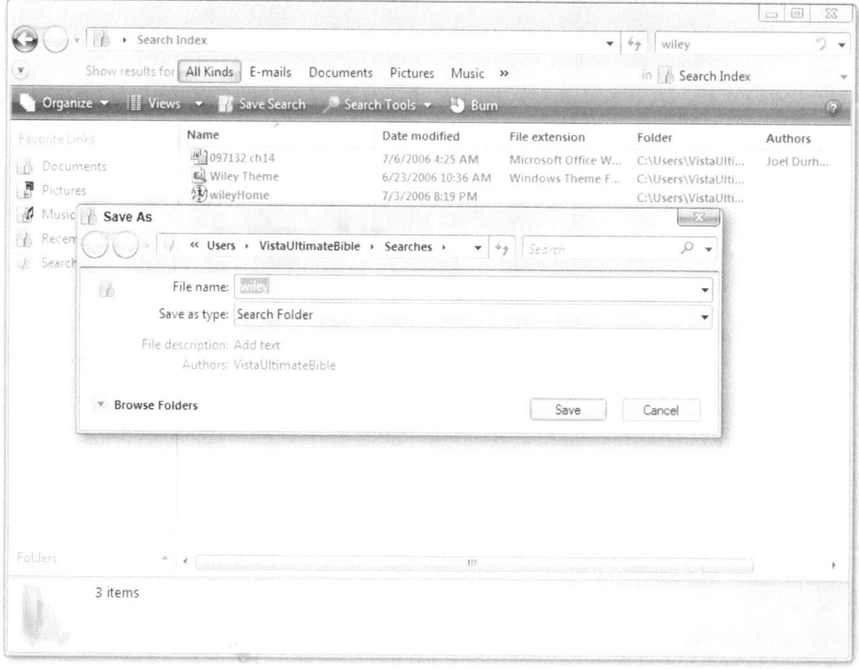

Summary

When I first cracked open Windows Vista, back in the days of the publicly released Beta 2, I was taken aback by the changes to its navigation interface. I didn't know about breadcrumbs, so I didn't know how to trek upwards to parent folders. I didn't know where my trusty drop-down menus were. I felt like I was experiencing . . . a whole new operating system. A Windows XP user, I was, for the first time since Windows 95 arrived, in a foreign land.

Once I became accustomed to the changes, however, I grew to love them. The contextual toolbar buttons, for instance, offer up the stuff I tend to do most often, so I don't have to sift through drop-down menus to perform common tasks. Breadcrumbs are cool, and once I found the file system tree view, I could navigate from one point to another in a matter of seconds. I'm absolutely bananas for the new, indexed search; it's past time that waiting, waiting, going and getting a cup of coffee, and waiting some more for a search to reach completion went away forever.

I'm duly impressed with the new shell, and if you give it a chance you probably will be, too. It's different, to be sure, but it really doesn't stray far from the established Windows conventions. In the end, it's more robust, more intuitive, and generally more user friendly, and the only obstacle in the path to embracing it is unlearning some old habits. You can always bring back the drop-down menus and the classic look and feel, but I'm of the opinion that you should give the new shell a good week or two and see if it doesn't grow on you.

Chapter 4

Basic Settings You Can't Overlook

IN THIS CHAPTER

Finding out where to make basic changes

Using the Control Panel

Setting display properties

Setting sound card and speaker properties

You've got it. Now customize it! One of the strengths of just about every Windows operating system is their strong propensity for customization. Through the centralized Control Panel menu, you can launch applets and properties dialog boxes for almost every aspect of Windows. Many of those settings pages are also attainable through shortcuts by right-clicking various objects, menus, and areas of the screen.

Windows Vista has made the Control Panel even more powerful and user-friendly, with a new format that groups the settings and controls better than Windows XP's Control Panel did. Lots of new areas lurk within the Control Panel, such as Solutions to Problems, Performance Rating and Tools, Backup and Restore Center, Windows Sidebar, Parental Controls, Windows Update, and more. Of course, the old standbys are there, too, like Device Manager, Administrative Tools, Printers, Keyboard, and Mouse.

Windows Vista takes care of the vast majority of the necessary settings automatically on installation. It sniffs out your network, looks for Internet access, detects as much of your hardware as it can with its default drivers, sets up background items like the paging file and Windows Firewall, and the list goes on. You'll have to set some basic options, however, such as the screen resolution and refresh rate, the sound card and speaker configuration, and a few other odds and ends.

I discuss many of the settings mentioned in this chapter in depth in later chapters — I refer you to those chapters for more details as necessary. Meanwhile, this chapter introduces you to the most basic and most necessary settings, the ones you really can't ignore to get the most out of your Vista Ultimate multimedia experience.

Changes You Can Make and Where to Make Them

Windows Vista Ultimate Edition is all about customization. It's ready to be the operating system you want it to be, and although it's packed with features (a great deal of which are enabled right from the start), you can change how most of them work and turn off those you don't need.

You can adjust and personalize almost every aspect of Windows Vista Ultimate Edition, from its visual appearance right down to its core set of services. Here are some of the minor and major items that you can change the properties or behavior of, along with the chapters of this book that explain them in detail:

- Visual appearance and theme (Chapter 5)
- The screen saver (Chapter 5)
- The taskbar and Start Menu (Chapter 5)
- The Sidebar and its gadgets (Chapter 8)
- The Windows Aero interface (Chapter 7)
- Networking basics (Chapter 12)
- File and printer sharing (Chapter 12)
- System performance (Chapter 28)
- Parental Controls (Chapter 11)
- Security features (Chapter 11)
- Backing up data (Chapter 10)
- Optimization features (Chapter 27)
- Display properties (This chapter)
- Audio properties (This chapter)

And that's not everything! It does give you an idea, however, of just how malleable this new operating system can be.

You can invoke property dialog boxes with selectable options for various Windows Vista items in all sorts of ways. In many cases, if you right-click something on the screen and click Properties or Settings, the pertinent dialog box will appear. Sometimes that dialog box contains multiple tabs for tweaking similar areas of the operating system.

If you're not sure where to start, head to the source. The Control Panel is ground-zero for customizing Windows Vista.

Customizing Windows Vista with the Control Panel

Click Start ➪ Control Panel. The Windows Vista Control Panel window, shown in Figure 4.1, appears.

FIGURE 4.1

The Windows Vista Control Panel

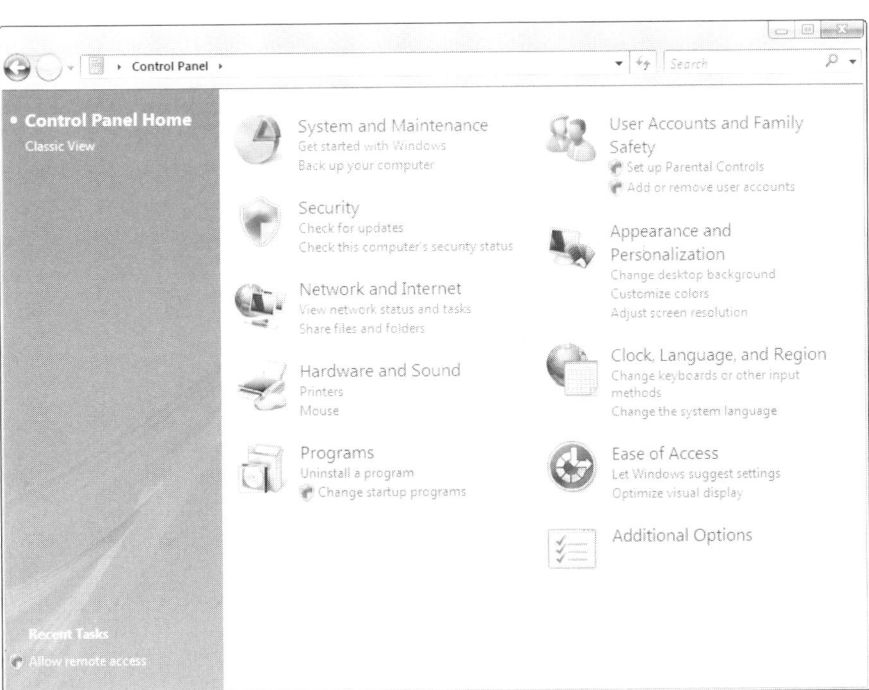

Take a few moments to read through the menu, which offers the following:

- **System and Maintenance** (Figure 4.2): This area contains controls for Windows Update, remote access, and backups and restores. It's also where you find Device Manager and Administrative Tools.

FIGURE 4.2

System and Maintenance

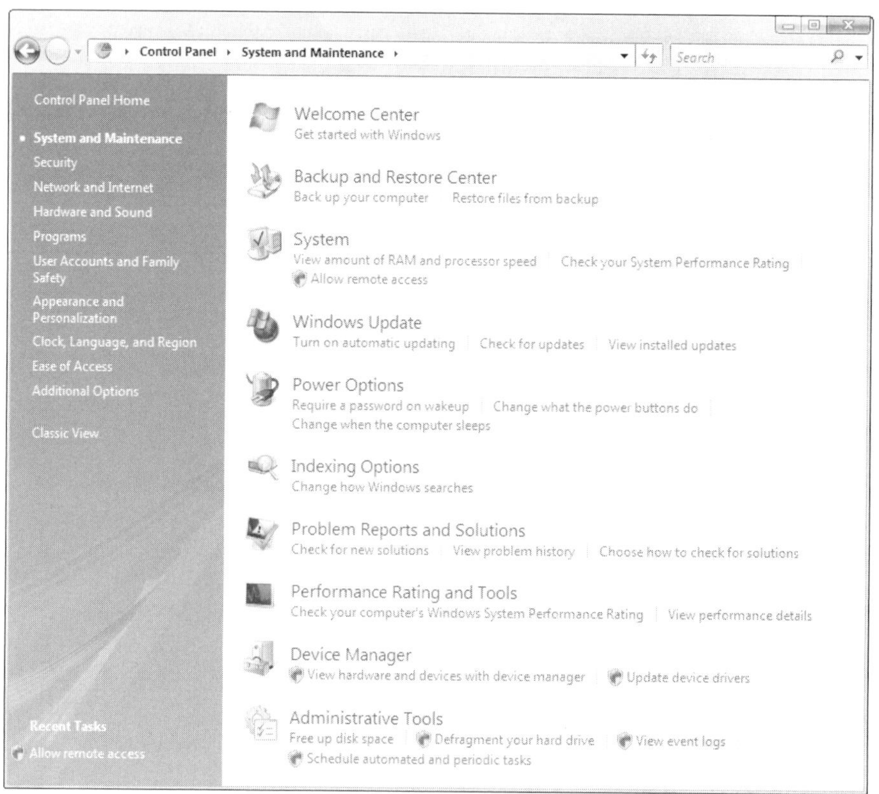

- **Security** (Figure 4.3): The Security page offers options for keeping your PC safe. You can control Windows Firewall and Windows Defender here, change Internet options, and tweak Parental Controls.

FIGURE 4.3

Security

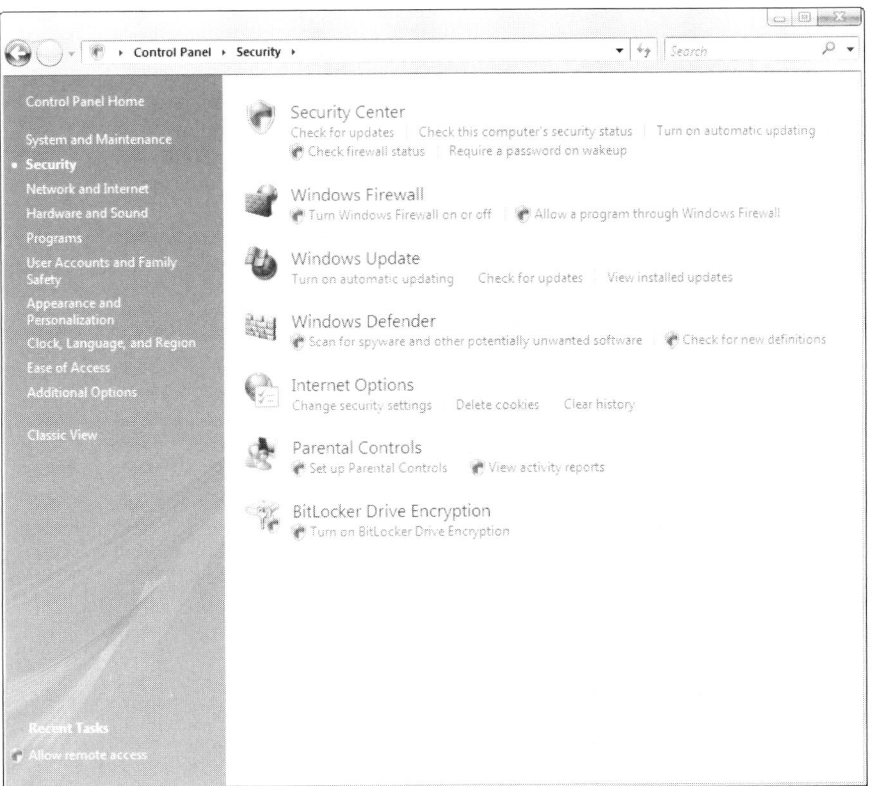

- **Network and Internet** (Figure 4.4): This page offers the Network Center, along with lots of network options. Windows Firewall appears on this page (note the overlap with Security; you'll notice lots of overlap in Control Panel), as does the Sync Center and Network File and Printer Sharing.

FIGURE 4.4

Network and Internet

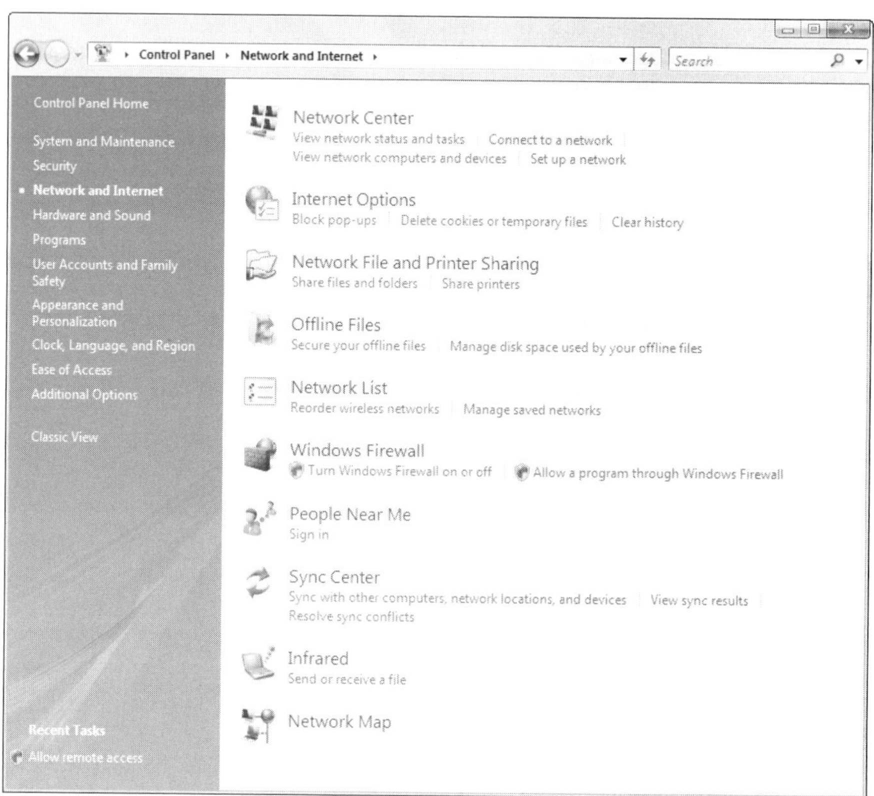

- **Hardware and Sound** (Figure 4.5): This page (which I focus on later in this chapter) is where you configure audio and video options as well as mouse, keyboard, modem, and game controller settings. Device Manager appears here as it does in System and Maintenance.

FIGURE 4.5

Hardware and Sound

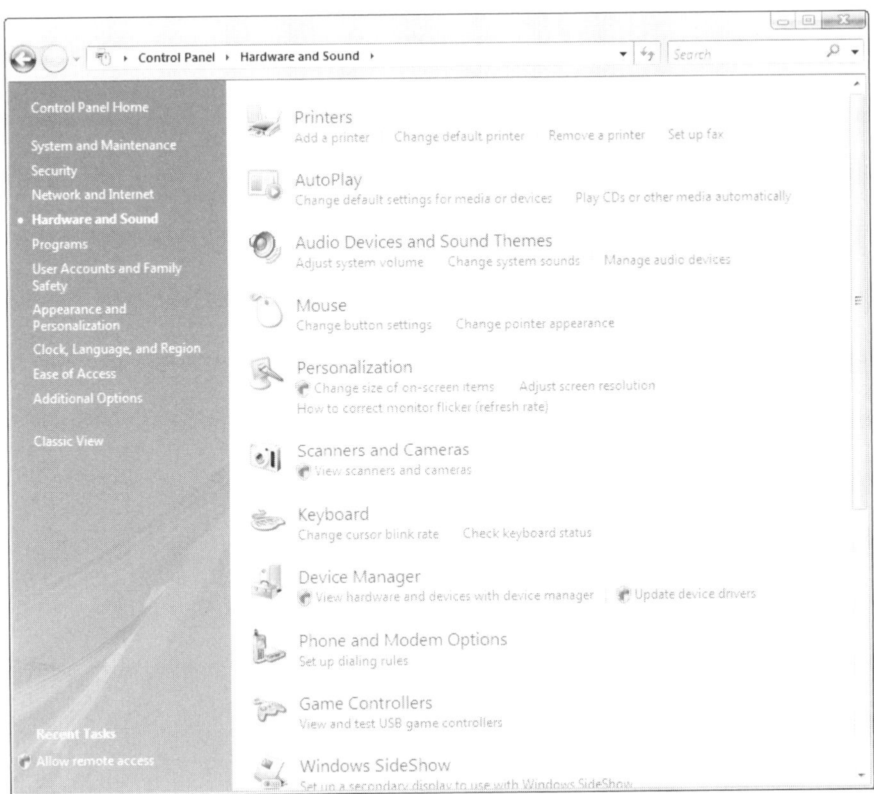

- **Programs** (Figure 4.6): The Programs page is a central location for controlling installed programs and installing new ones. This page is where you find the old Add/Remove Programs applet, now called Installed Programs. You can tweak Windows Defender on this page, and change programs that run when Windows starts.

FIGURE 4.6

Programs

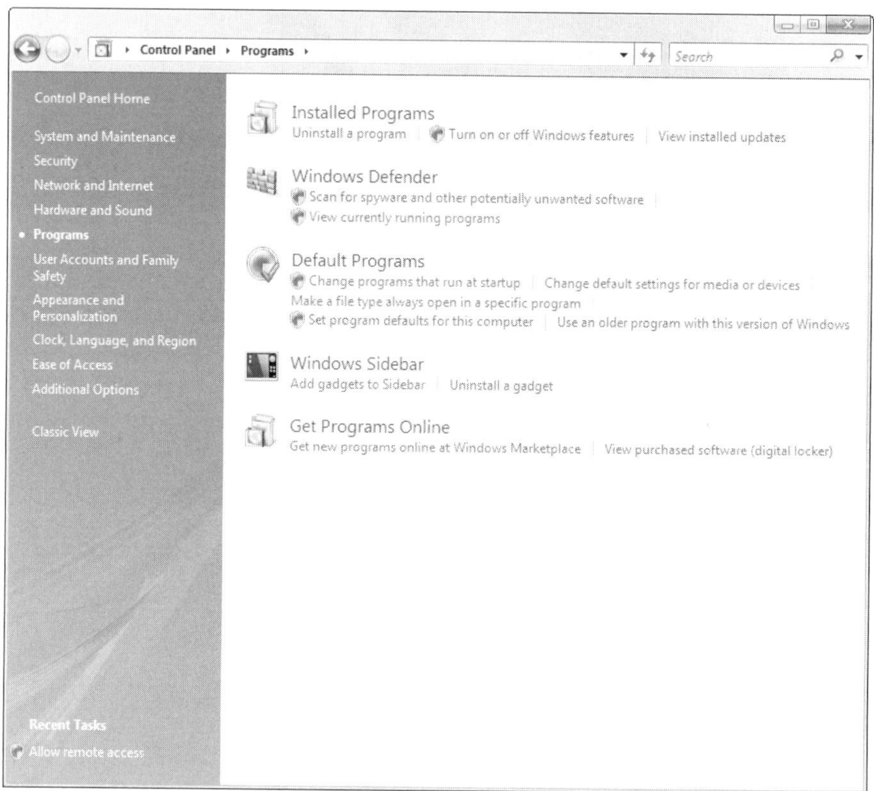

- **User Accounts and Family Safety** (Figure 4.7): You can configure user accounts on this page and tweak Parental Controls to dictate what the kids can and cannot access. You can also manage e-mail options and Digital Identities (through an applet currently code-named "InfoCard").

FIGURE 4.7

User Accounts and Family Safety

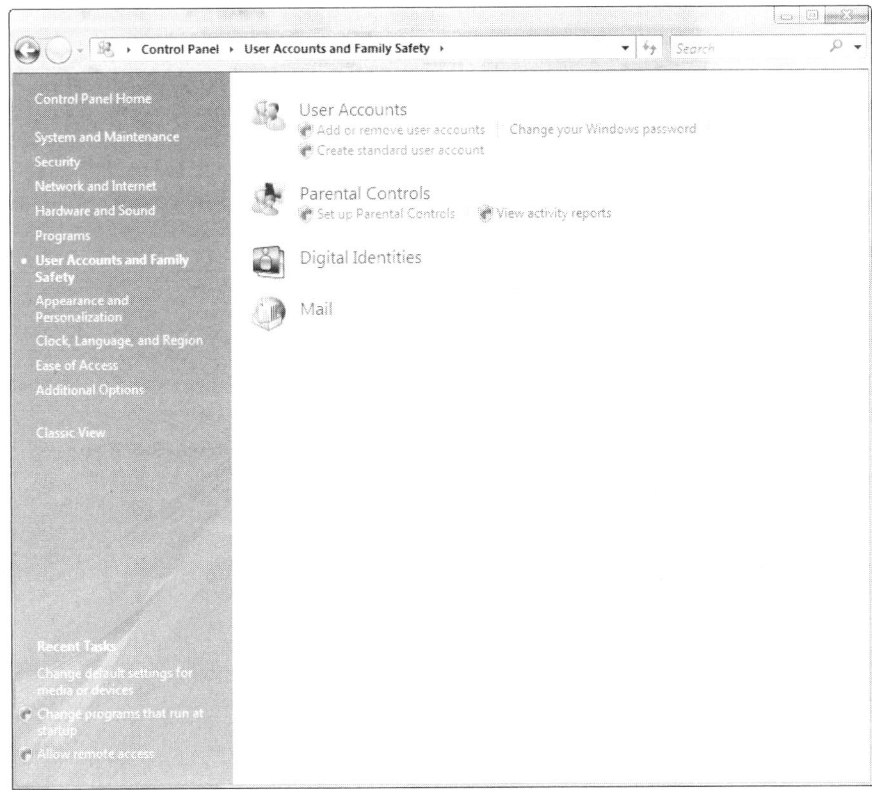

- **Appearance and Personalization** (Figure 4.8): In this Control Panel window, you can tweak things like the theme, desktop wallpaper, taskbar, and Start Menu, as well as control fonts and folder options. This page is another place to adjust the Sidebar, and the Ease of Access Center also appears here.

FIGURE 4.8

Appearance and Personalization

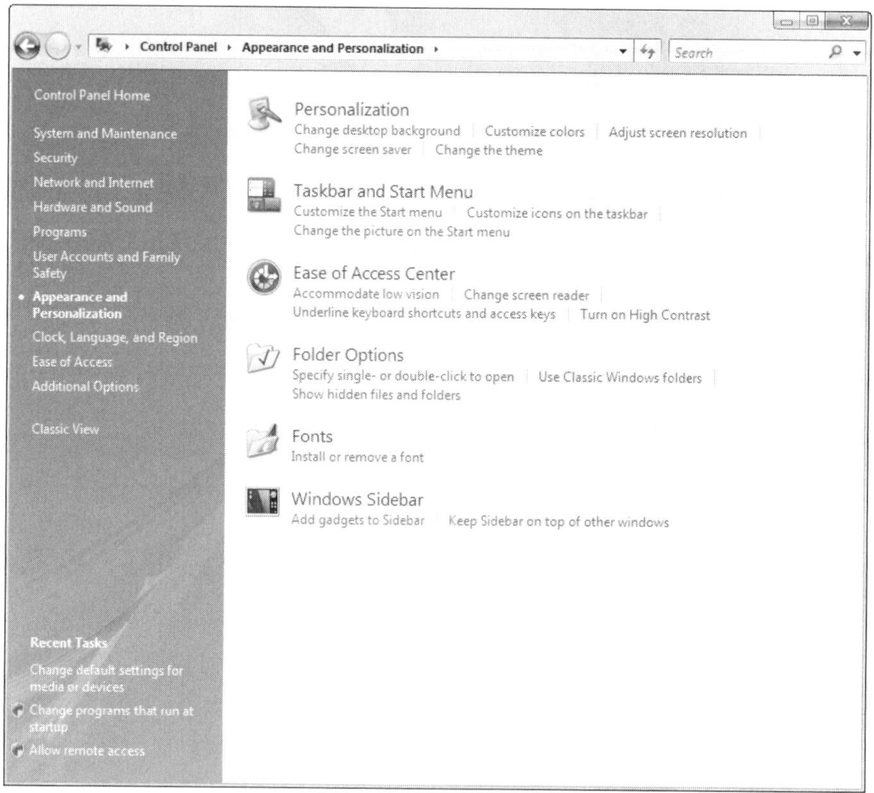

- **Clock, Language, and Region** (Figure 4.9): Set the date and time via this window, and add multiple clocks so you can view different time zones. You can also change the display language, adjust your country or geographical location, and tweak other regional settings.

FIGURE 4.9

Clock, Language, and Region

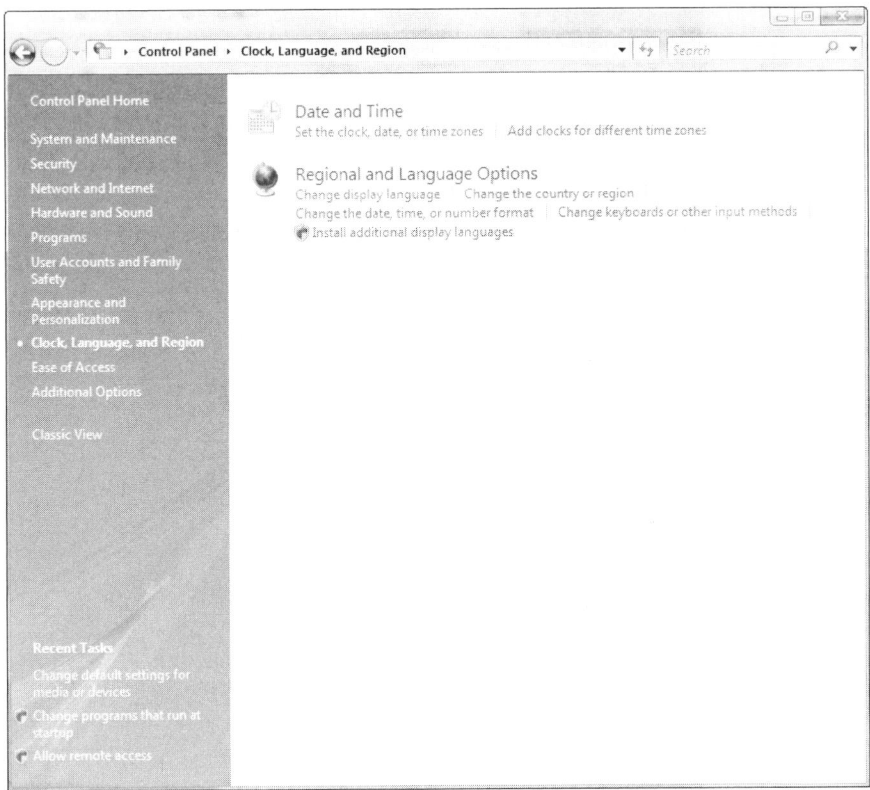

- **Ease of Access** (Figure 4.10): If you have special needs, Microsoft might have you covered. The Ease of Access Center lets you swap out sounds for visual cues, change how the keyboard and mouse work, and more. It's equivalent to the Accessibility Settings in previous versions of Windows but with more options.
- **Additional Options** (Figure 4.11): Programs and drivers might drop additional control applets in this area. As they say in the industry, it's "reserved for future use."

FIGURE 4.10

Ease of Access

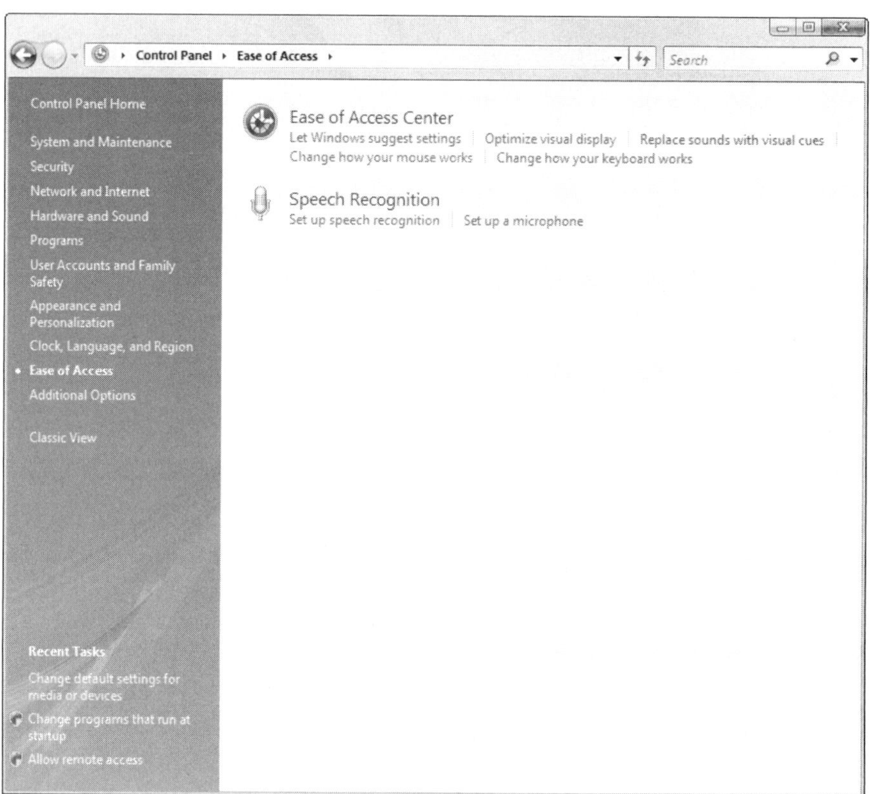

FIGURE 4.11

Additional Options

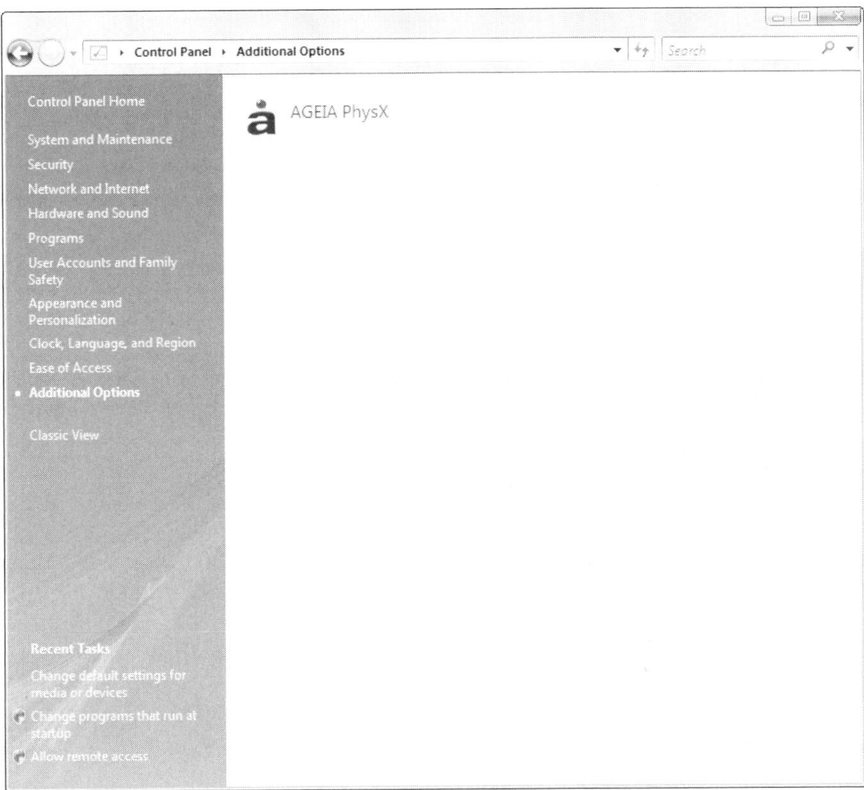

If the new Control Panel layout has got you down, you can switch to the icon-driven Classic View. Just click Classic View in the menu on the left (Figure 4.12). The icons are automatically arranged alphabetically. You can further tweak the Classic View as if it were any folder by right-clicking an empty area of the window (between icons) and selecting View options, Sort options, Grouping options, and more.

FIGURE 4.12

A Classic View of the Control Panel

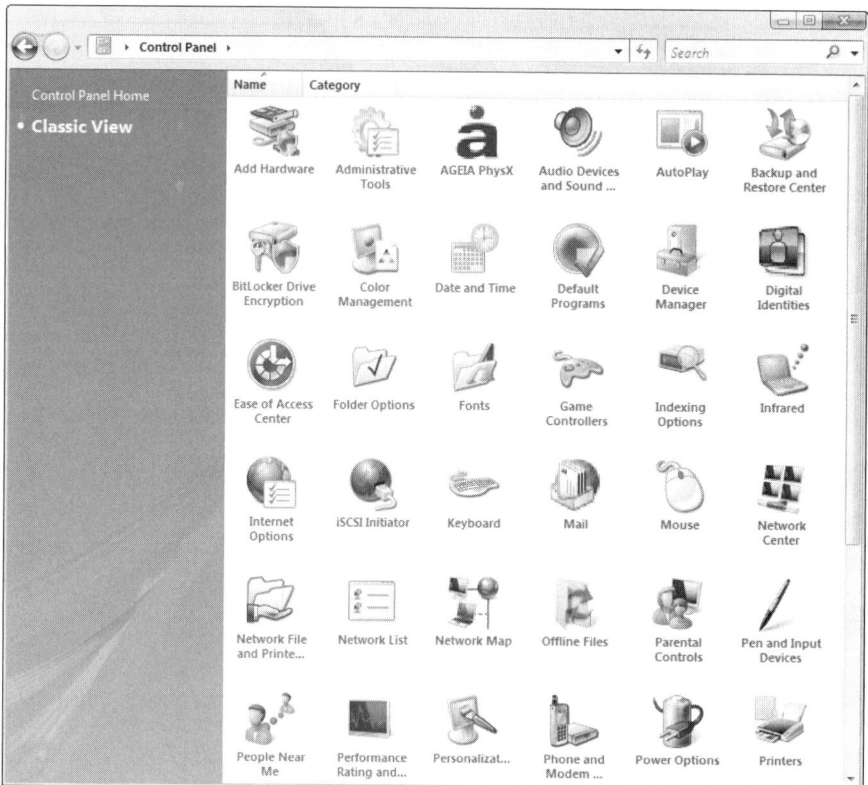

Using common shortcuts

If you're familiar with earlier versions of Windows, you'll probably suspect that Windows Vista has alternate routes to many of the properties dialog boxes offered through the Control Panel. You're absolutely right.

As in prior versions of Windows, Windows Vista features a context menu when you right-click. The word *context* in this sense means that the menu that appears depends on where or upon what you right-click. Furthermore, contextual menus on the navigation windows in Windows Explorer, as well as contextual toolbars in a large number of the special folders, allow you to jump to various settings and properties dialog boxes without ever having to open the Control Panel. Check out Table 4.1 for a list of these context menu shortcuts.

TABLE 4.1

Shortcuts to Settings Menus

Settings Menu	Shortcut to Invoke it	Shown in Figure
Customize the Start Menu	Click Start, right-click on an empty area of the Start Menu, and click Properties.	14.13
Customize the taskbar	Right-click an empty area of the taskbar, and click Properties.	14.14
Customize the Sidebar	Right-click an empty area of the Sidebar, and click Properties.	14.15
Configure certain system properties	Click Start, right-click Computer, and click Properties.	14.16
Alter or remove a program	Choose Start ➪ Computer ➪ Change or remove a program.	14.17
Adjust desktop appearance	Right-click an empty area of the desktop, and click Personalize.	14.18
Change Internet properties	Click Start, right-click Internet, and click Internet Properties.	14.19
Adjust time and date settings	Right-click the clock on the taskbar and click Adjust Time/Date.	14.20
Open Network Center	Choose Start ➪ Network ➪ Network Center.	Not shown
Configure power settings	Choose Start ➪ Control Panel ➪ Hardware and Sound. Then, scroll down and click Power Options	Not shown
Open Parental Controls	Choose Start ➪ Games ➪ Parental Controls.	Not shown

Customize the Start Menu

You can select one of two Start Menu styles in the Start Menu tab, shown in Figure 4.13: the standard Windows Vista style or the Classic (Windows 2000) style. The latter will be more familiar to users of older versions of Windows; it features menus that expand through fly-out submenus. It also has fewer direct shortcuts to commonly used applets and personal folders.

Two check boxes allow you to dictate whether you'd like Windows to keep lists of frequently opened files and frequently accessed programs handy in the Start Menu. In both cases, such commonly used items are presented to you for quick access, but if more than one person uses a particular user account the feature can compromise privacy. Use them at your discretion.

FIGURE 4.13

Here is where you can customize the Start Menu properties, including switching to the classic version.

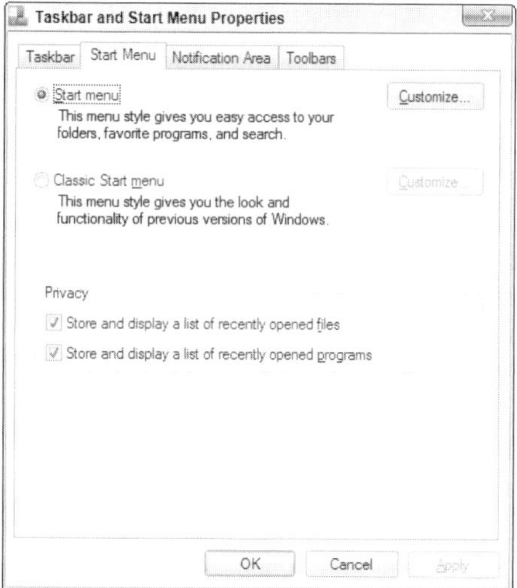

Customize the taskbar

The Taskbar tab, shown in Figure 4.14, presents a list of check box items that allow you to tweak the taskbar as you see fit. They include:

- **Lock the taskbar:** You can prevent the taskbar from being dragged and resized with the mouse by locking it.
- **Auto-hide the taskbar:** This causes the taskbar to disappear when it's not in use. If you move the mouse to the bottom of the screen, the taskbar reappears.
- **Keep the taskbar on top of other windows:** You can prevent other windows from obscuring the taskbar through this option.
- **Group similar taskbar buttons:** If you have several files open within the same program, each will have its own taskbar button. This option reduces clutter by grouping such items into a single button. If you click that button, Windows displays entire list of open files in that group.

- **Show Quick Launch:** The taskbar features a customizable Quick Launch bar, whose default location is on the left near the Start button. The bar shows small icons of programs that you can launch with a single click — you can drag items from desktop icons and the Start Menu to the Quick Launch bar to add them to it. This option tells Windows whether you want to see the Quick Launch bar or not.
- **Show Thumbnails:** If you hover over a button on the taskbar, Windows can display a live thumbnail of the program or file if this option is checked.

FIGURE 4.14

The Taskbar tab in the Taskbar and Start Menu Properties dialog box enables you to customize the look and behavior of your taskbar.

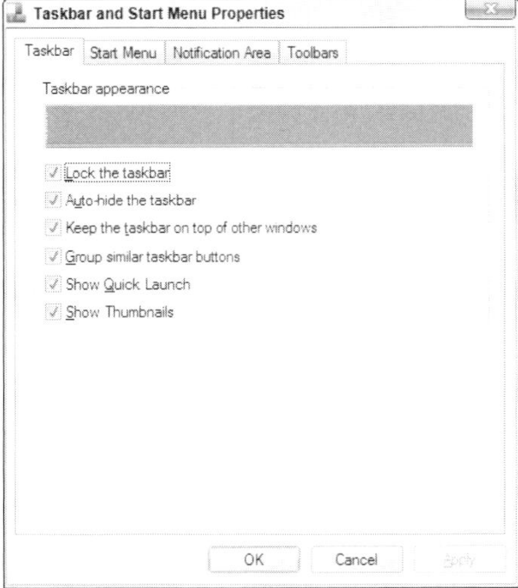

Customize the Sidebar

The Sidebar tab in the Windows Sidebar Properties dialog box allows you to set several Sidebar-related options (Figure 4.15).

At the top, you'll find a check box that allows you to determine whether the Sidebar is displayed when Windows starts. Next is a check box to let you decide whether the Sidebar is always on top of other applications. In other words, with this box checked, other windows will not obscure the sidebar.

Two radio buttons allow you to select whether the Sidebar is displayed on the left or right side of the screen. Another option lets you determine which monitor displays the Sidebar in multiple monitor environments.

Finally, you can click a button to view a list of running gadgets, and another, if it's not grayed out, to restore the default gadgets from when Windows Vista was first installed.

FIGURE 4.15

The Sidebar tab in the Windows Sidebar Properties dialog box enables you to customize the behavior of the Sidebar.

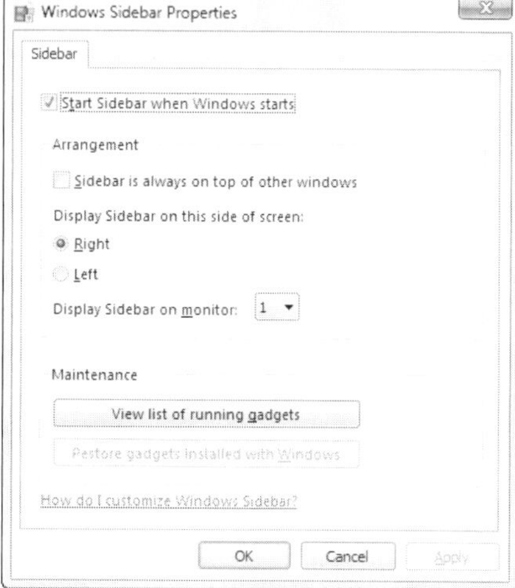

Configure system properties

You can configure certain system properties with a Control Panel applet called System. (The System pane is shown in Figure 4.16.) It allows you to configure many system-level items, such as hardware configurations and the computer's network name. The Control Panel's System pane is covered in detail in several chapters, including Chapters 2, 10, and 12.

Change or remove programs

Another Control Panel applet, the Change or Remove Program interface (Figure 4.17), lets you uninstall programs. For programs that allow various installation options, you can often change them through this interface. You might need the installation media if you choose to change a program's installation properties.

Change the desktop appearance

You can change the desktop appearance in the Control Panel's Personalization pane, shown in Figure 4.18. This Control Panel applet is covered extensively later in this chapter, and additionally in Chapter 5.

FIGURE 4.16

Note the Tasks pane on the left, which allows you to launch Device Manager and other applets.

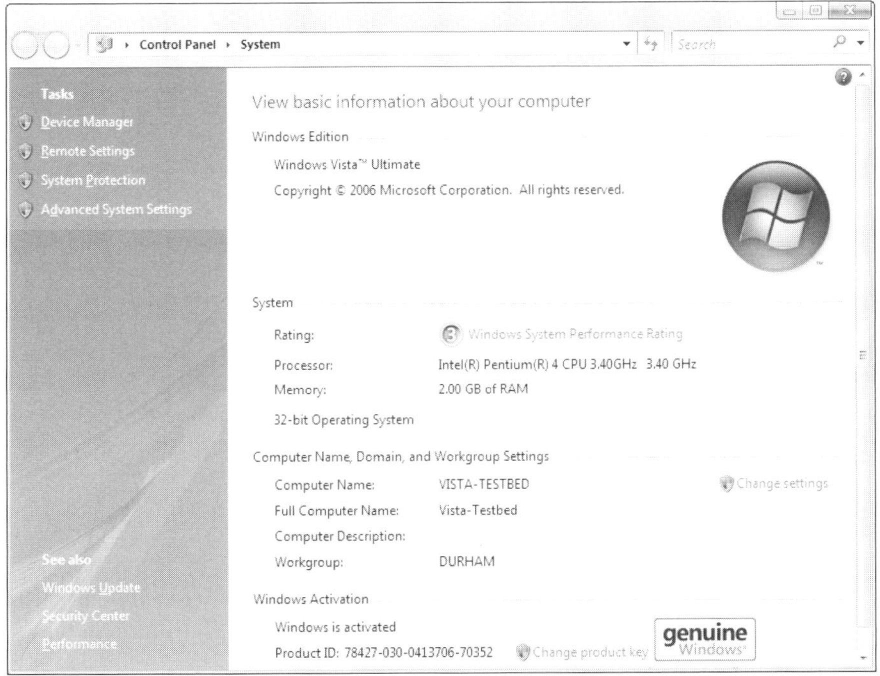

FIGURE 4.17

You can change or remove programs here.

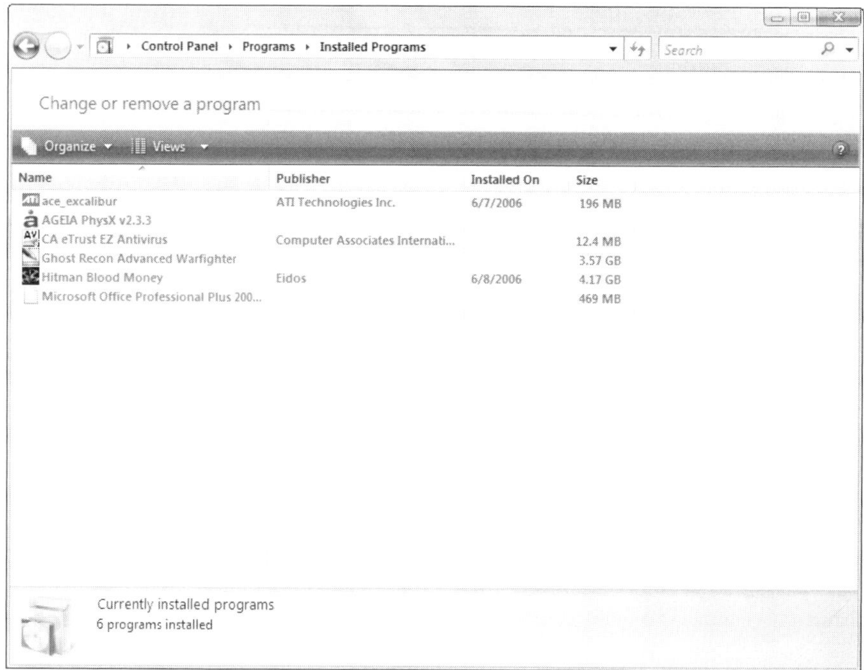

Customize Internet properties

Internet properties are customizable in the Internet Properties dialog box, shown in Figure 4.19. Another Control Panel applet, the networking and Internet properties are covered in Chapters 12 and 13.

Adjust time and date properties

You can change the computer's time, date, and time zone in the Date and Time Properties dialog box, shown in Figure 4.20. You can also add up to two additional clocks to the taskbar by clicking the Additional Clocks tab.

The third tab, Internet Time, lets you choose an Internet time server. Most time servers use atomic clocks for blindingly accurate time, and your computer will automatically sync with the time server of your choice when it's connected to the Internet.

FIGURE 4.18

You can customize your computer's audio and video here.

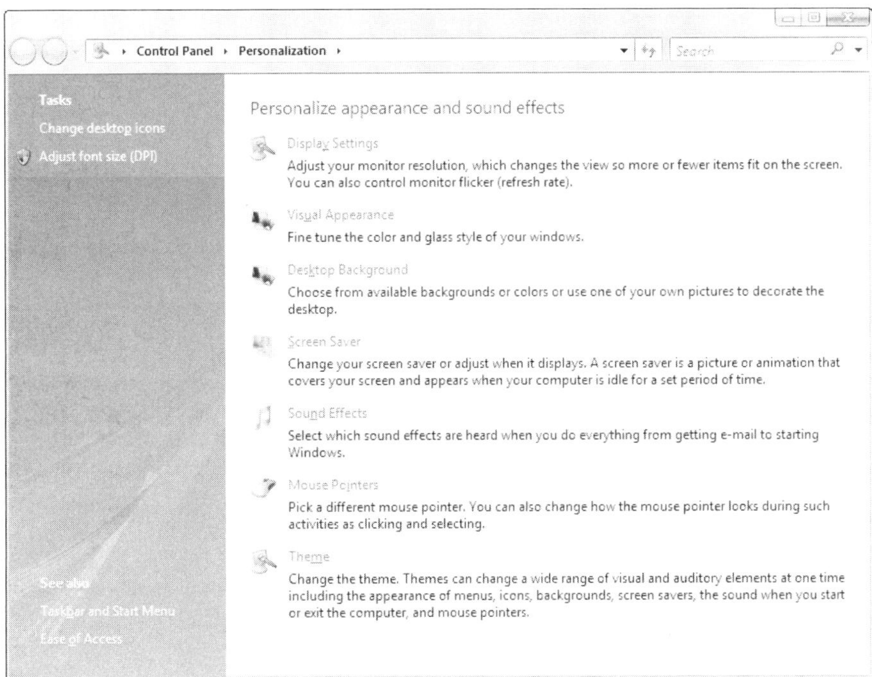

You'll probably discover even more shortcuts to various controls as you grow used to the new interface presented by Windows Vista.

NOTE The right-click context menu is universal; it's not only for shortcuts to the Control Panel settings windows. You can right-click on almost anything in Windows Vista and find a dialog box for it.

Windows features dozens of ways to do reach the same location, so find the way easiest for you to adjust the cornucopia of customization options that Windows has to offer. Whether it's through Control Panel or a context menu, as long as you find what you're looking for there's no wrong way to get there.

TIP Windows XP users will notice that the Power Settings dialog box is no longer intimately paired with the Screen Saver Properties tab. Wasn't that a weird place for it to begin with? You can find the power settings in the Control Panel's System and Maintenance area — although you can still launch the Power Settings window through the Screen Saver Settings dialog box. Old habits die hard.

FIGURE 4.19

The multi-tabbed Internet Properties dialog box enables you to customize your home page as well as security, privacy, and other settings.

FIGURE 4.20

Set your Date and Time properties here.

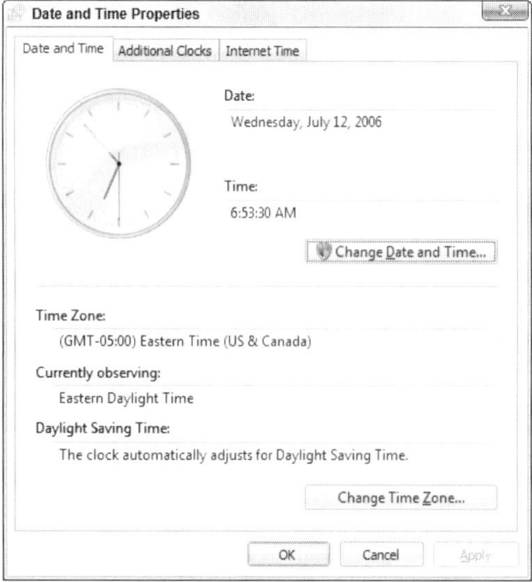

Multimedia Device Settings

I delve deeply into many of the settings presented in the bulleted list earlier in this chapter in later chapters; however, there are a couple of basic settings you need to tackle right away to get the best experience out of your multimedia applications. Those are your display settings and the settings for your sound card and speaker configuration.

Adjusting the display settings

When you install Windows Vista, it attempts to detect your computer's graphics card (also called display adapter) and monitor, and it tries to set the display properties to an optimal state. Three variables it tries to deal with are the desktop pixel resolution, the color bit depth, and the monitor's vertical refresh rate.

Open the display properties window by opening Control Panel (Start ➪ Control Panel), clicking Appearance and Visualization, clicking Personalization, and finally by clicking Display Settings. The screen should resemble the one shown in Figure 4.21.

FIGURE 4.21

The Display Settings dialog box

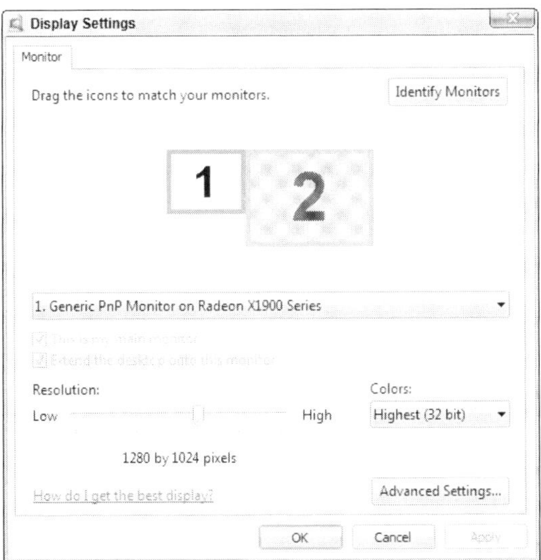

Resolution

The slider on the Display Settings dialog box allows you to adjust the pixel resolution. Below it, you'll see a measurement such as "1024 by 768 pixels." A *pixel* is the tiniest component of a computer image; everything you see on your computer screen is made up of a series of pixels. The resolution numbers indicate the number of pixels across the screen by the number of pixels down; thus, a resolution of 1024 x 768 is 1,024 pixels across and 768 pixels down. The higher you set your resolution, the sharper the screen will look and the more you'll be able to display on your Windows desktop— but everything will look a bit smaller. This notion is often referred to as "desktop real estate."

NOTE Windows Aero, the desktop interface used by Windows Vista, uses your system's 3D graphics card and its memory; the maximum displayable resolution depends upon the amount of video memory on the graphics card. Your computer needs at least 256MB of video memory to display a resolution of 1600 x 1200 and at least 64MB of memory to reach 1280 x 1024.

You can adjust the slider by dragging it with the mouse. Choose a pixel resolution and click Apply to see it in action. The screen will go blank for a moment and then reappear at the new resolution. If you hate it, adjust the slider again. Experiment with resolutions until you find one you prefer; I run my desktop at 1280 x 1024.

CAUTION Don't set the resolution to something higher than your monitor can handle. If the monitor drivers are installed properly, or if Windows has automatically detected the plug-and-play monitor, this shouldn't be an issue. If, however, you set the resolution too high, on the monitor, you may see a distorted image. It's even possible to overdrive an older CRT display and potentially damage it. Press the Escape key to return to the previous resolution.

Color depth

The monitor's color depth is also referred to as its *bit depth*, and it indicates how many colors each pixel can display. Your Windows Vista installation may have defaulted to 16 or 32 bits. Here's how they translate into actual colors.

Back in the olden days, computers had one color. They were called monochrome. You might remember black screens with green or amber lettering on them. Those computers were capable of exactly two bits per pixel. Each pixel was either turned on or turned off.

Each bit is a simple 0 or 1. Combining several bits results in more combinations. The more bits that are available, the greater number the number of combinations. A two-bit display has two combinations: green (or amber) or black.

Then came 16-color computers. They were capable of displaying 4 bits per pixel. Each bit has two combinations, so multiply those two combinations four times (2 x 2 x 2 x 2) and you arrive at the computers' capabilities of 16 colors.

Two hundred fifty-six color computers, therefore, were capable of 8 bits per pixel. Sixteen-bit display modes (sometimes called "high color") display 65,536 colors. Twenty-four-bit color is considered "true color"; each pixel can be 1 of 16,777,216 colors.

Now, 32-bit color modes are sort of confusing. They can't display pixels in 1 of 4,294,967,296 colors, as the arithmetic would seem to indicate. They actually operate at 24 bits per pixel, plus an 8-bit *alpha channel*. The alpha channel can be used to adjust the transparency of pixels.

To change the color depth of your display, simply click the drop-down menu under the word *Colors*. You'll probably see only two options: Highest (32-bit) and Medium (16-bit). I recommend running at 32-bit unless you have an extremely old graphics card that's not capable of 32-bit color. But then, what would you be doing reading *this* book?

Refresh rate

CRT monitors have variable *vertical refresh rates*. The refresh rate is the number of times per second the screen displays an image. It's measured in *hertz*, which means cycles per second. One hertz means once per second; 60Hz means 60 times each second.

It happens that 60Hz is the lowest refresh rate that most displays can achieve. The downside of a 60Hz refresh rate is that it causes a noticeable flicker, and if you stare at a CRT monitor set at 60Hz long enough you'll probably get a massive headache. Therefore, you want your monitor to be flicker-free. You want the highest refresh rate that your monitor can display at your chosen resolution and color depth.

Click Advanced Settings to see the dialog box shown in Figure 4.22. Note that everything's grayed out except for the List All Modes button. That's because I'm using very early beta drivers for my graphics card.

NOTE This is not an issue for LCD flat panel displays. Even if you set your LCD monitor to 60Hz, you won't see any flicker. LCD displays behave differently than CRTs, and refresh is not an issue for these types of monitors.

Click the List All Modes button and another, smaller window, shown in Figure 4.23, appears. The List All Modes window bears a list of every single resolution and color depth that Windows thinks your monitor can display. Each resolution and color depth is followed by a refresh rate in hertz.

FIGURE 4.22

The Advanced display settings properties dialog box

FIGURE 4.23

The List All Modes window

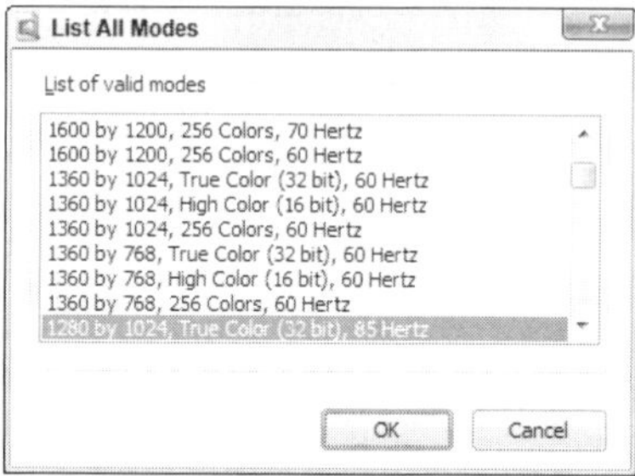

Your computer's current resolution, color depth, and refresh rate should be highlighted. Scroll the list and check out the options for the same resolution and color depth. If there's a higher refresh rate offered, click it and click OK. Then, click Apply on the advanced display settings dialog box. The refresh rate will change, and you should notice a more stable image with less flicker.

If, for some reason, the refresh rate makes your monitor go nuts, press the Escape key to revert to the previous refresh rate. As noted earlier in the section on resolution, Windows might think your monitor is capable of more than it actually is.

What's missing here?

You might notice that the advanced display settings properties dialog box looks pretty bare. If you're a gaming enthusiast, you'll notice that the graphics card's driver options tabs simply aren't there. That may change in the future, but for now, you'll have to invoke the graphics card driver applet either through the Start Menu or through the system tray icon if there is one.

For example, my computer is armed with an ATI Radeon X1900 series graphics card. The beta ATI drivers I'm using install CATALYST Control Center (Figure 4.24), but it's not available through the Display Setting's advanced properties dialog box as it was in Windows XP. Instead, I have to double-click a system tray icon to invoke it.

I talk about the deeper graphics card settings in Chapter 27.

FIGURE 4.24

ATI's CATALYST Control Center

Setting your sound card and speaker properties

When your display is all squared away, you should turn your attention to your ears. Your sound card may or may not have its own configuration applet (the current beta drivers for my SoundBlaster X-Fi doesn't), but Windows Vista has its own audio configuration interface.

You can invoke it in a couple of ways: Choose Start ➪ Control Panel ➪ Audio Devices and Sound Themes; the window shown in Figure 4.25 appears. You can also invoke that window by right-clicking the Speaker icon in the system tray and clicking Audio Devices.

The Audio Devices window shows what Windows Vista knows about the sound cards and their various features. Because at this point you're not as interested in this window as in the sound card's Properties dialog box, click once on the Audio Output (playback) Device listed, and then click Properties. The dialog box shown in Figure 4.26 appears.

Here, you can tell Windows about your speakers and set other audio options. Click the Configuration tab. This tab, shown in Figure 4.27, shows your speaker configuration. Click the Speaker Configuration drop-down menu and select the number of speakers you currently have around you. You can then click Test to hear a sound from each speaker while you watch the diagram, to ensure that each speaker is properly placed.

FIGURE 4.25

The Audio Devices window

FIGURE 4.26

The audio device's Properties dialog box

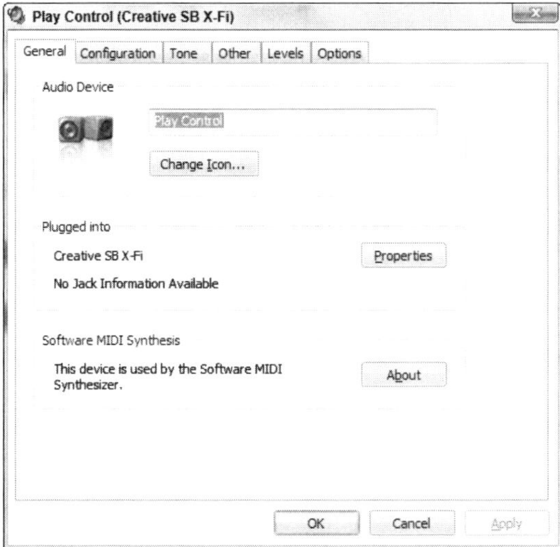

FIGURE 4.27

Tweak your speaker settings here.

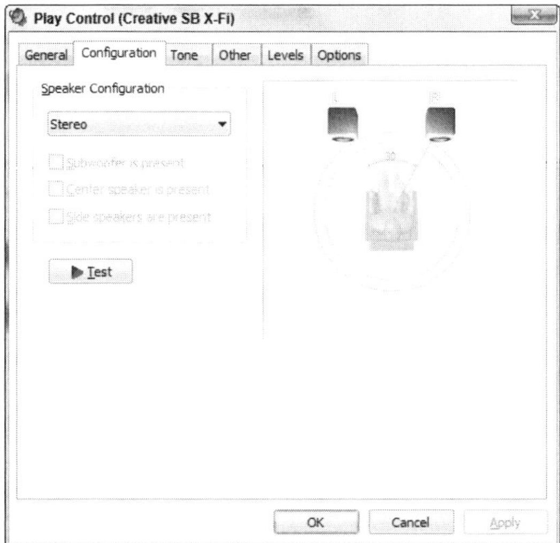

The rest of the tabs contain other settings. The Tone tab offers bass and treble controls. The Other tab might have an option to enable digital input/output, if your audio device has such capability. The Levels tab lets you adjust the gains for your audio device's various output and input ports.

The Options tab, shown in Figure 4.28, is important because it lets you select the sample rate and bit depth of your sound card's audio output. It defaults to 16/44,100, but if you have a 24-bit, 96,000Hz sound card such as a SoundBlaster Audigy or X-Fi, you'll want to set this option properly. Click the Default Format drop-down menu and select the highest sample rate and bit depth of which your sound card is capable. Then, click Test to be sure it works.

FIGURE 4.28

The Options tab of the audio device Properties dialog box

Summary

Windows Vista makes finding just about any setting that you want to adjust easy. If you can't find a shortcut, you can always go straight to the Control Panel, the central office of Vista adjustments.

I get into many, many settings changes and recommendations later in the book. You definitely want to set up the basic display and audio options before you proceed, however. They have an enormous impact on how well you'll enjoy your Windows Vista experience.

By making the proper resolution and color depth settings, you can tailor your desktop to your liking; you can ward off headaches if you have a CRT monitor by tweaking the refresh rate. You won't get the most out of your 5.1 or 7.1 speaker system unless you set the audio options. In fact, some games look directly at this setting to determine your speaker configuration, so you'll lose out on the surround gaming experience if you leave it at the default two-speaker configuration (unless, of course, you actually only have two speakers).

Chapter 5

Customizing Vista's Look and Feel

IN THIS CHAPTER

Customizing the Windows Vista interface

Working with themes

Tweaking the taskbar

Installing programs

Managing the desktop

Understanding the Notification Area (system tray)

Chapter 4 covered the customization basics. Windows operating systems have traditionally been vastly, incredibly customizable, and Windows Vista Ultimate Edition is even more so than previous versions of Microsoft's ubiquitous OS.

This chapter moves the discussion along to the overall appearance of Windows Vista. How you make this operating system look is totally up to you. You can customize everything you could in prior versions of Windows, including the desktop background (the wallpaper), the screen saver, the look of the Start Menu, the mouse pointers, and so on. Beyond these items, you can tweak the look of the new Aero interface and the color and translucency of "glass"; in other words, you can see through parts of the windows on the desktop. If you can't stand Aero, you can always switch to a classic Windows theme that looks more familiar and comfortable.

The taskbar and Start Menu in Windows Vista are similar to, but fundamentally different from those in Windows XP and other, earlier Windows operating systems. They, too, are fully customizable, and you're able, if you want, to transform them back in time to stylistically resemble those elements from earlier Windows operating systems.

Part of the appearance of Windows Vista is its icons, including those on the desktop, in the quick-launch area, and in the tray (also called the *notification area*). Those icons come from the programs that you install, which, of course, you can install where you want. You can customize the various icons however you desire, from hiding all the desktop icons (as the style guide for this book's screen shots requires me to do) and limiting other icons to embellishing the entire interface with icons anywhere and everywhere.

By the time you get to the end of this chapter, you'll be able to mold the general look and feel of Windows Vista to your whims and desires. Make it look like Windows 2000, or create something entirely new that reflects your personality. It's entirely up to you.

Possibly the best part of all is that you can change the appearance again and again, any time you want. When you get bored with the background or sick of the screen saver, change it! By working with themes, you can save a great deal of the visual configuration so that you can always revert back to a look and customization you enjoyed.

Tweaking the Appearance and Personalization Settings

Part of the Windows Vista Control Panel is dedicated to how Windows looks, sounds, and feels. You can get to that portion of Control Panel two ways:

- Choose Control Panel ➪ Appearance and Personalization.
- Right-click on an empty area of the desktop, click Personalize, and in the interactive path bar, click Appearance and Personalization.

The Appearance and Personalization window, shown in Figure 5.1, appears.

Each of the submenus contains options to make Windows look the way you want it to:

- **Personalization** is the most functional of all the menus, allowing you to customize the color scheme, the desktop background, and more.
- **Taskbar and Start Menu** lets you tweak the various aspects of those two key elements.
- **Ease of Access Center** is the equivalent of Windows XP's Accessibility options, with modes to help users overcome various disabilities and get the most out of their computing experiences.
- **Folder Options** lets you decide how Windows displays folders and subfolders, and the files within them.
- **Fonts** is the central location for installing and removing fonts.
- **Windows Sidebar** allows you to customize the Sidebar in various ways.

Through these submenus, you can mold and shape Windows Vista to your liking. The following sections run through each of these settings and show you how to tailor Vista to your taste.

FIGURE 5.1

The Control Panel's Appearance and Personalization window

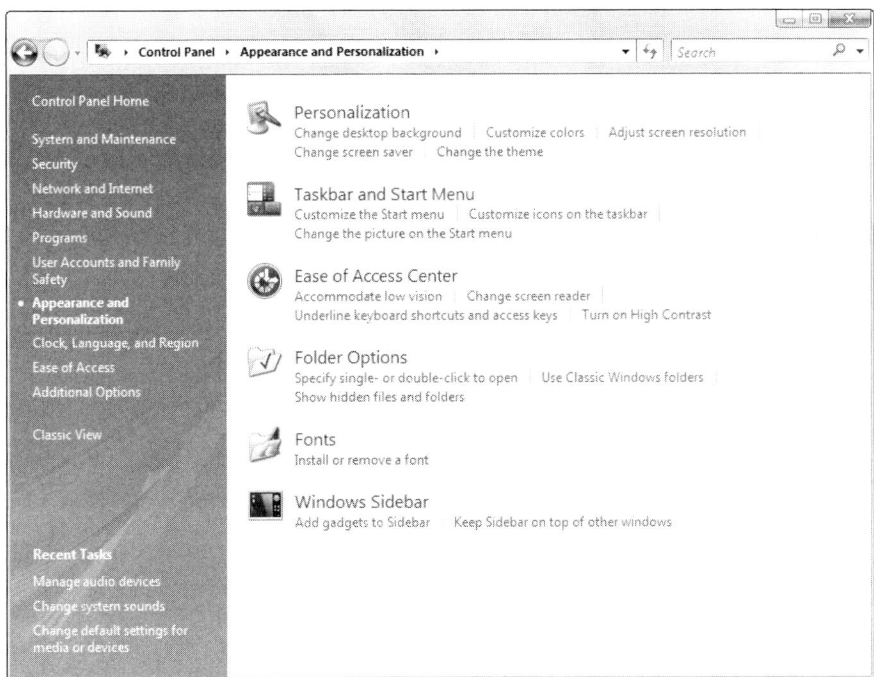

Display settings and appearance

In the Control Panel's Appearance and Personalization menu, click the Personalization submenu and then click Display Settings. The Display Settings dialog box, shown in Figure 5.2, appears. It allows you to set the screen resolution, the color bit depth, and if you click the Advanced button, the display's vertical refresh rate.

For more in-depth information on the Display Settings dialog box, see Chapter 4.

FIGURE 5.2

The Display Settings dialog box

The next submenu is called Visual Appearance. Click it to see the window shown in Figure 5.3. This simple-looking interface is more powerful than it appears.

You can customize the colors, fonts, and other aspects of the Windows interface here. The window offers several preselected colors for you to choose from, including the default Aero color. Below that the color options, you can manipulate a check box to select whether to enable the transparent property of the onscreen windows' glass areas. With this option enabled, you can control just how transparent the glass is via the Intensity slider.

To customize the color of Vista's Aero interface, click the down arrow next to Show Color Mixer. The window expands to that shown in Figure 5.4.

FIGURE 5.3

The color scheme window

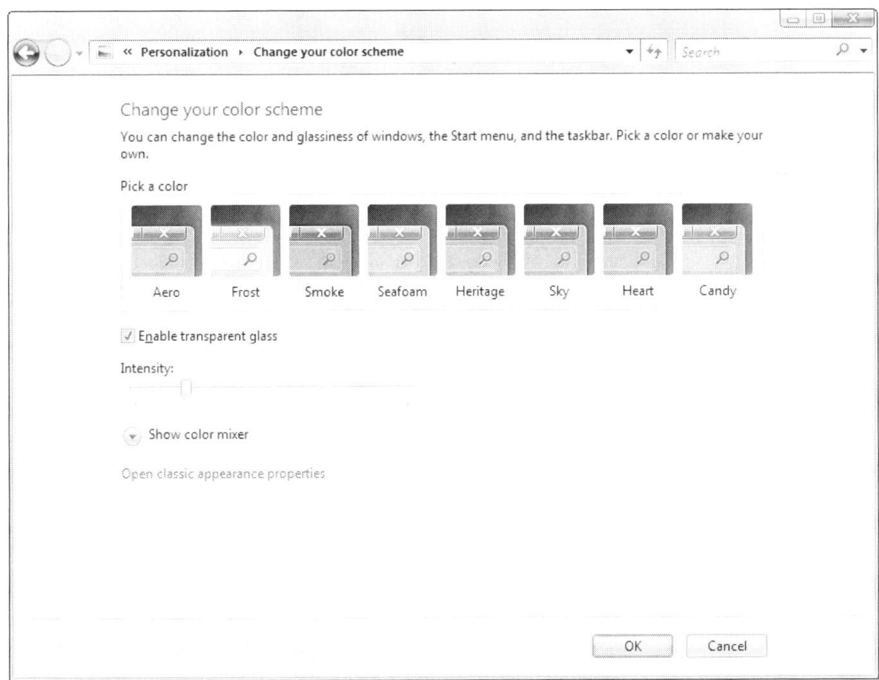

You can manipulate the color of the interface, as well as its saturation and brightness. By combining the power of these three sliders, you can achieve any color you want.

Although these global settings are usually sufficient, you can access a multitude of appearance options if you click Open Classic Appearance Properties, which opens a smaller window like that shown in Figure 5.5.

FIGURE 5.4

Note the color mixer on the bottom of the window.

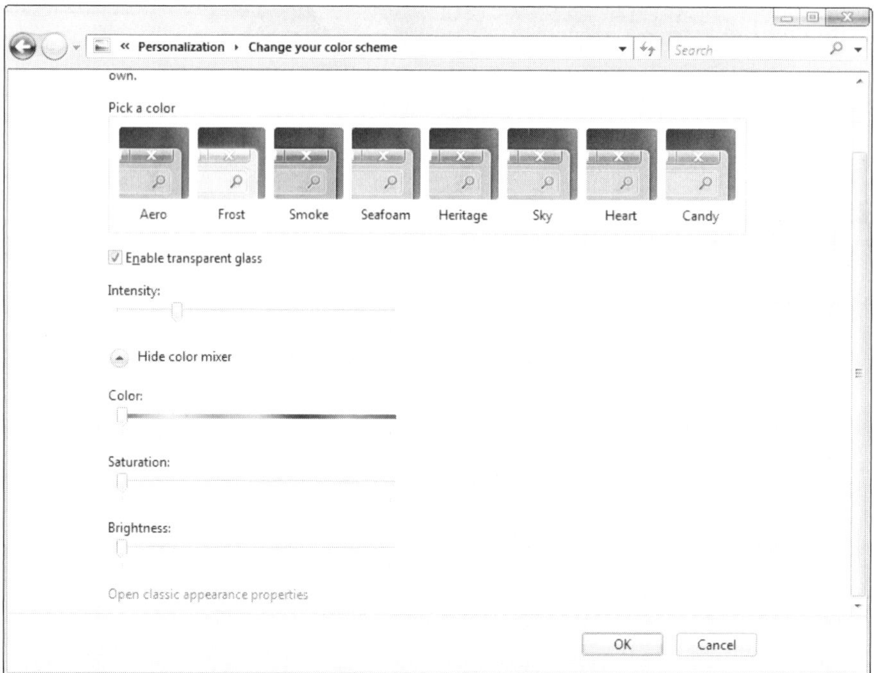

In this dialog box, you can do all kinds of stuff. You can choose a preset color scheme. Windows Aero is the default. You can also choose Basic for a less fancy version of Aero and Classic, and Standard and Classic for a couple of options closer to Windows XP's and Windows 2000's default color schemes.

Click the Effects button to choose whether to use screen font smoothing, for more eye-friendly, antialiased screen fonts. Two smoothing schemes include ClearType and Standard; if you're using an LCD monitor, ClearType looks fantastic and it's remarkably easy on the eyes. Standard looks more pixilated, but it provides more clarity on some monitors. You can also tweak whether to show shadows under menus and whether to display the contents of a window while you drag it around the screen.

FIGURE 5.5

The classic Appearance Settings dialog box

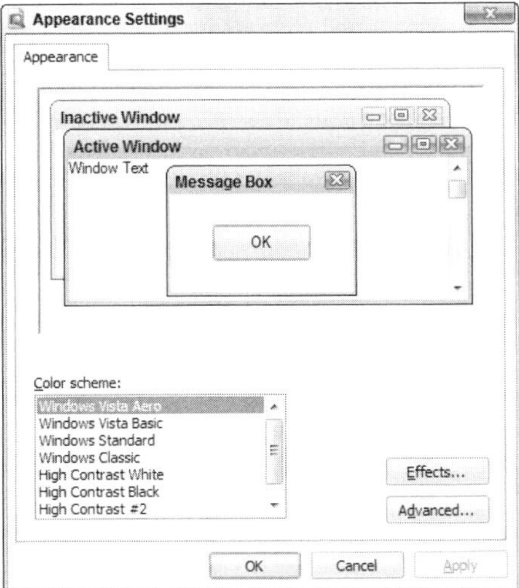

Click the Advanced button to invoke the Advanced Appearance dialog box shown in Figure 5.6. Here, you have complete control of every color and font displayed by Windows Vista. You can pull down the Item menu to find virtually any aspect of the Windows desktop that you want to tweak. Items you can customize include buttons, title bars, icons, menus, message boxes, tooltips, and so on.

For example, click Active Title Bar. You can choose the size of the title bar, its colors (it fades smoothly between Color 1 and Color 2), its font, the font size, the font color, and whether the font should be bolded and/or italicized.

FIGURE 5.6

Here you can change advanced visual appearance properties.

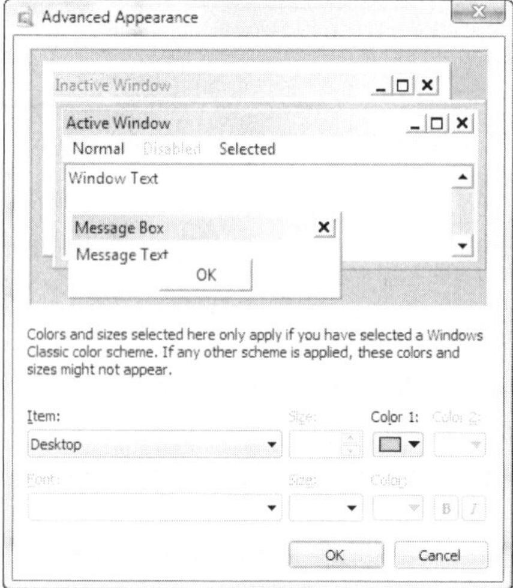

Desktop background and icons

Back in the Control Panel Personalization window, click Desktop Background. The dialog box shown in Figure 5.7 appears.

In the Desktop Background dialog box, you can choose a background for your desktop. The drop-down menu offers several options, allowing you to browse through various backgrounds included with Windows Vista. Categories for backgrounds include:

- **Black and White:** Here you'll find a selection of grayscale pictures.
- **Light Auras:** These nifty lighting effects make for cool, abstract background art.
- **Paintings:** Several backgrounds look like brush strokes, or oil on canvas.
- **Textures:** From blue pebbles to wood grain, these images are studies of interestingly textured objects.
- **Vistas:** These are mainly sweeping nature pictures.
- **Widescreen:** Especially for wide monitors, this category includes some of the light auras, vistas and textures in a different aspect ratio.

FIGURE 5.7

The Control Panel's Desktop Background dialog box

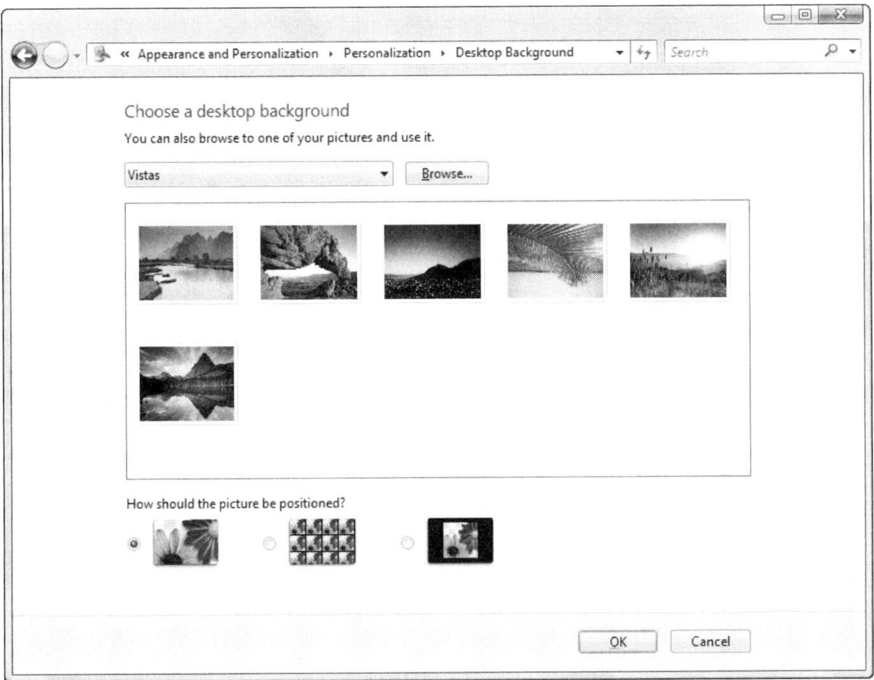

One of the options from the drop-down menu, Solid Colors, lets you choose a simple color for your desktop background; most of the screens you see in this book use a plain white background.

NOTE **If you choose an image, you can choose how to position it via the three radio buttons at the bottom of the screen. These are the equivalent of the earlier Windows' background options of Stretch, Tile, and Center, respectively. The first option resizes the image to take up the full screen, changing its aspect ratio if necessary. The second option tiles the image into a pattern. The third option centers the image; the rest of the desktop appears in a solid color that you can choose by clicking Change background color.**

You can browse your computer or your network to choose an image of your liking and make it your desktop background. Simply click the Browse button next to the drop-down menu in the Desktop Background dialog box (see Figure 5.8).

FIGURE 5.8

Here, I am browsing my network.

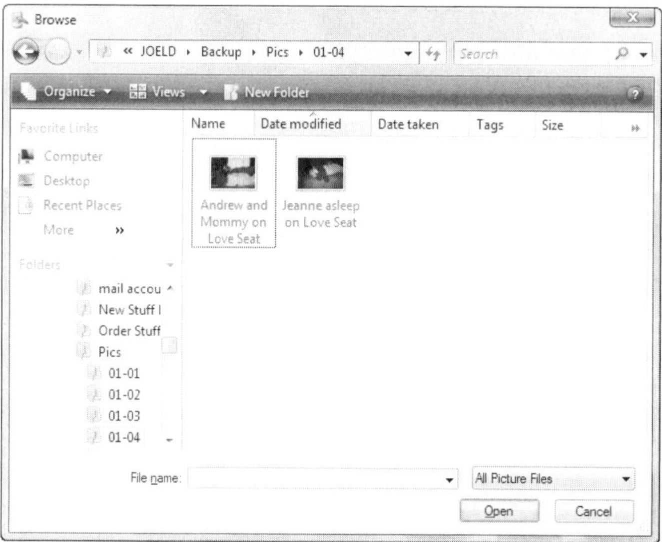

When you find a picture, click it. It immediately becomes the desktop background. Minimize your open windows to check it out (see Figure 5.9).

NOTE Instead of minimizing each open window individually, you can also click the "View Desktop" button in the Quick Launch bar, if it's available. Look on the left side of the Taskbar, just to the right of the Start button, for several Quick Launch buttons. By default, one of the Quick Launch buttons minimizes everything instantly and shows you the desktop background.

If you like the desktop picture you've chosen, bring the Desktop Background window back up from the taskbar and click OK. Otherwise, choose a different background.

Now, go back to the Personalization screen by clicking Personalization in the interactive path bar. Take a look at the Tasks pane on the left. Click Change desktop icons to invoke the window shown in Figure 5.10.

FIGURE 5.9

This background brings me a smile.

Here, you can customize the icons displayed on your computer's desktop. Choose the icons to be displayed from a bank of six system icons under the heading Desktop Icons. By default, only the Recycle Bin is displayed. Then, check out the actual icons. You can change each one, including Computer, Recycle Bin, and so on, by highlighting it and clicking Change Icon. Select an icon and click OK.

NOTE You can hide all the desktop icons easily right from the desktop. Right-click in an empty area of the desktop, hover the mouse over View, and then uncheck the menu item Show Desktop Icons. This selection overrides anything you select in the Desktop Icon dialog box.

FIGURE 5.10

Adjust the desktop icons here.

Screen saver selections

Head back to the Personalization screen by clicking Personalization in the interactive path bar. Now, click Screen Saver to invoke the Screen Saver Settings dialog box shown in Figure 5.11.

Windows Vista features a handful of all-new and updated screen savers. You can select them via the drop-down menu in the Screen saver section of the settings dialog box. The default is called Windows Logo, and it's a simple, black screen saver on which the Windows logo appears in different places.

FIGURE 5.11

The Screen Saver Settings dialog box

Click the drop-down menu and choose a screen saver; for example, Mystify, which is shown in Figure 5.12. Some screen savers offer control over how they display their images via the Settings button. The Preview button allows you to view the screen saver; the Windows desktop returns when you move the mouse or press a key.

FIGURE 5.12

The Mystify screen saver in action

The screen savers included with Windows Vista are:

- **Windows Logo:** Described earlier in this chapter.
- **None:** No screen saver. This effectively turns the screen saver feature off.
- **3D Text:** This screen saver shows text, which you can configure via the Settings button, in 3D. It moves in a manner you determine and displays whatever text you enter.
- **Aurora:** This cool screen saver shows what looks like the Northern Lights — eerie green and blue shimmering shapes on a black background.
- **Blank:** It's just what it sounds like, a blank, black screen.
- **Bubbles:** This screensaver superimposes colorful, bouncing, transparent bubbles over whatever is on the desktop when it comes on.
- **Mystify:** A funky series of lines careens around the screen on a black background.
- **Photos:** Use the Settings button to select a folder with photographs in it, and this screen saver displays them, one after another.

- **Ribbons:** Colorful ribbons of light flash across a black background with this screen saver, leaving fading trails.
- **Windows Energy:** This screensaver shows the Windows logo, and then what looks like lines of pure, pulsating electricity.

You can determine how long the system must remain idle before it displays the screen saver; simply change the time where it says Wait ... minutes. Next to that is a check box labeled On resume, display Welcome screen. If the box is selected, the screen saver will lock the current account and, when you resume Windows, you'll have to enter the account's password (if there is one) to return to the Windows desktop.

You can access the Power Management screen through the bottom of the Screen Saver Settings dialog box. Simply click Change power settings.

Sound effects

Back in the Personalization screen, click Sound Effects to invoke the window shown in Figure 5.13.

FIGURE 5.13

The Windows Sounds properties dialog box

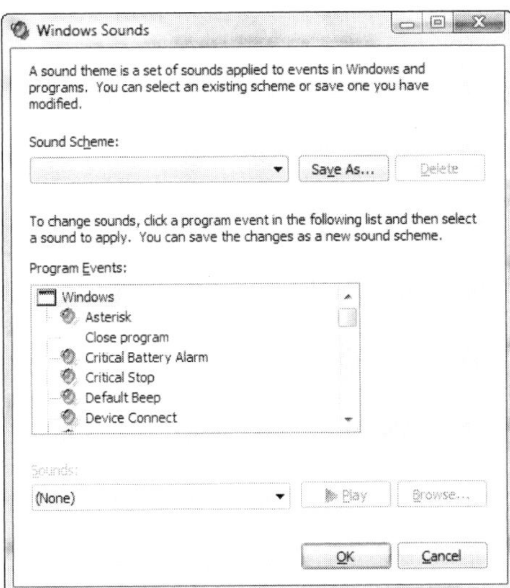

Here, you can define and save sound schemes. The Program Events box shows every system event that generates a sound. A little picture of a speaker next to an event means that a sound is already assigned to it. To hear the sound, highlight the event and click Play.

You can change the sound of an event highlighted in the Program Events box to another sound by pulling down the menu under the word *Sounds*. Select a sound to assign it to the highlighted system event. Click Play to hear the sound.

You may also use the Browse button to find your own sounds anywhere on your computer's hard drive. A browsing window, like the one shown in Figure 5.14, will appear, ready to find audio files in the .WAV format. It defaults to the C:\Windows\Media folder, where Windows stores its default sounds, but you can use any .WAV file for any system event.

FIGURE 5.14

Browsing for a sound

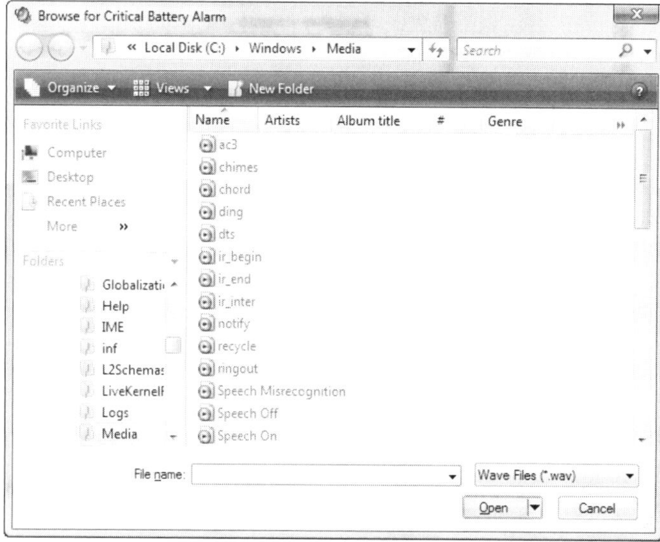

When you've tweaked the sounds to your liking, you can save your selections as a Sound Scheme. Click the Save As button and give your scheme a name. From this point on, your sound scheme will appear in the Sound Schemes drop-down menu.

Mouse pointers

Go to Control Panel ➪ Appearance and Personalization ➪ Personalization, and click Mouse Pointers. You'll see the Mouse Properties dialog box with the Pointers tab selected, as shown in Figure 5.15.

You can personalize the mouse in several ways through the Mouse Properties dialog box. You can select a pointer scheme with the drop-down menu under Scheme. You may also customize individual pointers by clicking on any of the pointers in the Customize window and browsing for a new pointer. Turn the pointer shadow off and on using the appropriate check box.

When you've customized your cursors, you can save them as your own cursor scheme. Just click Save As and give the scheme a name.

FIGURE 5.15

The Mouse Properties dialog box

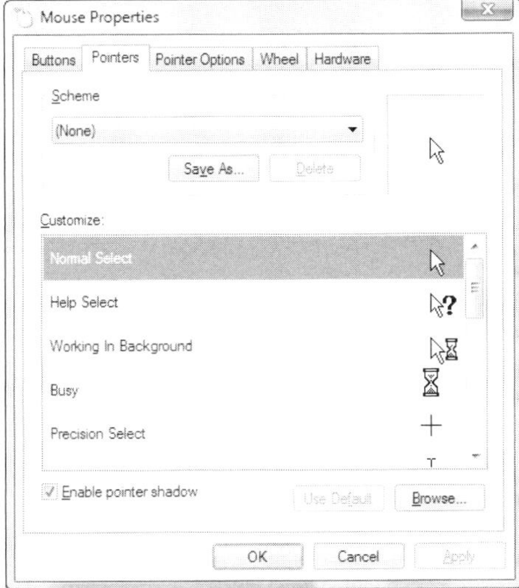

While you're at it, check out the other tabs in the Mouse Properties dialog box. You can customize some of the button properties on the Buttons tab, and determine how far the mouse wheel scrolls per notch on the Wheel tab. However, the most important tab is the Pointer Options tab (shown in Figure 5.16), which allows you to adjust the speed of the cursor in relation to mouse motion, and set other common options. Be sure to experiment with the settings on this tab to find the ideal feel and responsiveness for your mouse. This feature makes a massive difference in your Windows experience — Vista or otherwise! The Hardware tab shows information about your mouse and allows you to manually update the drivers, which you will probably never have to do as most mouse drivers come with automated installers.

FIGURE 5.16

The Mouse Pointer Options tab

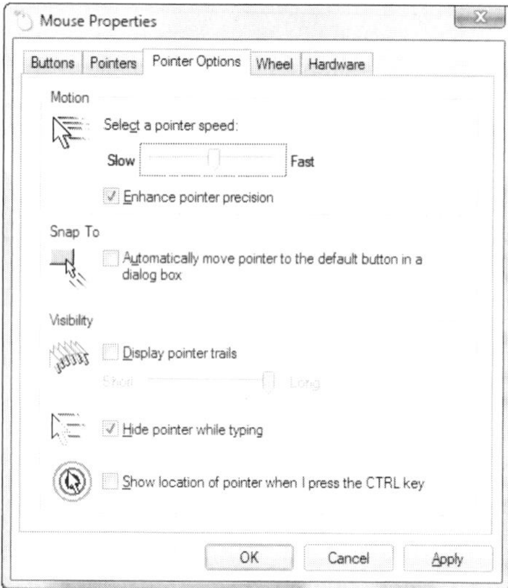

Themes

A Windows Vista theme is, more or less, a skin for your operating system. If you're familiar with Windows Media Player, WinAmp, or a number of other customizable programs, you know that a *skin* is an overall look and feel for the program.

Windows Vista themes incorporate most of what this chapter has covered so far: the desktop background and appearance, the screen saver, the desktop icons, the fonts, the sounds, the mouse pointers, and so on. You can create your own themes by customizing those elements, as discussed earlier, and then saving your current scheme as a theme.

Go to Control Panel ➪ Appearance and Personalization ➪ Personalization, and click Theme. The Theme Settings dialog box appears, as shown in Figure 5.17.

FIGURE 5.17

The Theme Settings dialog box

This window shows a sample of the current theme in the Sample box. Under Theme is a drop-down menu that shows all the themes that Windows Vista currently knows about. You can use the Save As button to save your current theme, and the Delete button to get rid of a selected theme.

If you pull down the menu, you'll see several default themes that come with Windows Vista. Windows Vista is the default Vista theme. Windows Classic resembles the interface used by Windows 2000 (see Figure 5.18).

The drop-down menu also has a Browse option. You can use it to browse the file system for other themes, which are files of the .THEME format.

TIP If you like your current desktop configuration, always save it as a theme. Doing so makes reverting back to it much easier if you change something and you don't care for the new look.

FIGURE 5.18

This is the Windows Classic theme. Note the lack of the Aero features.

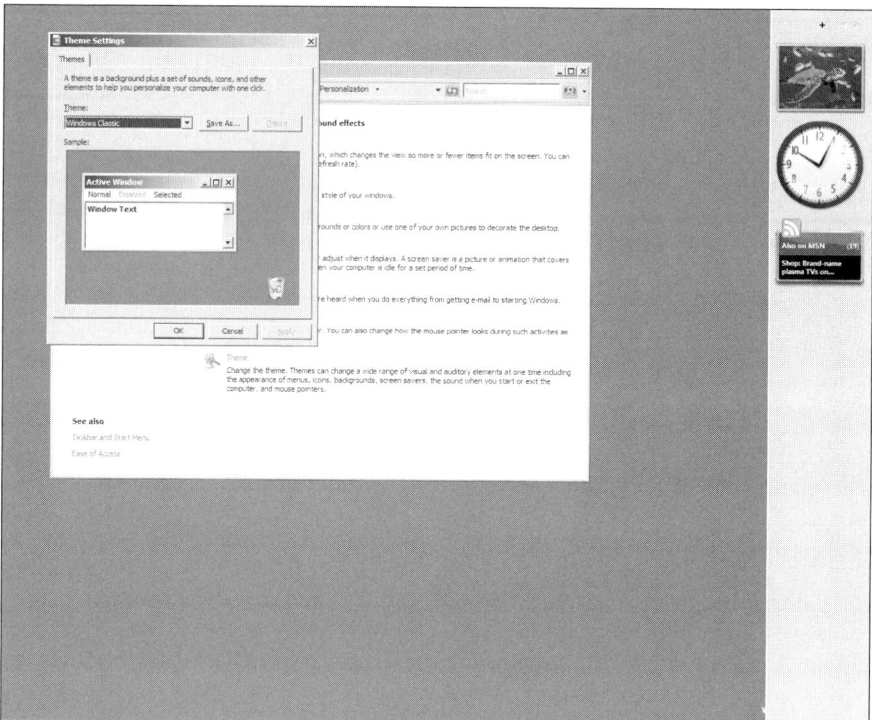

The Start Menu and taskbar

You can also customize the Start Menu and the taskbar (the bar across the bottom of the screen that shows things like the Start button, open programs, and the system notification area).

You can invoke the Taskbar and Start Menu Properties dialog box, shown in Figure 5.19, through the Control Panel under Appearance and Personalization, but a faster and easier way to do it is to right-click on an empty area of the taskbar and click Properties.

FIGURE 5.19

The Taskbar and Start Menu Properties dialog box

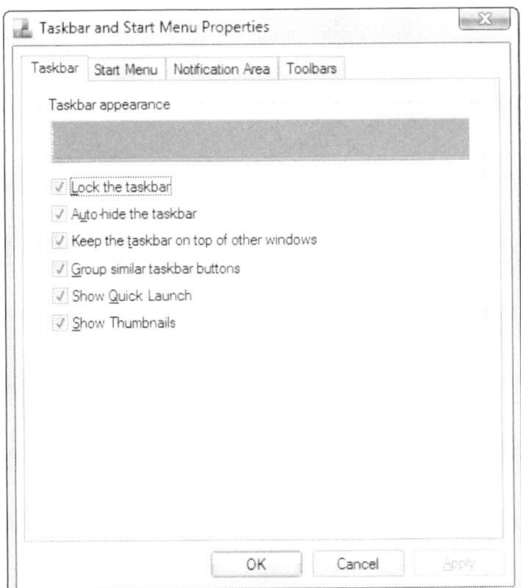

Each of the four tabs in this window enables you to customize the Start Menu and/or the taskbar in all kinds of ways. Let's look at them tab by tab:

- The **Taskbar tab** has the following options, all of which are check boxes:
  - Lock the taskbar keeps the taskbar from being resized or otherwise altered in shape.
  - Auto-hide the taskbar hides the taskbar, which reappears when you move the cursor over the bottom of the screen.
  - Keep the taskbar on top of other windows makes sure nothing obscures the taskbar.
  - Group similar taskbar buttons is for when you have several instances of one program open (for example, five Word files); the taskbar will group them into a single button.
  - Show Quick Launch displays the Quick Launch area of the taskbar, which contains single-click icons to launch programs.
  - Show Thumbnails is a new feature in Windows Vista that displays live thumbnails of the files represented by the taskbar buttons when you place the cursor over them (see Figure 5.20).

FIGURE 5.20

A thumbnail of the calculator, which is minimized to the taskbar

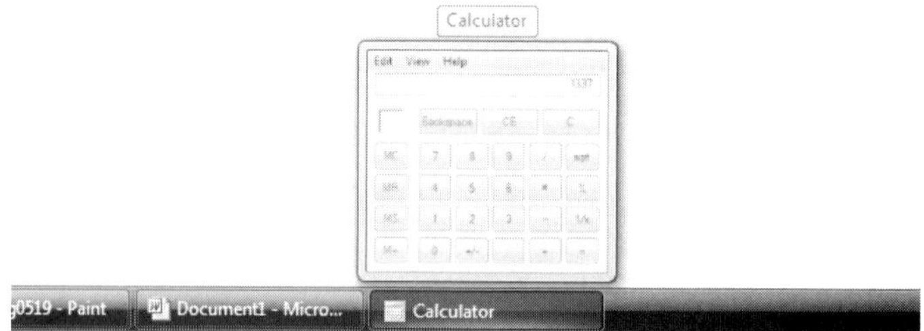

- The **Start Menu tab** has these options:
  - You can choose between Start Menu and Classic Start Menu to select the Windows Aero–style Start Menu or one more reminiscent of Windows 2000.
  - A Customize button lets you customize the Start Menu in many ways (discussed in more detail later in this section).
  - Privacy check boxes allow you to turn off the recently opened files and programs areas of the Start Menu.
- The **Notification Area tab** lets you customize the area known as the system tray:
  - You can allow it to hide icons that have been idle for some time, or customize specifically which icons to display or hide via the Customize button.
  - You can select from four items to show all the time, including the Clock, the Volume control, the Network status, and the Power status (for portable computers).

NOTE You can add additional clocks to the system tray! Click the clock, and then click Date and Time Settings. Click the Additional Clocks tab. There, you can add one or two additional clocks to the tray, and select their time zones. This feature is fantastic for people like me who work at home on the East Coast, and do lots of business with people in California!

- The **Toolbars tab** allows you to add a number of toolbars to the taskbar:
  - Address, for entering Web URLs or file system paths.
  - Windows Media Player, for controlling media right from the taskbar.
  - Links, for storing quick links to Web sites right on the taskbar.
  - Tablet PC Input Panel, for tablet PC users to write on their screens.
  - Desktop, which displays a handy menu of locations you might want to access.
  - Quick Launch (enabled by default), the Quick Launch icon area.

Customize the Start Menu

Don't close that Taskbar and Start Menu Properties dialog box yet! Click back to the Start Menu tab and click the Customize button to invoke the Customize Start Menu dialog box, shown in the following figure.

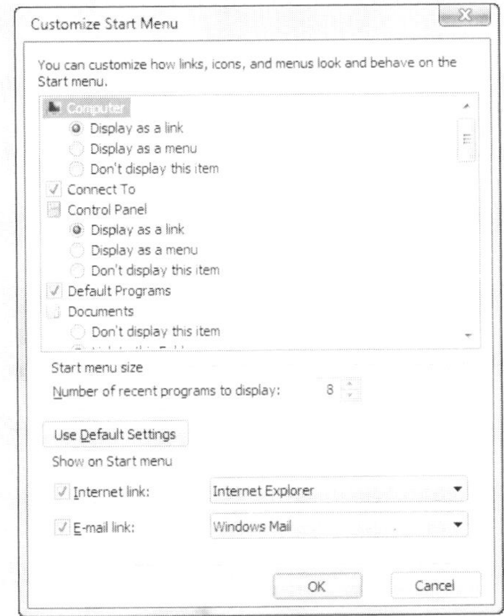

The Customize Start Menu dialog box

Here you can customize what appears in the Start Menu, and how many of the items are displayed. Check boxes let you selectively add or remove elements, like Computer, Connect To, Default Programs, Help, and so on. Some items have radio buttons that allow you to display the item as a link, or as a menu (which slides out when you move the cursor over the element).

You can customize the number of recently used programs that Windows Vista displays. It can go as high as 30, and as low as 0; the default is 8.

Finally, you can elect through check boxes to show the Internet and E-mail links, and even customize the default programs. For example, if you have both Outlook and Windows Mail installed, you can click the drop-down menu next to E-Mail link and select the program of your choice.

Folder options

You can tell Windows Vista how you want to view folders as you navigate through the file system. Open the Control Panel, click Appearance and Personalization, and then click Folder Options. The Folder Options dialog box opens, as shown in Figure 5.21.

FIGURE 5.21

The Folder Options dialog box

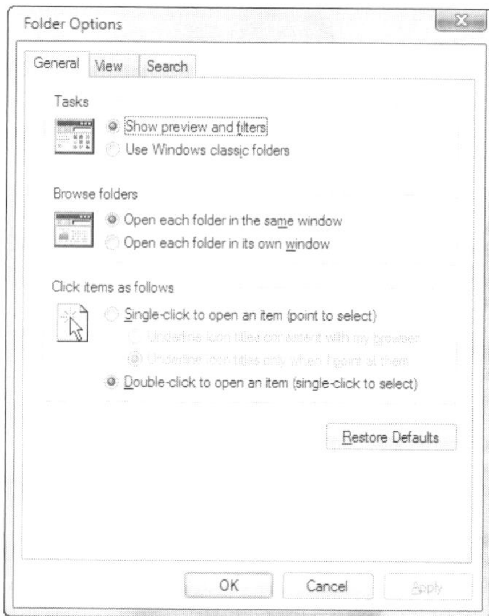

The General tab lets you choose how folders look and operate. Under Tasks, you can choose to use the new Vista folder style, or the Windows classic style. Compare the two in Figures 5.22 and 5.23.

Lower on the General tab you can tell Windows Vista to browse folders in a single window, or to open new windows as you browse. The latter can result in a cluttered desktop!

FIGURE 5.22

This is the Computer folder with the Vista interface. Note the Favorites links and the contextual buttons.

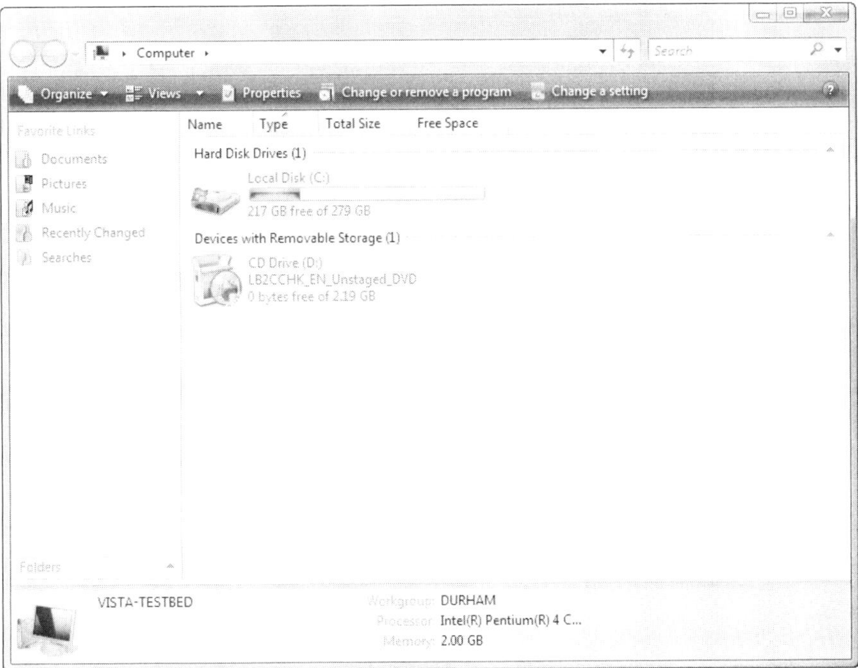

Finally, under Click items as follows, you can elect to double-click folder items to open them (which is the default), or single-click them as if they were Web-style hypertext links. You can also tell Windows to underline folder items that it'll open with a single click all the time, or to only underline them when you put the cursor over them.

FIGURE 5.23

This is the same Computer folder with the Windows classic interface. Though it still has Aero glass elements, it shows the traditional drop-down menus and lacks the tasks pane.

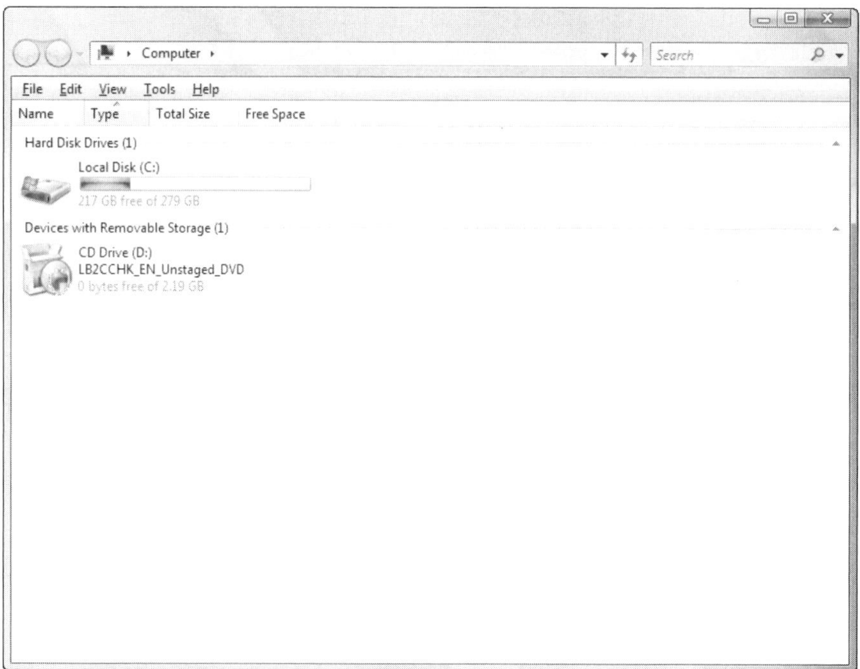

The next tab is the View tab, shown in Figure 5.24. This tab has two sections: Folder Views and Advanced Settings. If you make any changes to the folder settings, including the settings under any folder's Views button, you can apply those changes to *all* the folders in the file system. For example, if you open the Computer folder, click Views, and then select Details, the folder's view will change to show you the details of the items within it. You can then tell Windows to apply this view to all of its folders through the Folder Views section of the Folder Options' View tab.

If you've worked with the folder settings in Windows 9x, 2000, or XP, the Advanced Settings section will look hauntingly familiar. It contains a number of check box options and a few radio buttons. You can tell Windows Vista to show icons instead of thumbnails (mainly in media folders), to show hidden files and folders, to reveal the extensions of known files (which I find particularly handy), and so on.

FIGURE 5.24

The Folder Options View tab

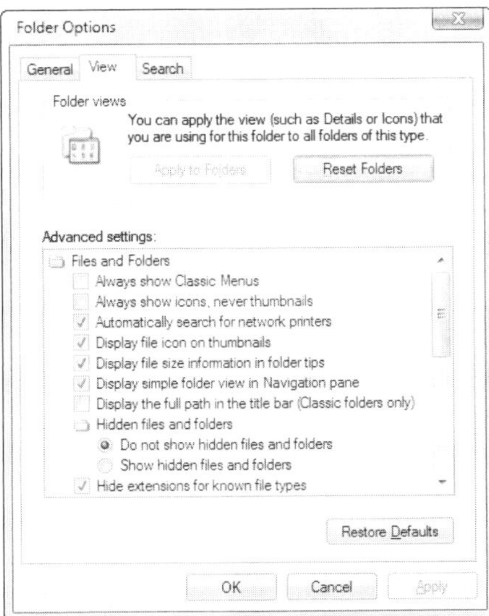

The Sidebar in Brief

I cover the Sidebar extensively in Chapter 8, but because it's a very visible desktop feature, I thought I would mention it here as well.

The Sidebar is that new thingie on the right side of the screen. By default, it contains a small slide show of the images in your Pictures folder, a clock, and an RSS feed notification applet. Those items are called *gadgets*.

The Sidebar is heavily customizable. If you right-click it, the context menu offers customizations. You can hide the Sidebar, bring the gadgets to the front of the screen, and even add and remove gadgets. Some of my favorite gadgets are the calculator and the notepad. You can get news about gadgets at `www.microsoftgadgets.com`, and you can score new gadgets online!

Summary

The look and feel of Windows Vista is nearly infinitely customizable. By surfing through the various Personalization options in Control Panel, you can transform Vista's look however you please, and you can save your creations as Themes. You can use any image file, including pictures you take with your own digital camera.

By saving themes, you can easily change from one set of visual and audio schemes to another with ease. Note that each user account can have its own look and feel, and its own set of themes; if you switch users, Vista automatically displays the new user's own theme. Themes include everything from desktop appearance settings to color and sound schemes.

Use Windows Vista's Personalization features to transform the operating system's look and feel to something you're truly pleased with. You have to stare at the computer all the time, so create a theme you're content with. I love my current theme (see Figure 5.25)!

FIGURE 5.25

My theme

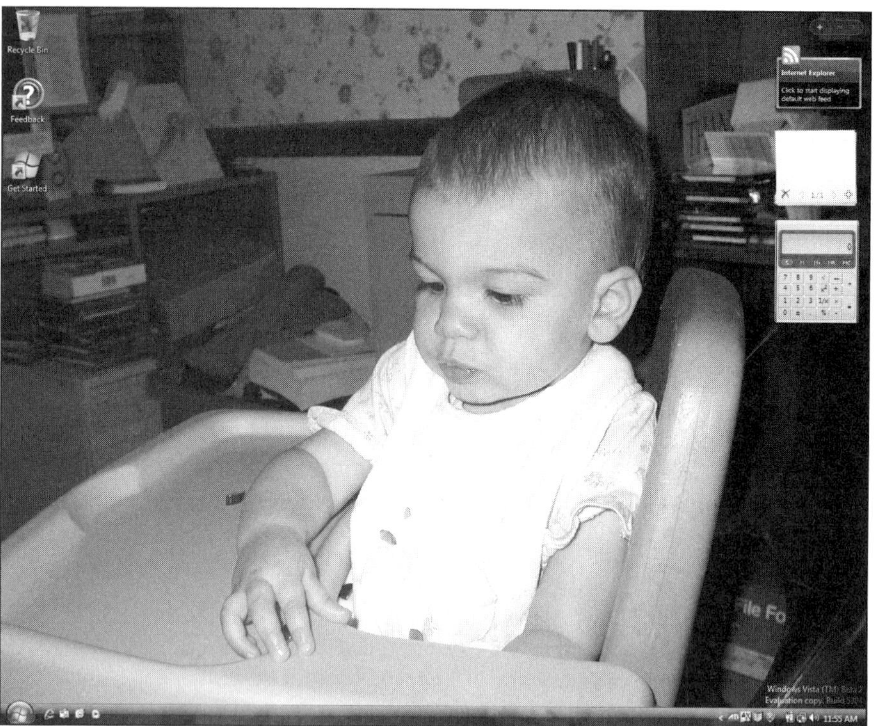

Chapter 6

Games and Programs Included with Windows Vista Ultimate

IN THIS CHAPTER

Playing the games included with Windows Vista Ultimate

Using other programs and utilities included with Windows Vista Ultimate

You might be bored during a long day of work and feel the need to refresh yourself, and kill some time, with a casual game. You might find your computer is overstuffed with junk you don't need, like temporary files and downloaded program files that you don't need anymore. You might want to view your myriad of images as a slide show, bang out a few notes in a simple text editor, or schedule some appointments that you really can't forget about.

Windows operating systems have a history of including a rich selection of games, applications, and utilities that make life as a Windows user easier and more fun.

I'm going to be brutally honest here: The Windows games aren't the best titles the world has to offer. They're strictly for casual gamers, and they pale in comparison to major release titles like *Doom* or *Tomb Raider* or titles in some other iconic franchise. Windows games are useful, however, for when you have a few minutes to kill or when you're stuck in the office and you can't load up those multiple-gigabyte monsters.

Games aside, Windows Vista Ultimate comes with all sorts of programs to help you accomplish a whole multitude of tasks before you even begin to load up third-party applications. As with games, many of these applications compare poorly to big-name commercial software products, but they're handy if you don't have access to a major title.

For example, Windows Calculator does just what it sets out to do; it's no spreadsheet, but it adds and subtracts like nobody's business. WordPad is a far cry from Microsoft Word, but it's better at formatting text than Notepad. But speaking of Notepad, some HTML gurus won't use anything else to create and edit Web pages.

This chapter looks at the games, applications, and utilities that come with Windows Vista Ultimate. They may not be at the top of the software food chain, but they're handy to have around and they're good at what they do.

Games Included with Windows Vista Ultimate

People become as addicted to Windows games as they do to the best commercial titles. Why is that? I think there are multiple reasons. For one, Windows games are universal; anywhere you go where you have access to a computer, you can most likely play Solitaire, Minesweeper, or Hearts.

Second, they're simple to play. Most of them take minutes to learn, and after that you can play for as long as you like. Windows games are terrific for killing small amounts of time. If you have to go to the dentist in ten minutes, you won't have the time to play through a level of *Hitman: Blood Money*, but you can get in a round of FreeCell.

Windows Vista Ultimate Edition includes most of the standard Windows games in its Games folder (see Figure 6.1), with the exception of the Internet-based games like Reversi and Backgammon. It also adds a few new titles, some of them classic and some innovative.

FIGURE 6.1

The Windows Vista Games folder

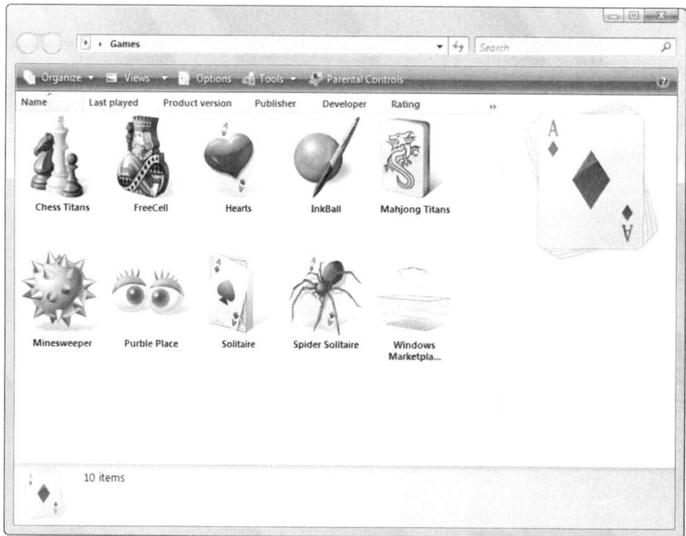

The old standards

If you're familiar with Windows operating systems, you know these games. Some of them go back as far as Windows 3.1. They've all been given a terrific facelift and Microsoft has updated their audio. Each has a Help file to assist you in learning the rules, and — this is new to Vista — they spawn pop-up help balloons when the computer thinks you need them. In addition, most of the games keep statistics of how often you play — and how often you win!

TIP Another new feature that the games boast is the ability to save your progress. If you have to leave a game in the middle, choose Game ⇨ Options, and then click in the check box next to Always save on exit. When you exit the game, Windows will offer to save it for you.

Solitaire

Solitaire, shown in Figure 6.2, is the standard in single-player card games. Arrange the cards in alternating suit color in the seven rows at the bottom of the screen. When you find an ace, move it to one of the four home stacks; then, stack cards of the same suit upon it in ascending order.

FIGURE 6.2

Classic, engaging, and maddening: Solitaire

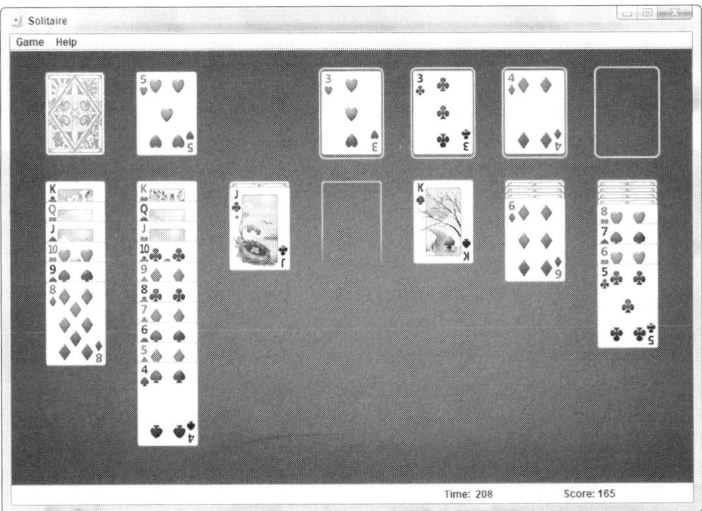

It sounds simple, but it can be frustrating. You can only flip cards over to put them in play when you've removed all the cards atop them; you can also, of course, flip cards up from the deck when you don't have any other moves. If an ace or a low card ends up buried (flipped down) so that you can't get to it, you're in trouble.

Solitaire has lots of options under the Game ➪ Options submenu. You can keep score standard or Vegas-style; draw one or three cards from the deck at once; and choose from a bunch of decks (choose Game ➪ Change appearance), as shown in Figure 6.3.

FIGURE 6.3

Customize your Solitaire deck's appearance here.

FreeCell

A cunning Solitaire variation, FreeCell, shown in Figure 6.4, features eight rows of cards, all face up. You can arrange them as you would in Solitaire: in descending order, alternating suit colors. On the upper left are four "cells" that serve as places to hold one card each for as long as you like. To the right of those free cells are the home cells, where you stack cards, ace first and ascending from there, of the same suit.

To win, you have to truly think ahead. A single move can have ramifications that affect the entire game until the end. Should you drop that five of clubs onto a free cell to free up the cards beneath it, not knowing when you'll be able to put the five back in play? Do you stack the jack of hearts onto the queen of spades, or will that screw you up later when you're trying to stack cards on the home cells?

FIGURE 6.4

FreeCell is tough; you have to think like a chess player.

As with Solitaire, you can customize the look of FreeCell through the Game ➪ Change appearance submenu. You can also play the exact same game, with the same card deal, more than once if you want: Through the Game ➪ Select game submenu, you can choose between games numbered between one and 1,000,000. Every game has a solution, but you probably couldn't win them all in a single lifetime!

Spider Solitaire

The most difficult of the Windows Solitaire games, Spider Solitaire (see Figure 6.5) has three difficulty levels: Beginner uses cards of only a single suit; Intermediate uses two suits, and Advanced uses all four suits (see Figure 6.6).

The goal sounds simple. Arrange the cards, dealt in ten rows, into stacks of the same suit from the king high to the ace low. Note that the game uses multiple decks, so you will see the same card more than once. Each move you make drops your score, which starts at 500, by a point. You score points by completing entire stacks from king to ace.

FIGURE 6.5

Spider Solitaire, with all four suits, can cause your head to explode.

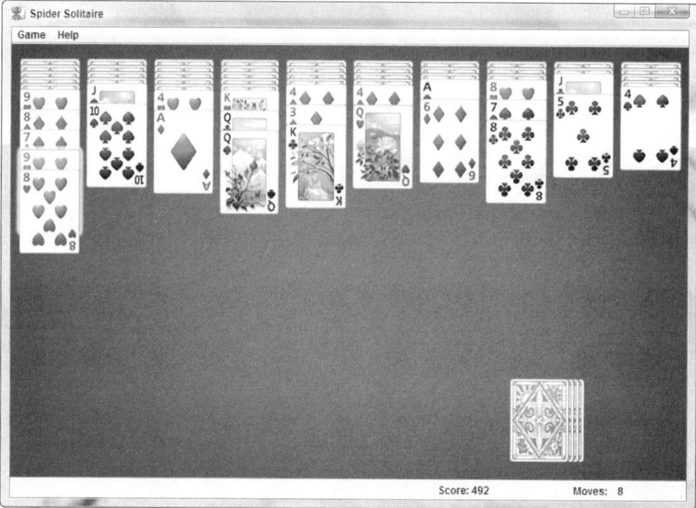

FIGURE 6.6

Choose a level when you start Spider Solitaire.

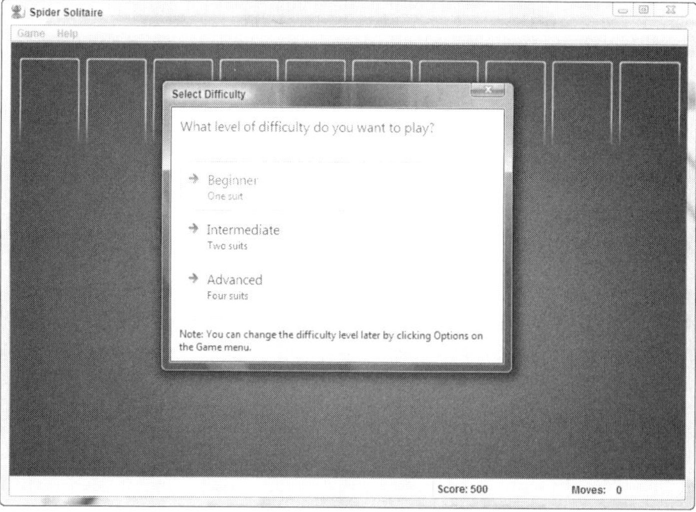

When you run out of moves, you can click the deck, which will deal out a new card onto each of the ten stacks. That can be a boon or a bust, throwing off sequences you' already had started with random cards. Even though 'winning on the beginner level is tough, Spider Solitaire with four suits is a maddening challenge that I know people would be happy to win *once in their lives*.

Hearts

Hearts, shown in Figure 6.7, is a great game to play with real cards and real people. It's a four-player card game far simpler than Bridge, which I've never come to understand, and it goes quickly. An equal number of cards is dealt to each of the four players. Before play starts, players are given a chance to examine their hands and choose three cards to pass to another player.

FIGURE 6.7

Hearts is a pleasant game of strategy.

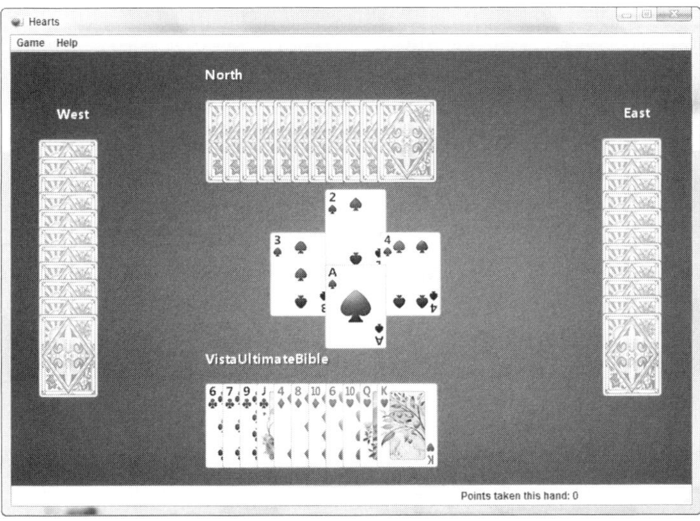

The player with the two of clubs starts the first trick. Players must follow suit; that is, they must each throw a card of the same suit that was lead, unless their hand lacks any cards of that suit. When each player has thrown a card, whoever threw the highest card of the suit that was lead takes all four cards.

If you happen to collect any hearts when you win the deck, you score a point for each one. The queen of spades is a special card, which counts as 13 points. Here's the twist: you *don't* want points. The first player to get to 100 points loses the game.

The only time you want to collect hearts and that nasty queen is when you're trying to *shoot the moon*. If you manage to collect *all* the hearts and the queen of spades, you get zero points — and everyone else scores 26!

Minesweeper

It's not a card game! Minesweeper, shown in Figure 6.8, is a challenge for the logically inclined. The game takes place on a grid, whose size you can customize through the Game ➪ Options submenu. A certain number of bombs is hidden within the grid. You uncover squares by clicking them.

FIGURE 6.8

Minesweeper challenges you to think before you act.

When you uncover each square, you'll reveal either a bomb, a black space, or a number. Numbers indicate how many bombs are adjacent to the square with the number in it. Using the configuration of the numbers you uncover, you must figure out where all the bombs are hidden.

It's up to you to mark all squares in which the mines are hidden by right-clicking them, without left-clicking a square with a bomb beneath it. If you click a bombed square, the game is over. To add to the fun, the game is timed; you not only try to win, but also to better your time and beat other peoples' best times.

The fresh faces

Windows Vista Ultimate Edition includes four brand-new titles for casual players of all ages. Two of these games, Chess Titans and Mahjong Titans, are classic board games dating back to medieval times. The other two, InkBall and Purble Place, are wholly original creations.

Chess Titans

The Game of Kings comes to Windows Vista Ultimate Edition in the form of Chess Titans (see Figure 6.9), a simple-to-play chess game that's smart enough to challenge all but the most serious of players. You can play this fully 3D game against the computer at any of ten difficulty levels, or against a person seated at the same computer.

FIGURE 6.9

Chess Titans is pretty...and pretty challenging.

Chess Titans allows you to rotate the board by right-clicking anywhere and dragging the mouse, so you can view it from any angle. A traditional top-down view is available through the Game ⇨ Options submenu. You can customize the look of the board and the pieces through the Game ⇨ Change Appearance submenu.

If you find yourself hopelessly outclassed and want to give up, Choose Game ⇨ Resign. There's no shame in resigning when you know you've been beaten!

Mahjong Titans

If you've never played mahjong, get ready for a new addiction. It seems like a simple tile-matching game, but Mahjong Titans, shown in Figure 6.10, is far more than that.

Play is easy enough. You choose from one of six tile layouts, as shown in Figure 6.11. You can customize the look of the tiles and the background through the Game ⇨ Change Appearance submenu. To play, match tiles that are not blocked horizontally on both sides. If one side or both sides of a tile is not blocked, and there's no tile atop it, that tile is available; if you can match it with another one that's similarly available, click on both tiles and they'll vanish.

FIGURE 6.10

Mahjong is a fiercely addictive game.

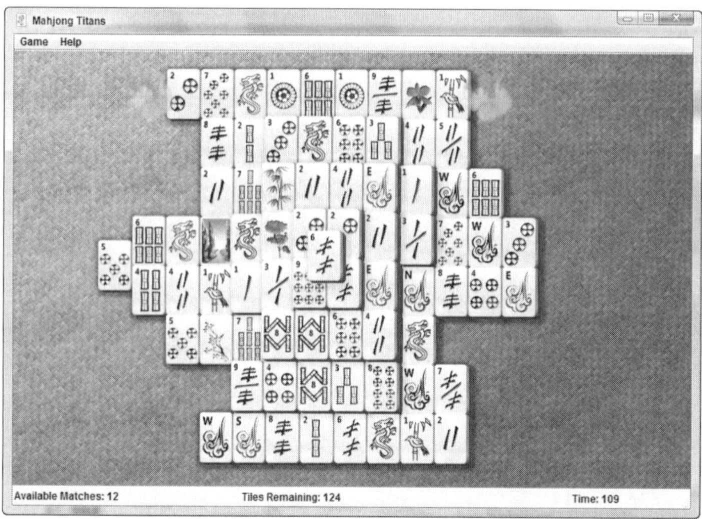

FIGURE 6.11

The more tiles are available from the start, the easier a layout is in Mahjong.

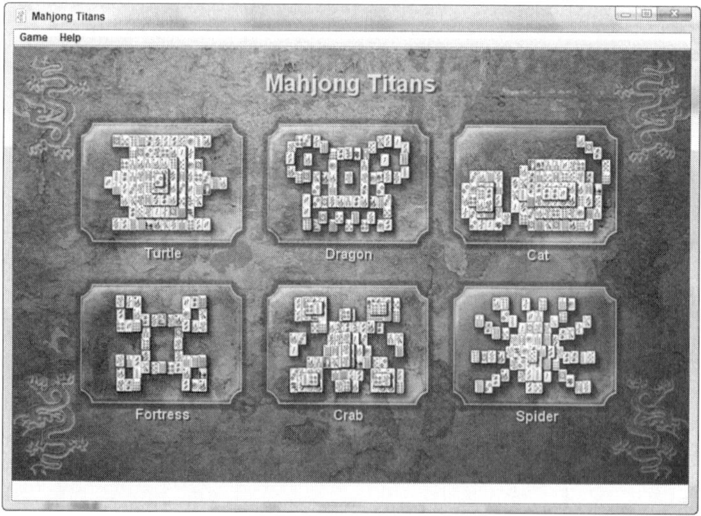

The board holds several copies of each tile, so be picky about the ones you remove. If you take the wrong pair, you could trap needed tiles beneath other tiles, resulting in a loss. Monitor the bottom left of the window, in the status bar, which shows the number of available matches remaining. If it falls to zero before you've cleared the board of tiles, you lose.

Right-click a tile if you think there's a match for it but you can't find one. The game will reveal any matches for that tile, or notify you if there are none.

InkBall

This wholly original game challenges you to knock balls into holes of the same color — with a pen. A cross between billiards, golf, and Microsoft Paint, InkBall, shown in Figure 6.12, is the first Windows action game.

FIGURE 6.12

Use ink to sink the balls.

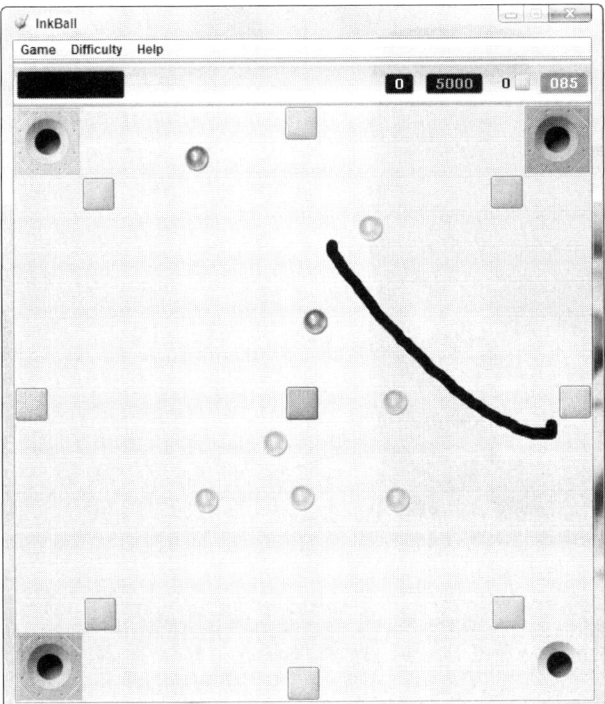

On each board, one or more balls is released. Each ball has a color-coordinated goal in the form of a hole. The balls bounce freely about. You can direct their paths by drawing lines; the angle of the line you draw indicates the trajectory of the ball after it bounces off. After a ball strikes a line you've drawn, the line disappears. You try to guide each ball into its proper hole as quickly as possible.

Draw simply by clicking and dragging the mouse cursor. Five difficulty levels determine the speed and number of balls, and also the obstacles in their way. Some obstacles can actually change the color of any ball that strikes them, so be careful!

Purble Place

Perfect for young children, Purble Place (see Figure 6.13) challenges tots with games of skill. For example, a cake-matching game challenges players to create cakes based on one shown; they must match the shape, the colors of the cake and frosting, and the toppings.

FIGURE 6.13

Youngsters will beg to play — er, *learn* — with Purble Place.

Purble Place also includes a memory game, in which players try to find pairs of cards by remembering the locations of cards they flip over on a grid. A third game is similar to Mastermind, in which players try to figure which facial features a character wants, first by guessing and then by deducing the proper features through clues (for example, "you got two features right; try again").

Complete with adorable animation and appealing, cartoonish art, Purble Place will have youngsters begging to play — that is, *learn* — using the computer.

Applications and Utilities Included with Windows Vista Ultimate

Vista lets you get a lot of things done right out of the box. When you install Windows Vista Ultimate, you're also installing a number of useful applications. Before you laugh, let me assure you that most of these applications really are useful; whereas a great deal of the Windows extras in the past have been half-realized, limited throw-ins that nobody really used, you'll probably find yourself actually appreciating the goodies that come with Vista Ultimate.

NOTE I cover many of these applications and utilities in depth in other chapters. If that's the case, the chapter in question is notated for you. The others are summed up right here in this chapter.

Applications

Applications, as opposed to games and utilities, are programs used to get stuff done: to communicate, to write, to read, to create, and so on. Windows Vista Ultimate includes more than a dozen applications to let you do everything from looking at pictures to authoring essays, and more.

You can launch most of the applications right through the Start Menu. Just click the Start button and hover the cursor over All Programs to see most of the applications listed. Click Accessories to view the rest. Launch any of them by clicking the application's name itself.

Windows Calendar

The two core elements of a PIM (personal information manager) are a contact manager and a calendar. Throw in an e-mail client and you practically have something as powerful as Microsoft Outlook.

With Windows Vista, you get Windows Calendar, Windows Contacts, and Windows Mail, a trifecta comprising a very promising PIM. You can take care of communications, keeping track of people you know, and meetings and appointments, all without installing a single third-party application.

Windows Calendar, shown in Figure 6.14, is a powerful creation that lets you schedule appointments, meetings, and whatever you want, as well as set pop-up reminders. Reminders can occur any time before the scheduled event that you want. If you need to drive across town for a doctor's appointment, you can schedule a reminder to appear an hour ahead of time, or if you're expecting a phone call you can have the reminder appear at the exact time of the appointment.

Windows Calendar is also a task manager; you can add to it stuff that you just need to get done. You can schedule Tasks, too, and assign them reminders, but only if you want to.

To add an appointment, simply click the New Appointment button in the toolbar; alternatively, you can navigate to the day and time you need to make the appointment and click right on the calendar itself. When you select an appointment, you can customize it with the interface that appears on the right side of the window, as shown in Figure 6.15. You can give it a name, details, a location, a URL, and a duration; set recurrences for reoccurring events; and even give it notes.

One powerful feature of the calendar is its ability to be shared. You can share your calendar with others on a network, and they can share theirs. Thus, if each family member has his or her own calendar, you can coordinate events to avoid scheduling little Julie's piano lesson during Mom's dentist appointment.

FIGURE 6.14

Windows Calendar remembers everything you need to know so you don't have to.

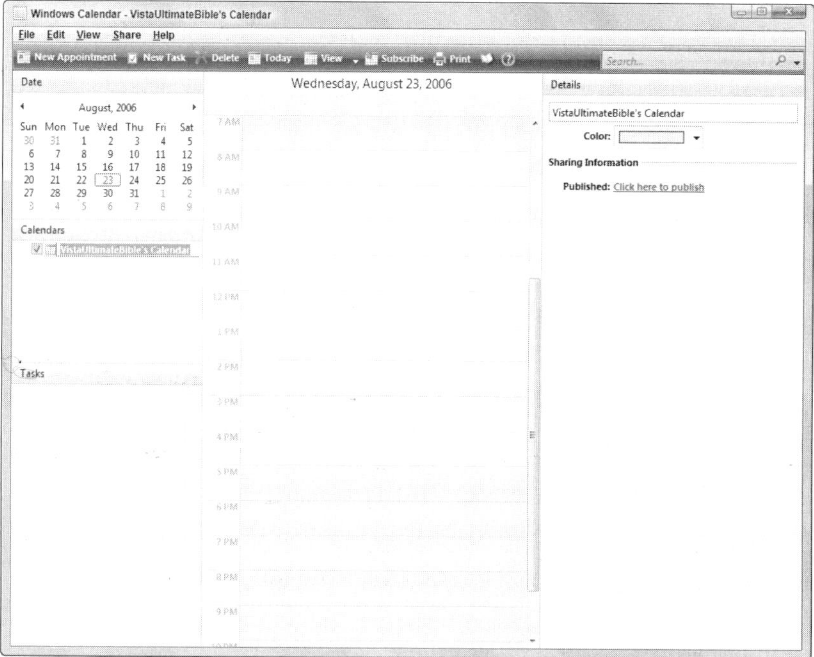

A Tour of Windows Vista

Our tour starts with a cool background and a customized sidebar on the Windows Vista desktop. This background is included with the operating system.

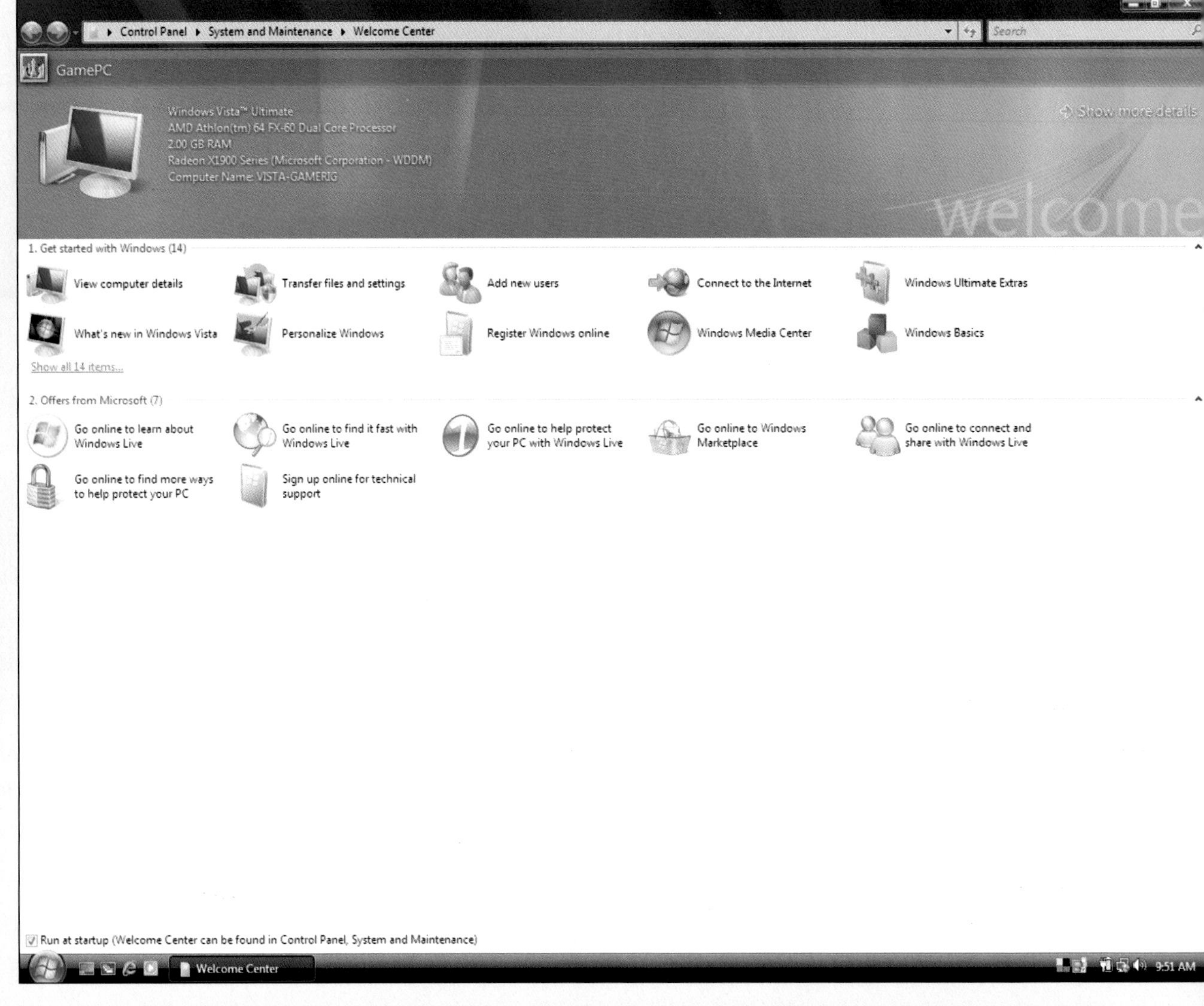

When Windows Vista first starts, it displays the helpful Welcome Center. You can click the check box at the bottom of the window to prevent it from starting every time Vista boots up.

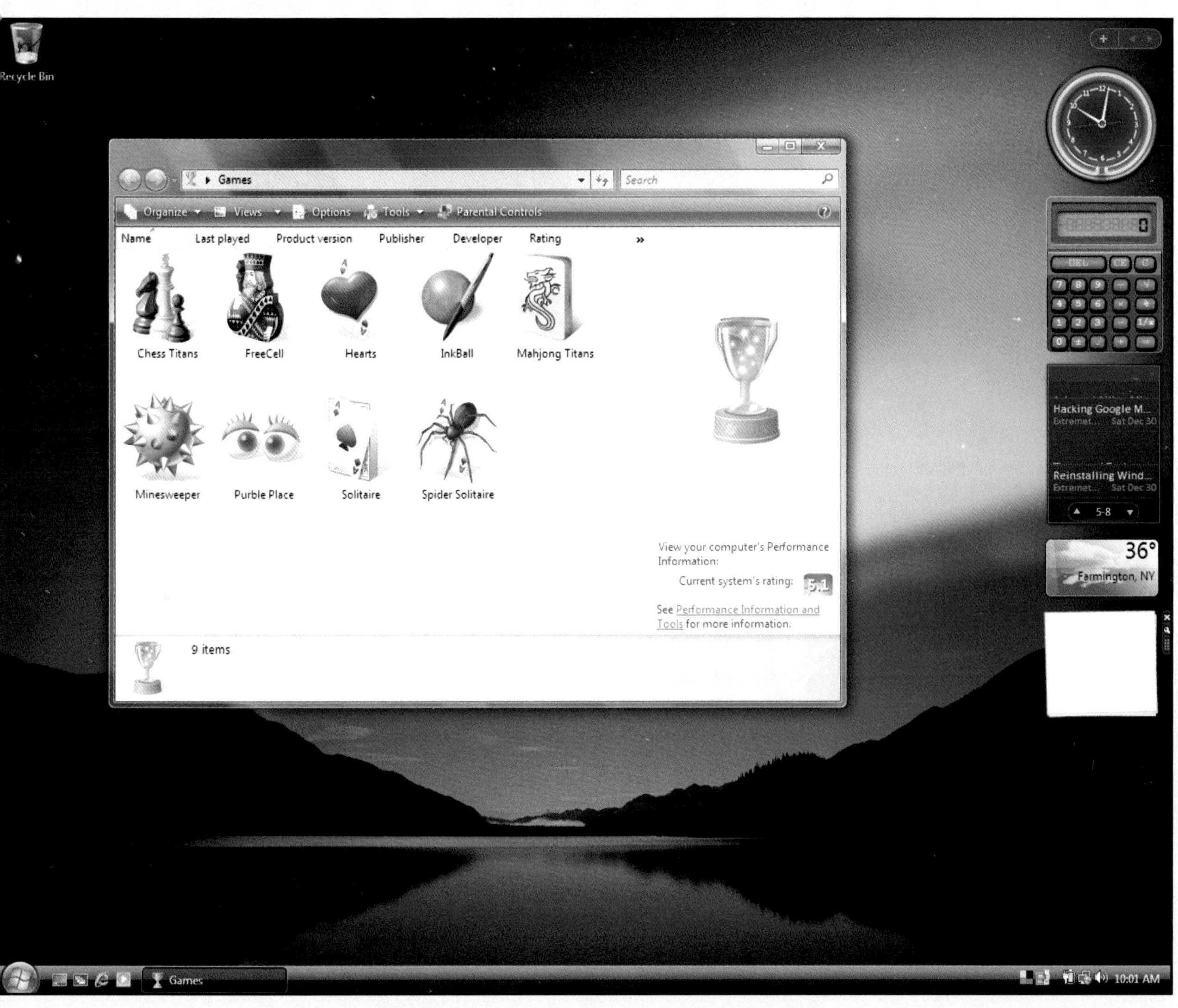

Of course, the first stop should be the Games folder, to check out the new games included with Windows Vista Ultimate.

Chess Titans is a cool, 3-D chess game included with Windows Vista Ultimate.

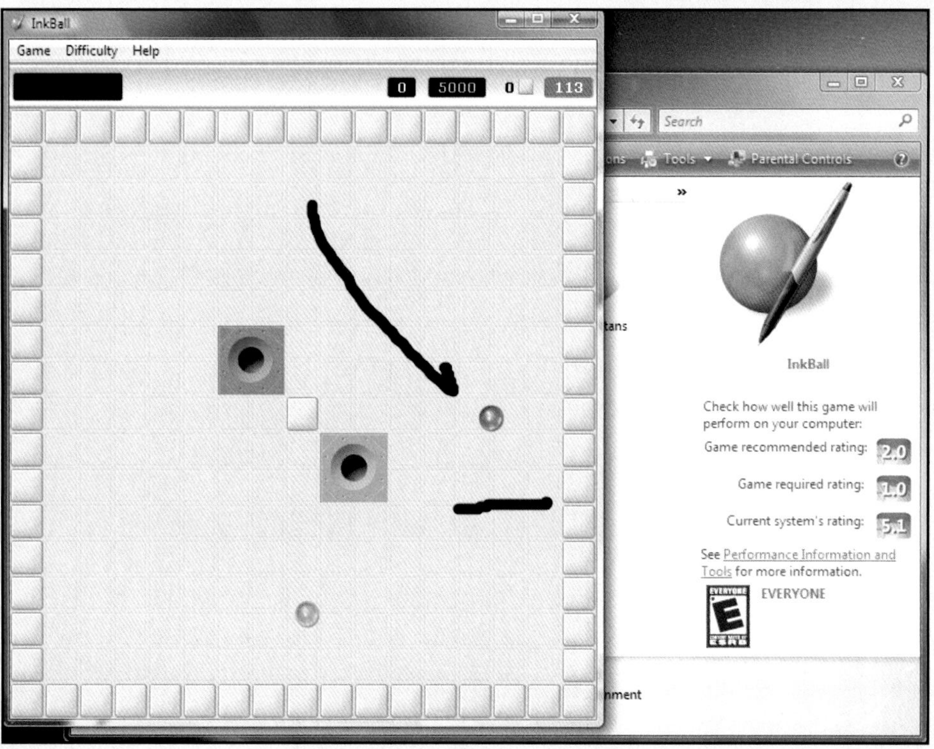

The action-puzzler InkBall will drive you nutty.

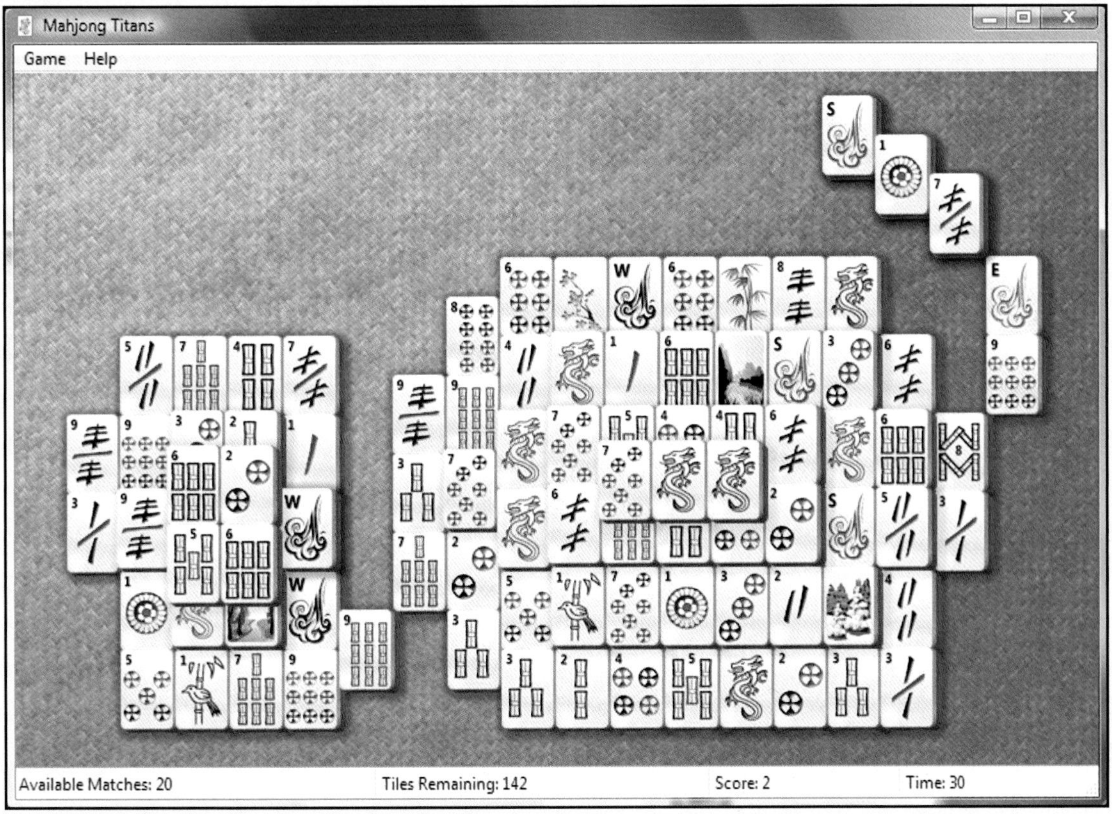

The popular Mahjong game is new to Windows Vista in the form of Mahjong Titans.

For the little ones, Windows Vista includes the edu-tainment title, Purble Place.

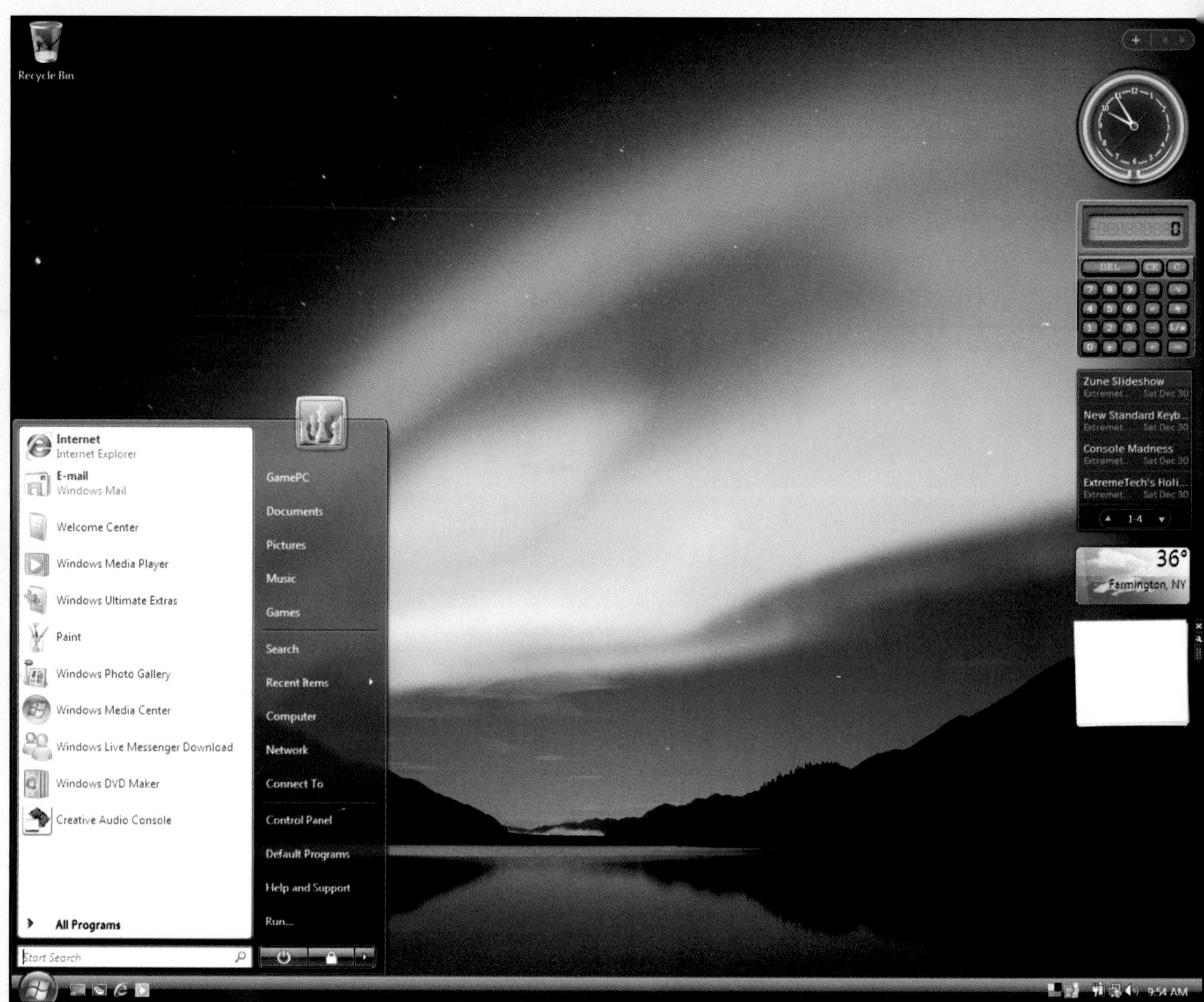

The Start Menu is both more useful and more graceful in the new Windows operating system.

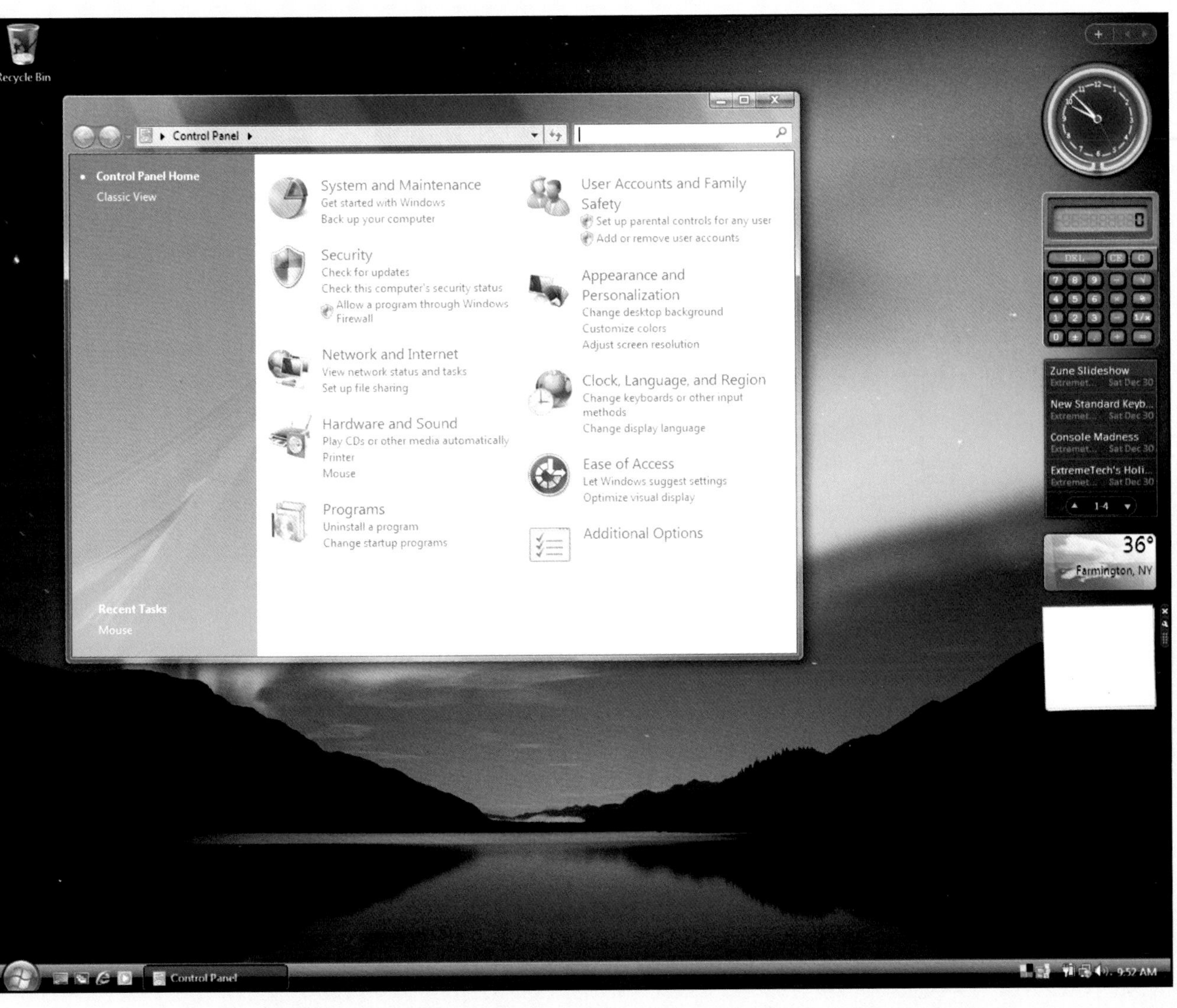

The Control Panel has an all-new look in Windows Vista.

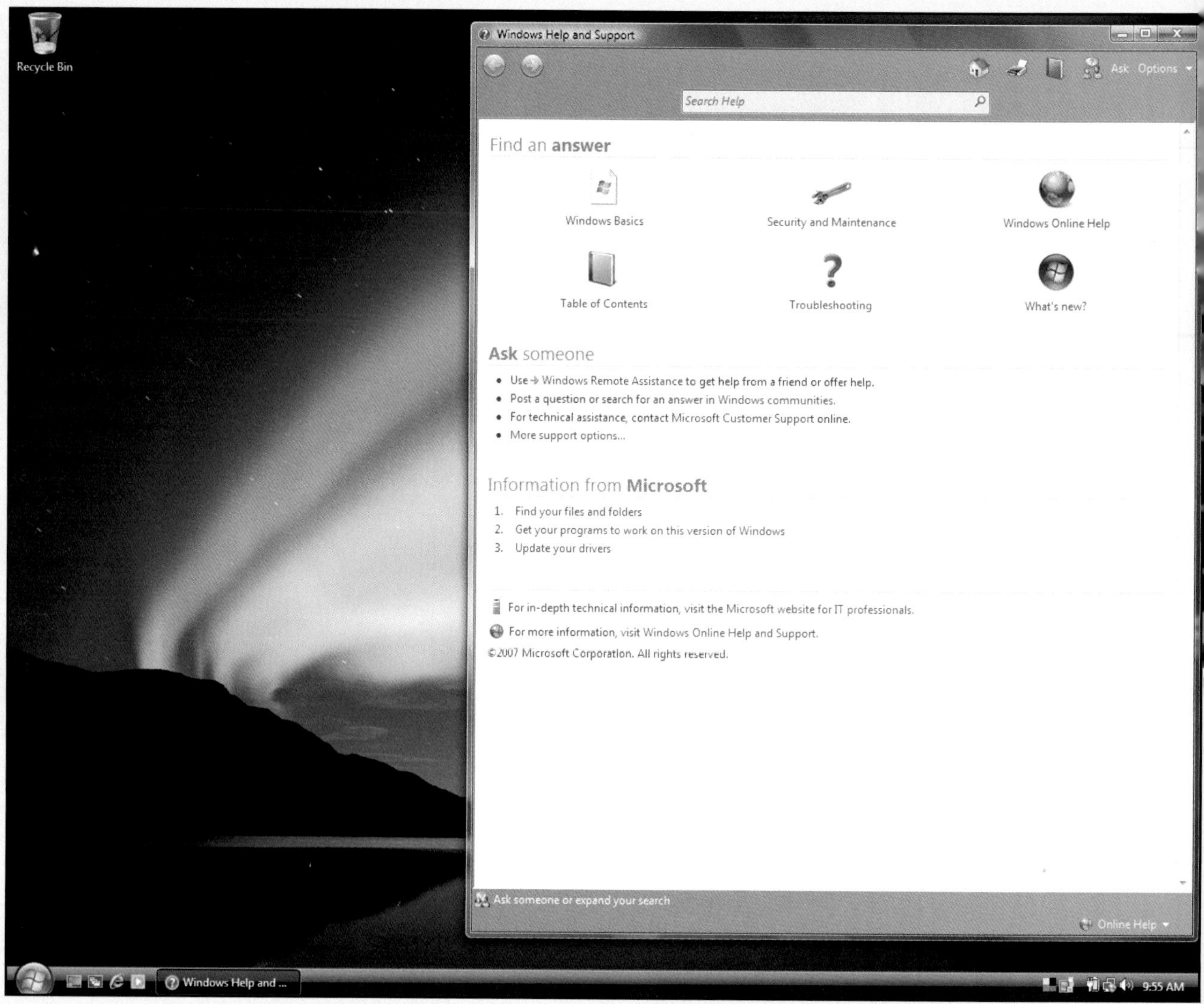

If you need help, check out the Help and Support window.

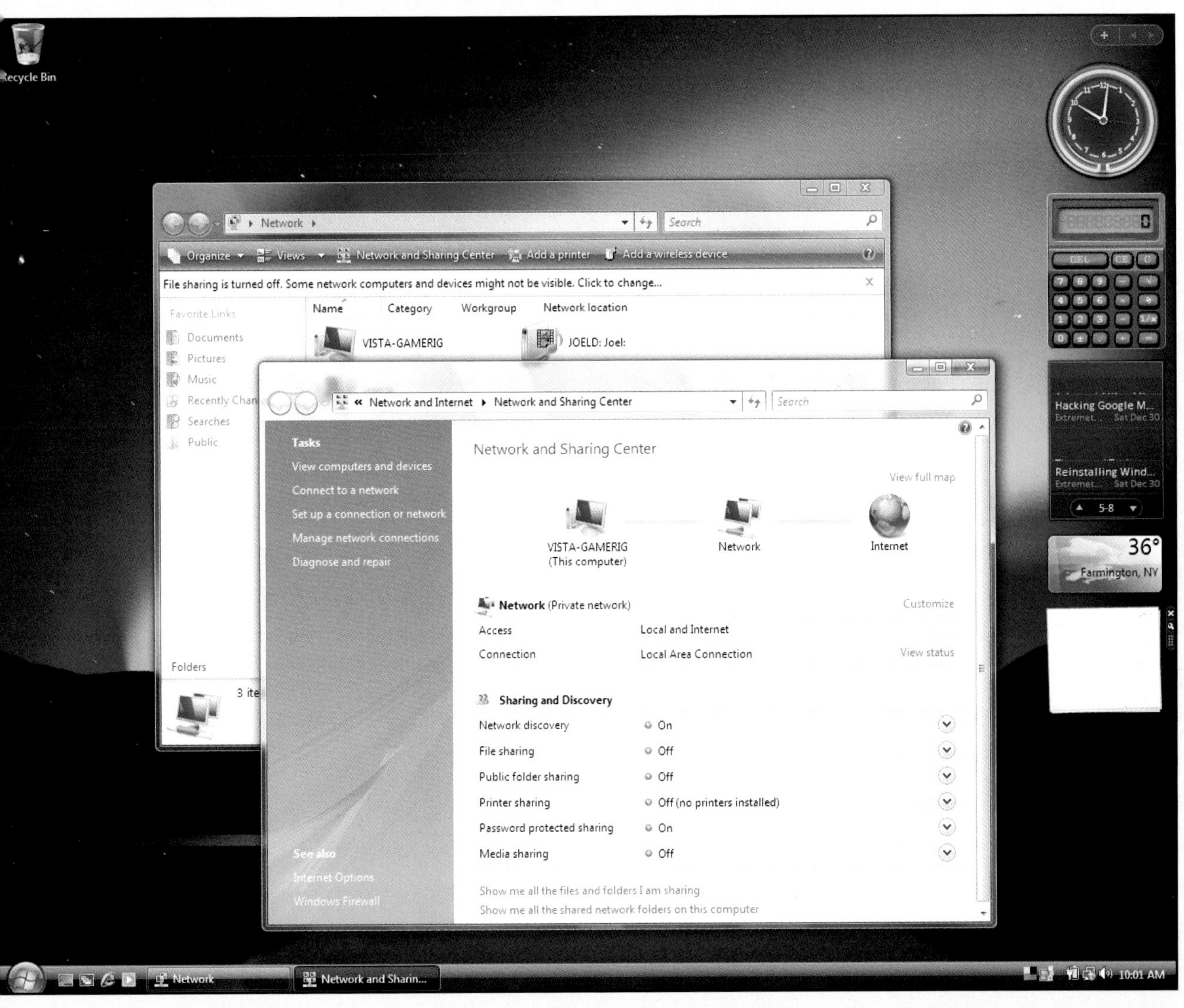

Networking is a cinch with the Windows Vista Network and Sharing Center.

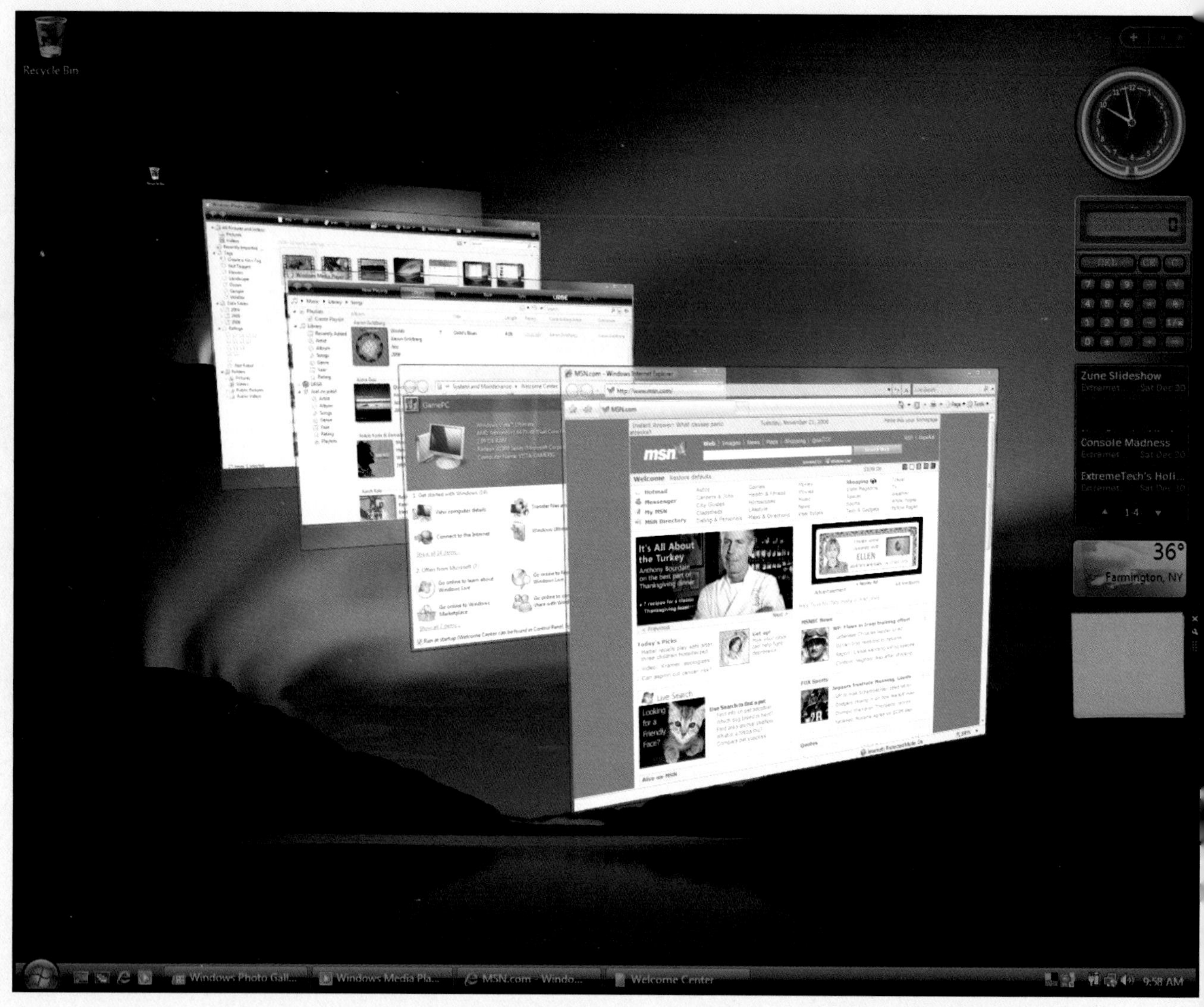

When you need to jump from one application to another, Flip 3D is ready. Just hold the Windows key on your keyboard and press the Tab key repeatedly to browse live representations of your open stuff.

For your multimedia pleasure, Windows Media Player 11 features icon-based organization and tons of enhancements over its predecessor.

Enjoy all of your digital photos and other images with the all-new Windows Photo Gallery.

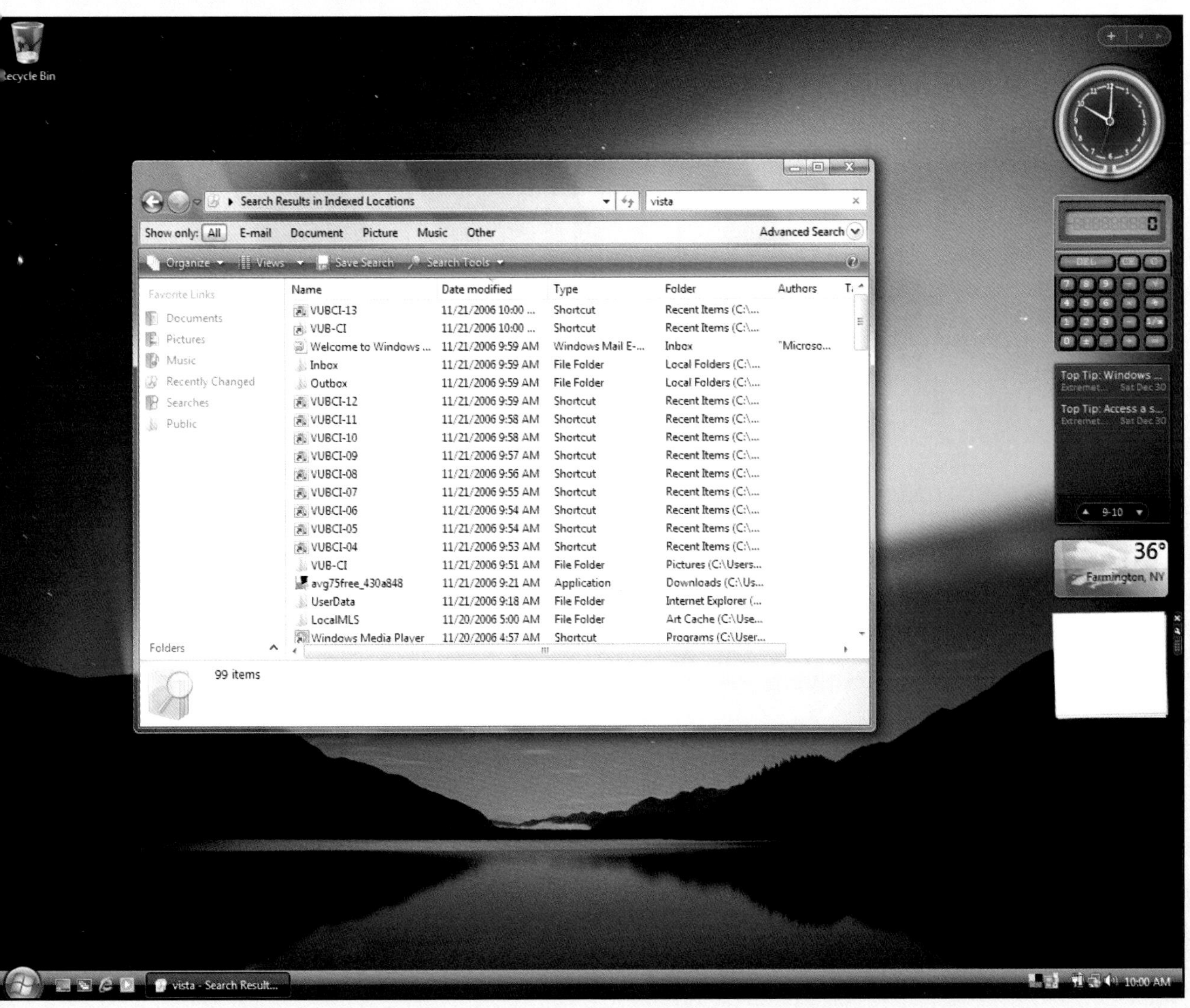

Looking for something? The new, indexed Search system finds files, e-mail messages, and other items all but instantly.

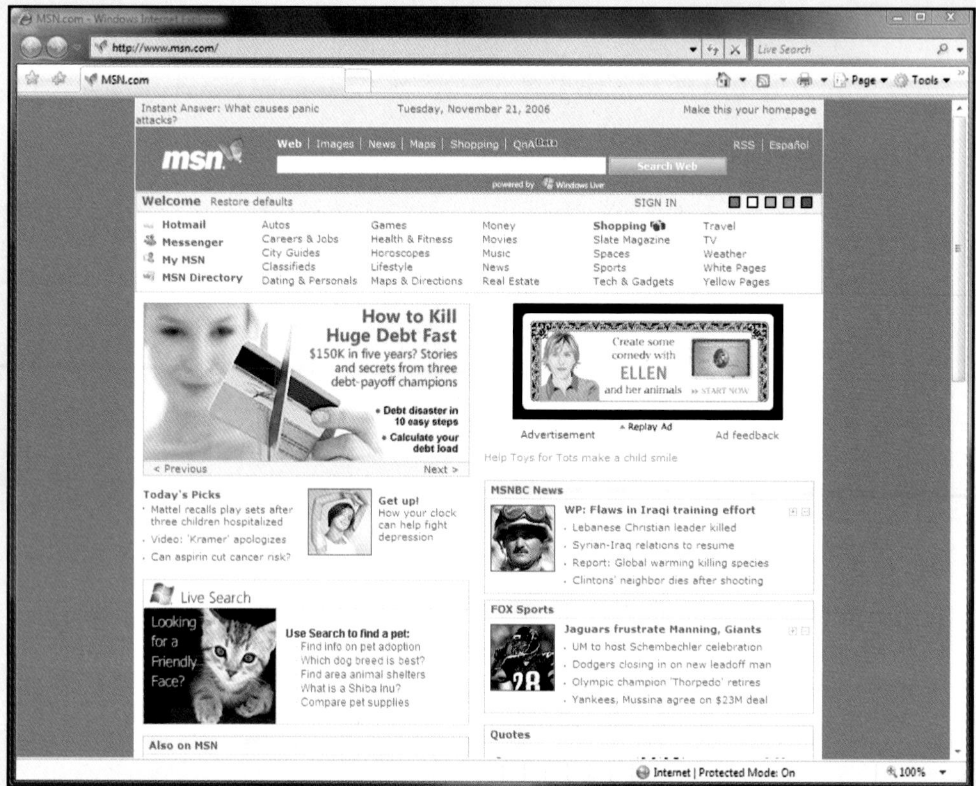

Internet applications are at your fingertips. The new Internet Explorer 7+ is a terrific browser . . .

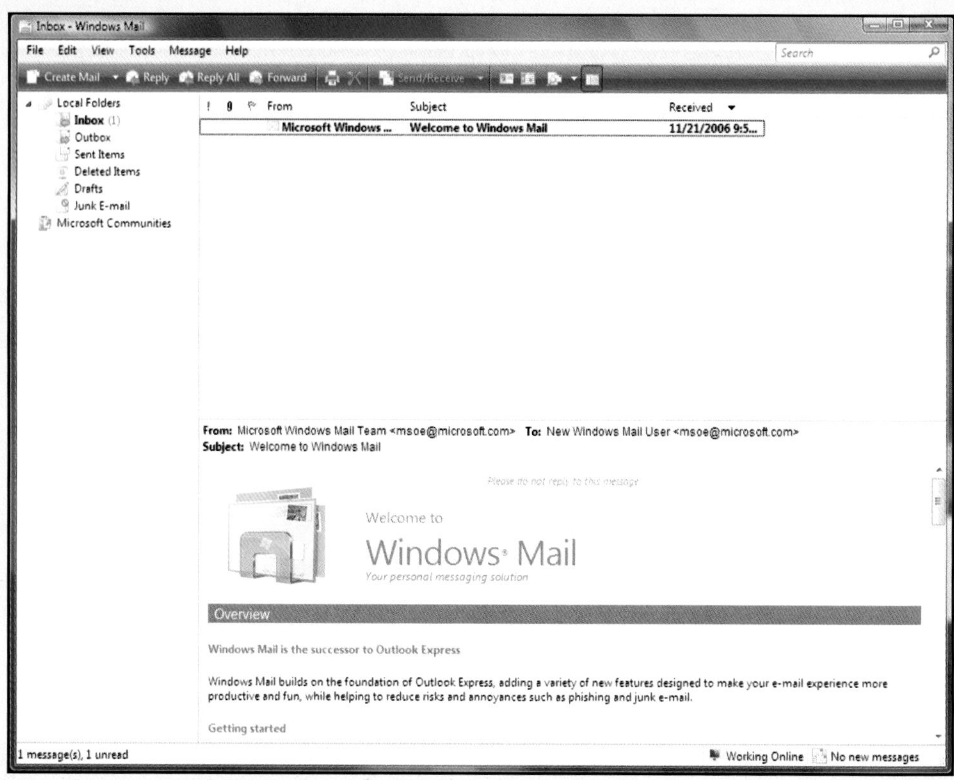

. . . and Windows Mail boasts several new features over its forerunner, Outlook Express.

Customize the Sidebar with a selection of gadgets included with Windows Vista . . .

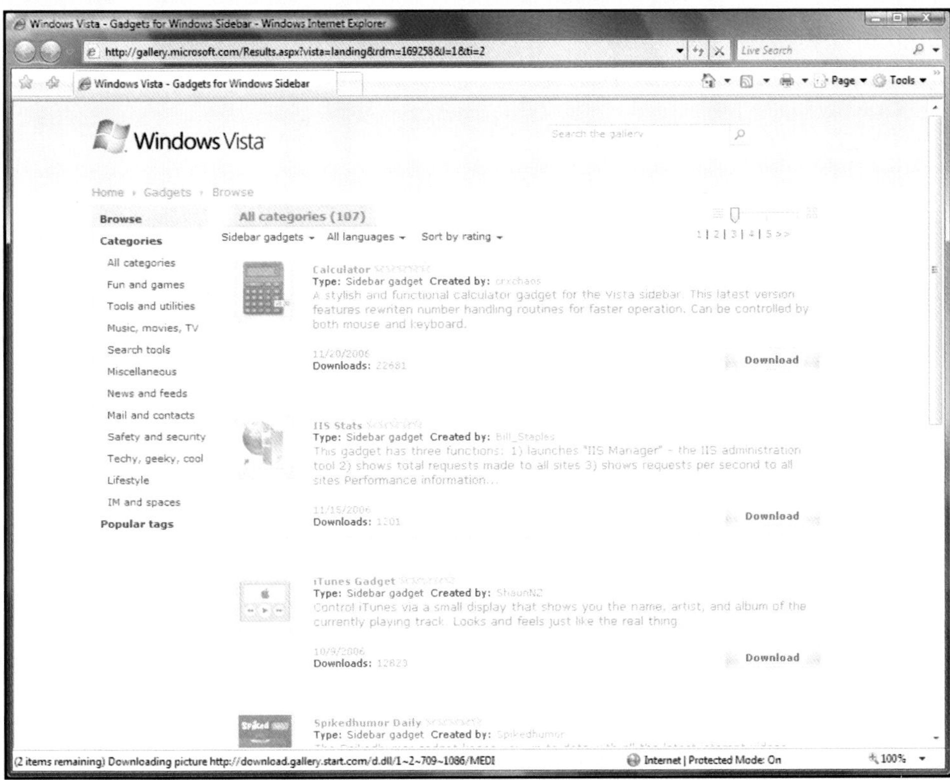

. . . and go online to find more gadgets.

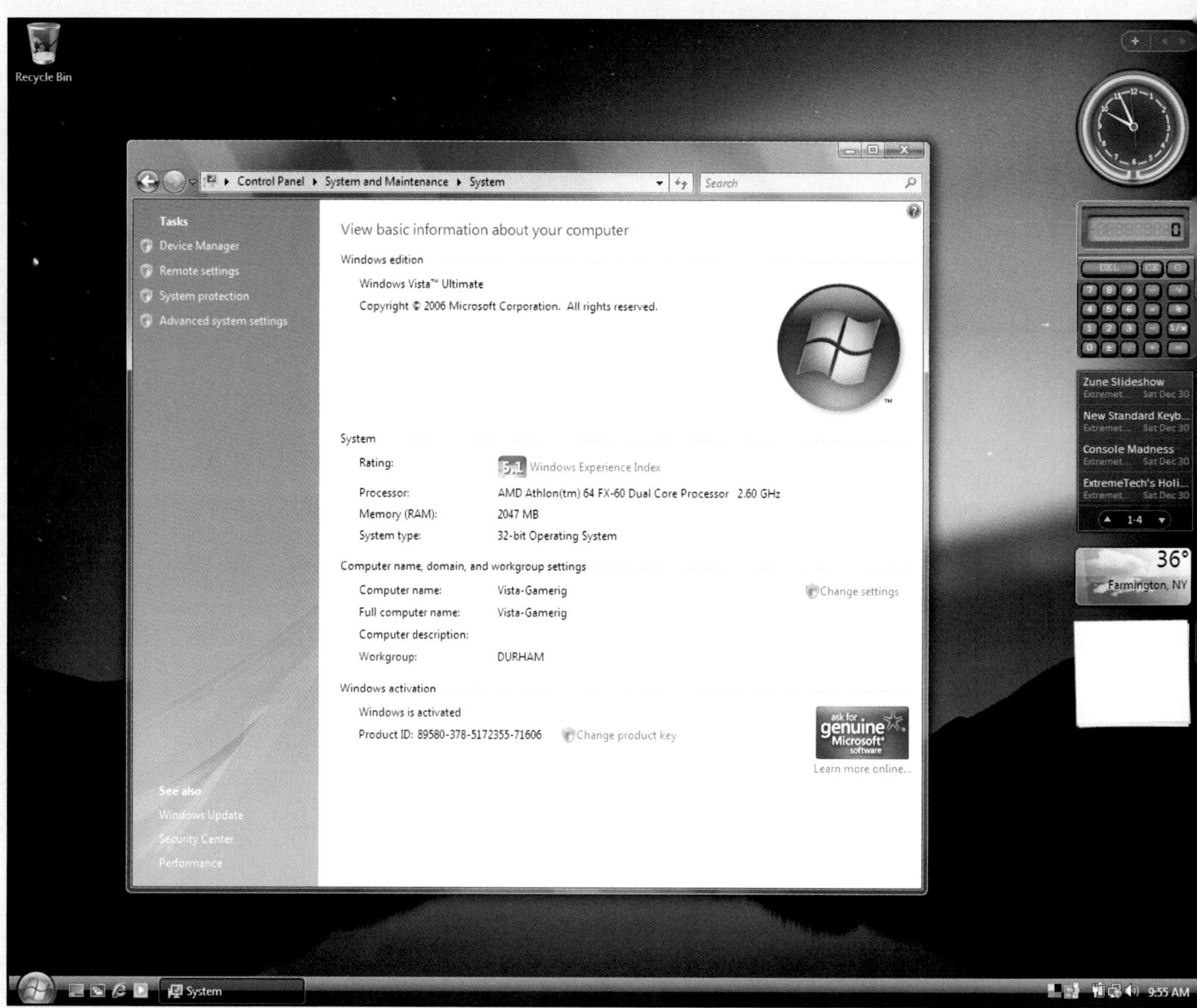

The System Information screen tells you all about your computer, including its performance score.

FIGURE 6.15

Customize the events in your calendar.

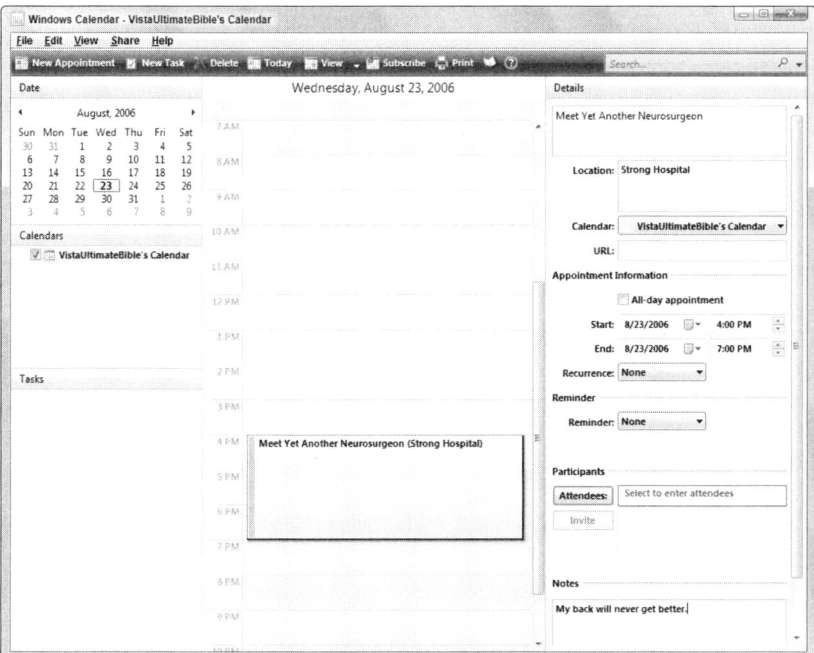

Tasks are like calendar events, but they can be kept in a simple list separate from the calendar. To add a task, simply click the New Task button on the toolbar or double-click in the Tasks area of Windows Calendar. Then, customize the task with the interface on the right.

Other buttons on the toolbar let you change the view settings of the calendar window, open Windows Contacts, print pages, and more. Of course, the universal Search field is available on the toolbar so you can find events at a moment's notice.

Windows Contacts

Interestingly, Windows Contacts (see Figure 6.16) isn't so much like a program that creates a file full of contact information. The contact manager, which allows you to save all sorts of data on everyone you know, functions more like a Windows Explorer folder with special buttons on the toolbar. It creates multiple files — one for each contact.

FIGURE 6.16

Windows Contacts

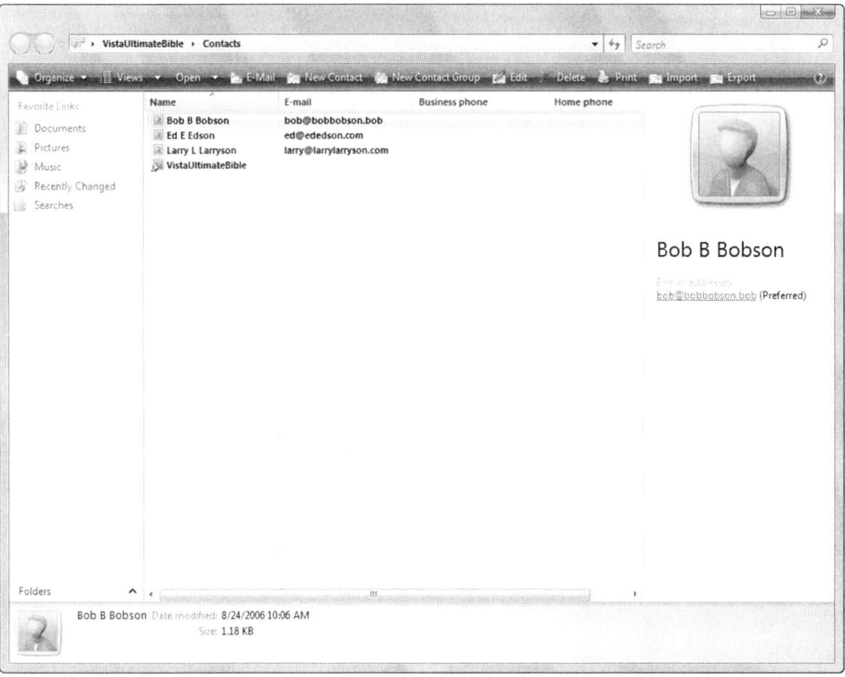

When you click the New Contact button, a dialog box like the one shown in Figure 6.17 appears. There, you can type in any information you want about the subject, including name, title, e-mail addresses, home address, work address, phone numbers, birthdays, and so on.

TIP **Check this out! You can even add a personalized picture to each contact's file. Click on the placeholder picture on the right in the properties window (like the one shown in Figure 6.16) and click Change Picture, then navigate to the one you want to use.**

You can group contacts for your convenience. I like to create groups of professional and personal contacts.

If you already have a batch of contacts in some other form, such as an Outlook Express address book, you can import it by clicking the Import button. This button also enables you to import vCards and lists in CSV (comma separated values). You can export your Vista contact list as vCards or a CSV file, as well.

FIGURE 6.17

A contact file in detail

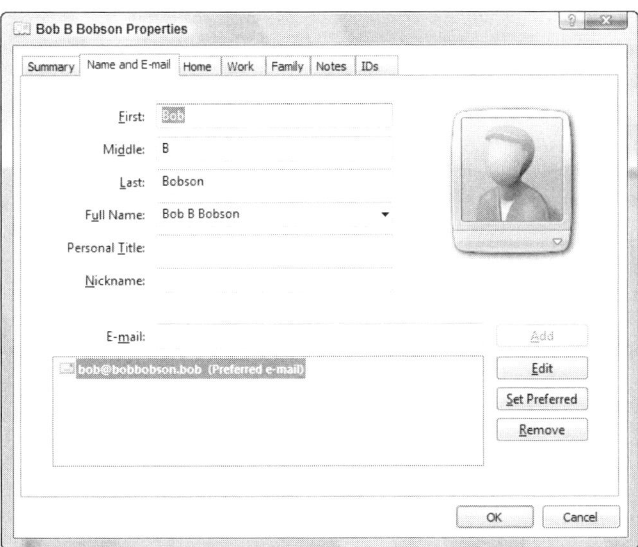

Windows Mail

Check out Chapter 13 for details on this fantastic, new version of Outlook Express.

Internet Explorer 7+

Chapter 13 covers this application, too. IE7+ is Microsoft's totally revamped Web browser, and it's armed with far better features and security than any of its predecessors.

Windows DVD Maker

While Windows XP boasted the ability to burn CDs, it couldn't handle DVD creation; users were forced to employ a third-party application like *Nero*. Windows Vista thankfully includes Windows DVD Maker, which allows you to create video and photo DVDs that can play on any machine, including DVD players, as long as it supports DVD-R or DVD-RW discs.

Launch Windows DVD Maker through the Start Menu. Click Start ➪ All Programs and click Windows DVD Maker. You'll see a screen like the one shown in Figure 6.18.

FIGURE 6.18

Windows DVD Maker

Click Add Items to browse your computer's file system and add photos and movie files. The files are represented in the Windows DVD Maker interface by thumbnails, as shown in Figure 6.19.

FIGURE 6.19

Windows Photo Gallery with a sample movie added

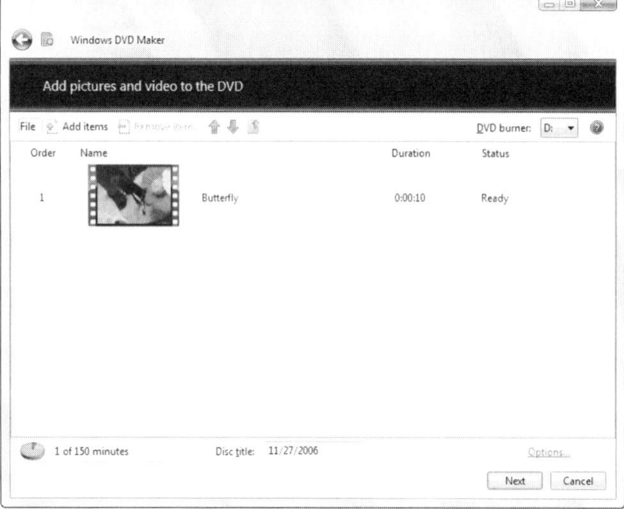

When you've added everything you wish to be on your DVD, click Next. You'll see a screen like the one shown in Figure 6.20.

FIGURE 6.20

Getting ready to burn

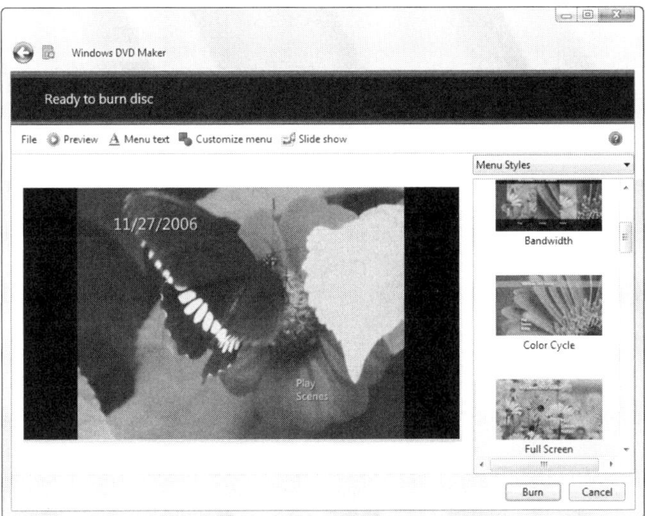

Here, you can preview the movie by clicking Preview. You can tweak the menu style with the interface on the right side of the window. You can also tweak the DVD menu that Windows DVD Maker will create for the DVD: click Menu Text to add the proper text to the menu, and click Customize Menu to see a screen like the one shown in Figure 6.21.

In this screen, you can choose the font of your DVD's menu and add foreground video, background video, and music, all from files on your hard drive. You can also choose the types of buttons for the scene selection screen. When you've made your changes, click Change Style to return to the DVD Maker interface (Figure 6.20). When you're done, make sure there's a blank DVD-R or a DVD-RW disc in the optical drive and then click Burn.

FIGURE 6.21

Customizing the DVD menu

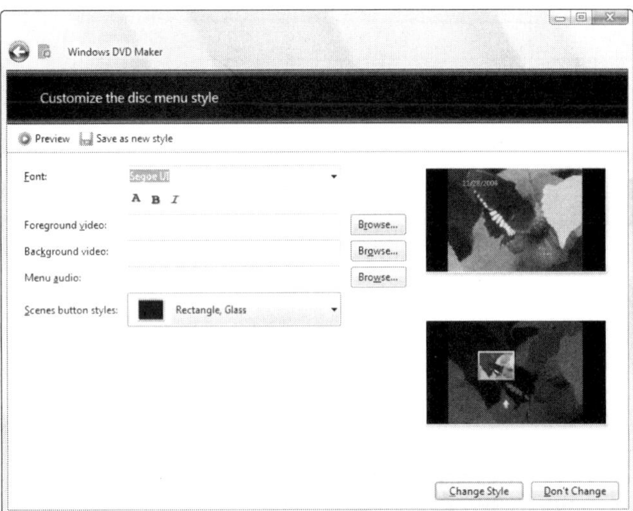

Of course, you might not want to create a visual masterpiece on DVD: you might wish only to store files on optical media. To do this, just head to a folder through the file system that contains the files you wish to burn to DVD, and click the Burn button on the toolbar. Windows will prompt you for a writable disc and burn the files to whatever writable media you put in the optical drive.

Windows Movie Maker

Chapter 20 contains an in-depth tutorial about this powerful movie-editing application.

Windows Photo Gallery

Viewing photos — and videos — is part of Windows Vista's multimedia experience, and with Windows Photo Gallery you can do it in a myriad of ways. When you first fire up the application, it looks around the hard drive for image files. It then instantly organizes them into a sheet of thumbnails that you can sort in a number of ways (see Figure 16.22).

FIGURE 6.22

Windows Photo Gallery

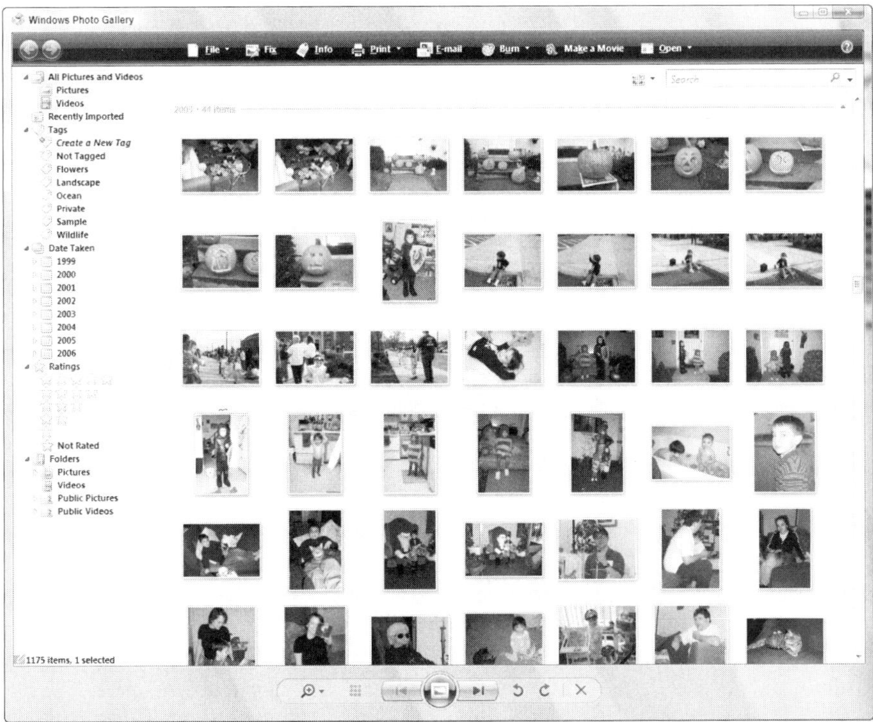

For example, you can sort the pictures by when they were taken according to their metadata; you can sort them by the folders they're stored in; you can sort them by their star rating (from one to five stars), which you can assign; and you can sort them by their tags, which you also define.

When you open a picture or video file, as shown in Figure 16.23, you'll see an information panel on the right. There, you can add a caption, add tags, give the file a rating, and so on.

FIGURE 6.23

Viewing a single photograph

NOTE If the information panel isn't visible, click the Info button on the toolbar.

In the Gallery view, you can select a number of photos to view as a slide show or burn to a data disc or even a video DVD. You can even work directly with Windows Movie Maker by selecting pictures or videos and clicking the Make a Movie button. You can open your selections with the image-editing application of your choice (the default is Paint). You can e-mail pictures via the E-mail button on the toolbar (Windows will offer to resize the pictures that you e-mail to make them more manageable for your recipients).

Windows Photo Gallery even features some simple photo-editing tools of its own. Using the Fix button, you can adjust the exposure and color of an image, crop the image (see Figure 16.24), and clean up red-eye effects. Alternatively, you simply click the Auto Adjust button and let Windows tweak the photo to what it thinks is ideal.

FIGURE 6.24

Cropping an image in Windows Photo Gallery

With Windows Photo Gallery, you no longer need a third-party, image-organizing application. It's simple and intuitive to use and makes viewing your pictures easier than ever.

Notepad and WordPad

This pair of text editors, shown in Figure 6.25, lets you get through basic word processing without a copy of Office. Although they lack truly powerful features like spell checkers and autoformatting, they're both useful in their own ways.

About Tags

In Windows Photo Gallery, you can create *tags* to add information to some of your media files. Tags are a recurring theme in Windows Vista, and they can make finding your files easier.

When you add tags to a photograph or a movie file, you create a new way to sort your work. As an example, I have about 1,000 photographs on just one of my many hard drives. Some are personal, some are work related; some are pictures of my wife, my kids, my friends, and some are other people. I can add one or more tags to each photograph to make sorting them easier.

If I encounter a photo of my wife and both of my children, I might add a tag for each of their names, another tag called *personal,* a tag called *kids,* and a tag called *family.* Then, I find a picture of just my son. I add the tag named after him, and the personal, kids, and family tags. Finally, I find a picture of a motherboard I reviewed in 1998. I add the tag *professional,* the tag *hardware,* and the tag *motherboard.*

If I keep all this up, eventually I can sort my pictures with amazing ease. When I'm looking for pictures of my kids, I simply look for the tag called *kids.* When I want all of my personal photos as opposed to professional stuff, I sort by the tag *personal.* When I'm looking for pictures of computer hardware, I click the *hardware* tag; when I need motherboards specifically, I click the *motherboard* tag.

Tags will give back as much as you put into them. The more organized and thoughtful your tagging system (and the more consistently you use it), the easier that sorting your media files will be.

Notepad, being a basic and, more important, a featureless text editor, is the program of choice for many a scripter and programmer. You can type anything you like into Notepad and save it as the most basic of text files, sans formatting of any sort. Experienced Web coders absolutely love Notepad; I know a few who, in fact, prefer it over Dreamweaver and FrontPage alike. You can type code of any sort into Notepad, save it as any file type you like, and then, if necessary, compile it with any compiler you please.

WordPad supports formatting and allows you to work with formatted text and plain text. It can save formatted text in rich text format (RTF). Although it's no substitute for Microsoft Word, it does let you do some basic word processing and even view Word document files without a more expensive application.

FIGURE 6.25

Empty pages in Notepad and WordPad

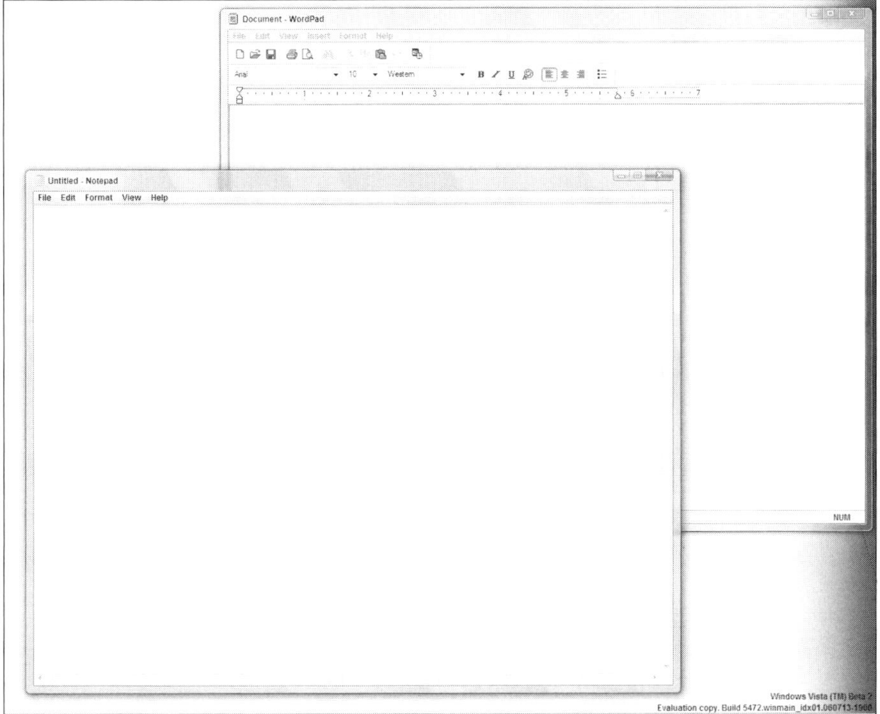

Paint

Many moons ago, this extremely simple image program was called *Paintbrush*. Nowadays, it's a much more accomplished program, but Paint, shown in Figure 6.26, is not going to win the hearts and minds of people who are used to Adobe Photoshop.

Paint features simple drawing tools like line and curve creators, brushes, fills, spray paint tools, and a full palette of colors. It doesn't allow you to work in layers or anything fancy like that, but it's okay for making very simple works of art.

FIGURE 6.26

A photograph in Paint

As a photo editor, it comes up short; it can handle basic tasks, like resizing, flipping, cropping, and rotating images, but don't expect to apply amazing effects. It allows you to work with images in a variety of formats, including BMP, TIF, PNG, and more, and even convert files from one format to another.

Sound Recorder

This simple application lets you record audio through a microphone attached to your primary audio device (e.g., your computer's sound card). When you launch it (Start ➪ All Programs ➪ Accessories ➪ Sound Recorder), its tiny interface, shown in Figure 6.27, pops up.

FIGURE 6.27

The Sound Recorder

Simply click Start Recording and speak into the microphone. When you're finished, click Stop Recording and a dialog box will appear allowing you to save the sound you've just recorded as a WMA file at a location of your choosing in the file system.

Snipping tool

This tool is brand new in Windows Vista. The Snipping tool, shown in Figure 6.28, lets you grab part or all of the desktop and turn it into an image, which you can then save.

The Snipping tool lets you send the snip as an e-mail; draw on it with pen and highlighter tools; save the snip as a JPEG, GIF, PNG, HTML, or other file; and copy the snip to the clipboard.

To use it, simply go to Start ➪ All Programs ➪ Accessories ➪ Snipping Tool. Windows may ask you if you want to add it to the Quick Launch bar. The little Snipping Tool interface appears, and you can then simply drag the cursor to create a square area of the desktop you wish to save as an image file. After you've dragged out a square, the Snipping Tool dialog box changes to show you the "snip" you've just created. It allows you to draw on it with a pen or a highlighter, send the snip to an e-mail recipient, or save it as an image file.

FIGURE 6.28

A browser, captured with the Snipping tool

Utilities

The Windows Vista utilities, such as Backup, Disk Cleanup, Disk Defragmenter, System Restore, and others, are discussed in Chapters 10 and 11 and in the book's appendix. They're there to help you maintain the operating system and your files; to keep your stuff safe, secure, and out of trouble; and to keep everything working well.

Summary

Windows Vista Ultimate includes an impressive array of both pastimes and tools to help you get through days of work and play. Old games that you're already hooked on have been given facelifts, and new addictions await your discovery. Sometimes, there's just no substitute for a game of Minesweeper!

Applications take Vista beyond gaming and into the realms of multimedia and productivity. You can keep track of your contacts, e-mail them, and schedule meetings with them through various PIM-inspired apps. You can sort, view, and tweak your photographs and movies, watch a slide show, take a snapshot of the desktop, and much more with the various goodies that Windows Vista Ultimate installs automatically for you.

Part II

The Windows Vista Interface

Out with the old! Windows Vista's interface is something unique, from its fantastic Aero desktop to its trendy Sidebar. Getting to know the interface is essential to making the most of this evolutionary — if not revolutionary — operating system. Whether you're a Windows veteran or a novice to all things Microsoft, you have to know the operating system's interface to get the most out of it.

Part II introduces you to the Windows Vista interface, including Aero. You can, if you wish, choose a more classic interface. Whether you use Aero or a different style, you can customize the interface in a variety of ways, all of which are laid out for you in the following chapters.

IN THIS PART

Chapter 7

Choosing an Interface

IN THIS CHAPTER

Exploring the Aero interface

Exploring the basic, standard, and classic interfaces

Choosing the interface that's right for you

If you're like me, your eyes probably flew clear out of your head when you first saw Windows Vista Ultimate.

That's a bit of an exaggeration, but the look and feel of Windows Vista is startling to longtime Windows users. That first look is a bit of a shock. It brought back memories of when I switched from Windows 3.1 to Windows 95; at first I didn't really feel that it was better or worse. It was just *different*.

Some of the old and familiar is still around. A taskbar runs across the bottom of the screen, complete with a clock and a notification area (better known as the tray). The Start Menu is there, even though it doesn't say "Start" anymore. There's a desktop, to which you can add all the icons you please.

Plenty of differences exist. The taskbar, the edges of various windows, and other elements are partially transparent. The mouse pointer is a little less like an arrow and more like an arrowhead. The menus in the navigation windows are gone, replaced by mysterious buttons. When you hover over a program's button on the taskbar, a little image of the program appears. Similarly, some icons display not just icons, but file contents.

You don't have to like it. If you're a Windows 2000 *grognard*, or if you miss the days of Windows 98, you can make Windows Vista Ultimate look and act more like those classic operating systems.

Some elements, however, you can't change. For example, Microsoft has issued new guidelines for dialog boxes that appear, often unexpectedly. They're supposed to be written more clearly, with more user-friendly explanations of what they're trying to tell you. In a nutshell, they should be a bit less maddening!

The new interface is called Aero, and you should give it a chance. It's pretty handy once you get used to it. This chapter can help with that, and also offer alternatives if you decide that transparent windows aren't your thing.

All About the Aero Interface

Aero is the interface of choice for Windows Vista. Although it's familiar enough for users of previous Windows operating systems to get around without getting lost (see a typical desktop in Figure 7.1), it's also unlike anything seen in computing thus far.

FIGURE 7.1

A Vista desktop looks a little different, but it's still recognizably Windows.

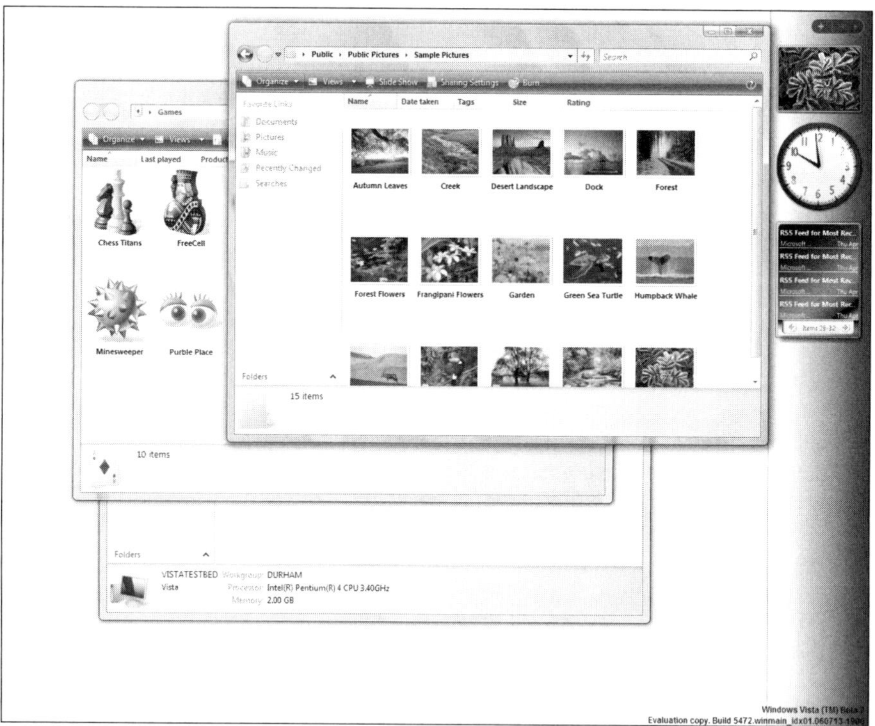

Vista's translucent window frames allow you to see through them and get a glimpse of what's behind them. Task swapping features live icons or even large representations of each task in a 3D view. Windows scale in size automatically to best display their content.

Aero versus XP

Stylistically and functionally, Windows Aero is quite different from Windows XP's interface. XP's overall look and feel was largely based on Windows 2000 and Windows 9x — even though XP added some friendly eye candy, a revamped Start Menu, and other features, it wasn't the breakaway from its predecessors that Windows Vista is.

However, good old XP and sparkling new Vista share a number of similarities:

- The desktop can hold or hide icons, as per your desires (see Figure 7.2). You can arrange them, drag them, and align them to a grid or sort them via the right-click context menu.
- Everything begins with the Start Menu. Although it looks significantly different, Vista's Start Menu functions in a way similar to XP's (see Figure 7.3).
- The taskbar, the bar along the bottom of the screen that contains buttons for open programs and files, is intact. Note that in Vista, if you hover the cursor over a taskbar icon, a live thumbnail displaying the contents of the task appears.
- The taskbar can contain a number of enhancements, such as the quick start icons and the system tray (or notification area), complete with a digital clock. Note that in Vista, however, you can add up to two more clocks.
- Program windows and Windows Explorer windows work the same way in Vista as they did in Windows XP, stacking on the desktop with the active window in front. You can still resize them by dragging a side or a corner around the screen.
- Other, minor conventions are carried over, like the maximize/minimize/close window area at the top right of open windows, scroll bars that dynamically appear when the content of a window is larger than the window itself, and so on.

Of course, a number of interface features have been introduced, and others have been enhanced or overhauled. Windows Vista's Aero interface is designed to look better, run more smoothly, and pack far more conveniences than earlier Windows interfaces did.

FIGURE 7.2

Desktop icons can be handy for launching frequently used applications.

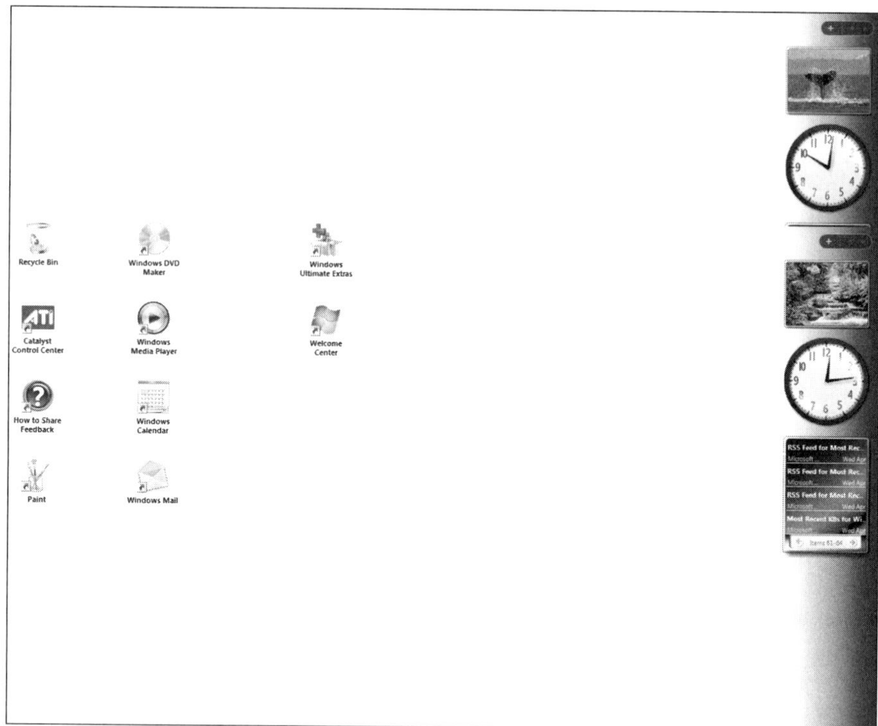

Glass and opacity

The much-hyped window transparencies truly set Windows Vista apart from its predecessors. You might not even notice them until you've opened more than one window, but once you get used to them you'll probably wonder how you ever did without them.

FIGURE 7.3

The Start Menu has a new look in Aero.

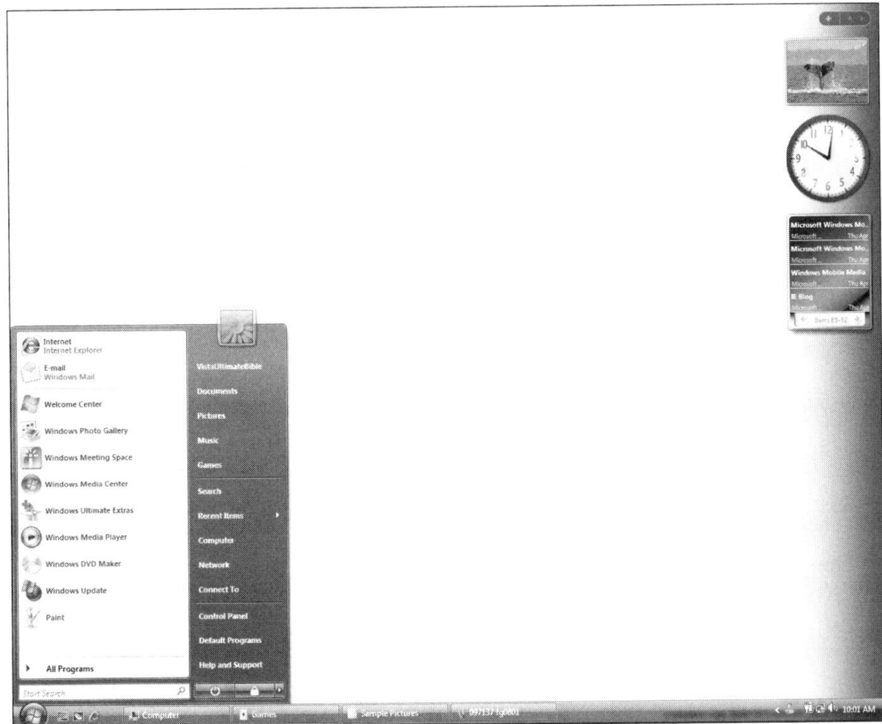

Windows Vista's Aero interface leverages the power of 3D graphics accelerators, which have been standard equipment in computers for at least half a decade. It uses them to render windows more gracefully, and to, among other things, use the power of the alpha channel to make the border of each window translucent, as shown in Figure 7.4.

NOTE Window borders in Vista aren't completely transparent, but they're far from the opaque windows in earlier versions of Windows operating systems. You can see through them, but the images behind them will be blurry and distorted, as if you were viewing them through murky water.

FIGURE 7.4

You can see the game icons through the top of the foreground window.

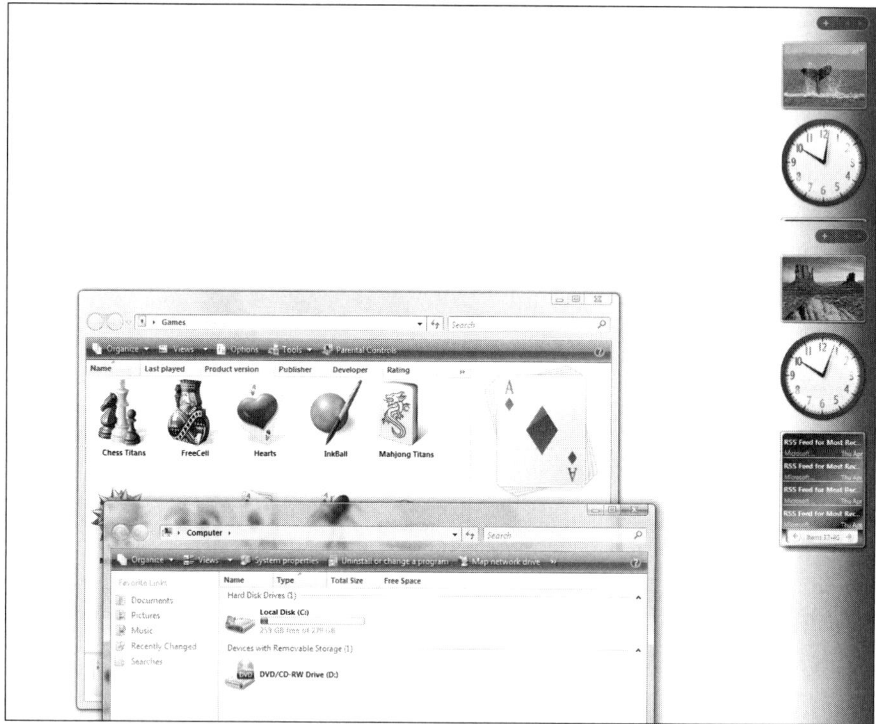

You can adjust the opacity of the window glass to make windows more transparent or less transparent. To do so, follow these steps:

1. **Right-click a blank area of the desktop.**
2. **Click Personalize.** The Control Panel's Personalization page opens, as shown in Figure 7.5.
3. **Click Window Color and Appearance.** A task pane like the one shown in Figure 7.6 appears.

   Here, you can tweak the look of your Windows Aero interface. You can choose a color at the top of the window, or open the color mixer at the bottom and find your own color. Toward the middle, just above a slider, is a check box labeled Transparency.

FIGURE 7.5

The Control Panel's Personalization window

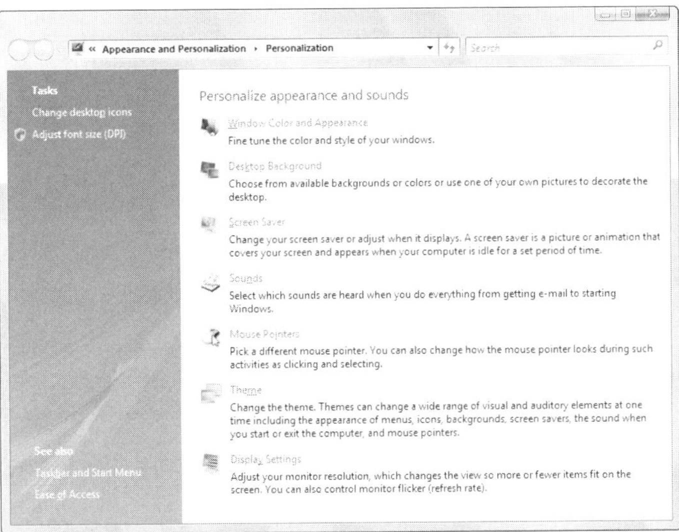

FIGURE 7.6

This is where you tweak Windows Aero's color scheme and transparency.

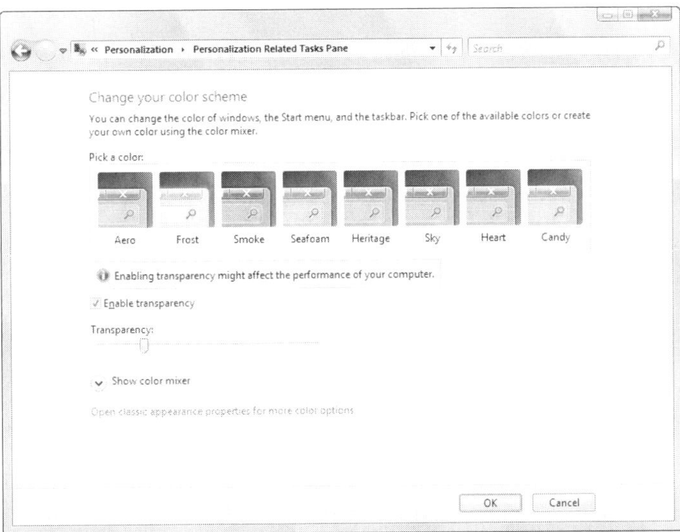

4. **Clear the check box to make window borders opaque.**
5. **Click the check box to make window borders translucent, as shown earlier in Figure 7.4.** You can use the slider to adjust the level of transparency. With the slide at the far left, window borders are almost clear (Figure 7.7); at the far right, they're almost perfectly opaque (Figure 7.8).

FIGURE 7.7

This figure shows the effect of moving the Opacity slider to the far left.

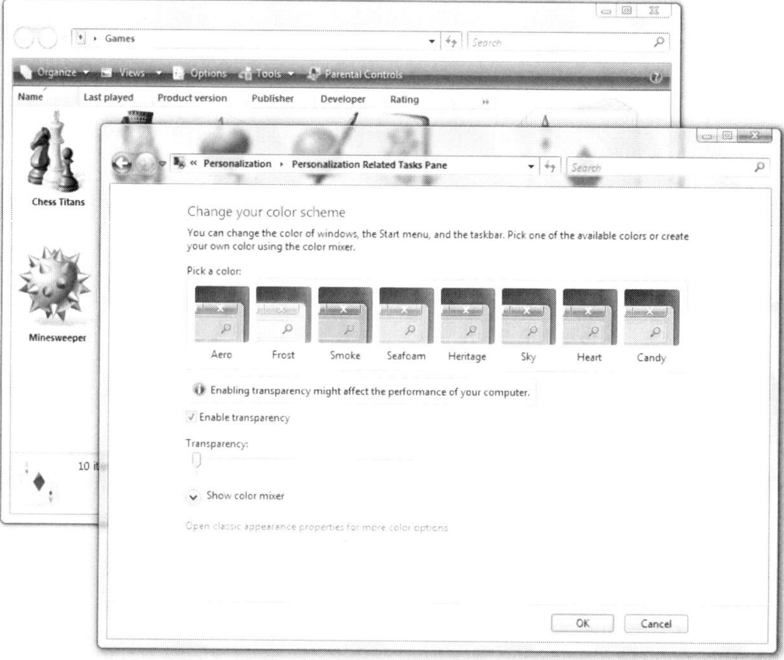

FIGURE 7.8

Here's how window borders look with the Opacity slider moved to the far right.

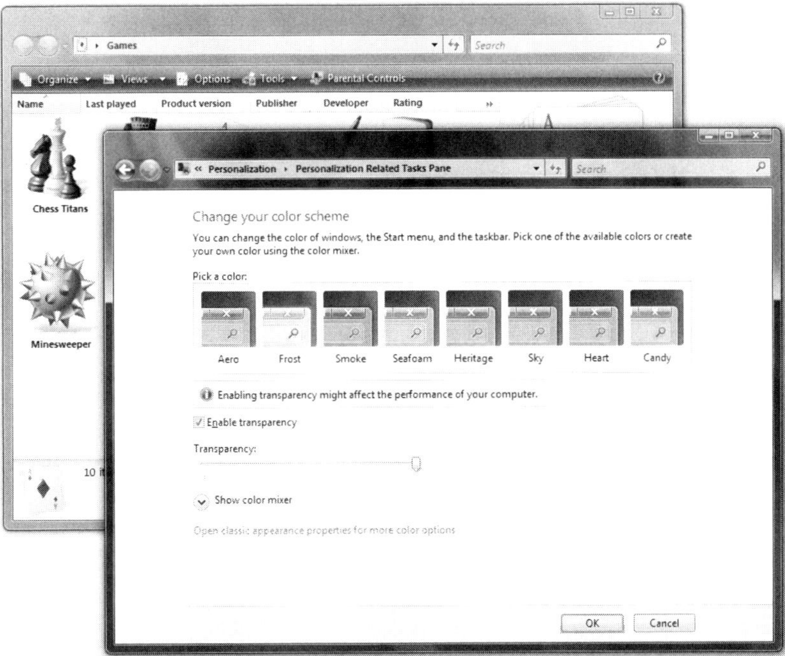

Flip!

When you have a bunch of tasks open, you can quickly rifle through them and choose the task you want to bring to the foreground. The most common way of doing this is by clicking the appropriate button on the taskbar, but Windows operating systems have long had another way.

If you hold down the Alt key and press Tab, you can see what is now called Flip (see Figure 7.9). Like prior versions of Windows, it shows a row of icons that represent the windows you currently have open. Unlike other Windows operating systems, it uses live thumbnails that show the actual contents of those windows. Keep holding the Alt key and repeatedly press Tab until you reach the task you want to work on.

That's one way to change tasks; another way is the brand-new Flip 3D, which is shown in Figure 7.10. Invoke Flip 3D by holding down the Windows key and pressing Tab. The desktop will warp into a three-dimensional space with flat, 3D versions of each task window floating. You toggle through each task with each press of the Tab key while holding the Windows key.

FIGURE 7.9

Windows Vista's Flip feature

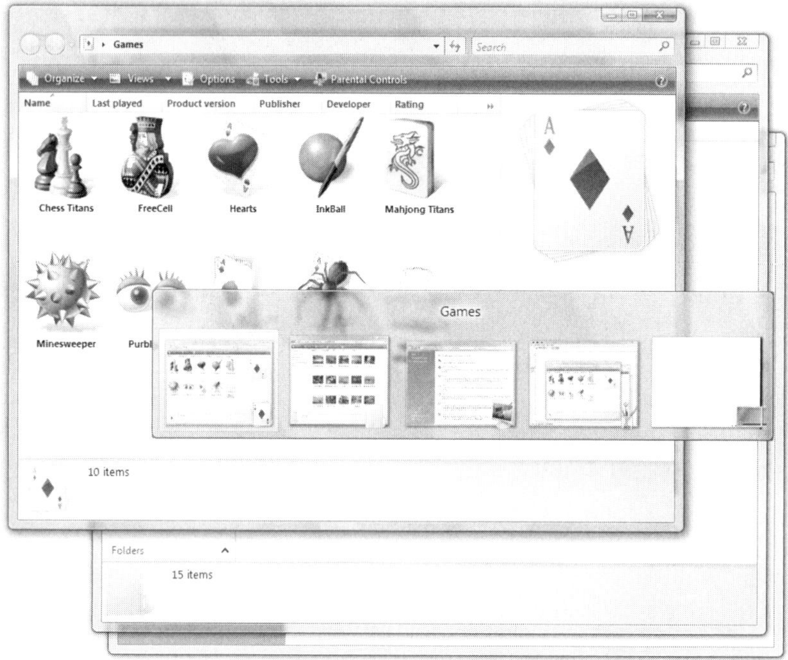

FIGURE 7.10

Flip 3D in action

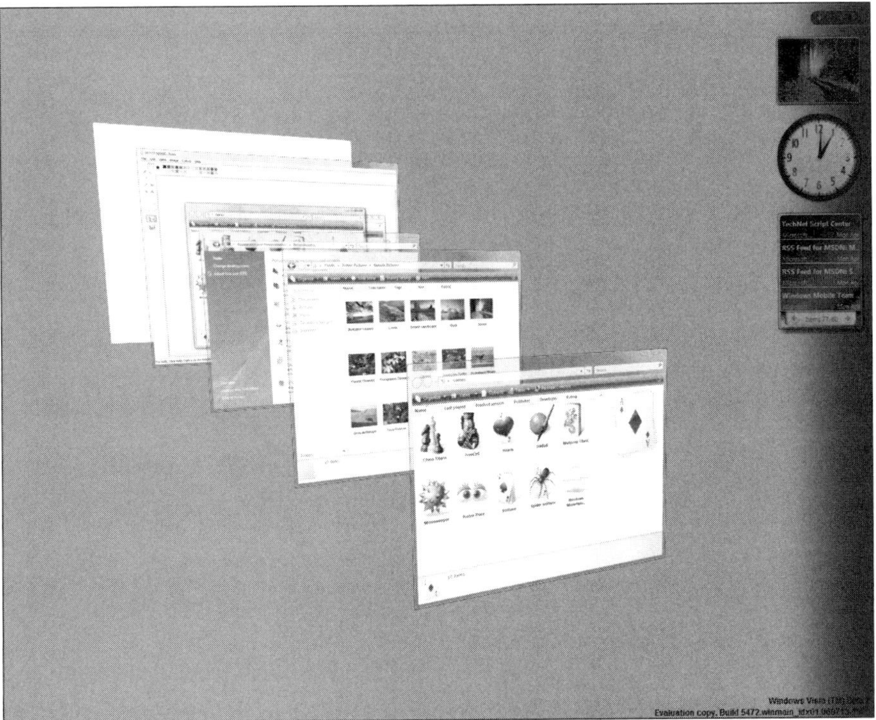

New window behavior and layouts

You'll notice right away that Windows Vista's windows don't behave the way windows do in other operating systems. They're more fluid, better animated, and more organic. When you minimize a window, it moves to the taskbar with such fluidity you expect to hear a satisfying *whoosh*!

Windows also have the ability to dynamically scale to show their content in the most logical manner. The best way to see dynamic scaling in action is to browse a text-heavy database, like the Help and Support menu. Choose Start ➪ Help and Support. The window shown in Figure 7.11 appears.

FIGURE 7.11

The Help and Support module starts with a window shaped like this...

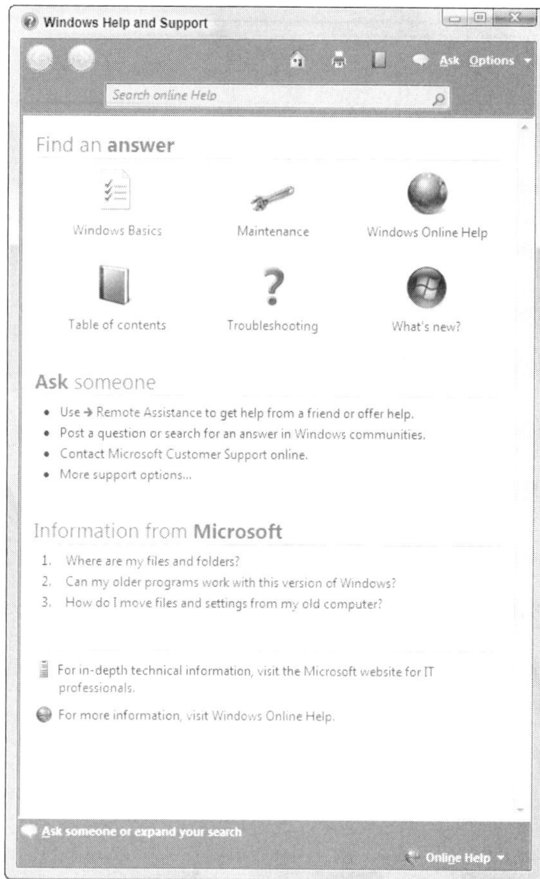

Now click on anything. It doesn't matter what. You're not looking for help right now; you're watching for the window to do something interesting. Click Windows Basics, for example, and the window suddenly molds itself into a new shape, as shown in Figure 7.12.

FIGURE 7.12

...and it morphs as needed to show different screens.

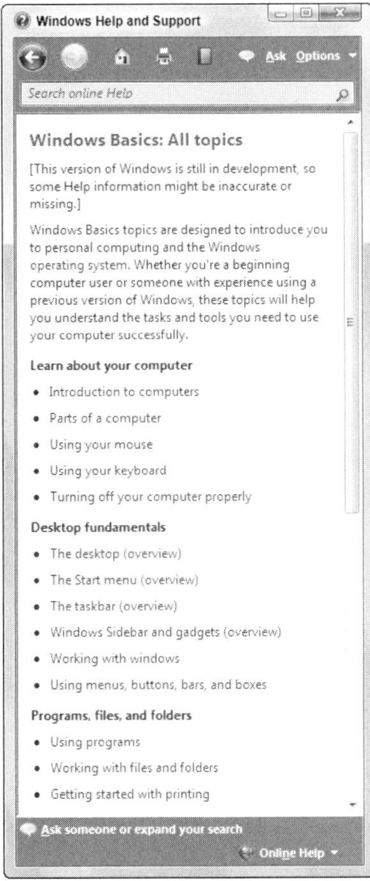

NOTE You can tweak some of the animations through the Performance Options dialog box. To get there, choose Start ➪ Control Panel ➪ System and Maintenance. Then choose System ➪ Advanced System Properties. You'll need administrator access privileges.

In the System Properties dialog box, under Performance, click the Settings button. Then, look at the list box. Each item bears a check box. You can turn off many animated elements through this dialog box by clicking to deselect the ones you don't want. Doing so can even increase performance on older machines by a small factor.

3D Graphics and Vista's Desktop

When you browsed the minimum requirements for Vista, whether on the box at the store, on a Web site, or right here in this book in Chapter 2, you may have noticed that Windows Vista demands 3D graphics acceleration. Does that make sense? Isn't the Windows desktop two-dimensional?

It used to be, but it's not anymore. Windows Vista uses an entirely new graphics subsystem to display everything you see, from the taskbar to the windows themselves. They're not merely two-dimensional constructs. Every window you see is a 3D surface.

So what does that mean? In 3D graphics, objects are made of polygons (flat shapes). When something looks like a fully three-dimensional object, it's really a series of polygons put together in a mesh called a *wireframe*. Each of those flat polygons has a surface overlaid with a texture (a two-dimensional image) to give the wireframe a solid look. After various effects such as lighting and bump mapping are applied to the 3D object, it takes on a realistic look.

Each window that you see on a Windows Vista desktop is a 3D surface — whether or not you use the Aero interface. Windows are processed through your computer's 3D graphics subsystems.

The 3D hardware in your computer, therefore, has a big effect on how well Windows Vista performs. Windows Vista uses the memory dedicated to your computer's graphics card to store surfaces. That's why it requires graphics cards with particular amounts of memory; that memory is as important to Windows Vista as the main system memory.

Surprisingly, a midrange graphics card with a ton of memory (say, 256MB) might outperform a high-end graphics card with less memory (say, 128MB) in Windows Vista. If you choose to upgrade your computer's graphics card specifically for Windows Vista, choose one with 256MB or more memory. You'll definitely see a performance improvement.

Not only do windows act differently, they look different as well. Each Explorer window has back and forward buttons. The classic menus are gone, replaced by contextual buttons. The status bar at the bottom of the window has been replaced by the Details pane, an information box that shows data about whatever you've selected within the window. The Search box appears in virtually every Explorer window. Take a gander at all those elements in the Games window in Figure 7.13.

CROSS-REF The new window elements affect how you navigate through the interface, so I explain them in greater detail in Chapter 3.

FIGURE 7.13

Here's how the Games folder looks with the Opacity slider moved to the far right.

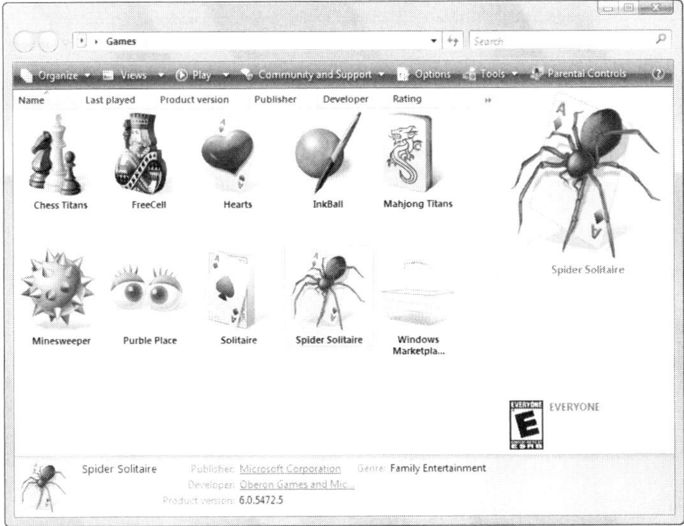

Other Interface Choices: Basic, Standard, and Classic

You don't have to love Aero. I know I do, but I've been tooling around with Windows Vista Ultimate for months. If you can't get used to the new look and feel of Windows, or if your computer is a bit older and doesn't have the horsepower to run the Aero interface (it requires a fairly powerful graphics subsystem), you don't have to.

You can choose a few other Windows display settings that may make you feel more like you're in familiar territory or that run better on older PCs:

1. **Right-click an empty area of the desktop.**
2. **Click Personalize.**
3. **In the Personalization window, click Window Color and Appearance.**
4. **At the bottom of that window, click the link called Open classic appearance properties for more color options.**

The little window in Figure 7.14 that appears may be familiar to you.

FIGURE 7.14

You can change the look of the Windows Vista interface here.

Under Color scheme are several options. Take a look at the first four, labeled Windows Vista Aero, Windows Vista Basic, Windows Standard, and Windows Classic. You can choose one of these to transform the look and feel of Windows Vista to a more basic, less fancy state.

Windows Vista Basic

If you click on Windows Vista Basic and click Apply, the screen will change to something similar to Figure 7.15.

Windows Vista Basic is still very much a Vista interface, but it doesn't rely as heavily on the 3D graphics card and its local memory. The Aero glass feature is not present, so all windows are opaque. Those nifty, live thumbnails don't appear when you hover over taskbar items, and Flip and Flip 3D don't work. If you hold down Alt and press Tab, you simply see icons that represent the open tasks.

Other elements, including those navigation nuances covered in Chapter 3, are still intact. The Start Menu works just like it does in Aero, and windows still have interactive path bars, search boxes, and the Details pane. Windows Vista Basic is not a complete reversion to Windows XP or 2000.

FIGURE 7.15

Windows Vista Basic

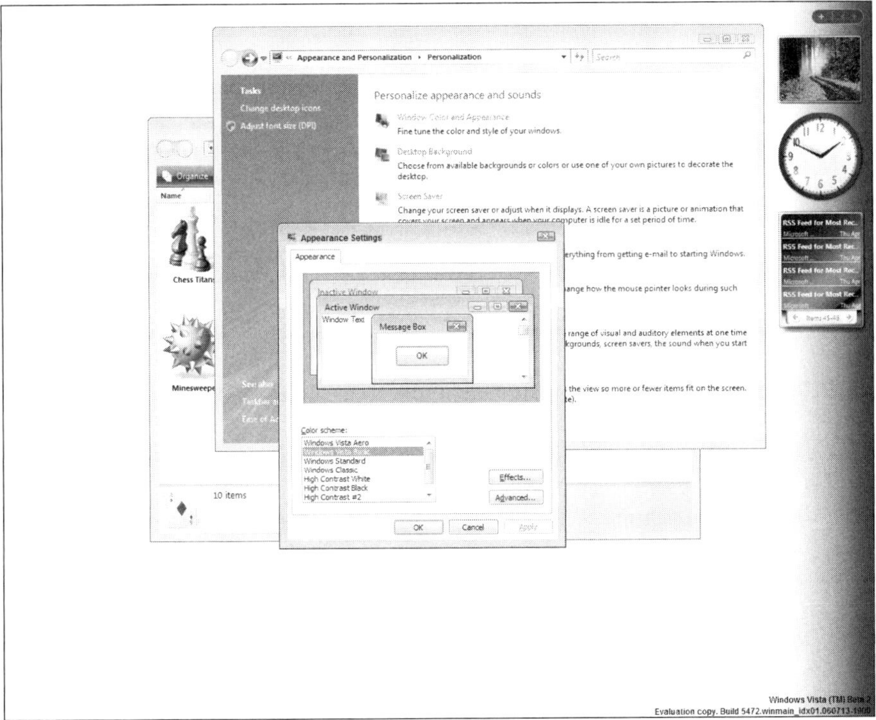

Windows Standard and Windows Classic

If you go back to the dialog box shown in Figure 7.14, two other options include Windows Standard and Windows Classic. Essentially similar, they further morph Windows Vista, in their case to the look and feel of Windows 2000 (see Figure 7.16).

As is the case with Vista Basic, in Windows Standard and Windows Classic the windows are opaque and the 3D features are gone. Flip and Flip 3D aren't available. The Start button says "Start" and isn't round and stylized. Even the Sidebar is flat and listless.

FIGURE 7.16

Windows Standard

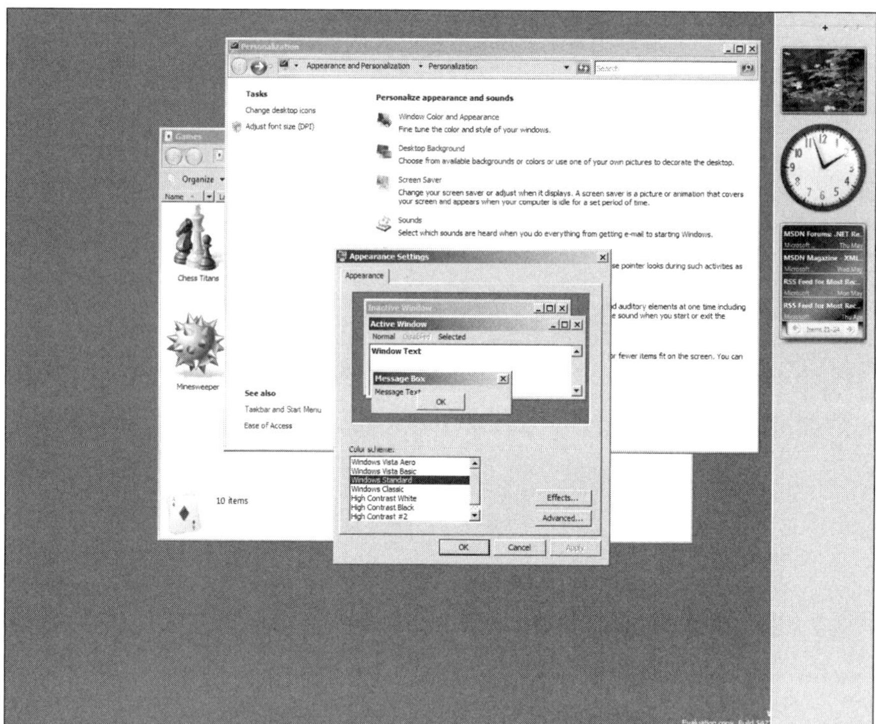

The window elements, however, remain in Vista style, with breadcrumb paths, search bars, and context buttons. You can change some of those features. For instance, to ensure that the classic pull-down menus always appear, do this:

1. **Click the Start button.**
2. **Click Control Panel.**
3. **Click Appearance and Personalization.**
4. **Click Folder Options.** A window like the one shown in Figure 7.17 appears.
5. **Click the View tab.** The window changes to the one shown in Figure 7.18.
6. **In the Advanced settings window, fill in the Always Show Menus check box.**
7. **Click Apply.**
8. **Click OK.**

FIGURE 7.17

The Folder Options window

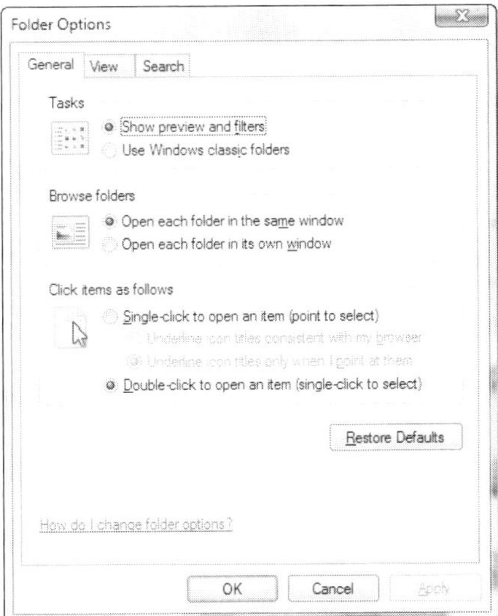

FIGURE 7.18

The View tab on the Folder Options window

To see the classic URL in the address bar, instead of the breadcrumb path, just click the down arrow on the right of the address bar. Figure 7.19 shows a breadcrumbs address bar, and Figure 7.20 shows one in the classic URL style.

FIGURE 7.19

Windows Vista's breadcrumb address

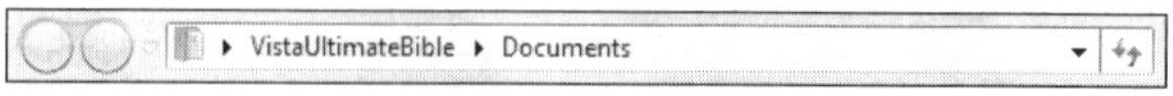

▸ VistaUltimateBible ▸ Documents

FIGURE 7.20

The more traditional URL address

C:\Users\VistaUltimateBible\Documents

Summary

Windows Vista brings a whole new look and feel to the Windows. Aero is a stunning new interface, complete with three-dimensional effects that bring the desktop to a whole new level of gloss and style.

Of course, if you're a longtime Windows user, you might be set in your ways. An associate of mine refused to upgrade from Windows 98SE to Windows XP because he didn't like the new, more colorful look of the operating system's default theme. I tried to convince him that he didn't have to use it; XP contains a classic scheme that resembles older Windows operating systems.

Similarly, Windows Vista is ready for users who don't want to bother with the new look and feel, or whose computers don't contain the graphics hardware to accelerate the Aero desktop. With Windows Vista Basic, the new look and feel are mostly intact, but they lack the translucent "glass" and other effects. Other styles take users back to the days of Windows 2000.

Chapter 8

Exploring Interface Features

IN THIS CHAPTER

Familiarizing yourself with the desktop

Exploring the new Start Menu

Using the Sidebar

Organizing your files

If you're used to Windows XP or any previous version of Windows, you know by now that Windows Vista Ultimate (or any version of Vista, for that matter) has changed dramatically from these earlier versions. Although all kinds of things are going on in the background that you can't see, the most striking alterations to the Windows meme are the changes in the interface.

In Chapter 7, I talked at length about Windows Vista's Aero interface. It's a sexy new way to view the amazing operating system, complete with transparencies, a new taskbar style, and other features. Aero isn't the only new sensation when it comes to the Windows Vista interface. Microsoft has added, updated, or changed a large number of other features, including the Start Menu, the search features, the incredible array of default folders for your various files, the desktop (complete with the brand-new Sidebar), and more.

The Start Menu's design, for example, though it echoes the XP Start Menu, is easier to use and puts all the games and applications installed in your computer at your fingertips. The menu is familiar enough to be natural, but its redesign is aimed at making it even more useful.

The Sidebar brings applets — little applications — right to your desktop where they're the most useful. It's customizable and comes with a number of useful gadgets, and even more are available via the Internet.

Windows Vista keeps track of all of your files, and even the contents of many of them, and stores them in its own little database to make searching incredibly fast and useful. The Search function, if you haven't already noticed, is universal: It's everywhere, it lets you search almost anything, and the results are nearly instantaneous.

Microsoft has also revamped the folders once known as My Pictures, My Music, and so on. Now, default locations store almost any type of document or media file you'll ever encounter. Being organized is so easy with Windows Vista you'll never look very hard for any of your stuff.

Little things in the interface, like built-in RSS support, make computing more informative and more useful. Support for a new type of document, known as XPS, is also built right in.

If all these new features seem a bit daunting, have no fear. It's all designed to be terrifically simple to understand and get started with, even if you're a complete novice to the Windows line of operating systems. Within a few clicks you'll be searching, organizing, using, and gaming on your computer with the expertise of a power user.

The Windows Vista interface isn't just a bunch of neat gizmos and eye candy. It's a conglomeration of truly useful technologies that will make your computing experience easier, smoother, and more intuitive than ever before. It will, that is, once you learn about and get used to all the new goodies, and that's what this chapter helps you do.

Vista's New Start Menu

Figure 8.1 shows the Windows Vista Start Menu. If you've used Windows XP in the past, it looks vaguely familiar, yet it's also strikingly different.

Notice that the little button that said "Start" on it is gone. Microsoft has replaced it with a circle with the Windows logo. That's where you click to invoke the Start Menu.

The menu itself contains a number of both old and new elements. The top-left side of the menu contains shortcuts to programs that have been "pinned" to the menu. By default, the only such programs are Internet Explorer and Windows Mail.

You can pin anything to the Start Menu by dragging its icon to this area of the menu.

Below that, still on the left side, is a row of shortcuts to programs. As you use the computer, Windows observes which programs you use the most and adds their shortcuts to this area, as well as removes those programs you use less frequently. Upon installation, Windows Vista Ultimate populates this area with a number of shortcuts it thinks you might use, such as Welcome Center, Windows Ultimate Extras, Media Player, and DVD Maker.

Moving on down the left side, notice the entry called All Programs. This item is the gateway to everything that's stored in your computer and has added a shortcut to the Start Menu. When you click it, it changes to show a number of other shortcuts plus a folder system, as shown in Figure 8.2.

FIGURE 8.1

The Windows Vista Start Menu

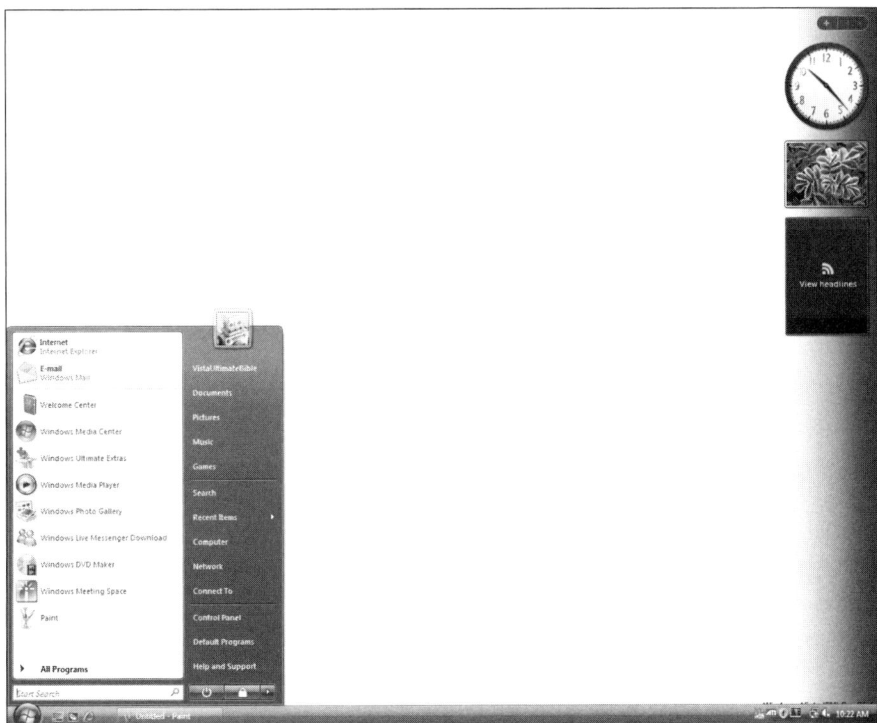

From this area, you can navigate through the various folders and subfolders to find the program that you want to launch. It functions much like the Start Menu in Windows XP, except it keeps the program selections inside the Start Menu area rather than expanding them out all over the desktop.

Below the Start Menu is the Search bar. This feature is completely new to the Windows Start Menu. Search, in fact, has been revamped to the point of being unrecognizable even to XP users. It's about a thousand times more useful than it has been in past versions of Windows. I talk more about the Search function later in this chapter.

On the right side of the Start Menu, at the top, is the icon you assigned to your user account. The right column contains shortcuts to all kinds of things you might be interested in, including your account's personal folders, the Search tool proper, recently opened items, the Computer window, the Network interface, Control Panel, and Help and Support.

FIGURE 8.2

The Start Menu, after clicking All Programs

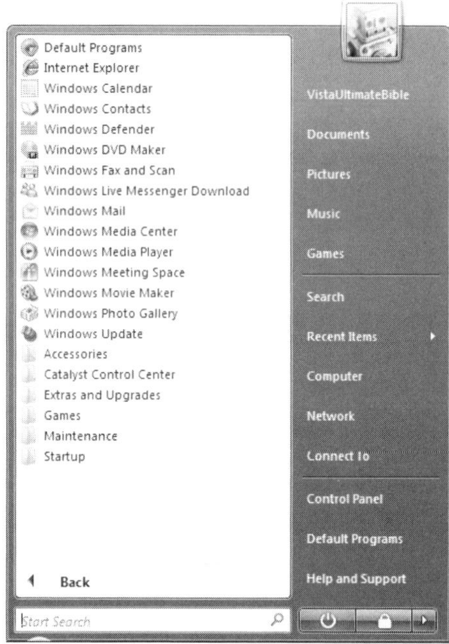

At the bottom right of the Start Menu is a trio of icons that you can use to power down the computer, hibernate it, switch user accounts, and otherwise end your session. On the left is a circle with a vertical line through it; click this circle to put the computer to sleep. It'll go into a low power state but recover much more quickly when you go to use it again than it would take to boot up from a complete power down. The button with the picture of the padlock locks your session; you'll be required to enter your password to get back into your account after you lock it.

TIP Locking your session is useful if you want to keep your stuff secure when you leave your computer for a few minutes. Only people with your password will be able to reenter your user account after you lock it. Don't share your password with anyone whom you do not want to have access to your files.

Clicking the last button, which is festooned with an arrow pointing to the right, invokes a little menu. Its options include the following:

- **Switch user:** Lets you allow another user to log onto the computer, while keeping your session open. The other user won't have access to your session.
- **Log off:** Closes your session and returns Windows to the login screen.

- **Lock:** Locks your session as described earlier in this section.
- **Restart:** Logs off all accounts and reboots the computer.
- **Sleep:** Puts the computer into a low power state.
- **Hibernate:** Saves everything in memory to the hard disk and essentially shuts down the computer. When you restart, Windows restores the data it saved back into memory and you can continue working from the point at which you hibernated the computer.
- **Shut down:** Logs off all accounts and turns off the computer.

Using the Classic Start Menu

Now suppose you gave the new Start Menu a try and you absolutely hate it. You don't like the way it looks, or you can't stand its transparency effect. It's ugly, it's pointless, and you wish it were Windows 98.

All is not lost. Right-click on the Start button and click Properties. The Taskbar and Start Menu Properties dialog box appears, with the Start Menu tab in front (see Figure 8.3).

FIGURE 8.3

Properties for the Start Menu

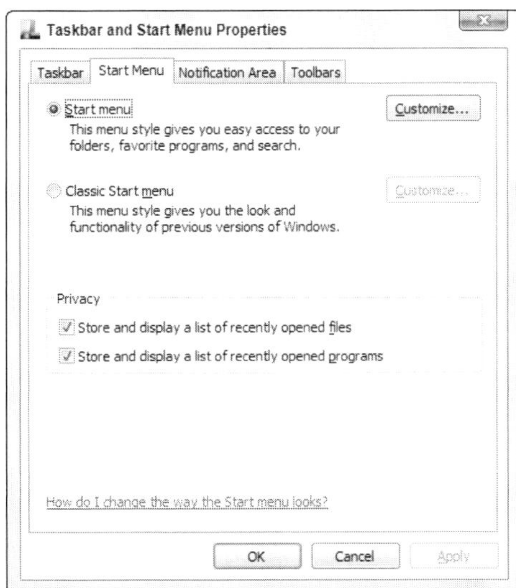

Click the radio button next to Classic Start Menu and click OK. Then, check out the Start Menu again. It looks remarkably like the Windows 98 Start Menu, complete with expanding menu trees (see Figure 8.4).

FIGURE 8.4

Windows Classic Start Menu

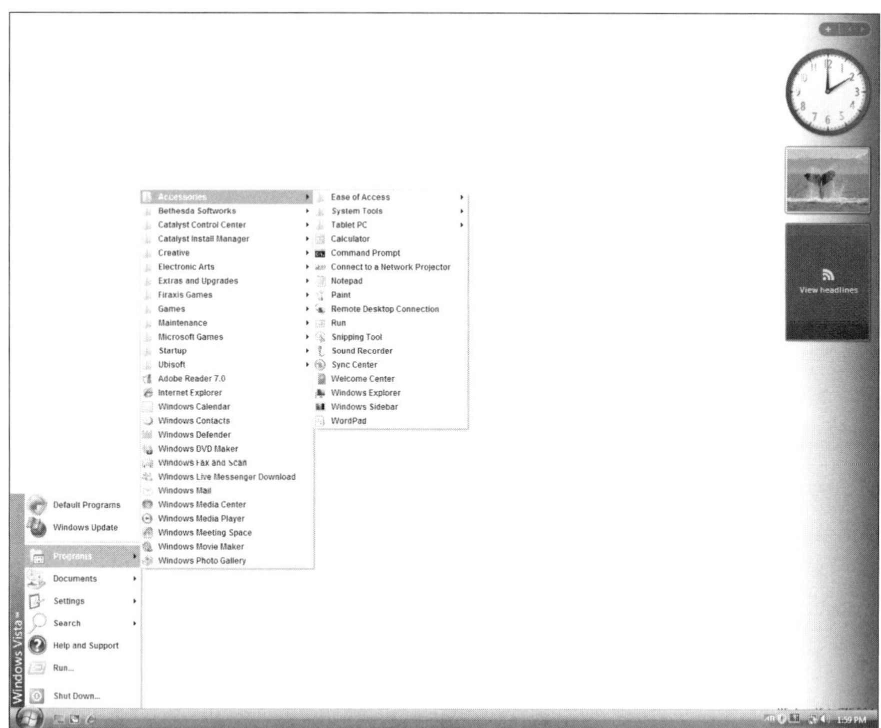

NOTE The Classic Start Menu isn't in the style of Windows Vista, whether or not you have the Aero features enabled. It won't be transparent, and it won't, by default, have all the handy shortcuts to commonly accessed areas of the storage system. If, however, you prefer it cosmetically and functionally, go for it.

Customizing the Start menus

You can customize both the Windows Vista Start Menu and the emergency backup classic-style Start Menu. Open the Taskbar and Start Menu Properties dialog box shown in Figure 8.3 by right-clicking the Start button and clicking Properties. Note that the Customize button (next to whichever Start Menu style you've selected) is active. Click it to open a smaller dialog box containing customization options.

Customizing the Vista Start Menu

If you click the Customize button with the default Vista Start Menu enabled, the Customize Start Menu dialog box, shown in Figure 8.5, appears.

FIGURE 8.5

Windows Vista Start Menu customization options

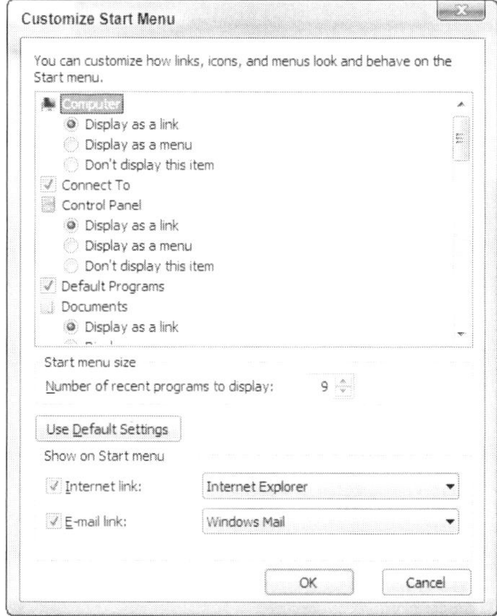

You can optimize the Vista Start Menu in a number of ways. Starting at the bottom, you can change the e-mail and Internet programs to those you desire. For example, if you have Microsoft Office installed, you might want to change the e-mail program to Outlook instead of Windows Mail. You might want to change the Internet browser to an IE alternative such as Firefox or Opera.

The next option up from the bottom enables you to set the number of recent programs for the Start Menu to display, from 0 to 30. The default is 8.

The biggest box in the window allows you to scroll through a wide array of options. You can choose different ways to display a number of the Start Menu components, or not to display them at all. The options include the following:

- **Computer:** You can display this item as a link (the default), a submenu, or remove it completely.
- **Connect To:** Use the check box to choose whether or not to display this item.
- **Control Panel:** You can display this item as a link (the default), a submenu, or remove it completely.

- **Default Programs:** Use the check box to choose whether or not to display this item.
- **Documents:** You can display this item as a link (the default), a submenu, or remove it completely.
- **Favorites menu:** Use the check box to choose whether or not to display this item.
- **Games:** Another item that you can display as a link, a menu, or not at all.
- **Help:** Use the check box to choose whether or not to display this item.
- **Highlight newly installed programs:** When you install a program and it makes an entry in the Start Menu, Windows can highlight it for you to make it easier to find the first time you run it.
- **Music:** You can display this item as a link (the default), a submenu, or remove it completely.
- **Network:** Use the check box to choose whether or not to display this item.
- **Open submenus when I pause on them with the mouse cursor:** With this item enabled, submenus will open as described; otherwise, you have to click them to get them to open.
- **Personal Folder:** You can display this item as a link (the default), a submenu, or remove it completely.
- **Pictures:** You can display this item as a link (the default), a submenu, or remove it completely.
- **Printers:** You can display the Printers item by checking this box; otherwise, you'll have to go to Control Panel to access Printers.
- **Search:** Several options let you customize how and what you can search through the Start Menu.
- **Sort All Programs by menu name:** Use the check box to choose whether or not to display this item.
- **System administrative tools:** You can display the Admin tools item by clicking this box; otherwise, you'll have to go to Control Panel to access the tools.
- **Use large icons:** Use the check box to choose whether or not to display this item.

Customizing the Classic Start Menu

Similarly, you can customize the Classic Start Menu. Enable it and click the Customize link in the Taskbar and Start Menu Properties dialog box to invoke the Customize Classic Start Menu dialog box shown in Figure 8.6.

This dialog box allows you to add programs to or remove programs from the Start Menu by searching the computer manually or with assistance from Windows. Click the Add or Advanced buttons to find programs to add to the Start Menu; click Remove to remove an item; and click Sort to sort them as you please.

FIGURE 8.6

Windows Classic Start Menu customization options

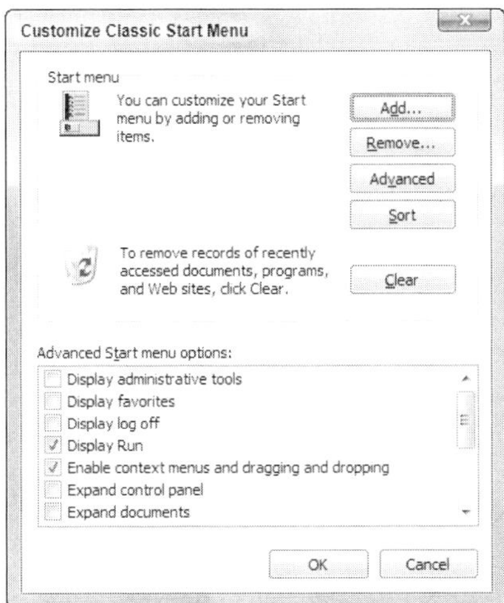

The lower part of the dialog box contains a scroll list with a number of check box options, which allow you to turn on or off various items that can be displayed in the Start Menu. They are:

- Display administrative tools (default: off)
- Display favorites (default: off)
- Display log off (default: off)
- Display Run (default: on)
- Enable context menus and dragging and dropping (default: on)
- Expand control panel (default: off)
- Expand documents (default: off)
- Expand network connections (default: off)
- Expand pictures (default: off)
- Expand printers (default: off)
- Scroll programs (default: off)
- Show small icons in Start Menu (default: off)
- Use personalized menus (default: on)

When you're satisfied with the look, feel, and functionality of the Start Menu, move on to the rest of the primary Windows Vista display: the desktop.

Customizing the Desktop

Like the Start Menu, the Windows Vista desktop is highly customizable. You can tweak everything from the background picture to the special icons (Computer, Recycle Bin, and so on) displayed. Furthermore, you can make fine adjustments to everything you see, such as window borders, scroll bars, title fonts, and much more.

The locations of the controls over these items is mostly centralized — more so, in fact, than they ever were in prior versions of Windows.

NOTE **Most of the Vista screen shots you see in this book are taken with the computer set up for a black-and-white book, and therefore the Windows desktop looks pretty plain. They are *not* representative of what you can do with Vista if you decide to get creative. Vista's desktop can look as fancy and colorful or as drab and plain as you want.**

Figures 8.7 and 8.8 show two desktops. The first is the Windows desktop as I'm required to set it up for this book, which makes seeing various elements in my screenshots easier for you but which, admittedly, is kind of dull. The second is a more typical Windows Vista desktop. (For more examples, see the color insert.)

FIGURE 8.7

A plain Vista desktop

FIGURE 8.8

A more colorful Vista desktop

These figures show just how utilitarian or charismatic you can make the Windows desktop. You can be as creative as you want to. You can even save and share some elements of your desktops with other people as *Themes*. The background, the colors, the opacity of the Aero glass elements, the styles of the system icons, and other things are included in a .THEME file that you can create, acquire, and share.

The quickest and easiest way to open the desktop customization screen is to right-click in a blank area of the desktop. In the resulting context menu, you can expand the View or Sort submenus, refresh the desktop, create new shortcuts, or click Personalize to call up the Personalization window.

The View submenu allows you to change the sizes of the desktop icons, turn on or off the option to snap the icons to an invisible grid and/or automatically arrange them, or hide them entirely.

The Sort submenu allows you to sort the icons in several different ways: by name, size, type, or date modified.

The Personalization window, shown in Figure 8.9, contains a number of options, some of which I explored in Chapter 7; the rest I cover in the rest of this chapter.

Changing Window Color and Appearance

Click Window Color and Appearance in the Personalization window to open the Window Color and Appearance pane shown in Figure 8.10. Here, you can change the color of windows, the opacity of their glass areas, and open the advanced appearance options.

FIGURE 8.9

The Personalization window

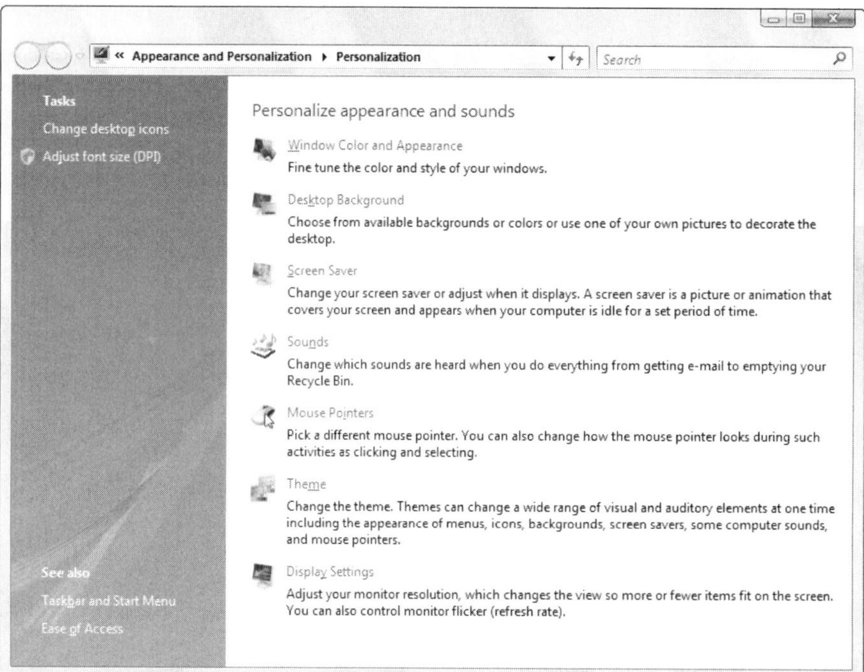

FIGURE 8.10

The Window Color and Appearance pane

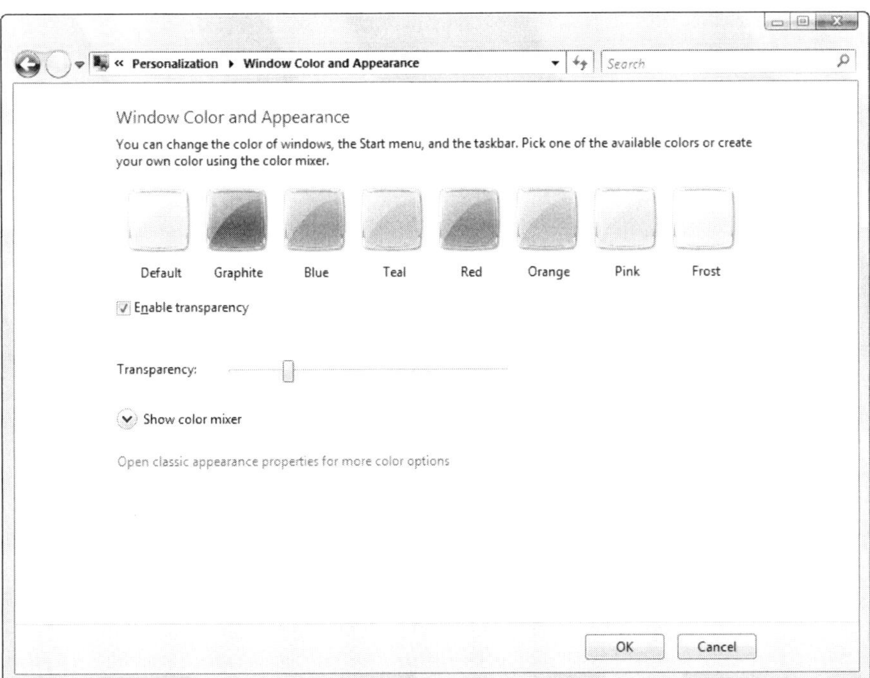

Vista provides a number of appealing, preselected colors for you to choose from. If you want, you can click Show Color Mixer to display a full palette of colors for complete control over the color of your windows (Figure 8.11). The color mixer features three sliders: one for hue, one for saturation, and one for brightness. With them, you can create any color you want within the scope of your desktop's color depth.

FIGURE 8.11

The Window Color and Appearance window with the color mixer shown

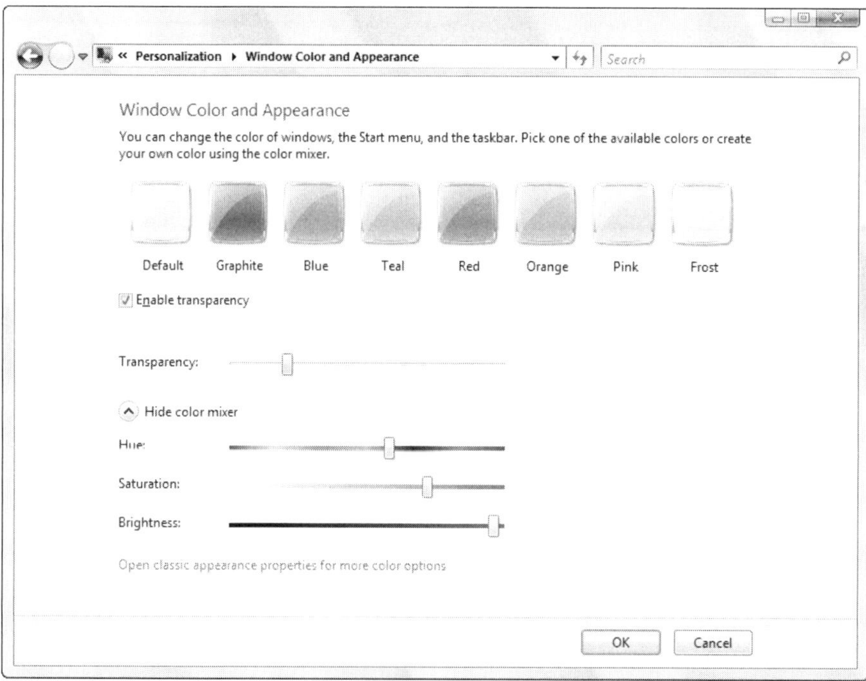

For even more drastic control over window appearance, click "Open classic appearance properties for more color options" at the bottom of the Window Color and Appearance pane. A new properties dialog box, shown in Figure 8.12, appears.

This window may be familiar to users of Windows XP and earlier Windows versions. You can pick a color scheme, or click the Advanced button to open the Advanced Appearance dialog box shown in Figure 8.13, which allows you not only to lord over the colors, but also to control many other options concerning the appearance of windows displayed on your Vista desktop.

Under Item, you can select basically anything that may ever appear on your desktop within the confines of the Windows conventions. Items include everything from the desktop and the windows themselves to 3D objects (buttons and such), scroll bars, tool tips, window borders, icon spacing, and more.

FIGURE 8.12

The classic Appearance Settings dialog box

FIGURE 8.13

The classic Advanced Appearance dialog box

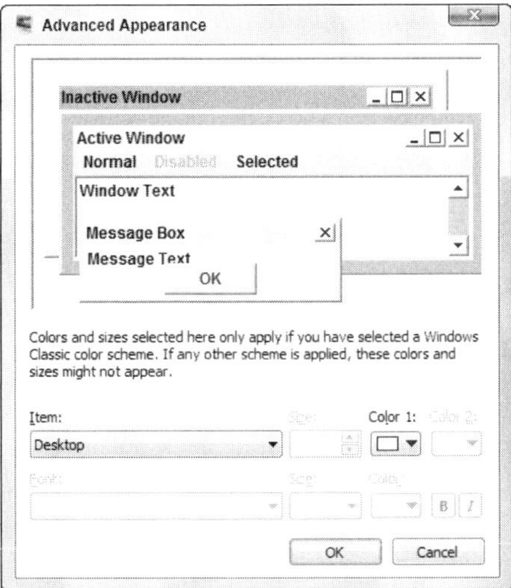

Select an item to govern its options. Options include, where appropriate, the color or colors of the item, its size, its font properties (including font, font size, font color, and bold and italic options). For example, if you select the Icon option, you can control the size of the icons on the desktop, the font in which icon text is displayed, the font's color, the font's size, and whether it's bolded or italicized.

The Advanced Appearance interface gives you a massive amount of control over the appearance of every element of the Windows desktop. You can change anything you like, from the thickness of the window borders to the colors of the active and inactive window title bars. What's more, when you deal with colors, you have the option to click an Advanced button that gives you a full palette of colors to choose from.

Changing the Desktop Background

The next option in the Personalization window is the Desktop Background item, which opens a window like the one shown in Figure 8.14. This is where you set the background of your desktop.

FIGURE 8.14

The desktop background personalization window

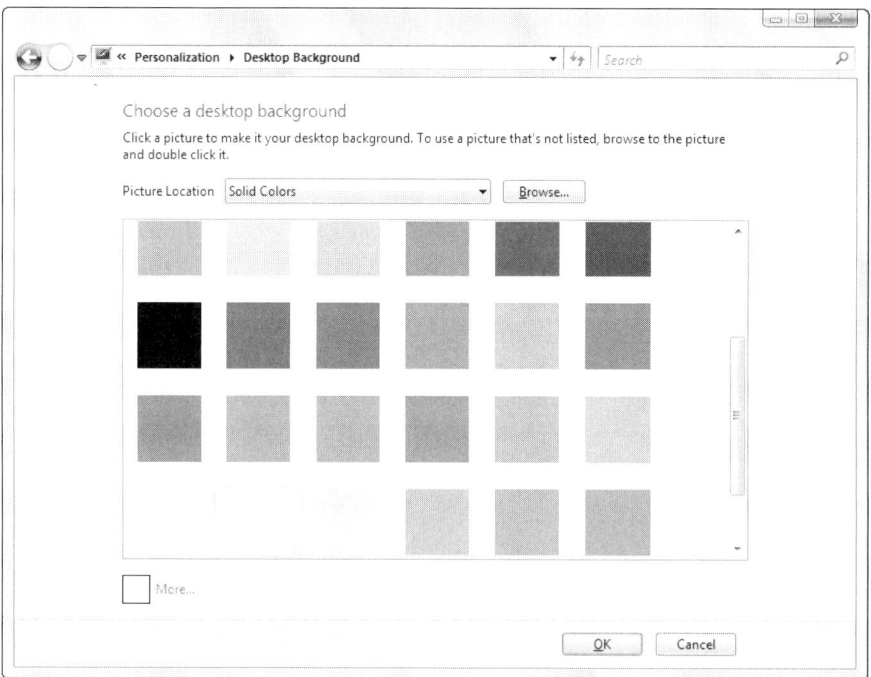

See Chapter 5 for more information on adjusting the desktop background and other appearance options.

The Sidebar

XP users, take note. Possibly the first thing you noticed when you laid fresh eyes on the Windows Vista desktop was a vertical bar that runs down the right side and has, by default, a clock, a little picture, and an RSS feed selector on it.

That's the Sidebar, shown in Figure 8.15. The Sidebar is a nifty new feature that puts little programs called gadgets at your fingertips. Windows Vista comes with a number of gadgets and a simple-to-use interface that allows you to download more from the Internet. You can arrange gadgets on the Sidebar however you please by dragging and dropping them.

Right-click somewhere on the Sidebar to see a context menu with several items:

- Bring Gadgets to Front
- Add Gadgets
- Properties
- Help
- Close Sidebar

If you happen to right-click on one of the gadgets, you may see other items as well, such as Options, Close Gadget, Detach from Sidebar, and Opacity.

Bring Gadgets to Front does just what it says: It brings the gadgets on the Sidebar to the front of the desktop, above any open windows that might have been obscuring them.

Add Gadgets invokes the Add Gadgets window shown in Figure 8.16. You can use it to drag any of the gadgets from this window to the sidebar. What's more, if you click the link on the window called Get More Gadgets Online, Internet Explorer will open and take you to a page like the one shown in Figure 8.17. Choose a gadget and click Download to add it to your collection.

Gadgets options allow you to close a gadget, to detach it from the Sidebar and move it around the desktop, to make the gadget more or less transparent, and so on. The options available vary with the gadget that you right-click on.

FIGURE 8.15

The default Vista Sidebar

FIGURE 8.16

The Add Gadgets window

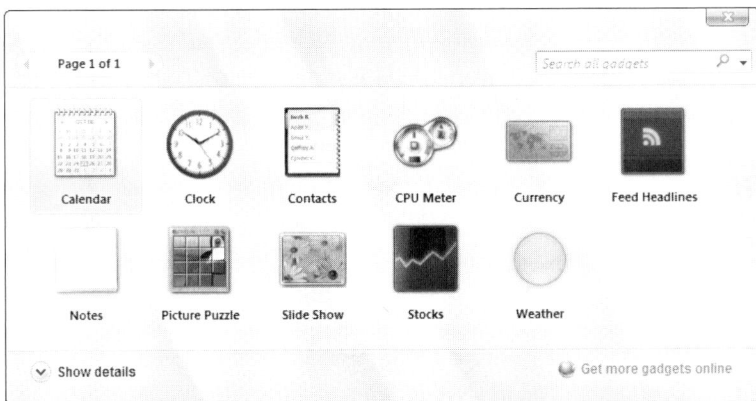

FIGURE 8.17

You can get more gadgets online.

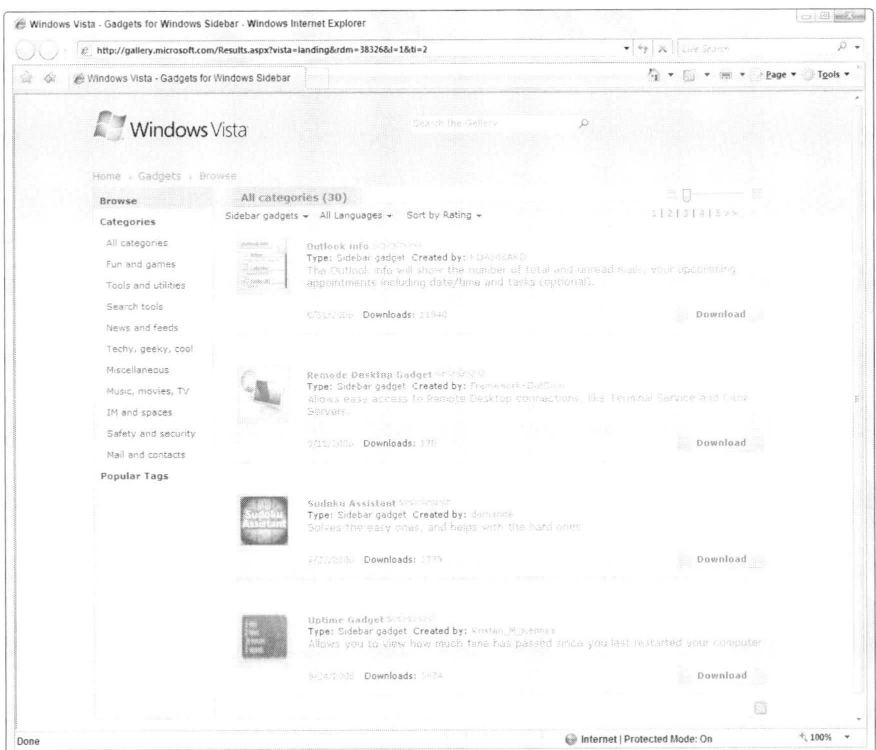

Properties invokes the Windows Sidebar Properties dialog box, shown in Figure 8.18. In it, you can:

- Use a check box at the top of the window to select whether to start the Sidebar when Windows starts.
- Use a check box to decree whether the Sidebar is always on top of other windows.
- Display the Sidebar on the left or right side of the desktop (the default is the right side).
- Determine which monitor on which to display the Sidebar, if your PC is connected to multiple monitors.
- View a list of gadgets currently running.
- Restore the gadgets originally installed with Windows Vista, should you have altered them.

FIGURE 8.18

The Windows Sidebar Properties dialog box

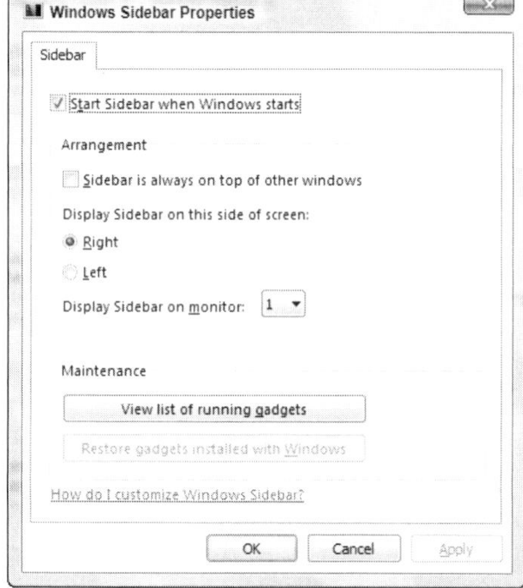

Windows Vista includes 11 gadgets, and they include a customizable, analog clock; a notepad; an RSS viewer; a mini-slideshow that can display the photos in your Pictures folder; a contacts list; a currency converter; a CPU meter; and more.

Customizing a gadget is usually self-explanatory. For example, right-click on the Slide Show gadget and click Options. The window shown in Figure 8.19 appears.

FIGURE 8.19

The Options panel for the Slide Show gadget

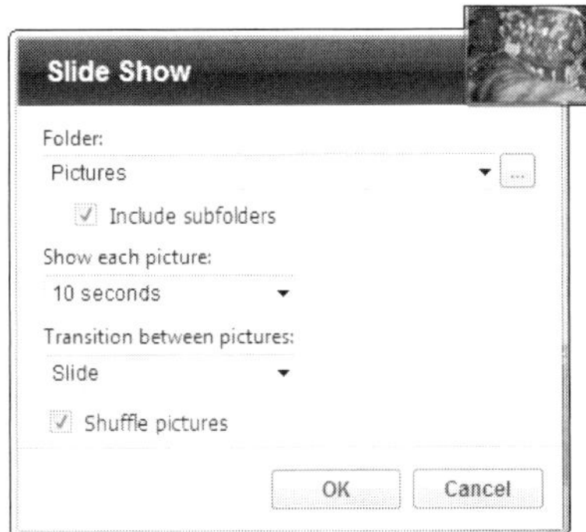

Here, you can use drop-down boxes and a check box to choose

- Which folder the Sidebar will display pictures from.
- How long to show each picture before displaying the next one.
- How to transition from picture to picture.
- Whether to shuffle the order in which the pictures are displayed.

NOTE Some of the gadgets use information from other areas of Windows Vista. For example, the Contacts gadget can display data from your Contacts folder; the RSS Feed Headlines gadget grabs feeds that you've configured through Internet Explorer; and so on.

The Sidebar is as useful as you make it. You can pick and choose from the gadgets you'll use the most, and place them in the order you desire. I love the notepad gadget, which is useful for typing quick notes for future reference, and the CPU Meter gadget to keep an eye on the health of my system's processor.

Some of my favorite downloadable gadgets from the Microsoft Gadget Gallery download link include:

- **Calculator:** This is an extremely handy tool for when you don't feel like opening the Calculator applet included with Windows. It's a simple adding machine that's always at your fingertips. Check it out in Figure 8.20.
- **Google-bar:** Search Google right from the desktop with this Sidebar gadget. It's simple and elegant, with a search box that opens a browser with a Google search of whatever you punch in (see Figure 8.21).

FIGURE 8.20

The Calculator applet

FIGURE 8.21

You can search Google with this applet.

- **Xbox Gamertag:** You can look up the Gamertag of anybody who has an Xbox Live account with this gadget. My Gamertag is shown in Figure 8.22.

FIGURE 8.22

My Gamertag is shown here.

- **MyDictionary:** I'm a writer, and sometimes I need to know a quick definition of a word. This gadget has a text box that lets you type in a word to look up on MyDictionary. It opens a browser with the definition all ready for you (see Figure 8.23).

FIGURE 8.23

You can search the dictionary with this applet.

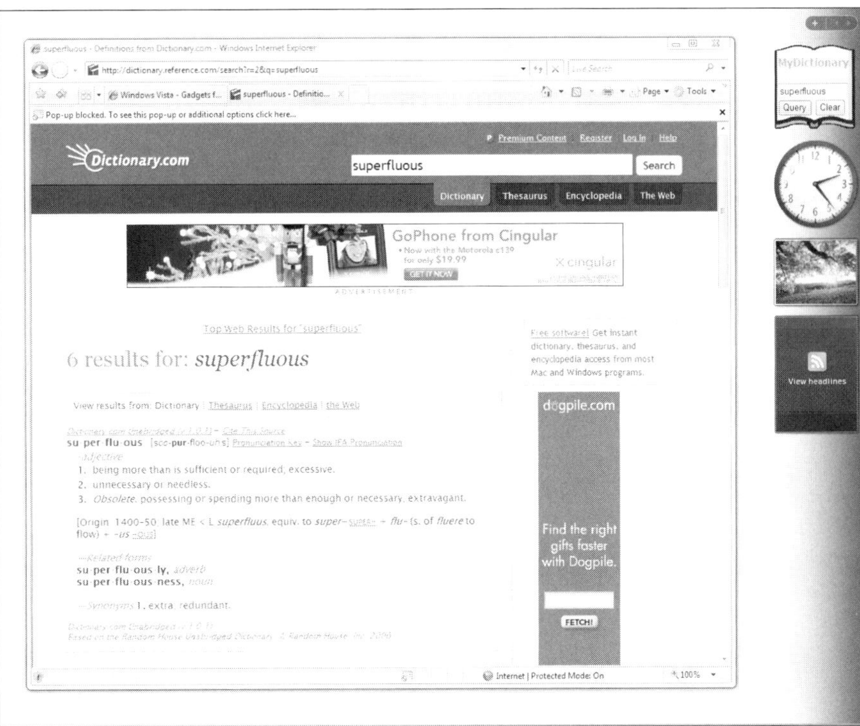

- **Poker:** This gadget is still in beta, but it's quite fun. It's a quick five-card game of jacks-or-better poker. Score by getting a great hand (see Figure 8.24).

FIGURE 8.24

Test your luck with the Poker applet.

Built-In Organization

Organizing your files is a big part of the computing experience. If you can't find what you create, download, or otherwise plop onto your computer's hard drive, you're in a bit of trouble.

Windows operating systems have made efforts in the past to make finding your stuff easy. The "My" series of folders in XP, for example, gave you a place to store movies, pictures, music, and more, in folders called My Movies, My Pictures, My Music, and so on.

Windows Vista has made organization even easier. It has a similar range of folders, which it creates for each user account on the computer. Vista features folders for videos, music, game saves, documents, pictures, downloads, and more.

Microsoft has eliminated the "My" prefix in the Windows Vista location folders. The folders are simply called Music, Videos, Pictures, and so on.

To see the full range of default locations, click the Start button and click the name of your user account. In my case, it's VistaUltimateBible. A folder like the one shown in Figure 8.25 appears.

FIGURE 8.25

Places for all of your files

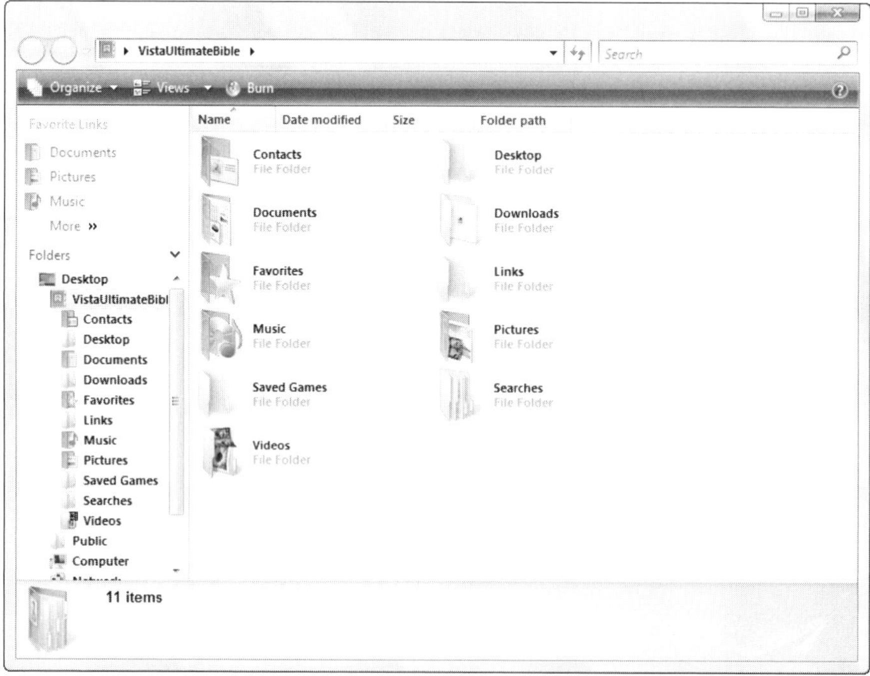

Check out all the subfolders. You can invoke many of them directly through links on the right side of the Start Menu. You can also open them by double-clicking them here.

Each folder has its own purpose, and many of the folders have special toolbar options.

Contacts

The Contacts folder, shown in Figure 8.26, stores all the contacts you create through Windows Contacts (mine's empty). You can add, edit, and remove contacts here.

The toolbar items include options to create new contacts and groups of contacts (which act like subfolders in the file system), to import contacts (from, for example, an Outlook Express address book), and to export your contacts.

FIGURE 8.26

The Contacts folder

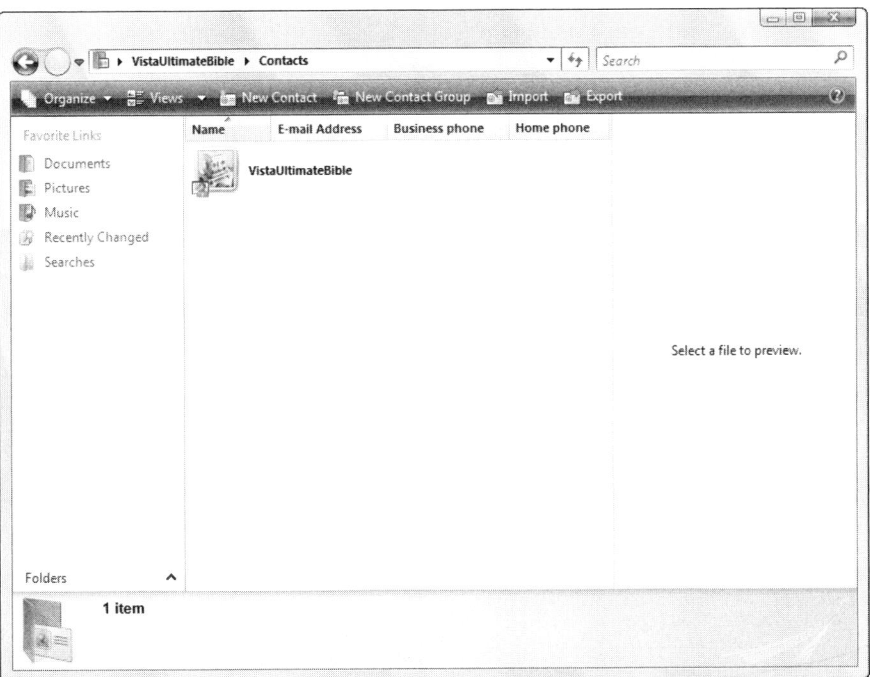

Documents

The Documents folder is for storing any documents and other miscellaneous files you create with various programs. Mine, shown in Figure 8.27, contains the theme I created for taking screen shots (I named it "wiley"). When you create documents in word processors, spreadsheet programs, and so on, the Documents folder is a fantastic place to store them.

Documents is a basic file system folder. You can and should create subfolders to organize your documents. For example, I'm a writer, and I write for many different companies. I might create a subfolder called "Submissions" for stuff I write professionally, and then create subfolders within it for each market that assigns me work. That way, all of my work isn't simply piled helter-skelter into the Documents folder.

FIGURE 8.27

The Documents folder

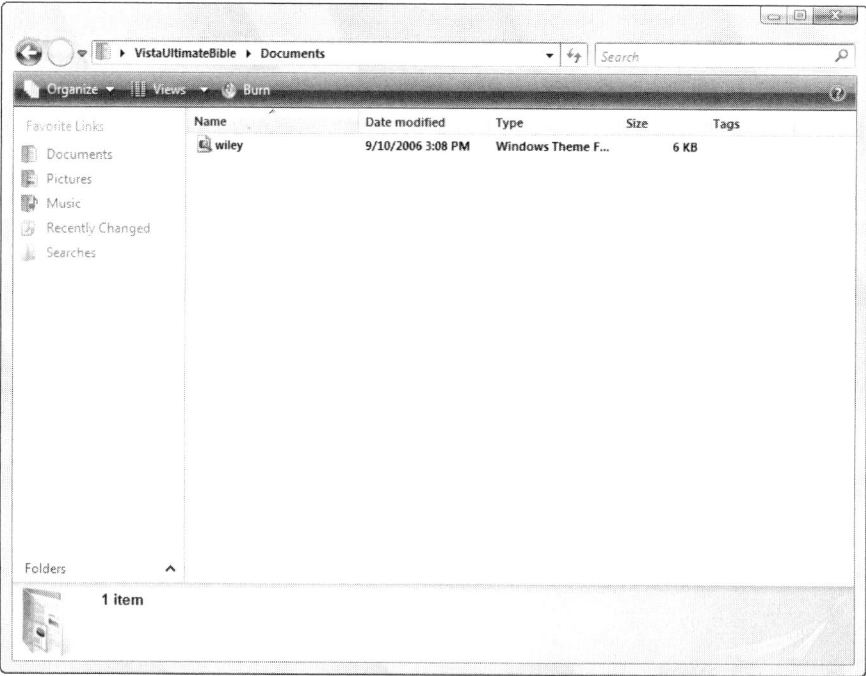

Favorites

The Favorites folder, shown in Figure 8.28, contains your Internet bookmarks. You can organize it like any folder in the file system, and invoke it through Internet Explorer's Favorites interface.

Although you'll probably encounter this folder through IE, you can go to any Web site stored within it by double-clicking on the link. Doing so launches IE and navigates you right to the page.

Music

The Music folder is intended for you to store all the music you rip, download, and otherwise acquire. Mine is full of tunes (see Figure 8.29).

Windows Media Player will look in this folder for music files. As you navigate through your music folders and subfolders, notice the Play All button on the toolbar; click it to play the songs in the folder currently displayed.

FIGURE 8.28

The Favorites folder

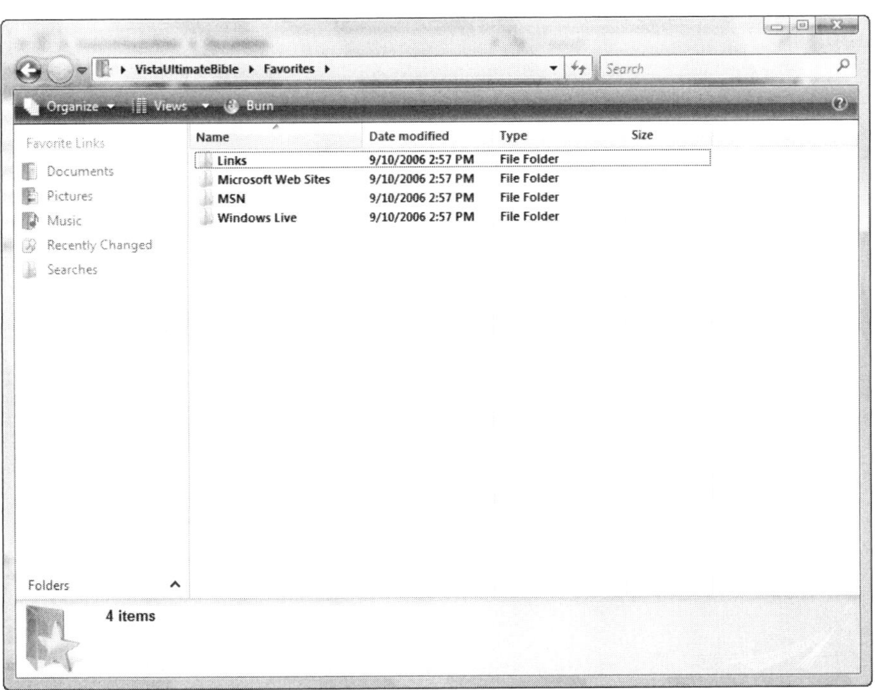

FIGURE 8.29

The Music folder

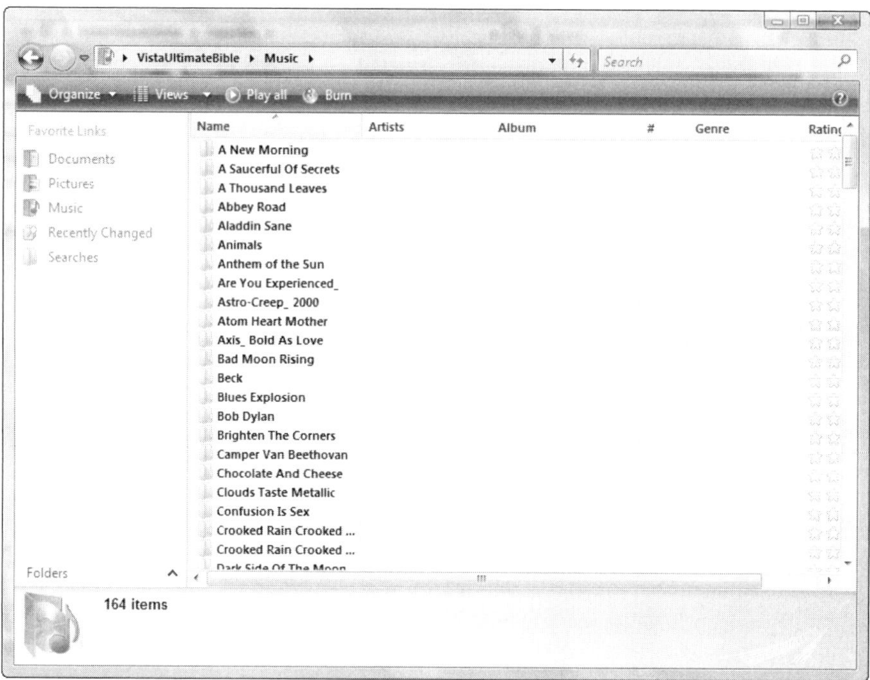

Saved Games

The Saved Games folder is for your game saves. Even though legacy games (games written before the coming of Windows Vista) save games wherever their programmers want them to, Vista-aware games will drop their saves into this folder. Otherwise, it operates like any file folder.

TIP Having a central location for game saves makes migrating to a new computer far easier than it ever has been in the past. Gamers tend to upgrade frequently, and one of the problems with moving to a new PC is that game saves tend to be all over the file system. Some saves are in the game folders themselves, others are in the My Documents folder, and so on. Look for that trend to evaporate as more and more games use the Vista Saved Games folder to store your saves.

Videos

The Videos folder works like the Music folder; Media Player looks here for video files. It's an ideal location to store any video you capture from your camcorder, download from the Web, or otherwise get your hands on.

Desktop

The Desktop folder is where your Windows Desktop gets its stuff from. Any icons or files stored on the desktop actually land here.

Downloads

A new folder in the Windows organization scheme, the Downloads folder is the default target location when you start a download through Internet Explorer. Figure 8.30 shows my Downloads folder, containing a display driver for Vista I've downloaded.

You can divide this folder into subfolders for organization, if you want. Make a folder for game demos, one for drivers, one for game patches, and so on.

Pictures

Like the Music and Videos folders, the Pictures folder is intended for media files: specifically, image files. I have a ton of them, as shown in Figure 8.31.

FIGURE 8.30

The Downloads folder

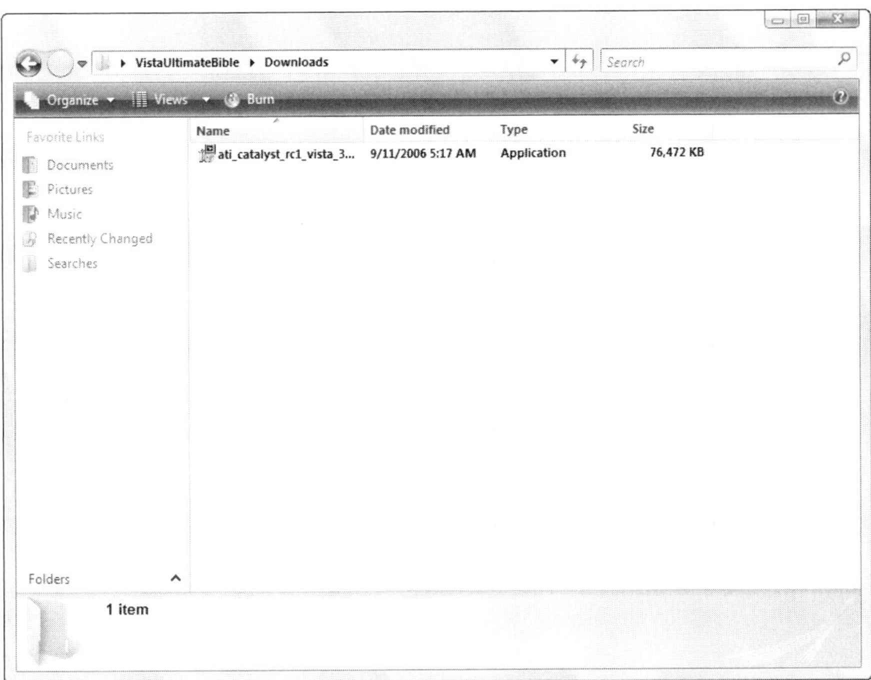

FIGURE 8.31

The Pictures folder, showing my pictures organized in subfolders by date

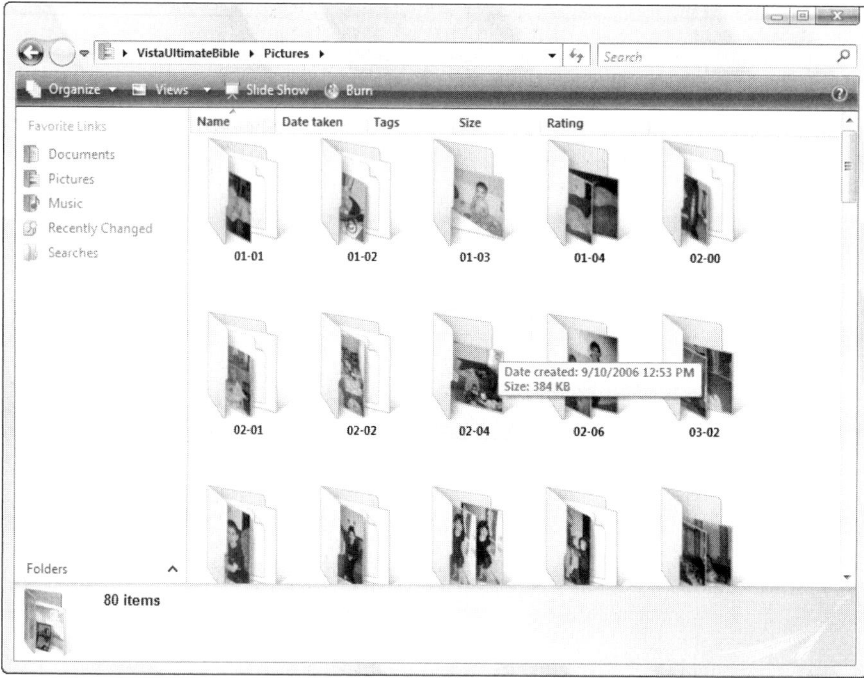

Note that, through the button on the toolbar, you can launch a slide show of your pictures (Figure 8.32). Windows shows the image files in the current folder. The slide show interface has a few buttons at the bottom so you can pause, play, and jump forward and backward through the selection of pictures.

Another button on the slide show interface lets you set a few options. You can loop the slide show and shuffle the order of the photos, and you can toggle the speed at which they're shown — fast, medium, or slow. On the other side of the interface, a Themes button lets you change the way Windows goes from picture to picture, and you can set a few other options.

Searches

This powerful folder allows you to save searches. If you search your computer frequently for the same items or file types, save the search — it'll end up here. You can invoke a search quickly by navigating to this folder and double-clicking the search you want.

FIGURE 8.32

A slide show in action

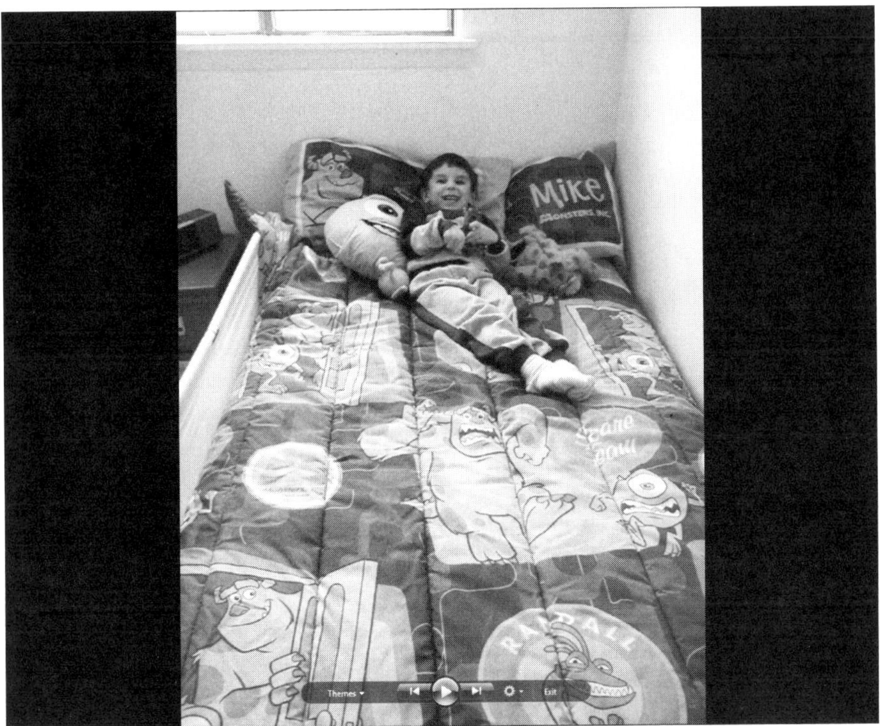

Summary

Windows Vista's interface melds elements both old and new for an amazing, intuitive, and efficient computing experience. Everything can be customized: the desktop, the Start Menu, and the Sidebar.

The Start Menu does away with expanding all over the screen and forcing you to drag your mouse cursor with annoying precision to get to the program you want to launch. It contains quick links to a powerful array of folders that enable you to organize your computer and your files quickly and with ease. The desktop and its window elements are subject to molding their appearance to your very whims. Meanwhile, the Sidebar keeps handy tools at the ready any time you need them.

Part III

Support, Stability, and Security

Before we move on to the fun and exciting stuff like gaming and multimedia, we have to deal with some important issues. Windows Vista was designed to be as secure and stable as possible, but you can take steps to enhance its foundation. Even so, sometimes something will fail or you'll find yourself faced with a dilemma; thankfully, Windows Vista is ready with offline and online help.

The chapters in Part III arm you with the knowledge you need to understand the security and stability features of the operating system, and how to make sure nobody has access to your files except the users you deem worthy. You'll also learn how to get assistance when you need it the most.

IN THIS PART

Chapter 9

Getting Help

IN THIS CHAPTER

Windows Vista has so many new and improved elements that you can easily get lost within its vast interface. However, once you get used to Vista, performing common tasks is a snap — more convenient, even, than in Windows XP.

Until you reach a comfortable level of familiarity with the operating system, however, or if you're brand new to Windows, you might get stuck. Don't feel badly even if the simplest tasks seem difficult; Windows Vista is a wide-reaching operating system stuffed with extras and features, and Windows Vista Ultimate is even more robust than the other Vista editions.

Windows operating systems in the past haven't exactly been renowned for their ability to deliver assistance when requested. To put it another way, the term *Windows Help* is widely considered an oxymoron. This perception changed somewhat with Windows XP, which included a much more robust help system than was found in earlier versions of Windows based on the Windows 95 kernel; Windows XP's help files often served up relevant information when confronted with a user's search. Windows Vista's help system is even better, complete with a comprehensive bank of information that really does assist users with their tasks.

As was the case with Windows XP, Vista's help system can also connect to the Internet, specifically Microsoft's own servers, to offer updated articles that may contain information newer than that within the offline, built-in help database. Switching between offline and online help is easy, and if the former doesn't have the solution you're looking for, the latter just might.

At last, you can feel confident that the help system has got your back.

The Help and Support Window

One of the cooler new elements of Windows Vista is the Sidebar. Its Gadgets let you do all kinds of stuff quickly and conveniently. The Sidebar is a new feature in Vista, however, and you might not know yet what to do with it.

For the sake of an example of the Windows Help and Support module of Windows Vista, let's say you want desperately to add or remove Gadgets from the Sidebar, but you have no idea how to go about it. (I know, some of you are rolling your eyes saying, "Jeez, it's pretty intuitive. Figure it out!" That doesn't always work for every user. Back in my days as the head of a support shop, I went on service calls to rescue people who had done something as simple as delete a folder from the Windows 95 Start Menu, but who believed they had rid their computers of the applications that the entries had pointed to!)

Before you tear into the Sidebar and do something you might not intend to do, such as turn it off or eliminate a gadget that you really like, fire up the help system. To do so, choose Start ➪ Help and Support.

NOTE The first time you invoke the Windows Help and Support system, a dialog box appears asking whether you want to include online help in your searches. I recommend clicking Yes, as you can easily toggle between online and offline help. Thus, even if you're on the road with your laptop computer and you become stranded in an archaic location that doesn't have wireless Internet access, you can tell Windows Help and Support to keep its searches limited to its local files (stuff stored on your hard drive).

After you call the Help and Support system into play, a window named, of all things, Windows Help and Support, appears. You have two ways to find the answer you're looking for: You can surf the help system or you can search it.

Surfing Windows Help and Support

Take a look at the Windows Help and Support window, shown in Figure 9.1. At the top are a bunch of navigation icons:

- On the left are the Back and Forward buttons, which work just like those in Internet Explorer or any browser.
- Near the center (well, maybe a little to the right) is the Home button, which brings you back to the Help and Support home page.
- Next is the Print button, which allows you to print the page currently displayed.
- Next is the Browse Help button, which invokes a contents page for the help database.
- Second to the last is the Ask button, which offers various types of online support, such as Remote Assistance or a search of the online Windows communities.

FIGURE 9.1

The Windows Help and Support window

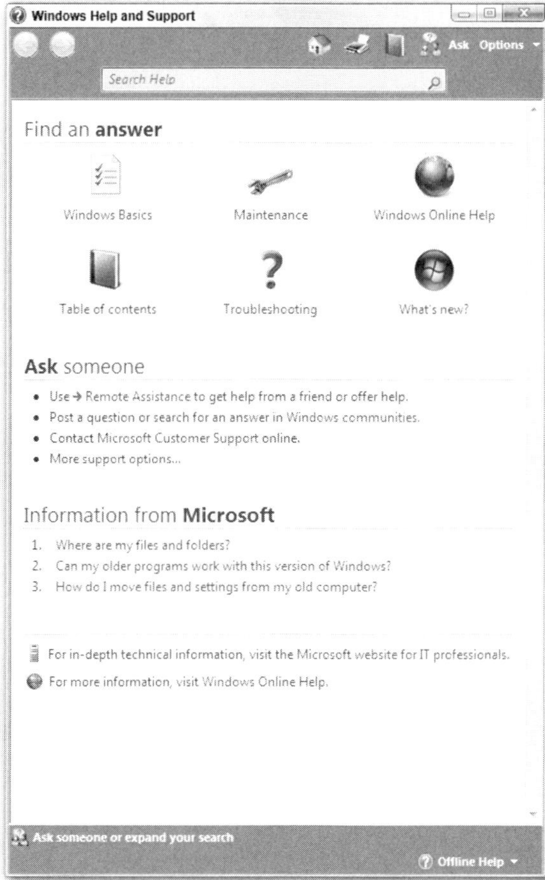

- Finally, the Options drop-down menu has entries for some of these very buttons, plus a settings option that invokes a settings dialog box that has two settings options within:
  - Include Windows Assistance Online when you search for help. Check this box to have your help searches include the online content from Microsoft's servers.
  - Join the Help experience improvement program. Check this box, to have Windows send your feedback anonymously back to Microsoft to ostentatiously help the company improve the Help and Support pages.

Beneath the buttons is a search text box. Below that is a series of icons that launch various topics within the Windows Vista help system. These icons are where you begin your surfing experience.

Because you're interested in learning about the Sidebar (remember?), the best place to start is Windows Basics. Click the icon once (it's a link, so you don't have to double-click it); the window morphs into the screen shown in Figure 9.2.

Give the headings a quick browse. The *Learn about your computer* section can teach you the very basics of computer usage, just in case that mouse next to the keyboard is a whole new experience for your hand.

Under the *Desktop fundamentals* section is the object of your query: *Windows Sidebar and gadgets (overview)*. Click it.

FIGURE 9.2

The Windows Basics section of the Help system

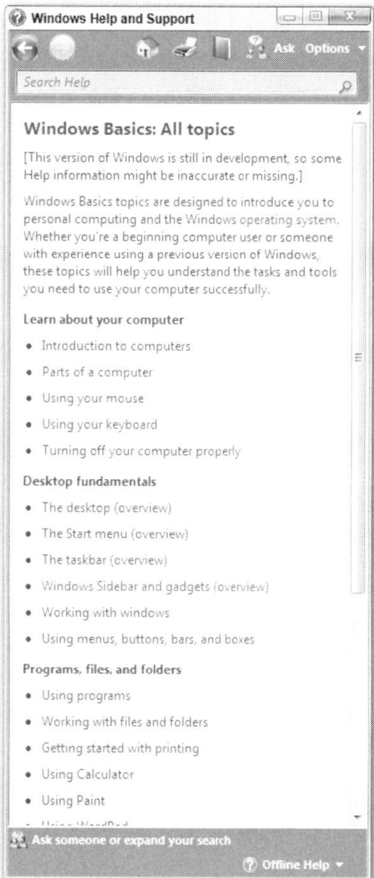

Again, the window magically resizes itself. It's a real shape shifter! New content appears, entitled *Windows sidebar and gadgets*. A nice introduction to the sidebar appears here, along with a picture of one (as if you can't just look on the right side of your desktop and see your Sidebar).

The upper-right corner of this window has a few links headed with the words, *In this article*. You can read any of them that you want simply by clicking them. For now, click the one that answers the question that drove you to the Help and Support database in the first place: *Adding and removing gadgets*.

The window turns to liquid yet again and emerges with new dimensions and contents as shown in Figure 9.3. There, in front of your waiting eyes, is the *Adding and removing gadgets* heading. Read up to learn all about how to place things onto your Sidebar and whisk them away.

FIGURE 9.3

Adding and removing gadgets

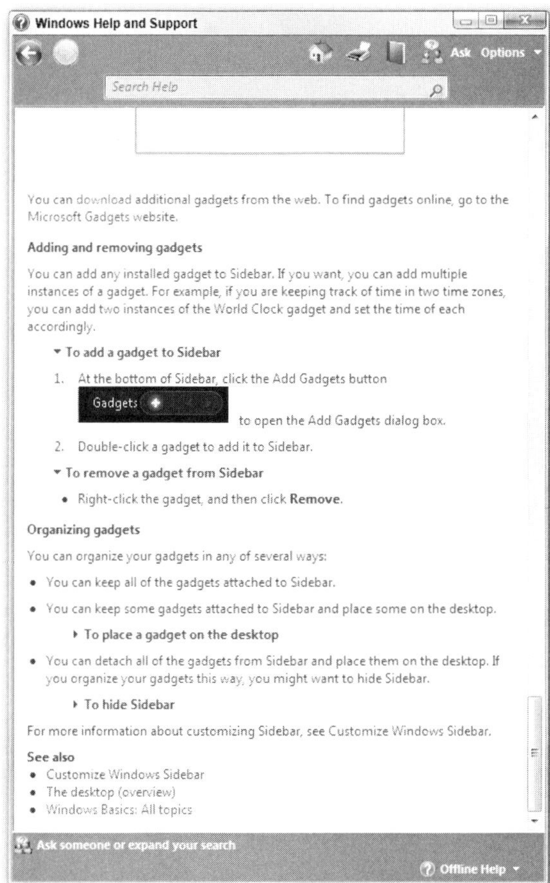

TIP Look at the instruction headings in the currently displayed help window (*To add a gadget to Sidebar*). If they have little arrows next to their left, you can hide the instructions or display them. Just click the tiny arrow to toggle between making them go away or come back.

That's how you surf through the Help and Support pages to find your way to information on a topic that's confounding you. The next section shows you how to search for the information instead.

Searching Windows Help and Support

Click the Home button to return to the Help and Support section's home page. Focus your eyes on the search text entry field. Then, sit back and think for a moment. Try to come up with the best search string you can on the subject of adding and removing gadgets to the Sidebar; for example, try using **add remove gadgets sidebar**. Click the text box, type it in, and press Enter.

With the online help system enabled, I scored 30 results with this query, as shown in Figure 9.4. Some of them, oddly, have little to do with the topic I was searching. For example, result number 16, *Installing new hardware: recommended links*, could lead to ruin if I didn't know what I was doing.

TIP Checking out the other entries in a help search after you've solved your problem is fun. You never know what you might learn if you check out the tangential information. Just like the Internet itself, the Windows Help and Support system is loaded with information, and unlike the Internet, the vast majority of it is true!

Of course, the more relevant results are closer to the top. I recommend you click result number four, *Windows Sidebar and gadgets (overview)*. If you do, you'll invoke the same window we eventually landed in while we were surfing the help system. Follow the *Adding and removing gadgets* link to see the window shown earlier in Figure 9.3. The problem, as they say, is solved.

Getting online and offline help

During my search for help with the Sidebar (see the preceding section), I used the Help system with the online help option enabled. My results would have varied if my computer hadn't been connected to the Internet, or if I had had the online help system turned off.

NOTE The online component has a proper name: Windows Assistance Online, as in WAO, or as in WAOwie-zowie! It also has its own Web site: `http://windowshelp.microsoft.com`.

Although you can use the Options menu's Settings dialog box to change the online/offline status of your Help queries, you can also use the drop-down menu on the very bottom of the help window. It shows the current status of the help system, and with a couple of clicks you can quickly toggle between online and offline help.

FIGURE 9.4

Results of my query in Windows Help and Support

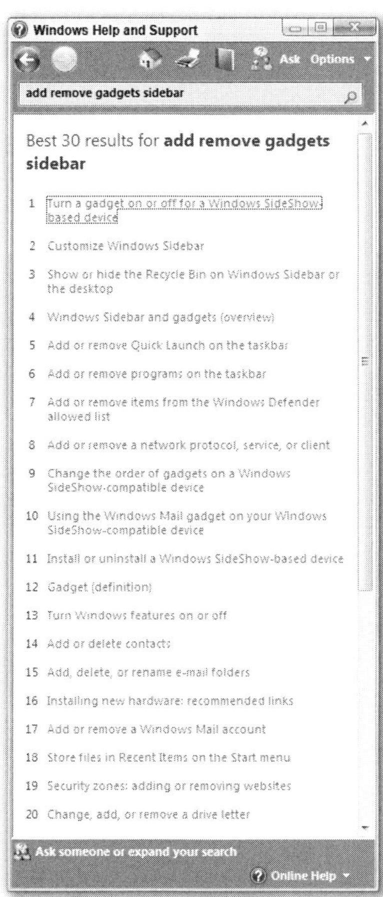

NOTE Try running a search of the same parameters first offline, and then online. Notice the differences in the search results. Sometimes, they'll be significantly different, and other times they'll be quite similar.

When you search with the online component enabled, the search includes both online and offline content. That means you search both your computer's local help files and Windows Assistance Online.

Microsoft's Centralized Support Tools

Sometimes, you need a little more help than the help system can provide. Say, for example, a particular program hurls a cryptic error code in your general direction and expects you to interpret its malfunction from information that wouldn't even make sense to someone who was raised to speak binary. What do you do then?

You can always go to Windows Help and Support. Search for the error message and see what comes up. Sometimes you'll get lucky; other times, you'll get results that appear to have been beamed in by space aliens from Mars, or no results at all.

That's when you launch Internet Explorer 7 and search the Microsoft Knowledge Base (`http://support.microsoft.com`), shown in Figure 9.5. Besides the Vista-only Windows Assistance Online, Microsoft offers to confused and annoyed Windows users a massive database of documents designed to report, comment on, and help solve problems relating to Windows.

FIGURE 9.5

The Microsoft Knowledge Base

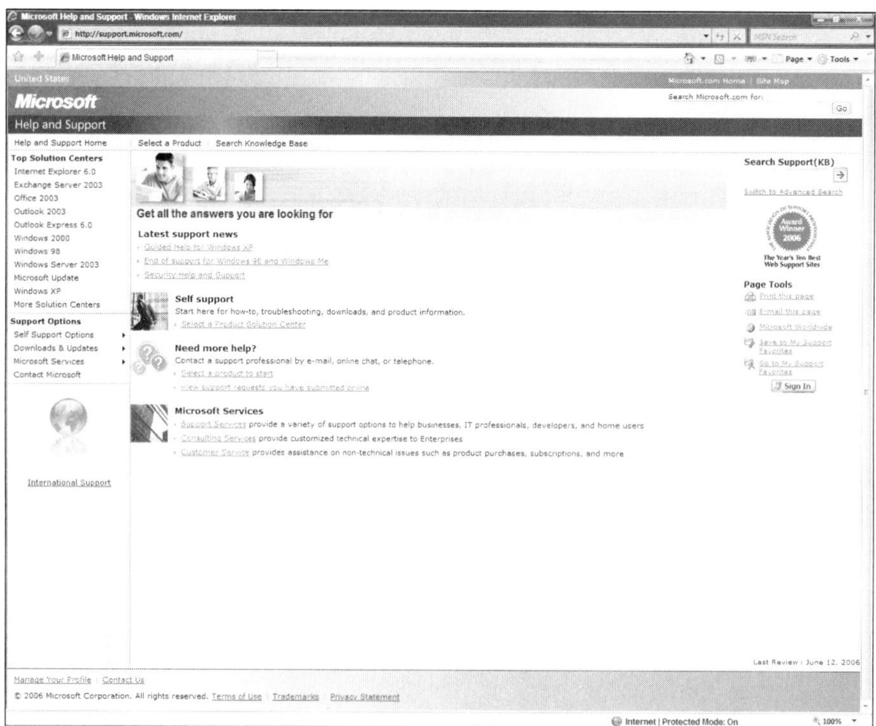

By *relating to Windows*, I mean that the Knowledge Base (KB for short) has data not only on Windows itself, but also on hundreds of programs and hardware parts and device drivers and so on. Although it's not intended to replace the support departments of third-party companies, the Microsoft KB should be your first stop whenever you encounter a technical problem within Windows. If your problem has been spotted in the wild, the KB will probably have a write-up all about it and, hopefully, a solution (or at least a workaround).

Although you can surf the KB in the same way you can surf the Help and Support system, the KB wasn't set up to be browsed. It is, however, very search-friendly, so you should start by thinking about the best search string to describe your problem to a computer.

TIP For the most precise results, use the advanced search (see Figure 9.6). Click the link just below the Search Support entry field on the right side of the Web site's window. You don't have to fill in every field in the advanced search page — only the ones that are pertinent to your search.

FIGURE 9.6

The KB's Advanced Search page

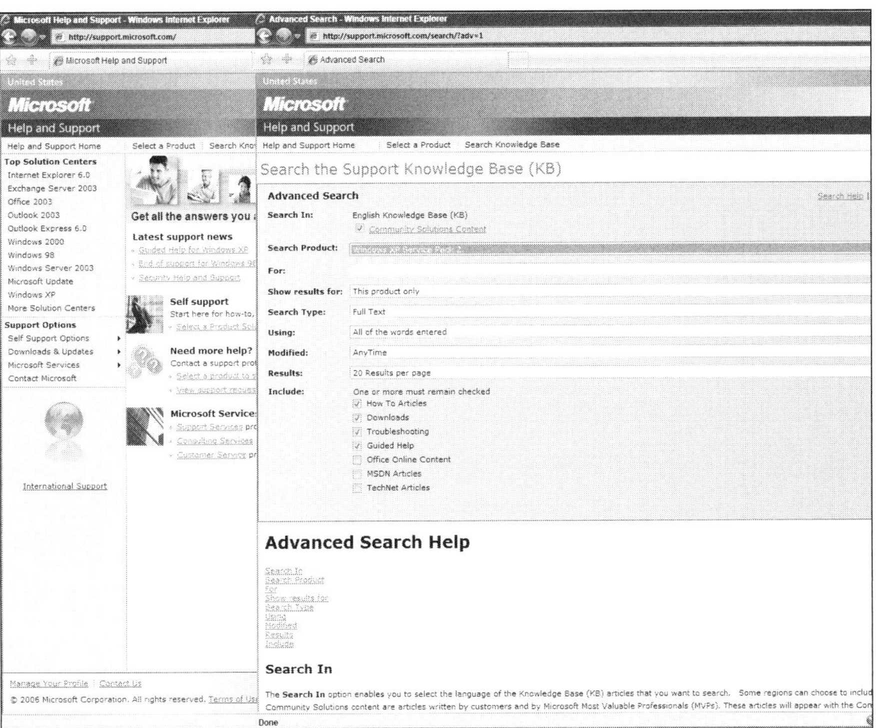

Let's do a search. Suppose you get an error trying to play Halo that says, "A problem occurred initializing Direct3D." Before you pop the disk out of the optical drive and hurl it across the room like a Frisbee, search the Microsoft KB:

1. **Open Internet Explorer 7.**
2. **Click the address bar.**
3. **Type** http://support.microsoft.com.
4. **Click the advanced search link beneath the search box on the site.**
5. **In the Search Product drop-down list, select [Windows XP Service Pack 2].**
6. **In the For text entry field, type** halo **followed by the error message verbatim.** That's the best way to search for a specific error message.
7. **Press Enter or click Search.** Check it out! Your problem is at the top of the results list (see Figure 9.7).
8. **Click it, and follow the instructions to solve your problem.**

FIGURE 9.7

The Windows Help and Support window

The KB is a powerful tool for all kinds of Windows errors and problems. It also covers most other Microsoft products, so if you find yourself fighting with an Office conundrum or a Money dilemma, check out the KB and see whether it has the solution you're looking for.

Remote Assistance

Sometimes you just need help. Not the kind of help you get from a cold computer, but real help from a real human being. You can invite someone you trust to give you assistance remotely, via the Internet, without having to drive over and get his germs all over your keyboard.

First, you have to generate an invitation to allow the person to log in to your computer. Before you do that, you have to enable Remote Assistance.

To enable Remote Assistance, follow these steps:

1. **Choose Start ⇨ Control Panel to open the Control Panel.**
2. **Click System and Maintenance.**
3. **Under System, click Allow remote access.** You'll need administrator privileges to do this. The System Properties window appears.
4. **Click Remote.**
5. **Fill in the check box next to "Remote assistance invitations can be sent."**
6. **Click OK.**
7. **Close Control Panel.**

Next, you have to invite someone to help you and generate a password.

Don't let just anybody into your computer. Only invite assistance from someone you trust not to steal your files or hose your system with a virus of some sort.

To invite remote assistance from someone, follow these steps:

1. **Open Help and Support.**
2. **Under the heading Ask someone, click Remote Assistance.** The Windows Remote Assistance window appears.
3. **Click Invite someone you trust to help you.**
4. **Choose a delivery option.** You can generate an e-mail to send to that person right now, or save the invitation as a file that you can attach to an e-mail or deliver another way.
5. **When prompted, select a password for your Remote Assistance session.** Your computer now waits for the incoming assistance.

Meanwhile, to offer remote assistance, the receiver of your S.O.S. must:

1. **Receive your invitation on a computer running an edition of Windows Vista.**
2. **Open Remote Assistance and browse for the invitation file.**
3. **Enter the password provided by the person who needs assistance.** The helper will now have full access to the other user's computer. A chat window on each desktop, shown in Figure 9.8, allows both users to chat and control the session.

FIGURE 9.8

The Remote Assistance control dialog box

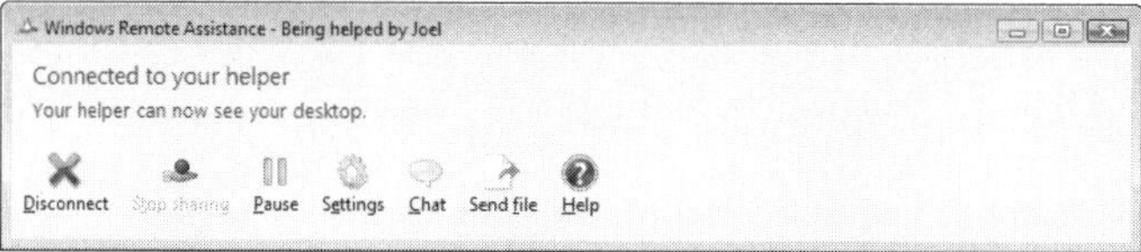

4. **When the problem is solved, the users can disconnect and close the incident.**

Summary

At last, Microsoft has made getting help with Windows easy, fast, and effective. In doing so, it's gone from the abysmal help file in Windows 3.1, through mediocre help databases in Windows 9x, on past the marginally acceptable help system in Windows XP, to a truly outstanding system that, for the first time in Windows history, will actually help people!

When you get stuck, you can search online and offline help, scope out the Internet (including the Microsoft Knowledge Base), and, if all else fails, invite someone to leap headlong into your computer from across the Net to dig you out of your situation.

Someday, when you're a Vista expert, you'll be able to help some other poor schlep whose games keep crashing or whose movies won't run at more than two frames per second. Just have that person e-mail you an invitation, and you'll know what to do.

Chapter 10

Keeping Windows Vista Stable

IN THIS CHAPTER

- Maintaining stability
- Understanding built-in stability enhancements
- Automating Windows updates
- Using the Reliability Monitor
- Backing up your stuff

Let's face it: Microsoft has taken some serious flack in the past for the stability (or its alleged lack thereof) of its operating systems. With each release since Windows 95, however — and barring Windows Me — the Windows family has actually gotten more reliable. Windows XP has been the most stable Microsoft operating system to date; that is, until Windows Vista.

Building an operating system for the PC environment isn't easy. The computer industry is clogged with thousands of pieces of current hardware at any given time, and an operating system has to somehow work on anything that a user might throw into her computer at any given time.

Windows Vista has a number of features built in to keep it from failing, and to prevent the operating system from going completely belly-up when something does crash. When an application goes down in flames, Vista can often close it gracefully without locking up or hanging, and often without even the need to reboot the operating system. Even when a driver doesn't cooperate or operate the way it should, Vista often manages to find a way to maintain reliability and prevent data loss.

Of course, one of the key elements to preventing data loss is backing up your data. Windows operating systems haven't provided much for backing up besides a cursory backup program, which in many versions wasn't even installed by default, until Vista. Vista itself comes with a powerful backup program that can save data to all sorts of media.

Windows also comes with a number of diagnostics and utilities to keep it running smoothly and to repair problems when something does go wrong. As with earlier operating systems, the market will soon be flooded with third-party applications that will claim to make Vista even more stable and to prevent potential problems.

Windows Vista will not be foolproof. Microsoft will release updates and, most likely, service packs that enhance not only stability but security and functionality. Updating Vista on a regular basis is more than necessary, it's mandatory.

This chapter can help you keep Vista up to date, teach you when to run diagnostics and repair programs, and show you how to back up your data. It also provides some information about the built-in stability enhancements that Vista boasts.

Challenges of Maintaining Stability

Nobody likes it when a program crashes.

It's even worse when the operating system itself hangs or reboots without warning. The absolute nastiest of all PC problems is data loss: when, for some reason, something on a drive becomes unreadable or disappears altogether.

When everything is working and happy, that doesn't happen. However, a PC is a conglomeration of scores of logic chips and data conduits, and they all have to cooperate for the computer to work properly — and every single one is subject to failure.

When a part fails, something bad happens. The symptoms cover a wide range: mild problems like video glitches or broken network connections; mysterious dialog boxes and program crashes; or complete failure and the loss of data.

Software, too, can be problematic. Device drivers — the code that tells Windows how to talk to the hardware in its system — must be written with precision; a bad driver can cause major problems. A poorly written program can hang, crash, or otherwise misbehave. An operating system bug can make life difficult in a myriad of ways.

Why do bad things happen to good computers?

As stated earlier, a PC is made up of many parts. The chips on those parts generally come from one company, and the actual part itself (for example, the graphics card, the hard drive, and the motherboard) come from different manufacturers. If you take all the chip makers and all the manufacturers and all the final products available and try to figure out how many permutations of hardware can make up a PC, you'll probably get a headache. The combinations are all but limitless.

People who make hardware, operating systems, and games/programs have to try their very best to make sure that their product works with all the other products that it might encounter in a PC. Although most software developers and hardware manufacturers do scads of testing before they release the product, they can't possibly test on every permutation of hardware in the world. It's not until a product hits the market that it's truly and thoroughly tested.

Microsoft has possibly the biggest burden of everyone involved in creating PC products. Windows operating systems provide the user the ability to run programs, which use hardware. If Windows isn't ready for all types of games and programs, and compatible with all types of hardware, unexpected results are inevitable.

Throughout the lifetimes of all the Windows products, Microsoft has released update after update — sometimes in major update conglomerations called *service packs*. They fix all sorts of problems, addressing compatibility, stability, and security. Expect the same in the case of Windows Vista. Although Microsoft did all it could to make sure Vista was stable and reliable before release, it is a new and ambitious product, and it will require updates to its code to reach its full potential.

What can you do to maintain stability?

Windows has a wealth of built-in features to keep it running at its best, and you can take a number of steps both to ensure it stays reliable and to troubleshoot it when problems to crop up.

Windows has a few utilities that you can use as stability tools, and it also has powerful diagnostics that can help you pin down the source of a problem if or when one comes along. It also has some recovery features that help you bring back stability after a change to the system wreaks havoc, and to recover data after a catastrophic failure.

Some of the stability tools are automatic — you don't even have to caress the mouse for them to help you — and some require a bit of basic work.

TIP Here's some advice to live by. If you can spend a few minutes a day to protect your data, you'll save yourself from a world of grief if something does go wrong. Heed the proactive advice in this chapter and you'll be much better off should your system fail at some point.

Microsoft *wants* you to love Windows Vista. Part of enjoying an operating system is knowing that it's reliable: When you turn on the computer, it should boot up; when you look for your data, it should be there; when you want to play a game, it should run smoothly; and so on. An operating system is, at its core, a tool that exists to enable you to use your computer. As with physical tools like screwdrivers and saws, if you take the time to maintain your operating system it'll work when you need it to.

Windows Vista's Built-in Stability Enhancements

Windows Vista is designed for stability and security. Microsoft's developers delved right down to the kernel — the deepest and most vital code of the operating system — to add stability enhancements that will elevate Windows Vista above the already very stable Windows XP.

To put it another way: Windows Vista does *not* want to crash.

All kinds of things can cause crashes, from operating system bugs to bad drivers. Windows Vista is ready to take on these faults and more, and keep on working the way it's supposed to.

Many of its stability enhancements are in the background. You're not aware of them as they quietly do their work to keep the operating system as reliable as possible. I discuss these enhancements in the following sections.

For more on security, see Chapter 10.

SuperFetch

Part of every Windows operating system going back more than a decade is *virtual memory* (Figure 10.1). Virtual memory is a way of extending the system's main memory by assigning applications hard drive space in a file known as the *paging file*. Windows Vista does this even if enough room exists in your computer's main memory for everything that's currently running.

NOTE Why use virtual memory when enough RAM is available? Virtual memory, after all, is slower than main memory; data stored in virtual memory take much longer to access because the computer needs to read them from the relatively slow hard drive rather than the far more efficient memory modules.

Windows operating systems, Vista included, uses virtual memory anyway, primarily because they don't know what you're going to do next. You might load an extremely memory-intensive application even as you're running your e-mail program, your Web browser, a game of Chess Titans, three IM programs, an antivirus program, and so on. If all that stuff clogged up main memory, Windows would go into a swapping frenzy when you launched the next program.

By using virtual memory efficiently, and employing the new SuperFetch feature, Windows Vista can keep your open apps running smoothly while being ready for anything else you toss at it.

FIGURE 10.1

Like Windows XP, Windows Vista uses Virtual Memory.

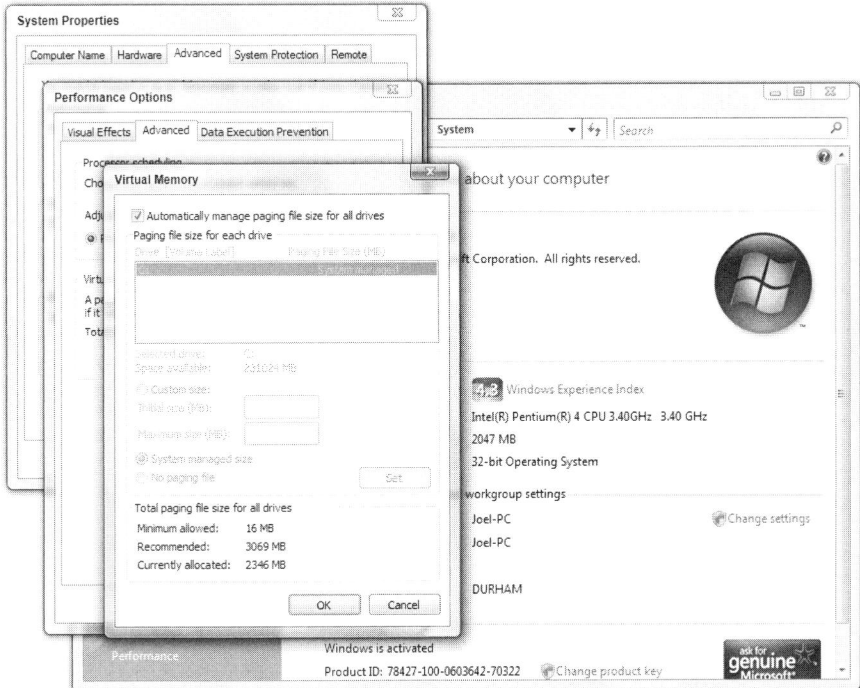

Windows XP used a feature called *Prefetch*, upon which the new SuperFetch feature is based. In Prefetch, a cache manager keeps track of everything that Windows moves from the hard disk into memory, everything that Windows moves between memory and the paging file, and so on, and creates maps of the operations as .PF files in the C:\Windows\Prefetch folder. When you do something that may require the use of data stored in virtual memory, Windows XP checks the \Prefetch folder for a pertinent map, and if it finds one uses it to quickly locate and restore the data.

Vista's SuperFetch takes this idea a step further. SuperFetch creates not only notations of the locations of data stored in virtual memory, but it also keeps track of which applications you use most and how you use them. It basically creates a profile of how you use your computer, and it uses this profile to try to guess what you'll do *next*, based on what you're doing *now*, and grab the data you may need before you even need it.

The end result is a far more responsive system that makes better and more efficient use of virtual memory than in any previous system. This efficiency creates a sense of stability: Your system is more responsive, so you spend less time waiting for programs to respond. You're less likely to suspect a program has begun to hang when in fact it's only waiting for the right data from the slow hard drive.

WDDM

WDDM stands for Windows Display Driver Model. It's the new engine that Windows Vista uses to display virtually everything you see. It's built to be stable and fast, and to make much better use of your computer's resources than any previous version of Windows ever did.

In older versions of Windows, a powerful graphics card and its local memory often went unused except when the user played a game. WDDM uses the graphics processing unit (GPU), which is the main chip on your computer's graphics device, and its memory as part of its display architecture. That's why the new operating system has such stringent graphics card requirements. Gamers who put a lot of money and faith into their computers' graphics hardware should love the fact that not only their games but Windows itself is making the most of it.

Windows achieves this efficient resource usage with two major components: a GPU memory manager and a GPU scheduler. The memory manager determines where in video memory Windows data are to be stored; the scheduler decides in what order data need to be processed to make the most efficient use of the computer's hardware and to offer the user the smoothest experience.

The WDDM also results in a vast improvement in computer stability. Display drivers — the drivers that arbitrate between Windows and the graphics hardware — are vast, unwieldy, and extremely important components of any computer system. Traditional display drivers operate at the kernel level, and one minor bug or glitch can cause the entire computer to hang, or even to cough up the dreaded blue screen of death.

WDDM drivers have two levels: a smaller, more streamlined, and more stable kernel mode driver, and the larger user mode driver, which takes care of most of the major calculations. Because most of the driver activity takes place *outside* the kernel, glitches are far less prone to result in catastrophic failures. In fact, the vast majority of driver problems should affect a single application or game, and not the entire computer.

WDDM also allows for all kinds of cool effects, like the Aero glass effects, Flip 3D (Figure 10.2), live icons and taskbar buttons, and more. It adds to the stability, usability, and appeal of the graphical user interface (GUI).

FIGURE 10.2

Flip 3D is possible because of the WDDM.

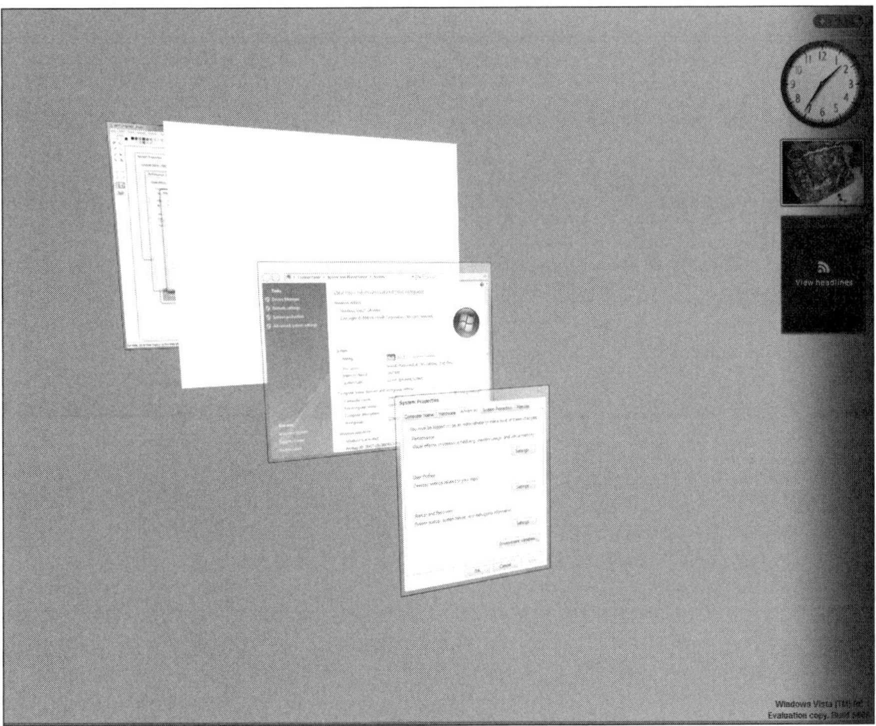

Windows Resource Protection

In the past, programs that felt the desire to alter critical operating system files and registry keys upon installation didn't have much trouble doing so. With Windows Vista's Windows Resource Protection (WRP), only a trusted installer is able to make such changes.

This means that programs that try to install themselves without your knowledge can't get away with corrupting your computer's operating system. WRP is actually a more robust and protective version of WFP (Windows File Protection), which was available for previous versions of Windows. WRP protects critical folders, files, and registry keys from being altered or overwritten entirely, which in turn keeps Windows Vista running smoothly at its core.

And more...

Vista has more stability features, but talking about them without getting into really dull tech jargon that only a software engineer would understand or appreciate is difficult. One other interesting tidbit, however, is both automated and available to the user to inspect. It's the Reliability and Performance Monitor, and I cover it later in this chapter.

Examples of other stability enhancements include:

- **A compartmentalized registry:** In older versions of Windows, the entire system registry, which contains deep and technical information about the computer's hardware and software, was fully open to any running process. Anything could modify any part of the registry, which made it vulnerable to abuse. Because the registry is such a core part of the operating system, a corrupt registry could bring the OS to its proverbial knees. The Windows Vista registry only allows programs to alter that which they need in order to function; other parts of the registry are off limits.
- **Automated diagnostics:** Windows Vista keeps tabs on the health of the system, ready to diagnose problems with hardware including the hard drive and memory. If it detects a problem, it can, in some cases, guide the user through a solution.
- **Automatic Recovery:** Windows Vista can recover from a number of failures all by itself—something no prior Windows operating system could do. If a service fails, Vista might try to restart it. A tool called the Startup Repair Tool detects problems that occur on boot and tries to fix them, right down to analyzing startup logs for answers. Windows does it so you don't have to.

Suffice it to say, much happens behind the scenes to keep Windows Vista working with stability and precision. It's an extremely large and multifaceted operating system, and it's built to be tough against crashes, hardware failures, driver glitches, and more.

Windows Vista Updates — A Must!

A major part of keeping Windows stable is to keep it up to date. Microsoft has always released stability fixes (as well as other software repairs) for all of its Windows operating systems, and you can expect it to update Windows Vista on a fairly regular basis.

Although Microsoft's goal was to make Windows Vista as stable as possible right from the start, the operating system will encounter more hardware combinations and third-party programs "in the wild" than the quality assurance people at Microsoft could have possibly tested it with in-house. Problems are bound to float to the surface, and Microsoft will stomp out the bugs as quickly as it can.

You *have* to keep Windows Vista up to date. The easiest way to do so is to enable Automatic Updates. This feature regularly checks Microsoft's servers for updates to the operating system, and when it finds them it can automatically download and install them.

Alternatively, you can manually check for Windows updates, provided you do so on a regular basis. If you don't, you could miss an important security or stability update that could make a difference in the performance, safety, and usability of your computer.

When in doubt, use Automatic Updates. The process doesn't take much memory at all, and you can set it to update the computer at whatever time of day you want.

Enabling Automatic Updates

Windows Update is accessible through Control Panel. Windows Update is essentially a file server at Microsoft that stores and serves up the latest updates for Vista. When you enable Automatic Updates, Vista periodically uses its Windows Update module to check the Windows Update site and automatically download the latest updates. Choose Start ➪ Control Panel. Then click System and Maintenance to invoke the System and Maintenance window shown in Figure 10.3.

FIGURE 10.3

The Control Panel's System and Maintenance window

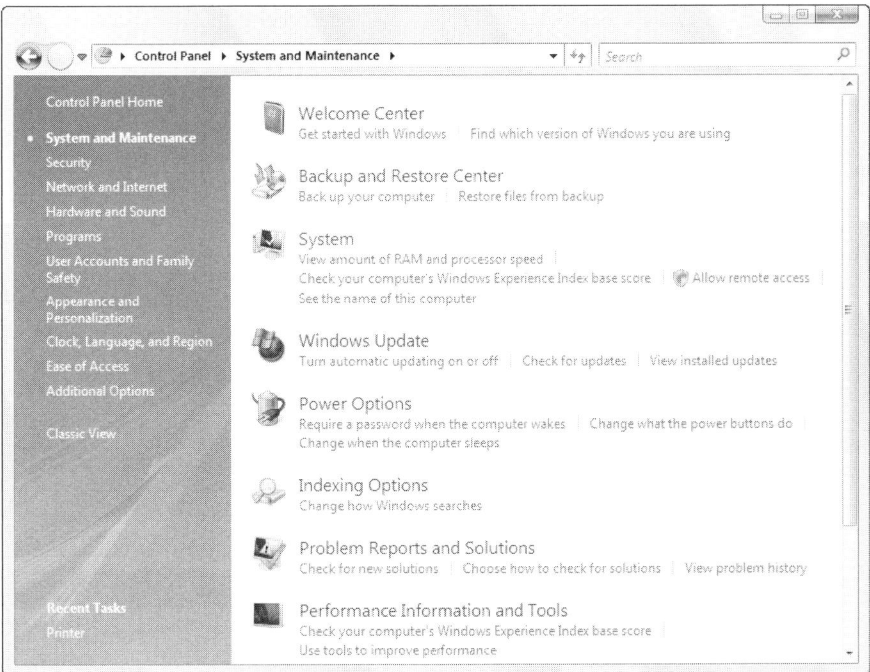

Windows Update is the fourth item down in the list of System and Maintenance links. Click it to start Windows Update, as shown in Figure 10.4.

NOTE Besides Windows Update, this window also contains Windows Ultimate Extras. You can use this window to check for Ultimate Extras, which are free programs from Microsoft available only to Windows Vista Ultimate Edition owners.

The screen in Figure 10.4 shows Windows being up to date. That's because I have Automatic Updates enabled, and my computer, which stays on all the time, checks for updates every morning at 3 a.m., which is the default recommended setting.

Part of the beauty of Automatic Updates is that you can set them to occur whenever you want them to. If you leave your computer on all the time like I do, updates can take place in the middle of the night when nobody is likely to be using the computer. You can also set them to take place at lunch time, early in the morning, or whenever else you want. If the computer is off when the update is scheduled, the program will check for updates the next time you turn on the computer.

FIGURE 10.4

The Windows Update screen

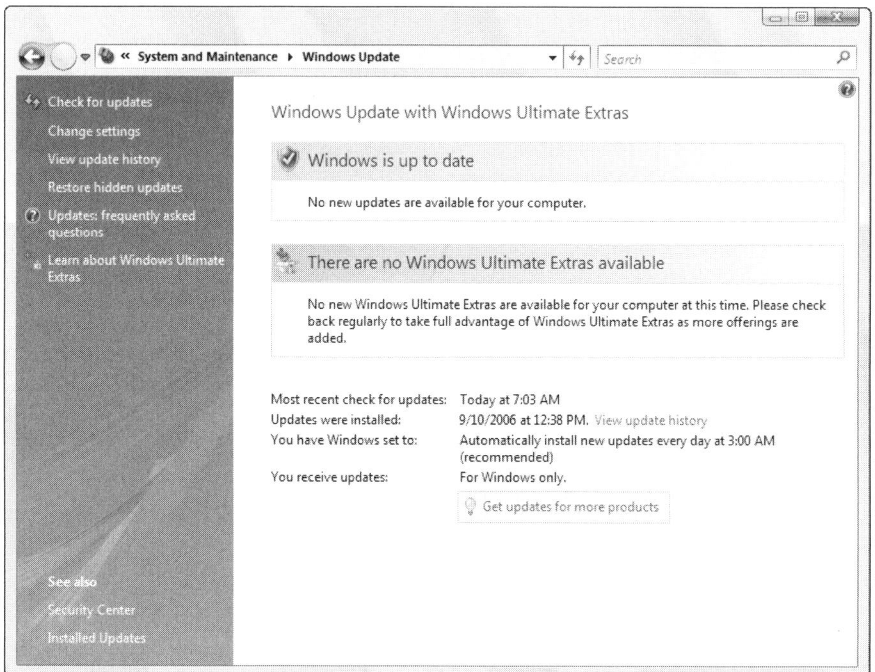

To ensure that Automatic Updates is enabled, and to schedule update sessions, click the Change Settings link on the left. The Change settings screen appears, as shown in Figure 10.5.

NOTE Upon installation (covered in Chapter 2), Windows will ask you about several preferences, and one of them includes security and updating. If you use the recommended settings, Windows will turn on Automatic Updates at that point. You should still check this area to ensure that Automatic Updates is, indeed, turned on, and to set your preferences.

This window contains several radio button options:

- **Install updates automatically (recommended):** Windows will check for updates as often as you specify. If it finds updates available, it will download and install them all by itself.
- **Download updates but let me choose whether to install them:** Windows will check for updates regularly and download them, and then notify you when an update has been downloaded. It's up to you to tell Windows to install it.

FIGURE 10.5

The Windows Update Change settings screen

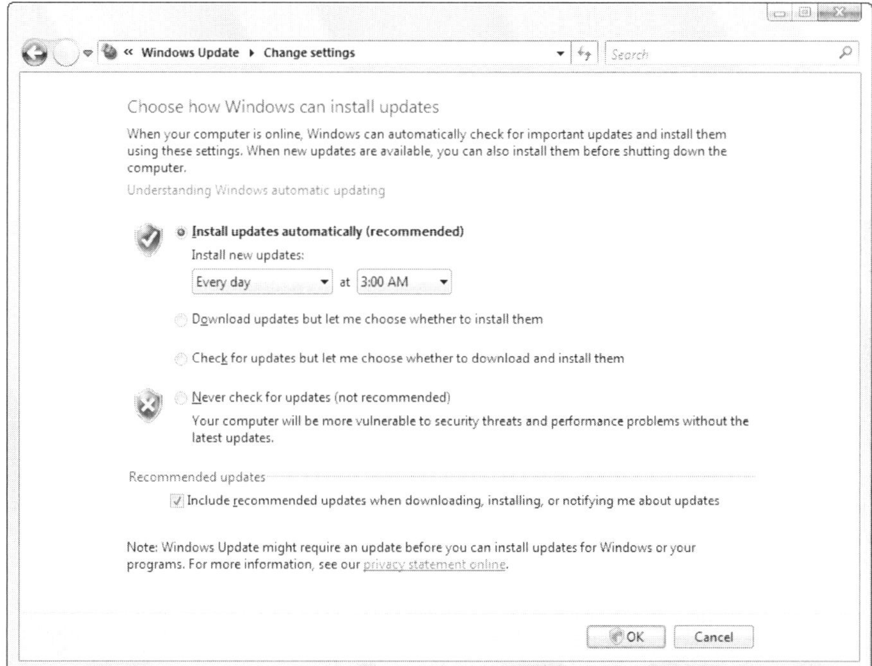

- **Check for updates but let me choose whether to download and install them:** Windows will check for updates and notify you if it finds any. You can then decide whether to download them or not, and whether to install them after downloading.
- **Never check for updates (not recommended):** Windows will not check for updates. You have to check for them manually.

A check box option lies beneath the radio button options. Select it to include not only critical but also recommended updates. Deselect it to include only critical updates.

Make your selections and click OK.

Checking manually for updates

You can check for updates whenever you please through Windows Update, whether Automatic Updates is turned on or not. Simply choose Start ➪ All Programs ➪ Windows Update to open the Windows Update window and click the link on the left labeled Check For Updates. A screen like the one shown in Figure 10.6 appears.

FIGURE 10.6

Windows is checking for updates.

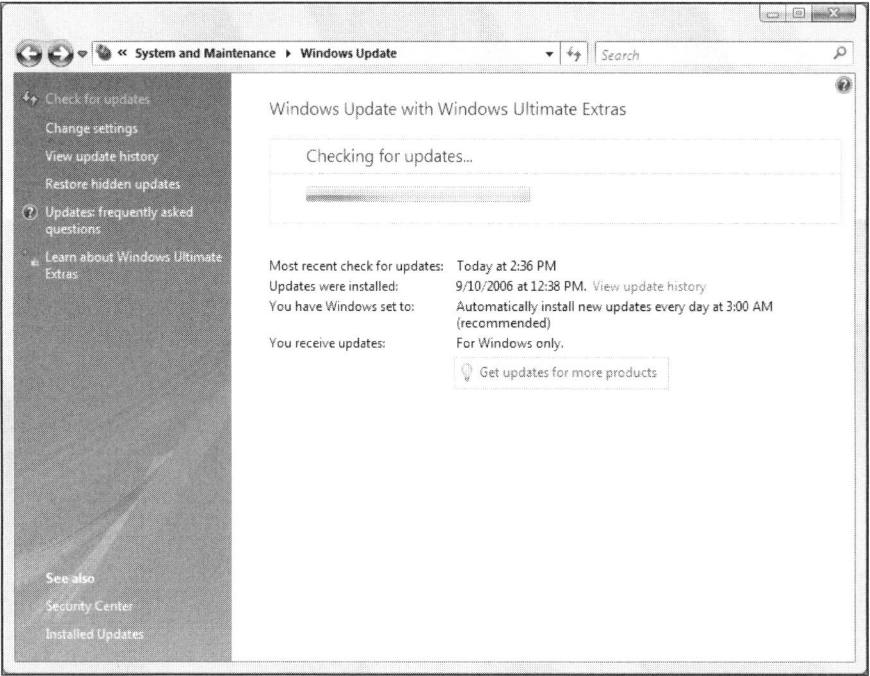

If Windows finds an update when you check manually, you'll have to indicate whether you want Windows to install it.

Upgrading to Microsoft Update

In the Windows Update window, on the left toward the bottom, it says that you're only getting updates for Windows. There you'll also find a link that says "Get updates for more products." If you click it, you can upgrade Windows Update to Microsoft Update, which looks for updates not only for Windows Vista but also for any Microsoft product installed on your computer that it recognizes.

Click the link and your browser will start up and navigate to a page like the one shown in Figure 10.7.

FIGURE 10.7

The Microsoft Update Web site

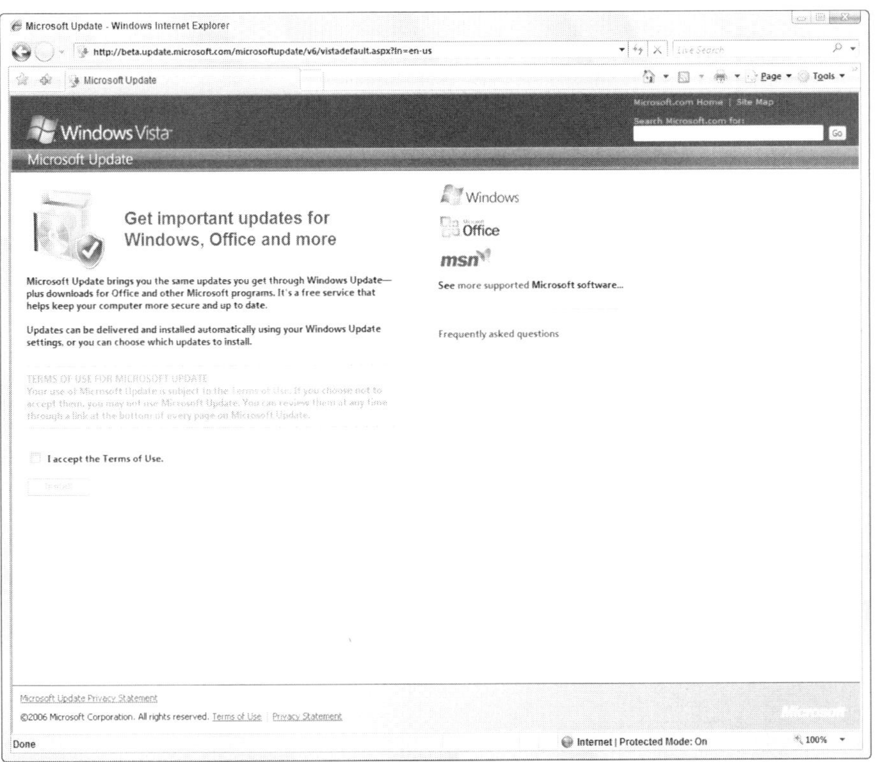

First, you need to click the check box that says you agree to the terms and conditions, which you should (but probably won't) read. Then, click Install.

The next screen that appears, shown in Figure 10.8, indicates that Microsoft Update was installed correctly. That's all there is to it — almost. This screen tells you to use your Start Menu to check for updates, as opposed to the Control Panel, which means you can launch Microsoft Update as you would any other program.

FIGURE 10.8

Microsoft Update has been installed.

The Reliability Monitor

If you suspect your computer is having a reliability problem, Windows Vista provides a powerful tool to help diagnose it. It's called Reliability Monitor, and it's available through the Microsoft Management Console (MMC).

You can launch the Reliability Monitor in several ways. The quickest way to access it is to choose Start ➪ Computer ➪ Manage. The MMC then opens, as shown in Figure 10.9.

In the left pane, double-click on Reliability and Performance. Then, click the Reliability Monitor option. The window changes to something like the one shown in Figure 10.10.

FIGURE 10.9

The Microsoft Management Console

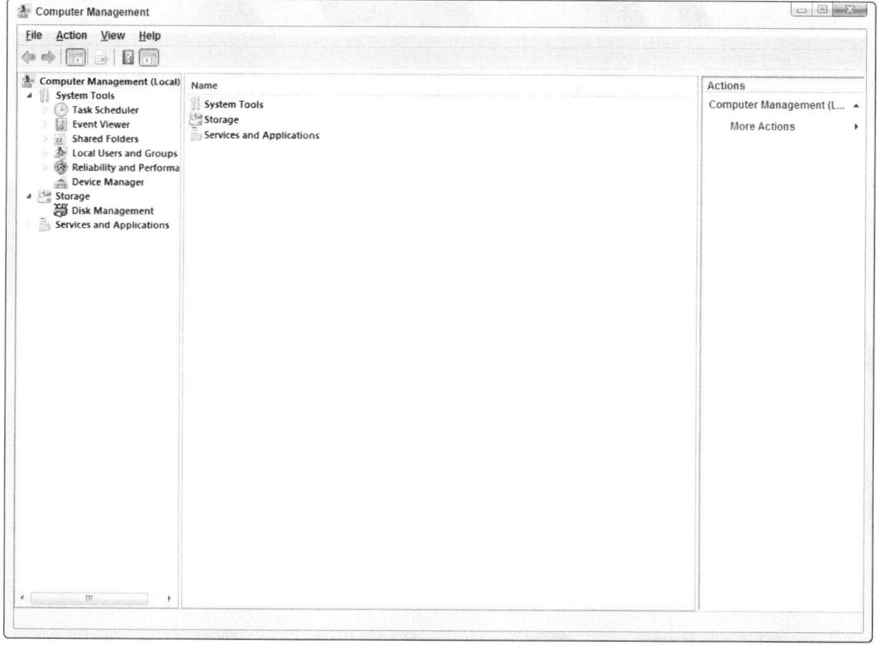

FIGURE 10.10

The Reliability Monitor

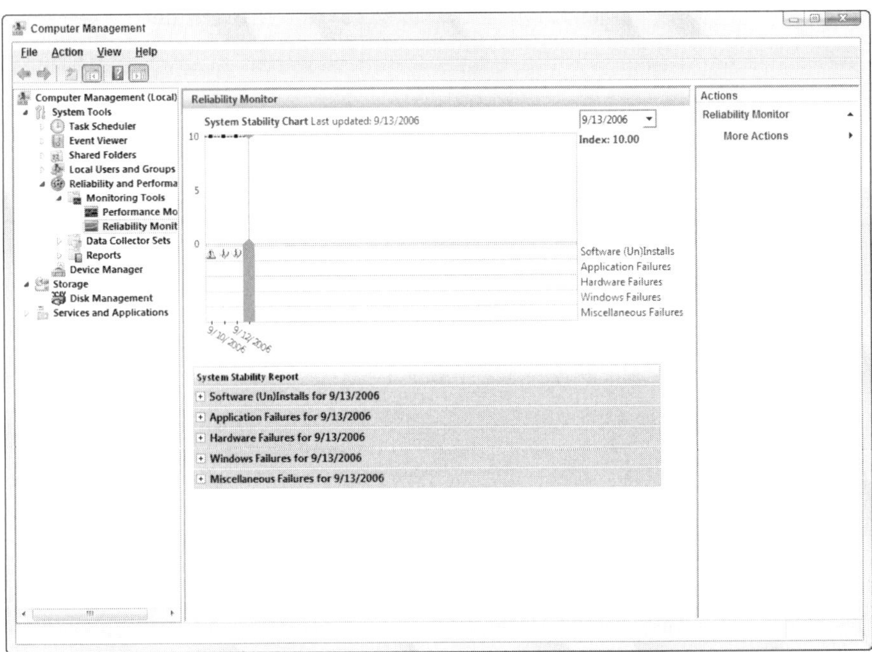

The Reliability Monitor keeps track of five types of events that may affect the reliability of your computer. They're at the bottom of the chart, represented by five horizontal lines. They are:

- Software installations
- Application failures
- Hardware failures
- Windows failures
- Miscellaneous failures

If one of these events occurs, it will be represented on the graph. Click the event's icon, or click the + sign next to the type of event it is. As an example, I've clicked next to Software installations to view the report shown in Figure 10.11.

If you encounter failures, you can use the data provided to help you or a tech support representative troubleshoot the problem.

FIGURE 10.11

The software installation report

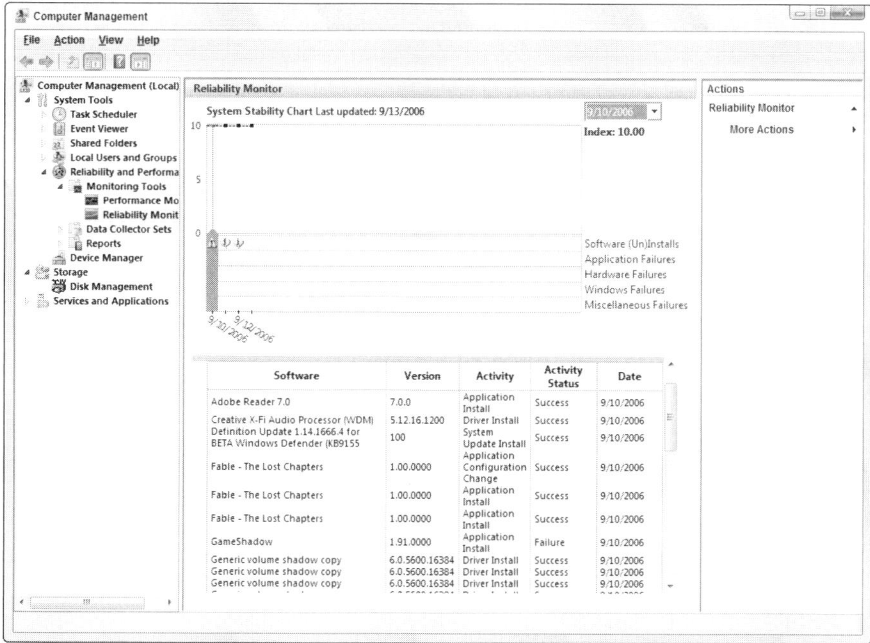

Backup and Restore Functions

Windows offers several ways to protect your data from all kinds of failure. System Restore, Shadow Copies, and Backup and Restore all keep your data as safe as it possibly can be. System Restore and Shadow Copies are automatic; they're turned on by default and do their thing in the background, ready to help you should you lose something important. Backup and Restore requires you to create a backup set and schedule backups.

Using System Restore

System Restore lets you revert the operating system to an earlier point in time, including its drivers, registry, and other critical files. It operates similarly to System Restore in Windows XP.

NOTE System Restore creates "restore points" on several occasions. Each time you install a program or driver or perform some other major task, Windows creates a system restore point; it also creates one automatically each day. You can also create them yourself. Restore points can take up as much space as 300MB, but Windows deletes the oldest restore points as you need the space.

To open System Restore, launch the Control Panel through the Start Menu (Start ➪ Control Panel). Click System and Maintenance, and then click Backup and Restore Center. The Backup and Restore window appears, shown in Figure 10.12.

On the left are two links for System Restore options. The top one is for actually reverting a system to a restore point, and the bottom one lets you create a restore point or shut off System Restore. The following sections show you how to do each of these tasks.

Creating a restore point

You might encounter a situation that prompts you to create a restore point manually. I do so when I swap out hardware. You might want to do it whenever you make a major change to the system.

To manually create a restore point, follow these steps:

1. **Open the Backup and Restore Center by choosing Start ➪ Control Panel ➪ System and Maintenance ➪ Backup and Restore Center.**

FIGURE 10.12

The Backup and Restore Center window

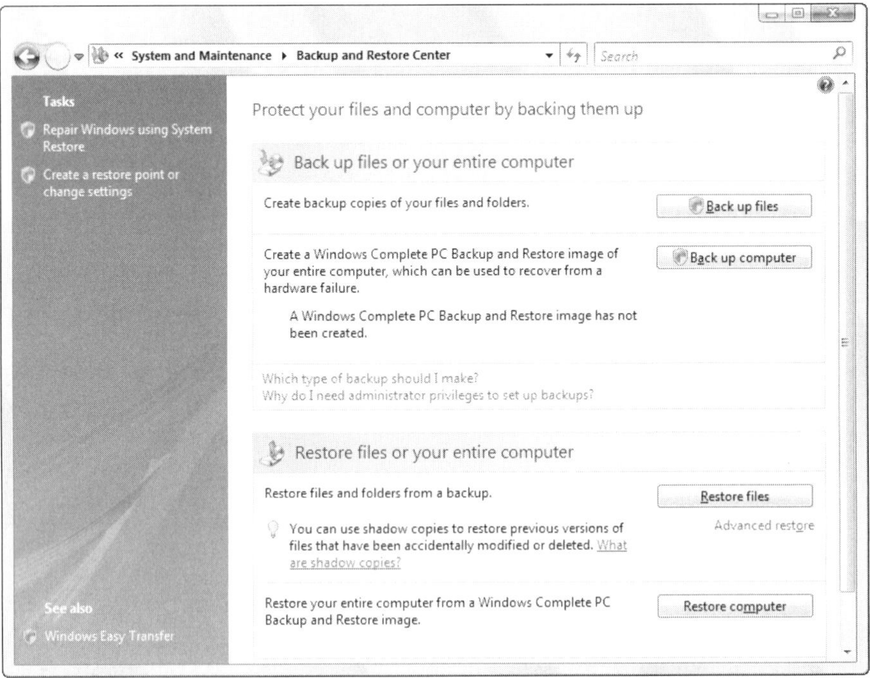

2. **Click Create a Restore Point or Change Settings.** The System Properties dialog box appears with the System Protection tab selected, as shown in Figure 10.13.
3. **Click Create.**
4. **Type in a name for your restore point.** Be descriptive (for example, Before Upgrading Graphics Card).
5. **Click Create.**
6. **Sit back and watch the progress bar.**
7. **When a dialog box confirms that the restore point has been created, click OK.**

FIGURE 10.13

Create a restore point or turn off System Restore via the System Protection tab.

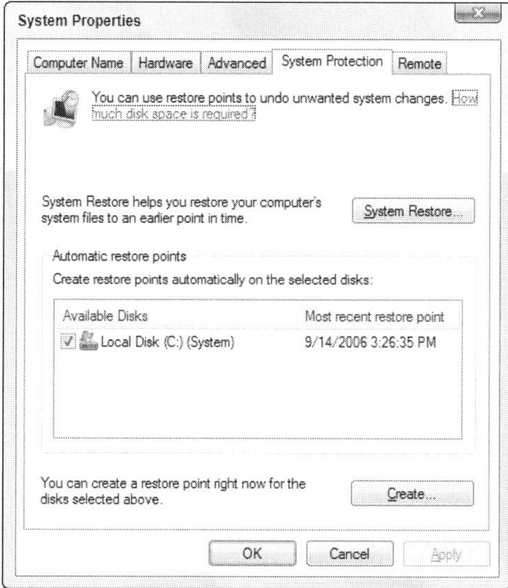

Restoring to a previously created restore point

Sometimes a program or a driver can trash Windows Vista's stability. Taking the system back in time to before you installed that software, or to any restore point currently stored on the hard drive, is easy. Just follow these steps:

1. **Open the Backup and Restore Center by choosing Start ➪ Control Panel ➪ System and Maintenance ➪ Backup and Restore Center.**
2. **Click Repair Windows Using System Restore.** The System Restore window, shown in Figure 10.14, appears.

FIGURE 10.14

You can restore a system to a previous restore point in the System Restore dialog box.

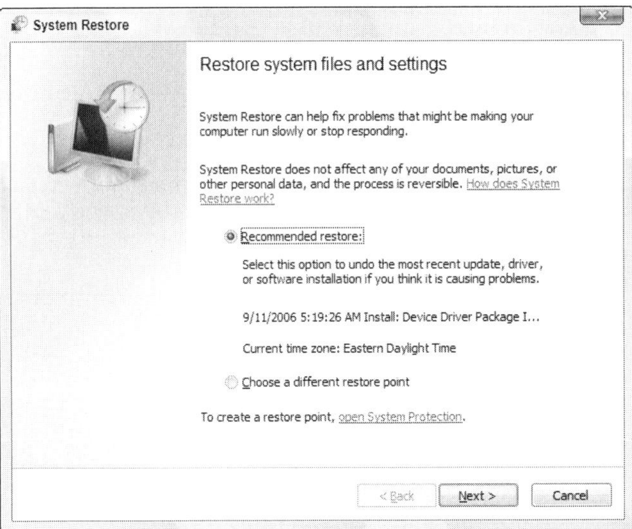

3. **Decide whether to use the recommended restore point or to choose a different one, and click Next.**
4. **Confirm the restore point and click Finish.** A warning dialog box appears, telling you that the restore cannot be undone; click OK to proceed.

   Windows reboots the computer. During the bootstrap, it restores the PC to your chosen restore point. When the boot cycle is complete and after you log on, a dialog box like the one shown in Figure 10.15 appears.

FIGURE 10.15

The hallmark of a successful System Restore operation

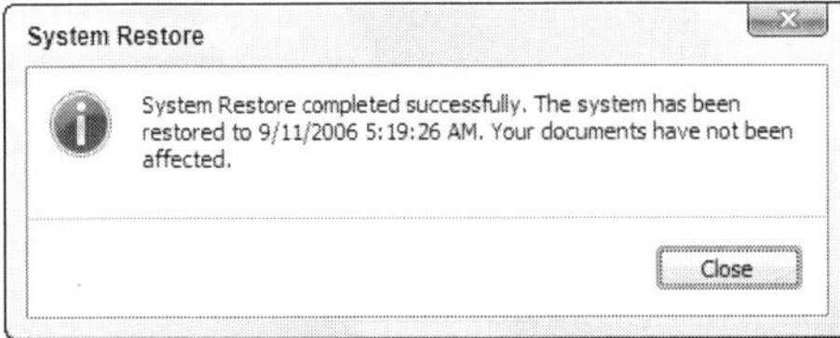

Turning off System Restore

I wouldn't recommend turning off System Restore. The System Restore service doesn't hurt Windows Vista's performance, and it provides an extra layer of protection beyond that of creating backup sets on removable media. To put it another way, System Restore works, and it works well. But if you want to shut it off, follow these steps:

1. **Open the Backup and Restore Center by choosing Start ➪ Control Panel ➪ System and Maintenance ➪ Backup and Restore Center.**
2. **Click Create a Restore Point or Change Settings.** The System Properties dialog box, shown earlier in Figure 10.13, appears.
3. **Click to deselect the box next to the drive designated for saving restore points.** In Figure 10.13, this drive is Local Disk (C:).
4. **Click OK.** A dialog box confirming your decision to turn off System Restore appears.
5. **Decide whether you really want to turn off System Restore, and click OK or Cancel.**

Restoring files from Shadow Copies

A second way to recover lost files is to restore them from what are known as *Shadow Copies*. Each time you alter and then resave a data file, Windows Vista keeps a copy of the overwritten version of the file. You can access the old versions of files when you need to.

TIP As a writer, I can honestly say that this feature alone is worth the upgrade. I don't know how many times I've accidentally overwritten a Word file that I meant to turn in to my publisher or editor, and then had to go to extraordinary means to recover the overwritten version. With Shadow Copies, I no longer have to worry about this problem.

To find a previous version of a file, you have to invoke its properties sheet. You can do so by navigating to a file, or a shortcut to the file, through the file system. Navigate to the folder, right-click on the file of which you want to fish up a previous version, and click Previous Versions.

Notice the tab on the properties sheet labeled Previous Versions. Click it, and Windows begins looking for Shadow Copies of the file.

For example, I cropped a picture of my son, Andrew. Let's say I wanted the uncropped version, but I overwrote it with the new version. I would just find the photo (through the Pictures folder, in this case), right-click the filename, and click Previous Versions. The Properties dialog box shown in Figure 10.16 appears. The computer automatically looks for shadow copies of the file and displays them in the dialog box.

The file in the Previous Versions window is the original version of the photo. I can treat it exactly like any data file; I can open it with an application, save it, and so on. In this case, I want to open it with a photo editor and save it with a different title. That way, I'll have both versions of the photograph in my Pictures folder.

FIGURE 10.16

Windows found a previous version of my photo.

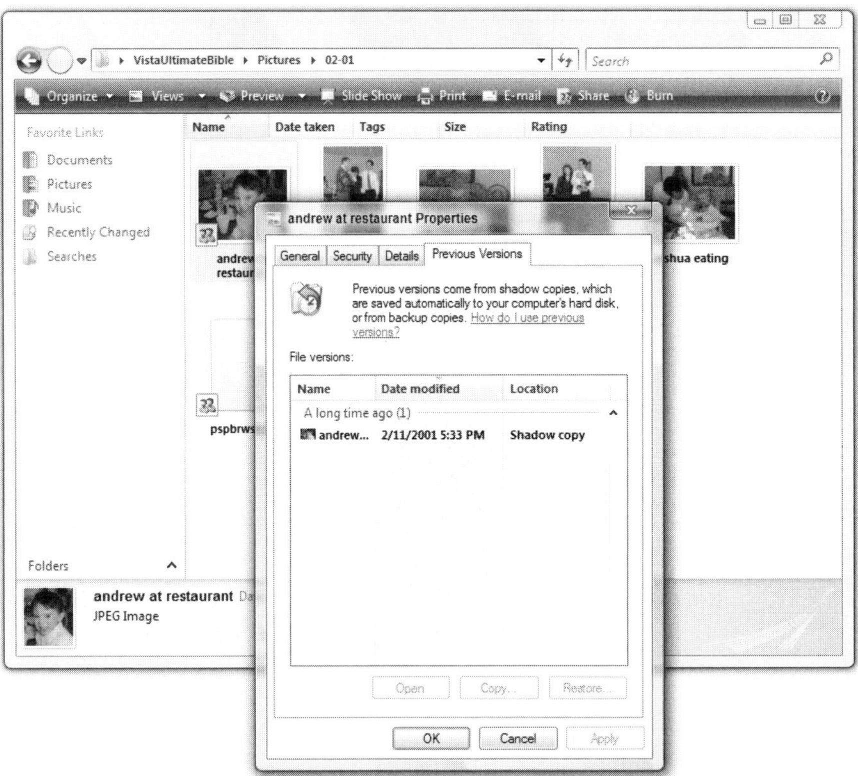

Backing up to external media or a network drive

System Restore and Shadow Copies are handy and reliable, but they won't save you from a complete and total hard drive failure. When that happens, unless you want to spend some serious coin getting the data retrieved by professionals, the only way to rescue your data is to restore it from a backup.

Of course, you have to *make* a backup to have one to restore. I am here to tell you, backups have saved my career more than once. I back up my important files religiously, to DVD+RW disks, every single night.

You should use the Backup and Restore Center, available through Control Panel's System and Maintenance page, to create backups of a file, a set of files, or your entire computer.

Backups and Consequences

This is a true anecdote that I'm printing here solely to scare you into backing up your important data. If you don't back your stuff up, it could be lost forever. That can be a pretty serious problem.

I worked for several years as the service manager of a local PC shop. I built PCs, I troubleshot PCs, I installed networks, and so on. Occasionally, the shop would get an emergency call, usually from someone who accidentally deleted a file and thought he'd wiped out his entire hard drive.

One client of ours ran a one-man pager store. He was the owner and the only employee. This was back when pagers were new and everyone had to have one, so he expected to turn a quick profit. He came to us for his computing needs, and we fixed him up with a single workstation that included a tape backup drive.

He called one day in a panic. His computer wouldn't boot up. I went to his store, expecting to find that he'd forgotten where the on/off switch was or something, and within a few minutes I diagnosed a seized hard drive. The drive was mechanically frozen; the platters wouldn't spin. The drive, in a nutshell, was dead.

I told him it wasn't a problem; I'd replace the drive and restore his most recent backup. He shook his head. "I haven't been backing up." I asked where his backup tapes were. He indicated that they were in a box somewhere in the back room and he had never once inserted one into the drive. The automated backups that I'd set up never happened.

I told him he'd have to manually punch in the important stuff from his paperwork. He said that he had no paperwork at all — he kept *everything* on the computer. The client data. The sales records. *The accounts receivables.* Without his computer data, *he couldn't even bill his customers.* The only things he ever printed out were receipts for customers.

He had nothing.

I looked into hard drive repair for him. There are companies with technicians who work in dust-free clean rooms that repair damaged hard drives and recover data. They charge a lot of money. I had to tell the pager guy that nobody would look at the drive without a generous non-refundable diagnostic fee, and the soonest he would get it back would be two weeks to a month.

Sadly, he had to close his store. He'd put thousands of dollars into it and was just about to break even. He didn't have the finances or the time to wait for the drive repair.

This is an extreme example of what happens when somebody with critical data does not make regular backups. From a business point of view, this person literally lost everything. Had he slid tapes into the backup drive each night at the end of the work day as he'd been instructed to, the recovery would have taken a matter of hours.

Instead, this failed entrepreneur had to go out and get a job working for someone else.

TIP People use all kinds of backup strategies. Some people do full system backups to a secondary hard drive every day; others only back up the files that they find to be the most essential. Make sure you back up everything you create with your computer that you wouldn't be able to recover. Programs are safe; you can always reinstall them from their media. Files you create or use with those programs, such as game saves, documents, spreadsheets, photographs, and so on, are prime for backing up.

Here is my backup strategy. I make sure to save everything into the folder bearing my login name. I save music into the Music folder, documents in the Documents folder, and so on. I then use Backup to make a backup of my primary folder and all of its subfolders. I back them up onto rewriteable DVD media each night. I have seven DVD+RW discs, one for each day of the week.

That way, I'll not only have one backup, but seven; in the event that one of my backup discs goes bad, I'll have six more to fall back on. The word to remember when backing up is *redundancy*: The more you have, the safer your files will be.

Making backups

You need to find someplace to back up data, preferably a removable media device such as an optical drive or a tape drive, or an external hard drive. You can also save to a network location, in the event your network has a dedicated backup server or an NAS device. To make a backup, follow these steps:

1. **Open the Backup and Restore Center by choosing Start ➪ Control Panel ➪ System and Maintenance ➪ Backup and Restore Center.**
2. **Decide whether you want to back up the entire computer (which will take up a lot of space) or only your important and unrecoverable files, and then click the appropriate button.**
3. **Pick a location (see Figure 10.17).** Use the wizard to choose a removable media device (such as a DVD+/-RW drive) or a network location.
4. **Click Next.** If you chose to back up the entire computer, one more screen appears to confirm the backup.
5. **Click Start Backup to proceed.**

If you chose to back up files, Windows will ask you to fill in check boxes for each file type you want to back up. You can then schedule regular backups and start the backup.

Restoring your data

You can restore individual files or your entire computer, if you have backed up your entire computer in the past. Restoring your data is as simple as backing it up.

Open the Backup and Restore Center (Start ➪ Control Panel ➪ System and Maintenance ➪ Backup and Restore Center). In the bottom half of the window, choose whether to restore the entire computer or only files and click the appropriate button. You'll rarely need to restore an entire PC unless the hard drive completely gave out.

FIGURE 10.17

Pick a place to which to back up.

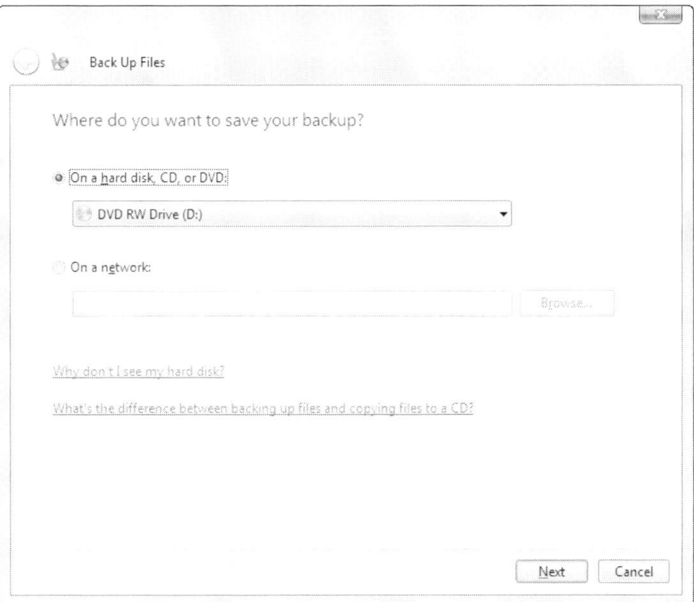

Summary

I wrote part of this book on a Windows XP system while running Vista on a nearby computer. I sort of wish I had been doing the writing at that time on the Vista PC. It might have detected the hard drive controller's impending death *before* I lost a chapter to file corruption and had to rewrite it.

Windows Vista has a myriad of ways to protect data and maintain stability throughout each day. Despite a number of obstacles to creating stable operating systems for the modern PC environment, Windows Vista is filled with stability tools, both active and passive. It also contains plenty of ways to recover data that you may lose due to any number of failures.

Several features run behind the scenes to keep Windows stable, like the WDDM and SuperFetch — which, incidentally, also makes computing faster and more responsive. You can use the Reliability Monitor to troubleshoot problems that Windows' own stability systems can't counteract.

Despite the fact that Windows does plenty of work to ensure stability and the safety of your files, the two things you absolutely have to do to keep your system healthy are to make sure it gets regular updates either through automated or manual updates, and back up your files. Windows can't prevent hardware, such as hard drives, from failing and losing all your data.

I'll say it again: Back up your data files. It's not an option; it's mandatory. When you upload that bank of photos from your digital camera to your computer, or as you work on each chapter of your Great American Novel, think what it would be like if you lost those files forever. Then think how relieved you would be if your hard drive destroyed them but you could pop in last night's DVD+RW disk and restore them. Back up your files. You won't regret doing it.

Chapter 11

Keeping Windows Vista Secure

IN THIS CHAPTER

- Maintaining security
- Understanding security features
- Using User Account Control
- Understanding firewalls
- Thwarting malware
- Learning strong security habits

When I think about computer security, I'm amused when I remember the Matthew Broderick/Ally Sheedy film *WarGames*. Imagine a defense department supercomputer that any high-school kid could dial into and cause it to want to blow up Russia. Even the supergenius who programmed it used his son's name as a back-door password. The humanity!

That was only a movie, but real vulnerabilities exist, and losers who call themselves "hackers" live to exploit them. Now that a vast number of computers are connected to the Internet (which wasn't much more than a neat idea when *WarGames* came out in 1983) whenever they're turned on via broadband, the need for secure systems is at an all-time high.

Even the staunchest Microsoft fan would have to admit that Windows security has been traditionally lax. Perhaps it's because the family of operating systems owns the vast majority of the market: Hackers and security experts constantly find vulnerabilities in Windows, and Microsoft constantly scrambles to patch them.

I won't be one to guarantee that Windows Vista will change all that, but Microsoft seems to have finally taken security as seriously as it should have years — or decades — ago. Windows Vista is loaded with security features to protect computers from intrusion, from both the Internet and from internal sources.

One of the cornerstones of Windows Vista's security is called User Account Control. It operates on what Microsoft calls the "Principle of Least Privilege," which means that programs and users only have the authority over the computer's files that they absolutely need to perform their tasks. If they try to exceed that authority, the operating system will demand authorization.

Windows Vista comes with a number of utilities intended to keep it secure, and third-party utilities have been in the works for the new OS since it was codenamed Longhorn. The built-in firewall, for example, is intended not only to keep intruders out, but also to prevent the computer itself from being used, unbeknownst to the user, as a pawn in an Internet attack. Windows Defender does its best to stop everything from popups to malicious software like spyware and adware.

Another source of threats is a computer that's not properly updated, that lacks antivirus software, or that's otherwise poorly protected joining your network. Many viruses and other malware are network-aware and can quickly spread from one computer to the next on a seemingly secure network. Windows Vista's Network Access Protection can protect you from such mayhem.

When you're surfing the Internet, the first line of defense is sometimes the browser itself. Internet Explorer 7+, the built-in Microsoft browser, has been beefed up to provide far more security than its previous version.

Of course, all the security programming in the world won't help you if you don't back it up with good habits. You have to know how to create powerful passwords, what software to purchase or acquire to add to Windows Vista's own security arsenal, and other ways to protect your computer yourself when its operating system can't do it for you.

Computer security isn't only for defense department supercomputers. Home users, gaming enthusiasts, multimedia fans, and anyone else who uses a computer all need some knowledge of security. This chapter introduces you to Windows Vista's security features and offers other tips for keeping your PC secure.

Whatever happened to Ally Sheedy, anyway?

Attacks from All Sides

Computer security threats are universal. Almost all computers are at risk. Many of the tasks you take for granted can lead to security breaches: meandering through the Web, installing software, and even walking away from the computer are all risky procedures. The only way to live without security threats is to move to a small island with your computer and live without Internet access, software to install, and other people; or to shut down the computer, unplug it, and find something else to do.

Those aren't necessarily the most convenient or fun suggestions, so you'll probably reject them. Instead, you should take some time to learn about computer security and to develop sensible security habits. A bit of foreknowledge and a dose of common sense can keep your computer free from intrusion for its lifetime.

Why Do Hackers Hack?

One thing a lot of less tech-savvy people ask me is, "Why?" Why is security such a big deal? Why do bad programs and worse people try to sabotage computers? What's the point?

Some computer security threats have reasons behind them: corporate or state espionage or sabotage, for example. Blasting advertisements to uninterested parties while hampering their computers' abilities to run efficiently is questionable at best. Infecting unsuspecting users' PCs with software to turn it into part of a "botnet," which is a network of computers that hackers can use for any purpose—including relaying spam.

Other motives are even fuzzier. Why, for example, would anyone want to invade some nameless Joe's computer from across the Internet and steal pictures from a family reunion? Why would someone want to cause a popular Web site to become inaccessible? Why would anyone want to spread software that arbitrarily harms every computer it spreads to?

Hacking can be defined as anything from maliciously damaging computer data to trying to find out more about a program or a system. It's a broad term, but it's largely associated with ill motives.

Not all hackers are evil. Some do good, like a group of hackers from a Usenet newsgroup who used to scour the newsgroups for people posting child pornography and collect data about them, which the hackers would then turn over to the proper authorities. Many hackers have gone on to drive computer security businesses, thwarting malicious hackers in the process. Hacking need not be criminal; sometimes, people hack simply to learn more about computer programs and security.

Unfortunately, the most notorious hackers are those who cause problems, often for people they don't even know.

Malicious hackers seem to think they've developed a culture of noble anarchy. They praise those among them who get caught and end up in jail, turning them into weird sorts of folk heroes. Encouraged by various media, from magazines to movies, they liken themselves to brave adventurers, while most are so "brave" they do all their work from their bedrooms. Are such people socially challenged? Are they full of rage at the world? Or do they simply lack the brainpower to comprehend the consequences of their actions?

Some malicious hackers claim to be doing the world a favor by exposing problematic code that's open to exploitation; they're helping perfect computer security. If that was their motive, however, they would report such problems and not wreak havoc with their knowledge. Without people like them we wouldn't need to implement drastic security measures. They cause damage. They do harm. I don't try or want to understand them; they're criminals and should be locked up with others of their type.

Viruses, worms, and Trojans

You've probably heard a lot about computer viruses, and subsets of viruses called *worms* and *Trojan horses*. For the most part, such programs are small bits of code that spread from one computer to another in any way that they're programmed to do so. Some are network-aware. Some use e-mail. In the old days, viruses used shared floppy disks to infect any system they came in contact with.

Viruses all have one thing in common: the ability to self-replicate. They're written to spread, to create copies of themselves, either through a user's unknowing intervention or, in the case of worms, through their own design.

Some do only that: spread. They don't have any malicious or destructive code, they simply want to infect other computers. Others deliver payloads of malicious instructions that can do anything from popping up a message to destroying data. A Trojan horse is a special type of virus that, once executed, enables distant computers to control the host computer.

Viruses can spread in a number of ways:

- **Older viruses spread through floppy disks.** They infected the boot sector of the disk, and if a computer was booted with an infected floppy in the drive, the virus could then infect the computer's hard drive. Every floppy inserted after that point would become infected with the virus.
- **Worms often spread through e-mail.** They come to a computer as an attachment in an executable file, or embedded in a document or image file. Once executed, they detect the host computer's e-mail program and send copies of themselves to everyone in the address book.
- **Some viruses are spread actively by malicious users.** They attach viruses to downloadable programs and post them for distribution on Web sites, FTP servers, Usenet newsgroups, or other sources.

Once released into "the wild," viruses continue to spread from computer to computer. Security companies watch for new viruses to become prevalent and then capture and analyze them. They catalog viruses by unique code traces. Antivirus programs use code traces to both detect viruses trying to install themselves and to find viruses as the antivirus program searches a hard drive.

Deadly DoS attacks

Web sites, both major and unknown, are often the targets of malevolent people. These people may try to crack the Web page's security and alter the home page, or they may try to prevent anyone from being able to use the page through a denial of service (DoS) attack. Web-oriented DoS attacks usually involve using a computer to send large amounts of data to a Web site, so that it cannot process legitimate data.

A popular tactic is to implement a distributed denial of service (DDoS) attack. Hackers do so by using Trojan horse programs to take control of as many Internet-connected computers as possible, without alerting the users to their presence. Such computers are referred to as *zombies*. At a specific point in time, all the zombies start sending huge amounts of data, such as page requests, to the same Web site. The site becomes overwhelmed and real traffic slows to a crawl. Many users who try to access the site find it impossibly slow — if they can access it at all.

NOTE DoS isn't relegated to the Web. Any attack that prevents someone from using a computer or a function of the computer, either local or across the 'Net, is a DoS attack. Using an automated script to flood a message board or a Usenet newsgroup is a DoS attack, as is sabotaging someone's computer's networking modules to prevent that person from accessing the Internet.

Spyware and adware

Hackers are associated with viruses and their subcategories. Another type of malware exists that tends to come from what are sometimes legitimate businesses. Spyware, and the similar adware, are programs that often come from trusted sources — or sources that claim that they can be trusted — but that perform tasks that the user either doesn't want or isn't aware of.

Spyware can be anything from a program running on a computer that a user doesn't know is there, to Internet cookies (little bits of code that Web sites drop onto your computer). Spyware tends to keep track of what a user does or what Web pages she visits, and reports such data to a distant computer. The data are often used for marketing or general data warehousing purposes.

Adware is software that blasts ads, sometimes seemingly out of nowhere, in front of the user's face. Ads from adware usually take the form of popup windows. Without warning, a window will appear urging the user to, for example, visit an online pharmacy or enjoy the pleasures of online gambling.

Not only can spyware and adware be unwanted, annoying, and deceitful, but it can also slow the responsiveness of legitimate programs. Spyware and adware often run in the background and, because they tend to consist of hastily and sometimes poorly written programs, they often hog resources that could be used by programs the user actually wants to run. Popups, especially, cause disruptions in a user's computing experience.

Spyware and adware often end up on a computer when a user installs a program, usually a freebie, that he downloads from the Web. As the program the user requested goes in, it installs other programs — spyware and/or adware — that the user doesn't know is part of the deal.

TIP A general rule is that if it seems too good to be true, assume it is. Those wacky banner ads promising 1,000 free smilies for your e-mail or free ringtones for download can be sources of spyware and adware. Free software does exist on the Net, but you have to be careful. Check the source. See what other people online are saying about it. Don't assume that just because it's advertised on a Web site you like to visit, that it's legit.

Spyware and adware can be really tricky to get rid of. Rarely do such programs include an uninstall component, and often when they do, it doesn't do a sufficient job. Antispyware programs treat spyware and adware the same way that antivirus programs treat viruses: They look for software traces of the malware and, at the user's discretion, quarantine or remove all traces of it from the system.

Attacks from inside

Not all computer problems come from the Internet connection or installation media. Sometimes, especially in office environments, seemingly trustworthy peers can be the source of security breaches.

When you walk away from your computer, how do you know that someone else doesn't take your seat and start digging for data? Corporate espionage is a major motivator of such infractions: When a computer may contain data that are valuable to competing companies, disgruntled workers may try to steal and sell it.

Even if you're a home user, do you have anything on your hard drive that you would rather other people in your family not see? Or if you take your computer to LAN parties (where people gather with their PCs to play local network games), where you may leave it running unattended, do you want people to have access to it?

Windows Vista is ready

Windows Vista doesn't have its own antivirus program. That said, it's ready for almost anything you can throw at it. Its security features can thwart viruses, even though it can't detect or remove them. Vista does contain programs to deal specifically with spyware and adware. Its security has been heavily fortified to deal with threats from the Net and from your side of the computer, as discussed in the remainder of this chapter.

User Account Control

One of the major security problems with earlier versions of Windows, all the way up to Windows XP, was that most user accounts provided full administrative privileges. That means, as long as a user was logged on, she could do virtually anything to the operating system with few, if any, warnings.

Worse, many programs and processes also ran with full administrative privileges, so they, too, could make all kinds of executive decisions with the PC's data, its core files, and so on, often without the user even knowing about it.

Malicious users had the ability to exploit this trait to run malicious code or even take full control of unsuspecting users' computers. If someone found a way to gain control of a module with administrative privileges through a buffer overrun or something, the person could suddenly do pretty much anything he or she wanted to the computer in question.

NOTE **Just what the heck is a buffer overrun? It's a complicated notion, but here's a simple definition. Computer programs, processes, and services often use small amounts of memory to store data. Those little hunks of memory are called *buffers*.**

A *buffer overrun* occurs when the process is instructed to write more to the buffer than there is actually memory space allocated for. For example, if a process creates an 8k buffer, and code told it to write 10k into that buffer, a buffer overrun (also known as a buffer overflow) is initiated.

Ideally, the program recognizes the problem and enters an error state. Sometimes, however, the program, through a bug or sloppy coding, doesn't respond properly and becomes compromised. Sometimes, this state results in other data in memory being overwritten; in some cases, the process can crash or be used to execute arbitrary code.

A malicious person could run destructive code, install Trojan horse programs, or otherwise compromise a computer's security. In the worst cases, security vulnerabilities could be automatically exploited by a phone Web site that blasted through Internet Explorer's somewhat weak defenses and wreak havoc on any computers whose browsers hit the site.

User Account Control (UAC) doesn't stop buffer overruns, and it doesn't fix bugs. What it does is use what is known as the Principle of Least Privilege to prevent arbitrary code from running, should such a vulnerability be found and an attempt made to exploit it.

Principle of Least Privilege

You may have noticed when you try to install a program or make system-level changes through Control Panel or Device Manager (Figure 11.1) that Windows Vista halts and tosses up a dialog box that asks you for permission to proceed. If you're not using an administrative account, you may even have to enter a password to get Windows to let you do what you set out to do.

Lots of critics call this an annoyance. Maybe it is, but it's there to protect your data. If code that you didn't know was running tries to make system-level changes or execute a program, you would receive the same message. Because you would be fairly sure you didn't actually try to make such changes, you could tell it "no" and, just like that, a dangerous exploitation is thwarted.

The Principle of Least Privilege says that no user, process, or program should have any more authority over the computer than it absolutely has to in order to accomplish its tasks. Thus, the vast majority of the operating system's major files and registry keys are constantly protected.

Standard and administrator accounts

Both standard and administrative accounts are subject to UAC, but there's a key difference. When a user is logged into an administrative account, changes to the operating system that require permission can be instructed to proceed with a mere click of the mouse. Standard account users, on the other hand, must enter an administrator's password to make such changes.

This feature gives the administrator more control over the computer. When an administrator enters the Control Panel's Manage Accounts interface (Figure 11.2), he or she can create or change account types as needed.

FIGURE 11.1

When you try to enter Device Manager, shown, Windows asks whether you're sure.

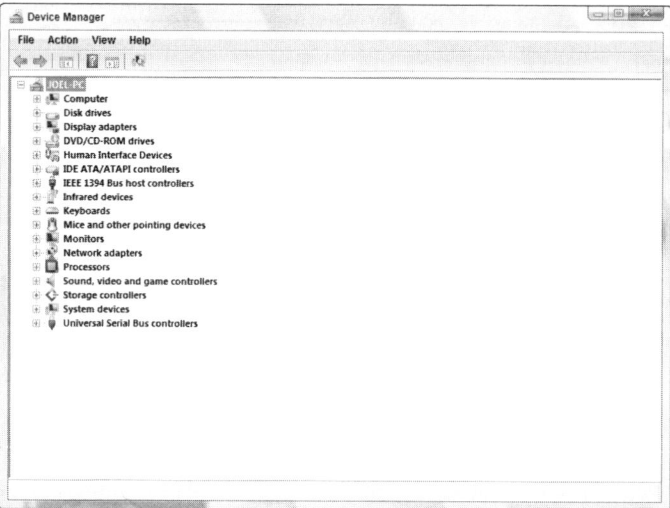

FIGURE 11.2

The User Accounts module is protected through User Account Control.

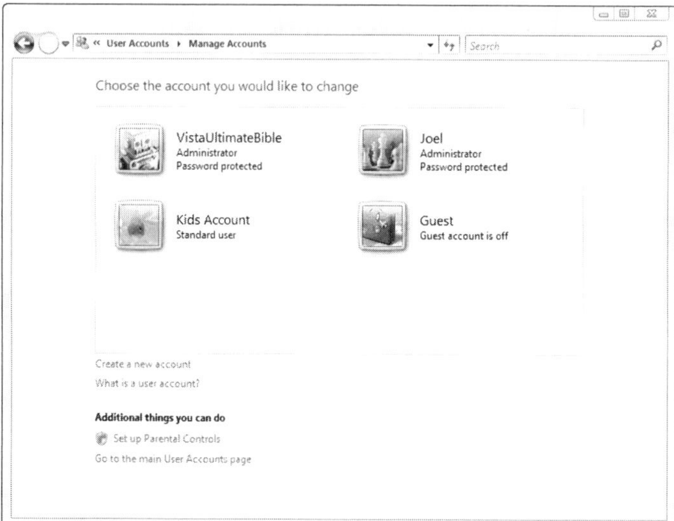

This feature can be handy in both office and home environments. For example, if you don't want your children messing about with installing programs or formatting hard drives, give them standard accounts and don't divulge any administrator account passwords to them. If they run into a UAC alert that requires an administrator's password, they can bother you for permission for whatever they're trying to do.

Windows Vista's Security Programs

As stated earlier, Windows Vista doesn't come with its own antivirus program. Why it doesn't is beyond me; probably some sort of antitrust thing. It does, however, include a firewall, an antispyware program, and a heavily fortified Web browser that's far less prone to exploitation than earlier Microsoft browsers were.

For an overview of Windows Vista's current security status, open Control Panel and click Security. Click Check this computer's security status; a Windows Security Center screen like the one shown in Figure 11.3 appears.

This screen tells you what it claims to: the status of the computer's security. If it detects a possible threatening situation (such as my computer's lack of an antivirus program, as shown in Figure 11.3) it alerts you to the problem. It also displays a small shield icon in the System Notification Area (on the right of the taskbar, near the clock).

FIGURE 11.3

Security status: Shame on me! I don't have an antivirus program running!

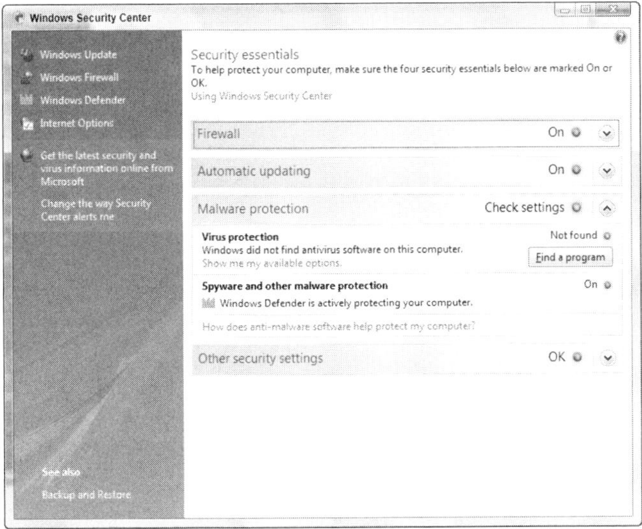

It keeps tabs on Windows Firewall, your antivirus program, Automatic Updates, Windows Defender, and other settings. Note that Automatic Updates is considered a security feature, as well as a feature to keep Windows Vista stable.

CROSS-REF **You can learn about updating Windows in Chapter 10.**

You can click on any of the security areas for more information. For example, if you click Other Security Settings, the window morphs into the one shown in Figure 11.4.

FIGURE 11.4

More security information

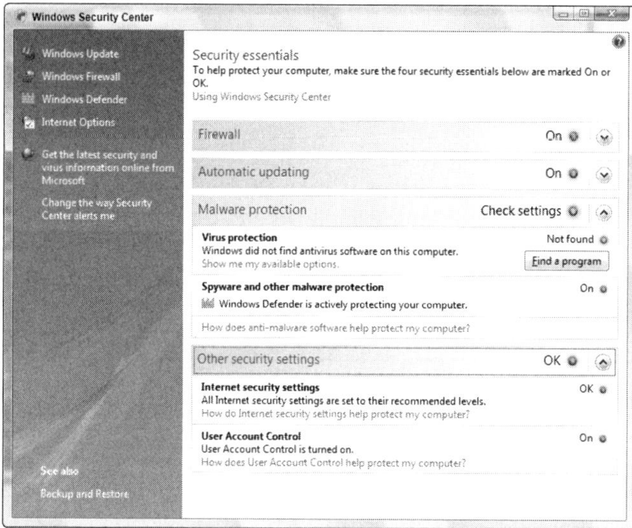

It shows that User Account Control is turned on, as it *always* should be, and that the Internet settings are the way Windows feels they should be.

Let's look at the various security programs included with Windows.

Windows Defender

Windows Defender is an anti-spyware application that can run in the background, looking for traces of malware that try to infect your computer, and that can also sweep the computer by your command or at regularly scheduled intervals, looking for spyware that somehow got past its memory resident module.

You can tweak its settings. Choose Control Panel ➪ Security ➪ Windows Defender. A screen like the one shown in Figure 11.5 appears.

FIGURE 11.5

You can control Windows Defender here.

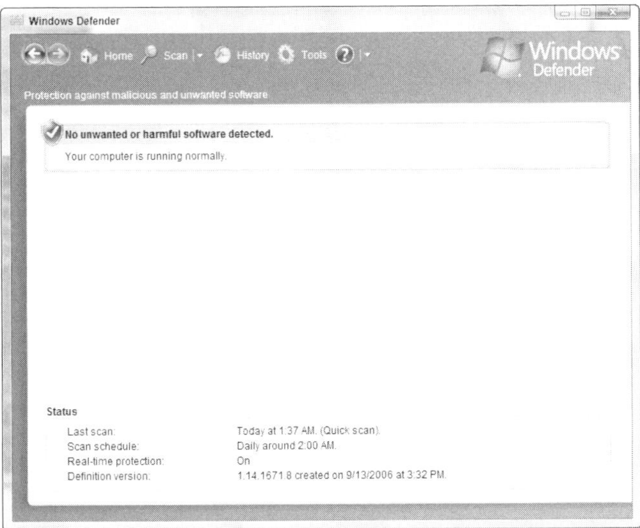

The Windows Defender dialog box has several pages. The home page shows a current status. If you click Scan, you'll see something like Figure 11.6. Windows Defender scans the computer's hard drive and memory for spyware traces.

Click the History button to see a dialog box like the one shown in Figure 11.7. It contains data about any spyware infestations your computer has experienced and what Windows Defender has done about them. You can click any item for more information.

Finally, you can click the Tools button to see additional options that offer more control over the program. Figure 11.8 shows the Tools display.

Options

The Options screen, shown in Figure 11.9, allows you to set up Windows Defender as you see fit. It contains a scrolling list of options with various setting controls, including list boxes, radio buttons, and check boxes.

FIGURE 11.6

Windows Defender is scanning for spyware.

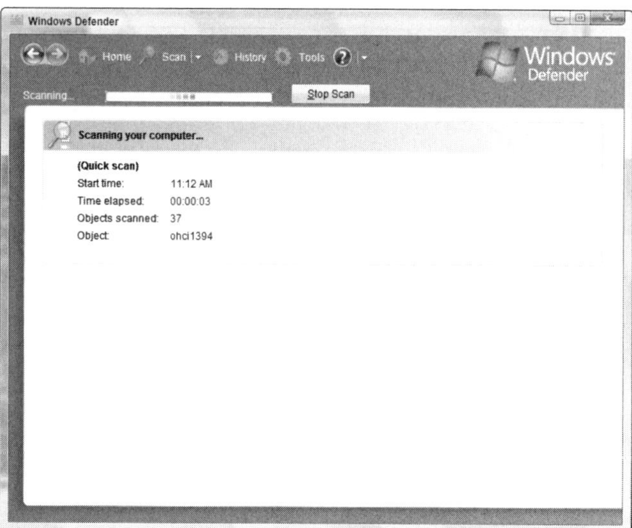

FIGURE 11.7

Windows Defender's history

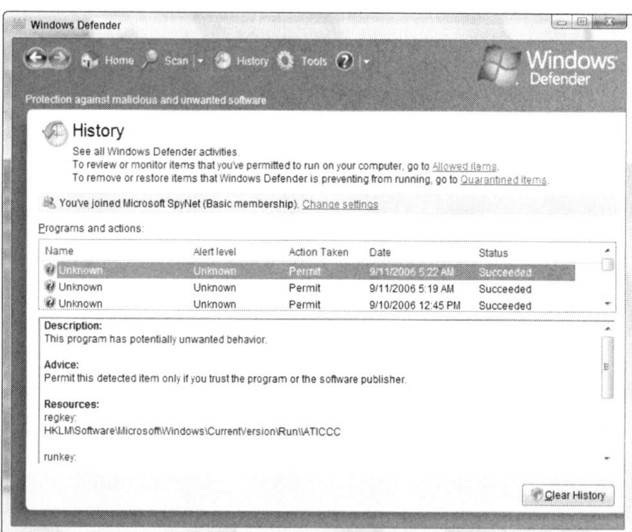

FIGURE 11.8

Windows Defender's Tools

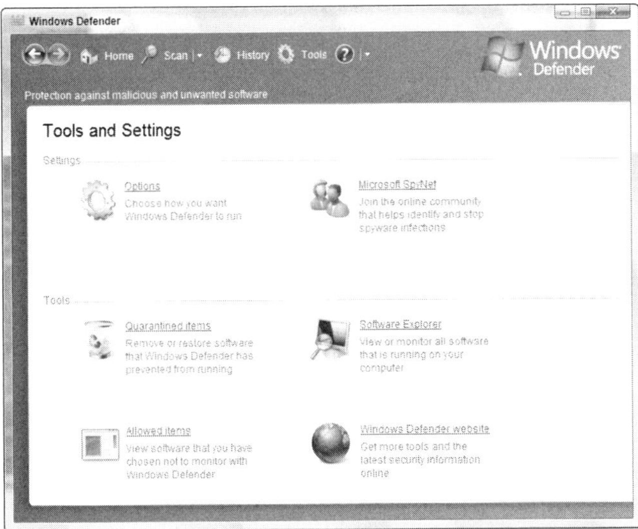

FIGURE 11.9

The Windows Defender's Options screen

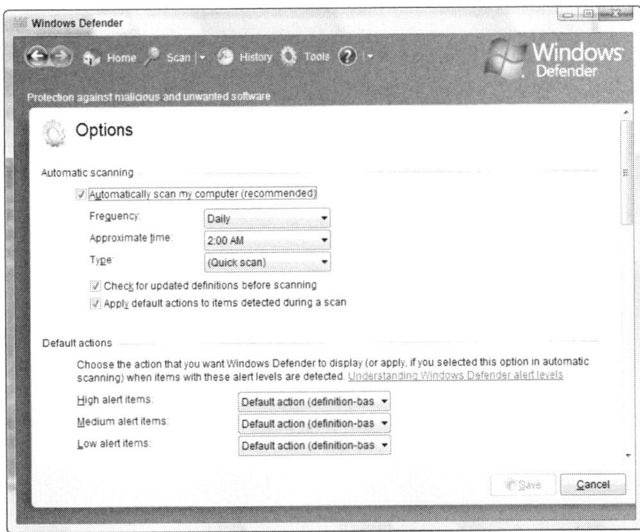

You can tell Windows Defender:

- When and how to perform scans of the computer. By default, it runs quick scans daily at 2 a.m. and checks for updated spyware definitions before it scans.
- What to do when it finds a problem. It has definition-based default actions it can perform, including ridding the computer of the offending item; or you can tell it to globally ignore or disable high, medium, and low security threats.
- How to use its memory-resident, real-time protection module (which is an independent part of Windows Defender that can run in the background). You can globally enable or disable real-time protection, or tweak it with a whole host of options including a number of security agents to run, when to notify you, and when to show the module's icon in the Notification Area.
- How to use advanced options, including creating restore points before performing various actions; using heuristics to detect unclassified threats; and defining a list of files and locations to ignore.
- Whether to run real-time protection at all, and whether to run for everyone on the computer or just the administrator.

The default options work very well in preventing spyware and adware from infiltrating the system. You should only change them if you are certain you need to.

You can also view quarantined programs, which Windows Defender has deemed harmful and rendered incapable of executing any commands.

From the Windows Defender Options screen, you can launch Software Explorer (Figure 11.10), which tells you everything that's running on the system and why it's allowed.

For more about Software Explorer, see Chapters 14 and 28.

You can also view software that's permitted to run on Windows Vista, and visit the Windows Defender Web site.

Microsoft SpyNet

Microsoft SpyNet offers community-based protection from malicious software. Windows Vista Ultimate automatically enables a basic membership. SpyNet allows Windows Defender to query a database when it detects a malicious trace and find out what other SpyNet members have done with it. It shares with the community whether its actions are successful or not. The advanced membership, selectable with a radio button, gives you more control over what to do with spyware that it detects that's not already in its database.

FIGURE 11.10

Software Explorer lets you see everything running on Windows Vista.

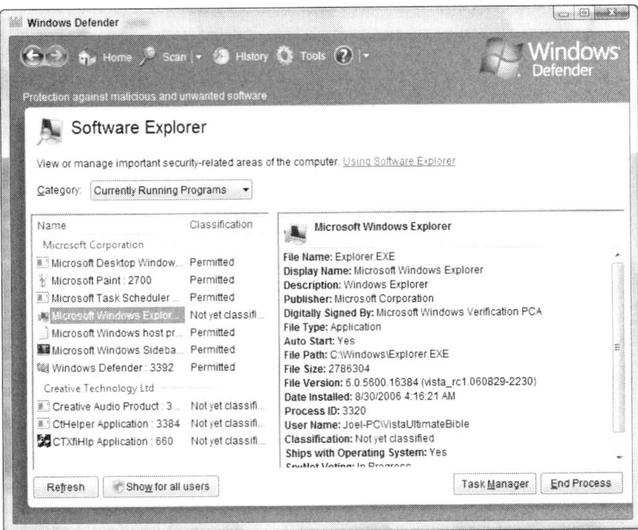

Note that both versions send information to Microsoft from your computer. SpyNet sends only anonymous information about programs that cause software changes, which helps the community to track down new and unknown threats. You can, however, turn it off if you don't want your computer to send information about spyware to Microsoft.

Windows Firewall

With Windows Vista, Windows Firewall is more powerful than ever. First introduced with Windows XP's Service Pack 2, it's a software firewall that traps any incoming Internet traffic that wasn't requested by a Windows Vista session.

In the Security Center, click Windows Firewall. A window like the one in Figure 11.11 appears.

The main page shows status information: namely whether the firewall is enabled. You have all kinds of control over the firewall, including whether to use it at all, which programs to allow to send or receive data through it, and which ports to open or close.

NOTE You shouldn't have any need to change the firewall settings. Most games and programs currently available are Windows Firewall aware and will ask you for permission to configure the firewall for them to work through it. If the firewall detects a new program trying to send or receive data through the firewall, Windows will pop up a message asking whether you want to block or unblock the program. Only in rare instances will you need to manually change the Windows Firewall settings.

FIGURE 11.11

Windows Firewall

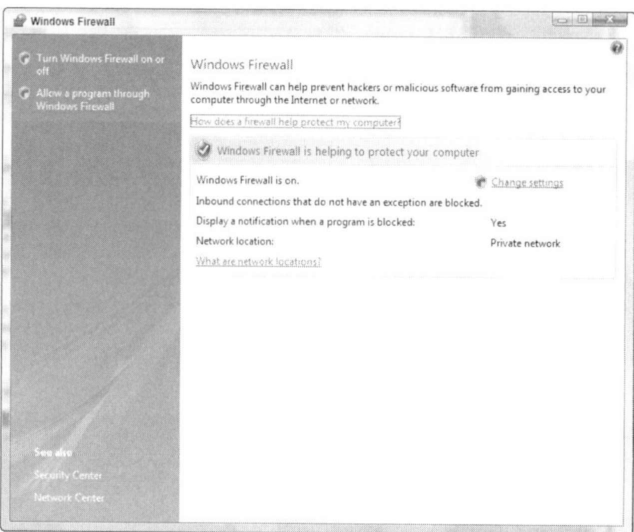

Two options on the left side of the window both open the same properties sheet, but to different tabs. If you click Turn Windows Firewall on or off, the General tab appears (Figure 11.12). If you click Allow a program through Windows Firewall, the Exceptions tab appears (Figure 11.13).

The General tab is simple: You can turn Windows Firewall on or off with radio buttons, or click a check box to block literally all Internet traffic to your computer (sort of a panic button, for when you think you might be under attack).

The Exceptions tab contains a list of programs that you can give permission to work through the firewall by clicking the check boxes next to them. You may notice games and other programs you install listed, as well as built-in Windows modules. You can add programs manually by clicking the Add Program button and finding it in a list or navigating to its executable.

You can also add specific ports. This feature might be handy for running game servers for legacy games that aren't Windows Firewall aware. Click Add Ports, enter the port, give it a name, and indicate whether it's a TCP or UDP port. You can find this data in the documentation of the program that you're trying to bestow Internet access upon.

FIGURE 11.12

You can turn Windows Firewall on or off via this tab.

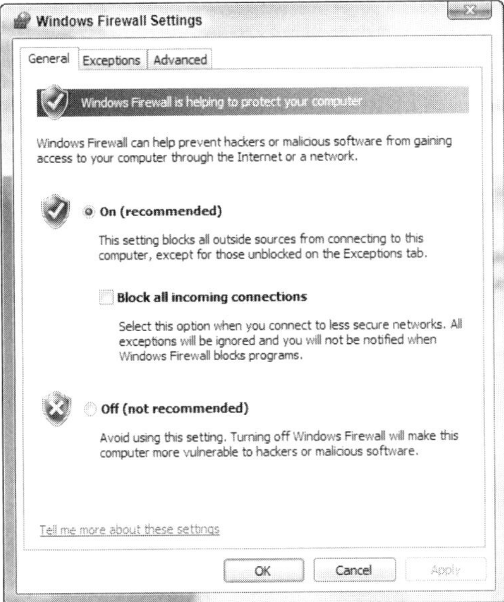

FIGURE 11.13

Tell Windows Firewall which programs to allow access via this tab.

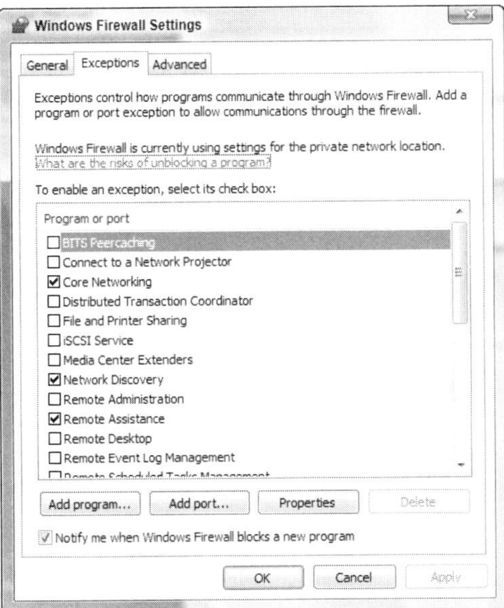

Secure Habits You Can Develop

With all of Windows Vista's built-in features, maintaining a secure computer should be far easier than ever before with a Windows operating system. There's more to keeping your computer secure, however, than simply trusting Windows to keep your PC safe.

The very habits you develop can make a massive difference in how secure your computer remains. You can take precautions to keep your data from theft or destruction, or you can ignore the warnings and go about your business without a care in the world — and find your system compromised.

The following sections offer some rules to live by to keep your computer from becoming a zombie, your data from becoming threatened, and your life from becoming complicated by computer security breaches.

Update windows frequently or use Automatic Updates

Visit Chapter 10 to find out all about updating Windows, including using Automatic Updates (Figure 11.14). Windows can update itself automatically on a regular basis, and you should let it.

FIGURE 11.14

Use Automatic Updates to keep Windows Vista secure.

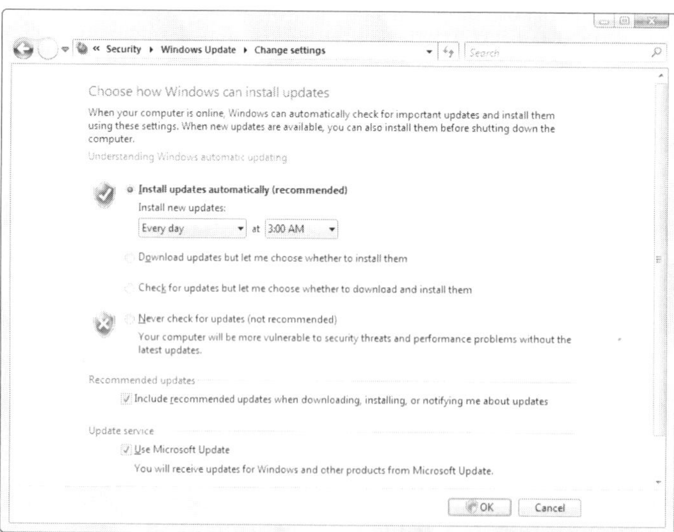

Windows security exploitations are like death and taxes. They're going to happen; it's just a matter of when. Microsoft tends to release updates as quickly as possible every time a Windows vulnerability is discovered. Even though UAC can help prevent malware from making harmful changes to your computer, the first line of defense is to patch the security hole immediately.

Use Automatic Updates to allow Windows to check for updates, download them, and install them every day. Besides security updates, Microsoft also releases stability updates, bug patches, and sometimes even new levels of program capabilities. If you don't update Windows Vista, you're not only preventing your computer from being as secure as possible, but you're also missing out on other updates.

Don't trust unknown e-mail

Check out Chapter 13 for a discussion of Windows Mail (Figure 11.15) and its new security features. Whether you're using that built-in e-mail program for your e-mail purposes, or another program such as Outlook or Mozilla Thunderbird, you should take a few precautions when you're dealing with e-mail.

FIGURE 11.15

Windows Mail has a phishing filter built-in.

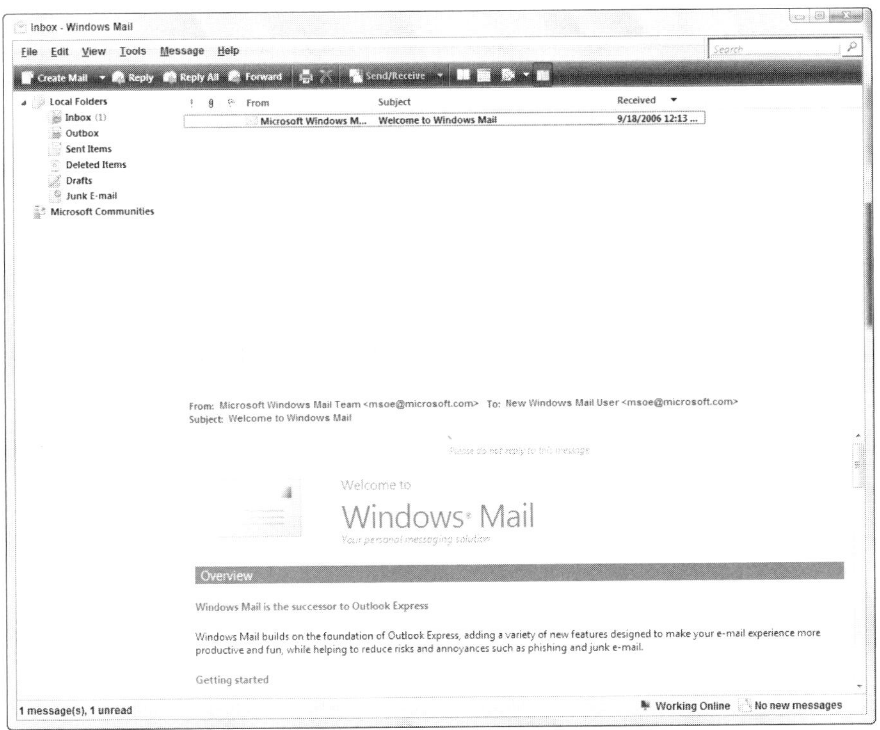

Phishing scams are everywhere. *Phishing* is an attempt by underhanded cretins to fool you into providing them with personal information, including stuff they could use to run up your credit cards or steal your identity. Phishing often comes in the form of e-mail claiming to be from a major financial institution, Web store, or other service asking you to click a link to "update your account information."

That link might take you to a phony Web site that looks almost exactly like the Web site of the actual institution. If you enter your personal data, well, congratulations: You've been phished.

Another threat from e-mail is attachments that contain viruses. These can come from anyone, including your friends who themselves have allowed their computers to become infected.

Do not trust such e-mail. If you get an attachment that you weren't expecting, notify the sender (if you know who it is) and ask whether it's legitimate. If you want to update your account information with your bank, launch a browser and manually type the URL into the address bar.

E-mail is a great thing, but it's also a wide-open door to getting scammed. Resist the urge to run attachments, even interesting ones, that you didn't expect. Don't get phished. Use caution when you communicate with the world through the Net.

Heed IE7+'s warnings

The Internet is like a big city. There are nice places, and there are not-so-nice places. Sometimes you're safe, sometimes you're in danger. It all depends on where you go.

Check out Chapter 13 for details about Internet Explorer 7+ and its new security features, including a utility that scans Web sites for phishing and phony links. Then, when IE tries to warn you not to deal with a site you're unfamiliar with, be very wary if you choose not to listen.

Phony sites exist to steal everything from your money to your identity; some can breach your PC's security and some track everything you do. If you encounter, for example, an online merchant that's not a well-known one like Amazon, Buy.com, or NewEgg, think for a second before you enter your credit card number.

Find message boards that discuss whatever it is you were shopping for and ask about the site. Look at the prices: Are they in line or a little lower than those on competitors' sites, or are they seemingly impossibly low?

Be careful while surfing, use common sense, and stay in the nice neighborhoods.

Create strong passwords

Sometimes, a password is the only thing standing between an intruder and your data. If someone guesses your administrator account password, he can then gain access to almost anything on your computer. He can also change the password to lock you out.

You need to create strong passwords. The sweet spot to aim for is a password that's easy for you to remember but impossible for anyone to guess. Ideally, it should contain letters in both uppercase and lowercase, and a few numbers for good measure.

Here are some tips to consider when choosing a password:

- Make it at least eight characters. The longer your password is, the longer it'll take password cracking software to defeat it.
- Try not to use a word that's in the dictionary. Password-cracking software often has ways to blast thousands of common words at a login screen in a matter of seconds.
- Stay away from obvious words or combinations, such as your childrens' names or your birth date. Anyone can guess them.
- If you must use real words, use two or three unrelated words in a row and some numbers, too. A bad password is "uncle." A better one is "uncle93blob20crease."
- The best passwords are series of random letters, but they're hard to remember. Something like "ZyhaLKvv87oPwrk" would be a terrific password, but you won't remember it without writing it down. And if you write it down, someone could find it.
- Don't use words that are visible from the location of your computer. For example, I wouldn't use "southPark" because I have a South Park calendar.

Use antivirus software

This is not an option.

Antivirus software is absolutely necessary, no matter how strongly you feel that your computer is impenetrable. It should run in the background at all times, check e-mail as it comes in, and regularly scan the computer for virus signatures.

I use a free antivirus program called GriSoft AVG Free Edition, shown in Figure 11.16. GriSoft is available at `http://free.grisoft.com` and is free for personal use. GriSoft also offers premium packages for business use.

If you wish to use it, download the Windows version of AVG Free Edition (I suggest placing it in your Downloads folder) and then run it. The program will install the AVG Free Edition to your computer. You can feel free to use the setup program's default, standard installation.

When the installation is complete, you'll see a screen like the one shown in Figure 11.17. Click OK to continue.

Several things happen. The antivirus program's main window appears and a small tutorial window appears on top of that. Meanwhile, you might see a Windows Security Alert in the System Notification Area telling you that your antivirus program is out of date. See Figure 11.18 for the chaotic screen.

FIGURE 11.16

Visit GriSoft's site for its free AVG program.

Click Next in the AVG Free "First Run" window. The first thing it will prompt you to do is check for updates. Click Check for Updates to proceed. Like Windows Updates, AVG will check its publisher's servers for updated versions of the antivirus program and its virus definitions, which it uses to flush out any viruses it finds on your computer. After you click Check for Updates, the screen in Figure 11.19 appears. Click Internet.

The program looks for updates, finds them, and installs them.

FIGURE 11.17

Click OK when AVG Free Edition is installed.

FIGURE 11.18

Don't panic! Just continue the AVG tutorial.

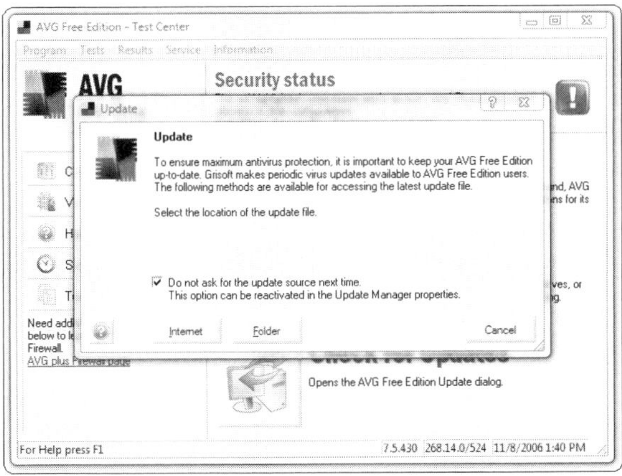

NOTE If, for some reason, the program can't find the update server, simply try again later. Open the program's main window by double-clicking its icon in the System Notification Area and click Check for Updates.

FIGURE 11.19

Check for updates.

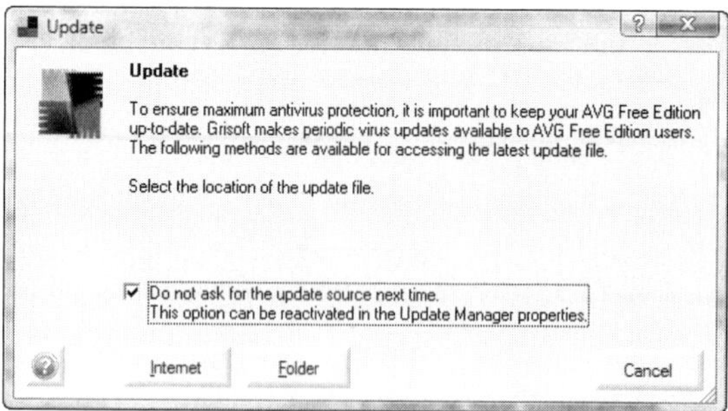

After the update, click Next. The window shown in Figure 11.20 appears. It offers options concerning daily antivirus system scans. Set them to Low Priority so they can scan the computer in the background as you work (High Priority would use more resources and slow down your computer's responsiveness), and do enable a scheduled scan. Click Next.

FIGURE 11.20

Enable system scans.

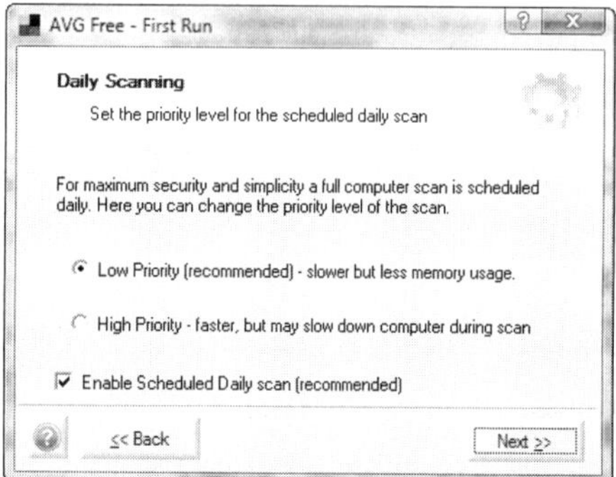

AVG will then offer to scan your computer right away (Figure 11.21). Click Scan Computer! if you wish it to do so. Because you've scheduled daily scans, a scan at this moment isn't critical unless you suspect your system is infected with a virus. Click Next to continue.

The last dialog box offers you the option to register the program by providing personal information to GriSoft. Click Next, and in the following dialog box, click Continue.

FIGURE 11.21

There's no need to scan now unless you think there's a reason to.

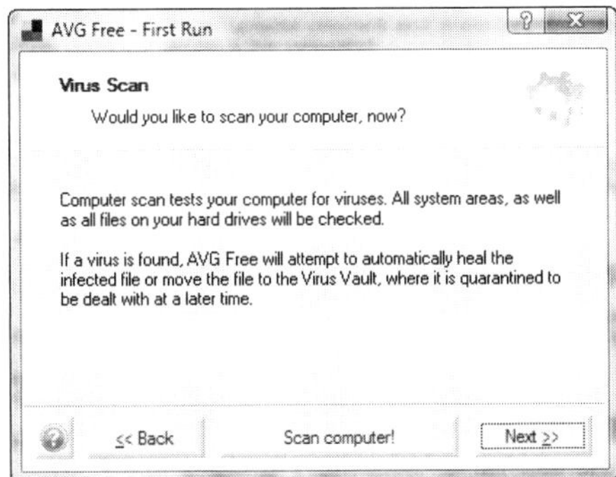

When you're done, the antivirus program's main window, shown in Figure 11.22, remains on the desktop. You can close it now; the antivirus program will remain in memory to watch for any incoming viruses.

FIGURE 11.22

AVG's main program window

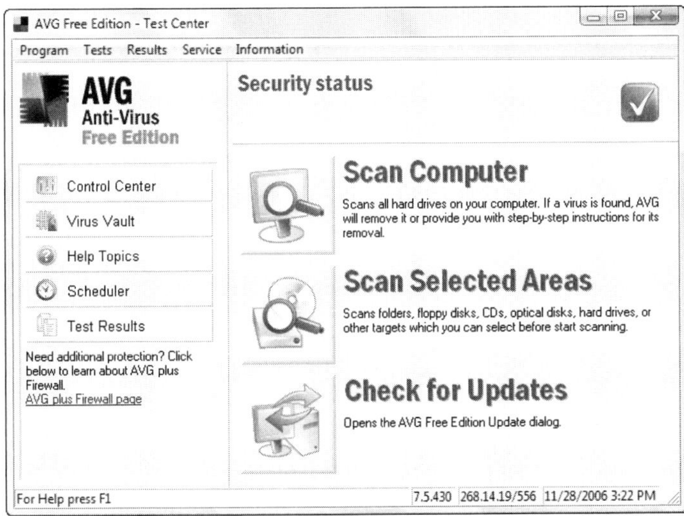

Other antivirus programs have similar installation routines. Whether you go with a downloadable free-for-personal-use program like AVG Free Edition or a commercial product in a box, be sure to equip your system with an antivirus program to protect it at all times.

Lock the operating system

Windows Vista can "lock" itself, requiring your account's password to get back in. In this regard, it's similar to the old-style Windows NT operating systems that power-users of yore will remember.

By default, when Windows Vista shows its screensaver, when you wake it up it'll display the login screen. You'll have to enter your password to regain access to the operating system. That state is called Windows being *locked*; you can lock it manually, too.

Get in the habit of locking Windows before you leave your desk, if you're in a place where other people might try to gain access to your computer.

Click the Start button and look for the little picture of a padlock on the bottom of the Start Menu (Figure 11.23). Click it to lock the computer. No one can use it anymore without a password.

FIGURE 11.23

Use the little padlock to lock the computer.

Lock the door

Of course, one way to secure your computer from intrusion has nothing to do with Windows features at all. If you don't want anyone gaining access to your computer, lock it up — physically!

Keep your computer in a room with a locking door. If you're in an office environment, lock your office door when you walk away. If it's a notebook computer, take it with you. Without physical access to a computer, nobody can gain access to it except through a network. You've read this chapter; you know how to protect Windows Vista from Internet attacks. Keep it safe from physical intrusions, too!

Summary

About a decade ago, I challenged a hacker to break into my little home computer. I was running Windows 95 with no third-party security features at all, but I thought hackers were full of baloney when they claimed to be able to breach Web-connected systems.

All he wanted was my cable modem's IP address. I gave it to him, left my system logged into the Internet, and went to bed; when I woke up there was a text file in the middle of my desktop with a message from him. It contained information he got from documents on my PC and from public record.

I've taken security much more seriously since then. Had he not been a friend, he could have taken steps to ruin my computer, or my life.

You should take security as seriously as I learned to that day. Your computer is vulnerable, and if it's Internet-connected then people do want to break into it — perhaps not your computer specifically, but *any* unsecured computer on the Net.

Even users of your computer whom you trust shouldn't necessarily have full access to every facet of your computer. User Account Control helps you keep users from sticking their noses where they don't belong; when they try to open Device Manager and find that they can't without a password, they'll know better than to try again.

Windows Vista's built-in security features are numerous and powerful, and they keep your data safe the best they can. You, too, have to take some responsibility and develop strong security habits. Between you and Windows Vista, your data should be as safe as if it were locked up in a titanium file cabinet.

Part IV

Networking and the Internet

A computer by itself is useful and powerful, but a computer connected to other PCs and the Internet can be a tool for nothing less than world domination. That might be an exaggeration, but networking and Internet connectivity are certainly very important parts of modern computing, enhancing the experience innumerably.

You'll learn how to build a home network in Part IV. It's easier than you think. With wireless networking equipment, you can connect every computer in your house without running cables all over the place. This part also introduces you to Windows Vista's Internet applications, including its rendition of Internet Explorer.

IN THIS PART

Chapter 12

Building a Home Network

IN THIS CHAPTER

- Networking computers together
- Acquiring the necessary hardware
- Connecting the computers
- Setting up Windows Vista for networking

You have 20GB of music files on one computer, a folder system full of family photos and videos on another, and a few games that simply demand to be played in multiplayer mode with opponents at different computers. One of your computers is connected to the entertainment center. Another is in the office. Of course, your laptop is wherever you last left it, which could be anywhere, and you wish you would take better care of it because it cost a fortune.

You want to be able to view those images and videos on the television.

You want to listen to that music wherever you please.

You're dying to school your siblings or children at some of those games.

These situations, my friend, call for a network. A home network is easy to establish, especially with wireless networking within financial reach of anyone who can afford a computer. Laying the necessary foundation for a network no longer involves running unsightly cables all over the house, or snaking them through the spider-filled gaps between the walls.

The software side of network construction has never been easier, thanks to Windows Vista. You can set up the network in minutes after you get the necessary hardware installed and configured. Vista works perfectly with wired and wireless networks, and it immediately recognizes those magical little boxes known as wireless routers.

Networking opens the doors to all kinds of things that make computing more efficient and enjoyable. With a network, you share an Internet connection with ease. You can designate one hard drive as the backup drive and avoid the need to have to back up individual computers on a regular basis. You can share multimedia all over the place. You can game until late in the night, diverting your attention from less important things like paying bills, making work deadlines, and sleeping.

This chapter helps you get started in creating your own home network the Vista way. Windows Vista is primed and ready for wireless networking on both desktop and portable PCs. Its Network Center makes it a snap to use and to monitor a network. Security features keep your network safe from computers that might be infected with various viruses.

After you've established a wireless network, adding computers to it is easy. Wireless networks are completely modular, so you can drop a new PC into the kids' room, the basement, or somewhere else, and provided it's in range of your network's access point or router, all you have to do is run a wizard and it'll become part of the network as if it had been there from the beginning.

If you're worried about the cost of networking, don't be. High-speed routers with Internet sharing built in are well under $100 (heck, the cheaper ones are under $50), and wireless networking adapter cards for the PCs cost even less. A great number of notebook computers come with wireless networking built right in, and you can fit those that don't with a PC Card (also known as PCMCIA) adapter to make portable networking a cinch.

The Windows Vista networking wizard takes all the guesswork out of configuring your computers. With it, you don't need to know the jargon-filled, technical side of the equation. Leave IP address, subnets, DHCP, and all that wacky stuff to your router and to Windows Vista. Of course, Vista gives power users the option to tweak and mold networks however they see fit. Beyond the wizards lies every setting a tweaker could want to tweak.

Introduction to Networking

All kinds of definitions exist for the concept of computer networking. Mine is simple. *Networking* is the act of getting computer A to talk to computer B (and computers C, D, and E if applicable).

This definition is pretty broad, but think about it. Networking causes computers to communicate with each other. Any number of reasons exist for why someone would want to get computers to do that. Most of them involve access to the same files from multiple computers. Sharing resources, like printers, is another big advantage. I've probably set up more than 100 networks for homes and small businesses alike. In almost every case, the users wanted to do something along those lines.

Most offices for which I built networks wanted shared access to data. Many offices use one or more database programs that simultaneously track inventory, pricing, revenue, debits, and so on, and everyone from the boss to the warehouse team needs access to this information. Offices also want to protect their data through regular backups, which is easier when the data are all saved on a file server — so they only have one machine to back up. Some offices invest in massive printers that handle documents in more ways than you probably realized was possible, and of course they only want to have to pay for one of those five-figure expenses; everybody shares the printer through a network.

Even network gaming basically involves moving data between a bunch of networked computers. One usually acts as a server and does most of the data crunching, and the other machines are clients through which players participate. The server shares data with the clients as needed, to tell them what's going on in the game and what effects their input is having.

NOTE **The Internet itself is a massive, global computer network. Web servers, FTP servers, and other places that you surf to all share data with your computer. They send, at your computer's request, Web pages, RSS feeds, files, and so on.**

Setting up a simple, home network has two sides: the hardware side and the software side. The hardware side involves procuring, installing, and configuring various equipment, such as a router and network adapter cards. The software side involves telling the operating system — Windows Vista — how to use the hardware and which files and resources to share across the network.

If it sounds simple, well, thanks to Windows Vista and some relatively recent networking standards, the process is easier than it ever has been.

If you're setting up your first home network, I strongly suggest you go with a wireless solution. Running cables through a house is not fun, and, with current wireless security, there's really no reason to do it.

Why go wireless?

Why not?

There are, of course, advantages and disadvantages to using a wireless solution versus going with a wired solution. Take a look at Table 12.1. The convenience of wireless networking clearly outweighs the hassles of wiring your house. Unless all of your computers are in the same room, you'll have to either run cables down corridors or through walls to connect the PCs.

TABLE 12.1

Wireless Networking Versus Wired Networking

Issue	Wireless	Wired
Connecting computers	Little if any wiring necessary	Every computer needs its own cable from a centralized hub
Hardware needed	Optional (but strongly suggested) router or access point; adapters for each computer	Centralized hub, switch, or router; adapters for each computer (but they're often built in); Category 5 (6 if you're planning on using Gigabit Ethernet) cables to connect to each PC; wall plates, boxes, and other hardware if you choose to run cable through the walls

continued

TABLE 12.1 *(continued)*

Issue	Wireless	Wired
Hardware cost	Network adapters are more expensive than wired equivalents	Switches for high-speed networking can be expensive; network adapter cards are cheap; cables and wall hardware can add up
Ease of installation	Nothing to it	Running cables through walls and terminating them properly can be complicated and require special tools
Ease of adding new computers	Nothing to it	A new cable must be run for each PC
Data transfer rate	54Mbps or less; faster with emerging 802.11n technology (plenty of bandwidth for home networking)	10/100/1000Mbps, depending on how much you're willing to spend
Bandwidth sharing	Yes; wi-fi shares bandwidth among multiple client computers so that 54Mbps becomes 27Mbps per computer for two attached PCs, 18Mbps for three PCs, and so on	No bandwidth sharing at the router level; however, some routers and switches may have maximum throughput ratings. If all the ports are connected, and all the PCs are trying to transfer data at the maximum speed, then no PC will see full network speed
Security	Iffy. Any data transferred through the air can be intercepted, and it's easy for strangers to join a non-secured network; but WPA-2 is a very secure encryption scheme that protects your data	Very secure. Intruder must defeat Web security, or enter your house and connect to your network physically, to access your data
Gaming concerns	Introduces some extra latency	Ideal for gaming
Other considerations	No unsightly cables; no drywall cutting, terminating wires, and installing wall boxes and plates; take your notebook PC anywhere within range of the wireless router/access point	Effectively tethers notebook PCs; cabling is a pain in the neck

Data transfer rates are in Mbps, which stands for ***megabits per second***. The current wireless standard (see the following section) provides more than enough bandwidth for home use. Emerging standards will provide speedier data transfers. Although wired networking can be faster, in day-to-day use you won't notice a difference.

Wired networks are obviously more secure than wireless networks, which send your data scurrying through the air like a radio broadcast. Anyone can intercept it. If you don't take the steps to secure your network, anyone with a wireless computing device who wanders within range of your router can join it. Wired networks are vulnerable through the Internet, should a shared connection exist on the network, but locally the only way to intrude on your network would be to break into your house.

Wireless security has gotten pretty darn secure, however. WPA-2, a security encryption scheme that scrambles the transmissions across your network, is exceedingly difficult to crack. A hacker would have to purposely target your home and put quite a bit of effort into attacking your network in order to succeed, provided you secured your network effectively.

Laptop freedom is a big issue for some people. What's the point of a portable computer in the home if you have to run a network cable to it to get onto the Internet? With a wireless network, you can whip open your laptop, sans cables, and crunch your data wherever you please.

Understanding the wireless standards

Most modern wireless networks conform to a set of standards that ensures that hardware from different brands will work with each other. You've probably heard of IEEE 802.11b, 802.11g, or maybe 802.11n. You may also have heard of and/or seen the label Wi-Fi. Here's what that stuff means.

IEEE stands for Institute of Electrical and Electronic Engineers. This international group creates and ratifies sets of standards for everything from wireless networking to how batteries are made. Without such standards, hardware producers could make any hardware however they pleased, without bothering to ensure that it worked with other hardware. For example, the IEEE 1394 standard defines how "FireWire" works. Any IEEE 1394–compliant device, such as a camcorder, should work with any IEEE 1394–compliant port on a computer. Standards of this nature greatly simplify things for end-users like you and me.

NOTE Without such standards, or when you use hardware that doesn't comply to any known standard, you end up with proprietary stuff that can cause headaches. For example, older scanners sometimes came with their own PC interface cards. You had to install the PC card into an expansion slot (back then, in the pre-PCI days, computers had ISA slots) and then connect the scanner to that card. If the company, for example, stopped making drivers for its scanner card and a new version of Windows came out that didn't support the legacy drivers, your scanner suddenly became a large and expensive paperweight. Similarly, if the scanner card became faulty and replacements weren't available, you couldn't use the scanner anymore.

Now most scanners use USB connectors. USB is a standardized external data bus that will be supported for a very long time. USB 2.0 is backward compatible to the earlier USB 1.1, as well, so your USB 1.1 scanner will still work with a computer that has a USB 2.0 controller.

IEEE 802.11 standards are the IEEE's wireless networking standards. IEEE 802.11 itself is an old, unused standard; 802.11a is rarely seen. 802.11b is the first widely used wireless networking standard, and 802.11g is its follow up. 802.11n is emerging as I write this book; products are already coming out, but the standard has yet to be ratified by the IEEE, so interoperability is in question.

The key difference between those standards is bandwidth. 802.11b transferred data at a maximum of 11Mbps, whereas 802.11g can hit 54Mbps in the right conditions. 802.11n can transfer data at more than 200Mbps.

TIP With wireless technology, a standard's bandwidth rating indicates a maximum data transfer rate; actual rates vary. Various environmental factors can cause the bandwidth to diminish, such as radio interference and increased distance between the networking device and the router.

The IEEE standards are the target of a unified group of wireless network hardware developers called the Wi-Fi Alliance. Wi-Fi stands for Wireless Fidelity, and its branding is intended to ensure that parts built by different manufacturers will work together seamlessly. For example, I can have a Linksys IEEE 802.11g wireless router, a desktop PC with a Netgear IEEE 802.11g network adapter installed, and a notebook computer with a built-in IEEE 802.11b Intel wireless adapter, and they'll all find each other and the Internet provided they're properly configured.

Right now, I use IEEE 802.11g equipment; it all works together. A faster standard, 802.11n, is in the works, promising bandwidth of 5-10x 802.11g. At this point, 802.11n probably won't be final until the end of 2007 or early 2008, but already "pre-N" routers are on the market. Be wary of these, as interoperability may be spotty, but the manufacturers are promising upgrades that will fully comply with the 802.11n standard when it's ratified. 802.11g equipment is inexpensive and more than speedy enough for a home network, but early adopters might demand the performance of 802.11n, regardless of the price and compatibility.

Building a Network: The Hardware Side

To build a home network, you need a few things. First and foremost, you need networking devices: computers, some PDAs, PlayStation Portables, Microsoft Zune MP3 players, and so on are networking devices.

For simplicity's sake, this part of the chapter covers setting up a wireless network of multiple Windows Vista computers. If you want to network in other devices, just read their instructions thoroughly. Provided they recognize Wi-Fi networks, the process shouldn't be too difficult.

Determining what you'll need

The two types of Wi-Fi networks are infrastructure mode networks, which are governed by devices called wireless access points (WAP); and ad-hoc networks, which lack the WAP and therefore some of the security it provides. I strongly suggest that, in a home networking situation, you use a WAP. In fact, if you want to share a broadband Internet connection, the easiest way by far is to use a wireless router (Figure 12.1) that also acts as a WAP.

Besides the wirelessness of it, the router will feature a switch with several ports for traditional cat 5 network cables terminated with RJ45 connectors. One of the computers on the network should connect to the router with a cat 5 cable (Figure 12.2), if only to set the router up. This shouldn't be a problem, considering that most wireless routers come with the necessary cable, and that most computers have Ethernet ports built right onto their motherboards.

FIGURE 12.1

A typical wireless router

FIGURE 12.2

A cat 5 network cable with RJ45 connectors on each end

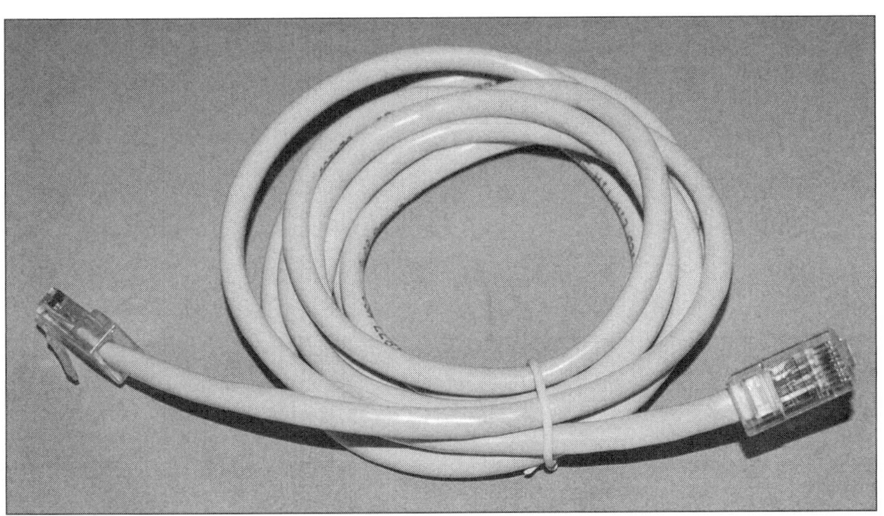

Each computer on the network will require a Wi-Fi compliant wireless networking adapter. You should fit desktop computers with PCI wireless cards, as shown in Figure 12.3.

Notebook computers will need PC Card wireless adapters like the one shown in Figure 12.4.

FIGURE 12.3

A PCI wireless network interface card

Finally, one of your computers will need a wired network interface card, provided none of your PCs has built-in Ethernet.

When you've assembled all this stuff, you're ready to set it up.

Setting up the hardware

To set up the hardware, you need everything that comes in the WAP or router's box, plus whatever tools you need to work on your desktop computers (probably nothing more than a medium-sized Philips head screwdriver).

If you're using a router, you are limited as to where you can put it by where the utility company installed your broadband Internet modem (whether it's cable, DSL, fiber, or whatever you have). You actually have to connect the data port of the broadband device to the specially labeled port on the rear of the router (see Figure 12.5) with a network cable.

FIGURE 12.4

A PC Card (PCMCIA) wireless network adapter

FIGURE 12.5

Connect the broadband modem's data port to this port on the router.

Ideally, the router should be in a central location in your home. If you plan to use a WAP without Internet-sharing capability, you have more freedom of where you can place it. You also need a PC within a network cable's distance from the WAP/router, as you have to configure the WAP/router through a wired connection.

Connect the PC nearest the WAP/router to the WAP/router with a second network cable. You can connect it to any of the RJ45 ports on the rear of the router, other than the one reserved for the broadband modem. See Figure 12.6.

Install the network adapters into each PC you want to join the network. If any of the computers has wireless networking built-in (as is the case, for example, with notebook PCs with Intel Centrino technology), you won't need to install extra equipment.

Then, install the drivers that came with the network adapters per the adapters instructions.

Configuring the router, if necessary

Before you continue, you should take some preliminary steps in setting up the router or WAP. Most routers and WAPs require you to open a browser and navigate to an internal IP address to access their configuration screens. Usually, the address is 192.168.1.1. You need to enter a default password, and possibly a user name, to access the router. You can find the necessary information in the router's instruction manual.

FIGURE 12.6

Connect the nearest computer to the router via one of these ports.

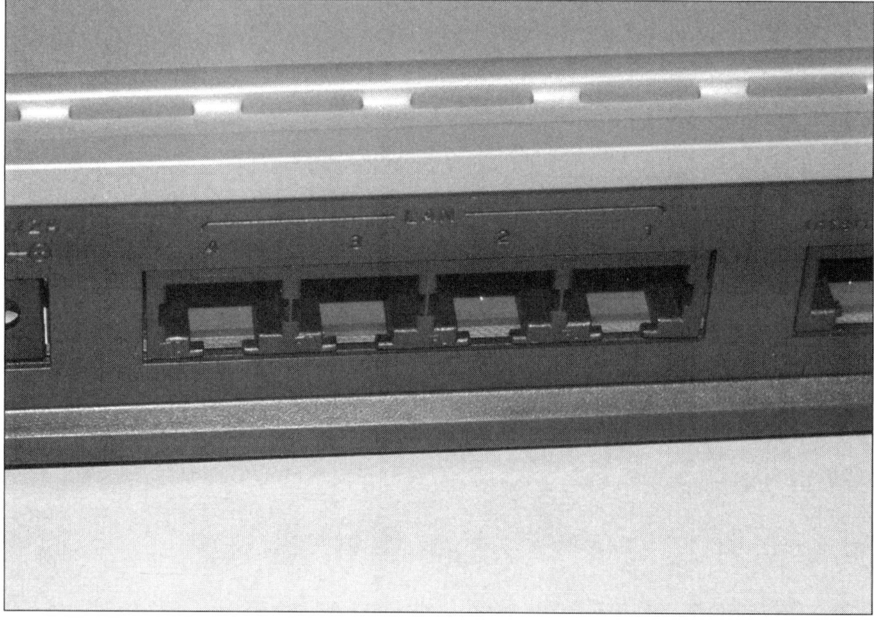

A router's configuration utility might look like the one pictured in Figure 12.7.

FIGURE 12.7

A configuration screen from a Linksys router

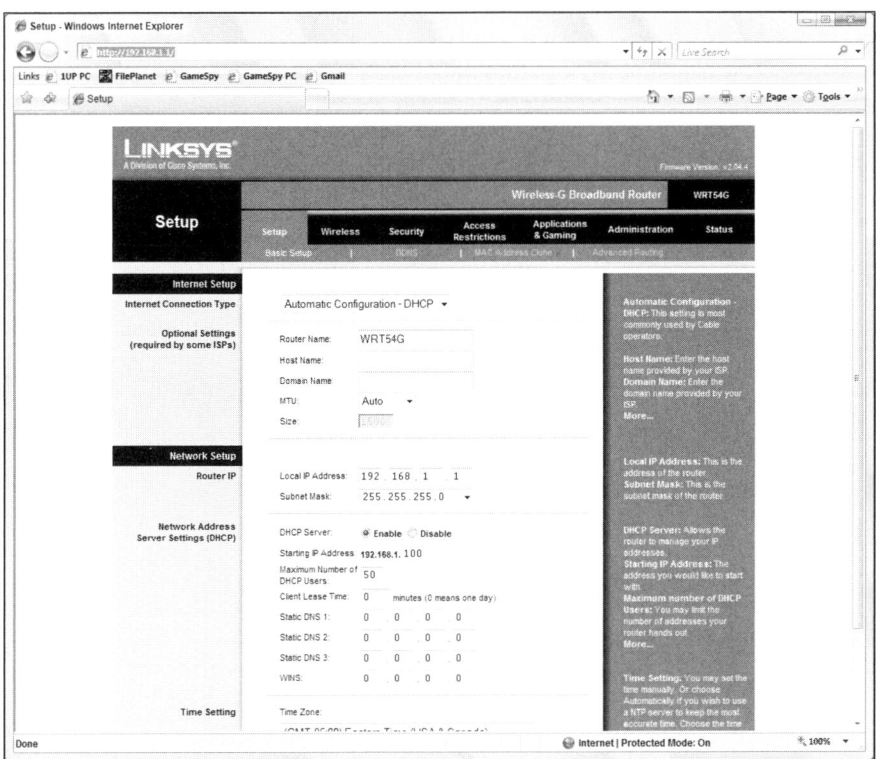

Most routers operate perfectly with the default configuration. Any configuring you'll do will probably have to do with security, but be sure to follow any preliminary instructions in the router's manual.

Setting Up a Network: The Software Side

Next, it's time to tell Windows Vista that you have a network. It may, in fact, automatically detect the network once you connect a computer to the router. You should still verify that the network is set up to your specifications.

Network and Sharing Center

Windows Vista is very good at detecting networks and figuring out what to do with them. Vista will probably find your WAP or router, determine that it has Internet access, and poke around the network for other computers that may or may not be sharing resources.

You can orchestrate its efforts through the Network and Sharing Center. Click the Start button, and click Network to see a window like the one shown in Figure 12.8. Click the Network and Sharing Center to invoke a window like the one shown in Figure 12.9.

Network and Sharing Center is the central repository for Windows Vista's network options. It's here that you can choose whether to share files, folders, and printers across the network; you can configure Internet connections; you can decide whether to require passwords for other people on the network to access your shares; and more.

FIGURE 12.8

The Network screen

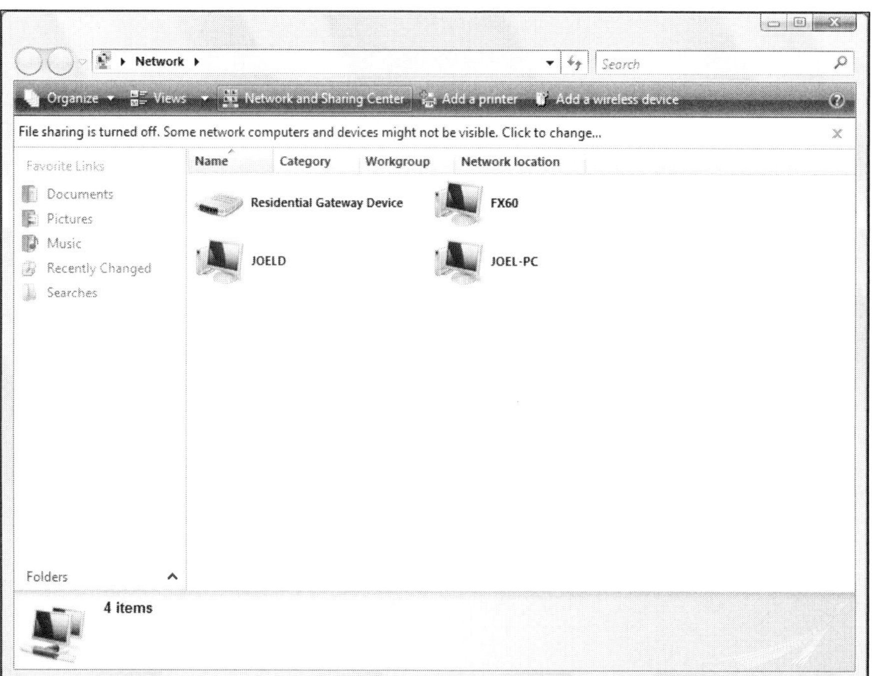

FIGURE 12.9

Network and Sharing Center

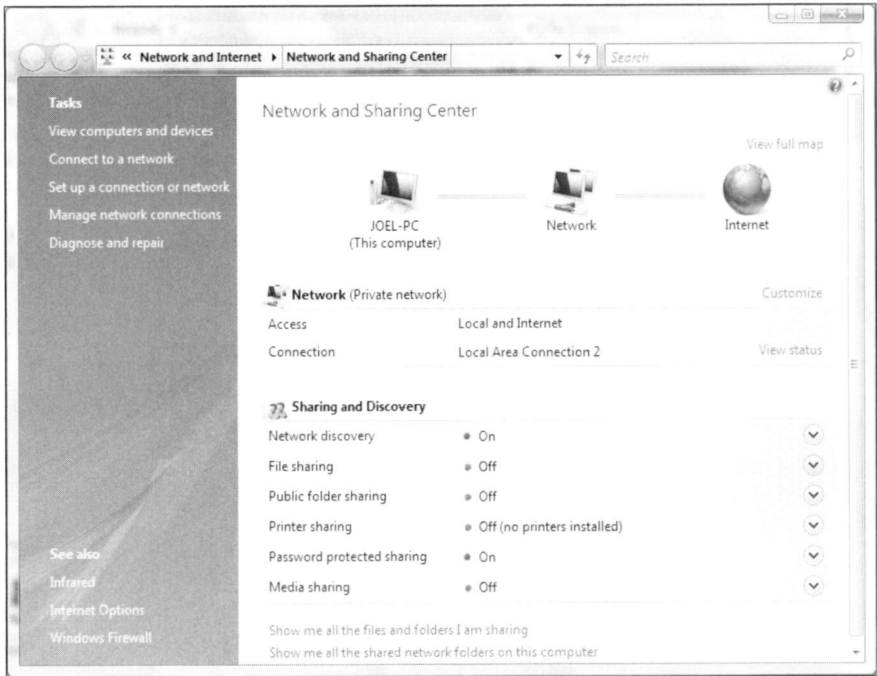

First, note the list at the bottom of the window. Its items include:

- **Network discovery:** Turn this option on for Windows Vista to sense networks automatically. This option also controls whether other computers can see your PC, and whether your PC can see other computers and resources on the network.
- **File sharing:** If you turn this option on, you can share files and folders with other computers on the network. With it off, none of your data are available to other PCs.
- **Public folder sharing:** Public folders are folders accessible to all users of a particular computer. You can elect to share them across the network in two ways: allowing others to open and read files; or allowing others to open, read, save, overwrite, delete, and otherwise have full file access to public folders. Turning it off hides your computer's public folders.
- **Printer sharing:** If printers are connected to your PC, you can share them across the network.

- **Password protected sharing:** When this option is on, only people with a user account and password on this particular computer can gain access to any of the items shared on the network. With it off, anyone on the network can access files.
- **Media sharing:** This option allows you to share movies, music, and other media files on the network. With it turned off, such files are off limits.

Below this list of options are two links. The first is called Show me all the files and folders I am sharing. If you click it, a list appears like the one shown in Figure 12.10.

This option presents all the files you're sharing on the network. The second option, Show me all the shared folders on this computer, shows a similar list (Figure 12.11) with only the folders you're sharing displayed.

FIGURE 12.10

A list of shared files

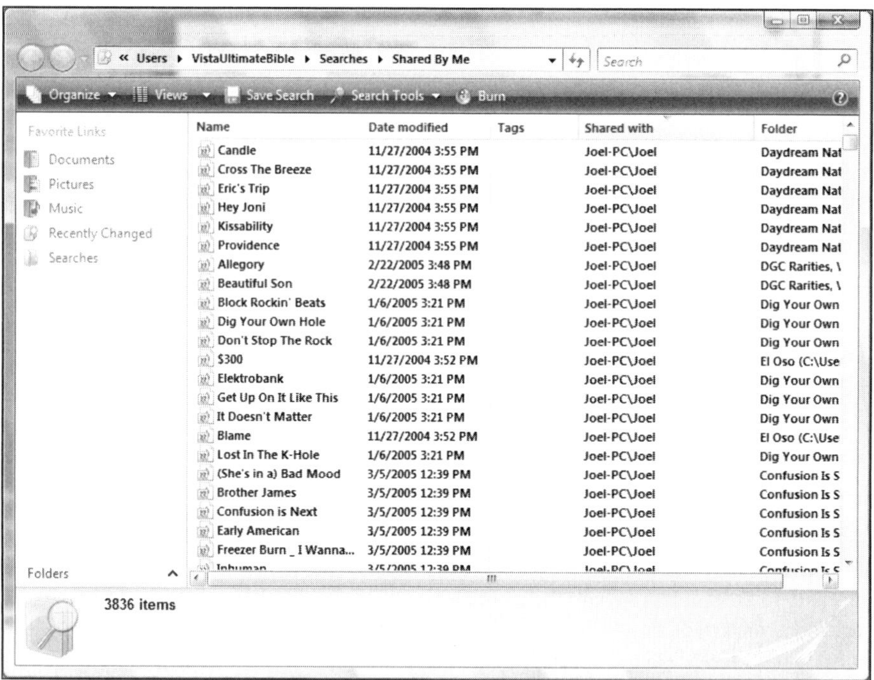

FIGURE 12.11

A list of shared folders

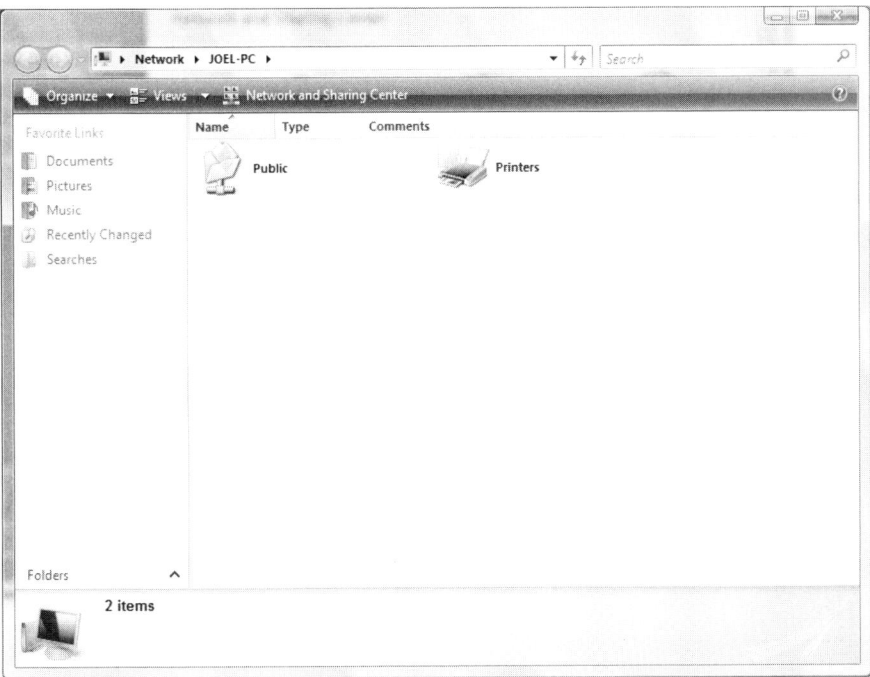

Now turn your attention to the links along the left of the Network and Sharing Center window. They are:

- **View computers and devices:** This option shows everything you can see on the network, including computers, printers, and other shares, in a window like the one shown in Figure 12.8.
- **Connect to a network:** Use this link to cause Windows Vista to look for networks to connect to. If you're already connected, a screen appears like the one shown in Figure 12.12.
- **Set up a connection or a network:** This option allows you to set up Internet or other network connections, should Windows not set them up automatically. See the following section for more information.
- **Manage network connections:** This option invokes a window that shows every network connection on the computer and its current status.
- **Diagnose and repair:** If a problem occurs, Windows will try to fix it when you click this link. If it can't find any problems, a window appears like the one shown in Figure 12.13.

FIGURE 12.12

It appears you're already connected to a network!

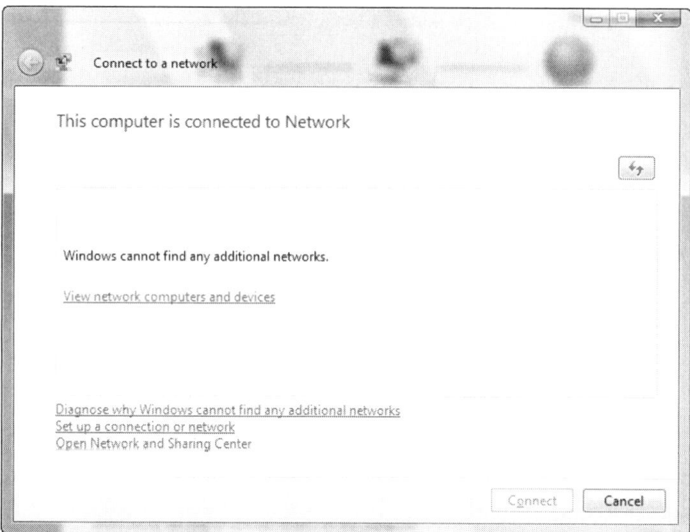

FIGURE 12.13

All systems go!

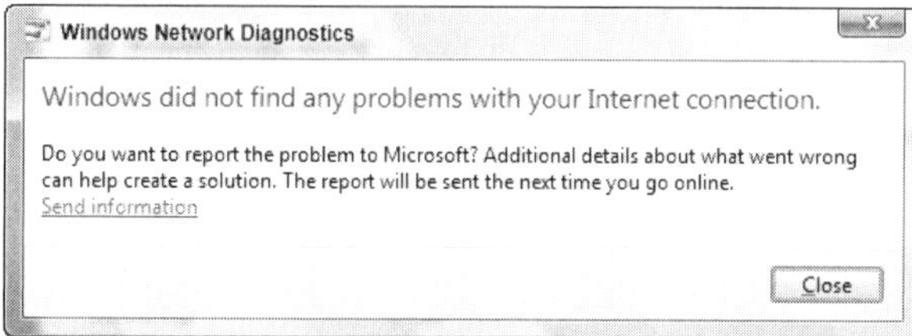

Setting up a connection or a network

Windows Vista includes a batch of wizards that help you set up networks and networking features in seconds rather than hours. Whereas in times past, setting up a network involved rolling up your sleeves and making a whole lot of manual configuration changes just to get a few PCs to recognize each other, Vista has made it so simple you don't even need to know what an IP address is.

NOTE In case you're wondering, IP stands for Internet Protocol. It's a networking protocol, which is a set of standards for transmitting information throughout a network. A routing protocol sends data to the particular computers that need it (rather than blast it to every computer on the network, as non-routing protocols do) and requires each computer on the network to have its own address: an IP address.

In most cases, a computer can receive an IP address automatically from a router or another computer on the network. You don't need to configure IP addresses. Large business networks might require someone to assign and regulate IP addresses, but small home networks work well with dynamically assigned IP addresses.

Note that two major categories of IP addresses exist: private (IP addresses relative to your local area network [LAN]) and public. Private IP addresses tell local computers how to communicate with each other, and public IP addresses allow data communication on the 'Net. Typically, a small network has a single public IP address, which your ISP assigns to your cable or DSL modem. Each computer or other device in your network has a private IP address. Network address translation (NAT) in a router or firewall routes data to and from the Internet between private and public IP addresses as needed.

IP addresses consist of four "octets" of numbers, each between 0 and 255. A typical public IP address might be 68.191.46.102 or something like that. Private IP addresses on small networks almost always start with either 192.168.x.x (used by most wireless routers and WAPs by default), 172.16.x.x through 172.31.x.x, and 10.x.x.x.

To see the wizards that Windows Vista offers, open the Network and Sharing Center and click Set up a connection or a network. A window like the one shown in Figure 12.14 appears.

FIGURE 12.14

Various networking setup wizards

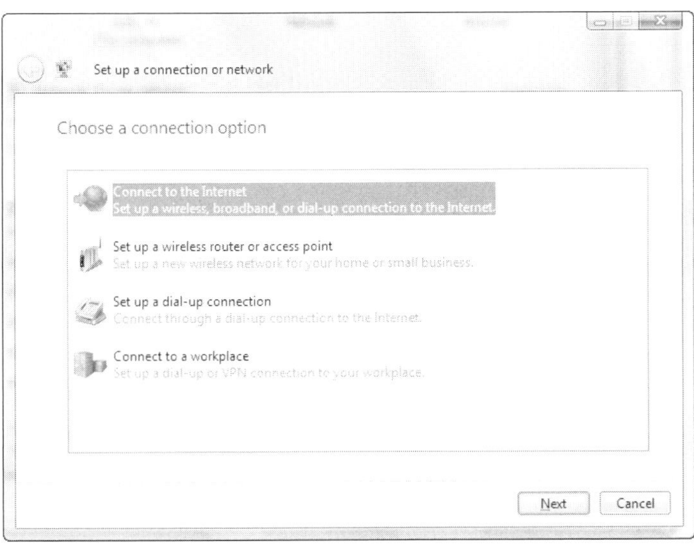

This window enables you to invoke one of four wizards to accomplish different networking tasks:

- **Connect to the Internet:** This option runs a wizard that helps you seek out an Internet connection from the PC on which you're working. It looks for a wireless Internet connection or a locally connected broadband connection, or enables you to set up a dialup connection.

This option is handy, for example, when you roll out of town with a laptop that's normally part of your home network and need to access a dialup account in some backwater hotel that doesn't have high-speed Internet access.

- **Set up a wireless router or access point:** This option lets you configure a compatible router or access point right from Windows Vista. It also helps you set up wireless networking in your home. You should only need to run this option if Windows Vista doesn't automatically detect your network.
- **Set up a dialup connection:** Use this option to create a dialup Internet connection.
- **Connect to a workplace:** Sometimes, you may have to join a private network from home. Telecommuters and other work-from-home types often need their PCs to become part of a network via the Internet through something called virtual private networking (VPN). VPN is basically a LAN-type network that can take place over the Internet, and only people with access credentials can join the network. When you click the Connect to a workplace option, a window appears like that shown in Figure 12.15. You can connect to a VPN through the Internet or dial in to it. You'll have to get the login credentials from the network administrator of the VPN you want to join.

FIGURE 12.15

Joining a VPN

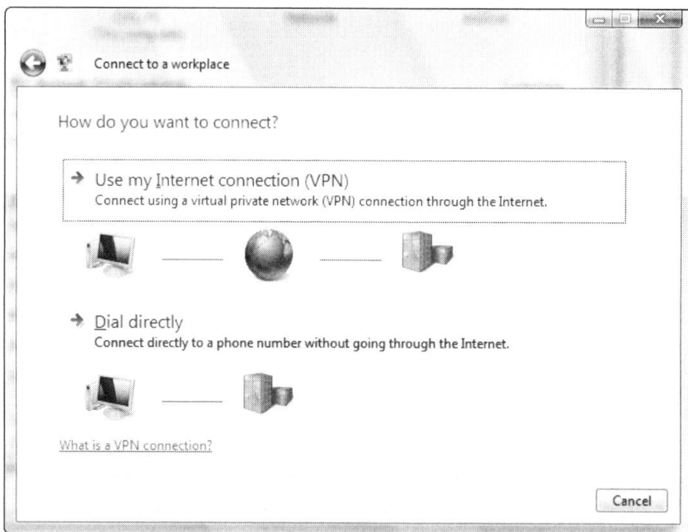

Wireless Network Security

A wireless network is only as secure as the steps you take to secure it. That sounds obvious, but you wouldn't believe the number of people who set up wireless networks and leave all the settings at their defaults.

An Example of Why Wireless Security Is Important

There are a lot of houses around where I live.

I've always been something of an early adopter. When cable modem service first came to my area, I was a beta tester. When Wi-Fi networking became widely available, I did away with the wires traversing the hallways of my home and set up a reasonably secure wireless LAN.

Recently, my wireless router froze up. It simply and suddenly died. Before I became aware of that, I fired up my Wi-Fi–equipped laptop computer and puzzled over why it spent so long looking for its network. It couldn't find *my* network's SSID, but it did find a bunch of other SSIDs.

Out of curiosity, I joined a few of these insecure networks. All of them had shared, broadband Internet access. I "borrowed" somebody's onramp to download diagnostics for my own network, and then I became curious.

I opened up the network browser on my Windows XP laptop and looked around. Most of the wireless networks I had found lacked any shares, but one of them had several folders open and unprotected. They weren't even password protected; they were flapping in the breeze.

Within one of the folders I found *Quicken* account data (which I didn't open); in another I discovered several versions of a resume (which I didn't read). A third, shared folder revealed hundreds of digital photographs (which I didn't view). Poking about some more, I found a shared printer.

Being a good Samaritan, I typed out a note to the effect of: "Hello, I must be your neighbor. I noticed you have a wireless network that's not terribly secure." I included numbered instructions on how to enable WPA protection and how to change the SSID, and stop broadcasting it.

A few days later, after I'd replaced my network's wireless router and forgotten the whole incident, I was outside when a neighbor approached me waving a piece of paper. He asked, "Did you do this?"

It was a copy of the security instructions. We had a good laugh and he thanked me.

It might not have worked out so well. Had the intruder on my neighbor's network not been such a fine upstanding gentleman, he could have stolen all of the *Quicken* data, sabotaged important documents like the resume files, and swiped a bunch of what I assume were private pictures taken by my neighbor and his family. The intruder could have used those files for all kinds of nefarious purposes I don't even like to think about.

If you have a wireless network, don't depend on the kindness of intruding strangers to help you secure it. You don't want to wake up one morning without any money in your bank account, or with a host of files gone from your computer, or with a warrant out for "your" arrest after your identity had been used by a perpetrator of a crime. Sure, those are extreme examples of what someone with access to your network could do, but is it worth the risk? Secure that network.

It's a new game the kids are all playing: Wardriving. That's when someone takes a wireless device, such as a notebook computer with Wi-Fi capability, and cruises through neighborhoods looking for wireless networks to break into. Once inside, they do whatever they please: steal files from unprotected shares, delete things, sabotage the WAP or router, and so on. Some people, unfortunately, make successful wardriving painfully easy by failing to secure their wireless networks.

In fact, I can go wardriving without leaving my house. If I instruct one of my computers to search for wireless networks, several unsecured networks appear. That means homes within range of my own house have unprotected wireless networks. I'm not so devious as to hunt for shares or borrow their Internet connections (called "leeching"), but it goes to show that unprotected wireless networks are all over the place.

Take steps to protect yours from wardrivers, leeches, and snoops. Wireless network safeguards have come a long way in just a few years, with a second-generation encryption technology in place and several other countermeasures that you can enable to keep your files safe.

Changing the password

The first thing you should do when you log in to your WAP or router is change its default administrator password. Don't get this confused with any Windows Vista passwords; I'm talking about the password you enter when you use a browser to navigate to the router's IP address.

NOTE If you don't change the router's password, you're basically allowing anyone with knowledge of wireless networks to waltz in and take over your router. Hackers and wardrivers usually have lists of default passwords for various router brands and model numbers. Sometimes the default router password is painfully simple to guess: It could be something as insecure as *admin.* If someone else figures out your router's password, he can enter your router's Settings menu and change anything he wants, locking you out in the process.

Navigate to the screen in your router's setup pages where you can change the password. It'll look something like the screen shown in Figure 12.16.

Make the password something easy to remember but hard for anyone else to guess.

CROSS-REF For tips on creating passwords, flip back to Chapter 11.

After you've set the password, save the changes. Then, don't forget the password. Every time you want to log in to the router, you'll need that password. Make sure it doesn't fall into untrustworthy hands.

Changing the SSID and not broadcasting it

SSID stands for Secure Station Identifier. It is, more or less, your router's name. When your computer detects wireless networks, the first thing shown on the detection screen is the SSID of the network.

Navigate to the screen that shows the SSID of your router as instructed by the router's manual, and change it. Changing the SSID forces any snoops to have to guess the name of your router. The screen on which you change the SSID might look something like that in Figure 12.17.

FIGURE 12.16

You can change the router's password in a screen like this one.

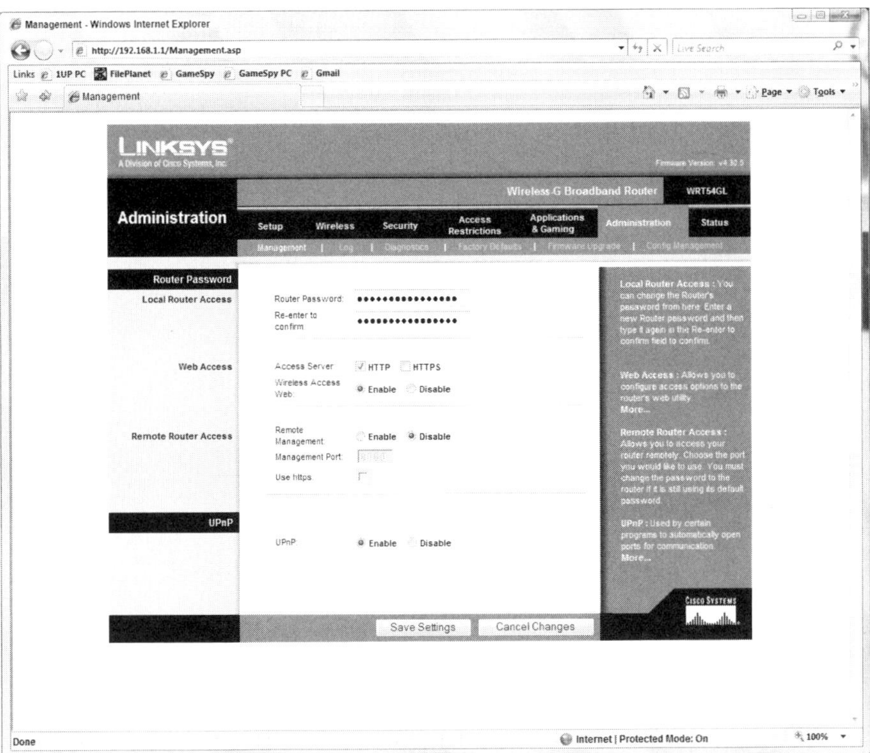

The SSID need not be as ridiculously secure as a password should be, but it shouldn't be something really easy for anyone to guess (like your dog's name).

Changing the SSID won't do a thing if your router broadcasts the new name to everyone who gets within range. You should also see an option on the SSID screen, or on a nearby screen, to disable the SSID broadcast.

Without a broadcasted SSID, nobody can detect your wireless router unless he or she already knows the SSID. It's not floating around the ether to be picked up by any PDA that drives by. With a newly secure SSID and with broadcasting turned off, your router is already relatively secure. The next step protects the integrity of your network's data.

Securing your network's transmissions

Long ago in computer time, which means just a few years ago in real people time, a wireless encryption scheme called WEP existed. WEP stands for Wired Equivalent Privacy, but as easy as it turned out WEP was to crack, it might have been called Without Encryption Protection or Wardriver's Entry Path. It didn't work. It was weak, it was flawed, and it was in need of a replacement.

The industry scrambled to make WPA (Wi-Fi Protected Access) available. Meanwhile, the IEEE continued working on a security standard called 802.11i. That, in essence, has become WPA2, and it's the one I suggest you use.

Navigate to the wireless security page in your router's setup interface. It might look something like the page shown in Figure 12.18.

Different flavors of WPA are available. The most secure is TKIP, which stands for temporal key integrity protocol, which just means it changes its encryption key at regular intervals. This feature makes WPA almost impossible to hack.

Select WPA2-TKIP (if your router doesn't support it, use WPA, *not* WEP), following which you'll have to enter a password of some sort. Make it long and strong, and remember what it is because you also have to enter it on each of the wireless computers or other devices on your network.

FIGURE 12.17

Change the SSID at a screen like this one. Note that the SSID is blurred. Sorry, wardrivers!

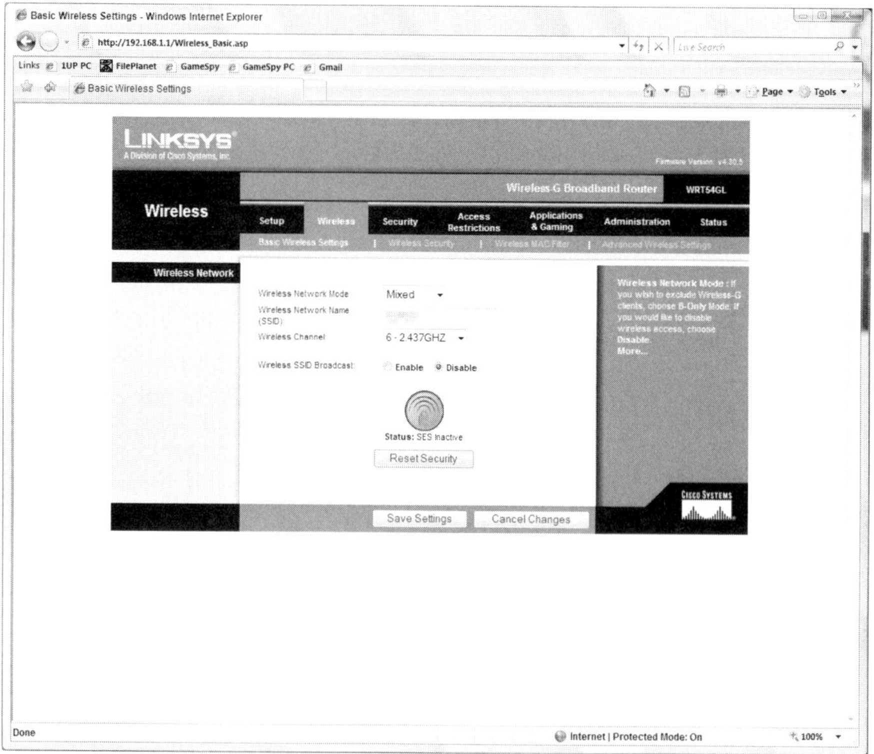

FIGURE 12.18

The security page

After you've changed the SSID, ceased its broadcast, and encrypted your network's transmissions, you have to go around to each computer or wireless device and set it up accordingly, instructing it as to the new SSID and the security password.

NOTE **For each computer on which you installed a wireless network adapter, you'll have to find out how to enter the SSID security password through the adapter's driver protocols. Different adapter drivers have different interfaces, so determining how, exactly, to get your wireless computers to work with your secured network is up to you. Make sure you enter the password exactly as you entered it in your router's setup interface or it won't work.**

With a private SSID and WPA or WPA2, your network is not impregnable. It's simply not worth the time for the average, casual wardriver to bother with it. If someone targets you, specifically, and decides to hack your network to pieces, she might find a way in. With these security measures, however, your network will be hard enough to crack that it'll be quite the challenge for anyone to steal your files or sabotage your network via its wireless router.

Network Activities

So you have a network. What do you do with it?

You can make life easier via a network in a number of ways. You can share stuff on a networked computer's hard drive with other computers on the network; you can share some peripherals, especially printers; you can make music and movies on your computer available for anyone else on the network; you can play network games; and more!

Sharing files and folders

I wouldn't be nearly as productive without my home computer network. I have several test computers, a main desktop PC where I do most of my writing, and my wife and I each have notebook PCs that enable us, thanks to my Wi-Fi network, to work anywhere in the house.

Because I work on a whole bunch of different projects, I need access to them from each of my computers. You might want to do the same. The way to make it happen is to share them across the network.

To share files, you must first enable file sharing. To do that, follow these steps:

1. **Open the Network and Sharing Center.**
2. **Look for the File Sharing option and click it.** The window should look like the one shown in Figure 12.19.
3. **Turn sharing on by clicking the radio button next to Turn on File Sharing and clicking Apply.**
4. **Close the Network and Sharing Center.**

Setting up shares

After you've turned on file sharing, you have to actually share files and/or folders. To do so, navigate through the file system to the file or folder you want to share.

When you find the file or folder you want to share, right-click it and click Share, or highlight it and click the Share button on the toolbar.

As an example, I'll follow these steps to share the folder that my Doom 3 files are in:

1. **Click Start.**
2. **Click Computer** (Figure 12.20).

FIGURE 12.19

Turn on File Sharing in the Network and Sharing Center.

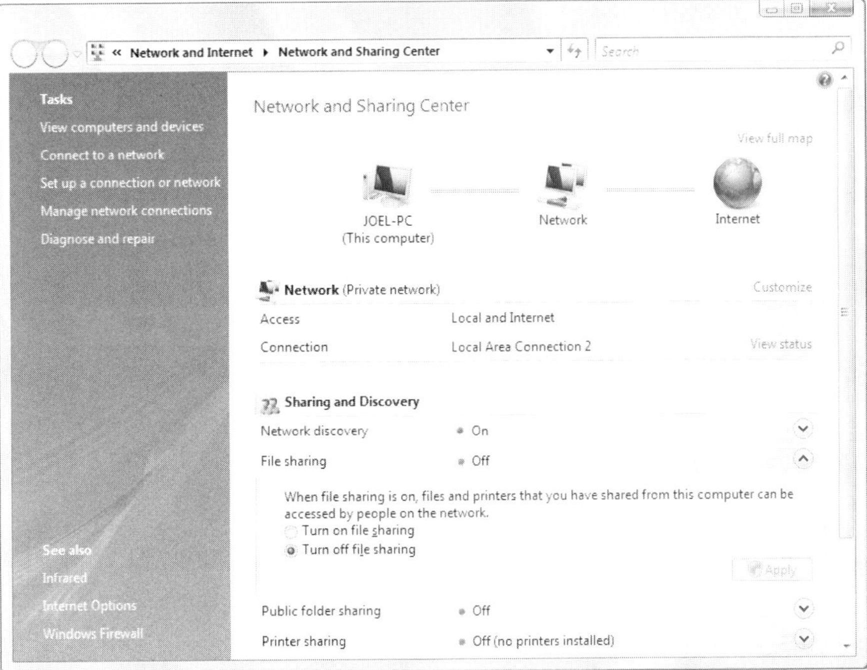

3. Double-click the C: drive and then double-click **Program Files** (Figure 12.21).
4. Locate the C:\DOOM 3 folder.

FIGURE 12.20

The Computer window

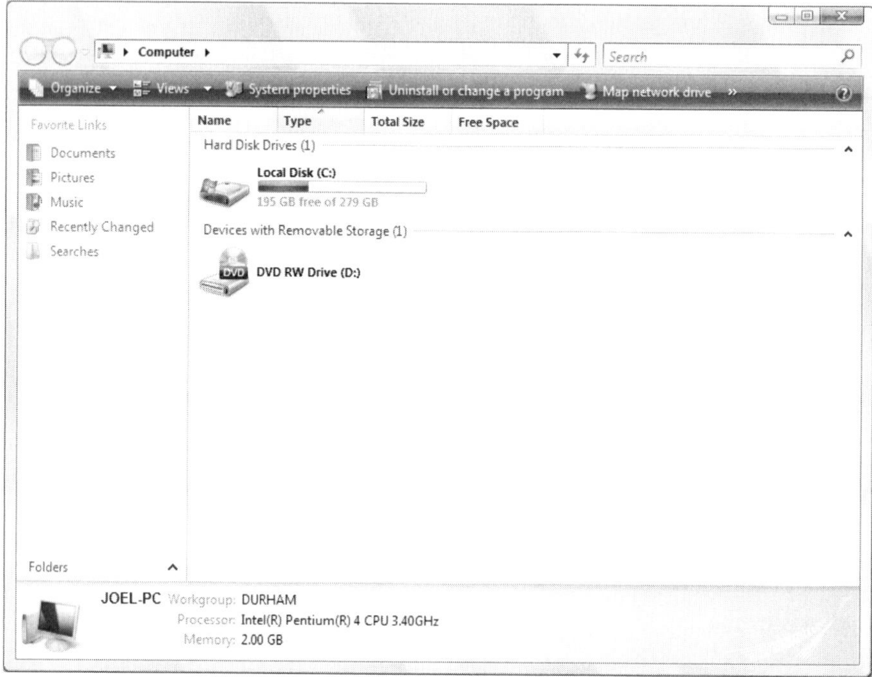

FIGURE 12.21

The DOOM 3 folder is in Program Files.

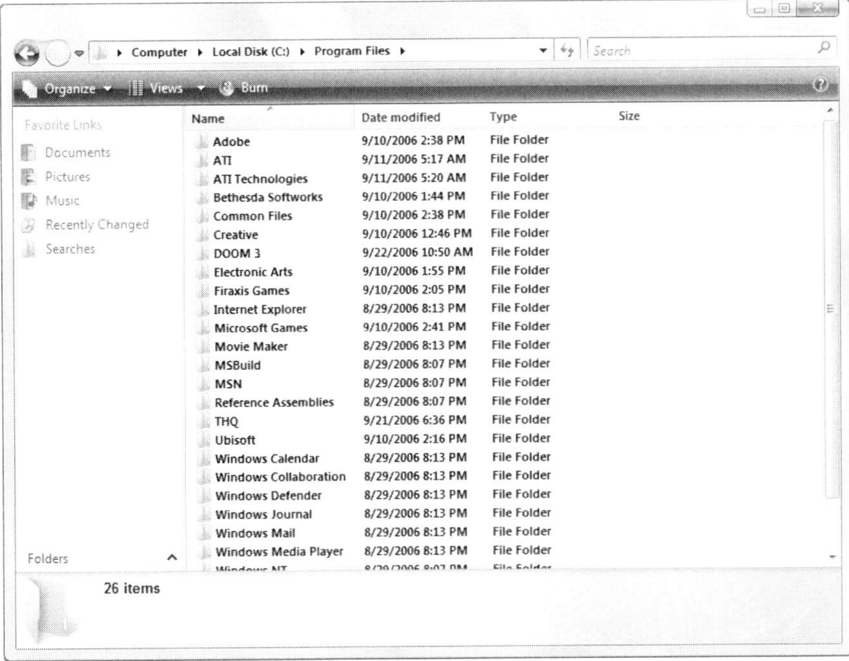

5. **Highlight it (click on it once) and click the toolbar's Share button** (Figure 12.22).
6. **Click Advanced Sharing** (Figure 12.23).

FIGURE 12.22

Sharing properties for the DOOM 3 folder

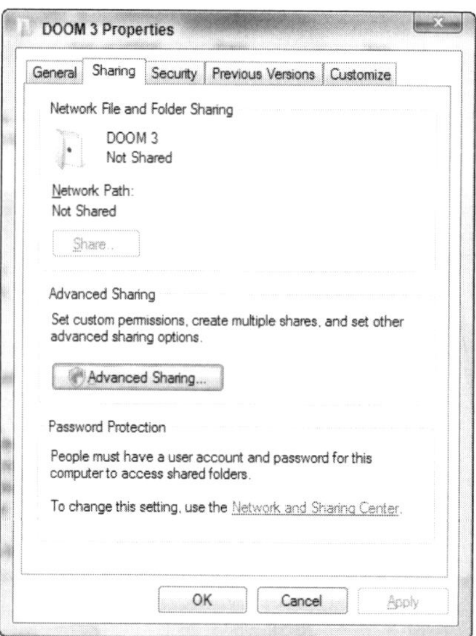

FIGURE 12.23

Preparing to share the folder

7. Click the Share this folder check box to select it.
8. Click OK.

I can now access the DOOM 3 folder from a different computer, provided I have a user name and password of an account on this PC. I have Password Protected Sharing turned on; if I wanted anyone with network access to be able to access my DOOM 3 folder, I could turn off Password Protected Sharing through the Sharing and Security Center.

Assigning permissions

I can control what different individuals are allowed to do with my files and folders. If I return to Step 6 (Figure 12.23), I can click on the Permissions button and decide who, exactly, can do what to this folder.

When I click the Permissions button, a Permissions window like that shown in Figure 12.24 appears. I can tweak the users who have permission to share this folder (right now Everyone — a user group that includes all users with network access — has access to it), and I can tweak their access levels. I can allow or deny full control (the ability to do anything they want in the shared folder), change control (the ability to change files), or read access (the ability to read files, but not to change anything).

I can also add users to the list. Click Add to invoke the Select Users or Groups window shown in Figure 12.25. Then, type in the user whose permissions you want to tweak. (I typed in VistaUltimateBible.)

FIGURE 12.24

This is the Permissions window for the DOOM 3 folder.

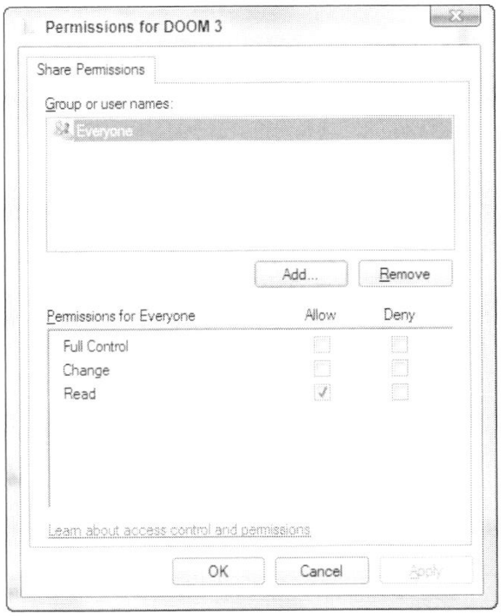

FIGURE 12.25

You can add users and tweak their permissions in the Select Users or Groups window.

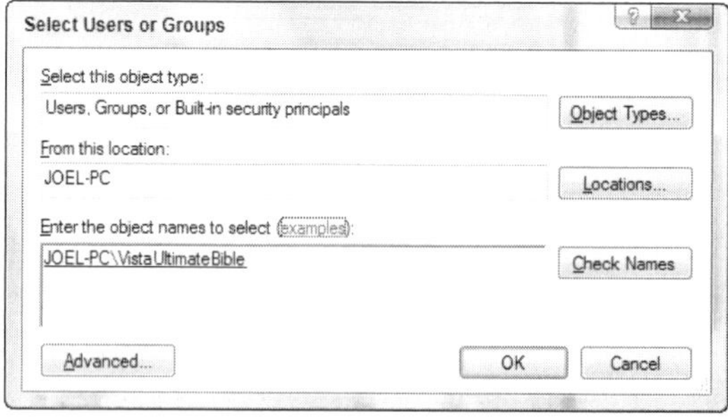

You can tweak permissions in this way for every file and every user. Permissions are a powerful way to customize sharing for your convenience and security.

When I click OK, VistaUltimateBible will be on the list in the permissions view, just beneath Everyone, as shown in Figure 12.26.

Because I happen to be VistaUltimateBible, I want full control over this folder. I click the Full Control check box under Allow. Now, Everyone has read-only access, but I have full access.

FIGURE 12.26

In the Permissions window you can tweak the permissions of multiple users.

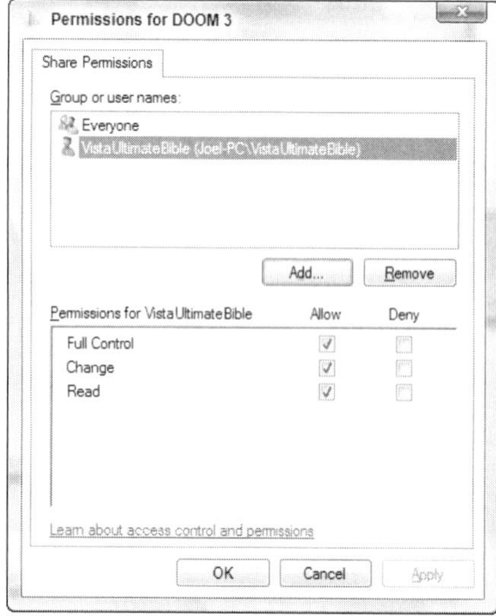

Finding files and printers on the network

Just as I can share files in Windows Vista, I can poke about the network for shared files, folders, and printers.

To do so, choose Start ➪ Network. Various computers on the network in the same workgroup as this computer should appear, as shown in Figure 12.27.

To find a shared file or folder, you can navigate this window just like the file system on your local computer. Double-click the networked computer to display its shares (Figure 12.28). You can then surf through them.

Shared printers also appear in the Network window. You can develop permanent connections to network printers through Control Panel, or by double-clicking the printer in the Network window. Windows Vista will prompt you to install drivers for the printer, and if they're available on the PC that's sharing the printer it'll grab them from there. Otherwise, you'll need the drivers that came with the printer.

After you've established a printer connection in the network, you can print to it any time that it, and the device that's serving it, is on.

FIGURE 12.27

The Network window changes as different computers become available or unavailable on the network.

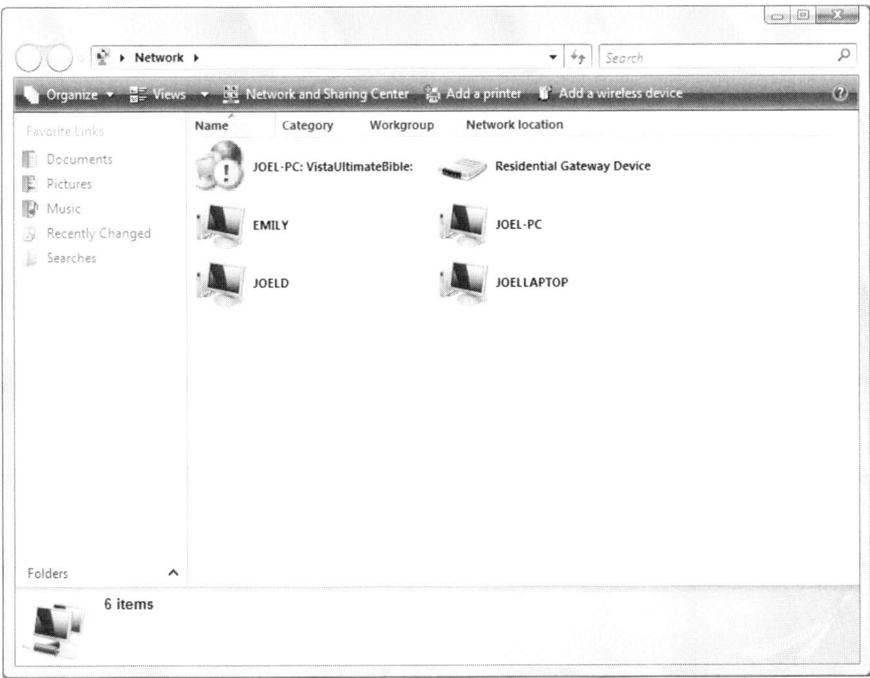

FIGURE 12.28

The shares on one of the computers in the network

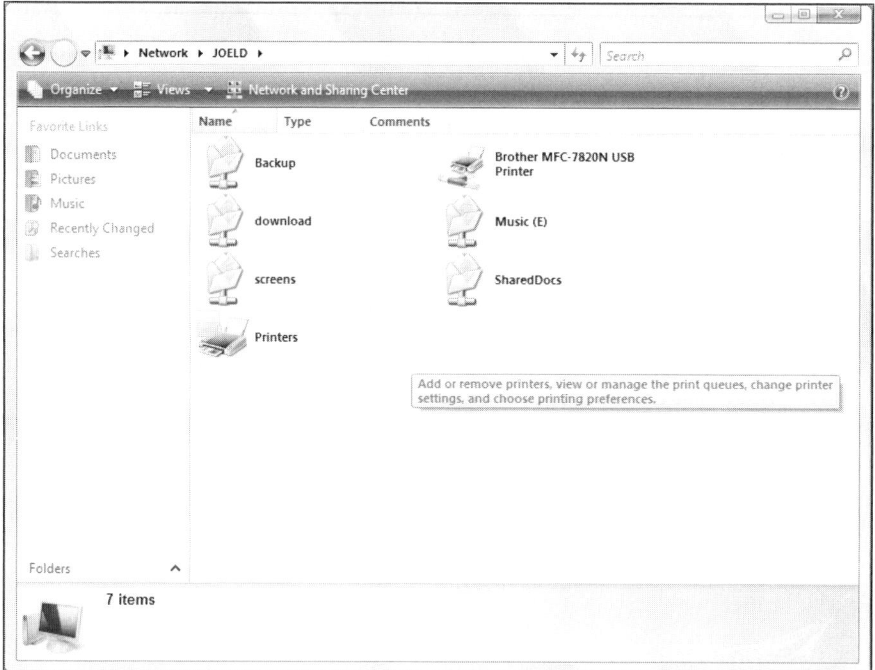

Summary

Networking is a powerful and absolutely necessary part of computing, and it's never been easier than it is now with Windows Vista. The operating system detects all kinds of network details all by itself, and you can tweak and manage your network however you see fit.

Connecting computers to form a network is gratuitously simple thanks to modern-day wireless networking. You no longer need to run cabling through your house to get computers to connect to each other. With the help of a router, you can share Internet access all over the house, and creating a network with a router, a few PCs, and Windows Vista can easily take less than an hour.

After you've gotten all the hardware you need, you simply install and configure it and then fire up the Windows Vista networking modules. Windows probably figured out what you were doing as you set the network up, with its network-sensing technology. It may have already discovered your shared broadband Internet gateway and configured itself properly without your intervention.

Of course, because your network data is floating through the air, wireless networks have security issues . You can sleep easy, however, by taking a few steps to safeguard your data from wardriving geeks and other intruders. New security encryption standards are incredibly difficult to crack, and enabling them is simple.

When you've set up and secured your network, you can finally share files, folders, and printers with permissions as specific as you require. You can allow anyone on the network to have any level of access that you want.

If your home contains multiple computers, you should network them to share resources, share media, and do more with what you already have.

Chapter 13

Internet Applications

IN THIS CHAPTER

- Exploring the new features of Internet Explorer 7
- Introducing Windows Mail
- Working with RSS

The Internet is such a major part of computing, few people even consider using a home computer without some sort of Internet connection, whether it's simple dialup or beefy broadband. Windows Vista Ultimate comes ready for online computing, with Internet-friendly features woven throughout its code. From its robust firewall and its built-in Automatic Updates system to its user-friendly browser and e-mail applications, Vista allows your computer to take part in a connected world, especially if it's wired to a DSL, cable, T1, or fiber Internet onramp.

Vista looks for network connections even as you install it. It automatically enables its firewall, enables Automatic Updates, and scopes your network for Internet connectivity, which it takes care of on its own. Assuming it recognizes your computer's network interface equipment and that a path to the Net exists (whether it's through another computer sharing an Internet connection or through a residential gateway like a broadband router), you can launch Internet Explorer 7 immediately after you install the operating system and get online in seconds.

Internet access is important. The Internet and its World Wide Web and e-mail infrastructures are so ingrained into what most people do with their computers, some folks just can't be without them. If you don't believe me, look at the proliferation of Web-friendly gadgetry: Some cell phones, most PDAs, all modern laptop computers, and even the Sony PlayStation Portable are all ready to surf the Web. Hotspots, places where you can get online through a Wi-Fi (wireless) network, are everywhere — in airports, coffee shops, bookstores, libraries, and so on. More and more homeowners are installing their own Wi-Fi, or at least wired Internet routers, so they can get online from anywhere in the house or yard. And I don't know about you, but when my power goes out or my broadband connection goes down, I feel naked and helpless when I am not able to get online.

Like many people, I get everything online. News? I haven't watched the six-o'clock news in years. Shopping? I can get virtually everything cheaper online with the exception of groceries. Socialization? I'm fighting to beat my upcoming deadline because the next day, people I've never met before but know intimately through a Web message board are coming to my house for the first time. Information? Whereas once I spent most of my time in libraries to research what I write, nowadays I can get most of my data online — it's more current, it's easier to find, and it's faster, and much of it can be tailored to my specific needs. Heck, the major downside of Internet proliferation is that I never leave the house anymore.

With Vista, my propensity to become a hermit will only become more dangerous. Windows Vista's Internet applications are vastly improved over those included with earlier versions of the operating system. Internet Explorer 7 might not even look familiar to IE6 users, as its entire interface has been torn down and built back up with a whole new look and feel. Outlook Express is gone, replaced by the far more robust Microsoft Mail. Windows Vista now includes RSS support, so you can subscribe to feeds and have them piped directly to your desktop via a Sidebar gadget. Now let's explore these exciting applications, starting with the new IE.

What's New in Internet Explorer 7+

Internet Explorer 7+ is the browser built right into Windows Vista Ultimate. It's also available as an add-on for Windows XP. Microsoft's first new version of Internet Explorer in almost six years, IE7+ is loaded with new features and security enhancements. Some of the features are inspired by competing browsers, such as tabbed browsing, which became popular thanks to the open source browser Mozilla and its offshoot Mozilla Firefox.

When you open Internet Explorer 7+, you'll notice that it looks completely different from any browser that you've ever used before, including IE6. At first, the look is almost as jarring as the new Vista interface; new trinkets are all over the place and some familiar interface items are missing. Let's take a look at the new interface.

The new interface: Where are all my menus?

Take a gander at Internet Explorer 7+ either by clicking the quick start button next to the Start button, or by choosing Start ➪ Internet. You'll see something like the screen shown in Figure 13.1.

NOTE By default, MSN.com is IE7+'s home page (the first page that IE7+ navigates to when you open the browser). You can change the browser's home page by navigating to a different page and clicking Tools, then Options, and then clicking the Use Current button. You can even use this method to make multiple pages your browser's home pages.

Immediately, you'll see some major differences if you're coming from an XP system running IE6. The menus at the top (File, Edit, View, and so on) are missing. A second text entry box is next to the address bar. The navigation buttons are all over the place. A star and a plus sign are to the left of some sort of tab, which itself displays not only the current Web page's title, but also its favicon (the little icon, displayed on the address bar, that represents the current page). Something about Protected Mode appears at the bottom of the browser, next to a little magnifying glass. What is all this?

FIGURE 13.1

Internet Explorer 7+, displaying its start page, MSN.com

You're looking at a fresh new face for IE. It's unfamiliar, but once you get used to it you'll realize it's a vast improvement over the old-style interface. Check out this maximized view in Figure 13.2.

Let's run through the new interface features, shall we? The new ones are explained later in this chapter.

- On the top of the window is, of course, is the title bar, and it displays the title of the Web page that's currently open followed by the application's name (Windows Internet Explorer).
- Below the title bar are the Back and Forward buttons, which, of course, take you back to pages you've visited in the current session and forward through your current browsing history. To the right of them is the address bar, with buttons on its right for refreshing the current page and stopping the loading of the current page. The last item on the right is the Search field, in which you can enter a string to search the Internet, using the engine of your choice (the default is MSN Search).
- Moving down to the next row and on the left are a star and a plus sign. The star opens your Favorites folder, whereas the plus sign lets you organize your Favorites. The tab is for tabbed browsing; you can open a whole bunch of Web pages in a single window with

tabs. The little subtab to the larger tab's right is the New Tab button. To the right of the tab is the customizable command bar, with, by default, buttons for Home, RSS, Print, Page options, a Tools menu, and, off the edge but accessible by clicking all the way to the right, the Help menu. If you have Office 2007 installed, a Research button is also available.

- Underneath the browser's main window is the status bar, and it includes two items: current security mode, which you can double-click to open the Security Settings menu (the default mode is Protected Mode), and the Zoom button, which you can use to zoom the browser's main window into and out of Web pages.

The new interface gives you all the functionality of the IE6 interface. In fact, if you have to have the drop-down menus, you can right-click the command bar and click Classic Menu. The comfortable old menus (File, Edit, View, Favorites, Tools, and Help) will appear below the address bar, but nothing is within them you can't do from the new interface's default configuration.

For example, if you want to send the current page by e-mail (an option under the File menu), you simply click the Page button and click Send this page under its menu. The Page menu also contains the options to save the page, edit the text size, and view the page source. Look at Table 13.1 for the new interface's methods for accessing the options found in the classic drop-down menus.

FIGURE 13.2

Internet Explorer 7+, maximized

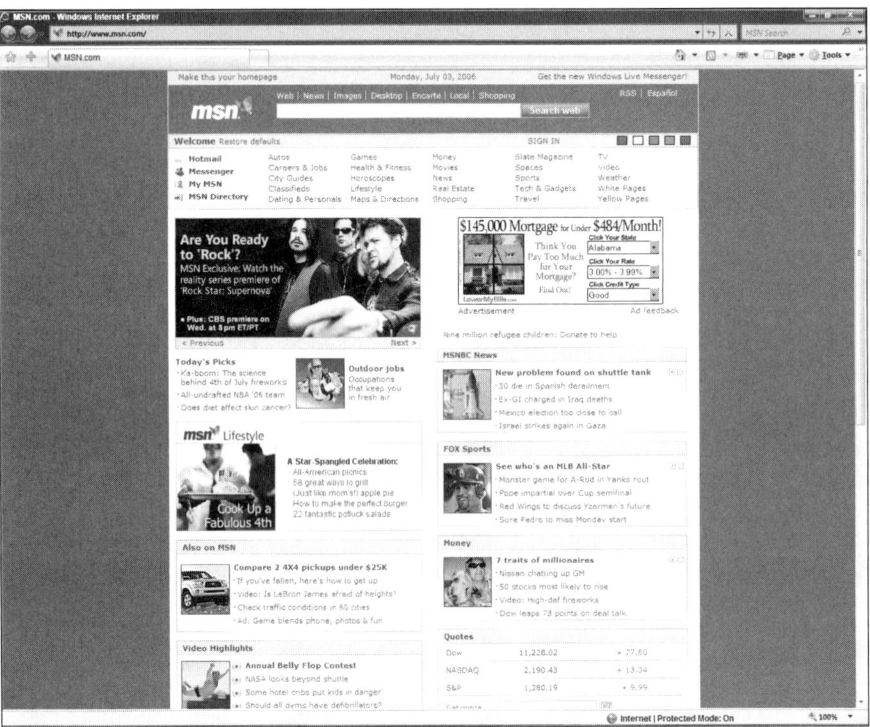

TABLE 13.1

Getting Things Done in IE7+'s New Interface

Classic Menu Command	How to Do It in IE7+
File ➪ New Window	Click the Page button and click New Window.
File ➪ Open	Hold down Ctrl and press the O key.
File ➪ Save As	Click the Page button and click Save As.
File ➪ Page Setup; File ➪ Print; File ➪ Print Preview	Click the Print button for these menu functions.
File ➪ Send options	Click the Page button and click Send this page.
File ➪ Import and Export	Click the plus sign and click Import and Export.
File ➪ Properties	Right-click the current page and click Properties.
File ➪ Work offline	Click the Tools button and click Work Offline.
File ➪ Exit	Click the X button in the browser's upper-right corner.
Edit ➪ Cut; Edit ➪ Copy; Edit ➪ Paste	Click the Page button for these menu functions.
Edit ➪ Select all	Hold down Ctrl and press the A key.
Edit ➪ Find on this page	Click the down arrow next to the Search field and click Find on this page.
View ➪ Toolbars	Click the Tools button and hover the mouse cursor over Toolbars.
View ➪ Go to (Back, Forward, Home Page, Current Page)	Use the appropriate buttons.
View ➪ Stop	Click the Stop button.
View ➪ Refresh	Click the Refresh button.
View ➪ Text Size	Click Page and hover over Text Size.
View ➪ Encoding	Right-click the current page and hover over Encoding.
View ➪ Source	Right-click the current page and click View Source.
View ➪ Full Screen	Click the Maximize button.
Favorites	Use the star and plus buttons to invoke the Favorites folder and manipulate Favorites, respectively.
Tools	All Tools options are available in the new Tools menu; click the Tools button.
Help	All Help options are available in the new Help menu; click the Help button.

New convenience features

When you get used to the interface, you'll be ready to take advantage of a whole plethora of new features, many of which are simply there for your convenience. Tabbed browsing, print scaling, a handy search field, and more pave the way for much more user-friendly Web surfing.

Tabbed browsing

Probably the most in-demand feature of modern browsers is tabbed browsing. A feature new to IE, it allows you to have many Web pages open at the same time without tracking browser windows all over your desktop. You can open dozens of Web sites in a single browser and easily jump from one site to another. Check out the tabs in the IE7+ tab bar shown in Figure 13.3.

FIGURE 13.3

Each one of those tabs in the tab bar represents an open Web site.

Tabbed browsing is easy and convenient. When you open IE7+, a single tab will display your browser's current home page. Its tab is displayed next to the star and plus sign buttons, which deal with your Favorites folder. When you develop the urge to open another page while keeping the current page open as well, stop yourself from opening IE again; simply click the New Tab button to the right of the current page's tab. A new, blank tab will open. Now you can treat it just like another browser window: You can type a URL into the address bar, you can search for whatever you please, and so on.

Each tab will display as much of its current page's title as it has room for. You can switch between tabs as quickly as you can click on the one you want. To close a tab, thus closing the Web site it displays, first click it to make it the currently selected tab, and then click the **X** on the right side of that tab.

Sometimes links on Web pages open their content in new browser windows. This still happens, unless you make a change in the Tabbed Browsing Settings of IE7+. To make sure that new content opens in new tabs and that pop-up windows open as they should, do the following:

1. **Click the Tools button.**
2. **Click Internet Options.** The Internet Options dialog box, shown in Figure 13.4, appears.
3. **Under Tabs, click the Settings button.** The Tabbed Browsing Settings dialog box, shown in Figure 13.5, appears.
4. **Under When a pop-up is encountered, click the radio button next to Let Internet Explorer decide how pop-ups should open.**
5. **Click OK.**
6. **Click OK again.**

FIGURE 13.4

The Internet Options dialog box

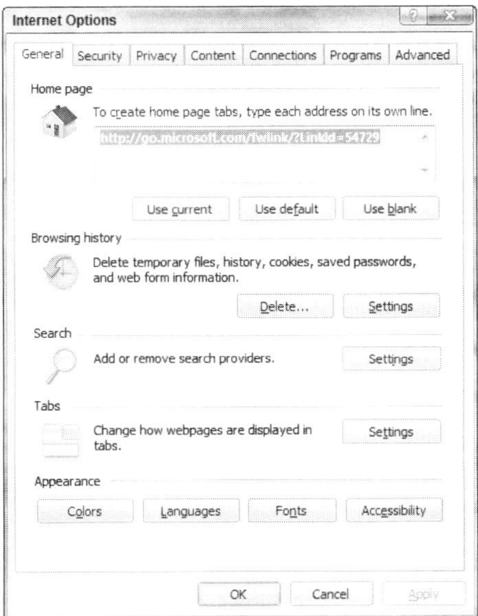

FIGURE 13.5

The Tabbed Browsing Settings dialog box

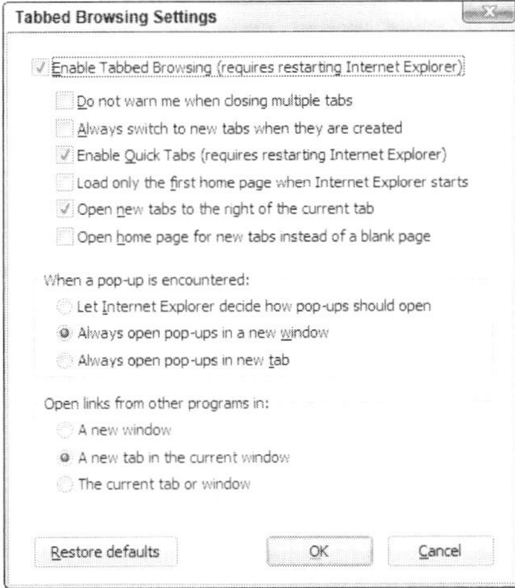

The Tabbed Browsing Settings dialog box also includes the following options:

- **Enable Tabbed Browsing:** Uncheck this box if you hate tabbed browsing and want it to go away. IE7+ will, in this aspect, act just like IE6.
- **Do not warn me when closing multiple tabs:** By default, IE7+ will pop up a warning dialog box when you try to shut it down with more than one tab open. To disable this warning, check this box.
- **Always switch to new tabs when they are created:** If you click a link and it opens content in a new tab, IE7+ will, if this box is checked, automatically switch to the new tab.
- **Enable Quick Tabs:** If you have multiple tabs open, a Quick Tabs button will appear next to the tab all the way on the left. If you click it, it will display thumbnails of all the open tabs, as shown in Figure 13.6. Uncheck the Enable Quick Tabs box to disable this feature.

FIGURE 13.6

Quick Tabs shows thumbnails of all the open tabs. Click one to jump to that tab.

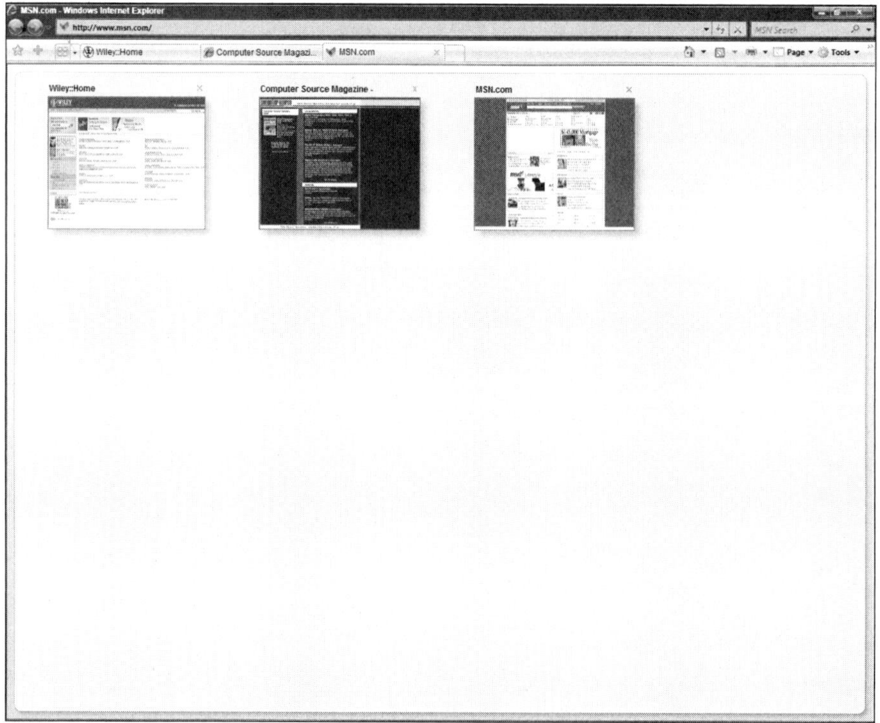

- **Load only the first home page when Internet Explorer starts:** You can save several pages as your "home pages" and have them all open in tabs when you start the browser — unless you check this box, in which case only the first home page will open.
- **Open new tabs to the right of the current tab:** Checked, this option ensures that when a new tab opens for any reason, it'll be to the *immediate* right of the current tab. If you uncheck it, new tabs will open to the far right of all open tabs.
- **Open home page for new tabs instead of a blank page:** With this option unchecked, new tabs that you create will be blank. With it checked, new tabs will open to the first home page in your list of tabbed home pages.
- **When a pop-up is encountered:** You can tell IE7+ what to do when popup content tries to open, forcing them to always open in new windows, always open in new tabs, or allowing IE to decide what to do with them.
- **Open links from other programs in:** When you click links in programs other than IE7+, this dictates whether they open in new tabs, new windows, or the current tab/window.

Toolbar search

If you're tired of navigating to a search engine or having an extra toolbar, such as the Google Toolbar, taking away space that could otherwise be used to display Web content, you'll dig this feature. Glance to the right of the address bar and you'll see a small text field with a little magnifying glass next to it. That's the Toolbar Search Box, and you can customize it.

To perform a Web search, simply type your search string into the box and press Enter. The current browser tab will leap over to the selected search engine's results page. By default, the search box shows the words *MSN Search*, meaning it will use Microsoft's search engine.

Let's face it: Most people use Google. You can tell the Toolbar Search Box to search Google, or one of several search engines, rather than MSN Search, by doing the following:

1. **Click the tiny, little down arrow next to the magnifying glass in the Toolbar Search Box.**
2. **Click Find More Providers.** IE navigates to the page shown in Figure 13.7.
3. **Click the provider of your choice (for example, Google).** The Add Search Provider dialog box appears, as shown in Figure 13.8.
4. **To add the provider, click Add Provider.**
5. **Click the little arrow in the Toolbar Search Box again.** Your new provider appears at the top of the menu.
6. **Click your new menu provider to select it.**
7. **To make your new provider the search default, click the down arrow yet again.**

FIGURE 13.7

This page shows search providers for the Toolbar Search Box.

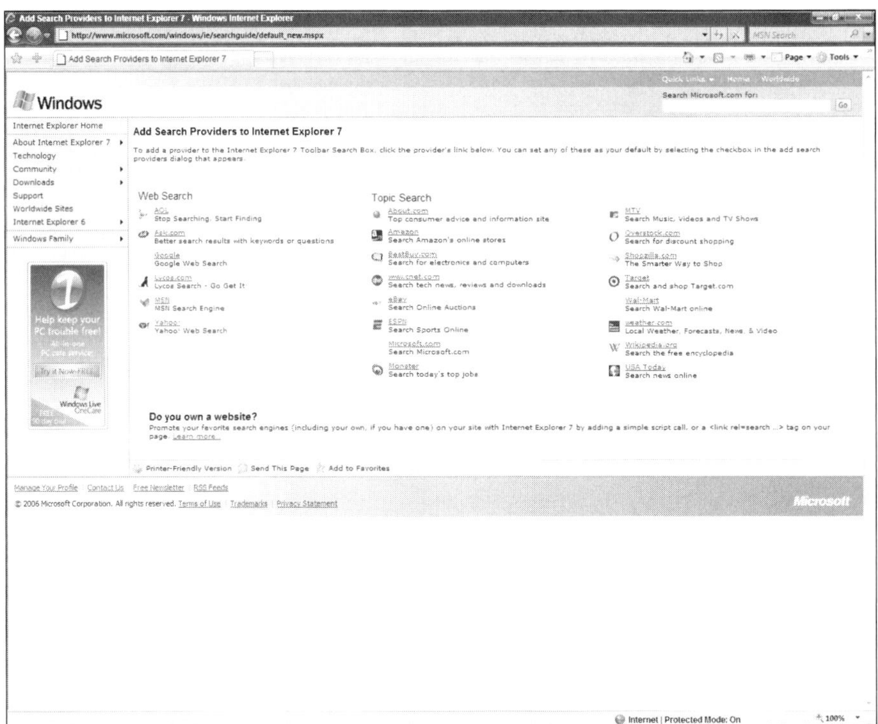

FIGURE 13.8

The Add Search Provider dialog box

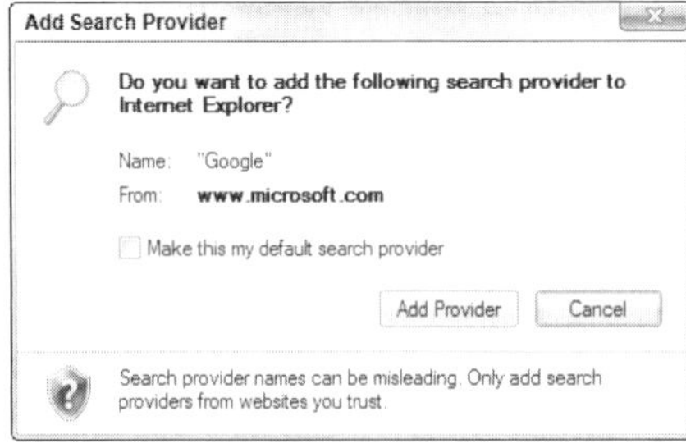

8. **Click Change Search Defaults.** The Change Search Defaults dialog box, shown in Figure 13.9, appears.

FIGURE 13.9

Set the default search provider in the Change Search Defaults dialog box.

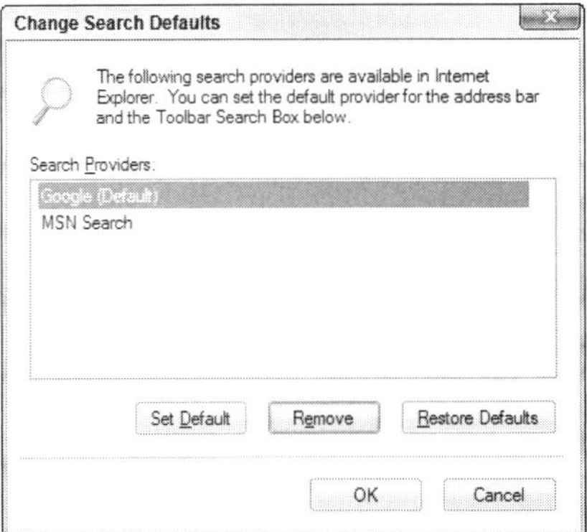

9. **Click the search provider you want to use by default and click Set Default.**
10. **Click OK.**

From now on, when you perform a search, IE7+ will use the new provider (in the example shown, Google) to search the Internet for you. Besides Web search engines, you can add selected Web sites, such as Amazon, ESPN, and eBay, so you can search them directly from the Toolbar Search Box.

Zoom

Care to get a closer look at a Web page, or get an idea of how the page looks overall — including the parts you can't see in the browser window? With IE7+'s new Zoom feature, you can do so.

Zooming in and out is as simple as holding the Ctrl key and clicking the = (equal sign) or (hyphen) keys. IE7+ zooms in 10 percent increments. To jump to various zoom levels, click the little down arrow next to the Zoom button on the bottom right of the browser. The Zoom button has a small magnifying glass next to a percentage.

Your options are 400%, 200%, 150%, 125%, 100%, 75%, and 50%. Click one to zoom to that level. If the Web content becomes larger than the browser window can accommodate, you can scroll around with scroll bars or the mouse wheel.

You can also specify the exact level to which you want to zoom. In the same drop-down menu as the fixed increments, click Custom and enter the level of your choice.

If you click the Zoom button itself, the browser cycles between 100%, 125%, and 150%.

Print scaling

Have you ever tried to print a Web page from a browser only to have it end up wider than the paper, cutting off the content at the right edge? With IE7+'s print scaling feature, the browser automatically scales the Web site to fit the width of the paper, and the Print Preview option is far more powerful than it was in previous IE releases.

Try this: Navigate to a Web site (such as `www.wiley.com`, as shown in Figure 13.10) and click the down arrow next to the Print button. Then, click Print Preview. A window like the one shown in Figure 13.11 appears. Notice how the entire width of the page fits on the "paper" shown.

FIGURE 13.10

A source of terrific books

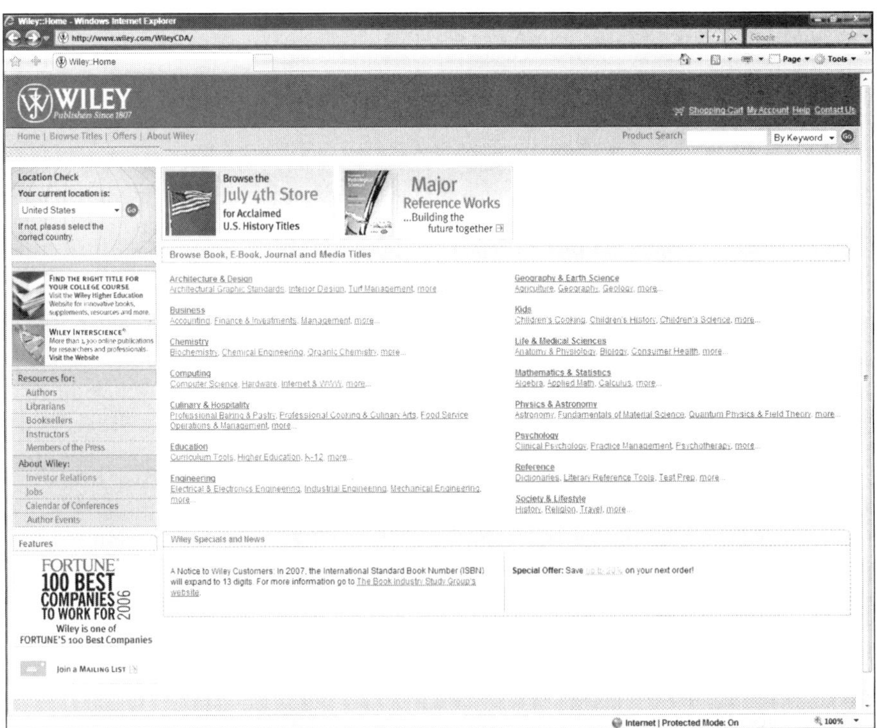

FIGURE 13.11

Print scaling squeezes a site into the margins of the paper you choose.

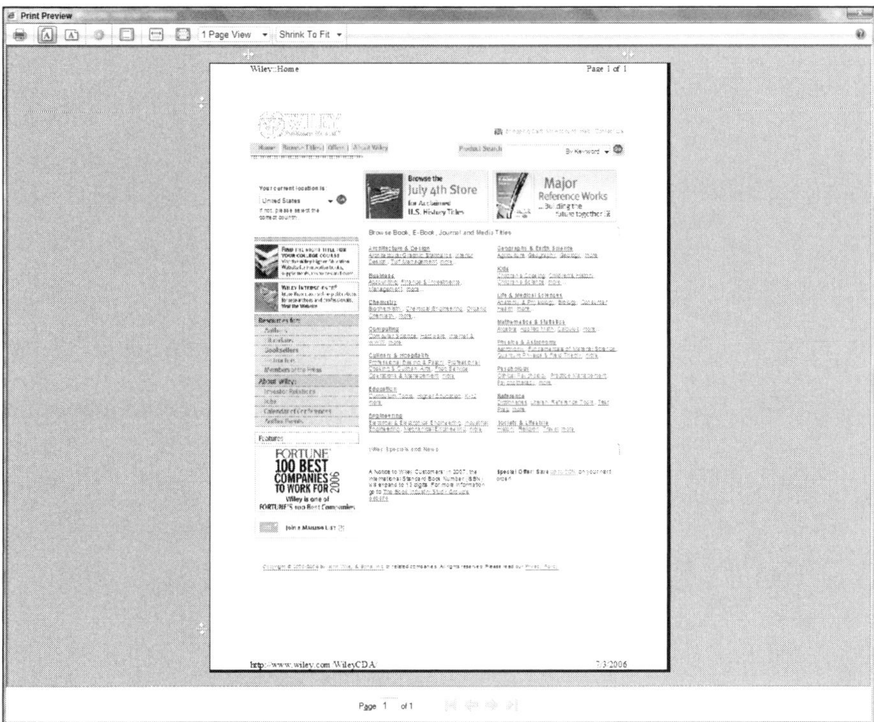

Now, look at the various options in the toolbar. The box on the right by default says *Shrink to fit*. Click it to pull it down and click 100%. The print preview re-scales the page, but this time, as shown in Figure 13.12, the right side may be cut off. With the option set to Shrink to fit, the browser automatically scales the page to fit on a page. Print scaling is an extremely handy feature when you're dealing with Web pages, receipts that aren't printer-friendly, large images you want to print without downloading and resizing, and a variety of other scenarios.

Favorites Center

Now let's look at the Favorites buttons, namely the star and plus sign buttons to the left of the tab bar. Clicking the plus sign invokes the Add to Favorites menu. From here you can add Web pages and entire sets of tabs to your Favorites folder; you can import and export your Favorites, cookies, and feeds from other applications or from files; and you can organize your Favorites.

To add a Web site to your Favorites folder, click the Add to Favorites option on the Add to Favorites menu. The Favorites Center dialog box appears, as shown in Figure 13.13. From here, you can decide which folder to add the Web site, or create a new one.

FIGURE 13.12

Without print scaling, the site may be cut off on the right. Notice how the words in the submenus on the right are cut off at the very edge.

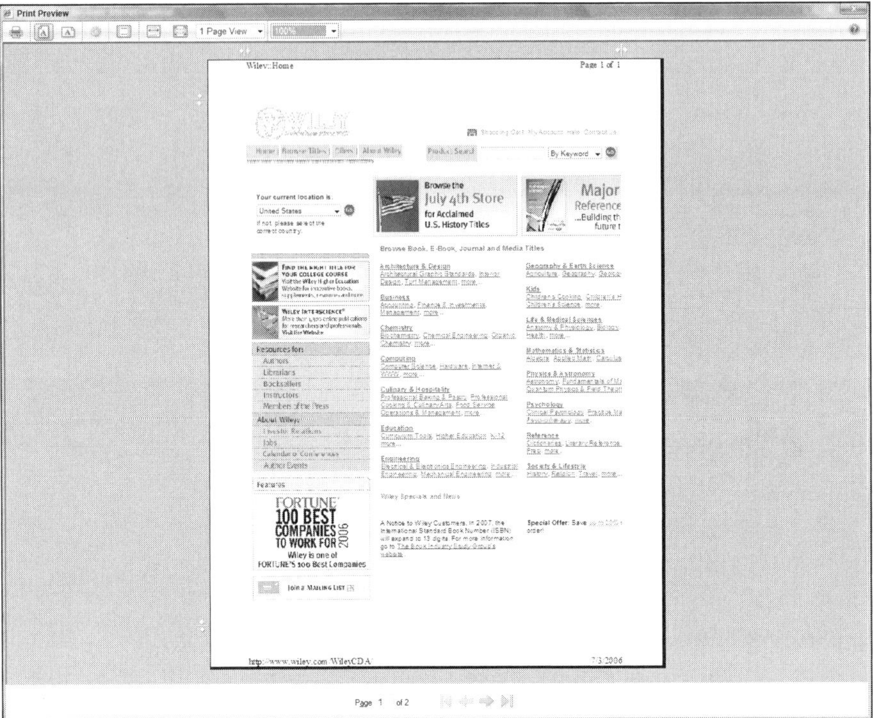

FIGURE 13.13

You can add a site to Favorites through the Favorites Center dialog box.

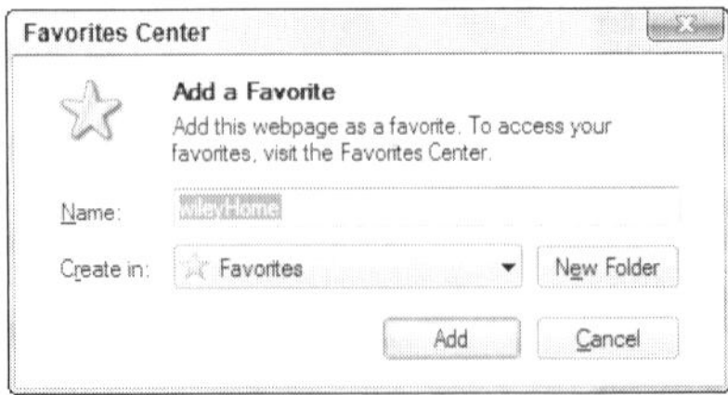

You can add all the open tabs to Favorites in one fell swoop by clicking the plus sign and then clicking Add Tab Group to Favorites. Type in a name for your tab group and click Add. A new Favorites subfolder by that name will be created.

To launch the Import/Export Wizard, click the plus sign and then click Import and Export. Follow the wizard to import favorites, cookies, and even RSS feeds from other applications or files of the appropriate type (Favorites files should be in HTML format, cookies in TXT, and RSS feeds in OPML), or to export them to other apps or files.

Finally, you can click the plus sign and then click Organize Favorites to create new Favorites folders, move favorites around, rename them, and delete those you no longer need.

Now, let's check out the Favorites Center proper. Click the star to invoke the Favorites Center, which contains three buttons: Favorites, Feeds, and History.

- The Favorites button, shown in Figure 13.14, displays all of your favorites and Favorites folders. Click on a folder once to display its contents.
- The Feeds button, shown in Figure 13.15, displays the RSS feeds to which you're currently subscribed. Click the feed of your choice to view the current content.

FIGURE 13.14

View your favorites here.

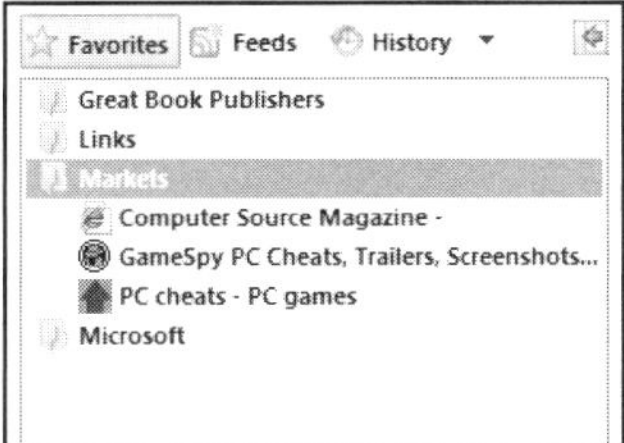

FIGURE 13.15

Check out your subscribed RSS feeds in the Favorites Center.

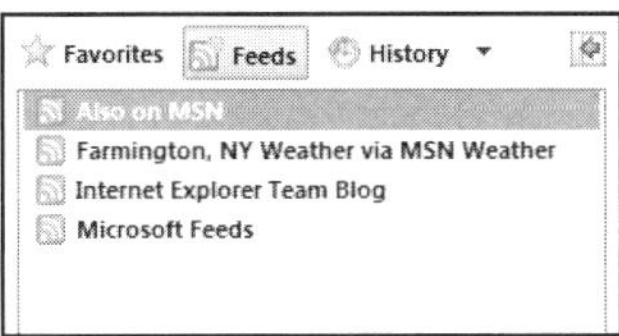

- The History button, shown in Figure 13.16, allows you to view your Internet history. You can view by how long ago you visited the various sites, and you can sort the list by clicking the down arrow next to the button.

FIGURE 13.16

Your Web history can be long and storied.

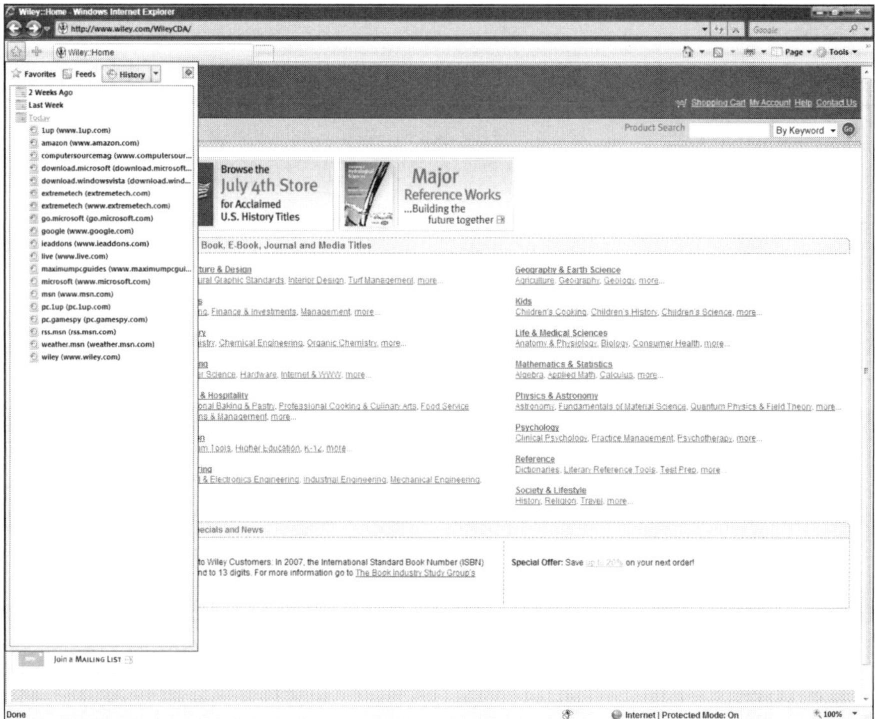

Centralized privacy interface

IE7+, like most browsers, saves a lot of data as you surf. This includes, among other things, your temporary Internet files, cookies, form data, history, and even passwords if you elect to allow it to save them. Sometimes, you don't want that stuff floating around. For privacy's sake, you can now delete any of these groups of data, or delete all of your browsing history in a single click

Click the Tools button and click Delete Browsing History. The Delete Browsing History dialog box, shown in Figure 13.17, appears. It's simple enough to use: To delete one of the groups of information shown, simply click the appropriate button.

After you click the button of your choice, a confirmation dialog box appears, allowing you one last chance to change your mind. If you go ahead with the deletion, IE7+ purges all the history in that category from your PC. To delete all the history at once, simply click the Delete all button at the bottom of the Delete Browsing History dialog box.

FIGURE 13.17

The Delete Browsing History dialog box

New security features

Along with its new convenience features, IE7+ unveils a number of new features to make browsing safer for you and everyone who uses your computer. Unsavory Web denizens often try to install malicious software or drop spyware on your PC without your consent. Scammers engage in what's called *phishing*, or ways to trick you into giving up valuable data ranging from user names and passwords to credit card and social security numbers.

Protected Mode

The most intricate and what might turn out to be the most effective new security feature of IE7+ is Protected Mode browsing. Protected Mode is enabled by default and although you can disable it, Microsoft doesn't recommend you do so.

TIP Want to disable Protected Mode anyway? Double-click the security portion of the status bar (at the bottom of the browser where it says the zone you're currently browsing followed by *Protected Mode: On*) to invoke the Internet Security window, shown in Figure 13.18. Under Security level for this zone, uncheck the Enable Protected Mode box. Click OK.

Protected Mode uses a trio of Windows Vista's new security technologies including User Account Control, Mandatory Integrity Control, and User Interface Privilege Isolation (see Chapter 11). Under Protected Mode, the IE process runs with low rights no matter what level of security the user's account is set with — even administrators' accounts are affected. Thus, if a Web site somehow exploits an IE7+ flaw and runs unauthorized code, it wouldn't be able to do much at all. It couldn't install software, for example, or perform critical alterations to the registry.

FIGURE 13.18

Enable or disable Protected Mode in the Internet Security window.

Even the browser's cache, temp directory, cookies folder, and history are isolated when the browser runs in Protected Mode. If you turn off Protected Mode or surf in the Trusted zone (the only zone in which Protected Mode is disabled by default), the browser won't access anything that was written during its time in Protected Mode except the Favorites folder.

For a detailed description of how Protected Mode works, visit this page on Microsoft's IEBlog site: `http://blogs.msdn.com/ie/archive/2006/02/09/528963.aspx`.

Phishing Filter

Phishing is using a ploy to try to get you to unknowingly give up personal information. Phishers might set up phony replicas of commonly used commerce or online shopping sites, like eBay or PayPal, in an attempt to get you to enter your login name, password, credit card numbers, and more, which they collect to use for their own purposes. They use e-mail and other Web sites to drive you to these suspicious sites, often by hiding a link to the phony site behind what appears to be a link to a reputable site.

For example, a phishing ploy on a Web site might include a link that looks like this:

```
https://www.amazon.com/gp/css/history/view.html
```

Understanding Security Zones

Security zones work in IE7+ the same way they work in IE6. There are four zones, each of which has its own, customizable security settings. You can see them represented in Figure 13.18. The zones are Internet (the one you'll spend most of your time in); Local Intranet (for office intranets, which are generally more secure than the Internet at large); Trusted Sites (which consists of Web sites that you trust not to attempt to exploit security flaws or otherwise compromise your computer); and Restricted (which is the opposite of the Trusted zone; sites in this zone are confirmed dangers).

You can manually add sites to each of the zones besides Internet and Local Intranet. To do so, invoke the Internet Security window by double-clicking the security area of the status bar and click the zone to which you want to add a site. Click the Sites button. Then, type the URL of the site you want to add in the Add this website to the zone box and click Add. The URL of the current Web site appears in the box by default, but you can change it if you want.

As for sites in the Local Intranet zone, the browser automatically detects intranet networks. You can, however, change its detection parameters by selecting it and clicking the Sites button. Clicking the Advanced button on that dialog allows you to manually add sites as you can with the Trusted and Restricted zones.

The Sites button is grayed out in the Internet zone. Pretty much *everything* is in the Internet zone, so adding sites manually is pointless.

You can set the security levels for each zone through the slider in the Internet Security window; each zone has its own, independent slider. You can also click the Custom level button to set custom security levels for each zone. Custom options include options to run such things as ActiveX code, .NET Framework components, JavaScript, and so on; and allowing such actions as file downloads, allowing Web sites to open windows without address and/or status bars, and more.

But the site actually leads to something more like:

```
http://153.183.96.260
```

I realize the preceding is an obviously phony IP address; you didn't think I would print the URL of a real phishing site, did you?

If you were to click the link, it would lead you to a site that looks identical to Amazon's login page, but if you were to enter your login ID and password, the phisher who set up the site would obtain it and could then use it to shop with your account.

Reputable sites like Amazon do everything they can to thwart phishing, but it remains a serious problem. One way to avoid phishing scams is to always type in the URL of any e-commerce or e-store site you want to visit in the address bar of the browser. Another way is to use IE7+'s Phishing Filter.

Phishing Filter is turned on by default. It sends Web sites you visit that aren't part of an automatically downloaded known-safe list to a master list on a Microsoft server for verification. What's more, it hunts through unknown sites for cloaked links like the previous example.

NOTE Does this feature sound creepy? Could Windows be phoning home? According to Microsoft, all data that IE7+ sends to the remote server is anonymous. Phishing Filter only checks sites that are *not* on the known-safe list, and URLs are stripped of extra data like query strings and account numbers before they're sent to Microsoft. They're sent over encrypted SSL connections for privacy.

You may get a warning when you visit a site that indicates that IE7+ suspects it of phishing. It'll give you an option to close the site or continue on. If you choose to enter the site, click the links at your own risk.

You can disable Phishing Filter through the Tools button. Click Tools, hover over Phishing Filter, and click Turn Off Automatic Web Site Checking. You'll see the Microsoft Phishing Filter dialog box, as shown in Figure 13.19, which advises you not to turn off Phishing Filter. To turn it off, make sure the radio button next to Turn off automatic Phishing Filter is selected and click OK.

FIGURE 13.19

Are you sure you want to turn off Phishing Filter?

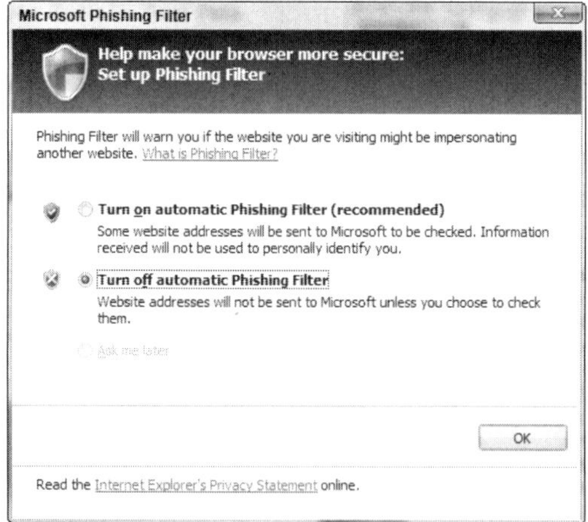

You can manually report Web sites by clicking Tools, hovering over Phishing Filter, and clicking Report this Web site. This option launches a new browser window and displays the screen shown in Figure 13.20. To report a site, click the box next to I think this is a phishing website and click Submit.

FIGURE 13.20

Report a Web site here. Of course, I'm not going to report MSN.com.

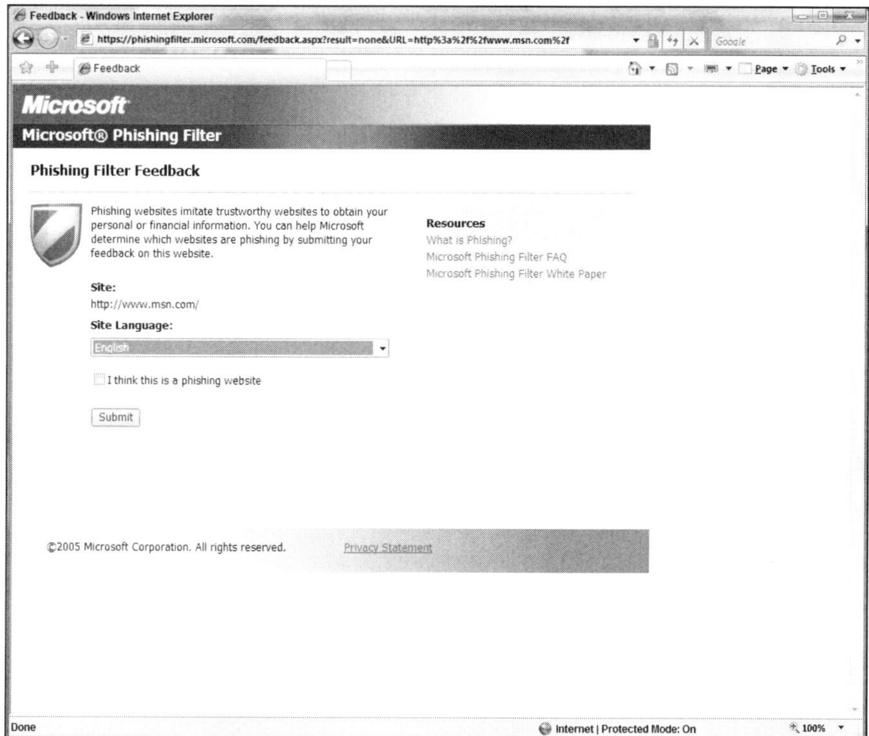

What's New in Windows Mail

It may look a lot like Outlook Express, but Windows Mail goes far beyond Microsoft's old freebie mail and news program with plenty of new features, both under the hood and in the interface itself.

In the good old days, Microsoft's Outlook Express stored mail messages in one huge file and account data in the system registry. This setup made porting your e-mail settings and account data to a different computer or backing up that information difficult. Under the new system, e-mail notes are stored individually, and account data is stored in files rather than the registry.

Windows Mail stores e-mail and account data in the hidden AppData folder within the C:\Users\<*username*>\ folder. Specifically, mail data is stored in C:\Users\<*username*>\AppData\Local\Microsoft\Windows Mail*.* so, in theory, backing up an entire swath of e-mail and then restoring it or moving it to a different computer should be a simple matter.

Meanwhile, the address book is stored in C:\Users\<*username*>\Contacts\. It uses the Windows Explorer shell with a few buttons to allow you to create, search, organize, and store your contacts.

On the surface, Windows Mail resembles Outlook Express. Its default layout, for example, is similar to the old style, and the Account Creation wizard has remained for the most part untouched. A few new features are obvious:

- A phishing filter, like the one in IE7+, is incorporated and it scans each e-mail for fraudulent links.
- A terrific Bayesian junk mail filter helps you filter out the spam from the legitimate e-mails.
- Message searching is almost instantaneous.

NOTE Bayesian filtering looks for particular text strings to identify junk mail. Many junk mail filters simply look for keywords in the subject line, but Bayesian is a contextual filtering method that can ward off junk e-mail that disguises typical junk mail words by misspelling the word or using alternate characters to represent a semblance of a given word (for example, replacing "porn" with "p.0rn").

Let's take a look at Windows Mail and its new twists.

The interface

Windows Mail (Figure 13.21) features an interface that's quite similar to that of Outlook Express, which was included with previous versions of Windows, but it's subtly different. Windows Mail includes the contextual toolbar found in most other Windows Vista applications, and it also has, by default, a folder for storing junk e-mail (Outlook Express didn't have a junk mail filter). Mail also includes the toolbar Search box, which allows you to quickly find words or phrases in e-mail subjects or other headers.

You can alter Mail's layout to your preference; for example, you can move the preview pane to a column to the right of the interface, as shown in Figure 13.22, or get rid of it altogether. You can also customize the toolbar and tweak which bars and lists are visible. All these options are available by choosing View ➪ Layout.

FIGURE 13.21

Windows Mail in its default configuration

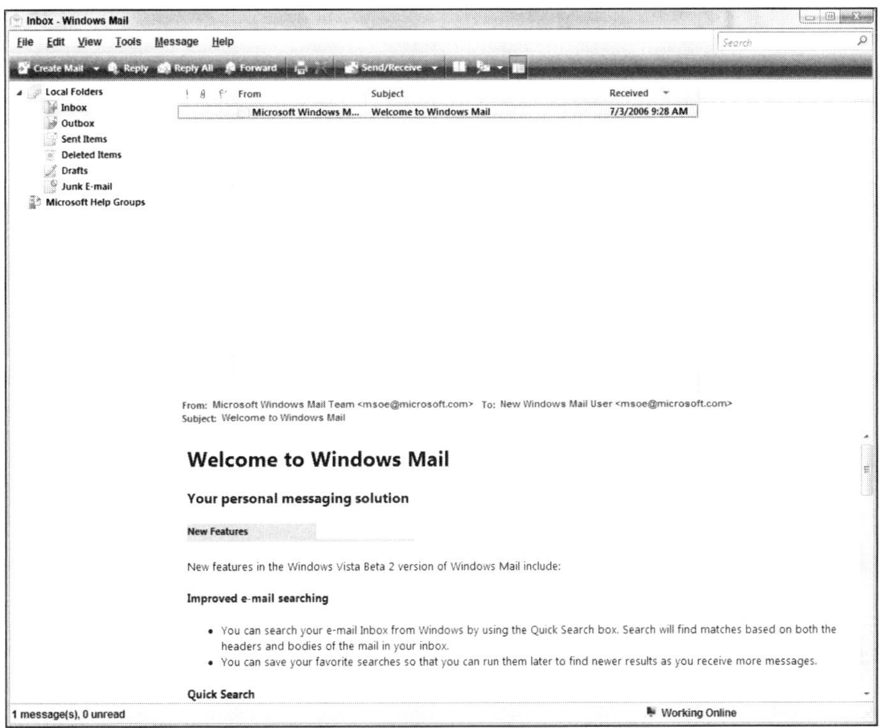

The rest of the interface is fairly straightforward. The drop-down menus are preserved from Outlook Express, and the toolbar buttons allow you to create mail, reply, reply to all, forward, print, and so on. A Toolbar Search Box has been added for you to take advantage of the new, blazing-fast search tool. For more advanced search options, click the Search button on the toolbar.

FIGURE 13.22

Move the preview pane for a different view.

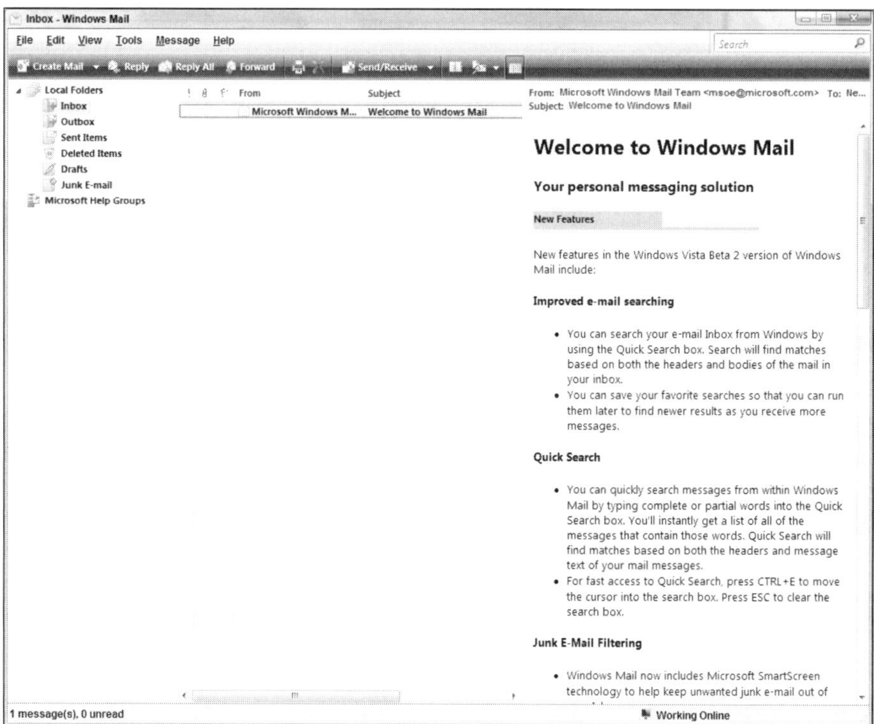

Filtering

Windows Mail can filter messages for both spam and phishing content. To set the filtering options, choose Tools ➪ Junk E-mail Options. The Junk E-mail Options window shown in Figure 13.23 appears.

This window has a bunch of tabs, each of which contains options that affect how Microsoft Mail filters messages:

- **Options tab:** Displayed by default, this tab lets you select the level of protection from junk e-mail (spam) you want Windows Mail to offer. You can select No Automatic Filtering, to turn junk mail filtering off; Low, for a moderate level of filtering; or High, for a high level but with a greater risk of filtering out legitimate e-mail. You can also choose Safe List Only, which allows you to receive e-mail only from senders on your Safe Sender list. By default, junk e-mail is relegated to the Junk E-mail folder, so you can check it periodically for legitimate e-mails that got dumped in there by accident; however, if you click the Permanently delete suspected junk e-mail box, Windows Mail will trash those e-mails instead.

- **Save Senders tab:** This tab lets you create and edit a list of e-mail addresses from which you always want the junk mail filter to allow mail. You can instruct Windows Mail to always trust people in the Windows Contacts list, and also to automatically add people to whom you send e-mail to the Safe Senders list.
- **Blocked Senders tab:** This tab is just the opposite of the Save Senders tab. You can add e-mail addresses to this tab's list to have mail from those addresses always flagged as junk.
- **International tab:** This tab allows you to block e-mail by top-level domain and by its international encoding. If you're getting lots of bizarre e-mail from, say, China, you can block e-mail encoded in Chinese and/or block e-mail from the .CN domain.
- **Phishing tab:** This tab allows you to turn on or off the Phishing Filter, which looks for signs of phishing (discussed earlier in this chapter) in incoming e-mail.

FIGURE 13.23

The Junk E-mail Options window

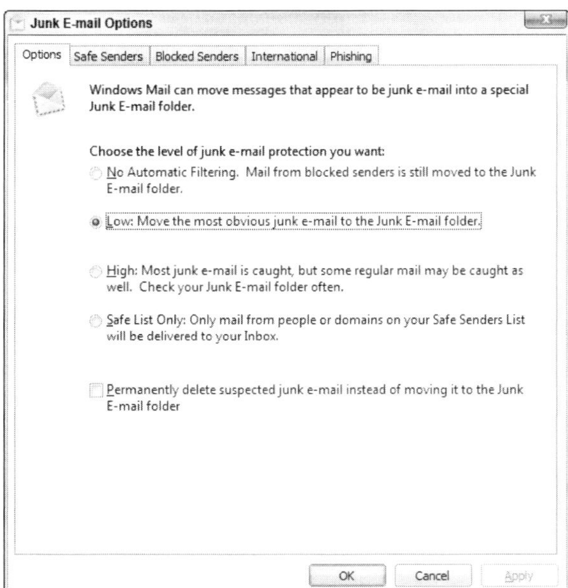

TIP You can add e-mail addresses to the safe or blocked senders list like this: Highlight an e-mail in the preview pane and right-click it. Hover the mouse cursor over Junk E-Mail (see Figure 13.24). Click one of the following: Add Sender to Safe Senders List, Add Sender's Domain (@example.com) to Safe Senders List, Add Sender to Blocked Senders List, or Add Sender's Domain (@example.com) to Block Senders List. Adding entire domains to the safe or blocked list causes everything from that domain to be considered safe or considered junk, respectively.

FIGURE 13.24

This is the easy way to add people to your safe and blocked lists.

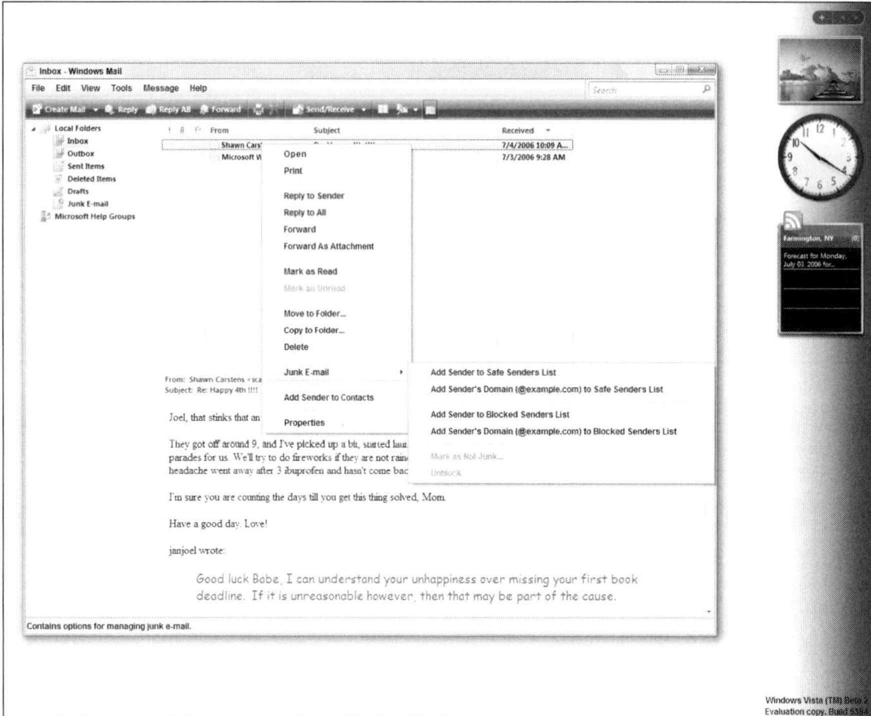

Windows Contacts

The Windows Contacts folder is, in Windows Vista, governed by the laws of the Windows Explorer shell. It looks and reads like a normal folder, rather than its own application.

You can open the Windows Contacts folder through the Start Menu or through Windows Mail. Click the Contacts button to open it. When you first start out with Windows Vista, it looks like Figure 13.25.

To add a contact, you can either right-click an e-mail in Windows Mail's preview pane and click Add Sender to Contacts, or open the Windows Contacts folder and click New Contact. The latter method opens a dialog box like the one shown in Figure 13.26 and allows you to fill in the various fields with data about your contact.

FIGURE 13.25

An empty Windows Contacts folder

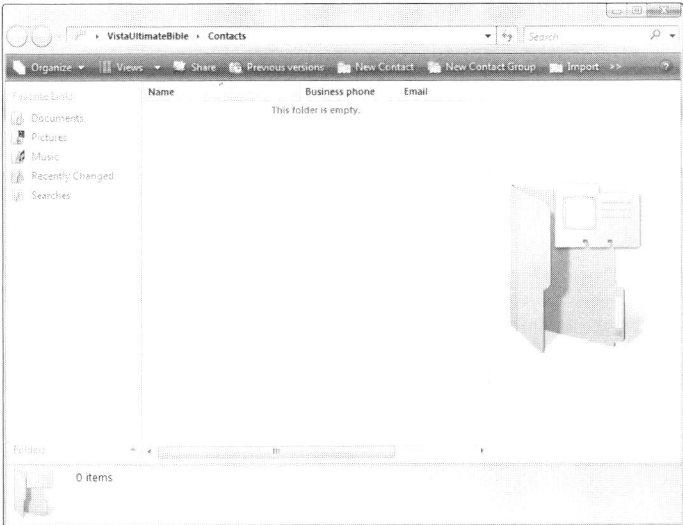

FIGURE 13.26

Adding good old Bob Bobson to my contact list. Everyone knows Bob!

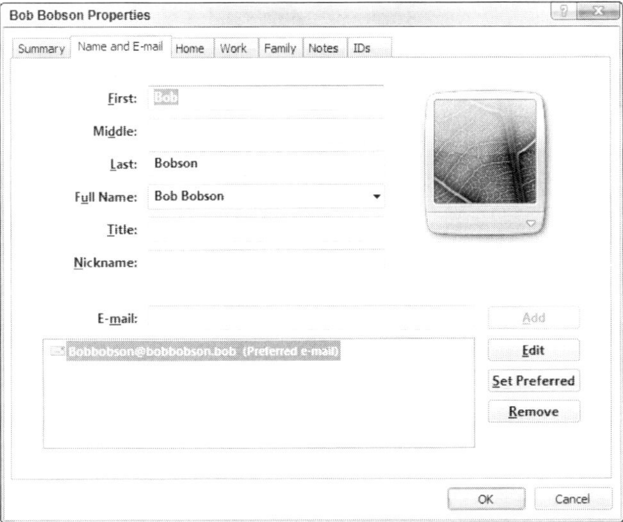

Using the other contacts-specific buttons on the toolbar, you can create new contact groups, which are basically subfolders into which you can group your contacts; and you can import and export your contact list. One handy option on the Import menu is to import contacts from an old-style Windows Address Book file (like the one used by Outlook Express).

Windows Vista's RSS Support

RSS stands for Really Simple Syndication. It's a way for Web pages, or parts of Web pages, that are frequently updated to deliver content to subscribers without the need for the subscriber to visit the page. RSS content is delivered through what are called *feeds*. An RSS feed can include anything, from simple headlines that link to articles to entire articles and even multimedia content like podcasts.

Windows Vista supports RSS through IE7+ and can even make podcast content available through a Toolbar gadget so the content is always right there on the desktop.

What is a feed?

An RSS feed (also called an XML feed) comes from a Web page and is usually a portion of the page that's frequently updated. For example, news sites and blogs often offer RSS feeds, as they're (hopefully) updated on a regular basis. Feeds can contain headlines, articles, links, and even attached content that you may choose to download.

Feeds usually come in RSS and Atom formats, and they're based on XML (which stands for Extensible Markup Language). XML is similar to HTML, in that it's used to dictate how documents (usually Web documents) appear and their various capabilities.

You can find feeds by looking for buttons or links on Web sites that say RSS or XML. For example, CNN.com has a whole host of RSS feeds, as shown in Figure 13.27.

Subscribing to feeds through IE7+

When you've found a feed that interests you, click the RSS or XML button or link on the page. A page similar to the one shown in Figure 13.28 appears. To subscribe to the feed, simply click the link that says Subscribe to this feed. A dialog box like the one shown in Figure 13.29 appears. Click Subscribe to subscribe to the feed.

FIGURE 13.27

This is CNN.com's generous offering of RSS feeds.

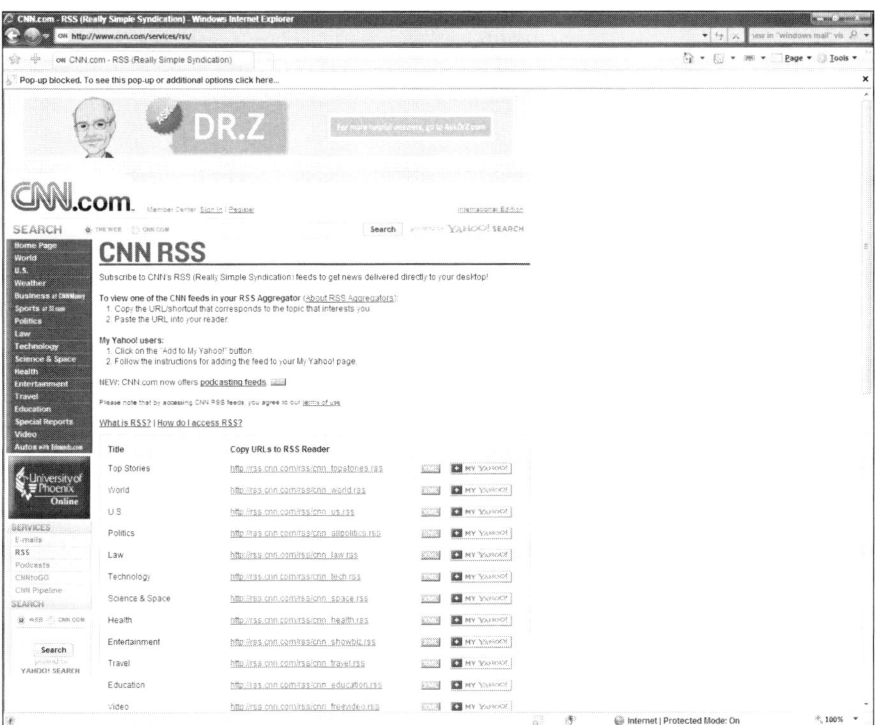

FIGURE 13.28

IE7+ displays this page after you click on an RSS link.

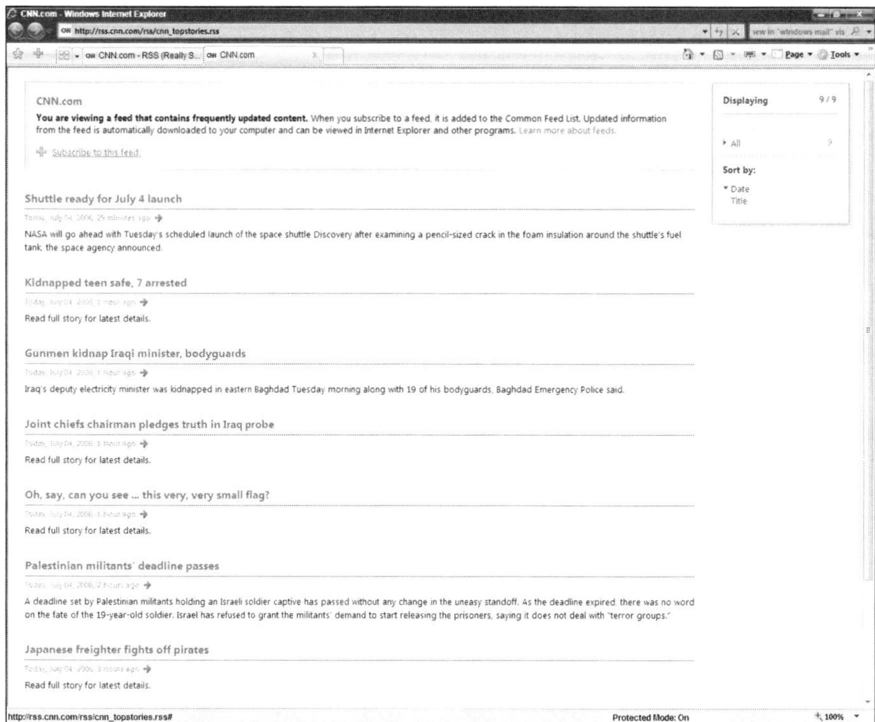

FIGURE 13.29

Subscribing to a feed

The feed page changes slightly. Now it shows a link called View my feeds, and to the right is a link called View feed properties. Click the former to launch the Favorites Center with the Feeds page displayed; click the latter to go to the current feed's options window.

RSS options

An RSS feed's options window looks like the one in Figure 13.30. It contains several options for the currently selected feed, including:

- **Name** and **Address:** You can tweak these properties if you want. Changing the name of the feed is no big deal, but altering the address can cause Windows Vista to be unable to find the feed.
- **Update schedule:** Here, you can alter how often Vista looks for new content in the feed. You can use the default or customize it. You can also tell Vista to automatically download files attached to the feed, and view those files. Through the Settings button you can tell Vista to play a sound when new content is found.
- **Archive:** This area lets you tell Vista how many content updates for a feed you should keep on the computer. The default is 200, the maximum is 2500, and you can configure it however you like.

FIGURE 13.30

The RSS feed's properties window

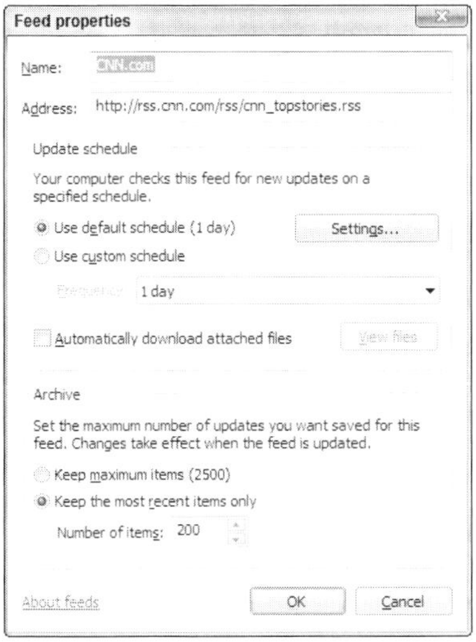

When you visit a Web page that features one or more RSS feeds, the RSS button on the IE7+ toolbar will change from being grayed out to a bright orange color. Click it to choose a feed to which to subscribe. For example, Figure 13.31 shows the popular site ExtremeTech (`www.extremetech.com`), which features several RSS feeds. Notice the orange button below the Search box.

FIGURE 13.31

ExtremeTech is a terrific tech site that features RSS feeds.

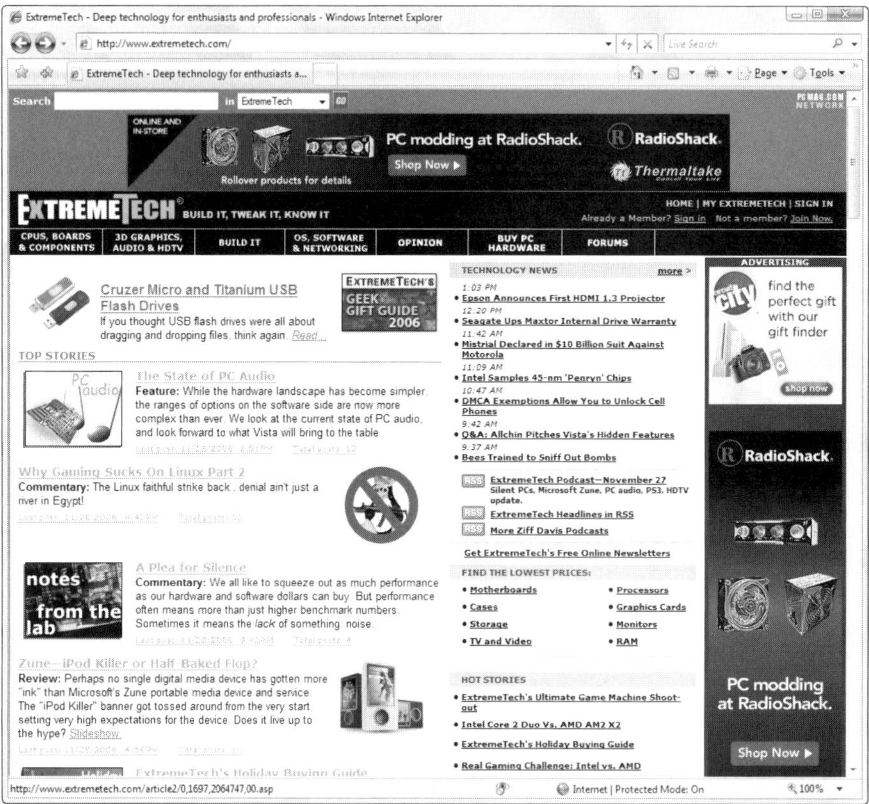

After clicking the RSS button, the page shown in Figure 13.32 appears.

From this page, you can subscribe to a feed, search the feed, sort it by date or by the titles of its articles, and browse through the current headlines.

FIGURE 13.32

Feed options offered by ExtremeTech's Web site

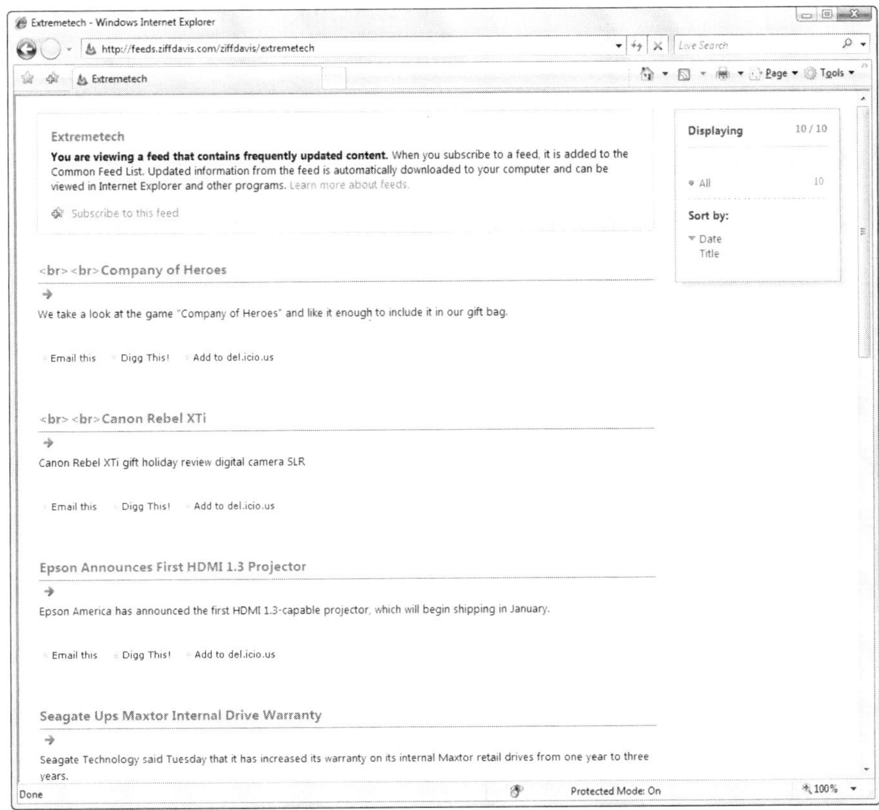

After you subscribe to a feed, you can check it out through several methods. First, you can open an IE7+ browser and click the Favorites button, and then click the Feeds button, as shown in Figure 13.33. Then, simply click the title of the feed you wish to view.

Thanks to the power of the Sidebar, there's another way to view your feeds. By default, the Sidebar features a gadget called Feed Headlines (Figure 13.34). It displays headlines of RSS feeds to which you've subscribed.

FIGURE 13.33

The interface on the left shows the feeds to which I've subscribed.

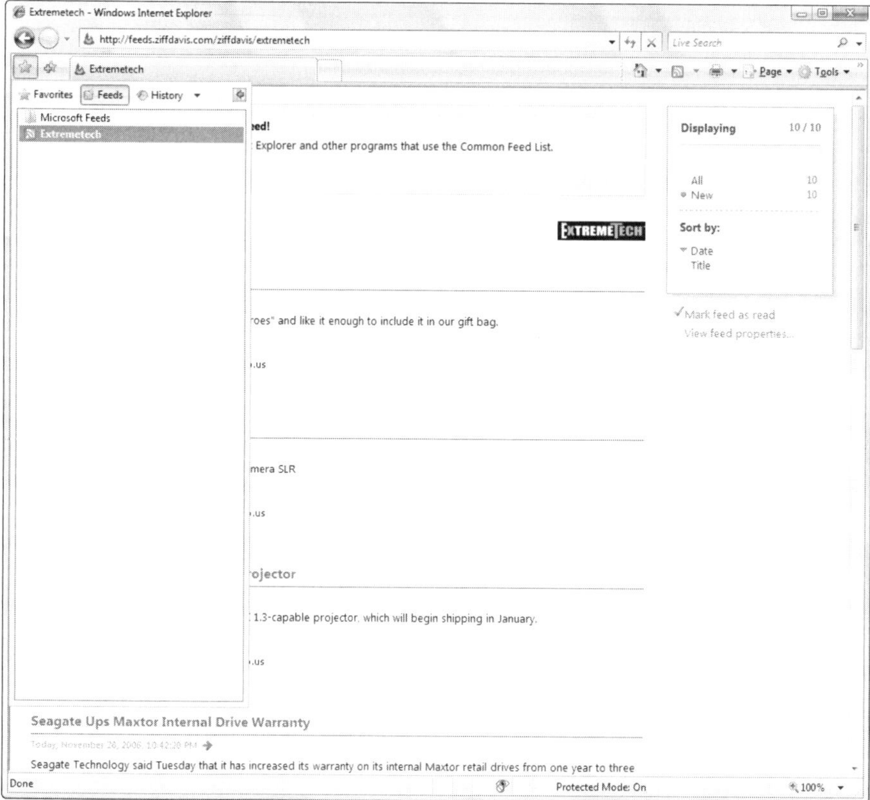

FIGURE 13.34

The Feed Headline gadget

You can click any headline currently displayed by the Feed Headline gadget to see a blurb, if the feed's originator provided one (Figure 13.35). If you enjoy the blurb and wish to see the actual article from which it originates, double-click it and a browser will appear dialed in to the page that displays the article.

FIGURE 13.35

A feed blurb, compliments of the Sidebar

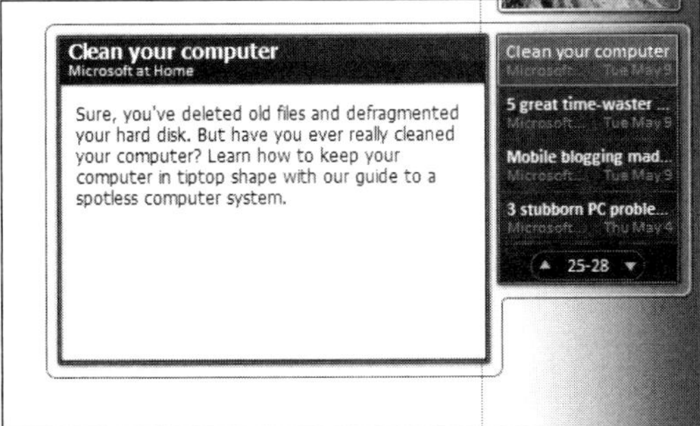

RSS feeds represent a powerful way to stay current with your favorite Web sites that receive frequent updates. Between IE7+ and the Feed Headline Sidebar gadget, you have no excuse for falling behind on the information you crave the most.

Summary

Windows Vista Ultimate is the most Web-ready operating system in the short history of the World Wide Web. Perhaps that's why an Internet connection is listed among its system requirements; you simply will not get the most out of your Vista-powered computing experience without 'Net access.

So much of the operating system is Internet dependant. A great deal of its modules require frequent updates, from Automatic Updates to Windows Defender. Of course, automated updating isn't the only reason to go online — Windows Vista Ultimate provides Internet Explorer 7+, Windows Mail, and powerful RSS support to keep you entertained, informed, and in touch.

Internet Explorer 7+ is beyond a simple evolutionary step past IE6; it's nothing short of revolutionary. Combining popular features of competing browsers, like tabbed browsing, with a streamlined interface, better Favorites management, multiple home page support, and more, it's among the finest browsers on the face of the Earth.

Windows Mail, meanwhile, is a step beyond the skeletal e-mail support offered by Outlook Express. While Windows Mail isn't quite as powerful as Microsoft Outlook or Mozilla Thunderbird, it's much better than its predecessor. Its most glaring new feature is a powerful, Bayesian junk mail filter. Its integration with Windows Contacts is top notch, too; contact management in Windows Vista is better than ever.

Windows Vista's RSS support is so streamlined it would be a shame if you don't try it out. Between the built-in RSS features of IE7+ and the Sidebar Feed Headline gadget, Windows Vista can blast you with information nonstop, and you don't even have to make the rounds to visit your favorite Web sites to keep up.

Part V

Gaming and Multimedia Enhancements

Windows Vista Ultimate is all about multimedia, and it's strongly enhanced to empower you to play, listen, watch, and otherwise entertain yourself at its keyboard. The newest version of the DirectX multimedia libraries is more powerful than ever, and when games arrive that take advantage of its abilities you won't believe your eyes or ears. Windows Media Center is built into this version of Vista, and it's better than ever.

Part V gives you the knowledge you need to understand the gaming and multimedia prowess of Windows Vista Ultimate. This *is* the operating system for visual, aural, and interactive gratification!

IN THIS PART

Chapter 14

Gaming and Audio Enhancements

Windows Vista is certainly welcome news for gamers; unfortunately, Windows operating systems haven't always been the gamer's best friend. With the superior graphical capability that Vista Premium computers offer over Windows XP–designed machines, as well as the introduction of ActiveX 10, Windows Vista finally steps into its own and becomes a legitimate option for gaming and entertainment possibilities.

This chapter provides a brief overview of some of the gaming enhancements available in Windows Vista, as well as an introduction to the new ActiveX 10. In this chapter I also discuss the new Windows Media Player 11, the Windows Experience Index (formerly known as WinSAT), as well as other audio enhancements now available in Windows Vista.

IN THIS CHAPTER

Looking at Vista's gaming enhancements

Introducing Media Player 11

Understanding the Windows Experience Index

Looking at Vista's audio enhancements

Gaming Enhancements in Windows Vista

Windows Vista provides a number of gaming enhancements. Some of these are available in the form of new features, such as a number of new games shipped with Windows Vista, new Parental Controls, the Games Explorer, and Microsoft DirectX 10.

A number of video game developers have announced plans for creating video games specifically for Windows Vista. While using Aero can only improve your gaming experience, remember that most games run on their own 3D surface or set of surfaces. In other words, you can run your games on any edition of Windows Vista; you're only limited by the quality of your hardware.

Two of the biggest operating system enhancements in Vista are the Games Explorer and Parental Controls. They are both designed to make your gaming experience easier and more comfortable.

Games Explorer

The Games Explorer, which is accessible from the Start Menu, is simply a window that includes all of the games bundled with Windows Vista, as shown in Figure 14.1. These include

- Chess Titans
- FreeCell
- Hearts
- InkBall
- Mahjong Titans
- Minesweeper
- Purble Place
- Solitaire
- Spider Solitaire

You can also access the Games Explorer by typing Games in the Start Menu Search box.

When you click on the icon of the game you want to play, information about the selected game appears on the right side of the Games Explorer. For example, if you click Mahjong Titans, the game icon appears, along with performance measurements for the game on your computer. Windows Vista provides a series of ratings — recommended game rating, minimum required rating, and the current system's rating. These ratings are based on the quality of your system's hardware. A link to the Performance Information and Tools window provides additional information about the Microsoft rating system, as well as scores for the other components of your computer. The Software Explorer also provides any ratings, if available, for your game, as shown on the right in Figure 14.2.

FIGURE 14.1

The Games Explorer is the central location for your games on Windows Vista.

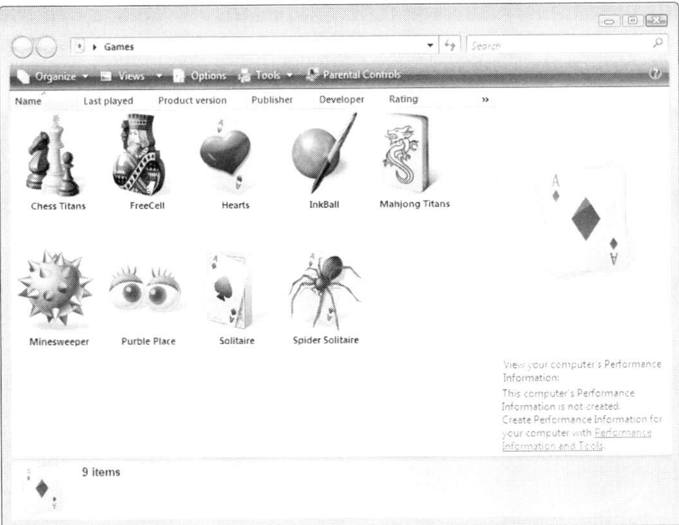

FIGURE 14.2

Game ratings help you determine which games are appropriate for your family.

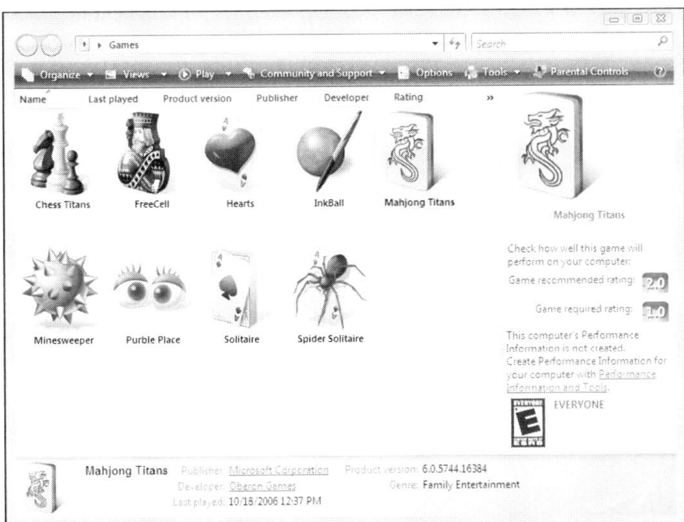

CROSS-REF For more information about the games and programs included with Windows Vista Ultimate, see Chapter 6.

Parental Controls

The ratings system is just one way to protect your computer from prying eyes. Parents will be happy to know that Vista includes a Parental Controls feature that goes far beyond any other sort of protection mechanism in previous versions of Windows. As an administrator, you have full leverage in deciding what other users on your computer can access. You can access the Parental Controls from either the Control Panel, or by clicking the link in the Games Explorer. From the Parental Controls page, select the user account to which you want to set restrictions; the Parental Control options appear for that user, as shown in Figure 14.3.

FIGURE 14.3

Set Parental Controls to determine how family members use the computer.

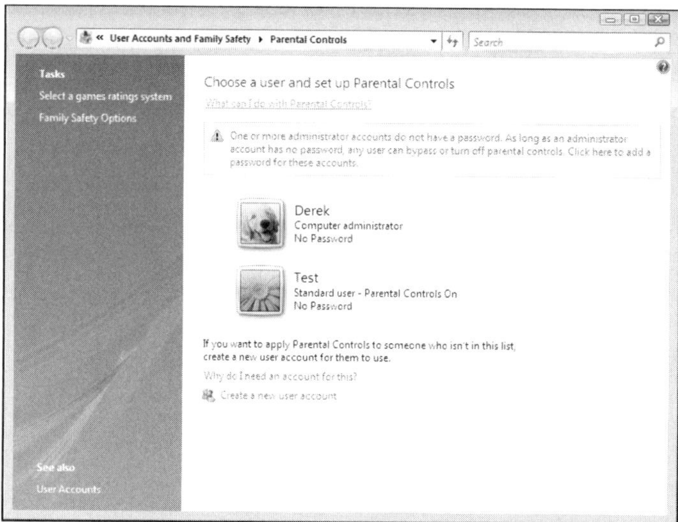

For example, as shown in Figure 14.4, you may want to set restrictions on what games are accessible to your children. The User Controls for each user has a number of different Windows settings, notably Games. By setting Parental Controls for Games, you can first decide whether or not to let that particular user play games.

You have two different ways of blocking games on your computer: by rating and content, and by selecting specific games to block. If you decide to block a game according to its rating and content, click the Set games ratings link (shown in Figure 14.4). The default maximum allowed rating appears just below the aforementioned Set game ratings link. By default, nothing is blocked. The status for blocked games (always blocked or always allowed) appears below the Block or Allow specific games link; by default, these are both set to None.

If you decide to block by ratings, you must first decide how to handle games that do not have an assigned rating; by default, these games are allowed. You can then decide which game rating level is appropriate for your user, as shown in Figure 14.5. Each rating has an applicable definition indicating the appropriate age group for each rating.

FIGURE 14.4

Parental Controls let you set security settings for games on your computer.

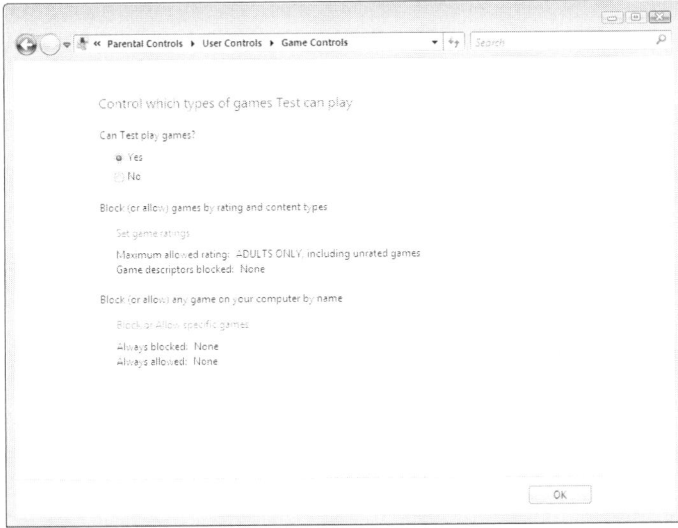

Of course, you may want to manually allow or block a specific game. By clicking Block or Allow specific games from the Game Controls page, you can view the current status for each of the games (Figure 14.6). By clicking the desired radio button for a particular game, you can decide whether or not to always allow or block a game. By default, these are all set to User Rating Setting, which uses the rating permissions that you set on the Game Restrictions page.

FIGURE 14.5

If a game doesn't have a rating, you can individually set whether to block or allow it.

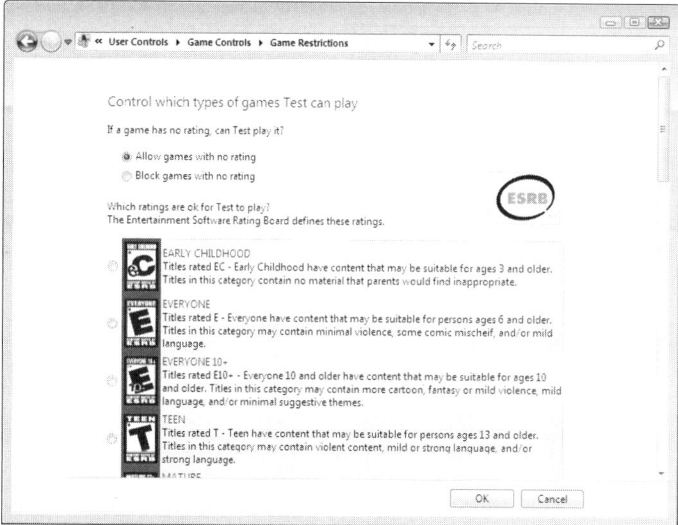

FIGURE 14.6

In the Games Overrides window you can manually allow or block specific games.

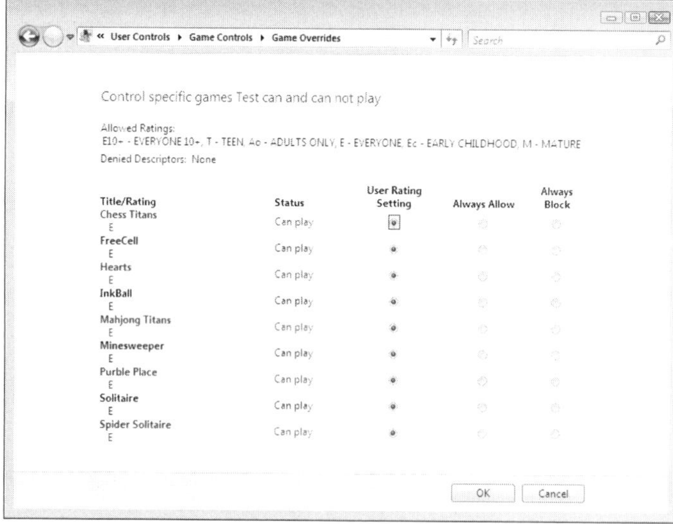

Microsoft DirectX 10

Windows users are probably familiar with DirectX, which has been a Windows staple since 1995. DirectX is a set of application programming interfaces (APIs) that are used in gaming, multimedia, and programming. Many Xbox, now Xbox 360, and Windows games are developed in DirectX.

DirectX 10 ships with Windows Vista, and runs alongside DirectX 9. It is not backward-compatible, which is why a version of DirectX 9, known as DirectX 9.0L, is also included. (Note that games written for earlier versions of DirectX should mostly run on Vista, using the built-in DirectX 9.0L.) Initially called the Windows Graphic Foundation (WGF), Microsoft eventually dropped the new name and stuck with the simple DirectX10.

NOTE The early games that use DirectX 10 will likely have a code path for DirectX 9 as well, as not everyone will have DirectX 10 capable graphics cards for several years.

What's new in DirectX 10? The API uses new and improved DLL libraries that offer much better performance — in other words, faster performance. This improved API should also help reduce the amount of system sources that the CPU runtime usually manages. DirectX 10 now also supports the latest Shader Model (currently 4.0). If you're not familiar with shaders, they are commonly used in 3D graphics; their purpose is to determine the final surface properties or attributes for an object.

NOTE DirectX 10 depends completely on the new Windows Vista device driver model (WDDM), so there are no plans to back port DirectX 10 to earlier versions of Windows. If you want DirectX 10, you'll need to have Vista.

CROSS-REF For full coverage of Microsoft DirectX 10, see Chapter 15.

Windows Media Player 11

Microsoft recently released Windows Media Player 11; currently available for Windows XP Service Pack 2, it also ships with Windows Vista (unless you are a resident of the European Union and are using an *N* edition). Although I discuss the Windows Media Player in full detail in Chapter 17, let's take a quick look at some of its new features.

Windows Media Player is more than a pretty new interface; it's easier to manage and is an overall improvement on Windows Media Player 10 (which was light years beyond the previous version). The improved interface, shown in Figure 14.7, makes media exploration easier than ever before. The layout is certainly more logical than in past versions of Windows Media Player.

Some of the new features in Windows Media Player 11 include:

- The Media Library, which displays content graphically using a thumbnail. This is a change from previous versions, which used category trees.
- Improved CD-burning capabilities. You can now see how much CD space remains when preparing a CD for burning.

- The ability to rip audio CDs to WAV format.
- The URGE music store, which is now part of Windows Media Player 11.

FIGURE 14.7

Windows Media Player 11 has a cleaner interface and, by extension, more easily navigated library.

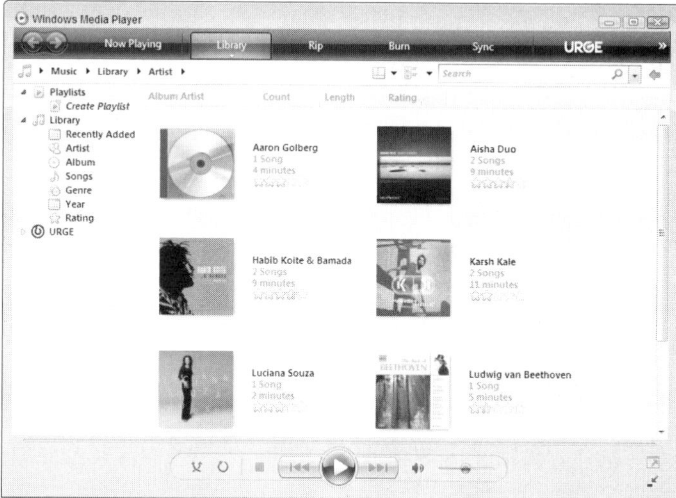

URGE online music store

URGE is a big component of the new and improved Windows Media Player. URGE is a joint Microsoft and MTV online music service; it is similar to Apple's iTunes or Napster. In order to use URGE, you must first download it from its Web site at `www.urge.com`, as shown in Figure 14.8 or directly from the Windows Media Player application. If you try to use URGE without the necessary installation, Windows Media Player will ask you to install it.

URGE is subscription based. For a flat monthly fee you can download unlimited songs and other multimedia. However, if you want to burn songs to a CD, you must purchase these songs individually.

Once installed, URGE integrates seamlessly into Windows Media Player 11. It features an extensive music catalog that rivals that of any of its competitors.

CROSS-REF **For more information about the URGE online music store, turn to Chapter 18.**

The Windows Experience Index

Formerly known as WinSAT (the Windows System Assessment Tool), the Windows Experience Index is a new feature in Windows Vista that is available in the Ultimate Edition. As its name might imply, it is a tool designed to optimize your computer for maximum results using Windows Vista. This very helpful, and important, tool is a command-line application that runs when you first log on to Vista. Every time you log on to your computer, the Windows Experience Index re-runs its tests and regenerates a new set of subscores and a base score.

FIGURE 14.8

You will need to download URGE before you can use it.

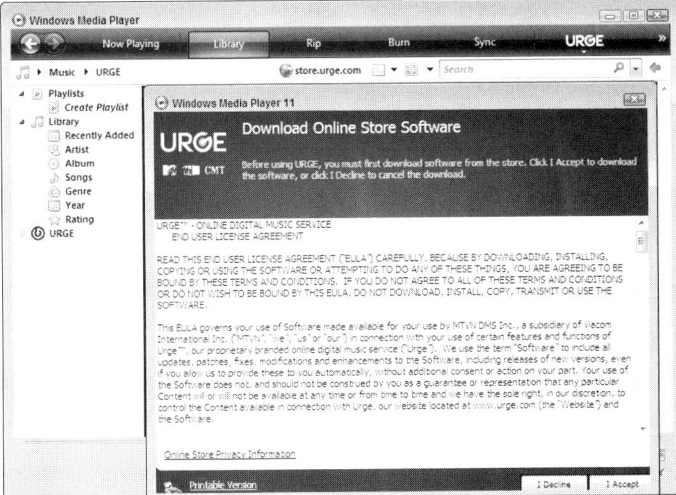

A built-in Windows benchmark

The Windows Experience Index is a fully integrated benchmark test for your Windows operating system. As mentioned earlier, it loads and runs every time you log on to Windows Vista. The inclusion of the Windows Experience Index in Vista is the first time that Windows has provided any sort of benchmarking application to see how your computer stacks up against the operating system requirements.

Given the number of changes in Windows Vista compared to Windows XP, as well as the potential upgrade requirements, the fact that such tests would be run on your computer is only appropriate and helpful.

Windows Experience Index runs a number of tests that determine your computer's readiness for Windows Vista; using the Performance Information and Tools window of the Control Panel, you can get an easy-to-understand breakdown of exactly where your computer stands, as shown in Figure 14.9.

FIGURE 14.9

Windows Vista lets you know how your computer stacks up.

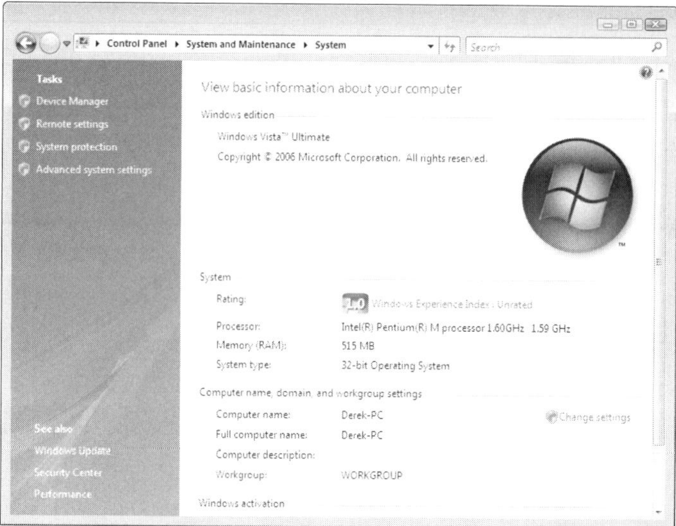

The tests rate your computer on the following five different components or aspects:

- Processor
- Memory (RAM)
- Graphics
- Gaming graphics
- Primary hard disk

Each component is given a rating; the higher the rating, the better performance that the component is capable of in Windows Vista. These components are detailed further in the section, "What the Windows Experience Index measures," later in this chapter.

Windows Vista spells out everything for you in the Performance Information and Tools page, so it's relatively easy to understand. However, the base score calculation may confuse users. The base score isn't an average of your component's subscore. In fact, it's simply the lowest subscore of the five components. For example, if four subscores are 4.2, but processor is 2.6, your base score is 2.6, as shown in Figure 14.10.

The Performance Information and Tools window provides additional information that can help you to better understand, or even increase, your score. By clicking the link at the top, located next to the lightbulb, you can access information in the Windows Help and Support that provides ideas on how to improve computer performance.

FIGURE 14.10

Your computer's base score is only as good (or bad) as your lowest component result.

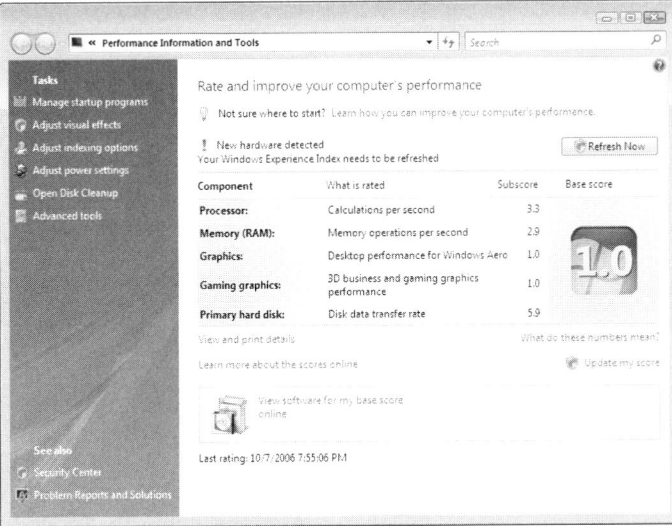

Beneath the table of subscores and base score are four actionable links:

- View and print details
- Learn more about the scores online
- What do these numbers mean?
- Update my score

The View and print details link displays your computer's scores (sub and base) in a printer-friendly format. It also provides information on your hardware; for example, you can see specific system, storage, graphics, and network information for your computer, as shown in Figure 14.11.

The Learn more about the scores online link, which requires an active Internet connection, takes you to the Microsoft Web site, shown in Figure 14.12, where you can get a more detailed explanation of the scores for your five components.

FIGURE 14.11

Get the 411 on your computer's system statistics here.

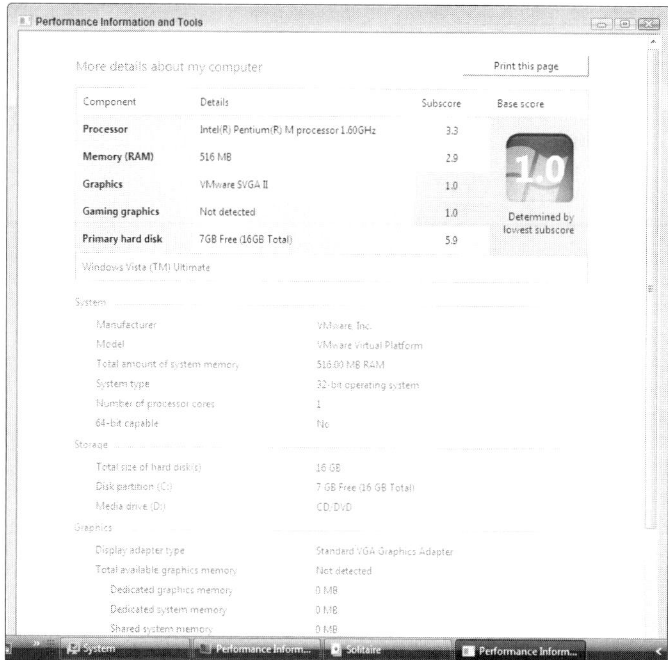

FIGURE 14.12

Windows Vista takes you to the Microsoft Web site for more information on ratings.

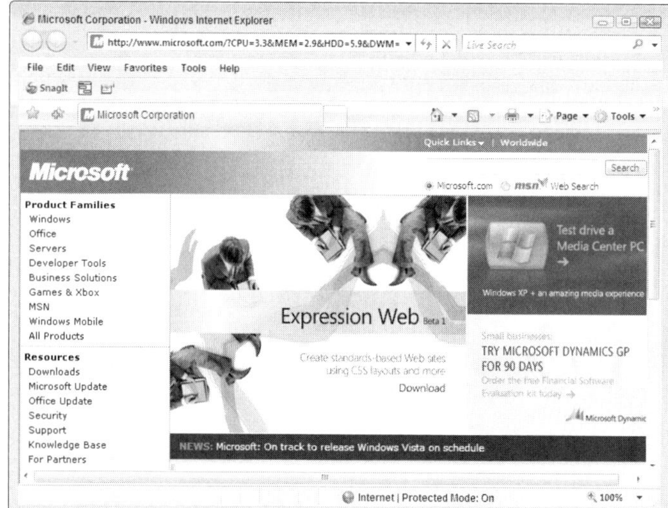

The What do these numbers mean? link takes you to the Windows Help and Support center, to the "What is the Windows Experience Index?" help topic. This page provides ample information on the Windows Experience Index. I recommend taking a few minutes to read this topic, as it provides good information on how the subscore and base score computation works.

Finally, the Update my score link lets your regenerate your score. If you've changed hardware or otherwise modified your computer in any way, you can tell Windows Vista to update your score for you. After you click Update my score, Windows Experience Index executes a battery of tests. Keep in mind that this calculation may last several minutes depending on your computer.

What the Windows Experience Index measures

The Windows Experience Index measures five components to determine your computer's ability to use Windows Vista effectively (as shown in Figure 14.13):

- **Processor:** This component sizes up the strength of your computer's processor. Specifically, it rates the number of calculations per second. In other words, it measures the speed.
- **Memory (RAM):** This component is tested and rated based on the number of memory options performed per second.
- **Graphics:** This component determines your computer's readiness for Windows Vista and how well your desktop performs to Aero standards.
- **Gaming graphics:** This component measures gaming graphics performance as well as 3D business; essentially, this component is a test of the quality of your video card.
- **Your primary hard disk and the disk data transfer rate:** Vista tests these items as well.

Vista generates a subscore for each of these components, where the lowest individual score is the base score of your computer. As I mention earlier in this chapter, if you click Update my score, Windows Vista regenerates your scores by running a battery of tests. These tests are:

- Aero Assessment
- Direct3D Alpha Blend Assessment
- Direct3D Texture Load Assessment
- Direct3D ALU Assessment
- Windows media playback
- CPU performance
- Memory performance
- Disk performance

After the assessment is complete (running these tests can take up to several minutes, depending on how powerful your computer is), Windows Vista displays the System page from the Control Panel with the new rating, as shown in Figure 14.14.

FIGURE 14.13

Windows Experience Index measures five distinct components.

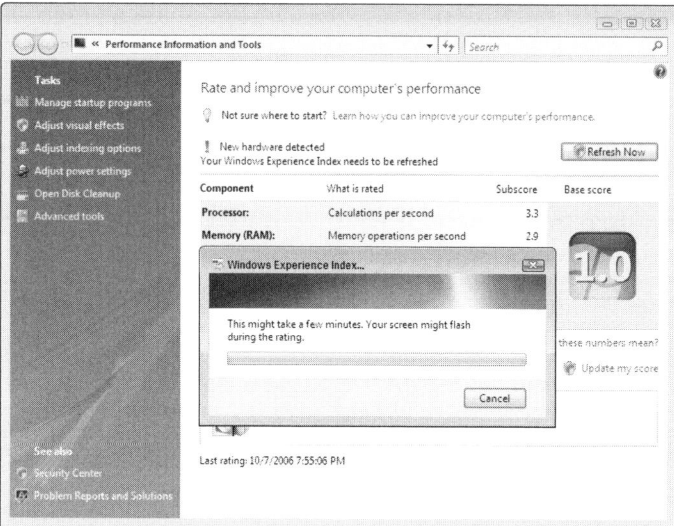

FIGURE 14.14

If your rating changes, Windows Vista displays it from the System page.

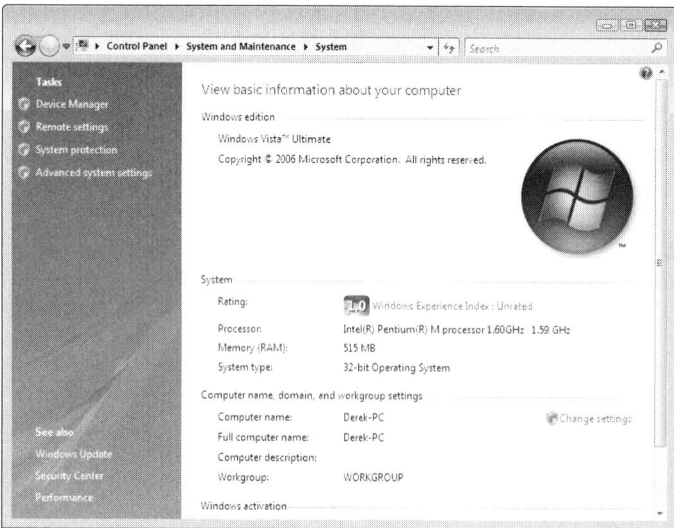

Audio Enhancements in Windows Vista

Multimedia enhancements in Windows Vista aren't limited to just video aspects of the operating system. The audio capabilities in Windows Vista are also greatly expanded and improved and give the user more control over the operating system and performance.

These changes include

- Individual audio control
- High-end audio playback
- Room correction
- Speaker fill
- Virtualization
- Advanced voice communication

Individual audio control

In Windows XP, you might remember that you had a master control using the Volume Control window. This window let you change volume controls for hardware, such as the overall computer volume, CD player volume, Wave, and SW Synth. Things are different now in Windows Vista; now you can set volume settings per application, and not just for your computer.

By right-clicking the speaker icon in the notification area, you can select Playback Devices to view the volume control for currently open applications, as shown in Figure 14.15.

FIGURE 14.15

The Windows Media Player sound level control

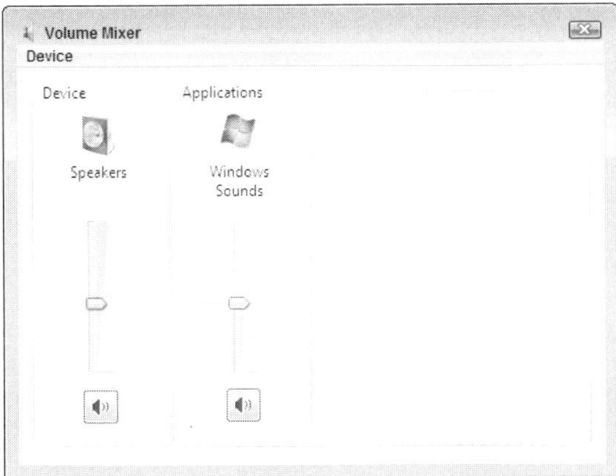

By default, two categories of sound controls exist: devices and applications. The Device section controls sounds for your machine, whereas Applications lets you set sound levels for Windows applications. The Applications section has a single application category by default: Windows applications. If you open another Windows application that uses sounds, for example, Windows Media Player, the icon appears in the Applications section of the Playback Devices window, as shown in Figure 14.16.

FIGURE 14.16

Here you can set the volume control for individual applications.

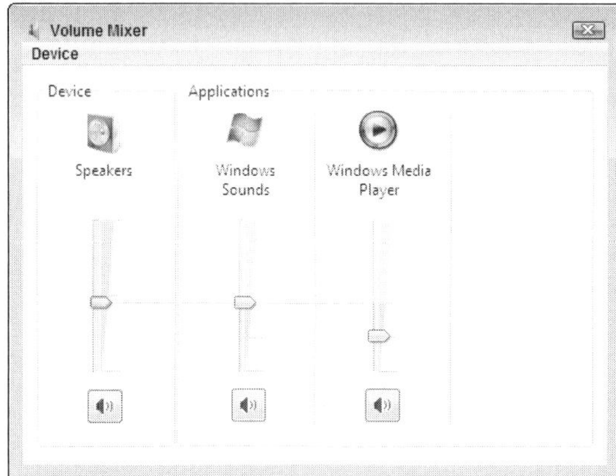

NOTE New applications do not appear on-the-fly; you must re-open the Playback Devices window in order for it to appear. You can then set sound levels for an individual application.

High-end audio playback

The Vista team took great care to improve audio standards for the new operating standards; even though the most intense gamers may or may not be impressed by the improvements, there's no denying that Microsoft clearly made significant progress in this respect.

CROSS-REF For more information about audio improvements in Windows Vista Ultimate, see Chapters 18 and 23.

Although I discuss most of these audio improvements in Chapters 18 and 23, for now I would like to talk about improvements to the supported playback devices for Windows Vista. Microsoft uses its Universal Audio Architecture, also referred to as UAA, as the lynchpin for the improved audio capabilities in Windows.

By relying on UAA technology, Windows Vista offers a far more stable and enjoyable audio experience. The use of UAA also means support for high-end audio playback; in other words, new and better ways of enjoying multimedia are available with Windows Vista. This new support includes

- Increased support for USB-devices
- IEEE 1394 support
- Intel High-Definition Audio support

Let's take a closer look at what these new options really mean for you.

Enhanced USB support

The improved support for USB audio devices means three major changes for Windows Vista users. First, Vista now decodes padded AC-3 (Dolby Digital), MP3, WMA, and WMA Pro streams, and outputting as S/PDIF (Sony/Philips Digital Interface). Simply put, Vista decodes these aforementioned audio formats and outputs them with S/PDIF, which allows digital audio signals to be sent from one device to another without having to first be transformed to an analog format. The advantage of this enhancement is that no loss of sound quality occurs during this process.

MIDI elements through USB are now supported in Windows Vista. An element is nothing more than a processing engine used in USB-MIDI functions.

Asynchronous endpoints are also supported in Windows Vista. These types of endpoints generate or process data at a rate that is locked to an internal or external clock.

IEEE 1394 support

Perhaps better known as FireWire, IEEE 1394 is now natively supported in Windows Vista. In other words, it is built into the operating system as a fully functioning driver. Any IEEE 1394–standard audio device is automatically supported. What is most interesting about this development is that this support is in reference to IEEE 1394b, which is the "next generation" high-speed version of the original IEEE 1394a standard. The IEEE 1394a standard could transport at speeds up to 400Mbps.

Intel High-Definition Audio support

Out with the old, in with the new! The AC97 audio standard, which you might remember from Windows XP, is not relegated to the trash bin. Microsoft has replaced it with Intel's latest audio standard, known as Intel High-Definition Audio (IHD). Even though this standard isn't exactly new — it was first released in 2004 — it is the *de facto* replacement for the AC97 standard. Any audio device that is designed to use this new standard is automatically compatible with Windows Vista. The IHD standard provides 192 kHz/32-bit sound quality for two channels; eight channels go to 96 kHz/32-bit sound quality.

Room correction

When regulating your speaker settings in Windows Vista for a high-definition audio device, you'll notice an Enhance tab in the device's properties window, as shown in Figure 14.17. Please note that this tab does not appear if you are not running a high-definition audio device. One of the enhancements available in this tab is the new room correction feature.

This feature works with very high end audio devices and also requires a high-end microphone in order to work properly. This is how it works: Vista, through the use of a microphone, scopes out the room in which you are using your computer and calibrates your audio settings to the ideal level through the use of a wizard. The wizard takes precise note of particularities, such as distance, frequency, gain, and so on. Another positive aspect, besides having the best sound possible for your conditions, is that this feature uses very little CPU.

FIGURE 14.17

An Enhance tab will appear if you are running a high-definition audio device.

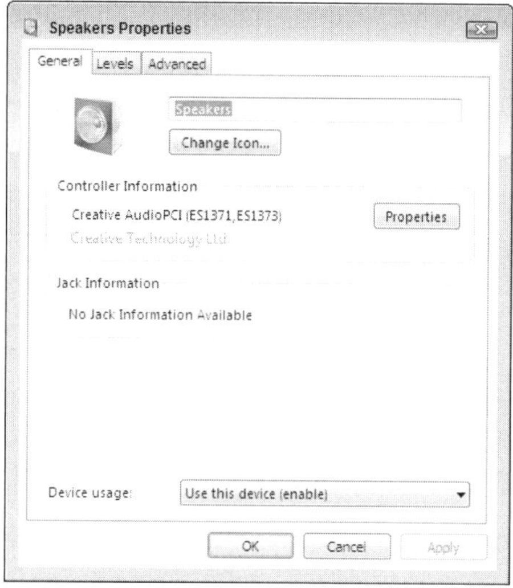

What Is the Universal Audio Architecture?

Universal Audio Architecture (UAA) is a new audio device driver concept that Microsoft announced in 2002; it makes its first public appearance with the release of Windows Vista. The point of UAA is very simple: reduce the dependency on third-party audio drivers for use with Windows operating systems. Vendors using this new class of audio device drivers will require less driver upgrades, meaning less code development and maintenance. For the user, UAA-compliant devices are easy to upgrade because you won't have to find or download drivers in order to install the device. Additionally, when you install Windows Vista on your computer, Vista automatically installs and configures UAA-compliant devices.

Speaker fill

The speaker fill feature is another enhancement available in the Enhancement tab. This feature is helpful to fill out the sound when you're listening to music recorded with few channels. It's entirely possible that you may have more speakers available for your system than there are actual channels for your music. For example, if you are listening to a recording that has two or four channels, the speaker fill feature creates virtual or synthetic channels for Vista to use and then send on to your speakers.

Virtualization

Windows Vista has also made wonderful advances in audio experience for laptop users. Working on the road is no excuse for having to endure subpar audio quality, and I'm glad to see that Microsoft recognizes this! One of the biggest improvements for the laptop audio experience is *virtualization*. Not to be confused with the notion of virtual machines, audio virtualization is a feature that works well with headphones. Windows Vista now allows for surround sound — virtual surround sound, that is — for use with headphones on Windows Vista.

Using virtualization, you can have a true home cinema experience. For example, you can literally distinguish sound from front to back, and left to right — just as when listening to your home cinema from the comfort of your living room. This new feature is thanks to a new technology called Head-Related Transfer Functions (HRTF), which works with the shape of the human head to create the most dynamic sound possible for the user.

Advanced voice communication

Windows Vista has considerably advanced voice communication features in a number of different arenas, especially in terms of accessibility.

For example, a voice recognition feature is now available that allows you to control your computer through voice commands, as shown in Figure 14.18. This feature is available for all editions of Windows Vista. Through the use of a wizard, you can literally teach Vista to recognize your voice. Once Vista learns your speaking pattern, you can almost literally say goodbye to your mouse and keyboard. This feature doesn't necessarily work with all applications, but it does work with all Windows Vista features and should work with Microsoft applications, such as Office 2007. This feature also works with an array of microphone types; these are particularly useful for this feature or with VoIP because they can distinguish voices among ambient noise. A number of demos and other support tools are also available to help you learn to use this feature effectively, as shown in Figure 14.19.

FIGURE 14.18

The Windows Voice Recognition feature lets you command your computer vocally.

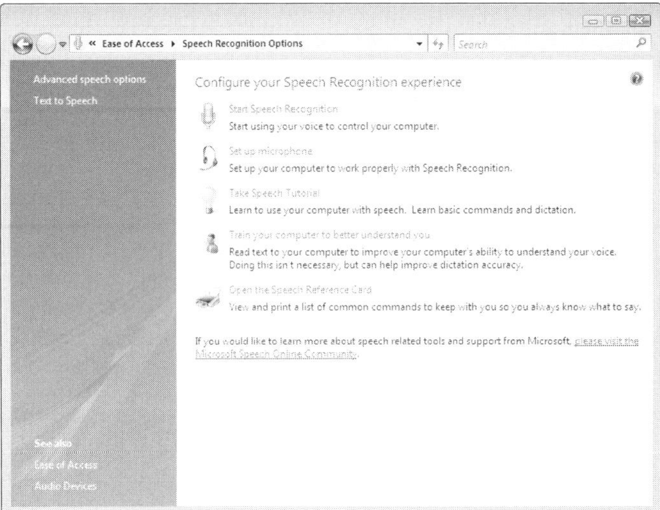

FIGURE 14.19

A number of demo and support tools are available to get you on your way.

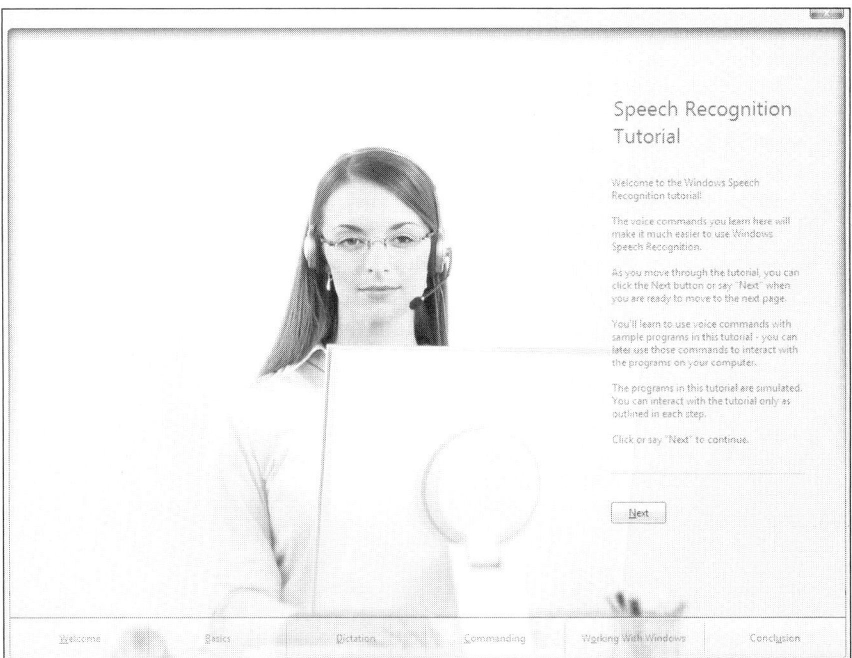

Summary

Microsoft can proudly boast of Windows Vista's impressive "out of the box" audio system. Of course, taking advantage of it means that you have to make sure that you have equally capable audio devices. What's great is that Vista can support most of these high-end audio devices out of the box without additional work on your part.

Gamers will also appreciate some of the newer features in Windows Vista, such as DirectX 10 and the Aero theme for high-end video games. Users who always felt that the Windows game bundle was lacking will be pleased to see a number of new games as well. If you're a parent, you may well appreciate the new security tools available to you to block inappropriate material from your children.

Windows Vista also includes on-board system benchmarking to help you determine how your computer stacks up against Windows Vista. This feature is particularly useful when you are considering whether or not to upgrade components of your computer. This benchmarking tool helps you find the weakest link.

The new audio enhancements, especially more high-end on-board support, will please users who want to take advantage of the possibilities that USB and FireWire can offer. Other users will appreciate that they can finally enjoy home cinema–quality surround sound over a laptop with headphones!

Windows Vista is certainly an improvement over Windows XP in all of these categories. Though many users might not use some of the higher-end audio features, those who do use their computer for multimedia will certainly enjoy the improved support and features.

Chapter 15

The New DirectX

IN THIS CHAPTER

- **Looking at DirectX's 32-bit floating-point audio**
- **Checking out DirectX's enhanced DLLs**
- **Looking at other new features**
- **Backward compatibility with DirectX 9.0L**

As discussed in Chapter 14, DirectX is a set of application programming interfaces (APIs) that are used in gaming, multimedia, and programming. It's no surprise that Microsoft included a new version of DirectX with Windows Vista, as this new version is geared toward the next generation of video games that are designed specifically for Vista.

A Windows staple since 1995, DirectX has been an integral part of the Windows gaming and multimedia experience. It has been revamped for Windows Vista; the final result is a bundle of APIs that are five to eight times more powerful than the DirectX 9 release.

Microsoft decided to stick with the familiar DirectX nomenclature, despite toying around with several ideas during development and the beta phase. For example, DirectX 10 was being touted as *Windows Graphics Foundation*. A bit long, Microsoft went with the more familiar *DirectX Next*. That idea later discarded; there was *Direct3D 10* before Microsoft stuck with good-old *DirectX 10*, whose logo is displayed in Figure 15.1.

FIGURE 15.1

The new face, or logo, of Microsoft DirectX 10

This chapter focuses solely on the release of Microsoft DirectX 10 and its impact on Windows Vista. In it I discuss important new features, such as the 32-bit floating-point audio, glitch resilience, improved DLLs, backward compatibility, and other new features in this release.

The Essential New Features

DirectX contains a number of important new features, but this chapter helps you take a closer look at the essential changes that will truly affect your Windows Vista experience. These changes include:

- 32-bit floating-point audio with 144 dB signal-to-noise (SNR) ratio
- Glitch resilience and prioritization of media applications
- Enhanced, high-speed DLLs

Although these features might not impact all Windows Vista users, those who are using the Windows Media Center or plan on playing next-generation games will certainly appreciate these new DirectX features.

32-bit floating-point audio with 144 dB SNR

Microsoft DirectX 10 helps take audio fidelity to a whole new level. Not only does it go far above and beyond Microsoft's offer in Windows XP (and previous DirectX versions), but it goes far above and beyond what current sound cards can support! The floating-point audio feature is just one such example.

In Windows Vista, with DirectX 10, 32-bit floating-point audio that supports signal-to-noise ratios of up to 144 decibels is now reality. This support extends to bit-for-bit sample-level accuracy. This capability is an on-board feature within the very core of the Windows Vista audio system. The advantages of this feature include the guarantee of improved-quality digital signal processing, as well as the fact that sound professionals and other users can enjoy the benefits of high-fidelity audio quality even with non-professional audio hardware generally used by the general public.

A Quick Word about DirectX

Perhaps you've never had to work with DirectX, at least to your knowledge, in previous versions of Windows. Perhaps your familiarity with DirectX ends at the information bar that displays in Internet Explorer informing you that you need to download Microsoft DirectX in order to properly view your Web page. Let's take a few minutes to discuss, or perhaps refresh your memory, as to what DirectX is and what it does.

Microsoft DirectX has been around since 1995. DirectX is a bundle of application programming interfaces (APIs) that are used to manage multimedia and game applications. It contains a number of Component Object Model (COM) components that each handle various aspects of your multimedia and gaming experience. Currently, Microsoft DirectX has eight components.

Dynamic link libraries, better known as DLLs, are literally libraries of data or executables that are used by Windows-based applications in order to run. For example, if you install an application for Windows, and you open its folder in the Windows Explorer, you may notice a number of files with a DLL extension. Each DLL file is critical; removing just a single file could very well take down the entire application and cause it to no longer work.

Back to DirectX 10, the collection of APIs used to comprise DirectX 10 depends on DLLs to execute applications. These DLLs are new and improved, literally, for DirectX 10, and users will notice the huge difference in gaming performance. Applications depending on DirectX 10 will also run much quicker and much more smoothly as a result of these new DLLs.

NOTE If you're not familiar with audio engineering, *signal-to-noise ratio* is the ratio of a transmitted signal to background noise. It is often referred to as SNR, S/N, or even as a D/U ratio (desired-to-undesired signal ratio).

Like a number of enhancements that Microsoft DirectX provides with Windows Vista, this feature is something that average home users might not appreciate as much as sound professionals or other users who really pay attention to audio quality.

Glitch resilience

The glitch resilience feature is another enhancement with DirectX 10 and Windows Vista that sound professionals or engineers will enjoy more than your typical home user will. Glitch resilience is designed to offer smooth audio playback that gives the listener the ultimate listening experience for even the most quality-demanding, high-definition audio content.

The glitch resilience feature is basically what its name suggests — it allows high-fidelity audio playback even in environments with limited or reduced resources. This performance is ensured for any application that is built using the new Multimedia Class Scheduler Service (MMCSS) technology.

Windows Vista raises the priority of your audio and video processes in order to deliver a more glitch-resilient platform. Part of this solution is offered through improved queuing latency control.

In other words, by giving the highest priority possible to any audio or video processes, streamed multimedia is guaranteed not to be interrupted by any other processes on your system that would create an interruption, or glitch, during delivery.

Enhanced, high-speed DLLs

Windows Vista, via Microsoft DirectX 10, now offers greatly improved (not to mention high-speed!) DLLs. What exactly does that mean?

Microsoft DirectX is actually a collection of APIs, which use dynamic link libraries (DLLs) to execute programs. If you're not familiar with the concept of the DLL, check out the nearby sidebar for a closer look at these basic components of computer science; knowing a bit about them will give you a better understanding of why these high-speed DLLs are so beneficial in Windows Vista!

Digging Deeper into Microsoft DirectX 10

The previous section detailed some of the more important updates to Microsoft's DirectX 10, but they are by no means the only differences. In fact, there are a number of other changes from the ground up that will affect how your computer and its software perform using Windows Vista.

These changes won't affect all users in their Windows Vista experience; however, multimedia junkies and gamers will really appreciate this latest version. Although this audience should appreciate the new features, there are some things that this same audience will not like.

Moving from Windows XP to Windows Vista affects more than just your operating system and sundry applications. Users who enjoy playing high-end video games (for example, graphics-intensive games for the PC) will have to see how their older games stack up in Vista. Initially, Microsoft intended to only use DirectX 10 with Windows Vista. The plan was to have virtually no backward compatibility whatsoever. Fortunately, cooler heads prevailed, and DirectX 9L is also included in Windows Vista in order for recent non–Vista-designed games and hardware to work with Vista.

NOTE **Keep in mind that DirectX 10 itself is not compatible with earlier versions of DirectX. That said, if you have games and hardware designed to work only with early versions of DirectX, you may need to investigate their performance under Windows Vista; in theory they won't work with the new operating system and the latest DirectX releases.**

Updated components

I mention earlier in this chapter that Microsoft DirectX currently has eight different components for handling multimedia and gaming applications. Most of these existing components change to some degree in DirectX 10 and Windows Vista. As you will see, Microsoft's Xbox had considerable influence over these updated components in DirectX 10 (see Figure 15.2).

FIGURE 15.2

Windows Vista and DirectX 10 were designed in part with Xbox 360 in mind.

- **DirectInput:** This component, which used to process data from game controllers, such as mice, keyboards, joysticks, and so on, is now replaced by the new XInput component (yes, as in Xbox). XInput is designed for Xbox 360 controllers. In other words, it is an API for next-generation game controllers.
- **DirectSound:** Until now the DirectSound component has managed playback and recording of waveform audio. It is now replaced with the Cross-Platform Audio Creation Tool (XACT) in DirectX 10. It was initially prepared for use with Xbox 360, but Microsoft decided to carry this over to Windows development.
- **DirectPlay:** The DirectPlay component was responsible for networked game communications and is now replaced by Xbox Live.
- **DirectShow:** For media management, DirectShow is now replaced with Media Foundation. This completely new set of APIs handles Windows Vista media playback (both audio and video). In addition to enhanced media quality, it also provides for high-definition capabilities.

XACT, as mentioned earlier, is designed to offer a more stable, consistent audio playback. One of its primary advantages is level balancing over a wide selection of audio hardware.

The cohesion among these updated or new components is the Windows and Xbox 360 commonality. These two systems require but a single API controller that is cross-platform. In other words, games designed for Xbox can also be used for Windows Vista. This saves time, money, and resources for video game developers.

Unified Architecture

So far this chapter has addressed 32-bit floating-point capability, glitch resilience, and those lightning-fast DLLs, but what really makes the difference? Is it the greatly improved and strengthened 3D graphics rendering feature? Could be. It could also be an interesting new technology called Unified Architecture (UA). The UA works to reduce the CPU workload, which in turn increases performance by combining several stages of the 3D graphics pipeline into one.

DirectX 10 is basically designed around the UA concept; by combining into a single stage the various APIs in DirectX with the graphics processing unit (GPU), less wear and tear occurs on the CPU, which in turn means higher performance. In the past, these units were each treated separately; this meant that a particular unit, or stage, might have to wait for another unit or stage to complete its process. As a result, performance was decreased and CPU workload was increased. The Unified Architecture concept within Microsoft DirectX 10 solves both of these issues.

Of course, you don't necessarily have to have a unified GPU to use DirectX 10, even though it is preferable. This means that you can still use older techniques, such as those detailed earlier (for example, running separate units) and still remain compliant with DirectX 10 requirements.

Nevertheless, the main idea behind the GPU and Unified Architecture is to make it into a true processor. This means not only rendering 3D graphics, but handling other gaming processes, such as animation. Working in tandem, DirectX and Unified Architecture turn your GPU into a true graphics and gaming powerhouse.

Microsoft DirectX 10 uses the GPU as a central point of its architecture by maximizing its power. By using the GPU and video cards to their fullest potential, the CPU enjoys a lighter workload, leaving more power for more resource-intensive games.

Other changes in DirectX 10

All the changes in Microsoft DirectX 10, detailed in this chapter, serve two primary purposes:

- To improve security
- To make using graphics easier for home users

Let's take a closer look at some of the essential changes that are featured in Microsoft DirectX 10. These are detailed in the following sections.

Scheduler

Microsoft made some changes to the driver model of past versions of DirectX. The new version for Windows Vista also includes a scheduler, as well as a memory virtualization system. The scheduler feature is designed to help developers schedule streaming content within an application.

In regards to development, DirectX 10 streamlines development and makes it easier to manage because Microsoft has removed the capability bits. Capability bits are used to indicate which features are active or available for a particular piece of hardware. In place of these bits, DirectX 10 clearly defines minimum requirements; verifying that your hardware is DirectX 10–compatible is a sufficient guarantee that your hardware is compatible with Windows Vista. This means that you can be sure of what features are supported and ensure game stability and performance.

Direct3D in DirectX 10

The core of the latest version of DirectX is the new enhancements to the 3D architecture. Central to this is Shader Model 4.0. ***Shaders*** are programs written in a language known as HLSL (high-level shader language) and perform a variety of different functions. Vertex shaders will operate on geometry, resizing or scaling the geometry as needed. Pixel shaders operate on individual pixels to change the color and other pixel attributes. Pixel shaders account for many of the dramatic lighting effects you see in modern 3D games. Pixel shaders are also used for some of the special Aero Glass effects on the Windows Vista desktop.

The Shader Model 4.0, also new to Microsoft DirectX 10, contains several new features or specifications that also facilitate development. These include:

- 32-bit color depth precision per pixel.
- A new shader type, known as a ***geometry shader*** has been added, to create or destroy geometry. In the past, the actual geometry of a 3D scene was created or modified on the CPU. Vertices (triangle information) were then fed to the graphics card, but the GPU could not actually change the amount of geometry. Now, new geometry can be created or destroyed on the graphics card, offering more flexibility and better performance for graphics programmers.
- Support for longer shaders. Previous shaders were limited to 512 instructions; Shader Model 4.0 boosts that to 64K (65,535) instructions.
- A unified shader architecture. In earlier versions of DirectX, pixel shader instructions were slightly different from vertex shader instructions. Shader Model 4.0 uses a single, unified programming language for all shaders.

The latter provides developers with more options in terms of audio processing and physics calculations by allowing them to use the GPU for these features.

Shader Model 4.0 is an integral part of DirectX and will prove to be very helpful for more technical, demanding users, such as CAD designers or other special effects developers or artists.

DirectX 10 also makes use of geometry shaders, which produce very visible results, including more realistic shadows for humans and objects. Humans also enjoy more human-like, or more realistic, facial features through the use of geometry shaders.

Developers or artists can perform operations on complete triangles and use complex primitives instead of simply using vertex points. Geometry shaders let developers take things further and make vertex operations a thing of the past. These shaders also allow for increased special effects without sacrificing performance or frame-rate speed. All of these characteristics make for more believable, life-like animations.

Microsoft DirectX 10 is the (or one of the) principal actors in the Windows Vista multimedia and gaming experience. If you're a game developer, this wonderful tool can help you create cutting-edge video graphics that enable you to take gaming to another level. Fortunately, Windows Vista gives users the operating system to take advantage of these graphically impressive creations.

DirectX Diagnostic Tool

If you aren't sure what version of Microsoft DirectX you are currently using under Windows Vista, or want to find out more about DirectX, you can use the DirectX Diagnostic Tool.

The easiest way to access the DirectX Diagnostic Tool is to type **dxdiag** in the Start Menu's live search box. The application appears in your Start Menu, as displayed in Figure 15.3.

After you click the icon, the tool appears and displays pertinent information about your various DirectX components and drivers. The Diagnostic Tool displays with four different tabs:

- System
- Display
- Sound
- Input

The System tab, which opens by default, displays important system information. It is also where you can find out what version of DirectX you are using, as shown in Figure 15.4.

FIGURE 15.3

The DirectX Diagnostic Tool is accessible from the Start Menu.

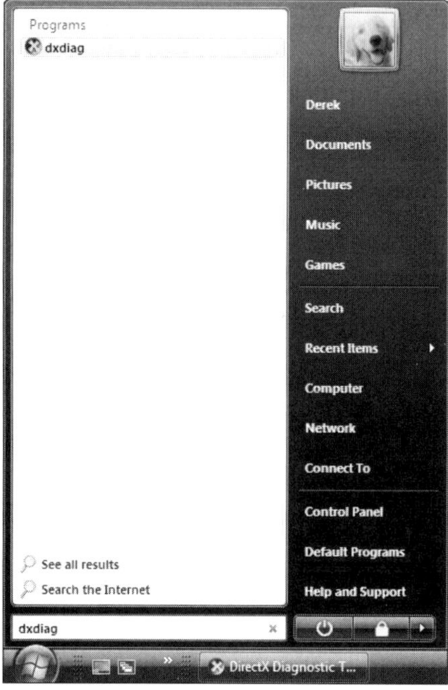

Customizing Windows Vista

Windows Vista Ultimate starts with a pretty plain desktop.

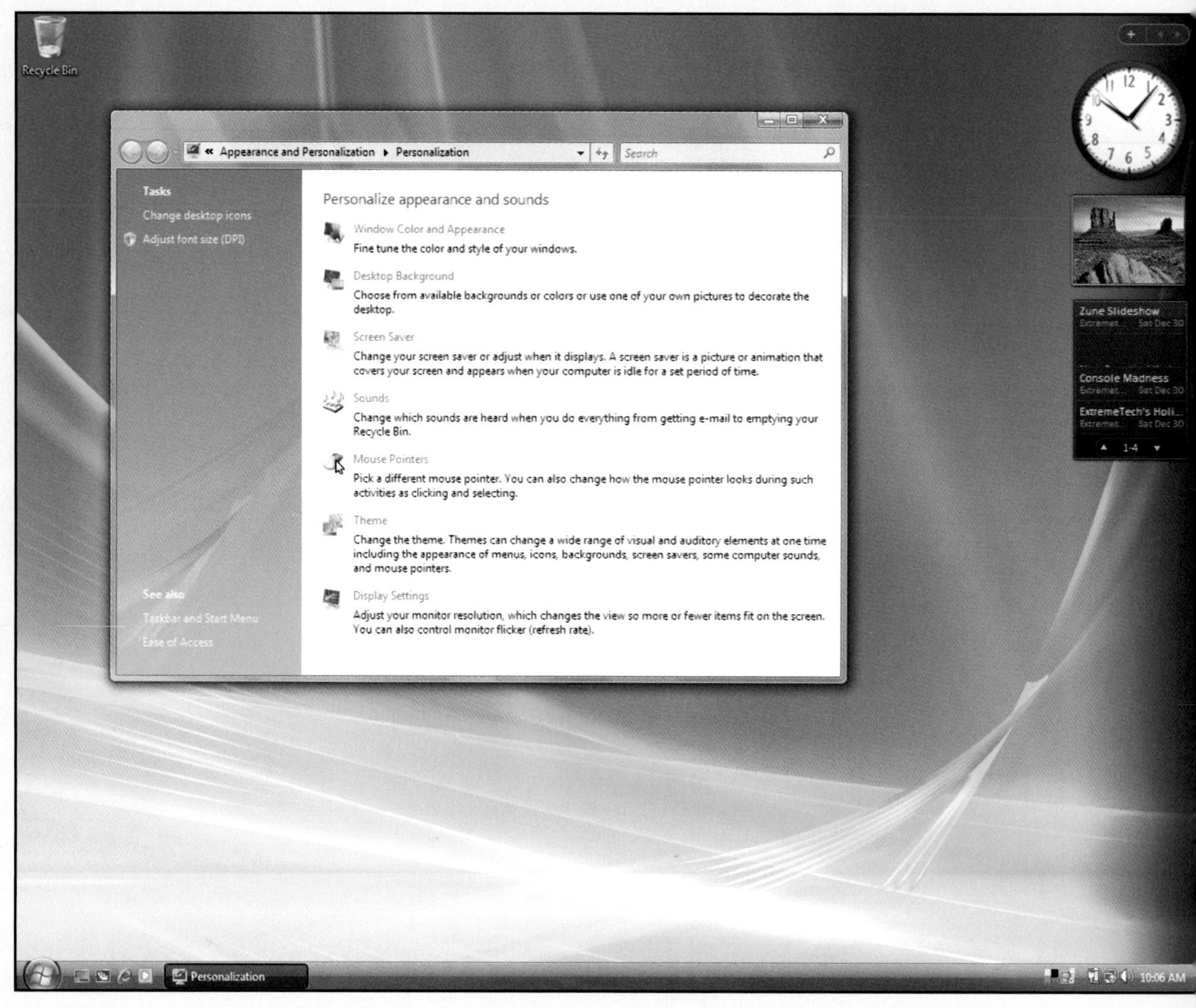

First, open the personalization options through the Control Panel.

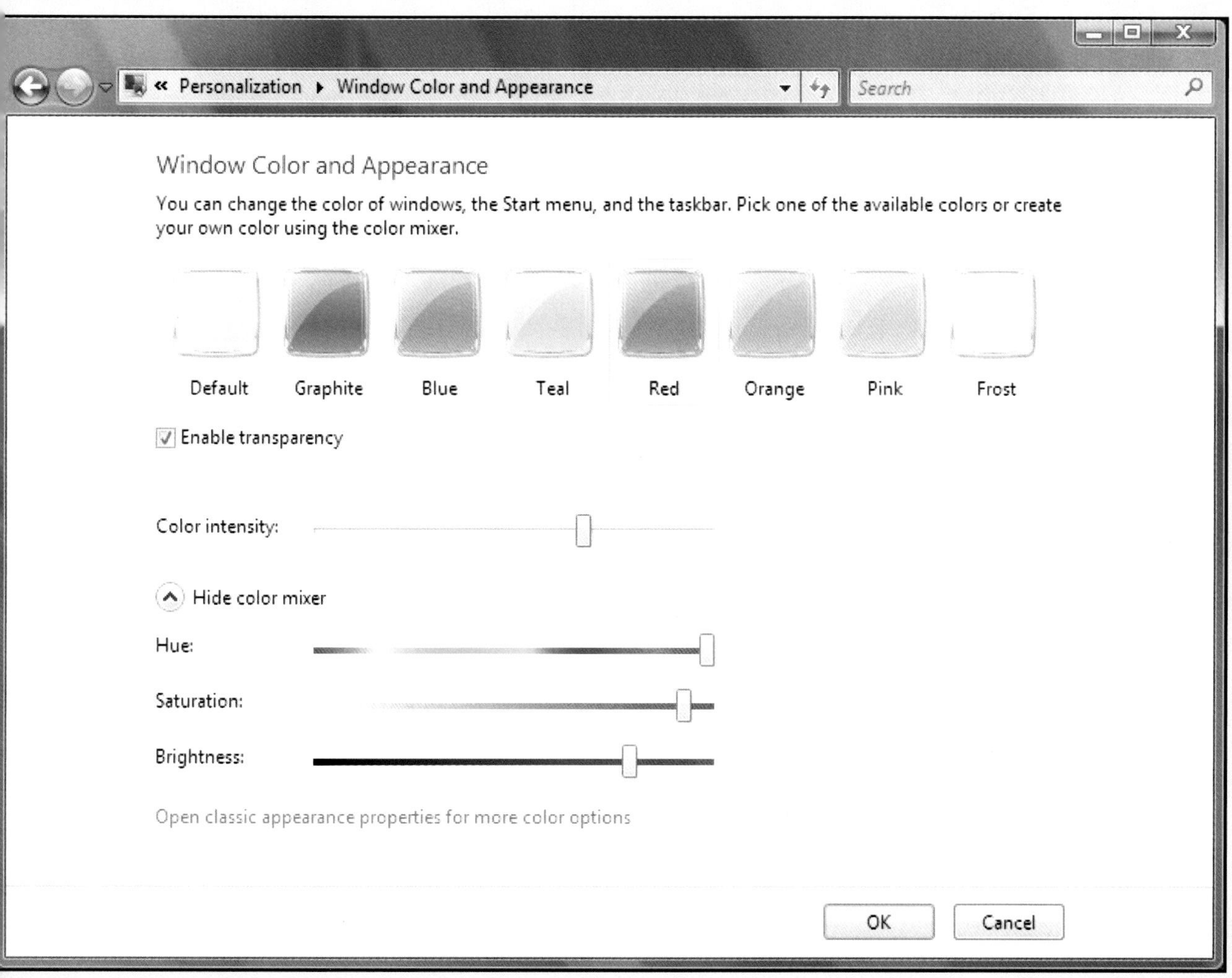

In the Window Color and Appearance pane you can change the color of the Aero-powered windows.

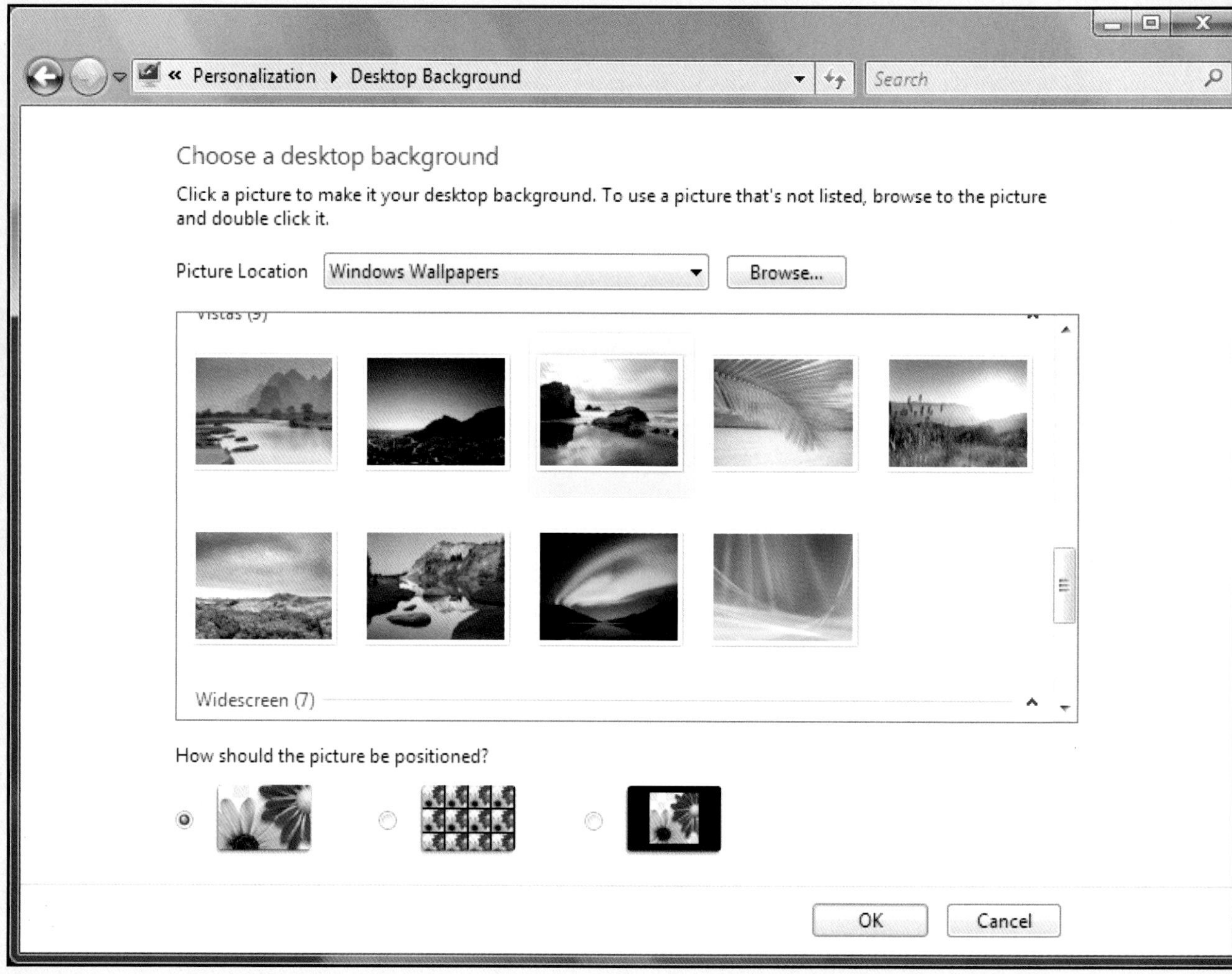

In the Desktop Background pane you can choose a new background. Windows Vista Ultimate offers a whole bunch to choose from.

You can also customize the Sidebar as you wish.
Windows comes with a number of gadgets.

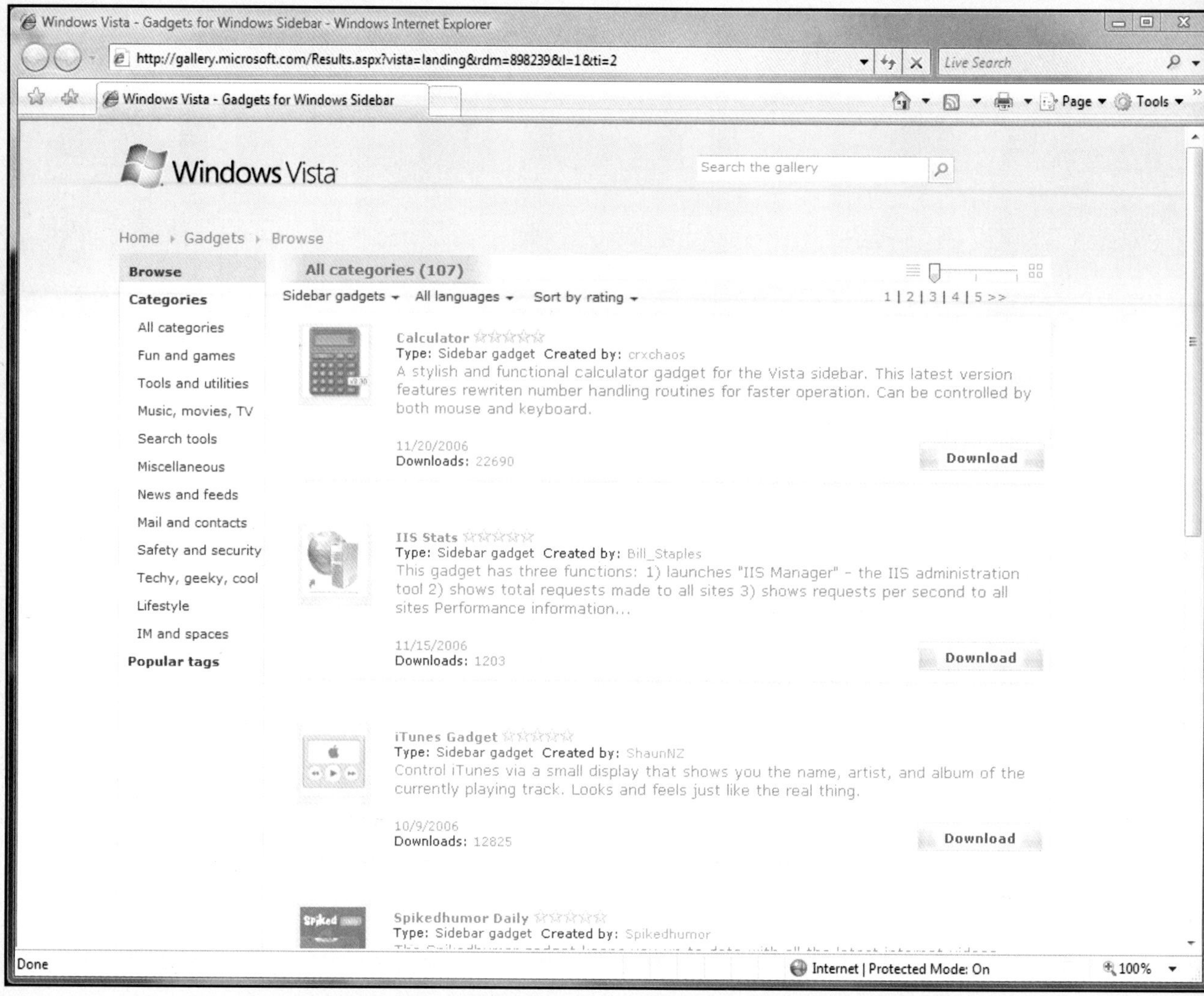

You can go online to choose from a wealth of Sidebar gadgets from Microsoft and from independent developers.

To add a gadget to the Sidebar, simply drag it from the Gadgets window.

Many gadgets have their own options. You can, for example, choose a different face for the Sidebar clock.

You can also drag and drop gadgets on the Sidebar to rearrange their order.

Add icons to the desktop as you desire. Here, I'm dragging the Games link to the desktop right from the Start Menu.

Here, you can create new User accounts for parental control through the Parental Controls window.

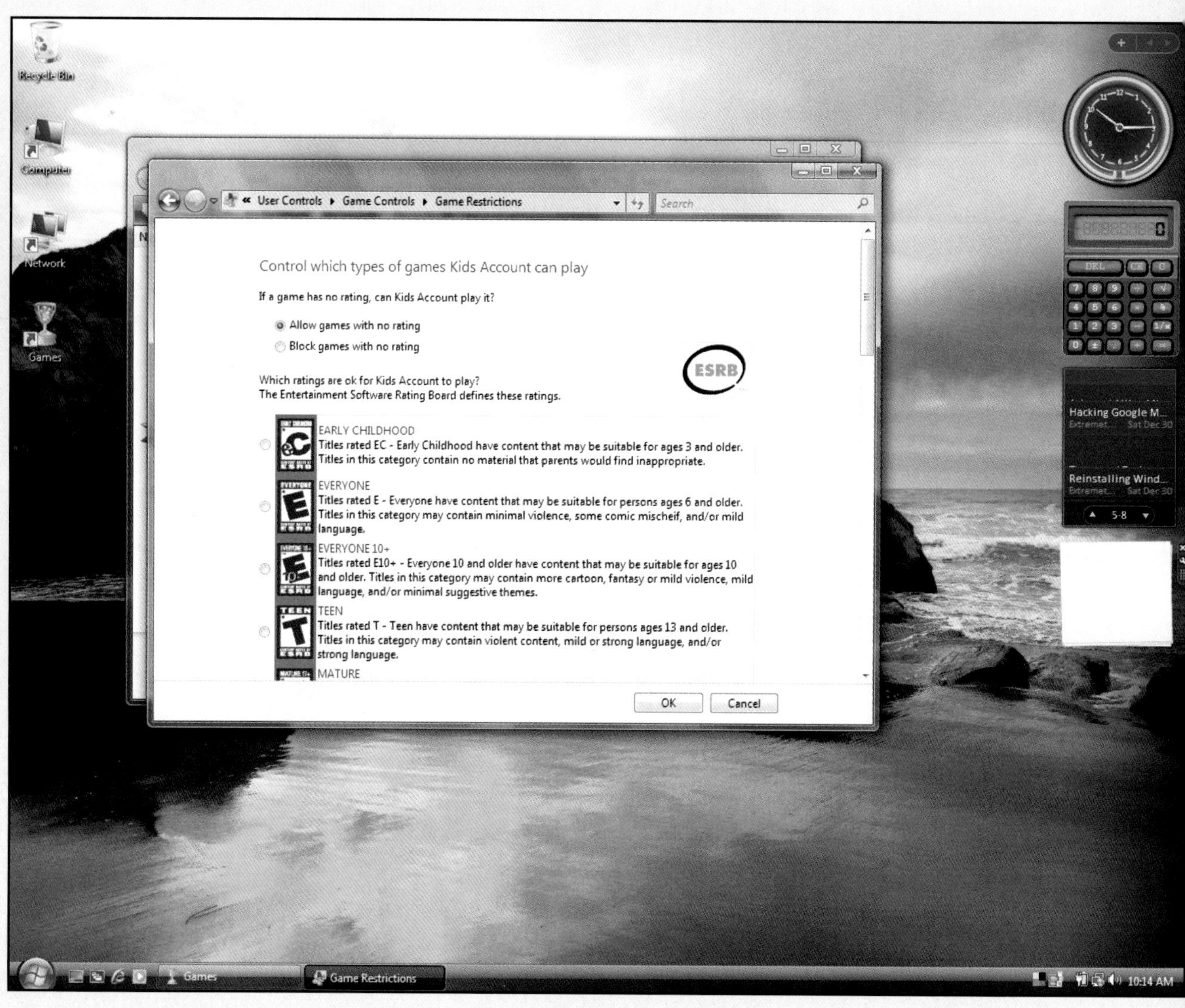

You can control the games, movies, the Web, and other content your computer's accounts can access.

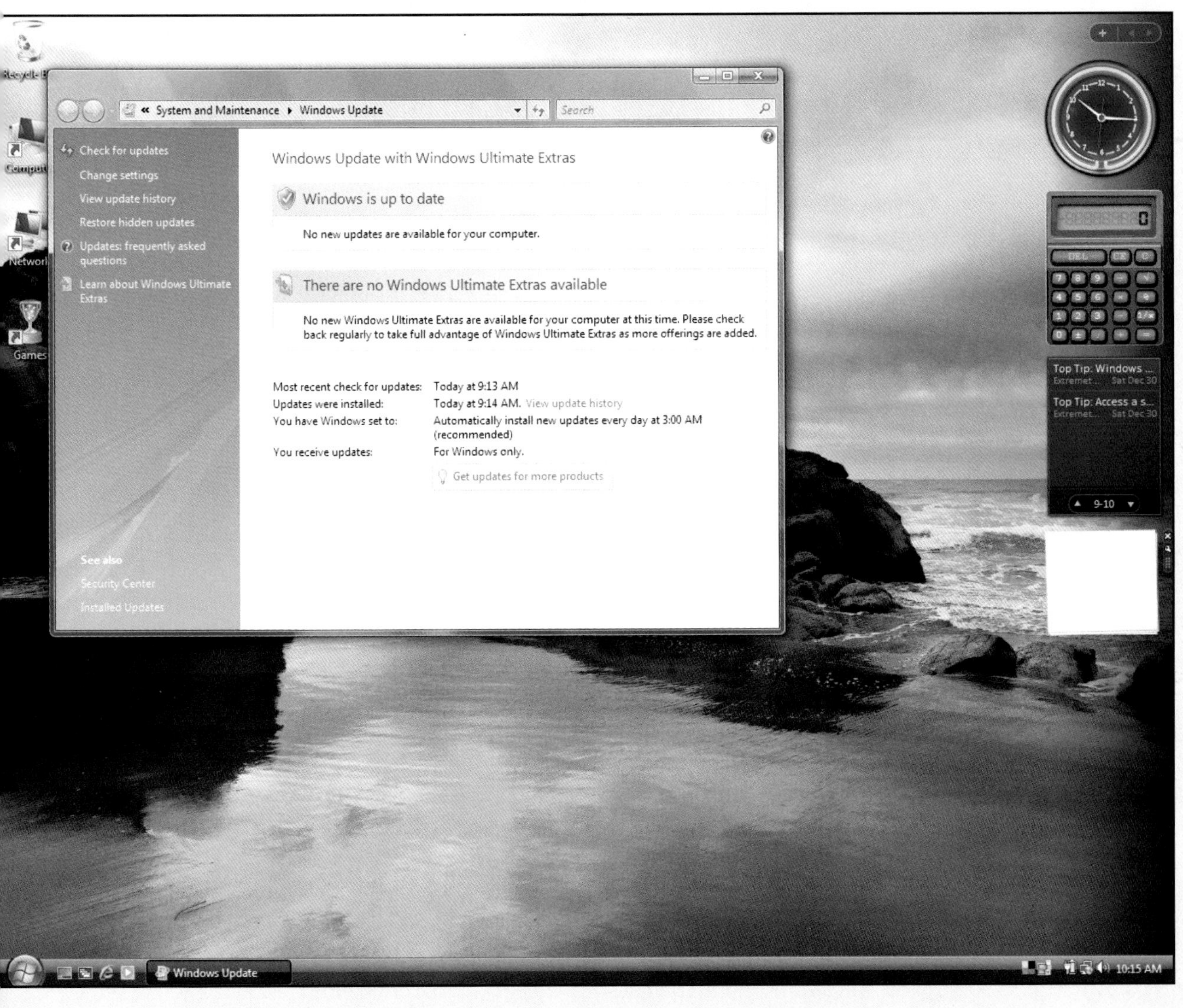

Microsoft will offer Windows Ultimate Extras to owners of Vista Ultimate.

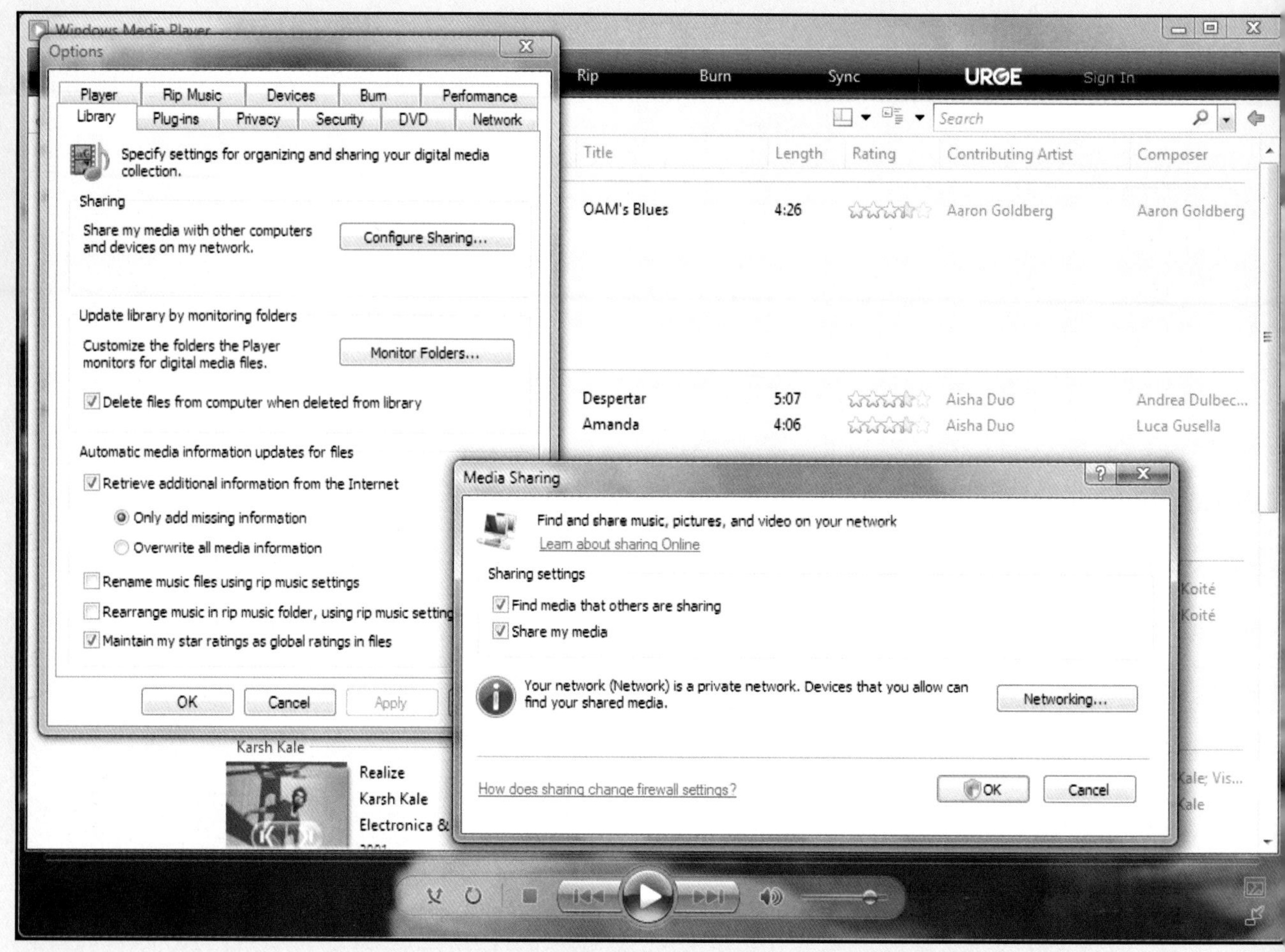

Share your computer's media files through the Library dialog box within Windows Media Player 11's Options screen. You can share them with other computers or with media extenders, including the Xbox 360.

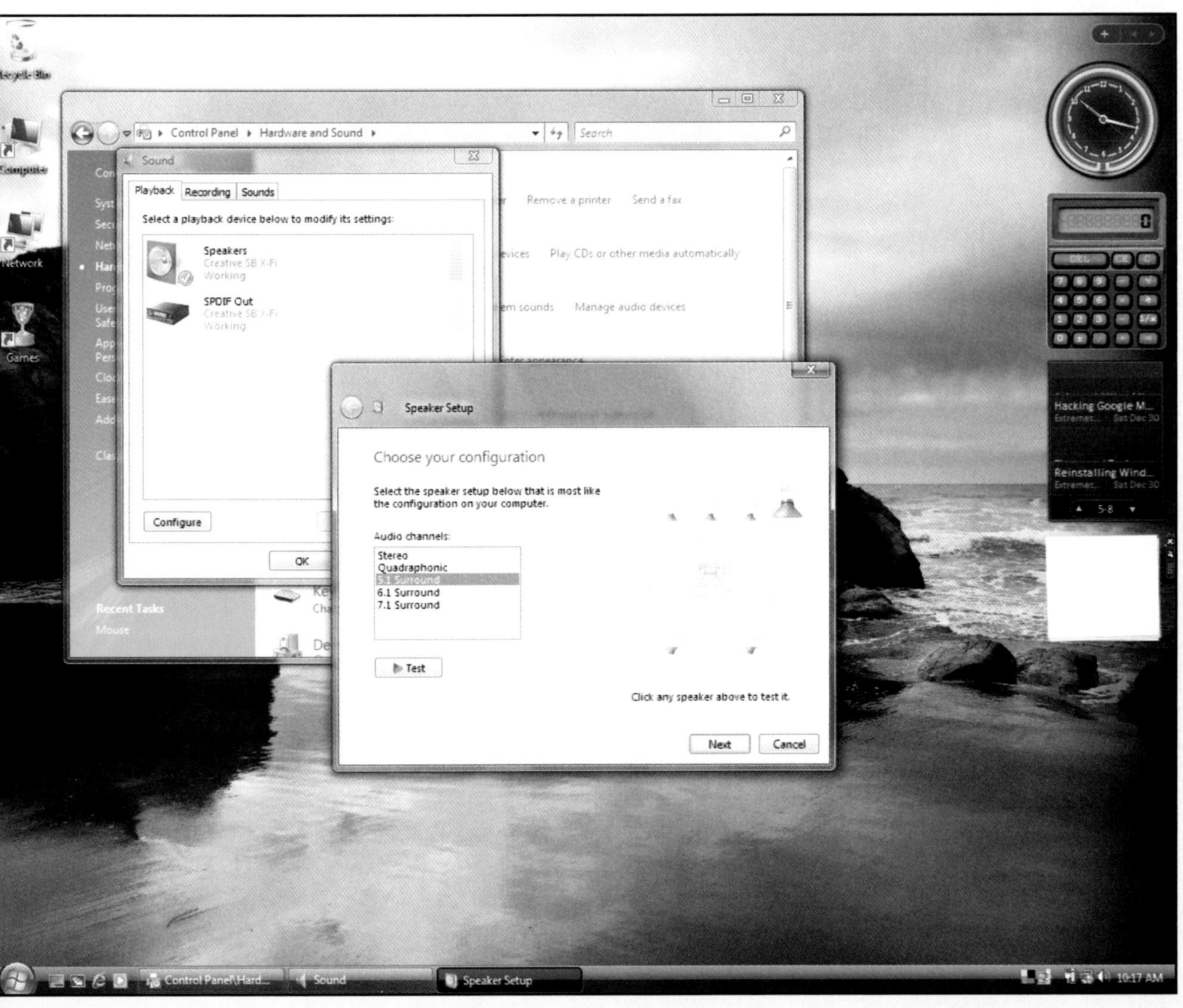

Be sure to set up your sound card and speakers through the Control Panel's Hardware and Sound pane.

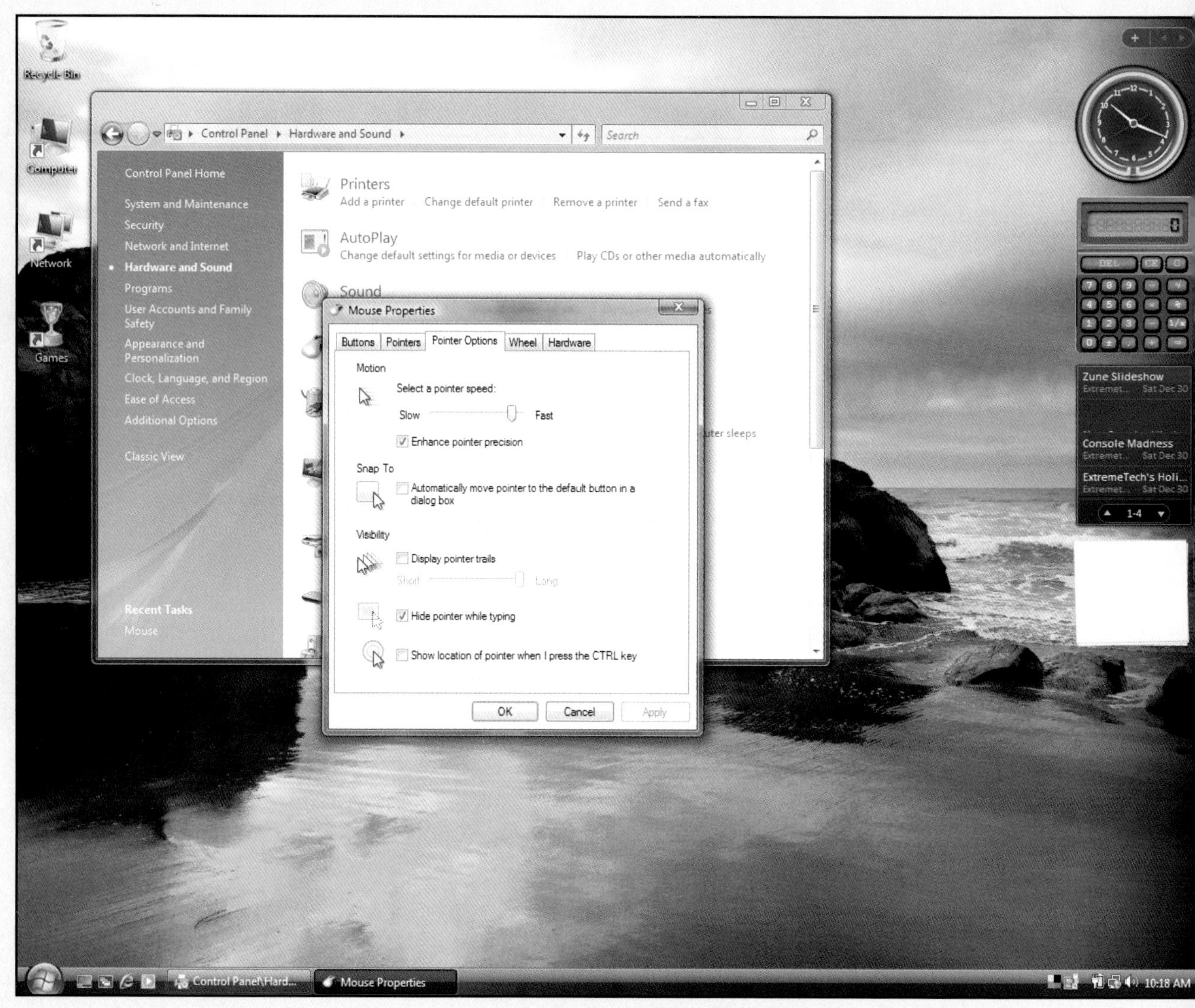

The last thing I do when customizing Windows is to set up my mouse via the Control Panel's Hardware and Sound pane.

FIGURE 15.4

The DirectX Diagnostic Tool lets you know which version of DirectX you are using.

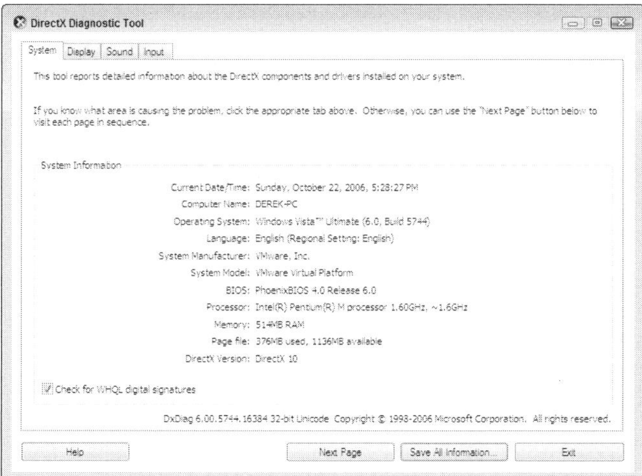

You can click the Display tab to find out various types of information about your graphics card. This tab also displays important information about installed graphics drivers. At the bottom of this screen, the DirectX Features area displays the status of various DirectX components, as shown in Figure 15.5. If any drivers are unsigned, or any other anomalies occur, information indicating as much appears at the bottom of the Display tab in the Notes section, as shown in Figure 15.6.

FIGURE 15.5

The DirectX Diagnostic Tool also displays information about the status of your DirectX components.

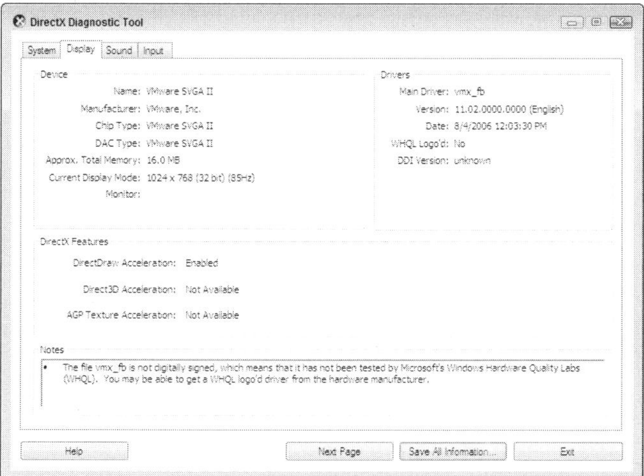

FIGURE 15.6

The Notes section displays driver or component information.

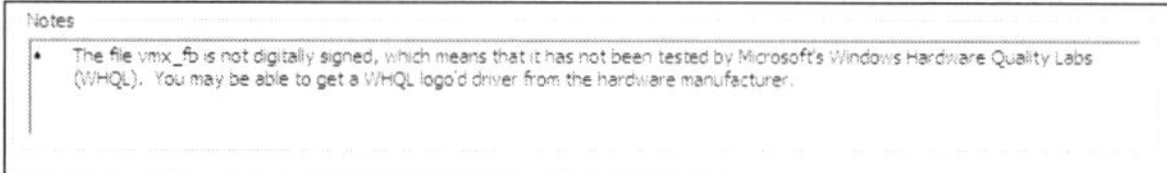

The Sound tab, predictably, displays information about your audio hardware and installed audio drivers, as shown in Figure 15.7. Similarly, any unsigned drivers or other anomalies appear in the Notes section.

FIGURE 15.7

The Sound tab in the DirectX Diagnostic Tool

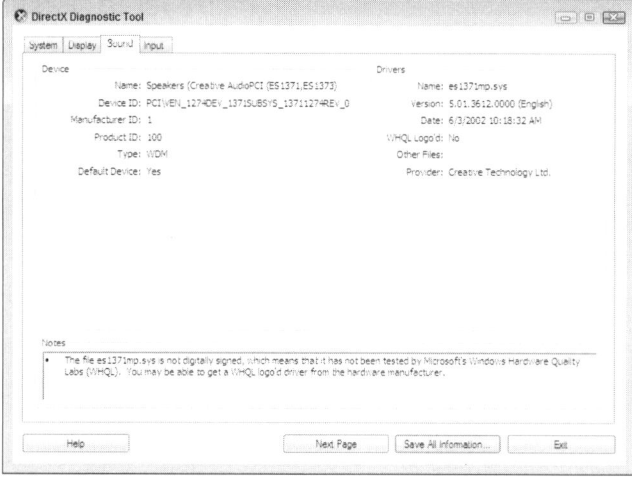

The final tab, Input, displays information about input devices, such as keyboards and mice, as well as installed drivers, as shown in Figure 15.8.

The DirectX Diagnostic Tool lets you save your report (the information recorded in the four tabs) as a text file for future reference. By default, Vista saves this file to the desktop, as shown in Figure 15.9.

FIGURE 15.8

The Input tab has driver information about input devices, such as keyboards.

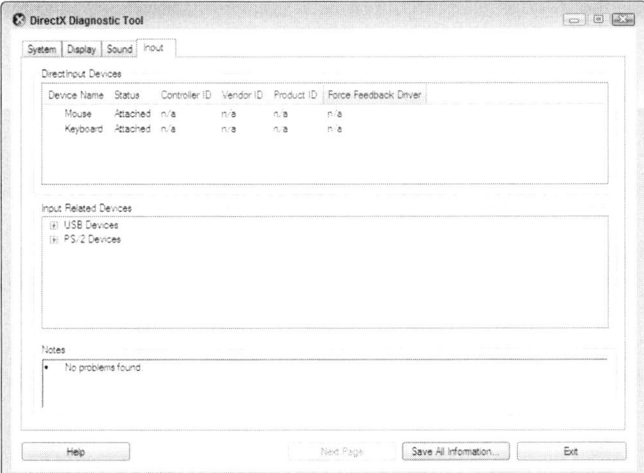

FIGURE 15.9

You can save DirectX Diagnostic Tool output as a report.

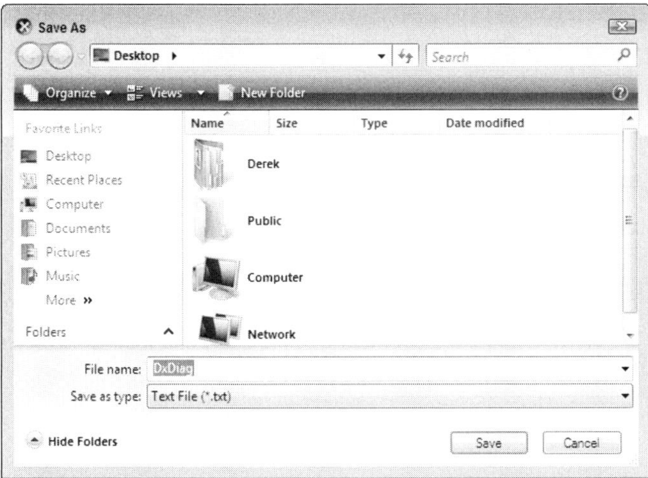

Windows Presentation Foundation

The Windows Presentation Foundation engine, which is built on top of Microsoft DirectX 10, demands top performance and full power from your graphics hardware. Applications can finally scale and use high-dpi monitors thanks to vector-based rendering. As far as developers are concerned, this engine provides a single runtime for multimedia creations, such as video, audio, graphics, browser and form-based applications, and so on. Unifying how developers experience multimedia enables them to continue creating groundbreaking applications and graphics without extra work.

DirectX 9.0L: Backward Compatibility

After much trepidation on the subject, Microsoft decided to also include Microsoft DirectX 9.0L (*L* for Longhorn) with Windows Vista.

If you've been used to working with Windows XP and kept your DirectX up to date, you're probably familiar with version 9.0C. The secondary version, 9.0L, is included with Windows Vista, but it is not available for download. In fact, its sole purpose is to be on hand in case you are using older hardware or applications that are not compatible with Microsoft DirectX 10.

As Windows Vista becomes the new Windows operating system standard, more and more of your favorite applications and games will be designed for use with Microsoft DirectX 10, if they haven't been designed as such already. In the meantime, you can still enjoy the benefits of DirectX 9 on Windows Vista if your situation or application (game) requires it. The 9.0L release simply provides the DirectX 9 API for Windows Vista.

NOTE If you are currently running Windows XP as your primary operating system, I want to clear up any potential misunderstandings based on various pieces of misinformation that have been reported elsewhere. First of all, DirectX 9.0L is not the same thing as DirectX 10. I also want to remind you that the DirectX 9.0L is not available for Windows XP. If you are still using Windows XP, you should use DirectX 9.0C.

Summary

Microsoft is releasing Microsoft DirectX 10 with its Windows Vista release. For multimedia and gaming fans, this alone may be sufficient reason to make the switch to Windows Vista. Despite several name changes leading up to its release, DirectX 10 delivers the goods.

As discussed earlier in this chapter, Microsoft DirectX 10 is a completely new API that takes multimedia and video game development to a whole new level. From 32-bit floating-point technology to glitch resilience that vastly improves your Windows Vista audio experience, the DLLs in DirectX 10 are lightning fast, which means greater game and multimedia performance. Microsoft includes DirectX 10 with Windows Vista installation; you cannot download it, nor can you uninstall it.

Microsoft DirectX 10 also features some new components to replace the more outdated aspects of DirectX. These changes were necessary to bring it in line with the new cross-platform capabilities that Windows Vista and Microsoft Xbox 360 share. These cross-platform commonalities will facilitate development for both PC and Xbox games.

Windows Vista also features a helpful tool known as the DirectX Diagnostic Tool. This tool is designed to help users find out more about their current DirectX version and components. The Diagnostic Tool also provides information on installed drivers and provides information on any anomalies or any unsigned drivers.

Despite concerns about backward compatibility, Microsoft also includes a version of Microsoft DirectX 9.0L, which is unique to Windows Vista. For users who are using applications or hardware that isn't DirectX 10 compatible, for example, to play a game that requires DirectX 9, you can use this Vista-only version for compatibility. As Windows Vista becomes a market and industry standard, games, applications, and hardware will be increasingly DirectX 10 compatible. Because Microsoft has decided to rid DirectX of its capability bits, anything labeled as DirectX 10 compatible is certain to work with Windows Vista and DirectX 10 at the highest performance levels possible.

Chapter 16

Windows Media Center

IN THIS CHAPTER

- Using your computer as a multimedia hub
- Using media extenders
- Using Windows Media Center as an all-in-one centralized media center

If you've been using Windows for the past couple of years, you may recall a different kind of Windows XP that was available in a number of retail stores, for example, BestBuy and Circuit City in the United States. If that rings a bell, then you are probably thinking about the Windows Media Center.

The Windows XP Media Center (WMC) Edition was created to serve as an all-in-one multimedia hub where you could enjoy the best in audio and video from a centralized location. The difference between standard Windows-operated computers and those with Windows Media Center Edition comes down to a single piece of pre-installed software called Media Center.

Microsoft released the WMC edition as a bundled package to retailers selling new computers. No way existed to upgrade to this edition; indeed, even buying it outside the United States proved to be difficult because Microsoft limited its sales to a limited number of countries worldwide.

When Windows XP Media Center Edition 2005 shipped, it became more widely available. In fact, you could even build your own WMC system if you so desired.

Jump forward to 2007 and the Windows Media Center is now an important part of the Windows Vista Ultimate Edition release. Microsoft has included this feature in the higher-end editions of Windows Vista instead of making it a separate bundle/purchase. Given the stringent requirements for Windows Vista in terms of multimedia/graphics, if your computer is Vista capable, you should be able to adequately enjoy the Windows Media Center.

This chapter details the latest edition of the Windows Media Center now available in Windows Vista. It also discusses how you can use it as your one-stop place for your Windows multimedia experience. In this chapter I also discuss media extenders, and how you can use them to enhance your Windows Vista experience.

CROSS-REF Media extenders are also detailed in depth in Chapter 26.

Using Your Computer as an At-Home Multimedia Hub

Windows Media Center is truly an at-home multimedia hub. As silly as that may sound, it is true — just take a quick tour of the various applications and multimedia formats that it handles and you'll see that you can pretty much take care of all your multimedia needs from a single application.

Of course, if you really want to take things further and truly take advantage of what Windows Media Center has to offer, you need to upgrade hardware above and beyond what Windows Vista requires. For example, if you want to use the television features, you need to make sure that you have a TV tuner card for your computer.

The Windows Media Center available for Windows Vista is quite different than it was in Windows XP. For example, the menu has been redesigned for Windows Vista and its improved graphics, as shown in Figure 16.1. Windows Media Center also offers support for CableCard, which is a recent technology created in response to FCC regulations in the United States. This support enables you to watch an HDTV broadcast on your computer. Finally, digital tuners used with the Windows Media Center no longer require the presence of a corresponding analog tuner.

However, you won't be able to buy a CableCard tuner for your PC after the fact. For the time being, if you want high-definition digital cable piped into your PC, you'll need to buy a complete system purpose-built with a digital tuner.

The following sections detail each of the various sections of the Windows Media Center in Windows Vista.

FIGURE 16.1

The menu in the Windows Media Center has a new look.

Setting up the Windows Media Center

First and foremost, you need to set up Windows Media Center to run on your Windows Vista computer. Before you can do so, you need to first find the application. One of the easiest applications to find in Vista, it's available in the Start Menu as soon as you click Start, as displayed in Figure 16.2. You can also click All Programs and it's also available in the next menu.

FIGURE 16.2

The Windows Media Center is easily accessible in the Start Menu.

When you open the Windows Media Center for the first time, it asks you to select one of the setup options, as shown in Figure 16.3:

- Express setup
- Custom setup
- Run setup later

You can, depending on your familiarity with Windows, choose either of the first two options. I show you how to walk through the Custom setup.

FIGURE 16.3

Choose a setup option in the Windows Media Center welcome screen.

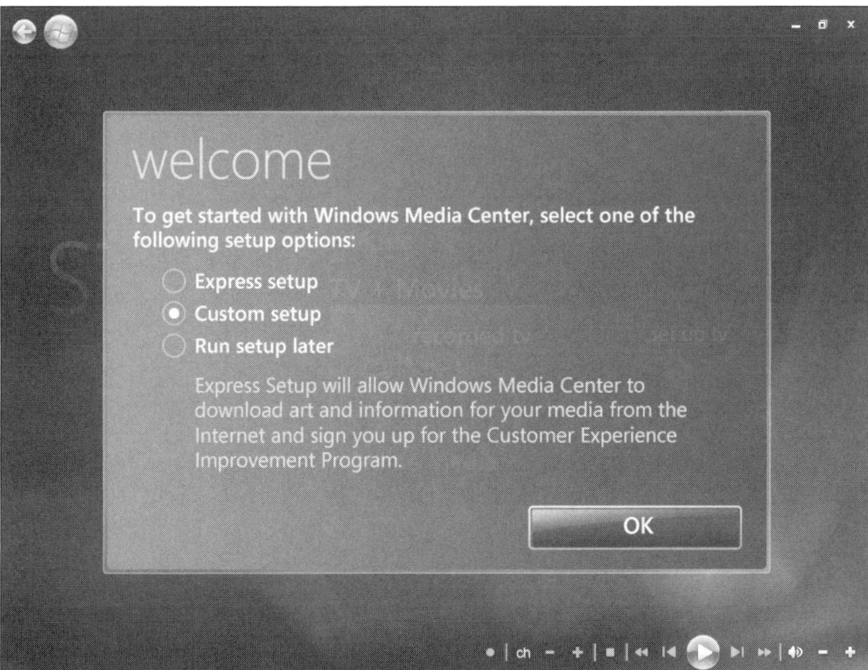

To set up Windows Media Center to run on Windows Vista, follow these steps:

1. **Open Windows Media Center by choosing Start ➪ Windows Media Center.**
2. **Select Custom setup from the welcome screen and click OK.** The Window Media Center Setup screen explains the setup process, as shown in Figure 16.4.
3. **Click Next when you have finished reading.** The Windows Media Center Privacy Statement appears.

FIGURE 16.4

The Windows Media Center Setup screen explains the setup process before performing it.

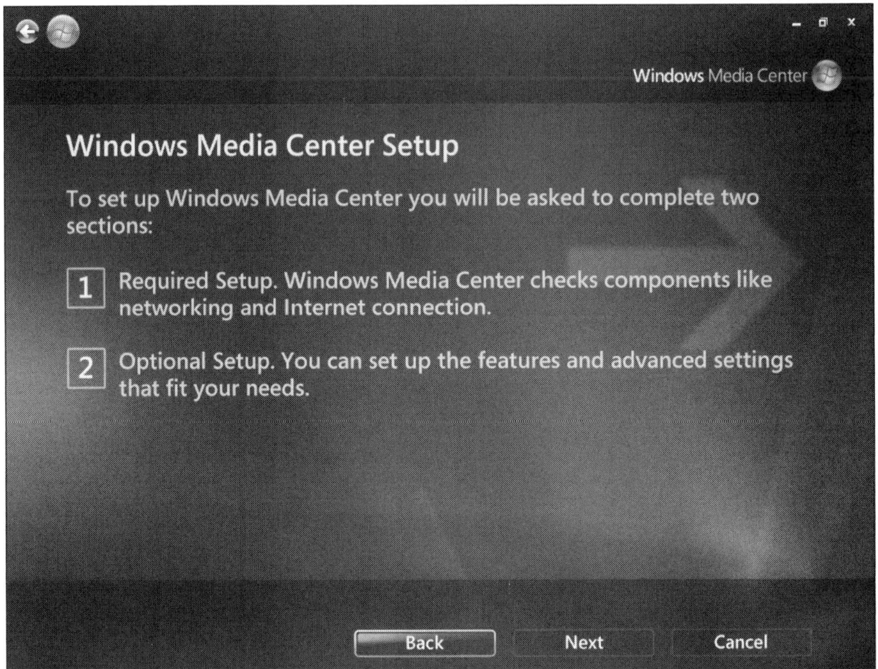

4. **Read the Privacy Statement and click Next.** If you don't agree with the Privacy Statement, you can click Cancel to end Setup.

If at any time you need to back up to a previous screen, you can click either Back or the back arrow at the upper left of the screen.

5. **Click Yes or No to indicate whether you want to participate in Microsoft's Customer Experience Improvement Program, and then click Next.**
6. **Click Yes or No to indicate whether you want Windows Media Center to connect to the Internet for album or video information, such as album or DVD art, track listings, TV program listings, and so on. Click Next.** This completes the required components section of Windows Media Center setup.
7. **Click Next.**

At this point, you can either complete the setup procedure, or you can ask Windows Media Center to set up your computer speakers or set up your audio and video libraries. (See Figure 16.5.) If you decide to do either, follow the next set of instructions in which I show you how to set up libraries.

FIGURE 16.5

Windows Media Center lets you set up how your speakers work in Windows Vista.

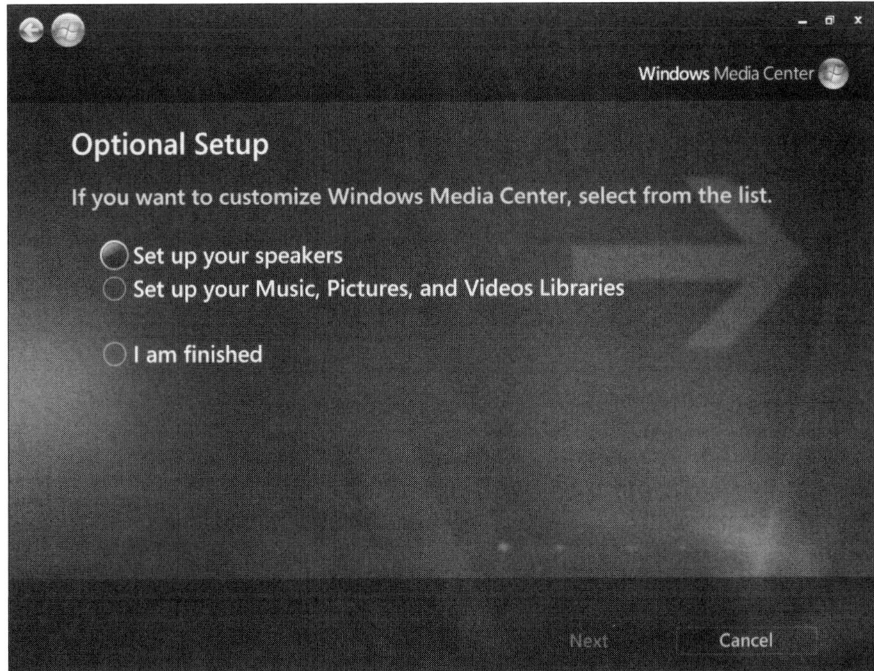

To set up your music, pictures, and video libraries in Windows Media Center, follow these steps:

1. In the Optional Setup window, select Set up your Music, Pictures, and Videos Libraries, and tell Windows Media Center to look at another folder or to stop scanning other folders.
2. Click Next.
3. In the screen that appears, click Add Folders if you want to choose which folders to add from your computer, shared folders on another computer, or both. Click Next.
4. Select the desired folder, as displayed in Figure 16.6. Click Next.

FIGURE 16.6

You can decide which folder(s) Media Center should scan for multimedia files.

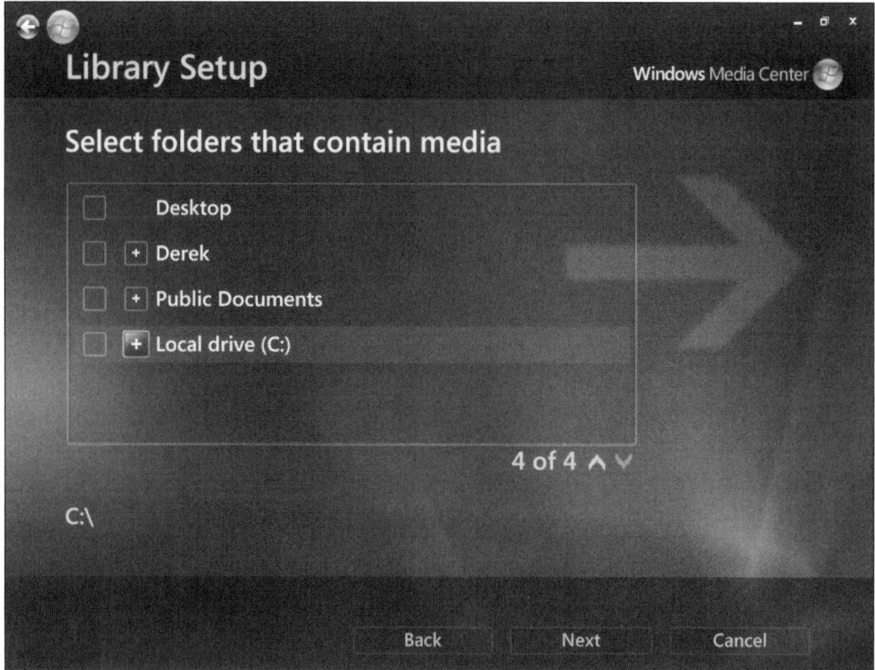

5. **Click Finish if the list of selected folder(s) appears correct.** Windows Media Center then scans for media files, as shown in Figure 16.7.

FIGURE 16.7

Windows Media Center scans for multimedia files to add to folders.

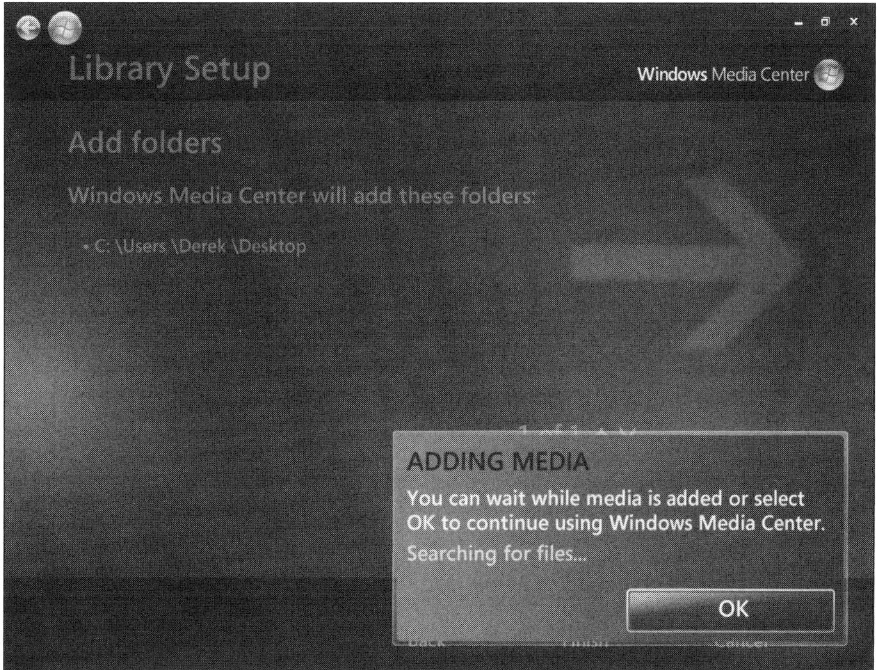

After you have set up your folders, WMC takes you back to the Setup screen. The screen now indicates that you have completed the media folder setup and lets you set up your computer speakers, as shown in Figure 16.8.

FIGURE 16.8

The Windows Media Center setup process keeps track of completed tasks.

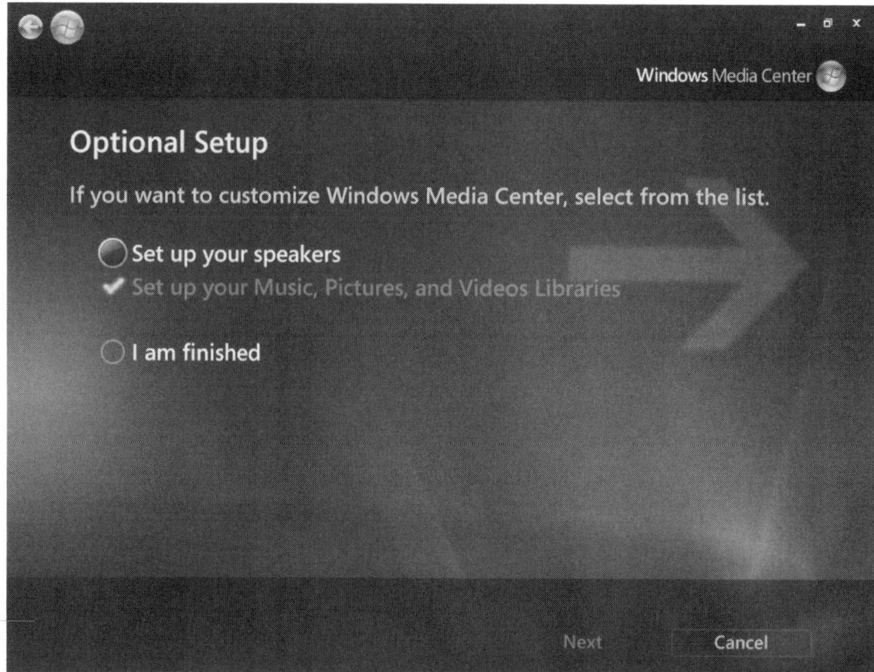

To set up your speakers in Windows Media Center, follow these steps:

1. **In the Optional Setup window, select Set up your speakers. Click Next.** The Speaker Setup window appears, explaining how speakers are set up in Windows Media Center.
2. **Click Next when you have finished reading.**
3. **Select the speaker configuration that best matches your computer, click Next.** The Test Speaker screen appears.
4. **Verify that your speakers are connected and turned on and then click the Test button.** Your computer should make a short sound.
5. **Select whether or not your heard the sound, as shown in Figure 16.9, and then click Next.**

FIGURE 16.9

The Windows Media Center speaker test options

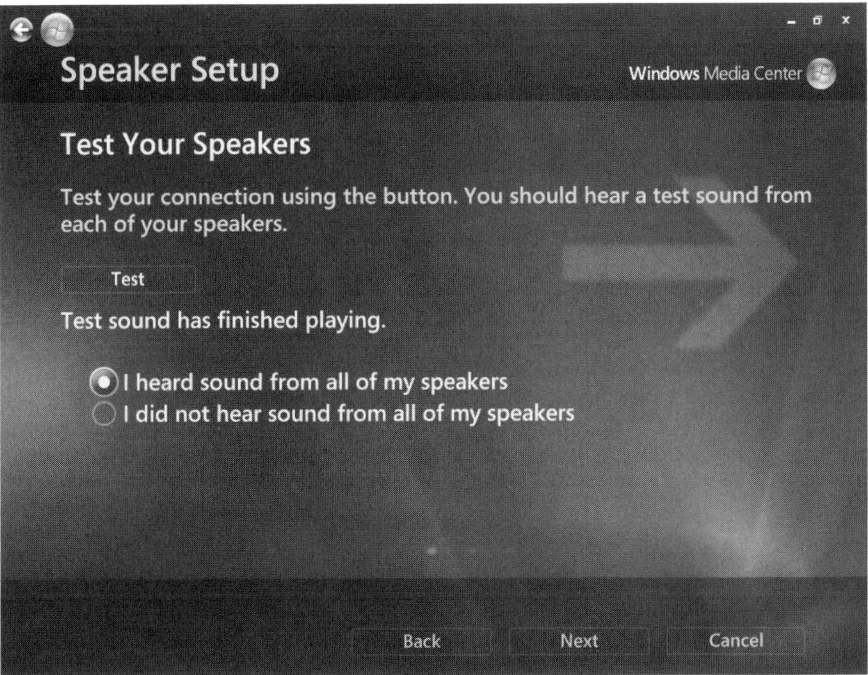

6. Click Finish in the "You are Done!" window.
7. Click "I am finished in the Windows Media Center setup" window.
8. Click Next.
9. Click Finish to complete the Windows Media Center setup.

Setting up recorded TV

The Windows Media Center menu can be somewhat confusing; in fact, it took me some time to fully understand where everything is. When you open up Windows Media Center, the first available option is the Recorded TV component.

If you click Recorded TV, WMC provides three different sample video clips to illustrate how Windows Media Center can handle recorded television, as shown in Figure 16.10.

FIGURE 16.10

The Windows Media Center contains sample clips in the Recorded TV component.

To set up Recorded TV, click "Set up tv from the recorded tv screen," under the main TV + Movies menu. In order to configure your TV signal, you must have compatible tuner hardware, otherwise the following screen displays, as shown in Figure 16.11.

FIGURE 16.11

Not having tuner hardware earns you this screen.

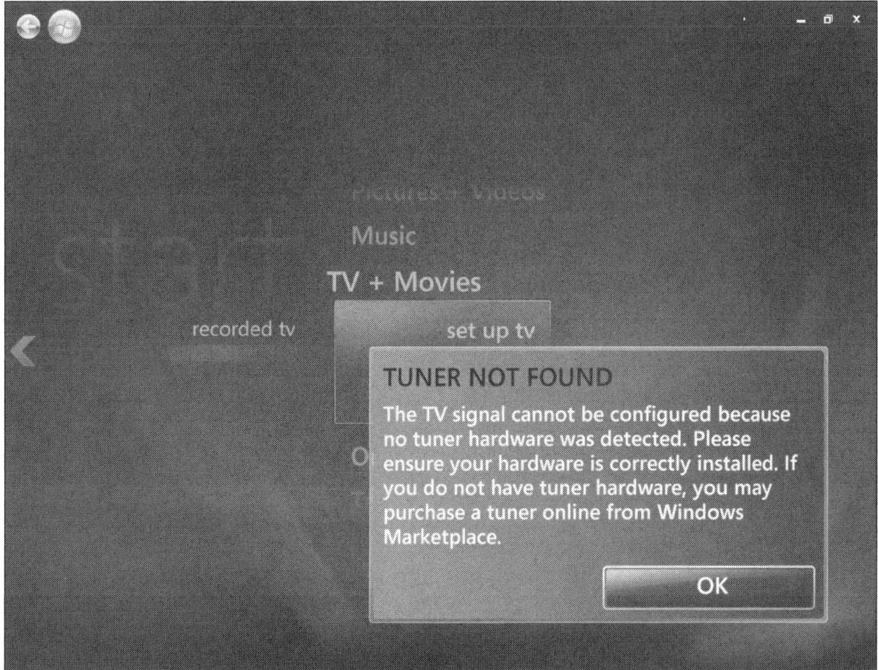

Accessing online media

The Online Media component of the Windows Media Center lets you access the program library. The program library displays media files by category, as displayed in Figure 16.12. The program library contains eight different categories:

- Programs by name
- TV + movies
- Music + radio
- Pictures
- News + sports
- Games
- Lifestyle
- Tasks

To access a program, just click on its icon.

FIGURE 16.12

Multimedia files are displayed by category in libraries.

Performing tasks

The Tasks feature is probably one of the most used features of the Windows Media Center. This component lets you perform a number of tasks related to media files, as displayed in Figure 16.13.

The Tasks component lets you do the following:

- Set and change settings
- Shut down programs
- Burn a CD/DVD
- Sync devices connected to Vista
- Add extenders to your home network
- Display Windows Media Center in full-screen mode

FIGURE 16.13

The Tasks feature enables you to perform a wide variety of multimedia tasks.

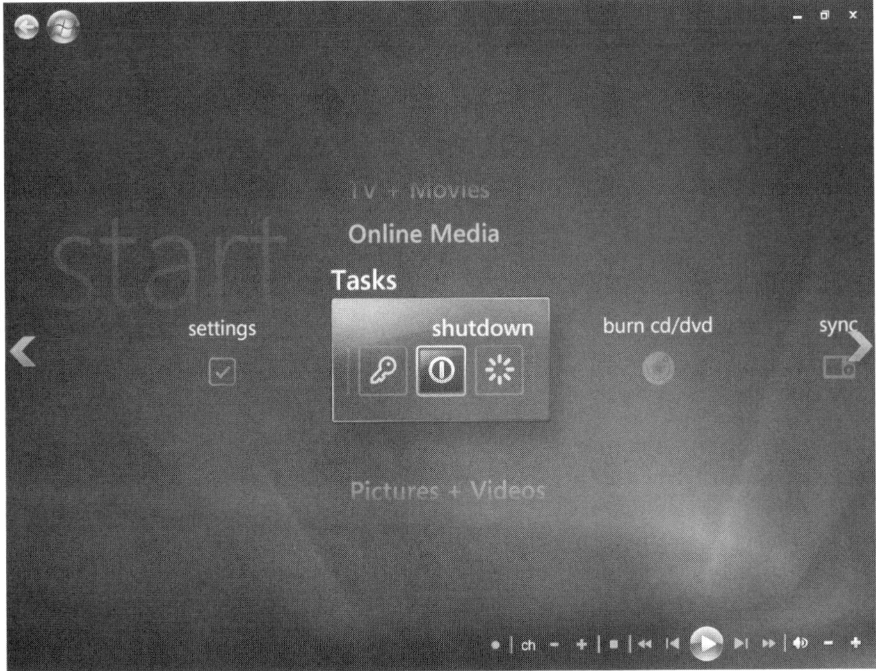

Settings

The Settings option of the Tasks component lets you set various options for Windows Media Center components; these include General, TV, Pictures, Music, Extenders, and Library Setup.

- **General:** If you are looking to set General settings, Windows Media Center includes a considerable number of settings such as Parental Controls, optimization, window behaviors, and visual and sound effects, as shown in Figure 16.14.
- **TV:** The TV settings let you set up your television signal and set various audio and closed captioning options.
- **Pictures:** Pictures settings let you determine how pictures are displayed in WMC and set details about song information appearance in slideshow presentations.
- **Music:** The Music settings let you determine what visualizations are available and how they appear.

- **Extenders:** The Extender options let you add new extenders or configure existing extenders. I talk about extenders later in this chapter, as well as in Chapter 26.
- **Library Setup:** The Library Setup option displays the same setup procedure discussed earlier in this chapter for setting up the Windows Media Center. You can add folders to scan for media or stop scanning folders.

FIGURE 16.14

The General component lets you set a number of Windows Media Center settings.

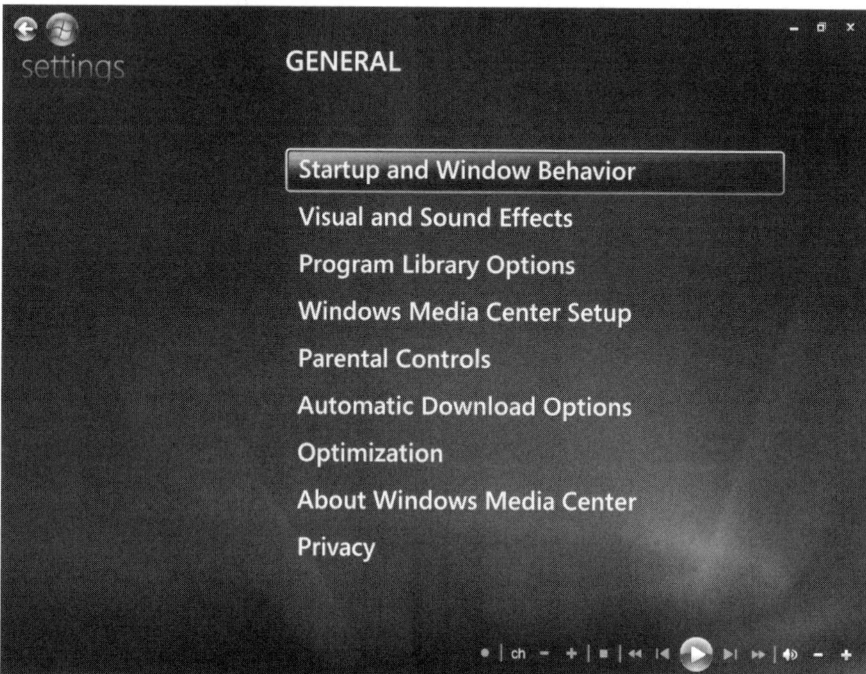

Shutdown

The Shutdown option is relatively self-explanatory; from this window you can close, log off, shut down, restart, or sleep. If you decide that you don't want to perform any of these tasks on your computer, you can click outside the box to go back to the Tasks window, as displayed in Figure 16.15.

FIGURE 16.15

You can cancel out of a window by clicking outside the box.

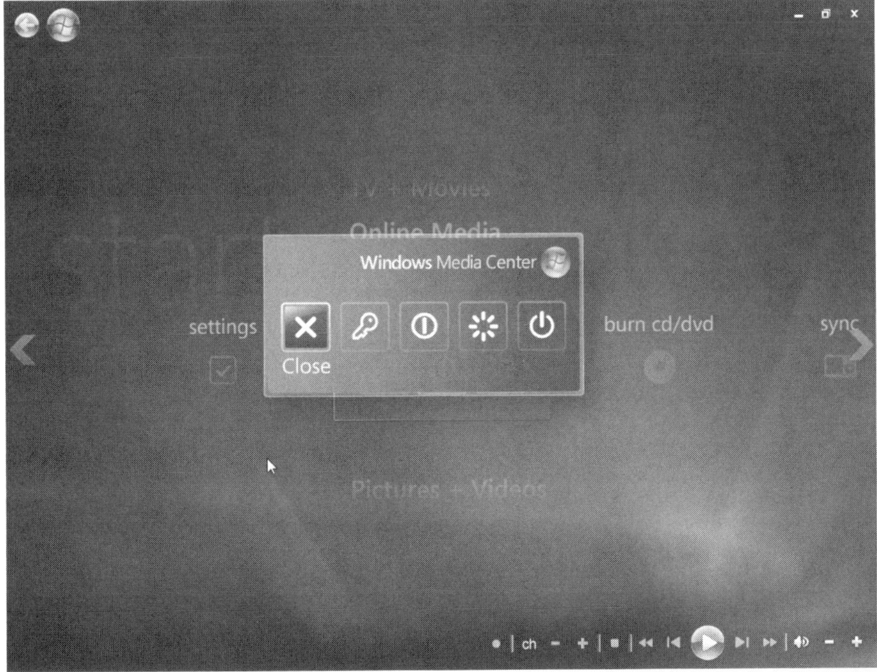

Burn CD/DVD

The Burn CD/DVD task lets you, predictably, burn a CD or DVD. In order to use this feature, you must have a writable CD/DVD player with a valid, writable CD/DVD in the player.

When you select the Burn CD/DVD option, the AutoPlay window appears, as shown in Figure 16.16, and lets you select the appropriate action to take.

FIGURE 16.16

The AutoPlay window appears when you prepare to burn a CD.

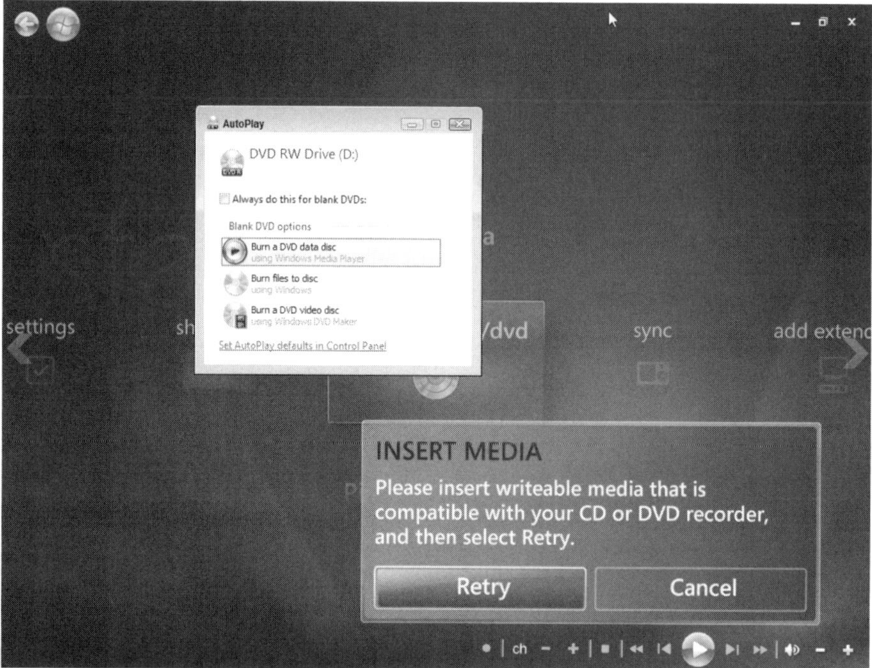

Sync

The Sync feature lets you sync any devices, such as PDAs or other handheld devices, connected to Windows Vista. If none are installed and connected, this feature will not work.

Add Extender

The Add Extender feature lets you add an extender to your home network. In order to use this feature, you must have an eight-digit key that is displayed on the television connected to the Windows Media Center.

For more information about media extenders, see the section "Using Media Extenders" later in this chapter as well as Chapter 26.

Media Only

The Media Only feature displays the Windows Media Center in full-screen mode. The minimize and close buttons are hidden when you use this feature.

Displaying pictures and videos

The Pictures + Videos component displays, as you might imagine, the available pictures and videos on your computer. This component features three different options:

- Picture library
- Play all
- Video library

The picture library displays a live view of folders with image files in them; you can change this default setting to view images by tags or date taken. If you click the folder, you can have a tile view of its content. However, you can also right-click the folder and perform a number of tasks: burn folder, view smaller icon, set up libraries, or access settings. Mousing over the folder tells you its last modification date, as well as the number of files in the folder.

If you open the folder, you can double-click a file to view it full size. Of course, you can always display your pictures as a slideshow by clicking the link, as shown in Figure 16.17.

FIGURE 16.17

Display pictures as a slideshow.

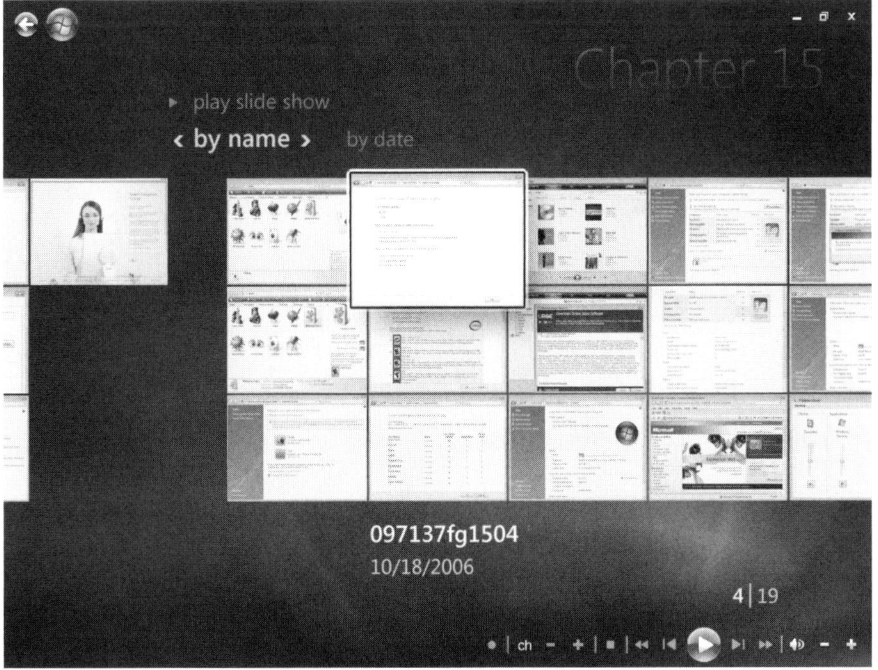

If you right-click a picture and select Picture Details, you can actually perform tasks on the picture; for example, you can rotate or edit pictures, as shown in Figure 16.18.

FIGURE 16.18

Edit pictures from the preview screen — a very helpful new feature.

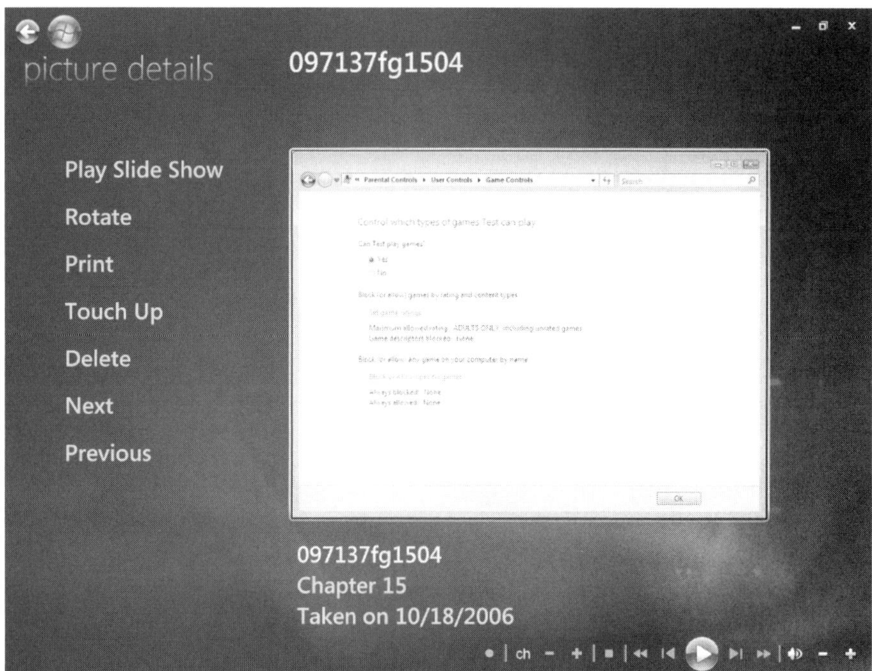

The Play all option displays everything, both video and pictures, in a slideshow fashion. The video library option works very similarly to the picture library option; the only difference is that it displays videos and not pictures.

Listening to music

The final component, Music, works similarly to the Pictures + Videos component. Like the aforementioned component, it contains a music library and a play all feature. It also has a radio feature that lets you set preset stations and listen to an online radio broadcast.

If you insert an audio CD into the player while using the Windows Media Center, you can go to the Music component and it appears in the Music library, designated with a CD icon in the lower portion of the album icon.

The Search feature lets you search for music by title or artist, as shown in Figure 16.19.

FIGURE 16.19

Search for artists or albums using the multimedia search feature.

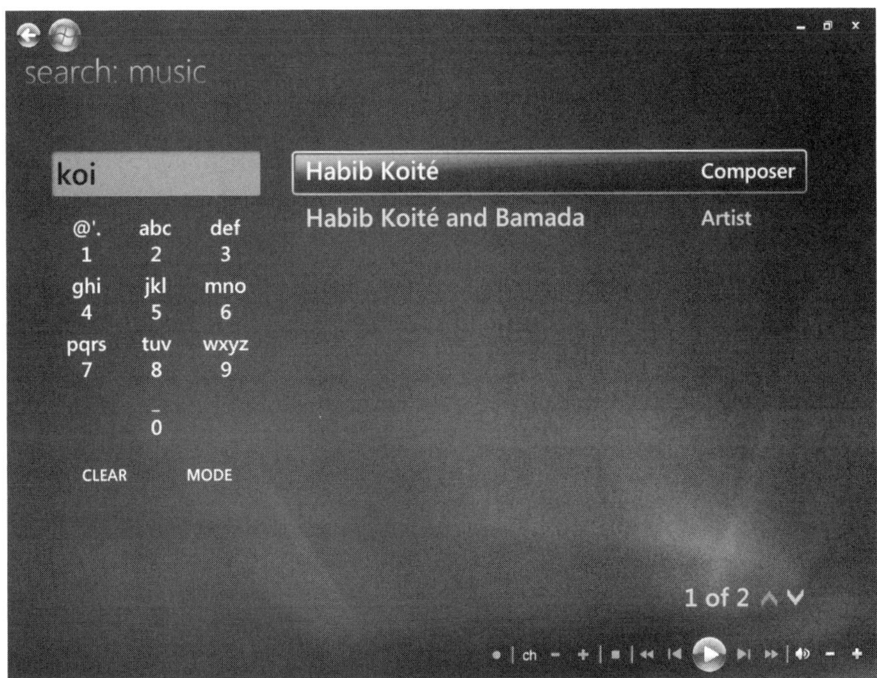

When you find the album or artist you're looking for, you can click the label and relevant information appears, as displayed in Figure 16.20.

FIGURE 16.20

Find all the information you want about an album or an artist.

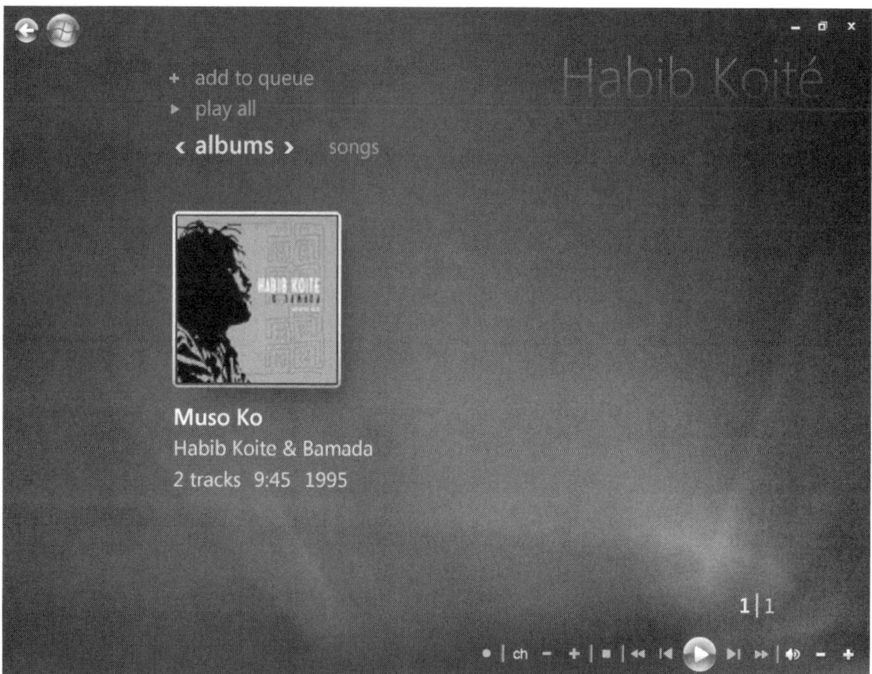

From the window displayed in the Figure 16.20, you can add the song to the Windows Media Center playlist or opt to play the entire album. By clicking the songs link, you can view the track listing for the album. If you click on the song title, you can find out more information on the song or choose to play it, as shown in Figure 16.21.

FIGURE 16.21

Clicking a song title reveals more information about the track.

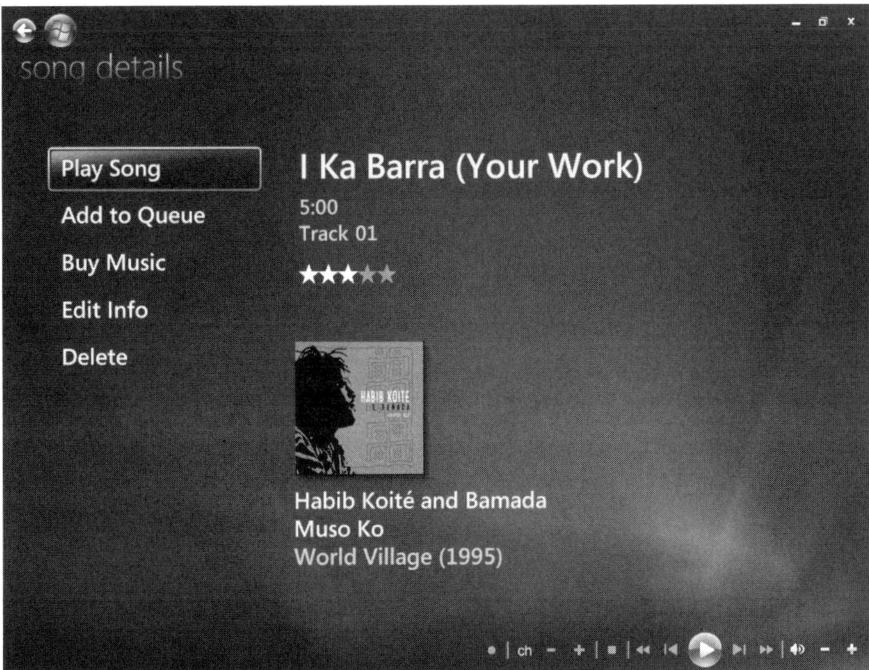

Using the remote control

I should also mention the very helpful remote control–like bar across the bottom of the Windows Media Center. This wonderful feature lets you handle a number of essential tasks such as changing channels, raising or lowering the volume, stopping playback, fast forwarding, or rewinding, when using the Windows Media Center (see Figure 16.22).

FIGURE 16.22

The remote control–like feature in Windows Media Center lets you handle a wide array of tasks.

Using Media Extenders

Windows Vista and the Windows Media Center continue to make use of media extenders. I discuss media extenders in greater detail in Chapter 26, but this section provides an overview as to what they are and how they can enhance your Vista experience.

A *media extender* is a set-top box that is used to connect either over a wireless connection or an Ethernet connection to your Windows Media Center. For example, you might use a media extender to use DVR functions with the Windows Media Center. These extenders were created with the advent of Windows Media Center edition for Windows XP.

Your computer acts as a host for the Windows Media Center; by using wireless connections, you can use extenders and Windows Media Center capabilities from convenient locations without having to lug your computer around from room to room in the process. As mentioned, you can use a wired Ethernet connection; however, Microsoft recommends using a wireless network in order to take full advantage of these benefits. A wireless network has the benefits of flexibility of placement or location. If performance is clearly your priority, I recommend using the wired connection, especially if you are using gigabit Ethernet.

The most popular example today of media extenders with Windows Vista is undoubtedly Microsoft's Xbox 360. It can be used with the Windows Media Center so that you can view pictures or audio media through your Xbox 360.

Setting up a media extender is quite straightforward; all you need is a wireless connection through a router (or Ethernet if you don't have wireless), Windows Vista Home Premium or Ultimate edition, and an Xbox 360 console or another media extender. By simply hooking up your media extender to your router or via wireless connection (if you do the latter, you'll need the Xbox 360 wireless adapter), you can use WMC through your television.

CROSS-REF See Chapter 26 for more information on setting up Xbox 360 as a media extender with Vista.

Windows Media Center as an All-in-one Media Center

Based on the features discussed in this chapter, you can easily see why Windows Media Center is literally an all-in-one media center. In addition to everything discussed in this chapter, you can also perform the simplest of multimedia tasks, such as playing an audio CD or watching a DVD.

One puzzling question is why continue to use Windows Media Player, when everything can be handled using WMC as its front-end application? I discuss the benefits of Windows Media Player in Chapter 17; however, it's true to say that the Windows Media Center is a full-service multimedia center that can serve most, if not all, of your audio and video expectations or needs.

Of course, the advantage of Windows Media Player is that you can use it while running other applications, such as web browsers, word processors and so on. Running office applications from WMCE isn't something you'd normally do.

In fact, with the integration of Microsoft DirectX 10, Windows Media Center can help you turn your personal computer into a virtual home cinema, let you VJ a party, or share your vacation pictures with friends — all from the same application.

Summary

Microsoft now includes the Windows Media Center in the Home Premium and Ultimate editions of Windows Vista. This feature, around which an entire system was released for Windows XP, is a true multimedia hub that allows you to go far beyond watching a movie or listening to a musical CD.

With the Windows Media Center, you can organize and catalog your multimedia collection as easily as you can watch or listen to it. Through its various libraries, you can organize multimedia by artist or title; you can even give each track a rating.

That's not where it ends; Windows Media Center is also a suitable resource for handling your pictures. Not only can you view pictures within their folders, but you can open a picture and edit it all from the picture preview.

Even more impressive, if you have the right hardware, is how the Windows Media Center lets you work with television. With new support for CableCard technology, you can even enjoy high-definition broadcasting. Television capabilities extend to DVR features, such as recording and saving. Consult the program guide to find out when your favorite show is on television.

Windows Vista and the Windows Media Center improve the use of media extenders. One of the most popular extenders currently available is Microsoft's Xbox 360. By connecting your Xbox 360 console to your wireless network, you can use Windows Media Center features through it over your television.

For multimedia fans, the Windows Media Center should be a welcome addition to Windows Vista. It's certainly a welcome addition to standard editions of Windows machines.

Chapter 17

Windows Media Player 11

IN THIS CHAPTER

Looking at the enhancements to the Windows Media Player

Sharing multimedia over the network

Organizing media files

If you thought that Windows Media Player was going to sit back and let Windows Media Center steal all of its thunder, think again! Microsoft recently introduced the Windows Media Player 11 (WMP11) for upgrade for Windows XP and is now the bundled version with Windows Vista.

NOTE If you live within the European Union, you will likely purchase a Vista *N* edition unique to the EU, which doesn't include Windows Media Player. You must manually download it if you want to use it with Windows.

If you are familiar with Windows Media Player 10, you probably thought that it was light years beyond the previous version, and you would be correct. Likewise, I can say the same for Windows Media Player 11. Not only does it blow away WMP 10, it even gives competitors such as iTunes a run for its money.

Windows Media Player 11 contains a whole new look and feel, which is the most superficial of its updates. It can now seamlessly handle various media file types, provide online store content, integrate its own online music venture called URGE, and provide far superior cataloging to anything I've seen yet from Microsoft and Windows Media Player.

This chapter provides a full rundown of all the many new and updated features in Windows Media Player 11 so that you can fully take advantage of this very capable media player. In this chapter I also discuss how you can use WMP11 and Windows Vista to share your media files with people over your network. Finally, I show you how to catalog media files in your libraries so that they are better organized and more accessible than in previous versions of the Windows Media Player.

A World of Enhancements

Windows Media Player 11 definitely lives up to its billing in light of its extensive list of enhancements. Just opening the application, as illustrated in Figure 17.1, shows how the Windows Media Player has evolved since the last edition.

FIGURE 17.1

The Windows Media Player 11 interface has changed dramatically.

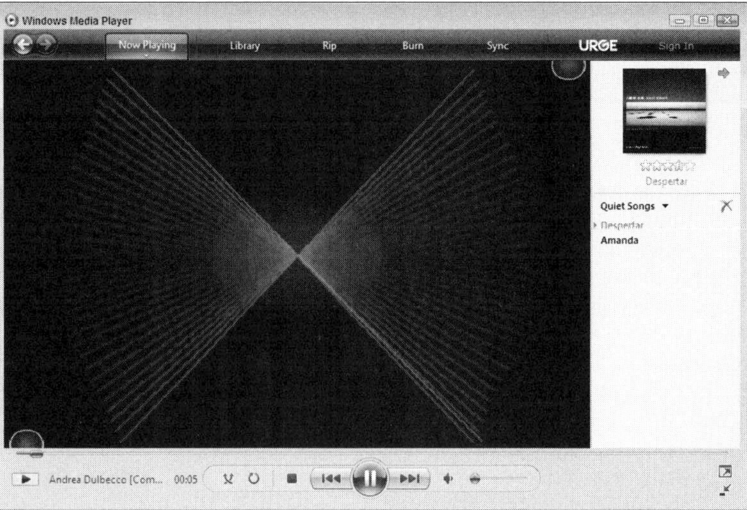

Reducing the Windows Media Player 11 to a simple interface update would be disingenuous and wrong. This following section walks you through the new enhancements in Windows Media Player 11 that will certainly grab your attention.

A new look for a new release

As shown in Figure 17.1, Windows Media Player 11 features a new interface and color scheme that is based on the Windows Vista color scheme. Of course, when you launch the WMP from the Start Menu, you may be disappointed to find the same old boring icon that we've grown used to over the years. Surprisingly, Microsoft didn't bother to update the icon, as shown in Figure 17.2.

FIGURE 17.2

Changes reign supreme in WMP 11, but just not in the Start Menu icon.

One of the first things I noticed beyond the sleek charcoal design is the new border in the Full view, which is a part of the new Windows Vista standard. I found that in the previous version of WMP that working with menus and accessing the features I needed could be difficult. Windows Media Player 11 moves past the text-oriented look and feel of previous versions and opts for a more visual, icon/thumbnail-oriented approach.

Toolbars are presented in a cleaner, more coherent way. They are displayed in a clear manner across the top of the WMP. This change is a welcome one from WMP 10, where you had the tabbed toolbar, and then more options, such as Radio, in the upper right of the application.

The new look toolbar at the bottom of the Windows Media Player 11 application that acts as a remote control, as shown in Figure 17.3, is easier to understand and use.

FIGURE 17.3

The Windows Media Player 11 playback toolbar is easy to understand and use.

Across the top toolbar, you may have noticed a new tab called URGE, which brings you to the new Microsoft and MTV joint online music store. I talk about URGE in greater detail later on in this section.

When it comes to playing music with WMP11, the interface is less cluttered and more congenial than in previous versions. For example, when you are playing a song, the Now Playing playlist in the List pane features the name of the song and the artist in a much clearer font. The current song is denoted by an arrow and appears in blue instead of black. Relevant song information, such as title, artist, album, and so on, displays at the bottom of the Windows Media Player, next to the playback toolbar mentioned earlier, as shown in Figure 17.4. Unlike in the previous version of WMP, album art appears at the top of the List pane, if available, along with the currently playing song.

TIP If you mouse over the blue arrow next to the album art, you can find information about the CD, such as the album title and artist, and musical genre. A link also appears to help you buy the album on URGE.

FIGURE 17.4

Song information appears in the Now Playing playlist and at the bottom of the Windows Media Player.

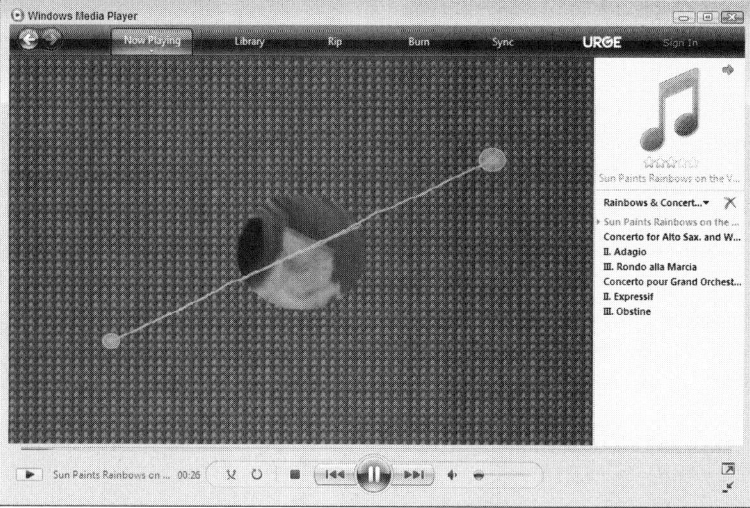

Windows Media Player 11 has considerably fewer visualizations than WMP 10. Personally, I don't find this to be a negative as the number of visualization varieties in the past started to be more than most people would use.

Of course, you can always customize the Windows Media Player application to match your desired look and feel. When you launch the application for the first time, WMP throws everything but the kitchen sink at you: It appears in Full view and includes both the List pane and Enhancements (which include features such as the graphic equalizer). You can make individual panes or components disappear simply by right-clicking the pane and deselecting it or clicking the close button. In the case of the Show List pane, you can simply click the aforementioned blue arrow.

List Pane

The List pane has a number of responsibilities in Windows Media Player 11. In addition to its normal duties as a sort of concierge for WMP and your multimedia files, it also has a number of additional features that helps you make sure your List pane is nice and neat. From the Now Playing menu in the List pane, you can clear the contents of your list. Also, having outdated files in your playlist is not uncommon. For example, you may have deleted some multimedia files, but they're still in the playlist; now, from the List pane, you can tell WMP how to handle such instances by either skipping over the missing files or having it ask you to remove them. You can also sort the content of your playlists or even save it. All in all, a very busy pane!

The Now Playing tab may be your best ally when customizing the WMP11 interface. You can handle all the options mentioned previously from this tab. You can also work with visualizations, which are detailed in the next section, or set other general application options.

Playing media

Let's get down to business. The real reason for using Windows Media Player 11 is not for nice colors or cool visualizations; it's so you can listen to music CDs or watch your favorite DVDs. In this regard, Windows Media Player doesn't disappoint.

The basics in WMP11 haven't changed. Simply put your musical CD in your CD-ROM and Windows Vista automatically loads the CD; an AutoPlay window may appear if activated, asking you to select an option. You can use either Windows Media Player 11 or the Windows Media Center. If you choose the former, WMP launches and loads your musical CD.

After Windows Media Player recognizes your CD, and assuming your computer is connected to the Internet, it populates the List pane, as shown in Figure 17.5.

If you are simply looking to play your CD without using any of the other features available in Windows Media Player 11, you will most likely work solely within the Now Playing tab of the toolbar. By right-clicking within the Center View of the WMP, you can perform a number of tasks, such as:

- Set the Info Center View
- Select a visualization
- Opt for no visualization
- Display full-screen view

Watching a DVD is just as easy as playing a CD. Windows Media Player 11 can play back your DVDs with all the standard features of your typical DVD player. When you put in a DVD, it loads in the WMP, and into the List pane, as shown in Figure 17.6.

FIGURE 17.5

If your computer is connected to the Internet, Windows Media Player automatically populates the List pane.

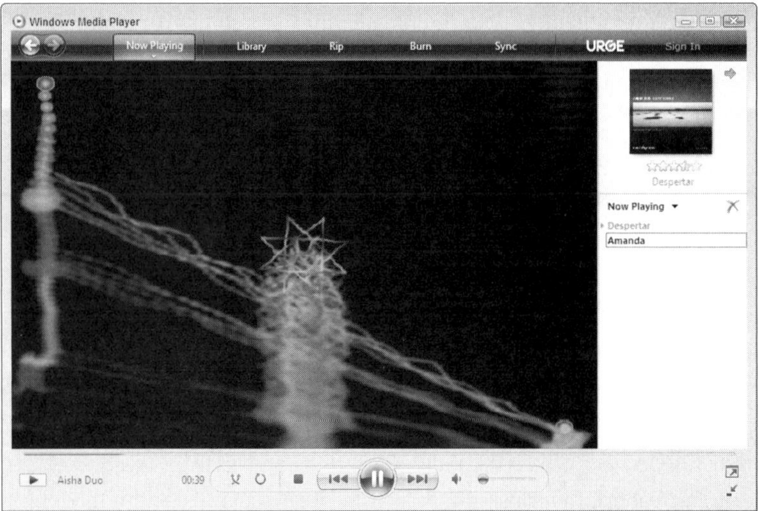

FIGURE 17.6

The various chapters of a DVD appear in the Windows Media Player Now Playing list in the List pane.

You can use the remote-like toolbar at the bottom of the Windows Media Player to handle DVD management. You can hold down the fast forward or rewind buttons to use these common DVD functions. If you hold down on the DVD button, which is shown in Figure 17.6, you can access more advanced DVD features, including:

- Audio and language options
- Captions and subtitle options
- Root and Title menus
- Camera angles
- Capture image

Windows Media Player 11 offers a solid option for DVD playback for Windows Vista Ultimate, especially if you are a laptop user or have great multimedia hardware.

Burning CDs and DVDs

I remember back in the day when copying computer files was limited to floppy disks with embarrassingly low disk capacities. Eventually, readable and writable CD-ROM drives became all the rage, and then it was rewritable CDs so that your disk wasn't condemned to be obsolete as soon as you completed burning. In the past couple of years, DVD burning has become the de facto standard simply because of the DVD's storage capacity.

Windows Media Player 11, as you might imagine, allows for burning CDs without your needing to download or buy additional software. Of course, making sure that you have the appropriate hardware for disk burning is up to you. Windows Media Player 11 does have its limitations in that it only allows for burning audio or data CDs or DVDs. Unfortunately, you cannot burn or copy a video DVD, using Windows Media Player. To work with DVDs, you can use the new Windows DVD Maker feature that is available in Windows Ultimate.

Although burning CDs and DVDs is not a new feature in Windows Media Player 11, it does have a helpful new aspect, as demonstrated in Figure 17.7. When you prepare a CD for burning, a progress bar illustrates how much space on the disk will be used for your burn compared to the size of the media. There is also a numeric indicator of exactly how much space is left.

FIGURE 17.7

You can now figure out how much space you have left on your CD to burn.

Although it's not an essential feature or update in WMP11, being able to gauge remaining disk space is certainly a very welcome addition to the application. In the past, it was hard to tell how much space was left, which made picking essential data difficult when deciding which files must absolutely be included when little space remained.

Improved rip and burn interfaces

This section builds on two improvements already discussed in this chapter: the improved interface and the improved burn process. One problem that some third-party burning applications suffer from is a difficult or cluttered interface.

Windows Media Player 11 doesn't have such issues due to a greatly improved cataloging system, as shown in Figure 17.8.

FIGURE 17.8

The improved cataloging interface means burning and ripping are easier than ever.

The following sections take a closer look at the ripping interface.

Rip interface

The Rip tab provides access not only to the rip interface, but also to a number of rip-related tasks and options that you can access by clicking the Rip menu tab, as shown in Figure 17.9.

These submenus let you set important audio ripping information; for example, you can select one of six audio output formats. The only new addition here is that you can rip audio CDs to WAV format. By default, WMP uses the Windows Media Audio. You can also set the bit rate for your media files in order to find the right balance for you between smallest file size and best audio quality.

FIGURE 17.9

The Rip menu tab opens up new worlds.

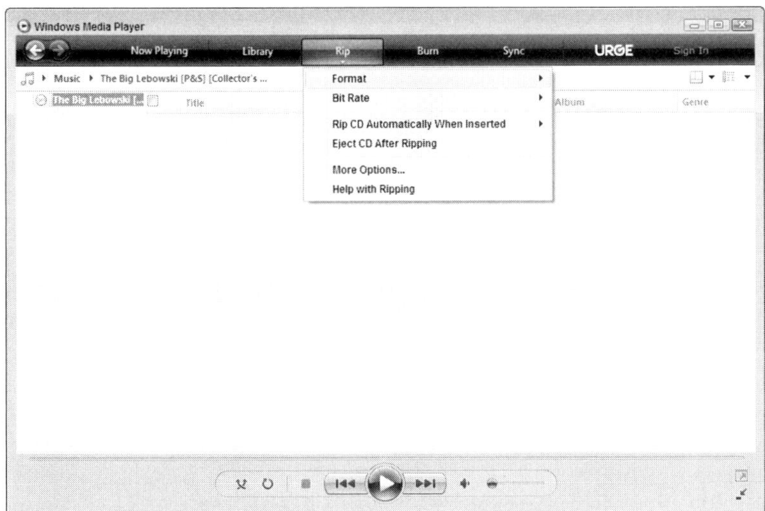

By default, the bit rate is set to 128Kbps.

The Rip submenu also lets you set other options. For example, you may want to enable automatic audio CD ripping. This option has three options: always, never, or when you click on the Rip tab. You can also set whether or not to eject the CD after ripping is complete. It also contains a command that links you to online help, and a More Options command that offers you general Windows Media Player options (it opens to the Rip Music tab).

After you insert an audio CD to rip and then click the Rip tab, the rip interface displays the content of the CD, including:

- Album art
- Album title
- Performer
- Genre
- Year of recording
- Rating (if applicable)
- Track listing

Each song has a check box next to it, indicating whether or not it should be ripped. By default, all songs are selected for ripping. The rip status provides a progress bar numeric indicator of a song's rip progress, as shown in Figure 17.10.

FIGURE 17.10

The Windows Media Player rip interface displays the status of your ripped audio CD.

The Global Status indicator, which is at the bottom of the Windows Media Player, provides status information on the state of the rip. This status is available for all actions that Windows Media Player 11 performs. When the CD rip is complete, you can view the ripped files in your library by clicking the Recently Added category in the Library tab, as shown in Figure 17.11.

FIGURE 17.11

The newly ripped files appear in the Library tab.

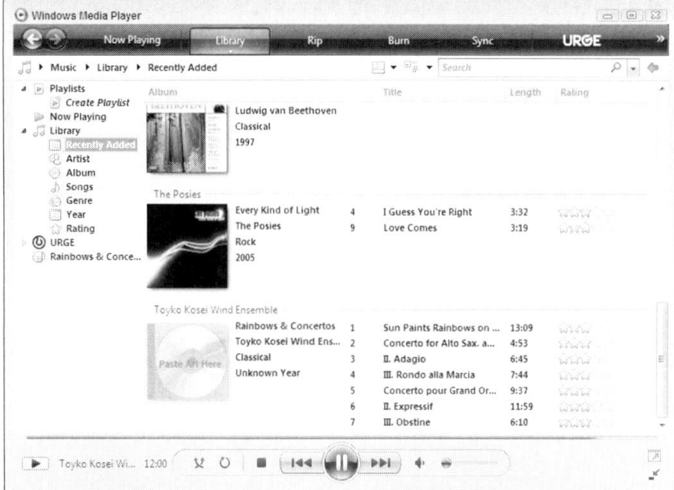

The following section takes a look at the burn interface and shows you how easy and simple it is to use.

Burn interface

The burn interface is slightly more crowded than the rip interface, but that's simply because you have considerably more options here. To access the burn interface, simply click the Burn tab. The screen is divided up into several sections:

- Library categories
- A graphical representation of albums in your library category
- A search feature
- Your burn list
- A graphical representation of your burn media with progress bar

Figure 17.12 illustrates this interface layout.

FIGURE 17.12

The burn interface in Windows Media Player 11

The track selection process is quite simple; you can use the categories in the library at the left of the burn interface to find the desired artist or album. Alternatively, you can use the search box at the top of the window to search. You can enter a letter or series of letters, and corresponding matches appear on the fly, as shown in Figure 17.13. This feature is called the *word wheel* and is new to Windows Vista and its applications.

FIGURE 17.13

The Search feature lets you find the music you want quickly.

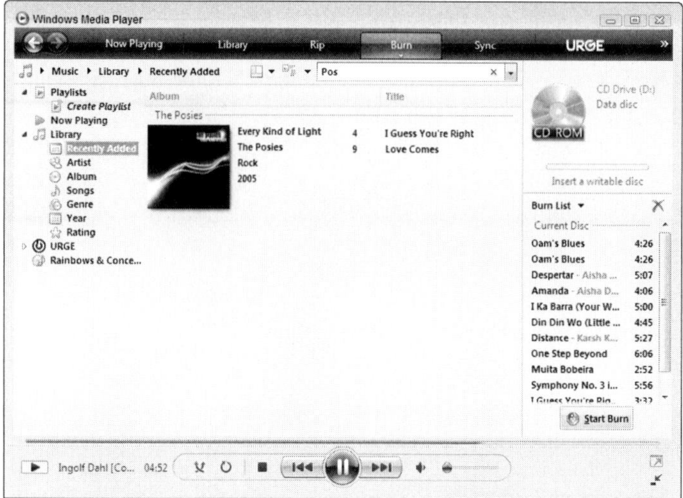

When you've located the album or songs that you would like to burn, you can drag and drop the multimedia files into the burn list in the List pane. If you have an extensive list of albums in your library, you'll notice that WMP now does what is called *stacking*—using a graphical representation, you can see how many albums are in a category. As you can imagine, the more albums there are, the bigger the pile of albums is.

NOTE **The burn list functions exactly like the playlist when you are listening to an album. You can use the Burn List drop-down menu to clear the list, shuffle or sort the list, rename, or save the playlist.**

What's more important here is the CD icon that appears just above the List pane. This icon displays a CD or DVD icon depending on the media in your drive; it indicates the media type, disk capacity, progress bar, and remaining disk space. As you add more and more files to the disk, the progress bar advances, showing both a graphic and numeric representation of how much disk space is used.

After you have prepared your disk for burning, simply click Start Burn.

Let's talk about the submenus in the Burn tab for a moment. Like the Rip tab, it features a number of actions relative to the task at hand, as shown in Figure 17.14.

FIGURE 17.14

Set a number of burn-related options from the Burn submenus.

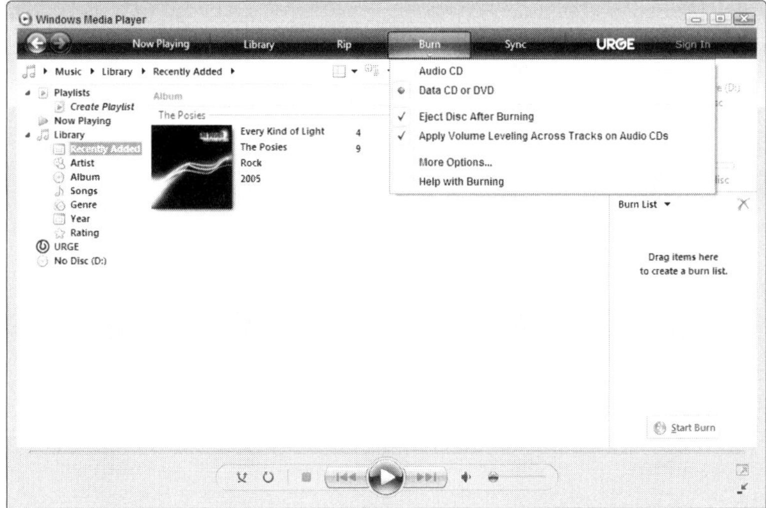

By clicking on the Burn tab down arrow, you can access options for performing a number of tasks, such as:

- Selecting whether you want to burn an audio CD or a data CD/DVD
- Setting whether to apply volume leveling across tracks on CD
- Deciding whether or not to eject CD when complete
- Accessing online help or setting general Windows Media Player 11 options (using the Burn tab)

Most of these features are self-explanatory except for volume leveling. By using this feature, you can rest assured that your songs are recorded at the same volume. This feature is particularly helpful if you are making a mix CD of songs recorded by different artists or formats. This feature guarantees that the perceived loudness is the same among all songs; in other words, a given song will not play louder or softer than another song, even at the same system volume.

Windows Media Player 11 also allows for disk spanning when burning disks. In other words, if your burn project goes beyond the available space for a CD or DVD, you can span it to a second CD or DVD in order for you to complete the project. This feature is new for WMP11 and Windows Vista.

Improved sync

Windows Vista and Windows Media Player 11 offer improved synching capabilities with external devices. Windows Media Player continues to let you sync your media files to external devices, such as portable music players, storage cards, or even external media centers such as a digital media player.

Most audio and video files, plus .JPG picture files can be synced; however, the kinds of files that can be synched depends more on your device and its compatibility. Windows Media Player lets you sync up to 16 different devices.

What has changed in the sync feature is the concept of reverse-synchronization. This feature lets you replicate media files on a handheld device onto the source machine. Windows Media Player 11 also works better with PlaysForSure-compatible MP3 players. The PlaysForSure concept is similar to the Vista-compatible concept; you can be sure that any device that has this logo displayed on it is compatible for use with Windows Media Player 11.

Clicking on the Sync tab sets up the sync interface, which looks similar to the rip and burn interfaces, as shown in Figure 17.15.

FIGURE 17.15

The Sync interface in Windows Media Player 11

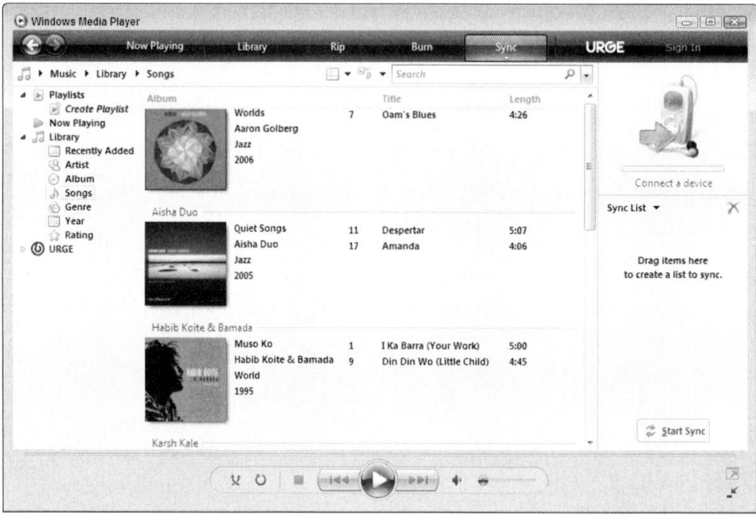

The List pane features a Sync List into which you can drag and drop media files. Similarly to when burning a CD, you click Start Sync when you are ready. The Sync List in the List pane has functions similar to the other tab interfaces; you can clear the list, shuffle/sort the playlist, or save the playlist.

The URGE music store

The biggest, or at least, most talked about change to Windows Media Player is the (semi) inclusion of the URGE online music store. This joint venture between Microsoft and MTV offers digital content (music and video) online for purchase and is integrated with Windows Media Player 11. Essentially, it's Microsoft's answer to Apple's iTunes or Napster.

Currently, URGE offers a catalog of more than 2 million titles for download, which is fairly impressive. Unlike other competitors, URGE is a subscription-based service with varying levels of access. Some plans are pay as you go with a lower monthly fee, whereas a more high-end subscription is available with unlimited access.

URGE is more than just downloads, though; it also features a radio service of approximately 130 channels that is akin to competitors such as Sirius or XM satellite radios.

As you have probably noticed, an URGE tab is available in Windows Media Player, as shown in Figure 17.16.

FIGURE 17.16

You can access URGE easily from Windows Media Player.

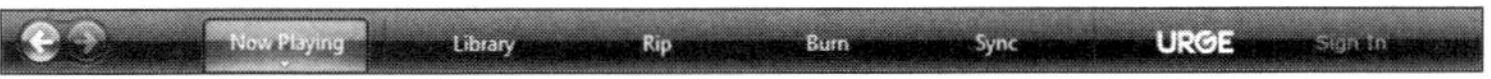

If you've never used URGE before, you need to perform a procedure before you can use it. Like Windows Live Messenger, URGE isn't actually installed on your computer when you install Windows Vista. Rather, you have to let Microsoft transfer you to a Web site and download the software. Keep in mind that you will need an Internet connection before you can use this feature.

After you click URGE, Windows Media Player takes you to the URGE home page, displays an error, and opens a new window with a license agreement.

Windows Media Player then downloads and installs the URGE software, integrating it into your Windows Media Player 11 application, as shown in Figure 17.17.

FIGURE 17.17

You can download and install URGE in a matter of minutes.

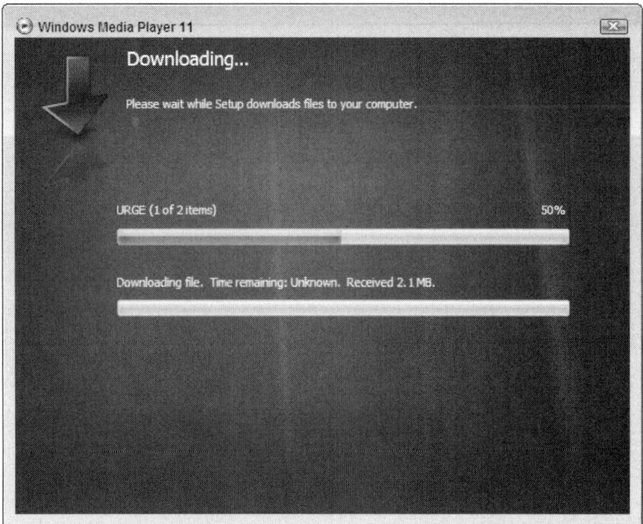

You need to authorize the installation by clicking Run and then Continue when the download is complete. After URGE is installed, you can click the URGE tab to load it within the browser.

You then need to sign up for an account in order to use it. However, once you buy or download tracks, they become available in your libraries. You can even use the category menus to view specific URGE features, such as music charts.

Using the down arrow on the URGE tab, you can find links to creating or managing your URGE account. From this same submenu, you can also access special sections for MTV, VH1, or CMT (all part of MTV Networks). There is also a media guide, similar to a program guide, with information on what's hot in music and entertainment. When you are finished with the media guide, you can use the down arrow to return to URGE. Finally, you can also view other online services (see the nearby Note) from the URGE submenu.

NOTE Before I finish with URGE, don't forget that it isn't the only online boutique available from Windows Media Player 11. Windows Media Player 11 offers links to third-party online boutiques. For example, you can visit Napster, XM, audible.com, and so on. These third-party sites are integrated within the Windows Media Player 11 browser.

Sharing Multimedia

Windows Vista is clearly an operating system that is designed to share information with others on your network. Windows Media Player is no different; in fact, it has a feature that allows you to share your multimedia files across your network.

Windows Media Player and Windows Vista let you take sharing one step further. When you think of sharing files, most of us think of letting others access files and use them on their own computers. Of course, you can do that, but you can also do more than that. For example, you can use sharing to:

- Play multimedia files from another computer in your house.
- Use a media extender, such as Xbox 360, to play multimedia files from your computer.

As mentioned earlier in this chapter, you can also let a user on your private network log into his or her account, access your files, and listen to them on his or her computer.

Sharing multimedia using Windows Vista is a simple and straightforward process. All you need to get started is a network (Ethernet or wireless), and one of two things:

- A remote computer running the same edition of Windows Vista as you
- A networked digital media player

After you have all the hardware requirements met, you're almost ready to start sharing files. This feature lets you share almost every digital media file imaginable. Most likely, if it is in your Player Library, you can share it. This sharing capability even goes for multimedia files with integrated protection; for example, if you buy a song from an online service, it may be protected so that you cannot share it across different forms of media. However, you need to make sure that your multimedia files are in an acceptable location. Acceptable locations are "monitored folders," such as Videos, Music, Pictures, and so on. The Windows Media Player scans these folders for media because they are the usual locations for storing media.

You can share any of the following types of media:

- **Audio:** WMA, MP3, and WAV
- **Video:** WMV, AVI, MPG, MPEG
- **Pictures:** JPEG, PNG
- **Playlists:** WPL, M3U

Unfortunately, you cannot share a DVD from your computer. If you are using one of the networked digital media players, you can watch a DVD on your computer or a television in another room from your home's DVD player.

Let's take a look at how to actually share your media files. You need to first make sure that Windows Media Player 11 is up and running.

Networked Digital Media Players

A relatively new concept, networked digital media players are hardware devices that connect to your network or router and allow you to transfer or share media files. For example, you can listen to digital music, watch DVDs, and share pictures over your television, another computer, even your stereo! These devices look similar to a wireless router. You can also connect these devices to your home media equipment using standard connection cables and connect to your wireless network. These devices can be somewhat expensive; don't be surprised to pay anywhere between $150–$200 for a networked digital media player. Before you buy one, be sure to visit the Microsoft PlaysForSure Web site at `www.playsforsure.com` to make sure your device is compatible.

To turn on sharing, follow these steps:

1. **Click the down arrow on the Library tab in the Windows Media Player.**
2. **Select Media Sharing.** The Media Sharing dialog box appears, as shown in Figure 17.18.
3. **In the Sharing settings section, select Share my media.**

FIGURE 17.18

The Media Sharing window lets you set basic sharing settings.

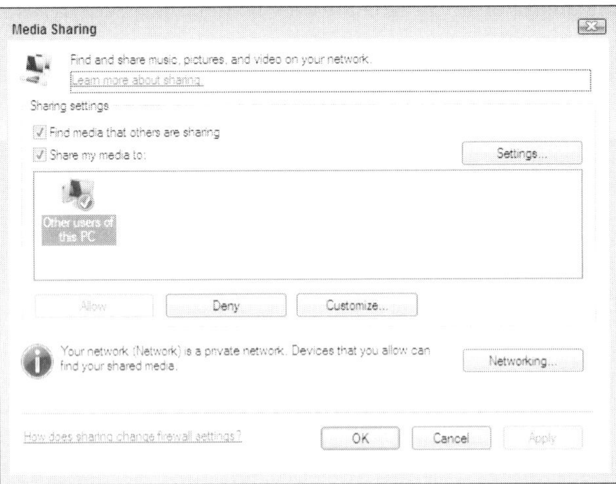

4. **In the window just below the Share my media to option, click the device(s), if any, that you are willing to share your media.** If you don't have any available media, the only "Other users of this PC" icon appears.

5. Click Allow for each device just underneath the device icon(s).
6. Click the Settings button just above the device icon(s).
7. Select your default sharing parameters in the Default Settings window, as shown in Figure 17.19.
8. Click OK.

FIGURE 17.19

You can set or limit what media to share with other users.

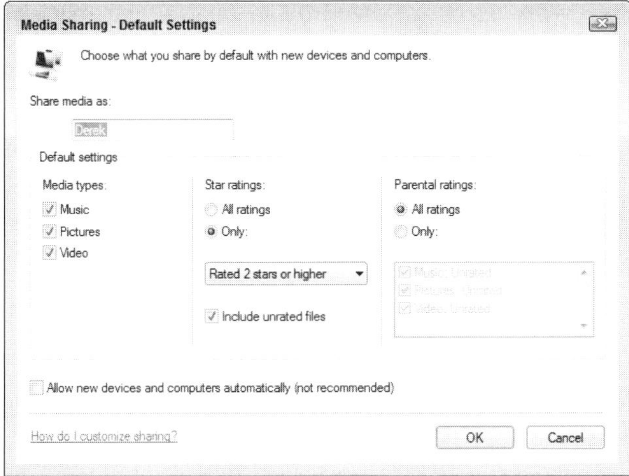

NOTE It's important to note that although you can share multimedia files over private networks, both wired and wireless, Windows Vista does not support media sharing over public networks. Examples of public networks include airports and cafés. If you are attempting to share media at work, please consult with your system administrator. Only your system administrator can enable this feature.

I should also mention another important aspect of media sharing, and that is the topic of *subnets*. Subnets are part of a network; they act as a separate identifier for a specific group of computers in a given location. If you're a home user, then this probably isn't an issue for you because most home networks use only a single subnet. However, if you're a hardcore networking guru and have several routers at home, be sure to connect your devices to the same router as your computer to avoid any connection complications.

If you are using a firewall, you may have to make changes in order to make media sharing work. If you are using the bundled Windows Firewall, you should not have to make any additional changes. Required ports are automatically opened when you enable media sharing. Windows Vista online help has helpful information on firewall port settings that should be opened.

Organizing Your Multimedia

Windows Vista, Windows Media Player, and Windows Media Center really make multimedia arrangement much more organized and efficient for users. Windows Vista helps by organizing your media folders within your Documents folder, as shown in Figure 17.20.

FIGURE 17.20

You can organize your media folders for clarity using Documents.

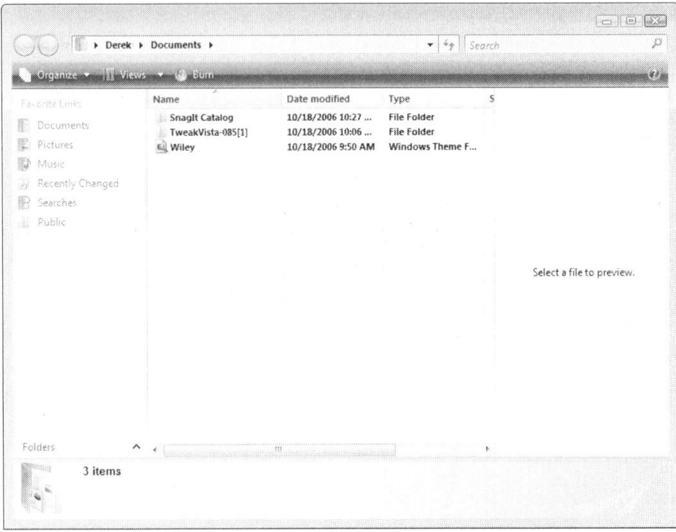

As you can see, your monitored folders are neatly displayed to the left of your Documents window; these include Pictures and Music. For some reason, Windows Vista doesn't include Video in this window, though it probably should.

However, if you go to Computer, go to User, and locate these folders, you'll notice that Video is there. You'll also notice that these folders are color-coded a shade of green or teal instead of the typical yellow folder color, making locating them easy, as shown in Figure 17.21.

Working with Windows Media Player 11 shows it to be even more efficient in terms of organizing your multimedia. As mentioned earlier, Microsoft abandoned the text-oriented interface of Windows Media Player for a much more graphical interface. Text is replaced with icons and thumbnails; a more readable font means easier reading on the eyes.

The categories are better organized, as shown in Figure 17.22. As the figure shows, you can quickly and easily access your multimedia by genre without having to hunt for it.

FIGURE 17.21

The Music, Video, and Pictures folders, as well as other monitored folders, appear differently.

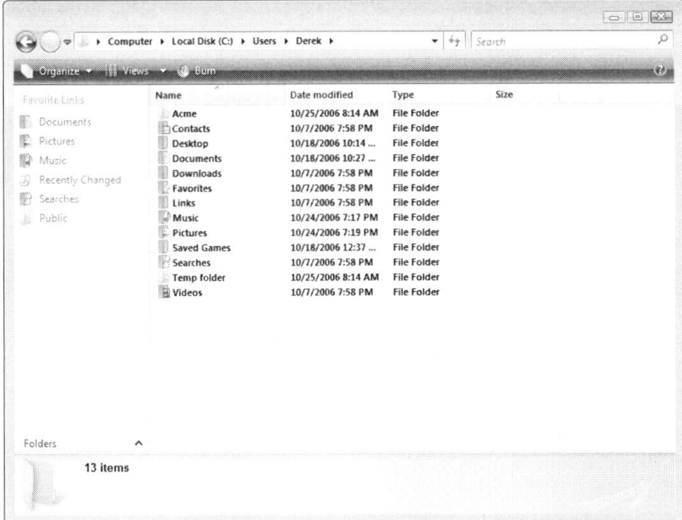

FIGURE 17.22

Windows Media Player 11 libraries are easy to manage.

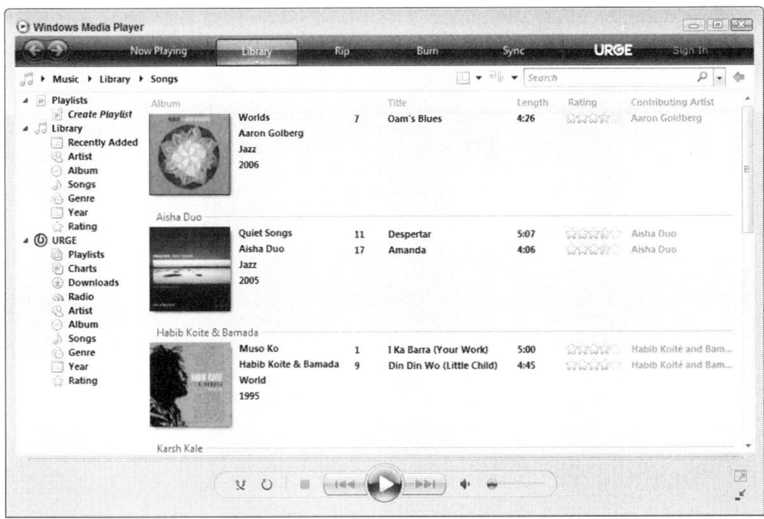

Everything is drag-and-drop or link oriented, which makes changing categories or performing other file operations simple.

Windows Media Center is equally as efficient. As mentioned earlier in this chapter, multimedia files are clearly and neatly displayed, along with relevant information. If you are working with pictures, you can locate pictures by folder with actual live representations of folder content to facilitate your search.

As shown in Figure 17.23, if you are working with music files, you can sort by categories by simply clicking the appropriate link at the top of the page. Once you select a category, you can view its content in full graphical representation, including artist name and title. If you select a file, the file details appear in full detail, as shown in Figure 17.24.

Compared to Windows XP, I find the entire Vista multimedia experience to be light years beyond, and, frankly, more enjoyable to use. This is due in large part to better use of screen real estate and better organization.

FIGURE 17.23

Windows Media Center is very well organized and makes your life easier, too.

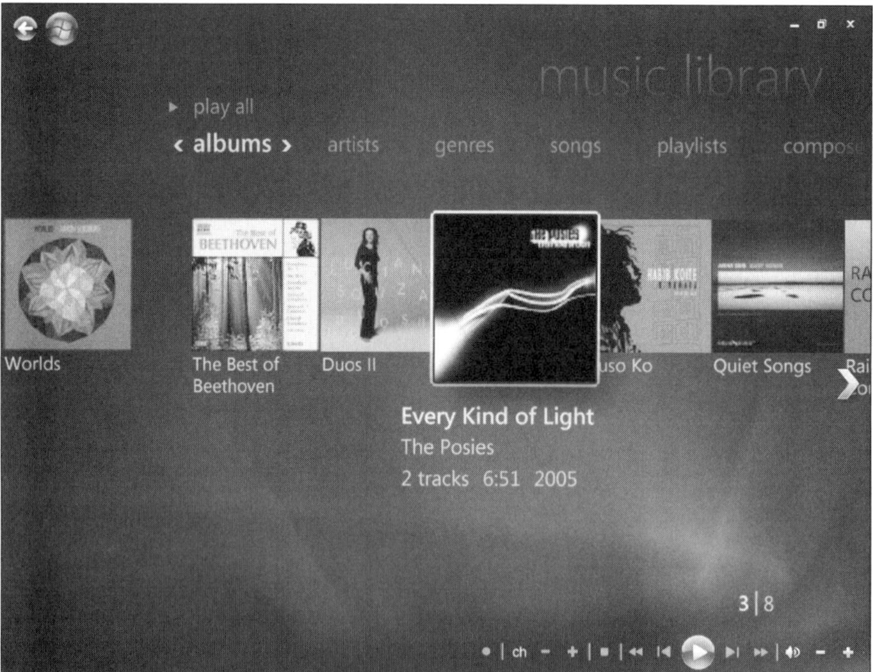

FIGURE 17.24

The Windows Media Center provides clean, well-organized file information.

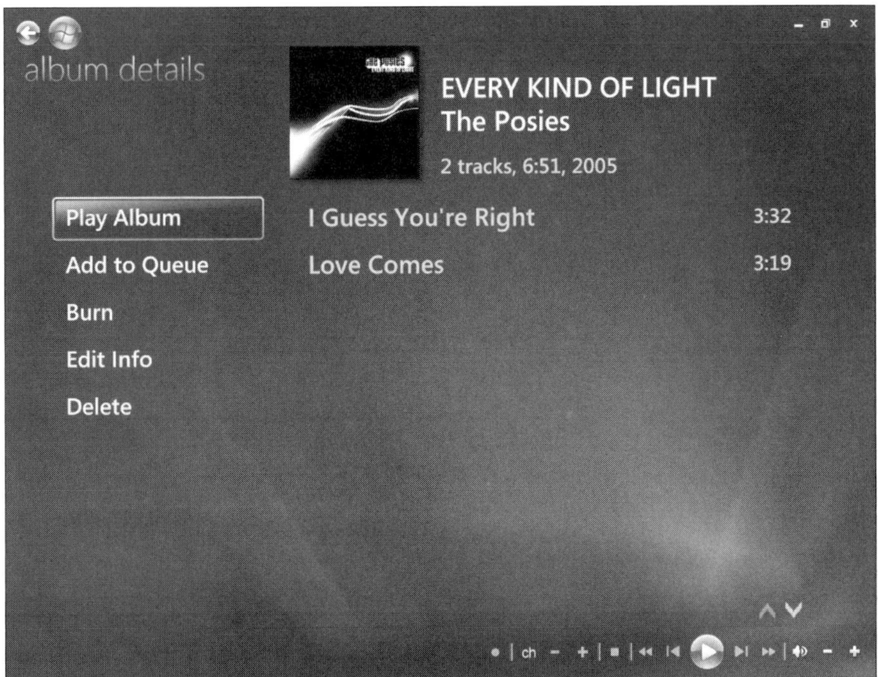

Summary

Windows Media Player 11, the latest and greatest version put forth by Microsoft for Windows Vista, is finally a competitor. After years of being a nuisance on our computers, while we sought out better alternatives, Microsoft finally gives us a reason to give it a shot.

Between the improved interface, better fonts, more graphics, and less text, better-organized libraries, improved DVD playback, and URGE, Microsoft may have a winner here! Windows Media Player 11 is finally ready to compete with the likes of iTunes.

The media share feature in Windows Vista is excellent. You can now easily share your media files — pictures, video, and music — over your private network. If you use a networked digital media player, you can even broadcast multimedia across your house, including your stereo, your TV, another computer, or media extenders like Xbox 360.

The superior organization of libraries makes finding your music even easier. Did I mention that the new search feature can help you find your multimedia files with the input of one or two letters?

There's little not to like about Windows Media Player 11, with the possible exception of its CD/DVD-burning capabilities. Then again, it's a media player, and we wouldn't realistically expect this application to make data DVDs or copy ISO files. However, Media Player gets the jobs done you need it to do, and it's free.

Overall, I think Windows Media Player may be one of the applications that Windows Vista users like best as they discover the new operating system.

Part VI

Music, Movies, Video, and Audio

Whether your computer is grafted to a set of multimedia super speakers or use your network or a direct connection to blast it through your living room entertainment center, you'll dig Part VI. It's all about how Windows Vista Ultimate gives you the power to watch and listen to your video files, audio files, DVDs, and more.

Learn all about Windows Media Player 11 here, including its video and audio prowess. It lets you play, enhance, and enjoy your movies and music as never before. Then, grab your camcorder and start shooting: Chapter 20 is a comprehensive guide to using Windows Movie Maker, a powerful video editing program included with Vista Ultimate. Create a masterpiece and share it with your friends via e-mail, the Web, or a DVD.

IN THIS PART

Chapter 18

Digital Music Guide

IN THIS CHAPTER

- Organizing your digital music
- Acquiring digital music
- Looking at Windows Media Player 11

In recent years, the computer has truly become a hub of musical activities. Whether you use it to buy music online, store your tunes for playback on the PC or connected devices, or sync up with a portable media player, the PC is a musical device.

Windows Vista Ultimate is right there to help with the effort. With everything from audio enhancements that make music sound fantastic to superior music organization, it's the music lover's operating system that dreams are made of. Vista can help you store your music and acquire more of it, play it how you want to, and share it across your home network.

The crux of Windows Vista's musical prowess is Windows Media Player 11. The new version of the age-old player is better than ever, with much better library organization, cooler visualizations, and built-in support for a very cool online music store. You can do everything with it that you could do with Media Player 10 and more: You can find music stored on your computer's hard drive in a flash; create playlists; sync with compatible, portable media players; rip songs from your CD collection; burn audio CDs; and a whole lot more.

I'm a longtime fan of Windows Media Player, especially versions 9 and later. There are those who swear by other media players (such as Nullsoft's Winamp) and they have their reasons, but for me, Windows Media Player has always been a trusted entertainment tool. I've been excited for Media Player 11 for some of its features, such as the ability to play tunes through my entertainment center via my Xbox 360; its ability to show album art in its library list; its library sorting in general; its new, tabbed toolbar; and so on.

Even the Music folder, which replaces Windows XP's "My Music" folder, is improved. You can organize and play files right from it via a toolbar option.

The icon view shows album covers, so you can spot the music you want right away (or, as I have been doing, discover music that you haven't listened to in a while that deserves a good listen).

The one thing you have to watch out for is the new, beefed-up digital rights management (DRM). This feature can make sharing music, restoring online music purchases if you change your computer's hardware, and moving files from one computer to another difficult. I have strong feelings about draconian rules governing how I can use my music, and my screed about it appears later in this chapter.

Regardless of DRM, Windows Vista Ultimate's music capabilities just may bring you to a whole new level of enjoyment in your music. Whether you're surfing your own library or seeking something new to brighten your aural day, Windows Vista Ultimate can help. This chapter shows you how to use Vista to acquire and organize your music, and it also takes a look at using Media Player 11 to optimize your musical experience as much as you can.

Music and Windows Vista Ultimate

You have tunes.

You might have a massive CD collection. You might be an online music shopping aficionado. You might be some of both.

Whether you're used to the way Windows XP handled your music or you're new to computerizing your wealth of songs, you're going to like Windows Vista Ultimate's way of helping you enjoy your music.

Vista wants you to be able to rip your CDs with ease. *Ripping* a CD means copying the contents of an audio CD into digital files, which you can then play on your computer, sync with your portable audio player, and otherwise enjoy.

Vista enables you to burn music as well. *Burning*, of course, means creating optical media (such as music CDs) with your computer, provided it's fitted with a CD-burning drive. You can create playlists with Vista's tools and burn your own mixes — sets of songs you pull from the wealth of your library.

With a Music Transport Protocol (MTP) music player, which includes any number of brands of portable media devices (also called MP3 players), you can sync up your tunes with your Vista-controlled library and carry them around with you. Whether you have a flash memory player with just a few gigabytes of storage or a hard drive player with 60GB, Vista is ready for you.

Storing and organizing your files are important, and Vista can help with those tasks, too. The Music folder (Figure 18.1) has several views, including the icon view shown, that let you organize music as you see fit.

FIGURE 18.1

The Vista Music folder

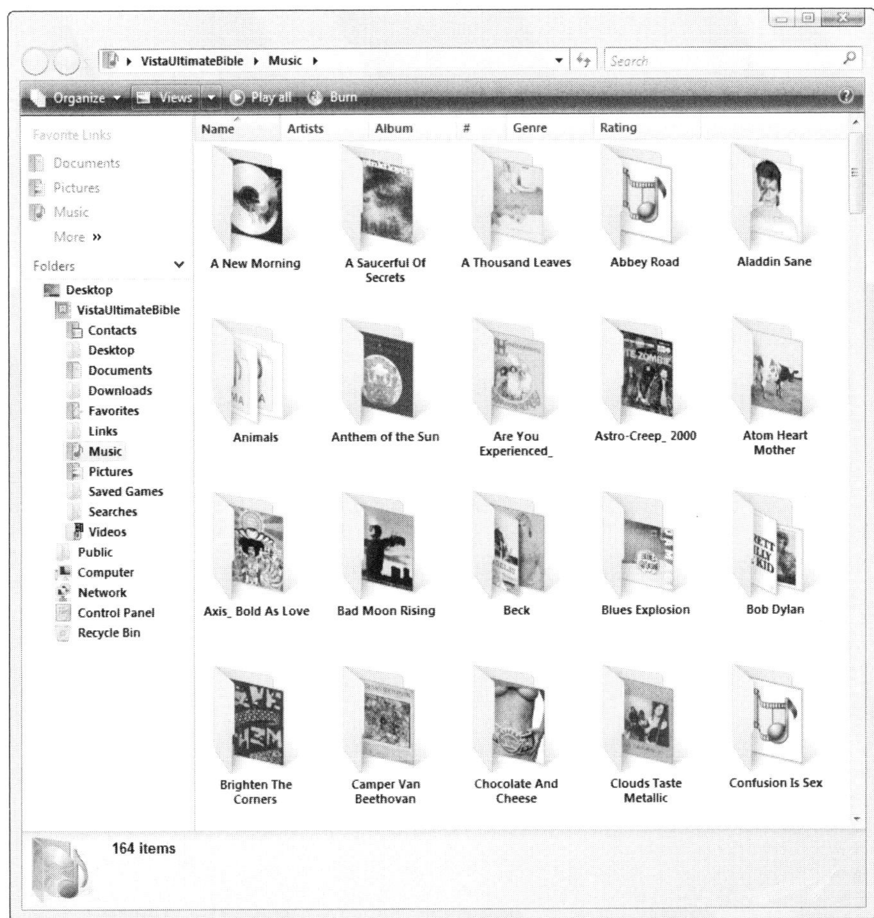

A big part of all this musical activity is Windows Media Player 11, shown in action in Figure 18.2. With its tabbed toolbar and multitude of uses, it's possibly the finest media player software on the planet.

Media Player 11 is the do-it-all tool that you'll use for about 90 percent of your music tasks in Windows Vista: You can use it to browse online music stores (including the new MTV URGE music service), to rip and burn CDs, to sync with portable media devices, to play music, and to do lots of other things.

Of course, Media Player 11 is handy for other media experiences as well. It's a complete movie player, capable of playing DVDs and digital movies in formats that it supports. Check out Chapter 19 for details.

FIGURE 18.2

Windows Media Player 11 playing a tune

You can share your music files with other computers on your network, and also with similar-minded devices called *media extenders*. (The Microsoft game console, the Xbox 360, is one such device.) With media extenders, you can play just about any media on your computer, music included, anywhere you want through your wired or wireless network. For example, if your Windows Vista computer is downstairs in the basement like the one in my office, and your Xbox 360 is usually connected to the television in the living room, like mine is, you can play your tunes and videos through your television and the deluxe speakers that you, of course, hooked up to it.

The question with Windows Vista Ultimate is not what you can do with your music, but what you *can't* do. It rips, it burns, it stores, it lets you get more, it lets you take it with you; what more do you need?

Organizing Your Digital Music

When you rip a CD or buy music, Windows, by default, puts it into the Music folder. Depending on the program you use to rip CDs, the music may be categorized in folders by album title or by artist. Media Player 11 places songs in folders named after the artists, and in subfolders named after album titles.

You can open the Music folder simply by clicking Start ➪ Music. The default view is shown in Figure 18.3.

FIGURE 18.3

The Music folder's default view

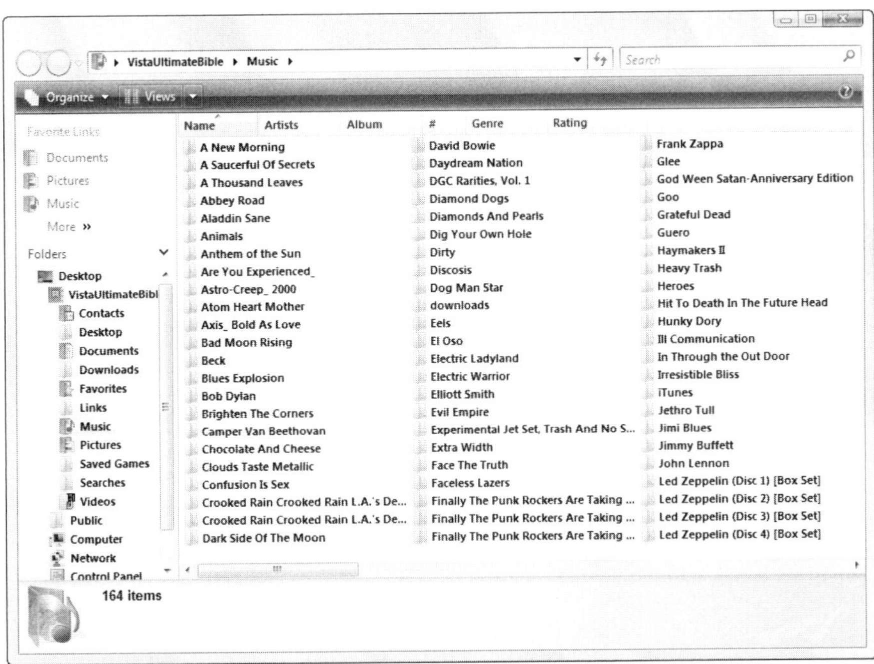

As you can see from the figure, I've built up a large (and, in my opinion, pretty decent) music library. This view is not the only way to display it. Look at the toolbar: In Figure 18.3, which shows the folder with nothing selected, the options are Organize and Views.

Clicking the Organize button opens the menu shown in Figure 18.4. It allows you to sort music in different ways; add various panes to the folder; and perform tasks such as cutting, copying, and pasting.

For example, if you want a search pane constantly displayed, click Organize, hover the cursor over Layout, and click Search Pane. The window transforms to one like that shown in Figure 18.5.

FIGURE 18.4

The Organize menu

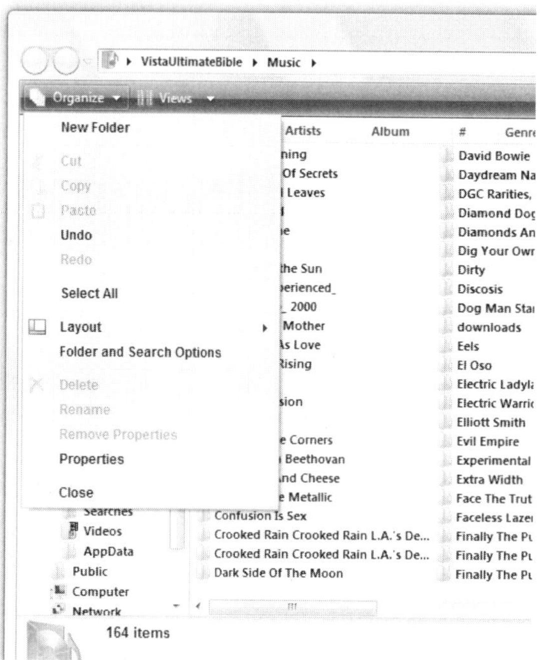

FIGURE 18.5

The Music folder with a search pane

You can click the Views button to see several options for viewing the folder, as shown in Figure 18.6. This handy feature can make finding your artists, albums, and songs easy. For example, you can select to display the contents with large icons (Figure 18.7), which show you actual album covers.

FIGURE 18.6

The Views menu

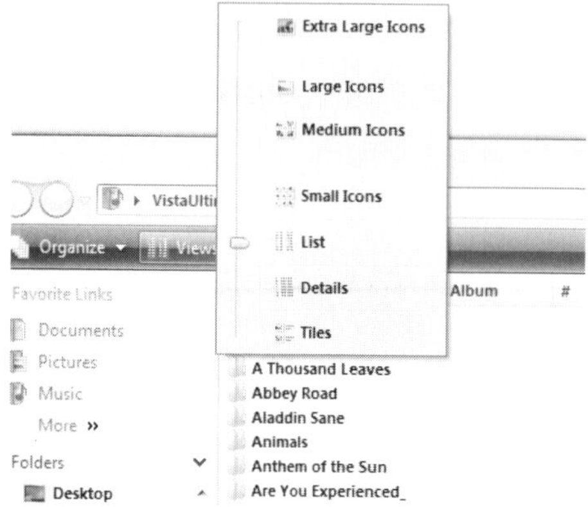

FIGURE 18.7

Large icons in the Music folder

If you select a folder, the toolbar changes slightly. Note in Figure 18.8 that I have selected a folder (containing Lou Reed's *Transformer*). New buttons on the toolbar include Explore, Play All, Share, and Burn.

FIGURE 18.8

New buttons on the toolbar

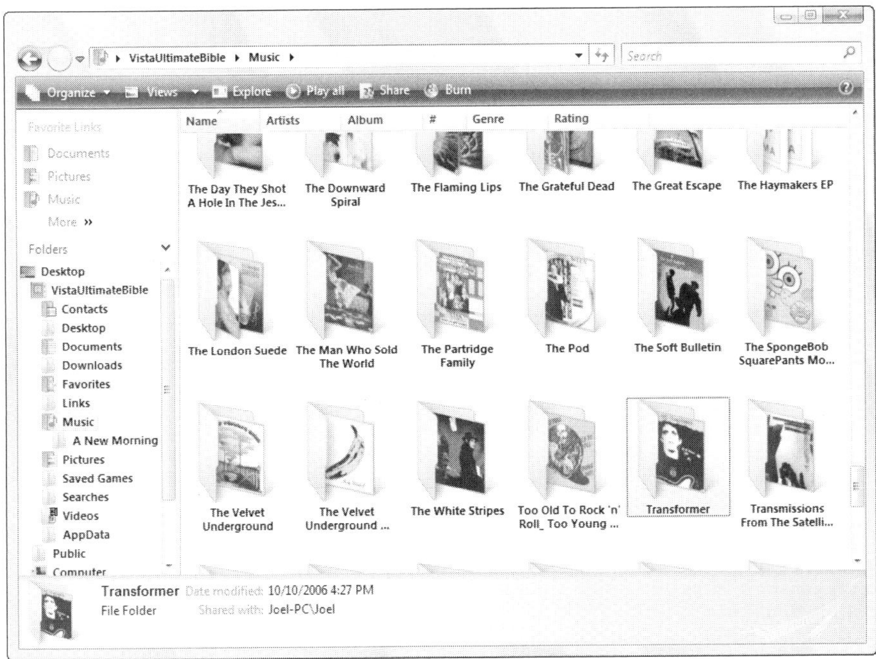

Clicking Explore simply takes you into the folder, which may contain songs or subfolders. Play All queues up the tracks in the folder and its subfolders and starts playing them, in alphabetical order, through Windows Media Player 11 (Figure 18.9). Clicking Share opens the sharing properties for the folder, which I cover in more detail in Chapter 12.

Finally, you can click Burn to launch a routine to burn the tracks to a writeable disc. If a disc isn't already in the optical drive, the drive will eject and Windows will ask for appropriate media.

NOTE This method burns the disc with the folder's contents as data files, as opposed to creating a music CD. If you want to burn a music CD, you have to do it through Media Player 11.

FIGURE 18.9

Windows Media Player 11 plays the tunes in my chosen folder.

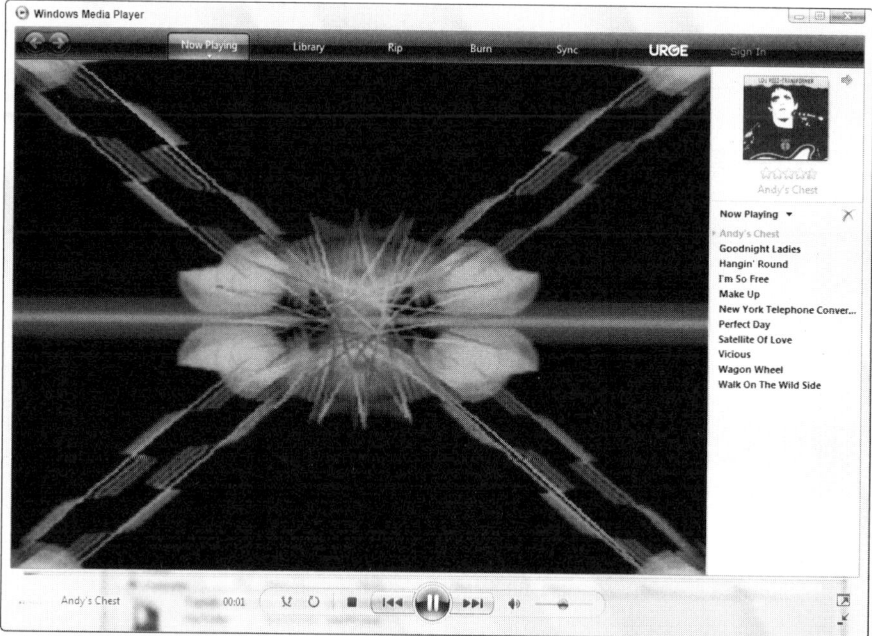

Acquiring Digital Music

Before you can start enjoying everything Windows Vista Ultimate has to offer as a digital music player, you have to actually cram some music onto your computer's hard drive. That task is easy enough. You can use Windows Media Player 11.

You have several ways to get music onto your PC. The two most common ways are to rip it from your CD collection and to buy it online.

NOTE You can, of course, download music illegally. I'm not going to tell you how to do that. In fact, I wish you wouldn't do that. If you like an artist's efforts, you should make sure he or she gets the royalties for them. Not all artists are millionaires, and many rely on royalties to get by — as well as to fund future endeavors. Stealing music *is* a crime, and it's also sleazy and cowardly.

If music isn't harshly copy protected, you can move it from an old computer to a Windows Vista computer, but if you bought it online you'll also have to find a way to move the licenses. You can find more on that topic later in this chapter.

Ripping your CD collection

Ripping a CD is simple enough, but you do need some knowledge of formats and bitrates (both covered in the "Nuts and Bolts: Windows Media Player 11" section later in this chapter). In this example, I use Beck's new-at-the-time-of-this-writing *The Information*. You can follow along with these steps:

1. **Insert a music CD into the drive.** An interface like the one shown in Figure 18.10 appears.
2. **Click the Rip music from CD option.** Windows Media Player 11 appears and immediately starts ripping the music, as shown in Figure 18.11.

FIGURE 18.10

AutoPlay options for a typical audio CD

Unfortunately, in this case Media Player doesn't recognize the CD. It didn't automatically fill in the album or song titles.

3. **If your CD isn't recognized either, click the Stop Rip button, right-click on the album cover, and click Find Album Information.** The window shown in Figure 18.12 appears.

FIGURE 18.11

Ripping music from a CD

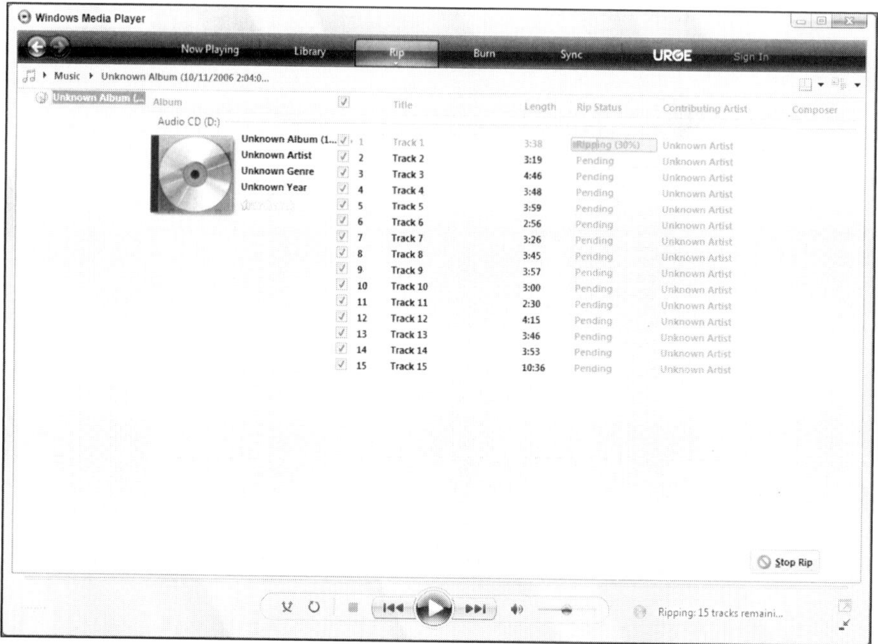

FIGURE 18.12

Getting ready to search for album information

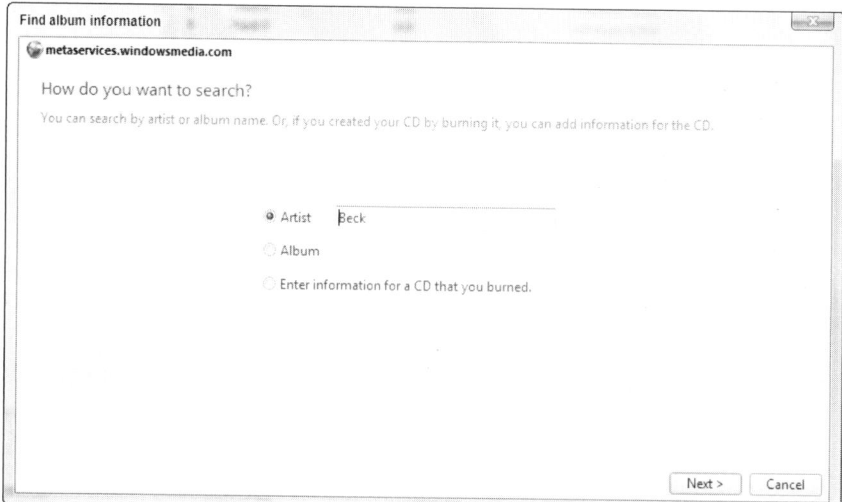

4. **Type in the artist's name under Artist (in this example, Beck), and click Next.** In my case, Windows goes online and finds about 130 artists with the letters B, E, C, K in them, and presents me with a list to choose one (Figure 18.13). I click the top choice, just plain old BECK.

FIGURE 18.13

Searching for Beck

5. **Click to make your selection, and then click Next.** In the screen that appears, choose the appropriate album entry for your artist, and click Next again. In this example, I scroll through the list of known Beck material. Note that this album came with a bonus DVD, so I choose the "The Information (2 Albums)" entry (Figure 18.14). Finally, I have found the proper album.

6. **In the final screen, tell Windows that the album you chose is correct by clicking Finish (Figure 18.15).** The view returns to Windows Media Player 11 (Figure 18.16).

NOTE Be sure to select the right album to avoid confusion. If you mislabel an album that Media Player didn't recognize by choosing the wrong one from its online search, your music library as shown in Media Player won't be accurate.

FIGURE 18.14

Zeroing in on *The Information*

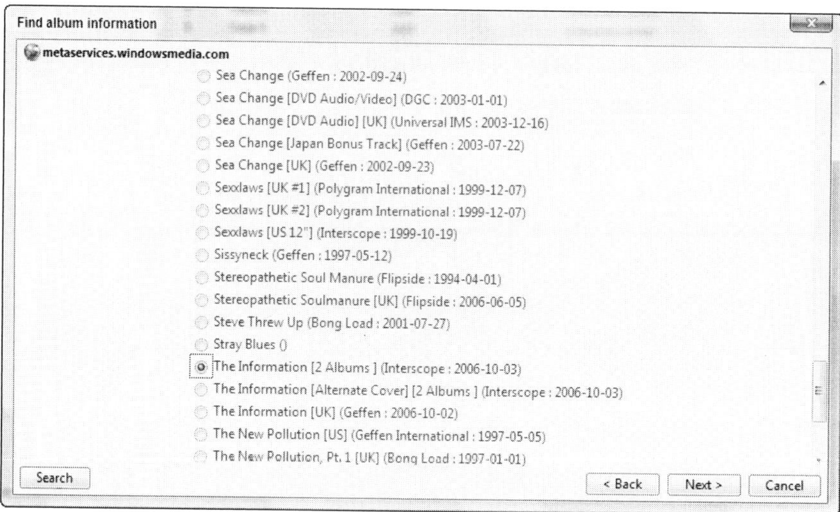

FIGURE 18.15

At last, I have *The Information.*

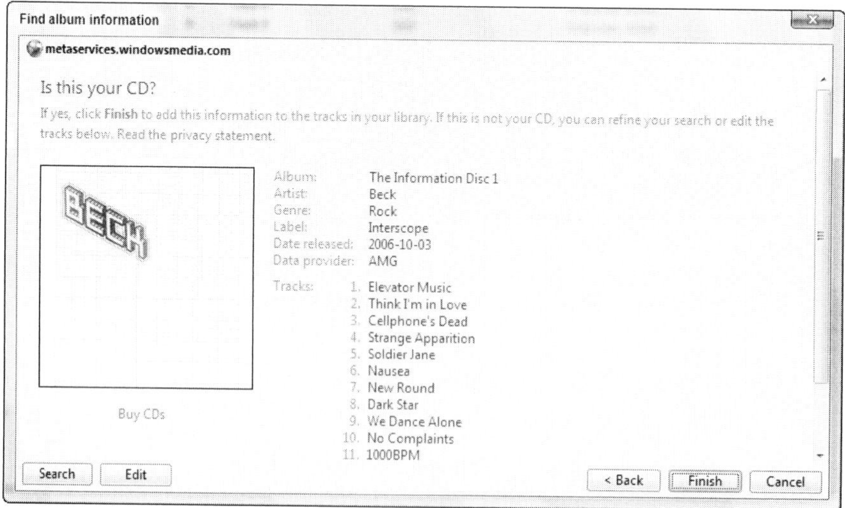

FIGURE 18.16

Ready to let 'er rip!

7. **Now that you have the proper album information in place, you can go ahead and rip the music into your library; just click Start Rip.** Media Player rips your selection onto your computer in the Music folder.

TIP You can circumvent the AutoPlay menu and prevent Media Player from ripping without first finding the album information. Simply start Media Player *before* you insert the album. Click the Rip tab, and go about getting the album information as described in the preceding steps. Then start your rip by clicking the Start Rip button.

The Beck album is ripped into my digital music collection as well, and I can verify this by heading to the Music folder and finding the album in the Beck subfolder (Figure 18.17).

TIP Keep reading! In the next section, you learn about the ripping options, including file format and audio quality, and also how to prevent DRM from infecting your ripped music.

FIGURE 18.17

Making sure *The Information* is in the right place

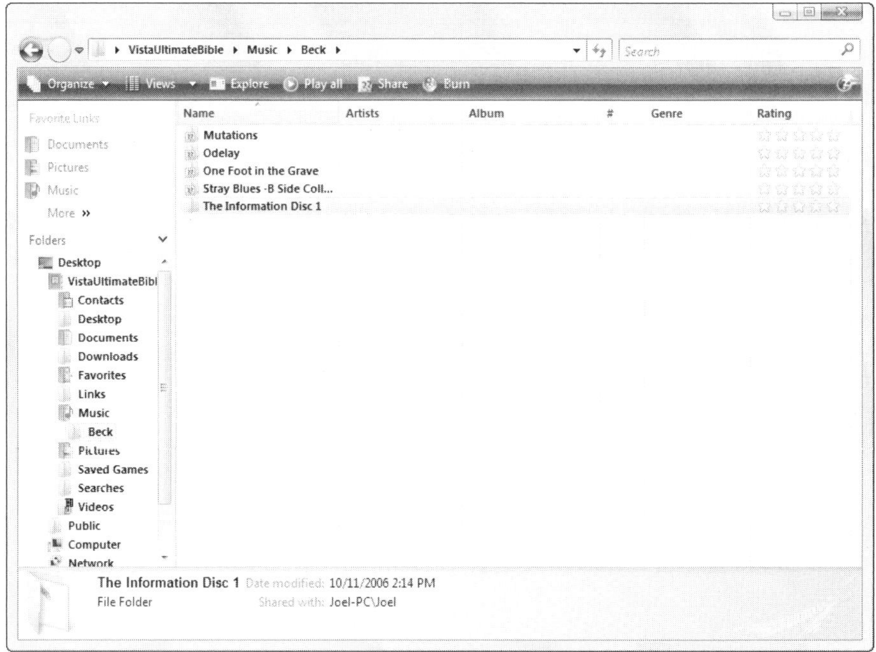

Procuring music online

You can surf through a variety of online music stores that are compatible with Windows Media Player 11 through the Media Player program itself. Windows Vista Ultimate offers the URGE music service, which I get to in a bit, but first take a look at other online stores.

Open Media Player 11 and right-click the URGE button. Note the option in the menu (Figure 18.18) to Browse All Online Stores; click it.

FIGURE 18.18

URGE alternatives

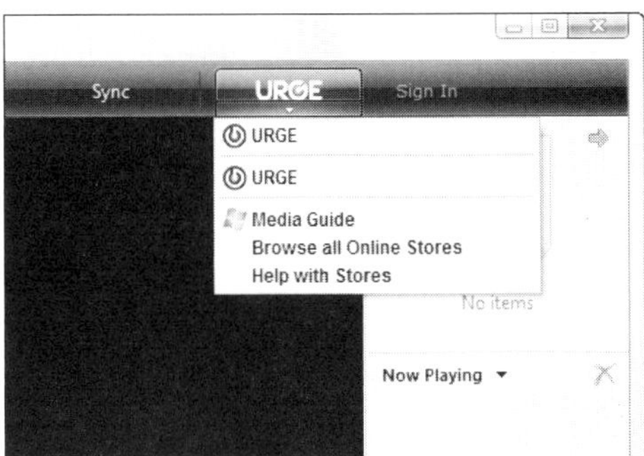

Media Player presents you with a window like the one shown in Figure 18.19, which is subject to change as more stores become available or, alternately, become unavailable for use with Media Player.

FIGURE 18.19

Online music stores

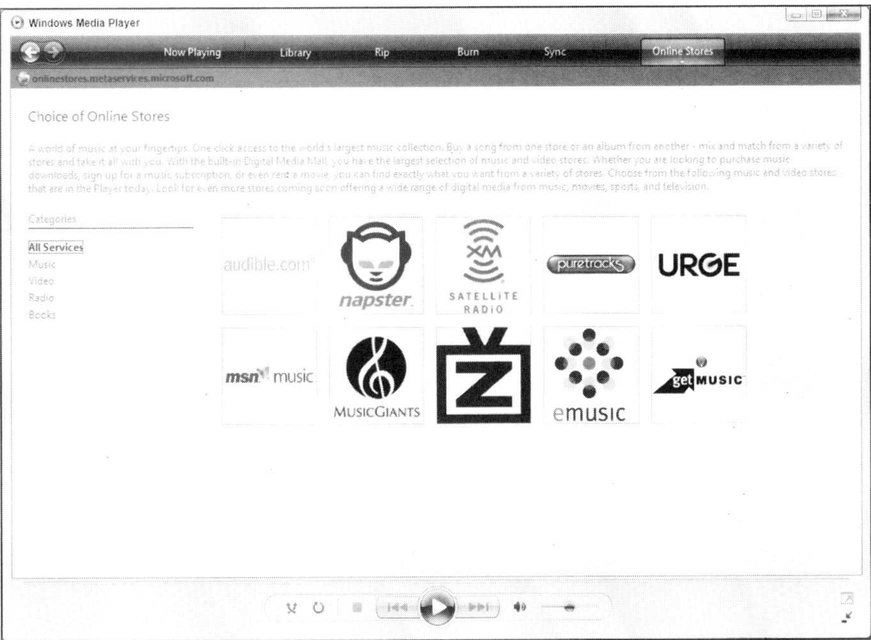

Some of these stores are actually services that for a monthly fee allow you to download any number of songs and use them as long as you're subscribed, whereas others let you purchase songs and albums permanently. MSN Music is one of the latter, and here's how you patronize it:

1. **Click MSN Music, and verify that it's the store you want.** The front page of the online store pops up.

2. **Browse or search for some music you want.** I've always wanted that Citizen Cope song, the one about the sun rising in a mile, so I decide to search for Citizen Cope. The results look good, as shown in Figure 18.20.

FIGURE 18.20

Lots of Citizen Cope

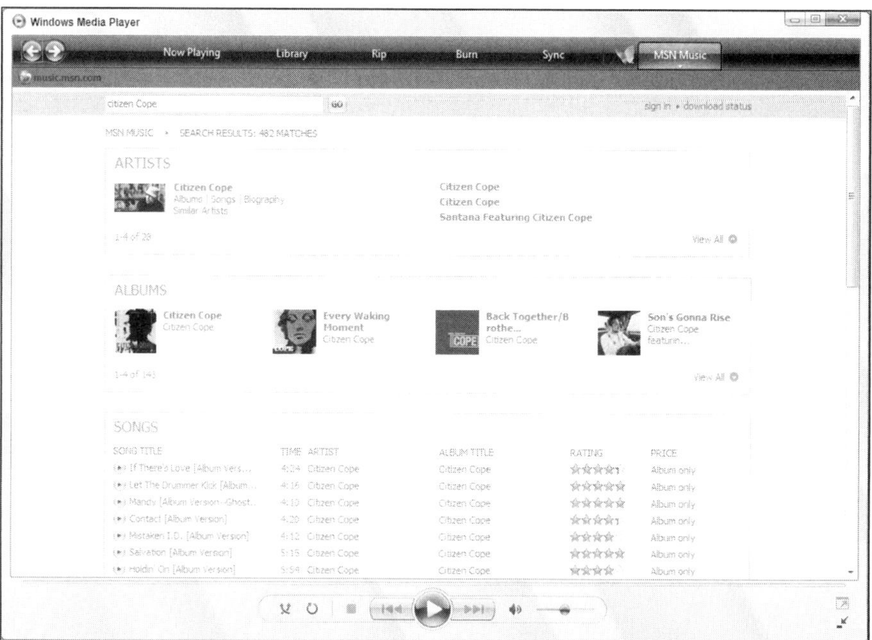

3. **After you locate the song you want, ensure you have the right one by clicking on it to hear a short clip. Click the Buy button if you want to purchase the song.** The song I want is only $0.99, so I buy it. It automatically downloads to my music library in my computer's Music folder. Figure 18.21 shows the store as it processes my request.

FIGURE 18.21

Buying "The Sun's Gonna Rise"

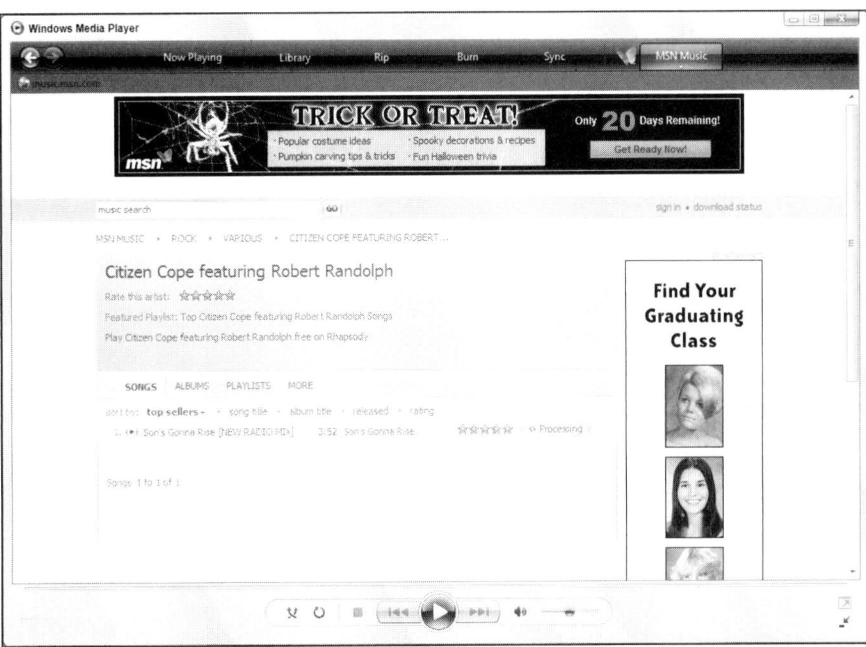

That's all there is to purchasing a song online. Windows Vista Ultimate features an online store from MTV called URGE, which is the default music store. Let's check it out.

Using the URGE music service

Click the URGE button in Windows Media Player 11's interface, or right-click on the music store button and choose URGE. Right away, an end user license agreement (EULA) appears, because the store's software has to be installed on your PC.

Follow the prompts to install the URGE music store software. When the installation is finally complete, the URGE front page appears.

You can also access the URGE music store at `www.urge.com`.

The iTunes Alternative

One problem with Microsoft's Media Player 11 and its various music stores is a total lack of compatibility with the most popular portable media player in the world, the iPod. Although at least a dozen other companies offer portable media players, Apple's iPod maintains a healthy lead in market share (even after the release of Microsoft's Zune).

To get the most out of an iPod, you'll need iTunes (as shown in the following figure), which you can download from `www.itunes.com`. The most recent version of iTunes, version 7, has garnered both praise and venom from iTunes users, many of whom prefer version 6.

The iTunes interface

Like URGE and MSN Music, iTunes allows you to purchase music online. It's also a replacement for Media Player 11 (using its own interface for organizing music and Apple's QuickTime for playing media files), but note that it's *only* compatible with Apple's iPod line of portable media players; it won't work with any other brand.

URGE works in two ways: First, like other music services such as Napster, it offers you subscription-based content. As long as you're subscribed, you can download any music you want from zillions of titles and even listen to it on your portable media player (if it's PlayForSure compatible), but if your subscription lapses you lose access to the content. Alternatively, you can buy songs and albums as demonstrated in the previous section.

To subscribe, just click the subscription link on the front page. You'll be treated to a 14-day trial (no credit card required at the time of this writing).

Through its subscription services, URGE offers songs, albums, radio stations, playlists, new music feeds, and all kinds of other stuff. because the plans and their fees are subject to change, I won't detail them here, but you can head over to `www.urge.com` and find out what services are currently offered.

Nuts and Bolts: Windows Media Player 11

Windows Media Player 11 is packed with options, many familiar and a few new, that give you total control over your Windows music experience. Although the interface is new, it has a multi-tabbed options sheet just like the vast majority of Windows programs, but getting to it is a little different.

To invoke the options window, you must right-click an empty area of the toolbar. When you do, a context menu, shown in Figure 18.22, appears. It contains the classic menu items (File, View, and so on).

FIGURE 18.22

The Windows Media Player 11 context menu contains the classic menu items.

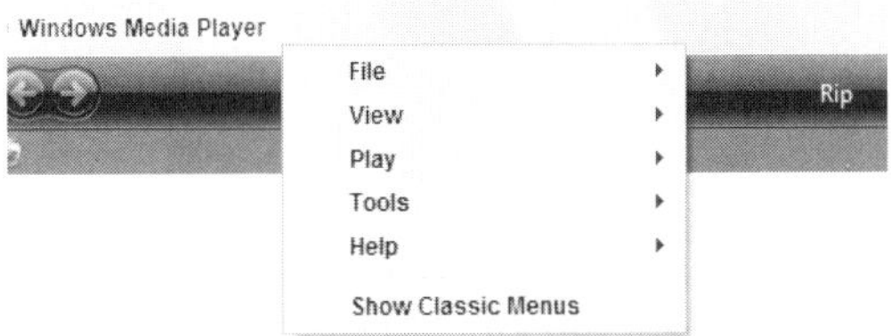

To invoke the options window, hover over Tools and click Options. A window like the one in Figure 18.23 appears.

This 11-tabbed sheet enables you to set the functionality of the player itself, the quality of CD rips, various music playback options, burning options, and so on. There isn't much about Windows Media Player 11 that you can't tweak in some way.

FIGURE 18.23

The Options menu with the Player tab open

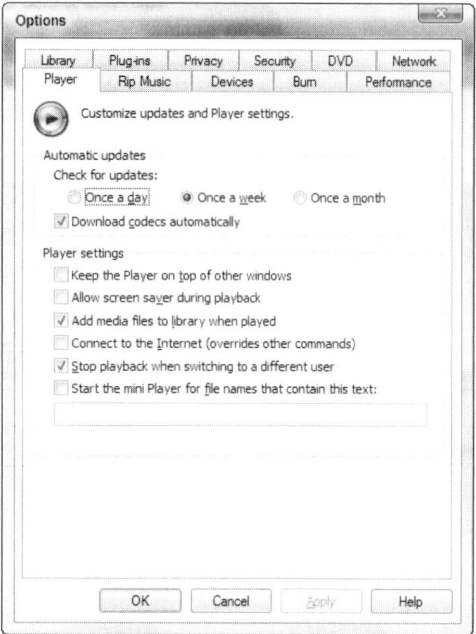

Basic options

The Player page of the Options window (Figure 18.23) lets you tell the software how you want to use the media player and how often to update it.

The top of the menu contains updating options. Windows Media Player 11 is an Internet-aware application that updates itself periodically; you simply choose how often you want it to check for updates. Choose a radio button for once a day, once a week, or once a month.

You can use a check box to elect whether to download codecs automatically. As Microsoft releases new codecs for Windows Media Player 11, the software can keep up automatically.

NOTE The word *codec* actually should be capitalized, because it's an acronym for COder/DECoder. In this case, it's a piece of software that allows you to use a particular means of compressing or decompressing a media file. Compression shrinks media to make it more portable, enabling Web transmissions or efficient storage. Audio codecs include familiar file types like MP3 and WMA, and you can download others such as Ogg Vorbis.

Sometimes, you may receive a message that Windows Media Player 11 is missing a codec that it needs to play a file. If you do, click on the Help link that appears with the message and look for the necessary codec online.

ON the WEB You can browse available codecs at www.wmplugins.com.

Other options in the player menu are check box–selectable, and they include

- **Keep the player on top of other windows:** This option does just what it says: keeps the player visible, and forces other windows to appear behind it.
- **Allow screen saver during playback:** Check this box to enable the screensaver while something is playing in Media Player 11. This feature can be inconvenient if you're watching a video or enjoying a visualization.
- **Add media files to library when played:** When you play a file anywhere on your PC or even from an online source, Media Player can add it to your library if you select this option. Note that it won't automatically add a file that it finds on removable media such as a CD or flash drive.
- **Connect to the Internet (overrides other commands):** This option forces an Internet connection any time Media Player is open.
- **Stop playback when switching to a different user:** Well, that's just obvious, isn't it?
- **Start the mini Player for filenames that contain this text:** If you enter text here, the player will switch to mini-mode when it encounters a file with that text.

TIP The mini player is a tiny version of Media Player 11. You can activate it any time by clicking the little arrow on the bottom right of the player window. Most of the media player program disappears, except for a small media control panel and any visual items you may be viewing.

Ripping, bit rate, and audio quality

The Rip Music tab of the Options window (Figure 18.24) enables you to configure where on the hard drive music you rip from CD will end up, the codec that will be used to compress it, and the quality of the ripped music.

The top of the window lets you configure the location in which you want Media Player 11 to store ripped music. You can select any folder you please. I suggest you leave it at its default setting, which is the user's Music folder, but of course it's up to you.

Under the Rip Settings section, you can set how Media Player 11 handles ripped content. The first option deals with the file format itself.

FIGURE 18.24

The Rip Music tab options

Choosing a format

Clicking the button under the word *Format:* actually pulls down a menu that shows all the available formats and codecs installed. By default, Media Player 11 includes four flavors of Windows Media Audio (WMA), MP3, and WAV (lossless, meaning uncompressed) formats.

The default is standard WMA. Also available are WMA Pro (a more aggressive form of compression that, although it results in smaller files, isn't compatible with all media devices); WMA Variable Bit Rate (compression that chooses its own bit rate so you don't have to), and WMA lossless (which doesn't compress the music much, resulting in high-quality but massive song files).

Choosing an audio quality

Let's head to the bottom of the window, where, depending on the format you chose, you may be able to manipulate a slider labeled Audio Quality. The slider is available with such formats as standard WMA, WMA Pro, and MP3.

As you can see by the labels on either side of the slider, you're trading off between the size of music files and the quality of the sound. Moving the slider to the left means your music will take up less space, but it won't sound as good; it may have "compression artifacts" such as a sizzling sound when it plays high notes. Moving the slider to the right results in larger files with better sound quality.

NOTE Moving the slider affects the music's bit rate. Bit rate is a measure of how much data is crammed into each second of audio to create the song file, in kilobits per second (Kbps). More data results in better sound but larger files, and vice versa.

You'll have to experiment to find your favorite format and sound quality. I find standard WMA compression to be superior to that of MP3, and if I rip my CDs at around 160 Kbps or higher, I don't notice much of a difference between digital song files and actual CD playback. Of course, you need to also take into consideration the capacity of your computer's hard drive and the formats that your portable media player supports.

On the other hand, if you ever plan on *transcoding* your music into other formats — burning audio CDs, for example — you may want to bite the bullet and rip on WMA Lossless format. Lossy codecs, like WMA and MP3, discard information during the compression process. But when you convert to a different format, errors can be introduced into the audio stream that can become audible after several transcode operations. While it consumes substantially more disk space, the fact that the compression is lossless eliminates these sorts of errors.

Setting other options

Three other check boxes allow you to set a few more ripping options:

- **Copy protect music:** I don't see why anyone would ever want to check this box. Doing so foists DRM (discussed in this chapter) upon your ripped tunes. I suggest leaving it unchecked for all eternity.
- **Rip CD when inserted:** Having this setting checked causes the computer to automatically rip CDs, without verification from you, either when you're in Media Player 11's Rip tab or whenever you insert an audio CD. I'm a manual ripper myself, so I leave it unchecked.
- **Eject CD when ripping is complete:** Select this box if you want Windows to automatically eject CDs after they're ripped.

Devices

The Devices tab, shown in Figure 18.25, gives you access to options regarding any media devices your computer is outfitted with. For example, Windows Media Player detects my computer's DVD+/-RW drive, its monitor, and its speakers as media devices.

I can highlight any device in the list and click Properties to nab a properties sheet. The optical drive has no properties sheet associated with it. If I highlight Display, however, and click Properties, I see the screen shown in Figure 18.26.

FIGURE 18.25

Device options

FIGURE 18.26

Display properties via Windows Media Player 11

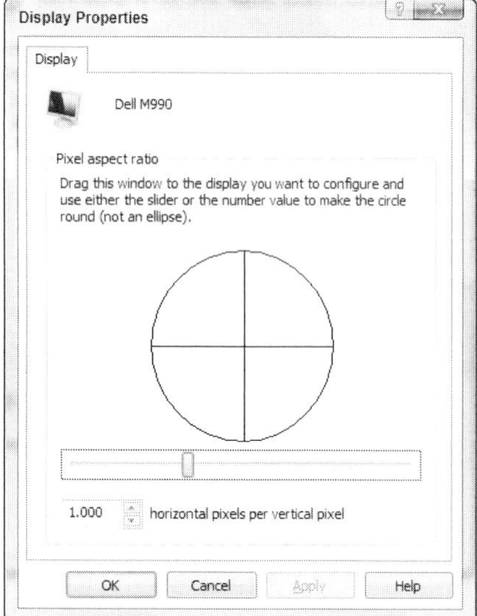

It informs me that I should calibrate the video playback by trying to make that circle as circular as possible (as in, not elliptical).

Similarly, if I click the Speakers item and click Properties, the window shown in Figure 18.27 appears.

FIGURE 18.27

The Speakers item properties

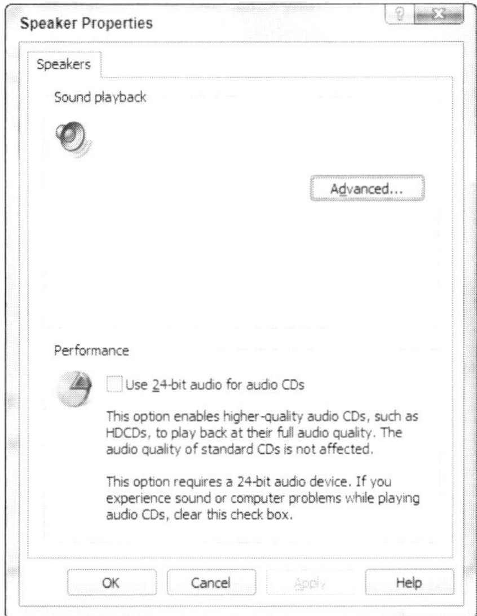

In this window I can enable 24-bit playback for CDs inserted into my computer's optical drive (if I have the necessary sound card, such as my Creative Labs SoundBlaster X-Fi) or click Advanced to launch the speaker configuration routine, which is also available through Control Panel (Figure 18.28).

CROSS-REF For more information on the speaker configuration routine, see Chapter 14.

Note the check box option back in the Devices tab called, When deleting playlists from devices, also remove their contents. This option, when checked, means that when you delete a playlist from, for example, a portable media player, the items in the playlist (that is, the songs) will be deleted from the player as well.

FIGURE 18.28

Sound properties

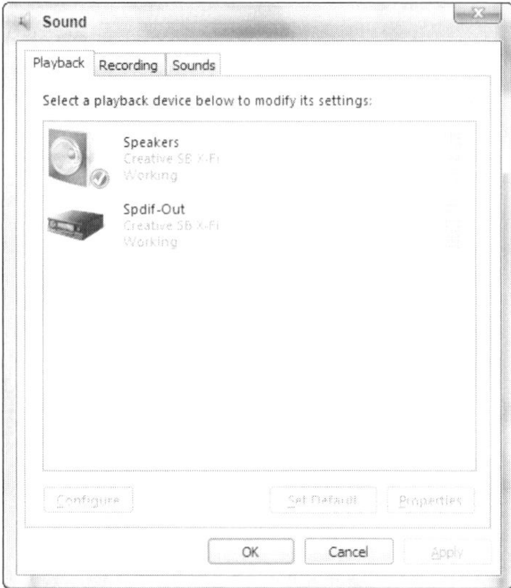

CD burning

The CD Burning tab of the Media Player 11 Options window (Figure 18.29) allows you to configure various options associated with creating your own music CDs, or data CDs with music on them.

In the General section of the tab, you can choose the speed at which discs are burned. Leaving this option alone is best (the default is simply *Fastest*) unless you encounter problems when you burn CDs and you end up with a bunch of useless coasters. If that's the case, then try reducing the burn speeds in increments until your computer starts producing useable CDs.

Also in the General section is a check box that allows you to dictate whether the optical drive ejects the disc automatically when the burn is complete.

In the Audio CDs section is one check box: Apply volume leveling across tracks on the CD. This handy feature compensates for a problem you may encounter when different songs have been mastered with different gains. A song ripped from one CD might be much louder than a song ripped from a different one. With this option checked, Windows will level out the volumes so that all the songs on a burned CD play at about the same level of loudness.

FIGURE 18.29

The Burn tab options

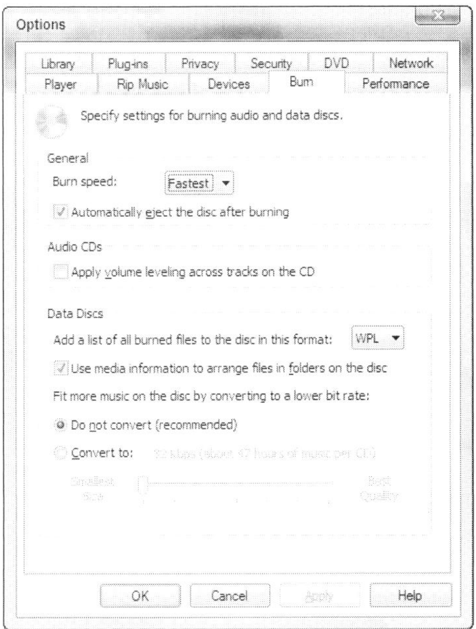

The Data Discs section contains options for when you elect to burn a disc full of songs as data files rather than a music CD. Its options are:

- **Add a list of all burned files to the disc in this format: WPL or M3U:** Select between these two options to determine the playlist file format. Some CD players that also recognize data discs with song files (such as MP3 or WMA files) also recognize certain formats of playlists. The playlist determines the order in which the songs are played. Use the playlist compatible with the device upon which you plan to play the CD.
- **Use media information to arrange files in folders on the disc:** If you want, rather than burn all the files to a single, root folder, you can use the information on the media to burn files into organized directories (<*disc root*>\Music\<*artist*>\<*album*>).
- **Fit more music on the disc by converting to a lower bit rate:** You can choose to automatically convert your song files to smaller files (with poorer audio quality) through this option. You can then choose the bit rate as discussed, earlier in this chapter. Windows doesn't recommend using this option, as it degrades the quality of your music, but if you really want to cram a lot of songs onto a disc and you don't care how they sound, it can come in handy.

Library options

If you click Media Player 11's Options window's Library tab, a window like the one shown in Figure 18.30 appears.

FIGURE 18.30

Library options

The top of the window contains a button called Configure Sharing. Click it to reveal a window like that shown in Figure 18.31.

The sharing settings in the Media Sharing dialog box allow your computer to search your Windows Vista network to look for shared media files, and also let you decide with whom you would like to share the media files on your computer. You can share with other accounts on the same computer as well as with other compatible devices on the network (such as other Windows Vista computers and media extenders).

The Share My Media To box shows every eligible device on the network you can share your media files with. To enable sharing, simply click the device and click the Allow button. You can also deny sharing, or customize it globally or for each sharing device.

If you click the Settings button, or highlight a device and click Customize, a window like the one shown in Figure 18.32 appears.

FIGURE 18.31

Sharing my media files

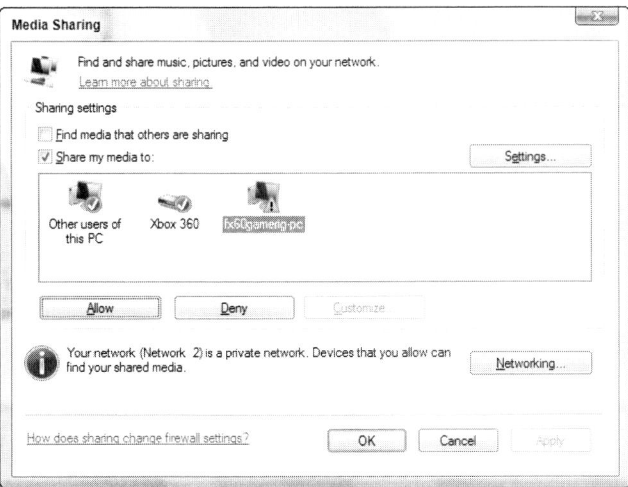

FIGURE 18.32

Customizing sharing

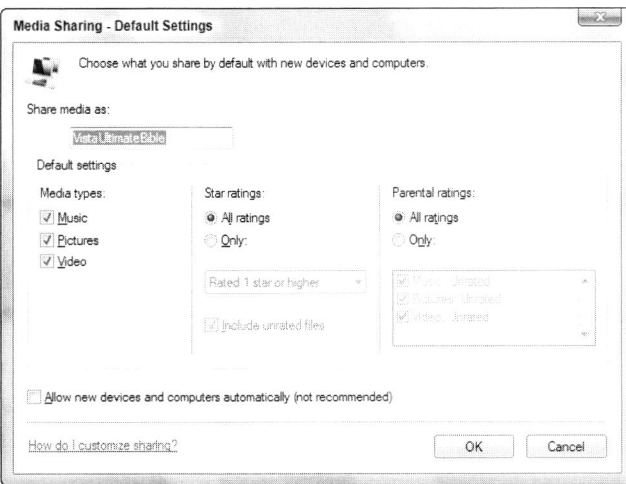

In this dialog box, you can choose to share music, pictures, and/or video via a series of check boxes. You can also select what to share by ratings. Star ratings are ratings that you give to your media manually. Parental ratings are ratings based on any parental guideline ratings that Windows detects.

NOTE You may notice that whenever your Media Player library is open, each song can be given a rating out of five stars. To assign ratings to your music, simply click the star rating you wish to give it. You can use star ratings to differentiate your favorite songs from your least favorite ones.

You can also elect to automatically allow new network devices access to your media files through a check box on the bottom of the window.

Going back to the Options window, the next section down in the Library tab is called Update library by monitoring folders. Click the Monitor Folders button to see a window like the one shown in Figure 18.33.

FIGURE 18.33

Deciding on which folders to monitor

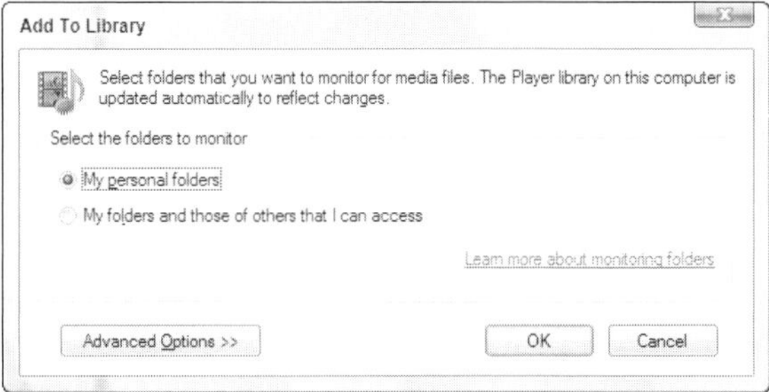

Windows Media Player can add items to its library automatically by checking the contents of folders when it launches. You can tell it where to look: in your personal folders, or in those folders plus folders of others that you can access.

If you click the Advanced Options button, the folder expands as shown in Figure 18.34.

In this dialog box, you can add folders to the list by browsing your computer and clicking the Add button. You can also choose whether to add items that you've deleted from the library, and add volume-leveling to all files. Furthermore, you can choose to skip small files by size, which is handy so you don't pick up tiny media files used by Windows or other programs as audio prompts.

Back in the Library tab of the Options window, beneath the Monitor Folders button is a check box option that allows you to delete files from the computer whenever you remove them from Windows Media Player's library. You might want to do that to keep your library in sync with the contents of your hard drive.

FIGURE 18.34

Monitoring folders — Advanced

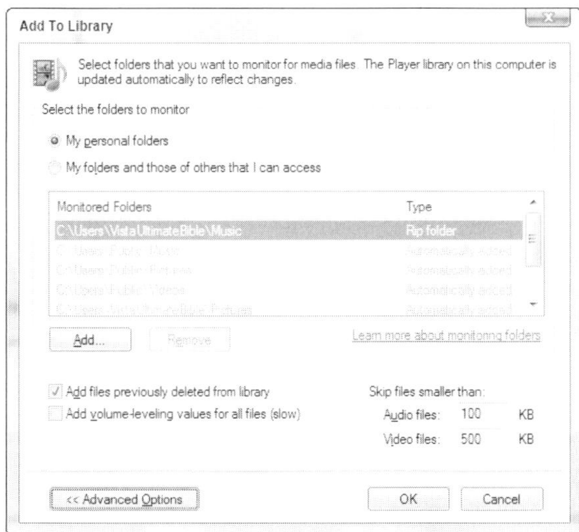

Lower in the window is a section called Automatic media information updates for files. It contains four check boxes:

- **Retrieve additional information from the Internet:** With this option checked, you can choose between the two sub-options. The first causes Media Player 11 to update media files with new information that it finds about them, leaving all other information intact. The second prompts the program to overwrite all the information about your media files whenever it finds new data.
- **Rename music files using rip music settings**
- **Rearrange music in rip music folder, using rip music settings**
- **Maintain my star ratings as global ratings in files:** You can rate music files with star ratings through the Library view.

Privacy and security

Privacy and security are two important items when it comes to an Internet-aware program like Media Player 11, and each has its own tab.

Privacy

The Privacy tab, shown in Figure 18.35, features four sections. The first contains five check boxes that indicate how much Windows Media Player will interact with the Internet:

- **Display media information from the Internet:** This option toggles whether you want to allow Media Player 11 to go online to retrieve information about your songs and other media.
- **Update music files by retrieving media info from the Internet:** Checking this box gives Media Player 11 permission to change your media information based on what it finds online.
- **Download usage rights automatically when I play or sync a file:** If you have DRM-riddled media, Media Player 11 can go online to get usage rights so that you are allowed to play it!
- **Automatically check if protected files need to be refreshed:** If you move a DRM-protected file from one computer to another, your right to play it might need to be re-enabled. Use this option to allow Media Player 11 to check this status automatically.
- **Set clock on devices automatically:** Media player will set the time on compatible devices if you enable it to with this option.

FIGURE 18.35

Privacy options

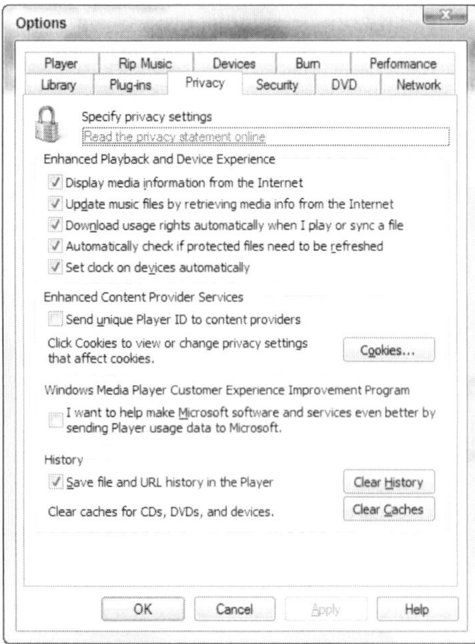

The next check box is entitled Send unique Player ID to content providers. Use this option to send an identification string from your Media Player software to sites from which you get your media. I don't see why you would want to do this; what you listen to is really none of their business.

The Windows Media Player Customer Experience Improvement Program is optional. By checking the box labeled "I want to help make Microsoft software and services even better by sending Player usage data to Microsoft," you're doing just that: sending allegedly anonymous data about how you use Media Player 11 to a Microsoft server somewhere on the Internet. I habitually uncheck this box, because Microsoft doesn't need to know what I'm doing with Media Player 11, anonymously or otherwise.

The last check box, under History, asks whether you want to save file and URL history in the Media Player. This feature is similar to other programs that show recently used or opened files, and if you don't want others on your computer, with access to your account, to know what media you've been accessing, you should uncheck this box.

Security

The Security tab presents a window like the one shown in Figure 18.36.

FIGURE 18.36

Security options

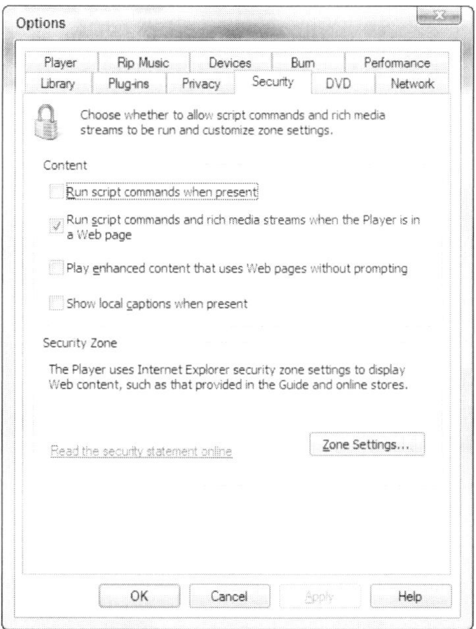

The Security tab contains four check boxes:

- **Run script commands when present:** Use this option to allow Media Player to run scripts (small programs) in media that contain them. Scripts are a great way for nefarious Internet predators to do things to your computer that you may not want them to, so leaving this option unchecked (as it is by default) is best.
- **Run script commands and rich media streams when the Player is in a Web page:** You may never encounter rich media streams, such as slideshows, but if you do, you need this option checked for them to run properly through Windows Media Player. It also allows script commands to run while the player is embedded in a Web page, which is normally safe.
- **Play enhanced content that uses Web pages without prompting:** Leaving this item unchecked causes Media Player 11 to prompt you before it loads a Web page called up by content it may be displaying. The best practice is to leave this option alone.
- **Show local captions when present:** Synchronized Accessible Media Interchange (SAMI) captions are an accessibility feature for the disabled that are turned off by default. You can turn them on by checking this box.

Finally, notice the Zone Settings button, which enables you to tweak Internet security zones, as you can do through Internet Explorer 7+ (Figure 18.37). Windows Media Player uses the Internet security zone, which is typically quite secure by default.

FIGURE 18.37

You can tweak Security Zone settings from this tab.

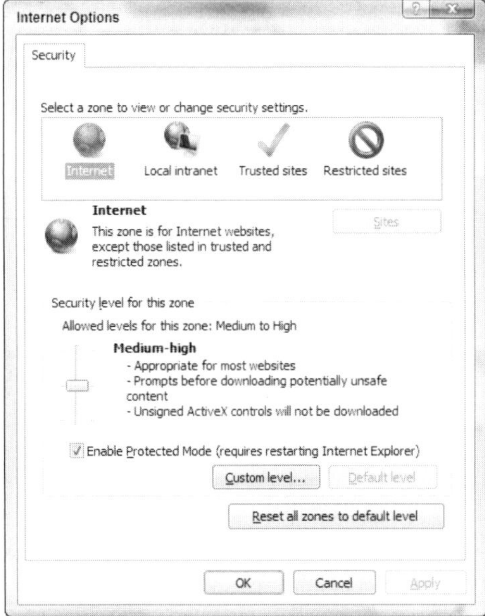

Performance settings

If you click the Performance tab, a window like the one shown in Figure 18.38 appears. Because it has mainly to do with video performance over the Internet, I explain it in detail in Chapter 19.

FIGURE 18.38

Performance options

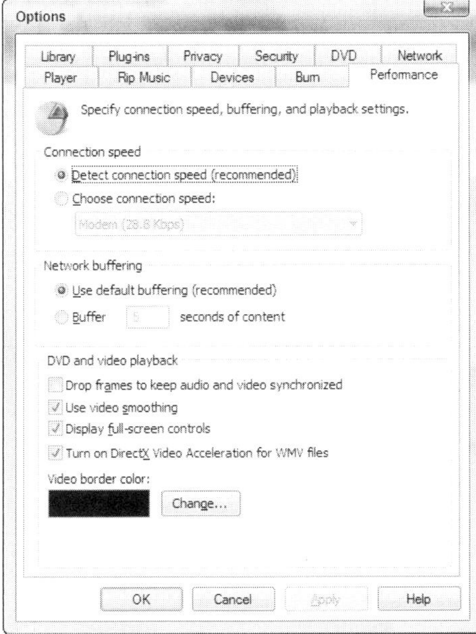

Enhancements

If you're familiar with prior versions of Media Player, you know most of the *enhancements*—those items that you can optionally display at the bottom of the window that include SRS WOW Effects, a color chooser, and a graphic equalizer, among others.

To view the enhancements, right-click in a blank area of the toolbar, hover over View, hover over Enhancements, and either click Show Enhancements or click the enhancement you want to view immediately. You can scroll through enhancements with the little left- and right-arrow buttons on the enhancement display.

The enhancements include:

- **Color Chooser:** This option simply lets you tweak the color appearance of Windows Media Player 11.

- **Crossfading and Auto Volume Leveling:** Auto volume leveling tries to keep songs from different CDs and artists from varying too much in volume, whereas crossfading smoothes the transitions between songs by fading out from one and overlapping with the next. You can adjust the amount of overlap that occurs with crossfading.

- **Graphic Equalizer:** This 10-band equalizer lets you adjust different frequencies of the sound, so you can increase or decrease bass, treble, or midranges. Clicking the Default item, opens a menu of a whole bunch of presets; or you can tweak the settings manually as you please.

- **Media Link for E-Mail:** You can e-mail a link to a media file you're viewing or listening to on the Internet with this item. Note that you can't use it with local media. Use Mark In to pinpoint where to start the link, and Mark Out to pinpoint where to stop it. You can control the playback speed with the Slow, Normal, and Fast links.

- **Play Speed Settings:** You can control the speed of a media file's playback with this tool. You can either use Slow, Normal, or Fast links, or use the slider itself to control playback rate.

- **Quiet Mode:** on Quiet Mode compresses the range of the audio sounds so that the loud sounds aren't too much louder than the quiet ones. This feature prevents large variations in volume from blowing your speakers or waking up the kids.

- **SRS WOW Effects:** SRS Labs is a company that makes various audio applications, including one called WOW. This application can enhance bass and stereo widening of the sound field in increments; you control it with the sliders.

- **Video Settings:** Like a television, you can control things like hue, saturation, brightness, and contrast of your video through Media Player with the sliders in this enhancement.

Enjoying Your Music

You have digital tunes packed into your PC. You've chosen the options you want in terms of ripping, burning, and playing CDs. Now it's time to crank up some tunes and have some fun!

You can play music anywhere in the house that has a Windows Vista-compatible media extender or a Windows Vista computer available. You can also take the music with you through burning it or syncing it with your portable music device.

Creating playlists and burning CDs

To create a playlist, simply browse through your library (by clicking the Library tab and clicking Create Playlist, which results in a window like the one in Figure 18.39) and then dragging songs onto the playlist area of the window, over on the right.

DRM and Piracy: A Screed

I still buy CDs. I'm anything but a Luddite, but digital music downloading has yet to really catch my fancy.

Part of the reason is that I don't think lossy compression does justice to the artists who put so much work and time into their compositions. I do own an MP3 player, and lossy compression is a necessary evil when using it, but I can rip my CDs to any bit rate I want; I don't have to settle for whatever the online music store deems acceptable.

Mostly, however, I buy CDs because with them, I can listen to my music anywhere I darn well please. I can rip them to any computer I want, and I don't have to worry about digital rights management (DRM) all that much. I don't have to create backups of my licenses, or worry that I might be unlocking my content too many times and have to repurchase it to make it work. I can rip CDs to any format I please, be it WMA, MP3, Ogg Vorbis, or something more exotic.

These are great reasons to buy CDs versus purchasing downloadable digital content, unless a publisher does something grossly underhanded like Sony did with dozens of CDs in late 2005. The CDs contained draconian copy protection that installed itself onto Windows computers without the users' knowledge, disabled some media programs, and dictated how users could play the CD.

Windows Vista won't let anyone install stuff onto your computer without your knowledge, which is a godsend. Windows Vista's Windows Media Player 11, on the other hand, is quite restrictive with its DRM practices. You can't back up the licenses to the content you purchase online, meaning that moving this content from computer to computer or using it after you've changed certain hardware in your PC is exceedingly difficult. Even music ripped from a CD may end up copy protected, if you don't disable that so-called feature.

Now, for the other side: A reason exists for why companies are going through such drastic means to protect music and media, and that's due to the rampant piracy that the Internet has fostered. Ever since Napster became mainstream (the *old* Napster, where you could download free MP3 files of just about any song on the planet), music artists have watched their royalties dissolve in a puff of cowardly piracy from kids who no longer had to go to music stores to steal music.

Piracy is *wrong*. You hear about the artists, the musicians, the software developers that make millionaires of themselves, but the vast number of them do not. They rely on royalties to feed themselves and their families, and when someone steals something — even through downloading it from a sharing network or Usenet — instead of buying it, that's food *off* the table.

I am not defending ridiculous DRM — I hate it. But piracy is equally unacceptable. By showing the world that they'll steal anything they can from the privacy of their own homes, pirates have brought forth an age of DRM that may infringe upon the rights of everyone, even people who get their stuff legally. If that becomes the case, everybody loses.

FIGURE 18.39

Creating a playlist

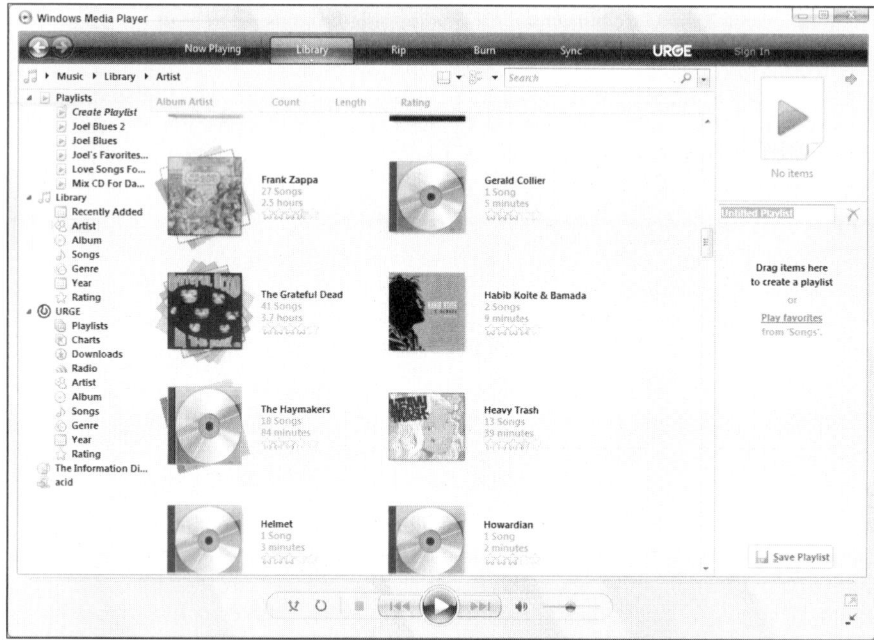

Give your playlist a name. Click on the Unnamed Playlist item on the right and click Rename Playlist. After you name it, click Save Playlist at the bottom. From this point on, you can find this playlist under the Playlists entry when you click the Library tab.

To burn a compilation CD, create a playlist, and then click the Burn tab, which invokes a window like the one shown in Figure 18.40.

FIGURE 18.40

Getting ready to burn

You can also create a burn list without creating a playlist first; just click the Burn tab and start dragging songs into the burn list (which replaces the playlist area) on the right.

You can drag songs up and down the list to change the order of the CD you plan to burn.

When you're ready, insert a blank CD and click Start Burn. The window changes to one like Figure 18.41 throughout the process, and depending on the option settings, your computer may eject the CD when the burn is done.

When Media Player is through burning your disc, the disc is done; it should play in any CD player that's CD-R compatible.

FIGURE 18.41

Burning a disc

Syncing to a portable media player

Windows Media Player 11 can sync media files to a portable media player; in other words, it can copy files to and from the player as you desire. It can sync to a vast variety of portable media players (but, importantly, it won't work with iPods), including any that conform to the standards set forth in the PlaysForSure initiative.

ON the WEB For information about which players Media Player 11 can synch with, visit `www.playsforsure.com`.

To sync a device, simply plug it in and start Media Player 11. If the sync option is set to automatic, Media Player 11 will copy your entire library to your portable media player. To prevent this from happening, click the arrow under the Sync button on the toolbar, point to the portable media player, click Advanced Options, and clear the check box labeled Start sync when device connects.

You may then decide what syncs to your device by creating a sync list. To do this, click the Sync button. Notice that the right side of the window has changed to display a sync list, as shown in Figure 18.42.

FIGURE 18.42

Note the sync list on the right.

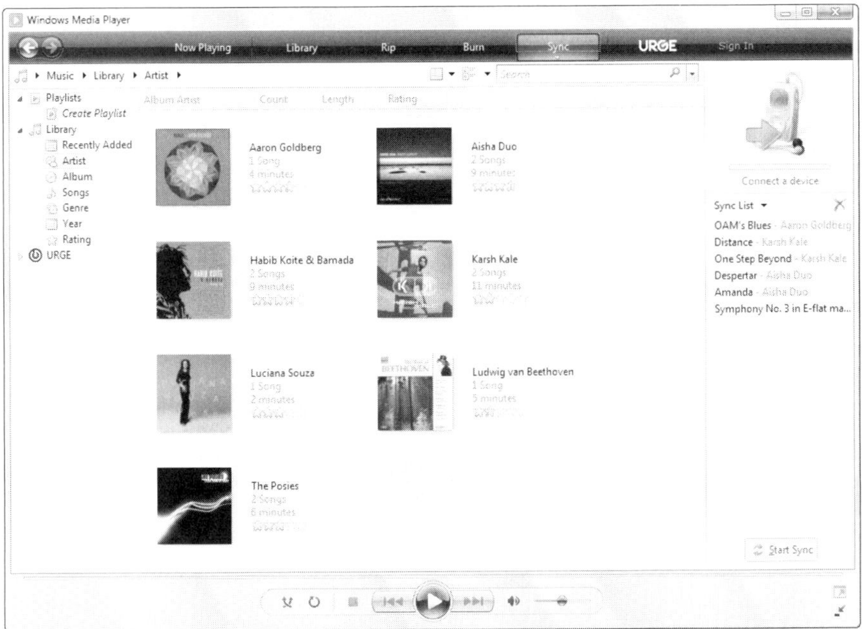

Drag items from your media library to the sync list. These items will be copied to your portable media player when you're ready. When you've completed the list, click the Start Sync button and Windows Media Player will perform the copying operation.

Automatic syncing is handy when you just want to plug a device in and ensure that your entire library is available when you grab your media player and hit the road, but smaller capacity media players, those which won't fit your entire library, make automatic syncing inconvenient. If you do have automatic sync turned on when you connect a device which can't contain your entire library, Media Player 11 will prioritize your library based on several criteria.

First, it will copy songs from playlists that you have created. Then, it'll include music that has a rating of five stars. Next, it syncs music that you've added to your library, by online purchase or by ripping from CD, in the past month. Following that, it syncs music that you've played in the last month. It continues down a line of criteria, eventually including pictures and video, until your player is full.

Summary

You have tunes.

When it comes to getting the most out of them, Windows Vista Ultimate has a whole lot to offer.

You can get tunes onto your computer in a lot of different ways. You can rip your CDs, you can buy music online, and you can subscribe to an online music service. For the latter two options, Microsoft has partnered with MTV to offer the URGE music store. Use it to buy songs and albums, or to subscribe and get unlimited content out of literally millions of songs, as long as you keep up your subscription.

Windows Vista stores your music faithfully and conveniently in your personal music folder, and it allows you to share it across your network with everything from other Windows Vista machines to Microsoft's Xbox 360 game console.

Sharing, along with setting a cornucopia of options controlling ripping, burning, security, privacy, and music quality, is a function of the vast and multi-tabbed Options menu. Getting everything set up the way you please might take a bit of time and understanding.

When you're done, you can play back music on your computer by selecting music from your library as it is, or by creating playlists. You can also burn your own music CDs from all the tunes you own — and have the rights to use.

Ah, there's the rub. The rights are becoming a big deal, as piracy has forced major music publishers — and indeed, publishers of all media and software — to take some drastic measures in terms of securing the rights to use their music. DRM is getting a little too draconian for my tastes, but if people hadn't been stealing music via the Internet for the past ten years, it wouldn't have been so obviously necessary. Do what I do: Buy music on CD and rip it as you please (just watch out for nasty, hidden software).

Then, with your music ripped into your computer, enjoy it however you want! Share it with other computers around the house, sync it up to your MP3 player, and take it with you. Windows Vista Ultimate and Media Player 11 make the computer the musical device it's always wanted to be.

Chapter 19

Watching Video Through Vista

IN THIS CHAPTER

- Understanding Vista's video capabilities
- Customizing your DVD watching experience
- Finding videos online
- Organizing your videos
- Other Video goodness

In the previous chapter, we explored the wonders of Windows Vista Ultimate's audio experience. The OS is terrific for enjoying your music any way you want to — and it also excels with video.

The computer, by nature, is a video device. Ever since the monitor replaced ticking printers and the keyboard replaced punch cards, computer users have been staring into the glow to get work done, to play games, and, more recently, to watch videos.

This latest version of Windows takes video enjoyment to the proverbial next level. With Media Center (discussed in Chapter 16) built in and Windows Media Player 11 at your service, Windows Vista lets you watch anything you want, from Web videos that you can watch online or download to DVDs. You can even queue up videos of your own creation.

CROSS-REF See Chapter 20 for video editing techniques.

You can do lots of things with your videos. Thanks to its wide range of features, Media Player 11 is a video powerhouse, allowing you to enjoy movies in all sorts of ways. Movies are both a visual and aural experience, and Media Player 11 lets you hear movies the way they're meant to be heard — through multi-channel speaker systems. The limits are only those of your sound card and speaker system.

You can, of course, share video media across your home network with other Windows Vista computers and also with media extenders (like Microsoft's own Xbox 360). This capability lets you watch videos pretty much anywhere in your house that you want.

Now I have to be honest: I didn't think of the computer as a video device until just a few years ago. I wasn't impressed with tiny video windows and the low-fi sound that I experienced on most computers; it wasn't until a technology demo that features full-screen DVD playback with a premium sound system that I decided that I could, and would, watch movies on my computer. In some cases, it's even better than sitting back in the living room to enjoy a DVD movie: My multimedia speakers are extremely high quality, and my monitor is much clearer and crisper than my prehistoric television.

Whether you're downloading television shows (legally, of course), watching DVD flicks, enjoying movies you shot and edited yourself, or otherwise digging video content, Windows Vista makes the experience better than ever.

This chapter introduces the wonders of watching video on Windows Vista Ultimate. You can customize the experience in several ways, organize your videos, and more. Read on.

Watching Video on Vista

The first video I watched on Windows Vista happened to be *The Crow*, a gut-wrenching film about a man who returns from the grave to avenge his own murder.

I enjoyed it through a 5.1 speaker audio system, and watched it letterboxed on my standard aspect ratio LCD monitor. It's a fantastic movie, made even better by the superior audio of Windows Vista and my SoundBlaster X-Fi sound card, awesome DVD quality thanks again to Vista, and my ATI X1900-based graphics card.

Of course, if you're not into such edgy fare, you can watch just about anything you want through Windows Vista. For example, on a lighter note, I watched a video I shot with my old digital camera in AVI format, of my wife dancing (Figure 19.1) on one of those arcade dance machines at one of those fun centers with the teenagers in oversized animal costumes roaming around.

The video quality wasn't as lofty, the monaural audio wasn't impressive, but it's a cute little movie and it reminds me of my son's birthday.

The point is, what you watch is up to you. Windows Vista and Media Player 11 make watching anything, provided it's in a compatible format, easy. Supported movie files are automatically associated with Media Player 11, so when you encounter one and launch it, the Media Player program starts up automatically and does everything for you. Videos in WMV format are enhanced even further, if your graphics card is compatible with DirectX 9 or later.

Configuring Media Player 11 can be as simple or as hands-on as you please; you can leave it at its default settings and get outstanding performance, or you can change it around, wield the power of its built-in enhancements, and tailor the experience to your desires.

FIGURE 19.1

My wife Emily plays a game with her feet.

For example, if your computer is on the older side and doesn't have the necessary power to crank out video as well as it should, you can configure Media Player 11 to drop frames to keep the audio in sync with the video. You can alter the look of the Player itself, including the border around the videos it displays. You can use enhancements to widen the sound field if you want, and you can even adjust the hue, brightness, and other aspects of the video just as you would on a standard television set.

When it comes to videos on Vista, you're in as much control as you want to be. The experience is limited only by your computer's hardware.

Organizing Your Video Files

Windows Vista has its own ideas about organizing your video files, and they're actually pretty handy. Although you can store any file anywhere in the file system you please, adhering to Vista's organizational guidelines for all-around ease of use is best.

The Videos folder

Back in the days of Windows XP, there was a folder called My Videos. It was nestled in the My Documents folder, and was intended to serve as a location to store video files.

Windows Vista has a similar folder, simply called Videos. Your personal Videos folder is in the folder named after your login name; for example, mine is in the VistaUltimateBible folder.

To get to it, click Start, and click the folder named after your account. A screen like the one shown in Figure 19.2 appears.

FIGURE 19.2

My personal folder

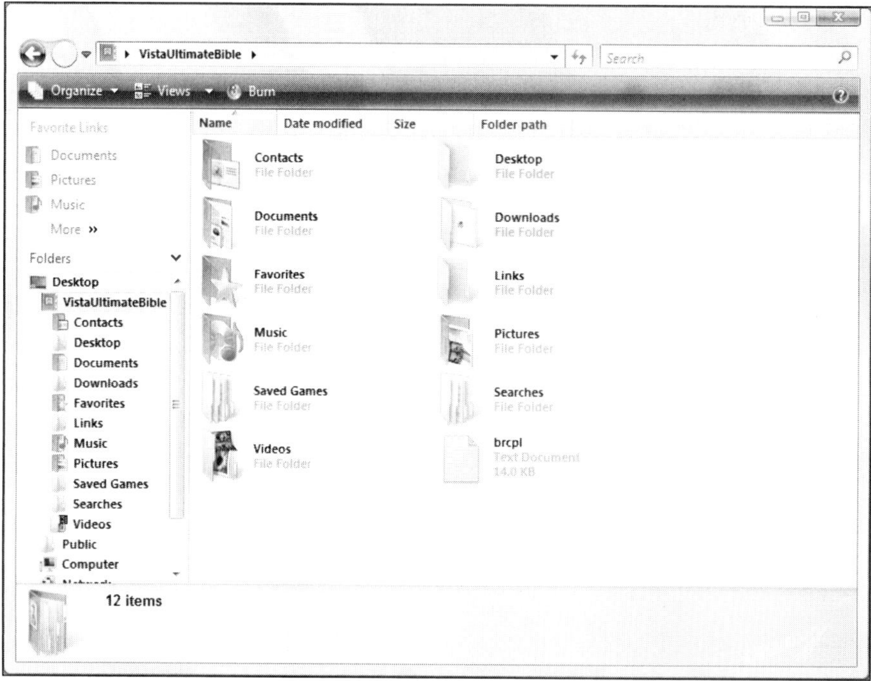

Then, double-click the folder called Videos. A folder like the one shown in Figure 19.3 appears.

FIGURE 19.3

My Videos folder

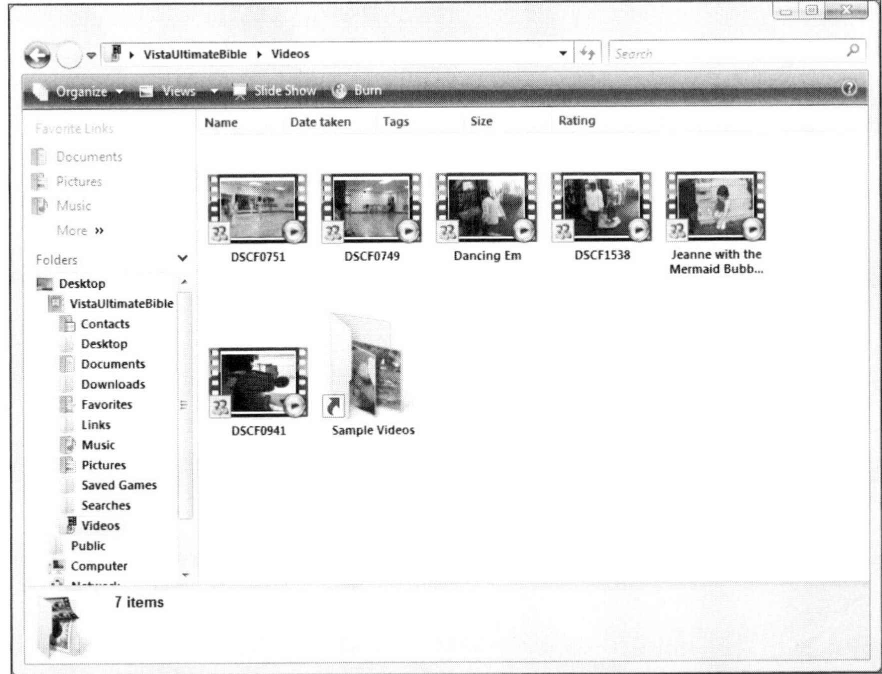

TIP If you want the Videos folder to appear in your Start Menu like the Music folder does, so you can access it in just a couple of clicks, you can make it do so — sort of. Navigate to your personal folder (Figure 19.2), and then drag the Videos folder to the Start button. When the Start Menu pops up, drag the folder to the area where the Internet and E-mail links are, as shown in Figure 19.4. Drop it there. When you're done, a shortcut to the Videos folder appears, pinned to the top of the Start Menu, as shown in Figure 19.5.

FIGURE 19.4

Dragging the Videos folder to the Start Menu

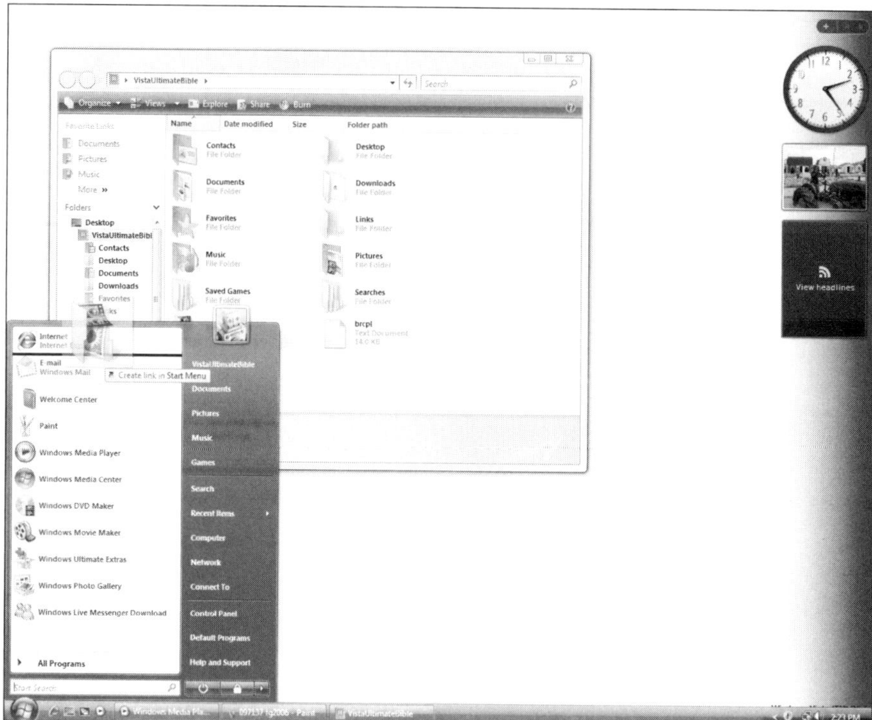

FIGURE 19.5

Note the Videos folder pinned to the menu.

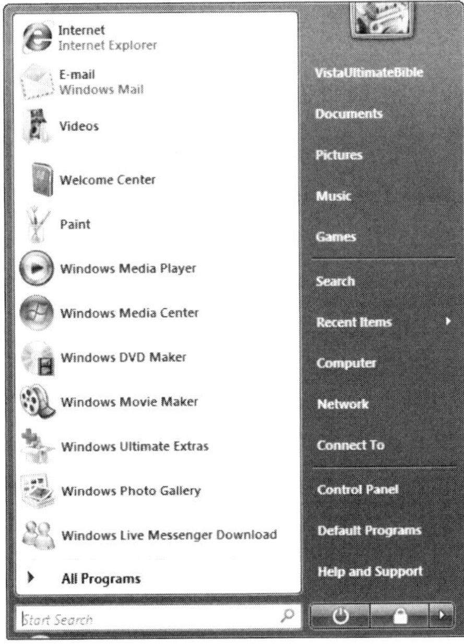

You can store videos in folders and subfolders within the Videos folder — or store them wherever you want in the file system. The Videos folder is there for your convenience, and it's also where Windows Media Player 11 looks automatically for video files.

File icons displayed in the Videos folder show still frames from the videos themselves, making it easier to find the videos. Of course, you must have the Views set to one of the icon view modes.

To check the mode, head to the Videos folder and click the Views button on the toolbar. You can choose list view, a details view that shows information about the files (Figure 19.6), and four icon views from small to extra-large (Figure 19.7).

FIGURE 19.6

The Details view in the Videos folder

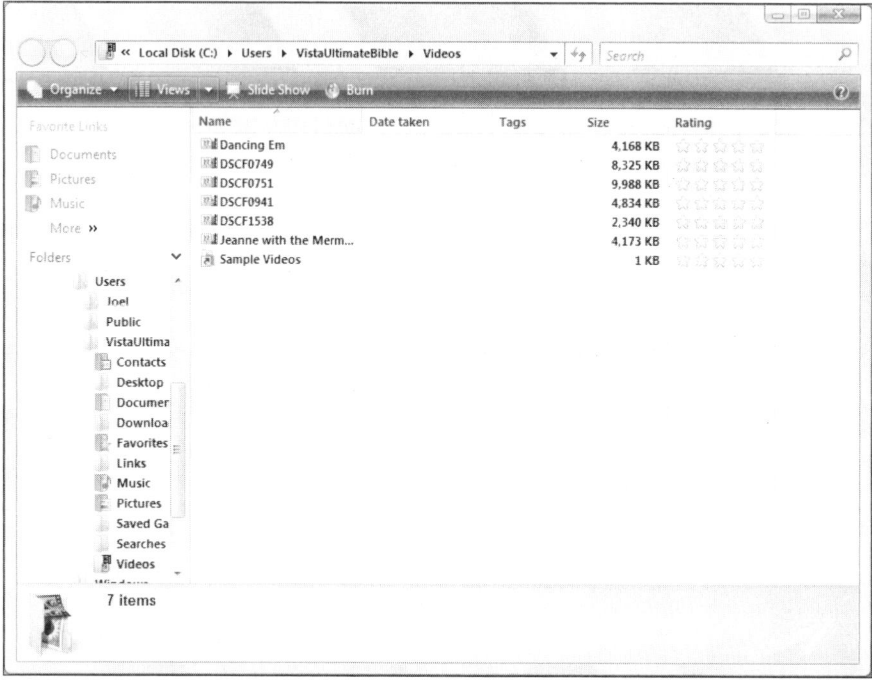

FIGURE 19.7

Extra large icons are easy to see.

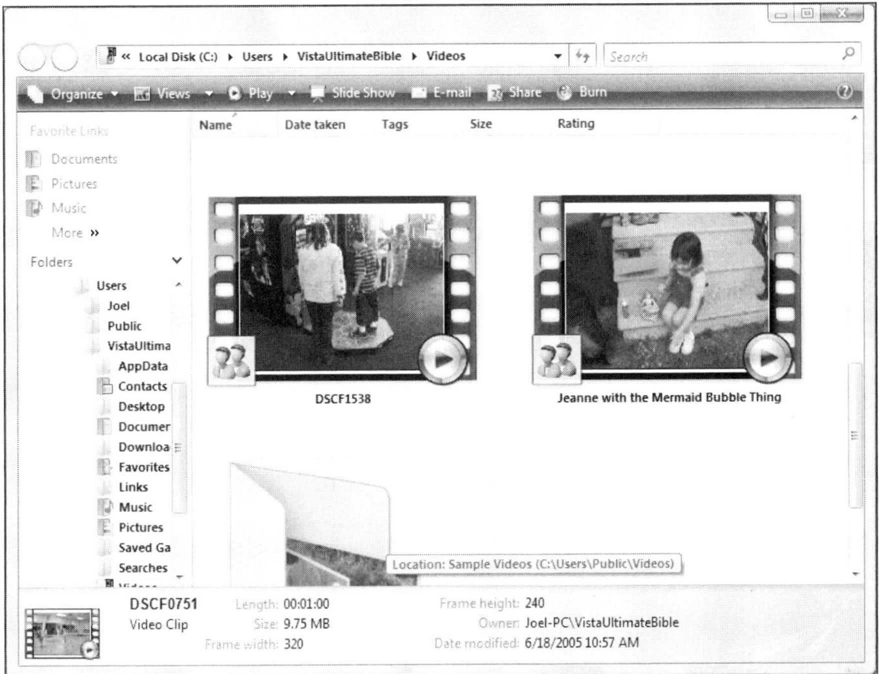

Other toolbar buttons include the standard Organize and Burn buttons, and if you highlight a video file the toolbar morphs to include a Play button, an E-mail button, and a Share button. The Play button launches Windows Media Player 11 and plays the video you've highlighted; the E-mail button allows you to send the file as an e-mail attachment (as shown in Figure 19.8); and the Share button lets you configure sharing options for the file.

FIGURE 19.8

E-mailing a small video

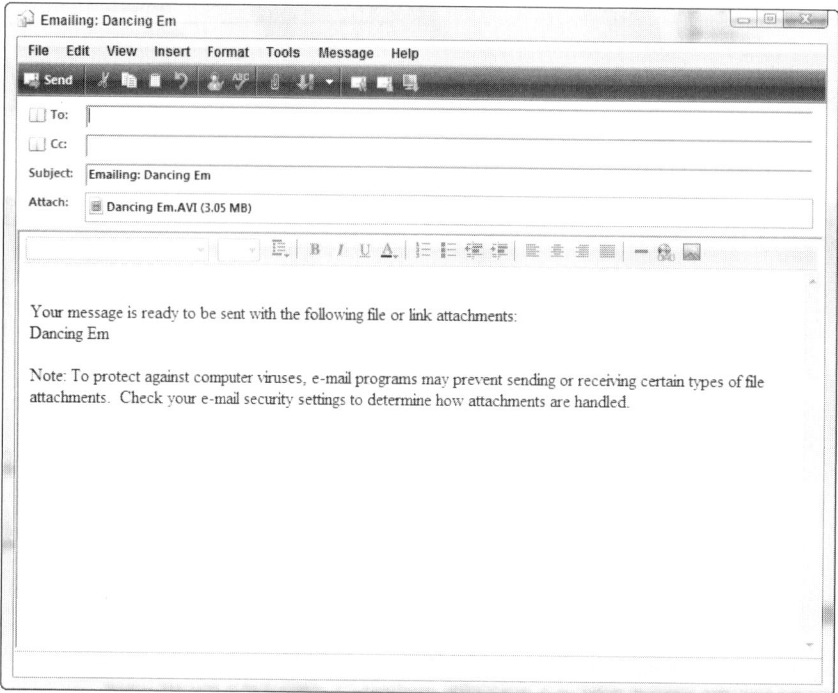

Windows Media Player 11

The Media Player helps organize your videos as well. It nicely displays video files it finds in the Videos folder.

To see your collection of videos, click the tiny icon on the upper left just below the back/forward buttons and choose Videos (see Figure 19.9).

Media Player 11 then looks in the Videos folder and its subfolders and displays still images as icons of all the videos it finds. You can then launch a video by double-clicking it, or by highlighting it and clicking the Play button at the bottom of the screen.

FIGURE 19.9

Viewing videos through Media Player 11

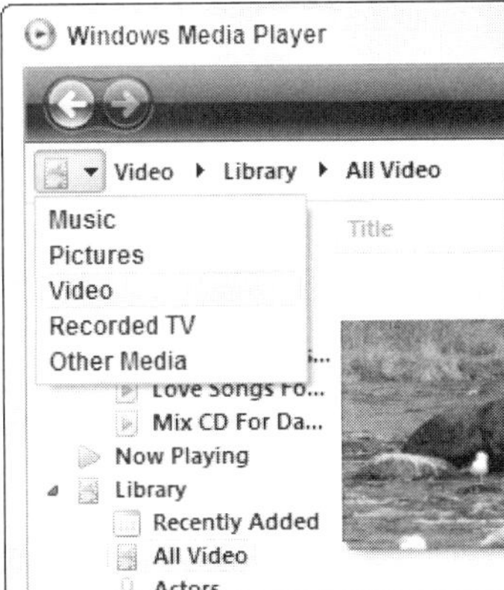

Configuring Windows Media Player 11 for Videos

I went over most of the Windows Media Player 11 settings in its options screen in Chapter 18, which covered music on Windows Vista. However, I want to discuss a few things specific to videos here.

For example, you can access a page in the Options screen on DVD options. Media Player 11 also has an enhancement especially for video viewing that allows you to control the hue, saturation, brightness, and contrast of the images you view with it.

DVD options

Invoke the options panel by right-clicking a blank area of the toolbar and hovering the mouse cursor over Tools (Figure 19.10). Click Options, and the Media Player 11 options sheet appears, as shown in Figure 19.11.

FIGURE 19.10

Navigating to the Options item

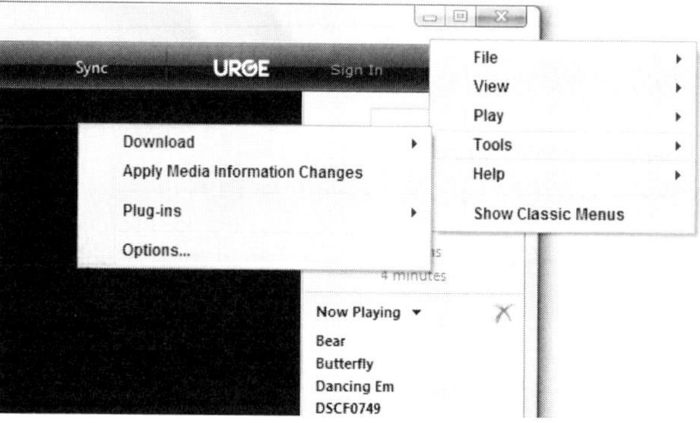

FIGURE 19.11

The Media Player Options window

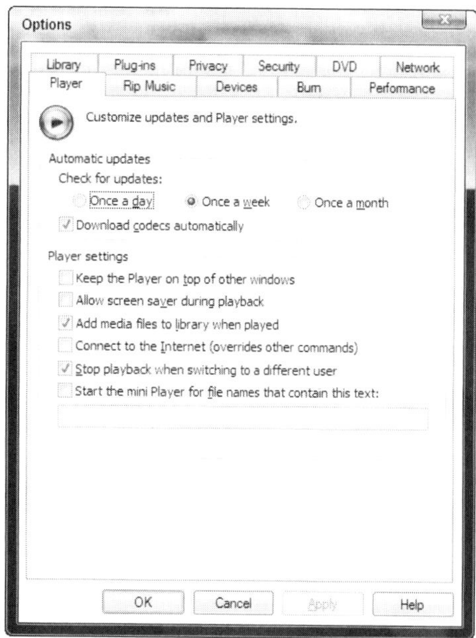

To see the DVD options, click the DVD tab. The window in Figure 19.12 appears.

FIGURE 19.12

DVD options

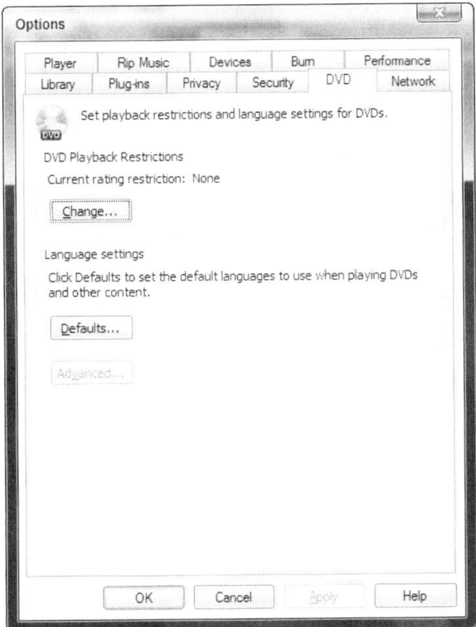

The top of the window shows your current DVD playback restriction level. Restrictions are a form of parental controls, which limit users of the computer from watching DVDs higher than a certain rating. If you click the Change button, a screen like the one shown in Figure 19.13 appears, with a dialog box in the middle of the screen that allows you to change the restriction. The dialog box itself is shown in Figure 19.14, with its menu pulled down.

FIGURE 19.13

The Windows desktop with the Change Rating Restriction dialog box invoked

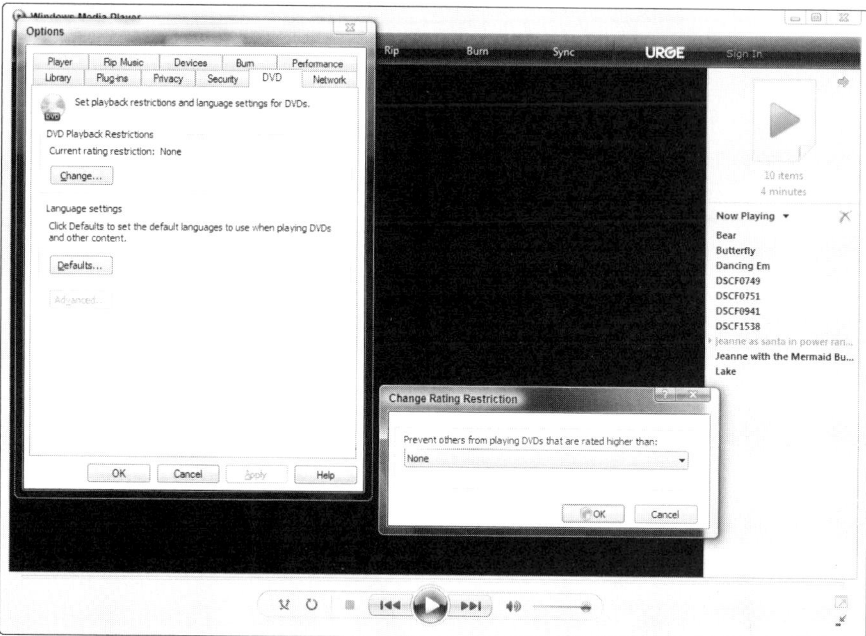

FIGURE 19.14

The Change Rating Restriction dialog box, with its options shown

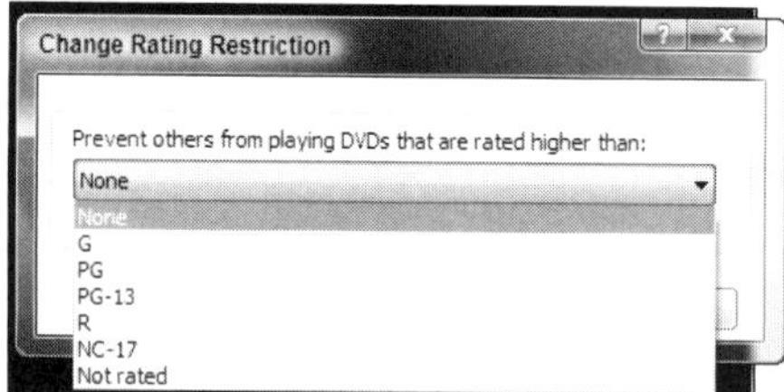

If you select a rating — for example, PG-13 — affected user accounts won't be able to play DVDs *higher than* that rating. So, for example, if you were to select PG-13, the user accounts subjected to that rating would be able to play PG-13 movies, but not movies rated R, NC-17, or unrated movies.

See Chapter 11 for details on family safety settings.

The next option on the DVD tab enables you to set the language defaults for DVD audio, subtitles, and the DVD menu system. Click the Defaults button to invoke the dialog box shown in Figure 19.15.

FIGURE 19.15

This is where you can change DVD language options.

You can pull down each of the menus to select a language for that aspect of the DVD. For example, if you pull down the Audio language button, you'll see part of a huge, scrolling menu of languages as shown in Figure 19.16.

FIGURE 19.16

Pick a language for DVD audio here.

The Video Settings enhancement

You can control the quality of the video displayed in Media Player 11 by displaying and manipulating the Video Settings enhancement. To display the enhancement, right-click an empty area of the toolbar, hover over View, hover over Enhancements, and click Video Settings. The enhancement appears at the bottom of the Media Player 11 interface, as shown in Figure 19.17.

FIGURE 19.17

The Video Settings enhancement is displayed.

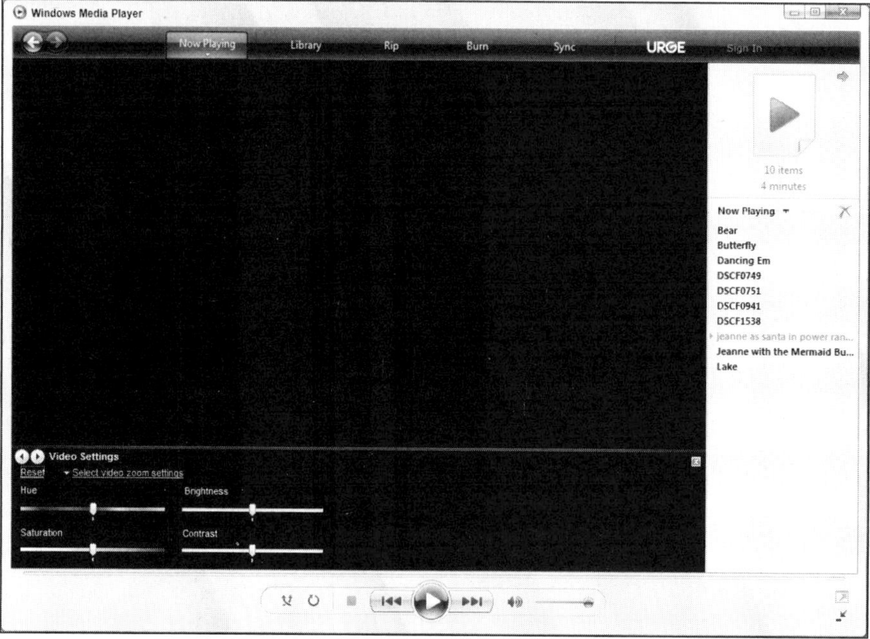

Invoke this enhancement when you want to change the look of a video, such as the Flaming Lips' tour-de-force, *The Fearless Freaks,* available at any fine music or movie store.

Other Media Player 11 tricks

Windows Media Player 11 has lots of video control goodness that may not be evident at first glance. Many third-party, DVD-playing applications suffer from overcomplicated control panels with too many buttons. Media Player 11 hides a lot of its functionality, but it's there.

Full-screen video

You can show a DVD video in full screen mode easily. Simply toggle full-screen video mode by pressing Alt+Enter. You can also achieve a full-screen mode by clicking a small button on the lower right of the interface, or by right-clicking in a video image, hovering over Video Size, and clicking Full Screen.

Viewing the picture at full screen makes a dramatic difference compared to viewing it in windowed mode. Compare the same scene in Figure 19.18 (windowed) and 19.19 (full screen).

FIGURE 19.18

Windowed

FIGURE 19.19

Full screen

Note that when you play a video full screen, the rest of the Media Player 11 interface disappears except for the control panel.

Full DVD controls

Wondering where the language, menu, and other buttons are that you're used to having on your DVD player's remote control? Those controls are all there; you access them simply by right-clicking a DVD movie while it's playing, which opens a context menu, shown in Figure 19.20.

Through this menu you can control languages, subtitles, and so on. The DVD features submenu contains links to go to the root and title menus of the DVD.

CROSS-REF Flip back to Chapter 18 to find out more things you can do with videos. They're subject to many of the fun things you can do with audio files, such as sharing across networks, tweaking their audio settings, and so on. Chapter 18 contains a solid look at all the rest of the Options menu tabs in Media Player 11 and contains important information on privacy and security.

FIGURE 19.20

Full control over your DVDs

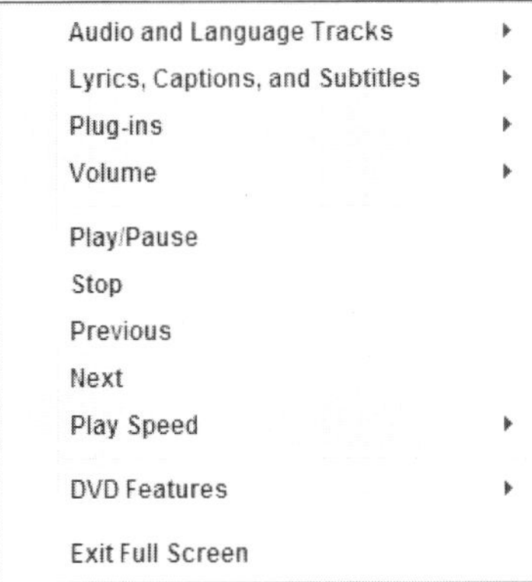

Summary

Windows Vista is full of features that make video viewing more enjoyable. About the only thing it *doesn't* let you do is rip video from DVDs; otherwise, there's not much it can't do to make your movie-watching experience first-rate.

Windows Vista organizes your videos effortlessly, allowing you to quickly find them through the Start Menu. The Videos folder even displays icons that show clips from within the video files themselves, so spotting the right video on your hard drive is lightning fast.

DVD viewing with Windows Vista is as exciting at your computer as it is using a set-top box (or a computer with Windows Vista running Media Center) with your television. You can tweak the language and parental usage restrictions with a few clicks, and even adjust hue, saturation, and other picture quality aspects.

Windows Vista is the best operating system on the planet for video viewing, whether your videos are Internet-based, locally stored, or on DVD. It's as simple as that.

Chapter 20

Editing Video with Windows Movie Maker

IN THIS CHAPTER

Exploring Windows Movie Maker's interface

Capturing video to edit

Editing video

Using effects, transitions, and more

Exporting video and creating DVDs

Here's a not-very-alarming truism: Nobody wants to sit through two hours of your boring family footage. Whether you're home from a vacation with a couple of digital video (DV) tapes packed with everything you saw the whole time or you just filmed little Tyler's first baseball game including every painful infield error, a *lot* of filler is in that video. Your neighbors will fall over themselves making excuses as to why they just can't come over and watch it any time soon.

They're likely to be much more open to the idea if you're able to tell them that you got rid of all the boring stuff and whittled down the entire experience to six-and-a-half action-packed minutes.

Why don't you? You probably have everything you need to make it happen. If you have a digital video camera (or an older camera and an analog video capture device) and Windows Vista, you can whip that footage into shape and produce something concise and compelling. Windows Movie Maker, included with Vista Ultimate, is powerful enough for most home video amateurs to get started.

To be honest, Movie Maker doesn't quite compare with aftermarket video-editing software. On the other hand, if you already own Vista, it won't set you back another $50 to $5,000 dollars, like video editing packages tend to do. Considering its freeness, you can do a lot of stuff with Windows Movie Maker: import video from a variety of sources; make pinpoint edits, cuts, and splices; incorporate titles and credits; add audio soundtracks; work in some pretty cool effects and transitions; and output video to DV, CD, DVD, and files for sharing via e-mail and the Web.

The best part is that you'll be surprised at how easy the whole process is. That's because Windows Movie Maker divides the entire process into tasks and helps you with each and every one. It can split a vast video into easy-to-manage clips and lets you drag and drop those clips through a friendly interface to create the groundwork for your magnum opus. Its wizards and templates make all of those tasks I mentioned in the preceding paragraph remarkably user-friendly.

In all honesty, making a decent movie is time-consuming and takes a lot of work and care, and the longer the film (and the more raw footage you've shot) the more of a time investment it will require. Windows Movie Maker won't turn you into Martin Scorsese. It will, however, give you the power to unleash your creativity in ways you may not have known you could.

This chapter shows you not only how to use Movie Maker, but also how to export your video and create DVDs so you can share your video masterpiece.

What You Need to Get Started

Whether you want to create a three-and-a-half hour masterpiece that will put *The Godfather* to shame or the aforementioned six-minute power flick of a home video event, you'll need equipment. In the case of home videos, the hardware doesn't have to be overwhelmingly costly. You can spend anywhere from under nothing to several thousand dollars, depending on what you already have, but even if you're lacking a camera and the necessary hard drive space, you can get away with spending a just a few hundred dollars.

TIP Shop wisely and do at least some research. I've found that online stores tend to charge much less than brick-and-mortar stores for things like camcorders and hard drives, unless the physical store is having a tremendous sale. You want equipment that you like, so read reviews before you buy. Lots of Web sites feature professional and customer reviews, and magazines like *Consumer Reports* and *PC Magazine* review camcorders on a regular basis.

Even if you have older equipment, you still might be able to make it work. For example, in a moment I'm going to recommend that you get a digital camcorder for your filming needs. If you have an older analog camcorder you might be able to get a video capture card — or use your existing video card — to capture video from it.

Besides a functioning computer with Windows Vista, you need a few other things, as discussed in the following sections.

A video camera

Obviously, you need footage. To that end, you need, at the very least, a Webcam or a digital camera that shoots videos, and ideally you want a digital camcorder.

Digital camcorders can cost anywhere from a couple hundred dollars to thousands of dollars. Characteristics that often set a cheap one apart from a deluxe one include the quality of the optics, the quality of the video it captures, its performance in different lighting situations, and its overall feature set.

If you're shopping for a DV camera, look for one that connects easily to a PC via USB or FireWire. The vast majority of modern DV cams handle both, but ensuring your camera supports an interface that's available on your PC is still a good idea.

Making sure that any DV camera you purchase is Windows Vista compatible is also important.

A way to capture video

If your DV cam supports a connector that your PC also supports, you need the proper cable. Some cams come with them, but you may need to purchase a USB or FireWire cable to connect the camera to the PC. Be sure to read the specification of the cable you need, as both types of cables can have a variety of connectors.

If you have an older camcorder with composite and/or s-video out ports but that lacks digital ports, you're not out of luck. You just need a device that can capture analog video and audio to a computer. Quite a few have this capability, known as "VIVO" (video-in, video-out), but they rarely come with the equipment you need to actually connect the camcorder to the computer. If your graphics card might have video-in/video-out (VIVO), check with the manufacturer to see whether it sells the connectors you need.

If your graphics card can't do capture video and audio, you can always get a USB-based video and audio capture device. Many support USB 2.0 and are amazingly simple to set up: You simply connect the device, install the drivers, and you're done.

Of course, once again, I must encourage you to ensure that any device you purchase is Windows Vista compatible.

Hard drive space

Video files can be cumbersome. To actually say how much hard drive space a minute of video occupies is impossible, because it varies by the video format and quality. I have a medium-quality, 25-minute WMV video that occupies 540MB of hard drive space (that's 20.6 megabytes per minute) but I've seen poor quality Web videos that cram 20 seconds of video into a single megabyte of space (that's 3 megabytes per minute). Regardless, you need plenty of room on the computer's hard drive to store lots of video.

Besides the raw footage that you capture from your camcorder, you need to have room to save the work in progress, possibly multiple times, and a finished product. This storage space can quickly add up from megabytes to gigabytes.

The good news is that at the time of this writing, massive, 500GB hard drives are relatively inexpensive, and terabyte hard drives are in development. Whereas hard drive space was once at a premium in the computer world, it's much cheaper per byte of data storage room than it used to be. If, however, you happen to be running low on space, you may want to install a second hard drive before you start importing video.

Getting to Know Windows Movie Maker

As discussed in the introduction to this chapter, Windows Movie Maker is a valuable addition to Vista. Making a compelling (or at least, not boring) home movie is now a reality for many home video beginners. Before moving on, you need to familiarize yourself with the enticing piece of software that is Windows Movie Maker (Figure 20.1).

FIGURE 20.1

Windows Movie Maker

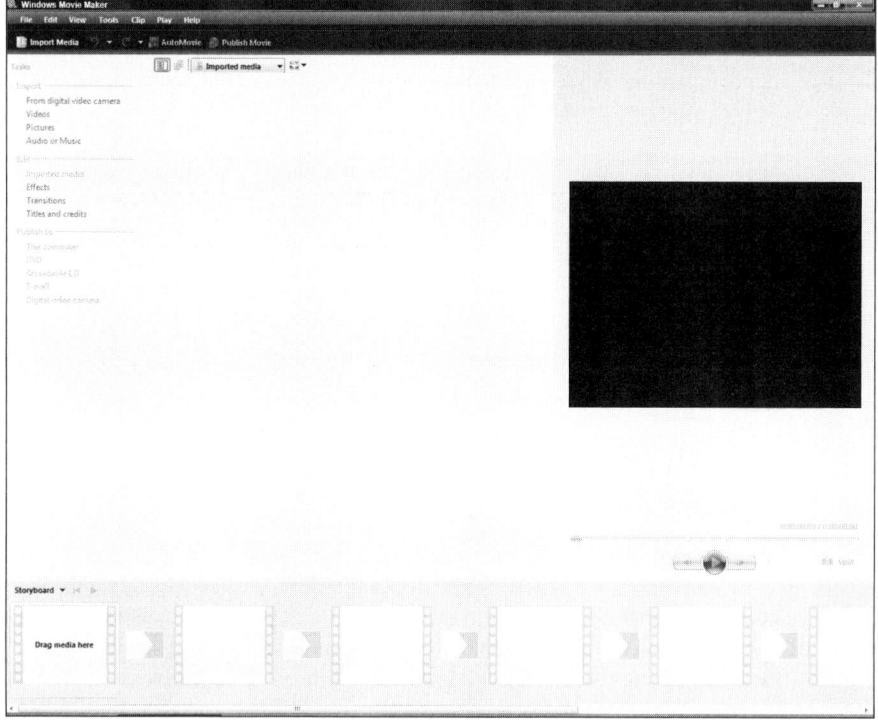

The interface

Launch the program by choosing Start ➪ All Programs ➪ Windows Movie Maker. If you've never worked on video editing before, Movie Maker's interface might look somewhat daunting, but don't be alarmed. The following list describes each part of the interface:

- The **menu bar** (Figure 20.2) runs along the top of the Windows Movie Maker window. This Windows Vista application uses traditional (File, Edit, View, and so on) menus, as opposed to a button-laden toolbar.
- The **Tasks pane** on the left (Figure 20.3) shows you the sequential steps you take in creating your movie, and it's complete with links to invoke each module you need to proceed. Although the commands on the task pane are also available elsewhere (that is, through the menu in the menu bar), invoking them through the Tasks pane is often easier for first-time users.

FIGURE 20.2

The menu bar is stocked with commands for making your movie.

FIGURE 20.3

The Tasks pane guides you through the process.

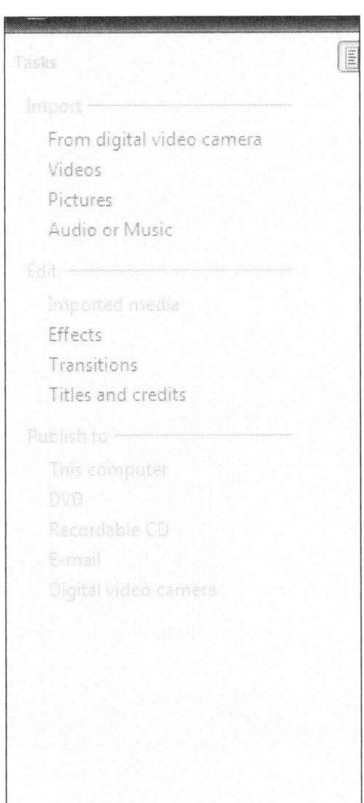

- The **contents pane** (Figure 20.4) is in the middle of the screen. Currently it's blank because I haven't imported any contents, but it would normally display clips from your movie (or transitions and effects, depending on what you toggle through its drop-down menu at the top).

FIGURE 20.4

The currently empty contents pane would normally contain your media clips.

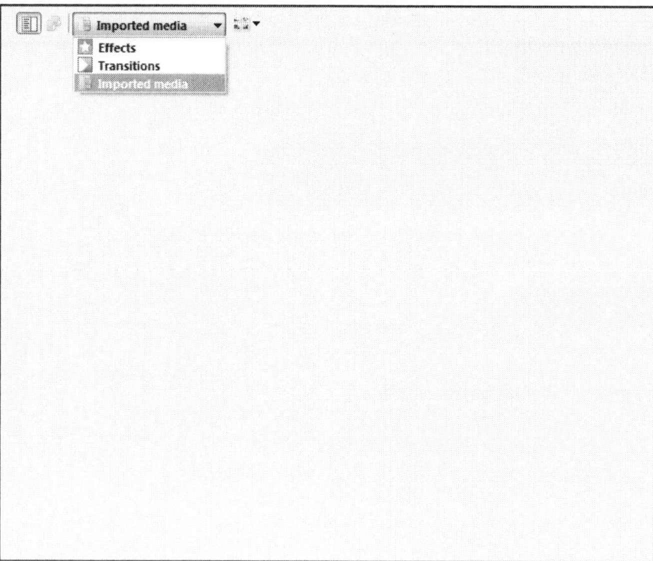

- The **preview panel** (Figure 20.5) is a handy viewer in which you can view any part of your movie at any time. You can view clips, transitions, and other portions of your film; it also contains a Split button for creating cuts where you want them.
- The **storyboard/timeline** (Figure 20.6; shown in Storyboard mode) is where most of the editing takes place. You drag clips to the Storyboard mode to create the foundation for your movie, and then use the Timeline mode for more precise cutting, splicing, and editing clip length.

FIGURE 20.5

The preview panel is where you view movie snippets.

FIGURE 20.6

The storyboard/timeline is your editing desk.

You can tweak the interface however you like. Through the View menu, you can turn on or off some of the elements in the interface; for example, if you don't like the Tasks pane, you can click View and then click Tasks to toggle it off.

AutoMovie

Notice the AutoMovie button below the menu bar. AutoMovie is a quick fix for people who want to watch something interesting very quickly. All you need to do to use it is to import at least 30 seconds of video clips, plus perhaps some still images and audio. Click the AutoMovie button and choose an editing style, and Windows will toss together a movie for you.

The obvious downside to AutoMovie is the complete lack of control you get over the editing process. You don't make cuts where you want them unless you do it beforehand; you can't tailor the movie to your whims. It's fully automated.

I find that AutoMovie works best when you want to set a short sequence to music. You can, through Movie Maker, import music and other audio files and use them as background sound for your films. AutoMovie is nice for creating an entertaining musical montage from a number of clips, and if you adjust the clip length to fit the personality of the song the result is even better. For example, a speedy dance track calls for short clips and quick cuts, while a slow rock anthem tends to work better with longer clips.

NOTE Although you can use any audio clips you want, including music you've ripped from your CD collection, you don't automatically have the right to publish movies with copyrighted music on the Web or otherwise use in public. If you plan to post a movie online, either use original music or get permission from the artist or publisher before you do so. Otherwise, you may be violating a copyright and you could end up in some sort of legal trouble. Use copyrighted media at your own risk!

Importing Media

Well, here's a problem. Because Windows Vista is still so new, I have yet to get a video capture device to work with it. Therefore, I can't show you how to import video from a video camera. In essence, it should be a matter of following a few simple steps:

1. **Connect the DV cam to your computer with USB or FireWire.** Alternately, connect an analog video camera to your video capture device.

Sometimes, USB connections result in slightly degraded video and/or audio quality compared to FireWire.

2. **Install the video capture drivers if you haven't already done so.**
3. **Set the camera to playback, streaming, export, or whatever mode its instructions tell you is correct for transporting video to your computer.**
4. **Start Windows Movie Maker.**
5. **In the Tasks pane, under Import, click From digital video camera.**
6. **Follow the prompts until Windows Movie Maker allows you to start importing video.**

7. **Start the import on the computer, and then start the camera's playback of your video.**
8. **Sit back and wait until your camera reaches the end of the movie you want to import.**
9. **Stop the camera and then stop the import process in Windows Movie Maker.**

Instead of demonstrating importation with a camera, I show you how to import video using a movie file. What I did was import video from my DV cam through a Windows XP computer; the DV cam has working drivers for XP. I saved the movie and transferred it through my computer network to my Windows Vista computer.

The first step is to import the movie from a file. To do so, follow these steps:

1. **In the Tasks pane under Import, click Videos.** A file system navigation interface appears (Figure 20.7) that shows my Movies folder by default.
2. **Click the movie you want to import and click Import.** The movie appears in the contents pane, as shown in Figure 20.8.

FIGURE 20.7

Importing a video from a file

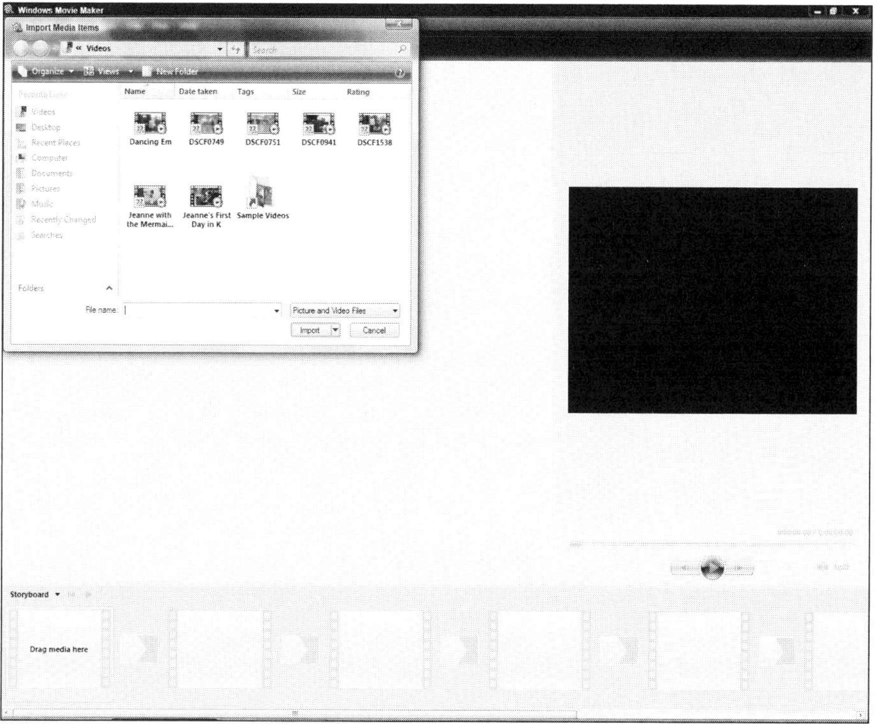

FIGURE 20.8

The movie I imported is represented by an icon in the contents pane.

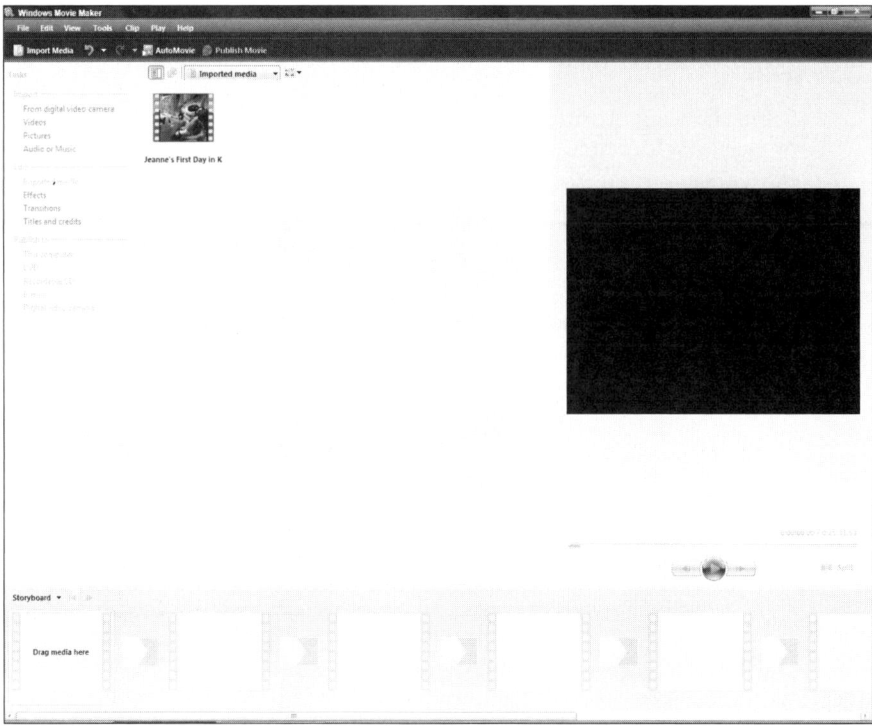

Big, contiguous movie files are difficult to work with. It's much easier to sequence a movie if they're broken up into a variety of clips, usually designated by places in the film where the camera stops filming and starts up again. You can allow Movie Maker to split your work into clips by itself, or you can create your own clips. Ideally, you'll employ a bit of both methods.

Letting Windows Movie Maker create clips

Now, I want the movie split into clips. Windows Movie Maker can do this task automatically for video imported from a camera, but not for video files.

I can either create my own clips from the video, or I can let Windows Movie Maker split it into clips automatically. To do the latter , I simply right-click the icon in the contents pane and click Create Clips. Windows Movie Maker analyzes the video and creates clips based on where it detects transitions.

NOTE Clip creation is a time-consuming process. For my 20-minute file of raw video, Movie Maker took 28 minutes to create a series of clips. If you don't elect to create clips automatically during an import from a DV cam but want to do it later, be prepared to do something else for a while as Windows works away.

When Windows Movie Maker creates clips for you, it populates the contents pane with an image from each clip (Figure 20.9), each representing the clip itself. To view the clip in the preview panel, simply double-click it.

FIGURE 20.9

Now I have a wealth of clips to work with.

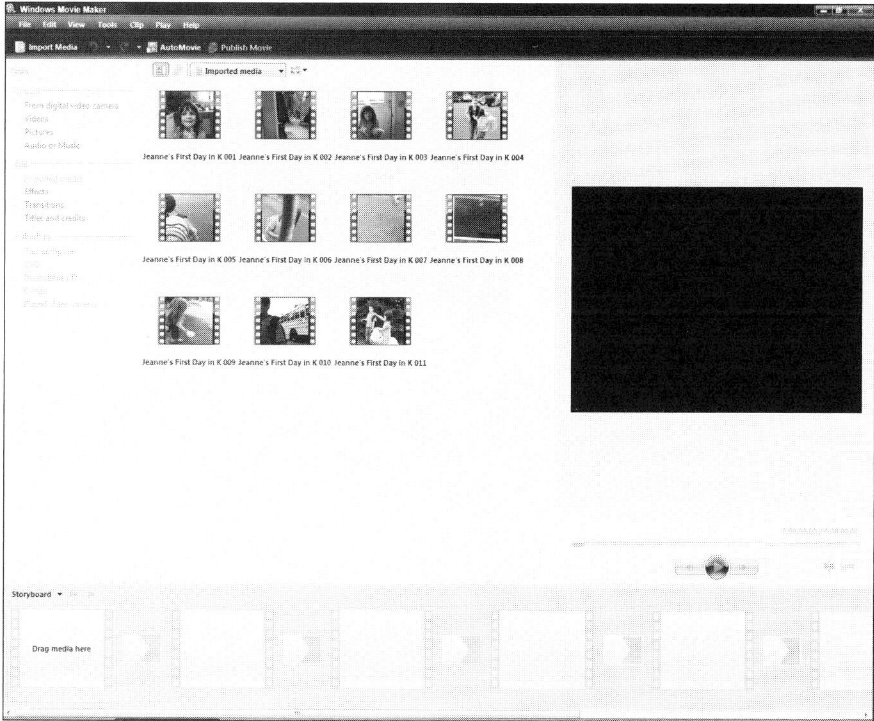

For an alternate view of the clips that shows more details about them, choose View ➪ Details. The thumbnails of your clips are then replaced with a details list, similar to that in any file system navigation window. Movie Maker shows data about each clip including the length of the clip, the start time, the stop time, and the resolution of the imagery.

Creating your own clips

If you want to create your own clips from the imported video, you need to work in the timeline mode of the storyboard/timeline interface. You must first drag your video from the contents pane to the storyboard, as shown in Figure 20.10.

FIGURE 20.10

A film, dragged to the storyboard

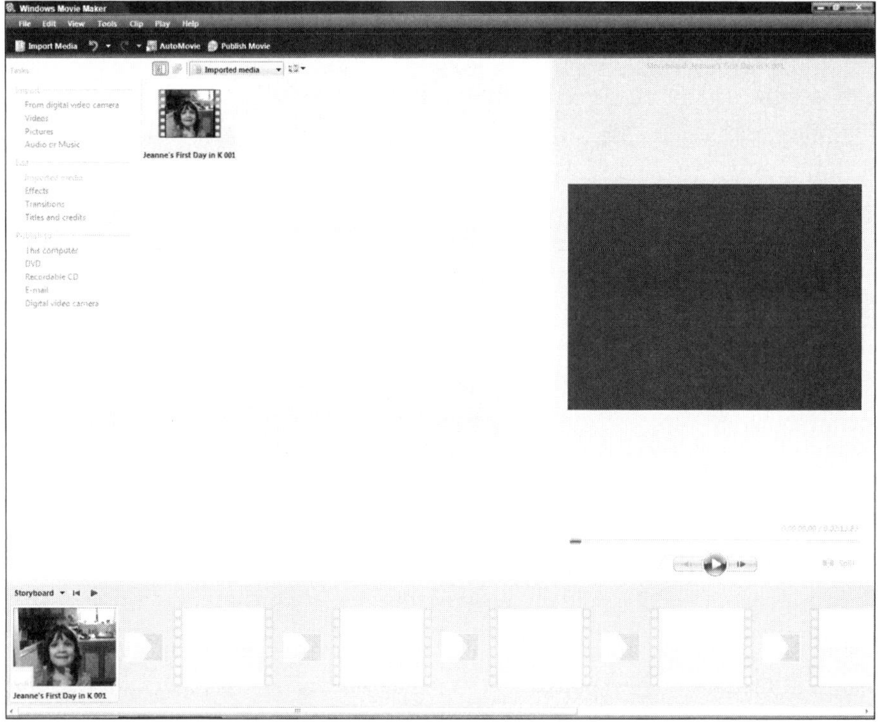

Switch to Timeline mode by choosing View ➪ Timeline (Figure 20.11).

The small bar at the top of the timeline interface, ticked with seconds and fractions of seconds, is itself a timeline. You can click on any part of that bar to move a green, vertical editing line called the ***seek bar*** to that moment of the video. The preview panel shows the current frame of video. You can play the video in the preview panel to advance the seek bar to the exact place you want to divide the movie into clips.

FIGURE 20.11

Now I'm in Timeline mode.

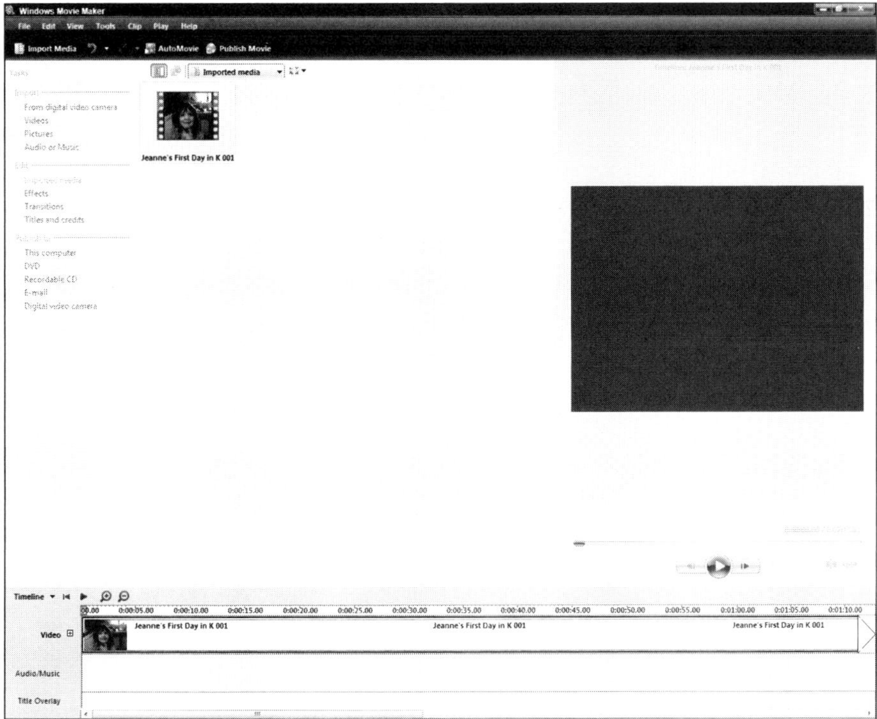

To divide the current clip or raw footage into two clips at that very point, click the Split button in the preview panel, which is shown in Figure 20.12.

Now, if you switch back to storyboard mode (View ➪ Storyboard), you'll see two clips on the board (Figure 20.13).

You can continue splitting the movie into as many clips as you like. The only downside of creating clips this way is that you cannot add them to the contents pane (if you let Windows Movie Maker create clips automatically, it drops thumbnails there).

FIGURE 20.12

I've split the movie right at this point.

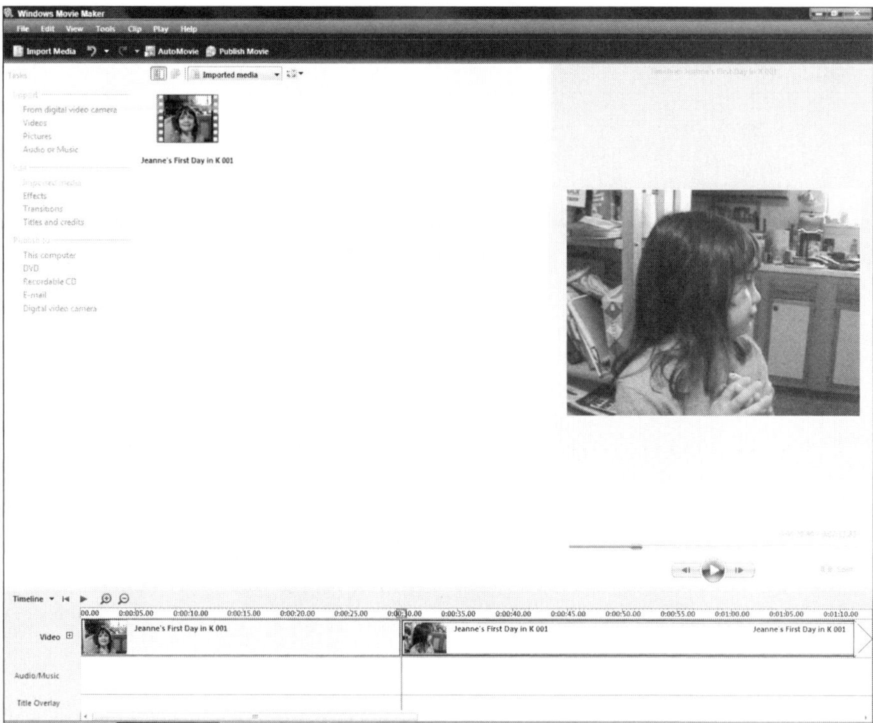

FIGURE 20.13

Now my movie has two clips.

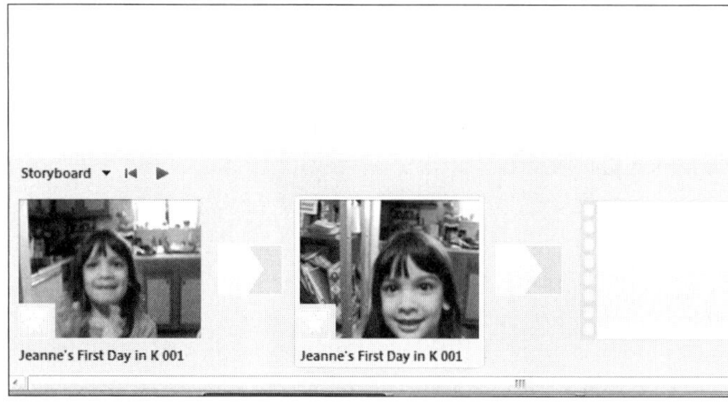

Importing audio and images

In addition to creating your own clips, you can also import audio files and pictures to add to your movie. You can find a link for each in the Tasks pane in the Import section.

Simply click the proper link, navigate to the file you want to import, and import it. When you elect to import audio files, the navigation interface defaults to your Music folder; images default to your Pictures folder. Find the file you're looking for and click Import; and it then appears in the contents pane, as shown in Figure 20.14.

FIGURE 20.14

Note the contents pane: I've imported two songs and a photograph.

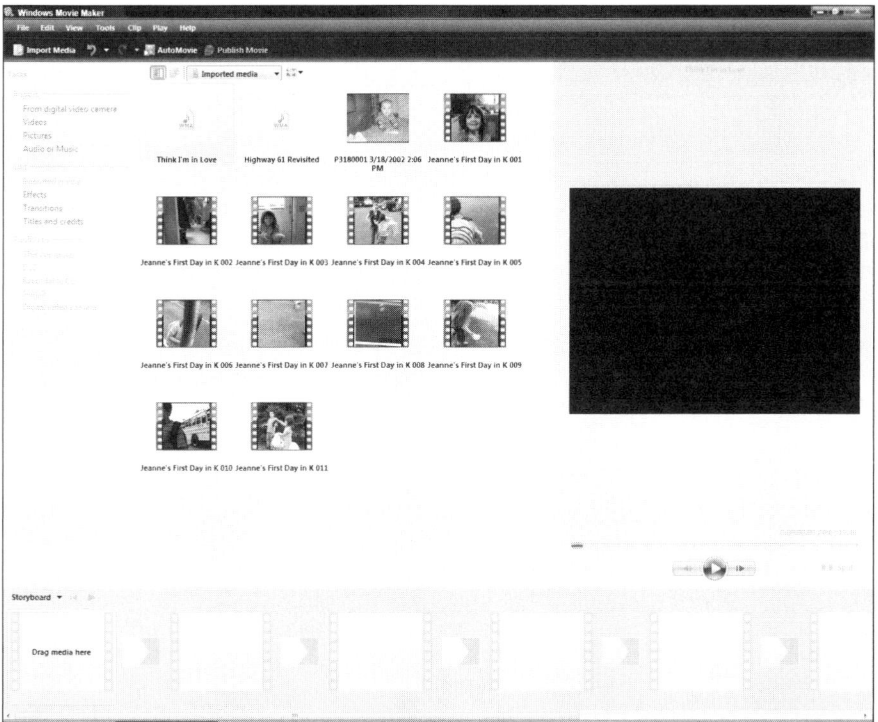

The Editing Process

The easiest way to edit a movie is to start by allowing Windows to divide raw footage into a series of clips (see the section, "Letting Windows Movie Maker create clips," earlier in this chapter). With clips in the contents hopper, creating the backbone of a film is simple.

Don't Be a Hero

The first few times you edit a movie, you'll probably take some time to become familiar with the process of editing and with the art of snipping clips and creating scenes. It's not an easy endeavor, and you can compound the difficulty by expecting too much too soon.

You are not Spielberg. Maybe someday your talent will rival his, but if you're editing your very first video project, keep it short and simple.

When I worked for a gaming magazine several years ago, a company competition challenged anyone who wanted to participate in a video contest. Whichever group created the coolest music video would win a nice prize. Of course, several associates and I formed a group with delusions of grandeur, and spent several days running around with a camcorder shooting what we thought would be the greatest music video in the history of mankind.

We waited to do the editing until the night before the entries were due. This was back in the 1990s, when computers weren't nearly as powerful as they are today. The poor guy who volunteered to edit the video spent a sleepless night putting together what turned out to be the most horrendous piece of work I've ever seen. Worse, he insisted on making it an electronic file, rather than export it to a video tape as everyone else did.

The publisher had a special day of viewing and voting, and everyone was invited. Some of the other videos looked relatively interesting, but then it came time to show ours. It was choppy. It was not synchronized with the music. It ran about two frames per second. The cuts were botched. Nobody could tell what was going on, or what the audience was supposed to perceive.

When our video finished its painful three minutes, there was silence. Then some laughter. The publisher, who was emceeing the event, was clearly embarrassed for my group. He mumbled something about it being "interesting" and then suggested we move on to the next video.

That happened because we bit off more than we could chew, or even fit into our mouths. Don't make our mistake. When you do your first project, start with maybe 20 minutes of footage and shoot for a final product of less than 5. Give yourself plenty of time to get it completed. Don't expect to make the next *Godfather* movie your first time out; instead, try to make your vacation look interesting for a few minutes. Once you've learned the ins and outs of editing, you can shoot for loftier heights.

You'll, of course, want to do some cutting, trimming, and even possibly some rearranging, all of which falls under the topic of editing. *Editing* a movie means taking lots of raw footage and trimming it down into a sensible film.

TIP Don't worry that you're losing little pieces of your life if you eliminate parts of your movie. The contents collections are imported from the whole; the raw footage still exists on the tape or in the file you imported it from. You won't delete anything from your original footage by removing bits from the storyboard/timeline or even from the contents pane itself.

Starting the editing process

The best way to get started editing is to familiarize yourself with your work. If you had Windows Movie Maker split the raw video into clips, play each one and decide whether you want part of it to be in your movie. If you do, drag the clip onto the storyboard. Note that the storyboard has boxes for each clip you drag; the storyboard continues off the screen and can stretch as long as you need it to.

After you've dragged several clips to the storyboard, it looks something like Figure 20.15.

FIGURE 20.15

I now have the skeleton for a movie on the storyboard.

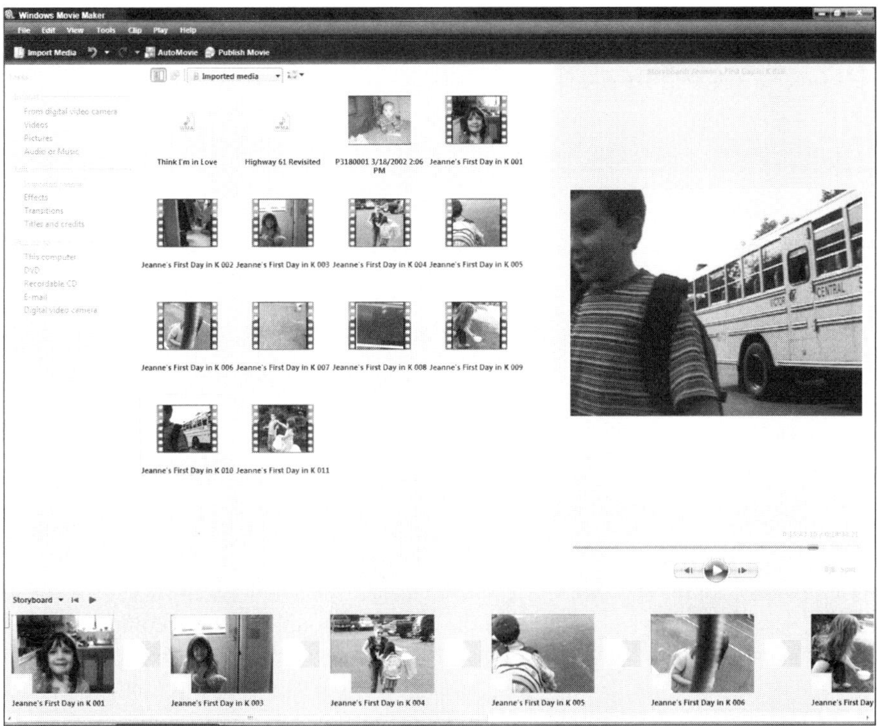

To remove a clip from the storyboard, simply right-click it and click Remove, or highlight it and press your keyboard's Delete button.

If you have still images you want to use for parts of the film, drag them onto the storyboard. You can adjust their duration in Timeline mode. The default duration that Movie Maker displays a still image is five seconds.

Snipping and trimming clips

After you've created the outline of your movie by dragging clips to the storyboard, it's time to get down to the precise acts of cutting and trimming clips.

Switch to Timeline mode. Take a look at the timeline (Figure 20.16). Notice how each clip is displayed along it, as long as graphically necessary to match its duration with the timer that runs along the top of the timeline.

FIGURE 20.16

A close-up of the timeline

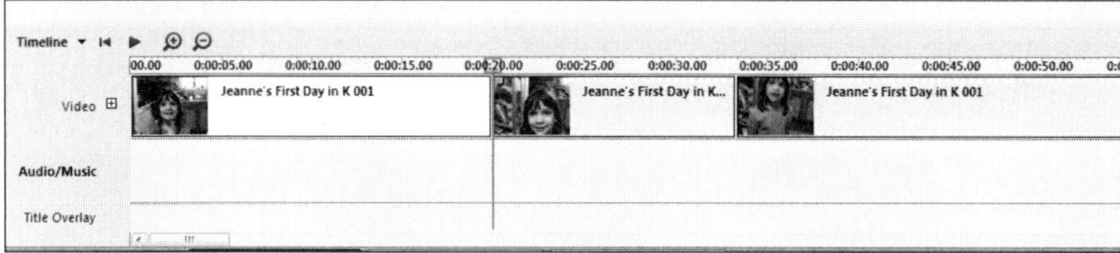

Each clip has a beginning, an end, and a duration. If you need to split a clip into two separate entities, follow these steps:

1. **Click the timer where you want to split the movie.** The green editing line appears at that point in the clip.
2. **Drag the editing line to a point just before where you need to cut, and play the movie in the preview panel.**
3. **Pause the movie exactly where you want to make the split, and click the Split button on the preview panel.** The affected clip splits into two clips, divided exactly where you split it.

You can also trim the parts of the clip that Movie Maker will actually play without cutting up a clip. Notice how, if you click on a clip, each side of the graphical representation is terminated by a black bar with a small arrow in the center of it (Figure 20.17). You can drag the arrows on either side of the clip to trim it (Figure 20.18). Doing so causes Movie Maker to play everything inside the arrows and ignore anything outside them. This feature is a handy way to pare down the clips without actually cutting them.

FIGURE 20.17

The trim lines are the black lines on either side of a clip.

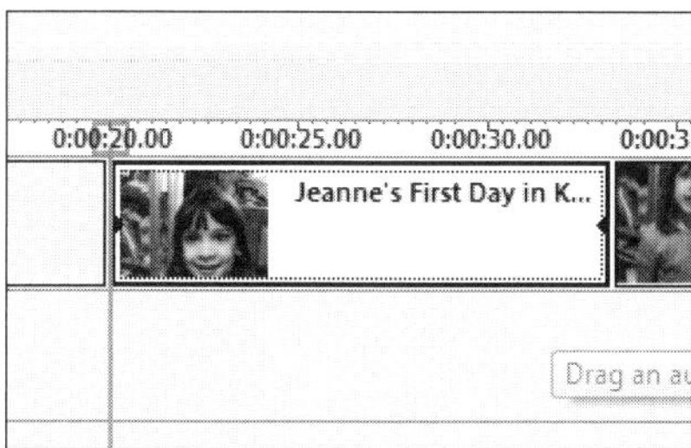

FIGURE 20.18

Drag the black lines inward to instruct Movie Maker on which parts of the clip to play and which parts to ignore.

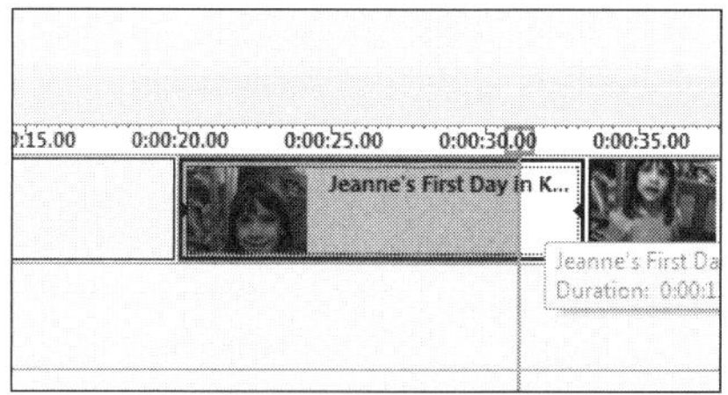

While editing your movie, bear the following points in mind:

- If you split a clip and need to remove part of it, simply right-click the part that you want to remove and click Remove.
- You can undo everything. If you make a mistake, choose Edit ➪ Undo. Alternatively, you can hold down the Ctrl key your keyboard and press Z to undo your most recent action.
- To adjust the duration of a still image, just drag the right border to make it longer or shorter.
- Editing takes time. Even culling 20 minutes of raw footage into a 3-minute movie can take hours.
- Save your project often. Click File, click Save Project, and give it a name. A project file is not a finished movie; it's the state of your project including all of your work on the storyboard and timeline.
- To play a portion of the movie, simply position the editing line where you want to start it and click the Play button in the preview panel. Click the Pause button to cease playback. Notice that there isn't a Stop button; the preview panel always shows the frame where the editing line appears on the timeline.

Using audio

If you imported audio, you can use it similarly to the way you use a video clip. The timeline has a line for audio. It shows the title of the audio file and the beginning and end of it, as shown in Figure 20.19.

FIGURE 20.19

You can use audio files as background music, and they also appear in the timeline.

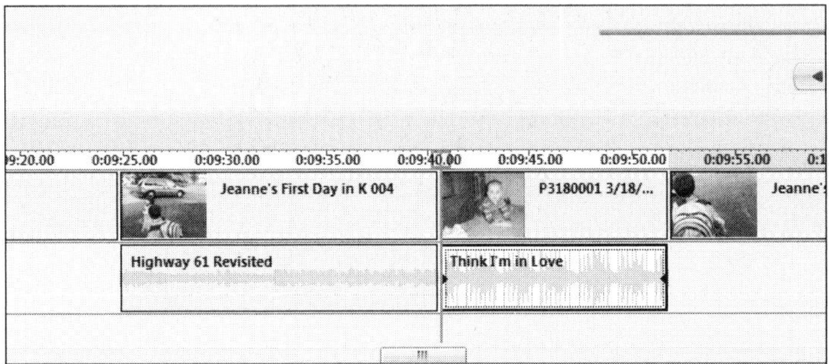

Although you can't split audio files like you can split video clips, you can trim them by dragging the left and right borders inward or outward as needed. In this way, you can trim off the beginning or ending of a song, or narrow it right down to a few seconds of a sound file that you want to use with a particular scene of your video.

When you play the video through the preview pane, you'll also hear any sound files that you played at the same time. You can use the preview pane and your ears to narrow down the audio file to exactly the part you need.

You can also add a narration track, if your computer has a microphone. To view the narration interface, choose Tools ➪ Narrate Timeline. The narration interface appears, as shown in Figure 20.20.

Move the edit line in the timeline to the exact point at which you want to start your narration. Then, click the Start Narration button, say what you have to say, and click Stop Narration to end that portion of your narration. You can narrate any scene this way.

FIGURE 20.20

The narration interface

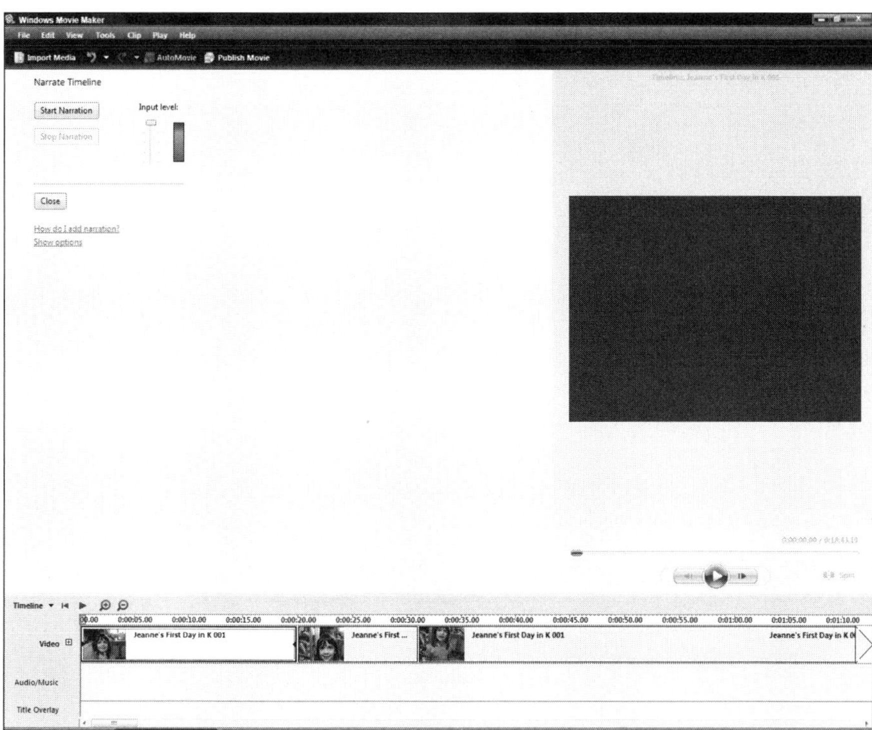

Adding fades, transitions, and effects

Windows Movie Maker has many cool tools that you can use to add professional polish to your films. You can fade into and out of scenes, transition between scenes, and even include interesting tricks from a whole array of cool effects.

Fades

Fades are easy enough to accomplish. Simply click the clip that you want to fade into and/or out of. Right-click it, and click Fade In or Fade Out. Movie Maker marks the clip with a star (Figure 20.21).

The star means that the clip has an effect of some sort. Fading in from black and out to black are actually special effects (see "Effects," later in this chapter). You can even elect to fade into and out of a white screen instead of a black screen through the Effects interface.

FIGURE 20.21

The star indicates that this clip has a special effect.

Transitions

A *transition* is a special way of moving from scene to scene. Windows Movie Maker offers a whole bunch of transition effects. To see them in the contents panel, click Transitions in the Tasks pane (Figure 20.22).

FIGURE 20.22

The transitions available through Windows Movie Maker

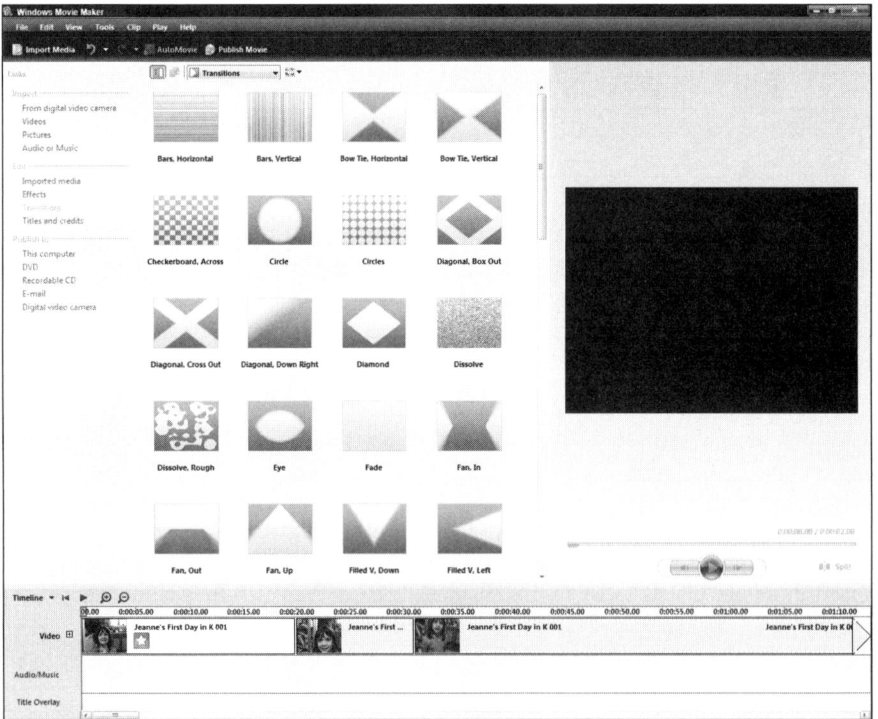

You can preview the effect of any transition by clicking it, and then clicking Play in the preview pane. Windows Movie Maker then shows a sample image transition to another sample image. For example, check out Figure 20.23 to see a Diagonal, Box Out transition in progress.

FIGURE 20.23

The Diagonal, Box Out transition

The easiest way to use a transition is to flip back to storyboard mode (View ➪ Storyboard). Notice that a transition box resides between each box representing a clip, as shown in Figure 20.24.

FIGURE 20.24

An empty transition box between two clips

To use a transition, just drag it from the contents pane to the transition box between the clips you want to transition out of and into. The box changes slightly, as shown in Figure 20.25.

FIGURE 20.25

This transition box indicates that these clips have a transition from one to the next.

You can drag transitions, from checkerboard fades to star wipes, between any and all of the clips in your film.

TIP Try not to get transition happy. Transitions can be interesting once in a while, but using fancy wipes between every single change in camera angle can distract your audience. If you look at most professionally-created videos, you'll see that they use transitions infrequently, and that those transitions are often simple. Well, except maybe for ESPN.

Effects

Click Effects in the Tasks pane to see the various visual effects you can add to your clips (Figure 20.26).

Effects include everything that changes the look of a clip, such as showing a clip in a different color variant (such as grayscale or sepia tone), showing it in slow motion, applying a mirror effect, and much more. Windows Movie Maker has plenty of effects you can use.

If you want to preview an effect, do it the same way you preview a transition: Right-click the effect and click Play Clip.

FIGURE 20.26

The contents pane displays the various visual effects.

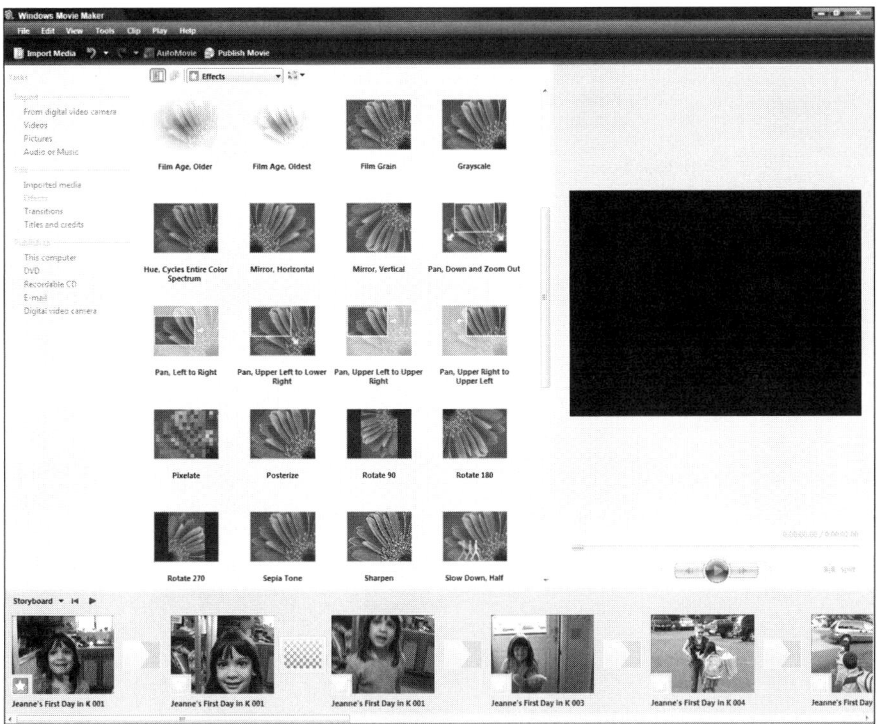

You can add an effect to a clip by dragging the effect onto it in either Storyboard or Timeline mode. Effects that build gradually, such as the Pixelate effect, shown in Figure 20.27, stretch their duration across the entire clip. Time-independent effects, like an old film look or a weird color effect, apply to the entire clip.

FIGURE 20.27

The Pixelate effect, in progress

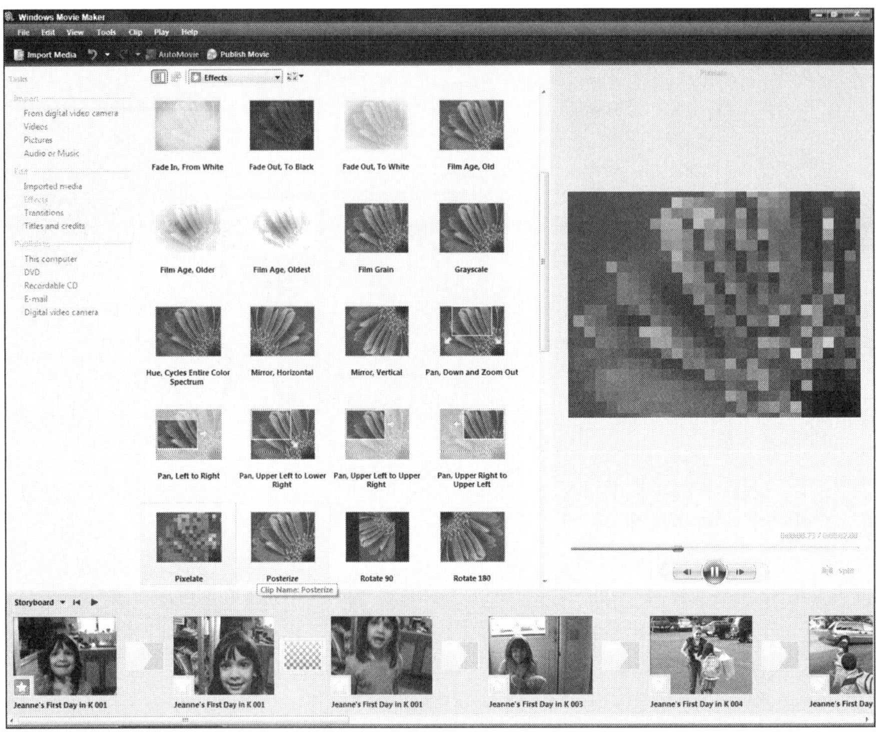

NOTE Use effects wisely. They can either add to a movie or distract from it, depending on how you use them. An effect that appears suddenly and out of context won't benefit your film.

Adding titles and text

You can add text, titles, and credits to your film with ease. To do so, follow these steps:

1. **Click on Titles and Credits in the Tasks pane to see the start of the various text wizards (Figure 20.28).** You're greeted with four options: Title at the beginning, Text before the selected clip, Title overlay on the selected clip, and Credits at the end.

FIGURE 20.28

You can add titles, text, and credits.

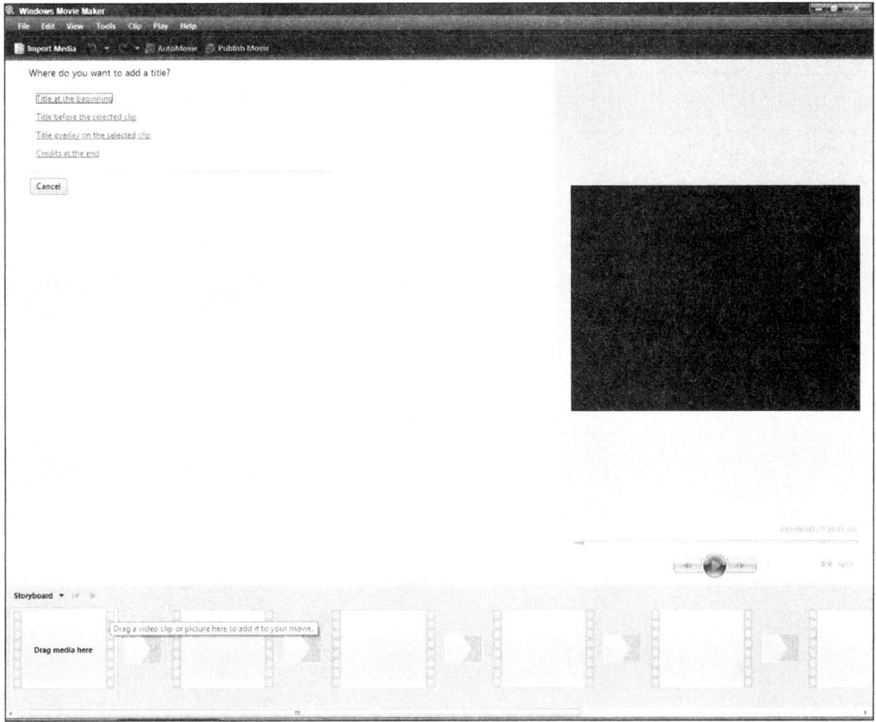

2. **Select the clip you want to affect (which is only necessary for the middle two options, text before the selected clip and title overlay on the selected clip) and click the option you want.** A wizard appears to guide you through the rest. For example, I want to start my movie with a title. When I click Title at the beginning, the screen shown in Figure 20.29 appears.

FIGURE 20.29

The Title at the beginning interface

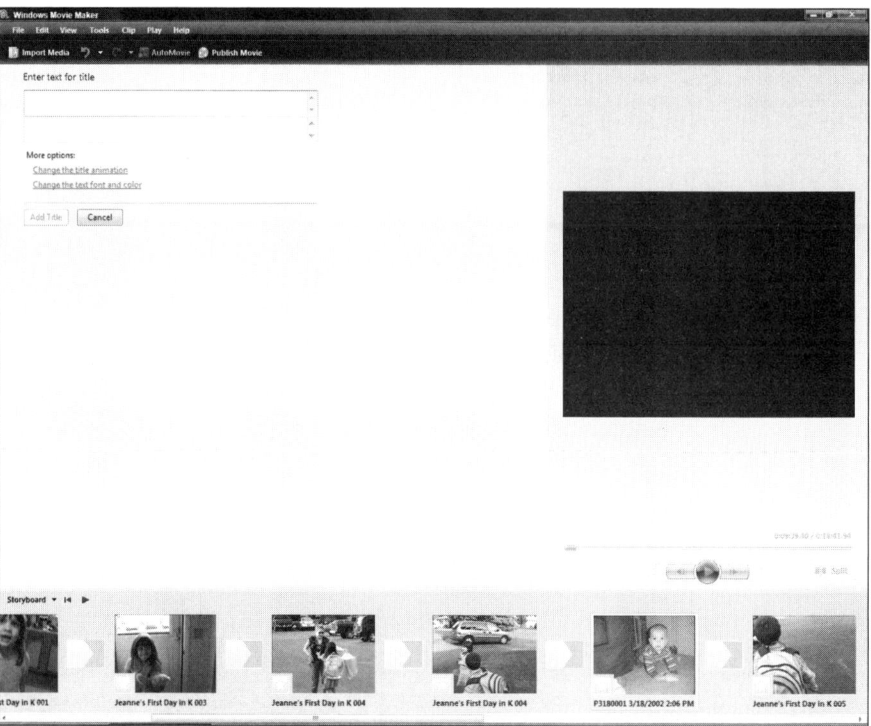

3. **Type in the text you want to appear in the clip.** Note that you can use the two options below the text box (if desired) to change the animation of the text (Figure 20.30), and change the font and color of the text.

FIGURE 20.30

You can change the text animation.

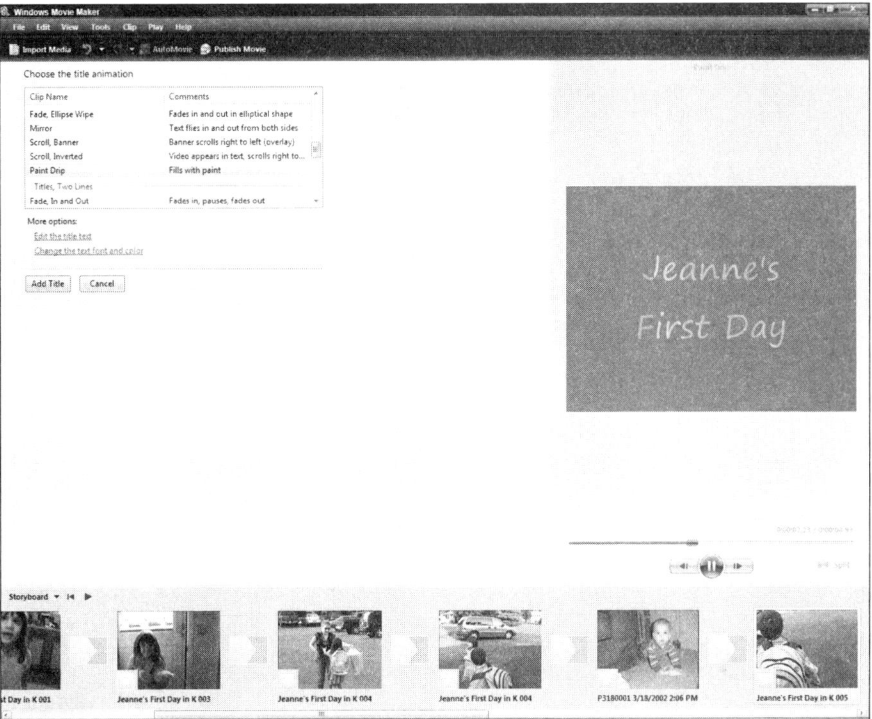

You can use titles and text for all kinds of purposes, from entitling your movie to captioning it.

Publishing the Finished Product

You've clipped, snipped, split, and trimmed your movie; loaded it with transitions; added a few nifty effects; put in a groovy title sequence; and faded to black at the end. The time has come to publish your film.

You can do so in any number of ways. The last entries in the Tasks pane offer options to publish it to your computer, to a DVD, to a CD, as an e-mail attachment, or to a digital video camera. Each option is wizard-based and incredibly easy, but I run through a couple for you in the following sections.

Publishing to a file

Sometimes, you'll wish to publish your clips to a file on your computer. Your movie would then take the form of a media file. Depending on the quality settings you choose and its overall length, it can wind up a small file or a massive one, or anything in between.

If you're creating a video of substantial length (more than, for instance, ten minutes long), you should check the space availability of your computer's hard drive before you proceed. Make sure you have plenty of hard drive space available. You can get an idea of how much space your film will take by initiating the publishing process and checking the interface you'll see in Figure 20.32 as discussed below.

Also, since you're creating an original work, it's important to realize that it's a unique file that can't be replaced — at least, not without a lot of effort. Make sure you include it when you back up your computer (as discussed in Chapter 11).

To publish your movie as a video file on your PC, follow these steps:

1. **Click This computer in the Tasks pane.** The first screen prompts you to choose a title for your film and choose a folder to create it in, as shown in Figure 20.31.

FIGURE 20.31

Publishing to a file step 1: Name your movie.

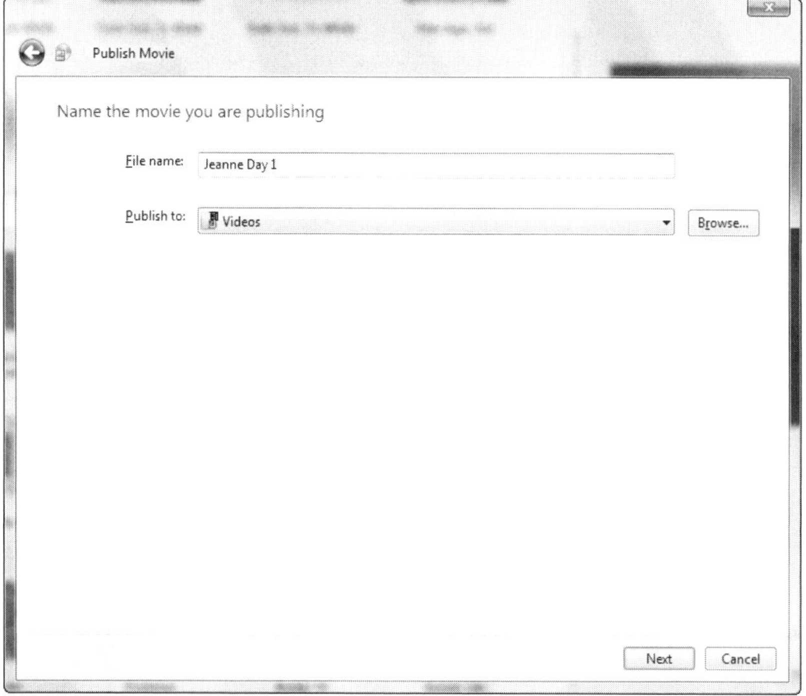

2. **Name your film, choose a folder (by default, Windows will choose the Movies folder), and click Next.** The screen shown in Figure 20.32 appears, prompting you to choose a format for your film.

FIGURE 20.32

Step 2: Choose a format.

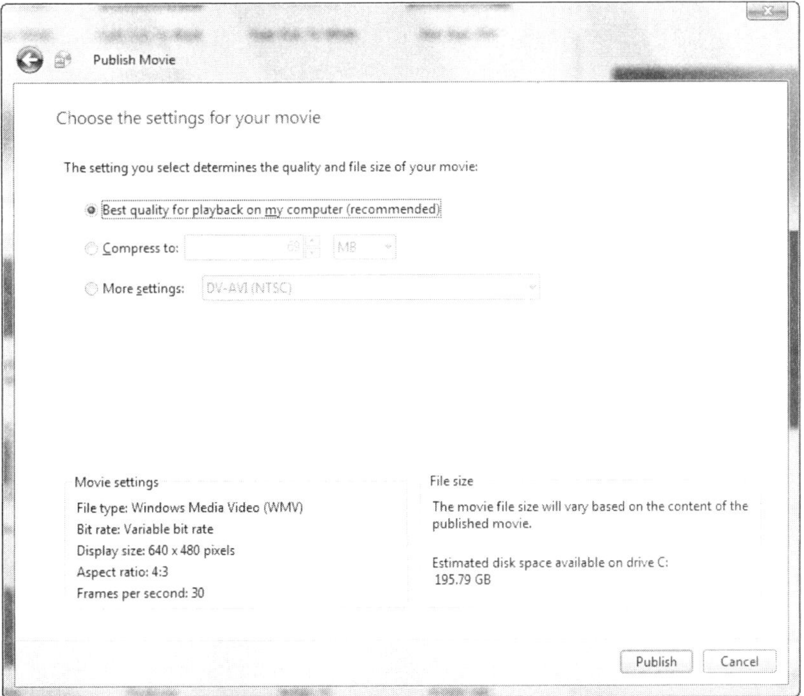

Three radio buttons allow you to choose from the following:

- **Best quality for playback on my computer (recommended):** This option formats the movie in the best possible quality. The file's attributes appear at the bottom of the window.
- **Compress to [*input a size in megabytes*]:** With this option, Windows shrinks the movie to a size you determine and displays the resulting attributes at the bottom of the window.
- **More settings:** You can choose from a wealth of formats by quality. Quality is shown in resolution and in bandwidth (megabits or kilobits per second). Windows can save movies in high definition (HD) or standard definition in different resolutions.

Note that most files are automatically published in the WMV format.

3. **After you make your selection, click Publish.** Windows displays a progress bar (Figure 20.33).

FIGURE 20.33

Step 3: Publish!

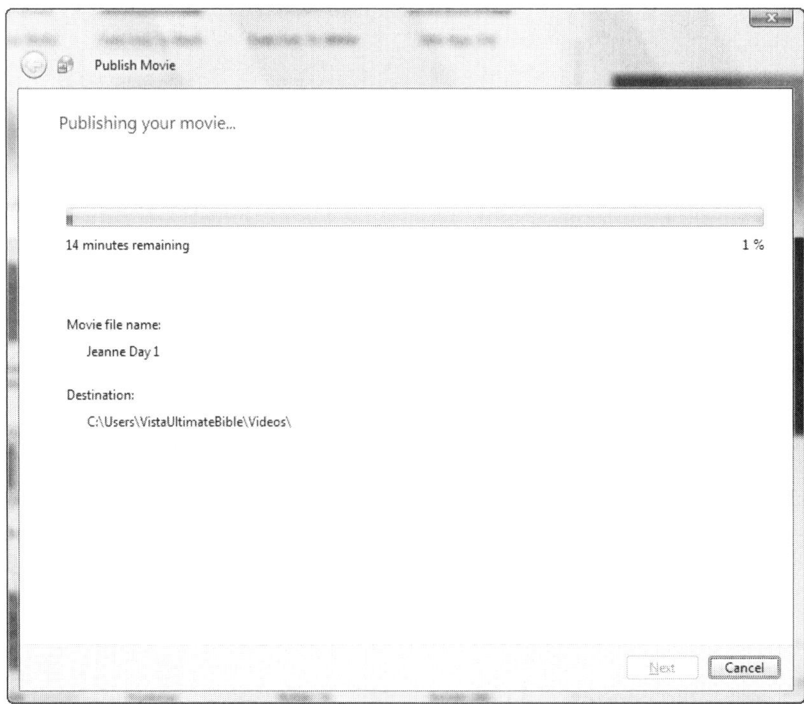

When the movie is done, it appears as a file in the folder you selected. You can watch it through Windows Media Player.

CROSS-REF See Chapter 19 for more information on watching video through Windows Media Player on Vista.

Publishing to a DVD

You can also publish your movie to a DVD. DVDs are handy because you can play them in any DVD player that can handle writeable or rewritable media. You can carry them with you, give them to friends, and not have to worry about e-mailing a massive file across the Internet.

Be sure to create at least two copies of your movie. Although, if you save your project before you publish, you can re-publish it at any time, you don't want to risk losing the movie if you part with the DVD and your computer crashes.

If you plan to distribute the movie on DVD, make at least one copy to store on your own shelf!

To publish your movie to a DVD, follow these steps:

1. **Click DVD in the Tasks pane.** Windows prompts you that it will open Windows DVD Maker.
2. **Insert a blank writeable or rewritable DVD into your computer's optical drive.** Windows DVD maker starts, as shown in Figure 20.34. Note that you don't need to add anything manually; in fact, you shouldn't if you wish only to publish your current video project to this DVD.

FIGURE 20.34

Windows DVD Maker adds your movie to its burn list automatically.

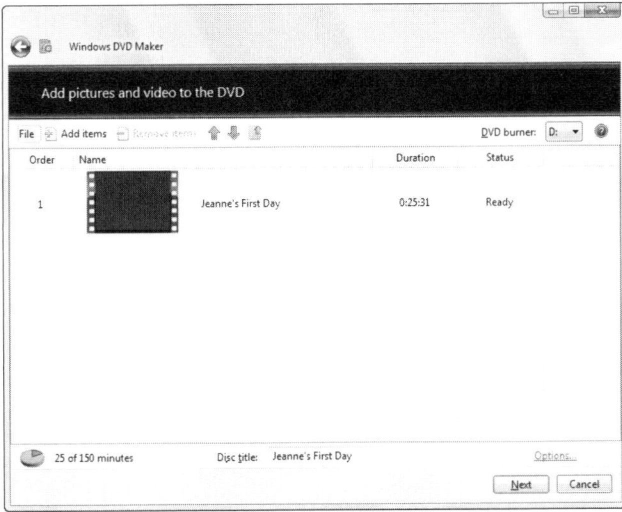

3. **Click Next.** Windows DVD Maker will display a Ready to Burn Disc screen, as shown in Figure 20.35. Don't click the Burn button yet! You might wish to customize the film.
4. **Click Menu Text.** A screen like the one in Figure 20.36 appears.
5. **Check the font, title, and other text and edit it as you wish.** When you're done, click Change Text to return to the Ready to Burn screen.

FIGURE 20.35

Ready to burn? Not quite.

FIGURE 20.36

DVD Maker fills in some of the text automatically, but you can change it.

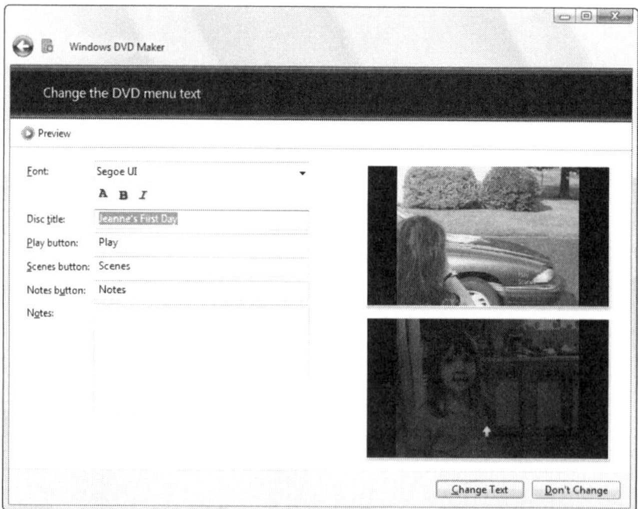

6. **Click Customize Menu to see a screen like the one shown in Figure 20.37.** Here, you can tweak the DVD menu that appears when you play the disc as you wish. Choose a font, select any video you wish to play in the foreground and background of the menu, select an audio file to play as the menu is displayed, and choose buttons for the scenes screen.

7. **When you're done, click Change Style.**

FIGURE 20.37

You can, if you wish, change the menu style of the disc.

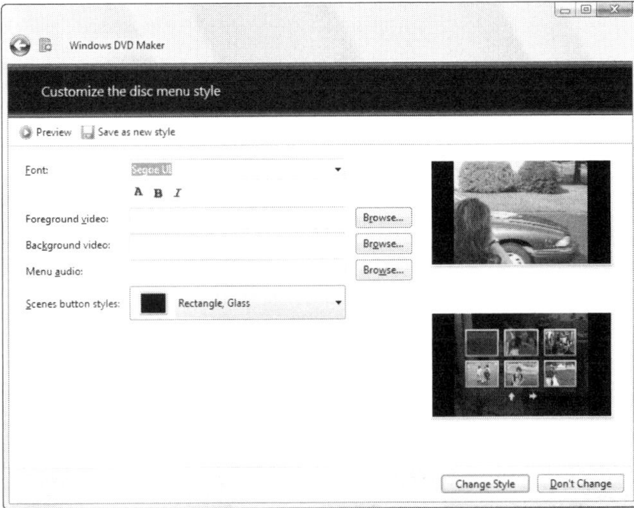

8. **Finally, when you're satisfied with everything, click Burn.** The burning process begins, and Windows displays a small dialog box with a progress indicator (Figure 20.38). Depending on the length of the DVD, it could take several minutes to more than an hour to create the final product.

FIGURE 20.38

Windows is creating the DVD.

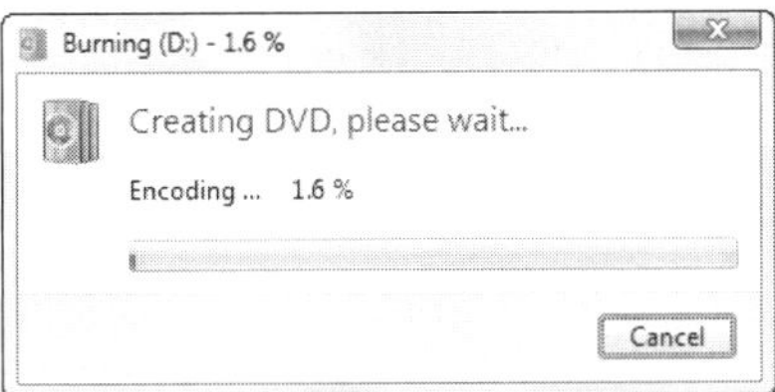

Summary

Figure 20.39 shows a movie that I created from raw footage via Windows Movie Maker. It's a short movie of my daughter's first day going to kindergarten.

FIGURE 20.39

Jeanne's First Day in Kindergarten.

I'm proud enough of it to show it to select friends and family, and I'm pretty sure their eyes won't glaze over with boredom — at least, I hope they won't. They're less likely to because I cut away the dull footage that won't mean anything to anyone besides my immediate family (such as the kids walking to the bus stop, and waiting idly for the bus).

Windows Movie Maker is surprisingly powerful for free, value-added software. It lets you edit movie recordings any way you want, by dividing them into clips and trimming them down to the exact footage you need.

Not only that, but you can also add interesting transitions and effects, fades and text, to complement your movie scenes. Movie Maker includes scores of transitions and effects: fades, wipes, color tricks, zooms, and much more.

When you're done in the editing room, you can publish your movie as a file or on removable media including DVD or even back to the DV cam that the footage came from. Windows Movie Maker might not be the choice of Hollywood film editors, but it's powerful enough for home users to get started with a new, creative hobby.

Part VII

Gaming on Windows Vista Ultimate

Gamers, start your engines. Part VII is nothing short of a crash course on all things gaming in Windows Vista Ultimate. You'll learn everything you need to know about gaming, from general game conventions and options to streamlining your games for performance and peak visual quality. This part contains info on calibrating your controllers, organizing games using the new Games folder, and integrating Windows Vista with Microsoft's Xbox 360, the first of the next-generation gaming consoles.

IN THIS PART

Chapter 21

Introduction to Windows Vista Gaming

IN THIS CHAPTER

Gaming on Windows Vista

Understanding DirectX 10

Exploring the Games folder

Setting parental controls

Sleep is for the weak. Sometimes, due to deadlines, I tend to make sleep a relatively low priority. Most of the time, however, my sleep deficit is due to the reason I firmly believe computers were invented: gaming. I play games every day. I review games for money, and also for the pleasure of partaking in this fantastic, modern diversion. You can do all kinds of things with a computer, but as far as I'm concerned, all other PC-centric activities take a back seat to gaming.

Windows Vista Ultimate, in speaking to the staunchest computer enthusiast, is truly a gamer's operating system. Microsoft packed a lot of gaming muscle into this operating system, focusing more on the pastime than it ever has in prior versions of Windows. Perhaps this focus is overkill for the casual gamer, the one to whom *Mahjong* or *The Sims* is the pinnacle of computer entertainment, but all gamers, casual and hardcore alike, will appreciate at least some of Vista's gaming features.

Hardcore gamers — who are they? They are the people who play games that bring computers to their knees. Not everyone grows visibly excited when they read the capabilities of a new graphics engine, but a gaming enthusiast sees features like support for advanced shader models and emerging physics engines as enticements to invest in the latest titles.

Hardcore gamers are the people who would rather spend their money on computer equipment than food. They are PC gearheads not because they care so much about electronics or logic circuitry, but because they want to be able to run their games with all the graphics detail turned up and still achieve high frame rates. They're the people who buy those graphics cards that cost more than some entire computer systems. They learn to work on PCs inside and out so that they can upgrade components as soon as something better comes along than what they currently own. They download new drivers for graphics, audio, and other hardware the day the manufacturer releases them.

Windows Vista Ultimate has features especially for these hardcore gamers. It also has features for casual gamers, for families, and for people who are just starting to discover the wonders of computer gaming (and, of course, how superior the PC gaming experience is compared to console gaming).

Games are graphics-intensive, and Windows Vista contains a whole new graphics model that's intended to make 3D animations smoother and more fluid than ever before. Microsoft has also upgraded the aural side of Windows, making audio a top priority. The Games folder provides a central location for managing and launching games, as well as a place for parents to monitor the kinds of games their children play. Parents and administrators can even automate controls to prevent young children from encountering game content that might not be appropriate for them.

Read on to learn about the wonders of Windows Vista's gaming enhancements, how to make sure the kids don't stumble upon *Grand Theft Auto* or some other unsuitable game, and more.

Gaming in Windows Vista Ultimate

In the Stone Age of personal computers, Windows wasn't anything like it is today. The first truly widespread version of the operating system, Windows 3.1, barely managed to handle any multimedia. PCs back then were considered tools, not gaming platforms.

But that wasn't the case. Windows 3.1 ran on top of the command-line interface DOS. Games, some truly fantastic games, did exist and they required the user to close Windows completely and run them from DOS.

Windows 95 changed everything. Designed to run as a complete operating system (although it still had plenty of DOS elements), it included a feature called *DirectX*. DirectX is a series of application programming interfaces (APIs) that were designed to allow multimedia and gaming to take place from within Windows. DirectX 1.0 was pretty awful, but it eventually evolved into an excellent gaming platform.

Vista includes DirectX 10.0, which packs some revolutionary features intended to make the Windows multimedia experience far better than it ever has been. Ever since Windows 95, Microsoft has taken steps to make gaming in Windows possible, but the company has, at last, truly embraced the gaming community.

How DirectX 10 benefits gamers

Until the release of Windows Vista, gaming has seemingly taken a back seat to other tasks in Windows. In fact, when Microsoft released the Xbox TV gaming console in 2001, worried speculation spread around the gaming community that Microsoft might cease to focus on Windows as a gaming platform. Happily, that idea turned out to be pretty far from the truth.

Microsoft, in fact, beefed up DirectX. With Windows XP, DirectX had entered version 8.1, and version 9.0 wasn't far behind. With each release, DirectX supported more advanced features, especially in terms of 3D graphics. As I write this book, DirectX for Windows XP is in version 9.0c and receiving updates about every other month.

Windows Vista introduces DirectX 10. Chapter 15 covers DirectX 10 in detail. To review, it includes a whole swath of new features. Most importantly, it's fitted with a new graphics driver model that uses optimized, high-speed DLLs (dynamic link libraries) designed to be far more responsive than earlier versions. If Microsoft is correct, DirectX 10 will display graphics eight times faster than DirectX 9.0c can. Check out Figure 21.1; a utility included in Windows Vista called DXDiag shows DirectX 10 information.

FIGURE 21.1

The DXDiag utility shows DirectX 10 system information.

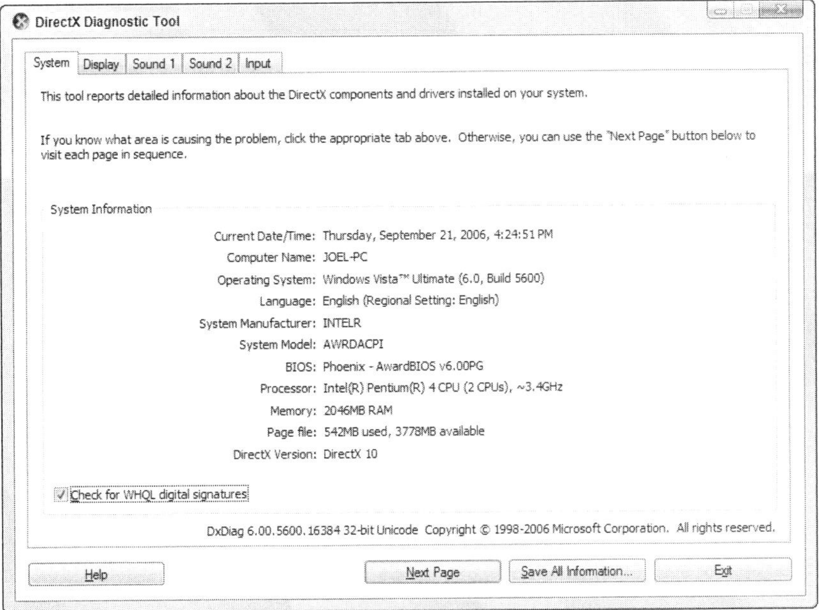

Unlike previous versions of DirectX, DirectX 10 is not backward-compatible with earlier versions of the API suite. Its code is too different. The graphical subset of DirectX 10, called Direct3D 10 (formerly codenamed Windows Graphics Foundation) will not work with hardware that doesn't meet its minimum requirements.

NOTE DirectX's non–backward compatibility raises a question: If DirectX 10 doesn't work with past versions, how does Windows Vista run pre-DirectX 10 games (like *Company of Heroes,* shown in Figure 21.2) and support pre-DirectX 10 hardware? The answer is that Vista also includes DirectX 9L, a version of DirectX 9.0c that Microsoft included for backward compatibility.

FIGURE 21.2

Company of Heroes runs on Vista thanks to DirectX 9L.

Microsoft is implementing a system that will tell graphics hardware manufacturers the minimum specifications that Direct3D 10 will support. Compliant hardware will certainly be marketed as Direct3D 10 compatible. Graphics hardware is either DirectX 10 compliant, or it isn't; the graphics hardware, to be considered DirectX 10 compliant, *must* support all but a very few optional features. This is different from older versions of DirectX, where some cards were considered compliant even though they couldn't support all of the features.

DirectX 10 features include things like the ability to swap graphics data to and from a paging file, which allows the data currently in demand to occupy graphics memory while other unneeded data reside elsewhere; Shader Model 4.0, a powerful engine for realistic lighting, reflections, and other lighting features; the ability to swap textures independently from the system CPU in the graphics card's processor (called the GPU, or the graphics processing unit); the ability to ignore some rendering calls to prevent the graphics hardware from having to draw items that aren't visible; and more.

CROSS-REF Check out Chapter 15 for the lowdown on DirectX 10.

The Games Folder

When you install a game, whether it's a brand-new game designed for Windows Vista or a pre-Vista Windows game, Windows Vista tries to detect it and, if it recognizes that it's a gaming title, it drops a shortcut icon into the Games folder, shown in Figure 21.3.

FIGURE 21.3

The Games folder, containing the Windows Vista games and other titles

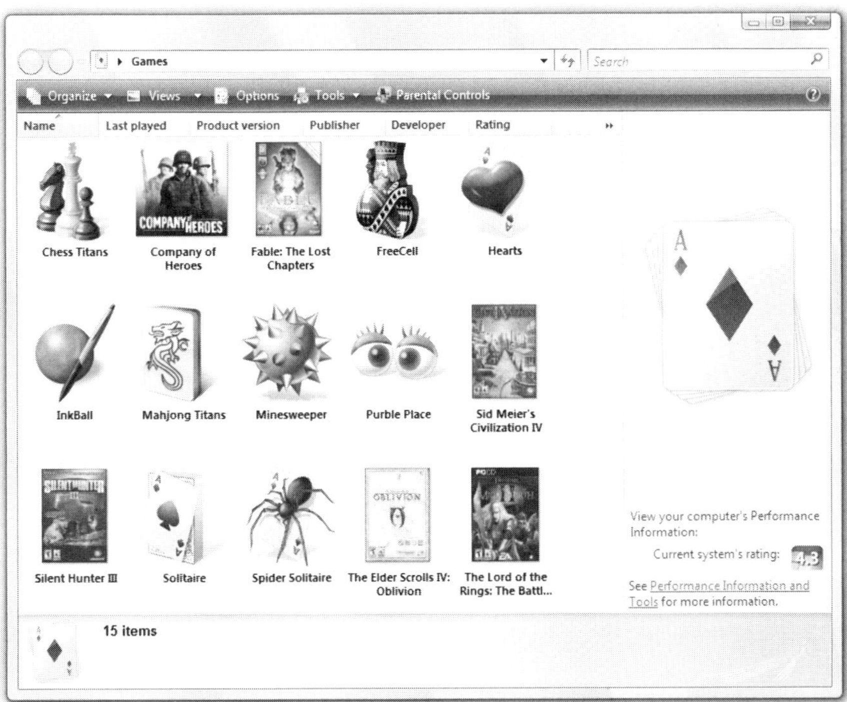

The Games folder is a tool to centralize your gaming experience. It doesn't matter where in the Windows Vista file system you install your games — whether you install them all in their default locations or whether you use a special folder like C:\GAMES — the Games folder keeps shortcuts for launching games, game data, parental controls, and even a system performance rating right at your fingertips.

Features of the Games folder

Invoke the Games folder by choosing Start ➪ Games. Everything you see in the folder is a shortcut; these icons don't represent the actual executable files.

Each game is either represented by its icon or by a picture of the game's box art. The toolbar contains standard buttons for organizing the files, changing views, and other items, and it also contains a number of items specific to this folder.

When you first launch the Games folder, a dialog box appears offering two check box–controlled options: One allows Windows to download information about the games you install from Microsoft's servers, and the other keeps track of the most recently played games. You can change these options through the Options toolbar button, shown in Figure 21.4.

FIGURE 21.4

The Games folder options dialog box

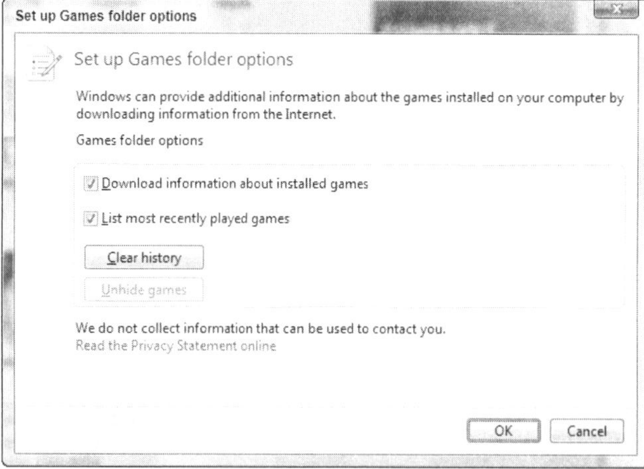

In addition to the two options described, the Games options dialog box allows you to clear the history of your playing habits, and to cease hiding any games you decided to hide (if any).

Other toolbar buttons specific to the Games folder include:

- **Play:** This button launches the highlighted game.
- **Community and Support:** If the necessary information is provided, this button, which invokes a drop-down menu, allows you to visit the Web home page, support page, and/or other pages associated with the currently highlighted game.
- **Parental Controls:** This button invokes the Parental Controls window.

If you right-click on one of the games in the Games folder, the context menu offers these options:

- **Play:** Launches the game.
- **Home Page, Support, Register, and other options:** These options are the same as those offered by the Community and Support toolbar button (see the preceding bulleted list).
- **Saved Games:** Launches your Saved Games folder.
- **Copy:** Copies the shortcut to the clipboard.
- **Pin to Start Menu and Add to Quick Launch:** Self-explanatory.
- **Customize:** Launches an interface for customizing the game's properties page and launch options.
- **Hide This Game:** Removes the game's shortcut from the Games folder until you unhide it as described earlier in this section.

Customize a game

If you right-click on a game and click Customize, a dialog box like the one shown in Figure 21.5 appears.

FIGURE 21.5

The Customize window for *Company of Heroes*

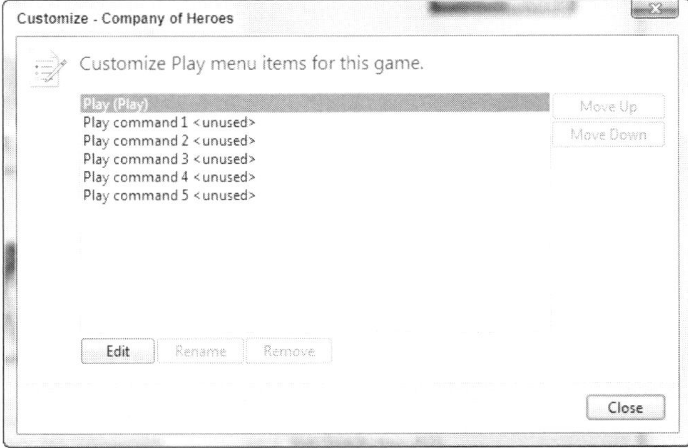

It lists several commands regarding the game's shortcut. If you highlight a command (for example, Play) and click Edit, a properties page will appear, as shown in Figure 21.6.

FIGURE 21.6

The Play Properties for *Company of Heroes*

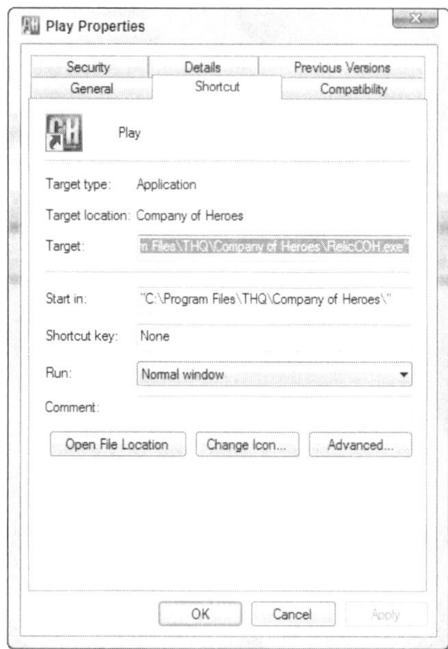

The properties page resembles the properties page for any shortcut or executable file. The tabs include the following:

- **General:** Contains information about the file, and allows you to change some of its attributes such as Read Only and Hidden.
- **Shortcut:** Allows you to change the location of the executable file associated with the shortcut, change the icon, and, through the Advanced button, select whether to run this game as an administrator (if you have the privilege).
- **Compatibility:** These compatibility options enable you to try to get Vista to run games written for earlier versions of Windows.

CROSS-REF For more information on compatibility options, see Chapter 25.

- **Security:** Allows you to edit the file's permissions regarding who can access it.

- **Details:** Shows details about the command in the Customize window that you're editing.
- **Previous Versions:** Shows any prior versions of the shortcut or its associated file that Windows has copies of.

System performance rating

Benchmarks — they're the tool of the PC enthusiast press and their bane, as well. Benchmarks are tests that result in numbers that supposedly reveal a computer system's performance capability, or that of a component such as a graphics card.

If you read reviews of computer hardware on the Internet or in print, you've likely encountered benchmarks. When a new graphics card becomes available, editorial markets all over the place run benchmark tests on it in a variety of configurations. They run synthetic benchmarks that pump theoretical pixels and polygons through the rendering pipeline, and they run real-world games that have frame rate counters built in.

The purported purpose is to tell readers how muscular, how powerful, or how impressive a piece of equipment, or a whole system, is. Most benchmarks are created for comparison. For example, is graphics card A really that much better than B? Benchmarks tend to be run in perfect circumstances: The systems are brand new, they lack many background applications that a typical reader might run (such as antivirus applications, instant messaging or chat utilities, and so on), and the conditions are heavily controlled.

Unfortunately, readers tend to look at benchmarks as predictions as to how well a given game will run on their systems. I can't begin to tell you how many times I've gotten letters from angry readers, after publishing a review of a graphics card, who shout that *their* Doom3 frame rates aren't nearly as high as mine were, and therefore I must have made them up. I explain that their systems aren't configured the same as mine was for the tests: They might not have the same CPU, the same graphics drivers, the same anything, and that the tests are there for comparison, not prediction.

If you're wondering how a game might perform on your system, you might want to check out Windows Vista's system performance ratings. Vista generates a performance rating for your system when you first install it, and then again whenever you request one. Once codenamed WinSAT, the system performance rating is a built-in synthetic benchmark that generates a number. You may have noticed that if you click a game in the Games folder, the right side of the window presents information about it including, if Windows has the data, a recommended system performance score, a required system performance score, and *your* system performance score. These data can be helpful if you know what to do with them.

Obtaining a performance rating

At the end of a Windows Vista installation, Windows will pause and try to entertain you with slides about its capabilities while it runs a few tests. It says it's measuring your system's performance, but it doesn't immediately give you any results. You can get them in the Performance and Information Tools window, shown in Figure 21.7. To invoke this window, click the link on the right side of the Games folder, or go to Control Panel, then click System ➪ System Performance and Information.

FIGURE 21.7

Performance Information and Tools

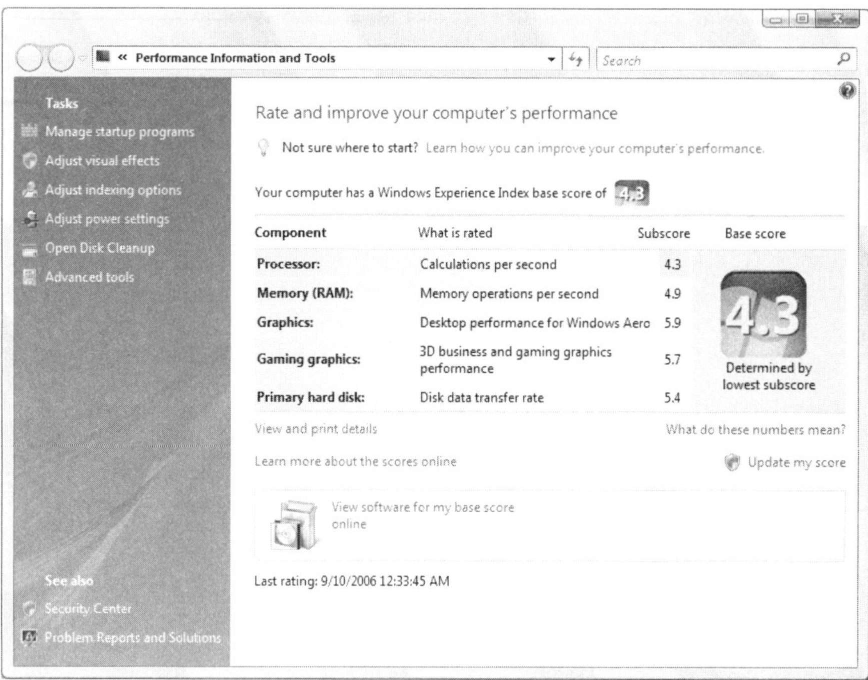

Take a look at the Performance Information and Tools window. The score is actually the lowest result for five performance subscores:

- The system's CPU is tested for its capability in calculations per second.
- System memory is tested for operations per second.
- The graphics memory is tested for overall Windows Aero performance.
- 3D graphics (for gaming and, well, business) is tested for overall performance.
- The hard drive transfer rate is tested.

You can obtain an updated system performance score if you have administrative privileges by clicking Update My Score. Windows doesn't show a graphical representation of any of the tests as they are performed, only a progress bar as shown in Figure 21.8.

FIGURE 21.8

A progress bar lets you know Windows is testing system performance.

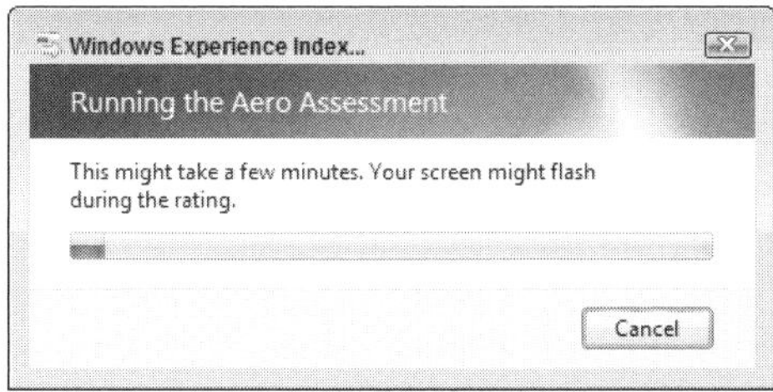

You should grab a new score whenever you update your system's major drivers (such as motherboard, CPU, or graphics card drivers) and whenever you upgrade any hardware. Your score could improve with such events.

The scale for the System Performance Rating isn't fixed. Right now, it goes from 0 to 5.9, but Microsoft might expand the scale as more powerful computer hardware is released.

Interpreting and using the performance rating

Your system's score is the lowest of all the subscores. Why the lowest? Because the score is not used to compare your system to anyone else's, or for bragging rights of any kind: It's there for you to get the best gaming experience you can.

Microsoft is implementing a new branding system in which games will be assigned required and recommended scores based on how demanding they are in terms of system performance. If your system score meets or exceeds those scores, your system should do the game justice. If not, you might want to upgrade something before you purchase the game.

Note the link in Figure 21.7 labeled View Software for my Base Score Online. It leads you to Windows Marketplace (Figure 21.9) via Internet Explorer. At the time of this writing, I can't find score data online, but hopefully you'll be able to choose games based on their recommended and required scores versus your own system's score in the future.

FIGURE 21.9

Windows Marketplace should have game score data sometime soon...

Parental Controls

From the Games folder, assuming your account has administrative privileges, you can invoke the parental controls and govern which games other accounts have access to. Click the Parental Controls button to invoke the window shown in Figure 21.10.

With Parental Controls, you can dictate not only which games other user accounts can access, but also enforce computer time limits, enable and configure a Web content filter, and determine which other programs other user accounts have access to.

FIGURE 21.10

The Parental Controls window

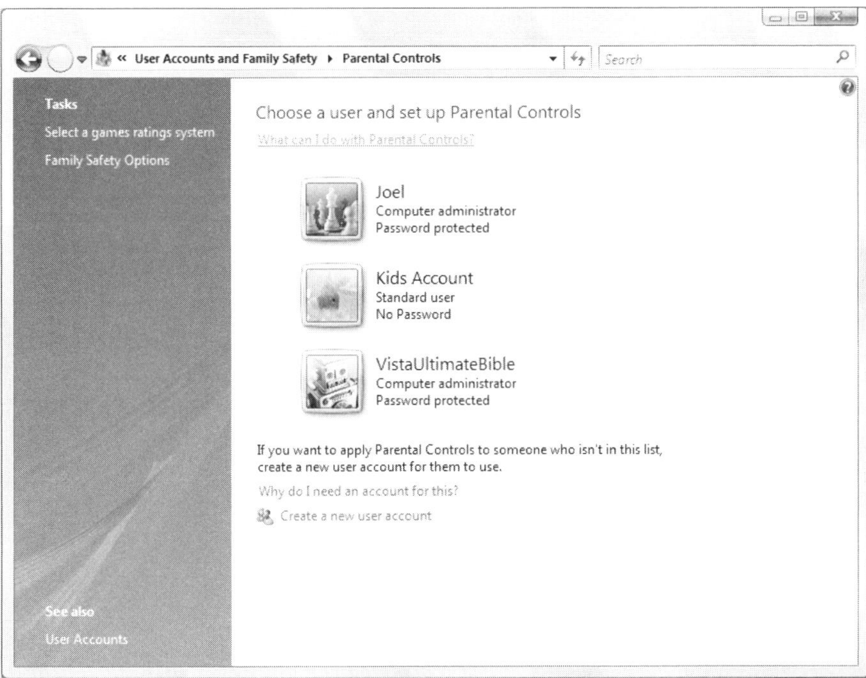

To start, click a standard user account. A window like the one shown in Figure 21.11 appears.

Parental Controls are turned off by default, which means even standard users have access to everything not protected by User Account Control (see Chapter 11). You have to turn Parental Controls on by clicking the radio button next to On, enforce current settings.

NOTE The Activity Reporting radio buttons allow you to enable activity reports. You can view what other users do with the computer in the form of reports. Activity reports include which Web sites the user visited; which Web sites Windows blocked access to; any downloads the user initiated; the number of times the user logged on; the applications and games the user launched; and e-mail, instant messaging, and e-mail reports.

Access an activity report by visiting Control Panel, clicking User Accounts and Family Safety, and then clicking View activity reports.

Now, take a look at the settings you can choose to enforce user restrictions.

FIGURE 21.11

Preparing to govern a user account

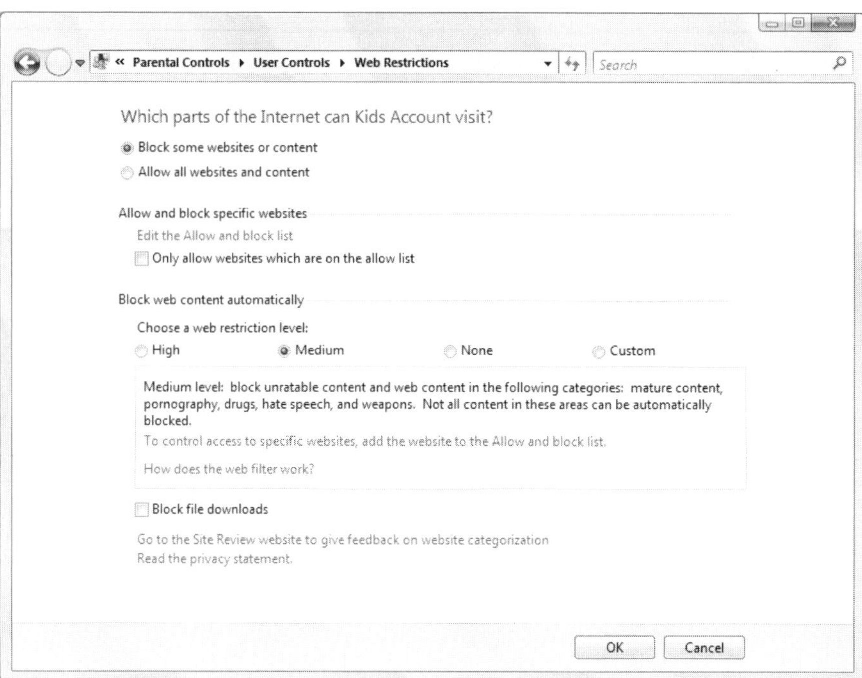

Windows Vista Web filter

Click the Windows Vista Web Filter link to invoke a window like the one shown in Figure 21.12. You can govern the user's Web access as closely as you like.

Through radio buttons, you can elect to block some Web content or allow access to all of it. A check box enables you to determine whether or not to block all Web access except for sites you *specifically* allow (click the Edit and Allow Block List link to allow certain Web sites, or restrict specific sites).

You can also choose from four automated settings by clicking a restriction level. High restrictions block all Web sites except those approved for children. Medium restrictions are more lax, but still block sites that contain porn, hate speech, and weapon-related content. The None option blocks, predictably, nothing, and Custom gives you a list of check box items you can choose to block, which is shown in Figure 21.13.

Finally, you can enable a wholesale restriction on file downloads by selecting the Block file downloads check box.

FIGURE 21.12

The Windows Vista Web filter

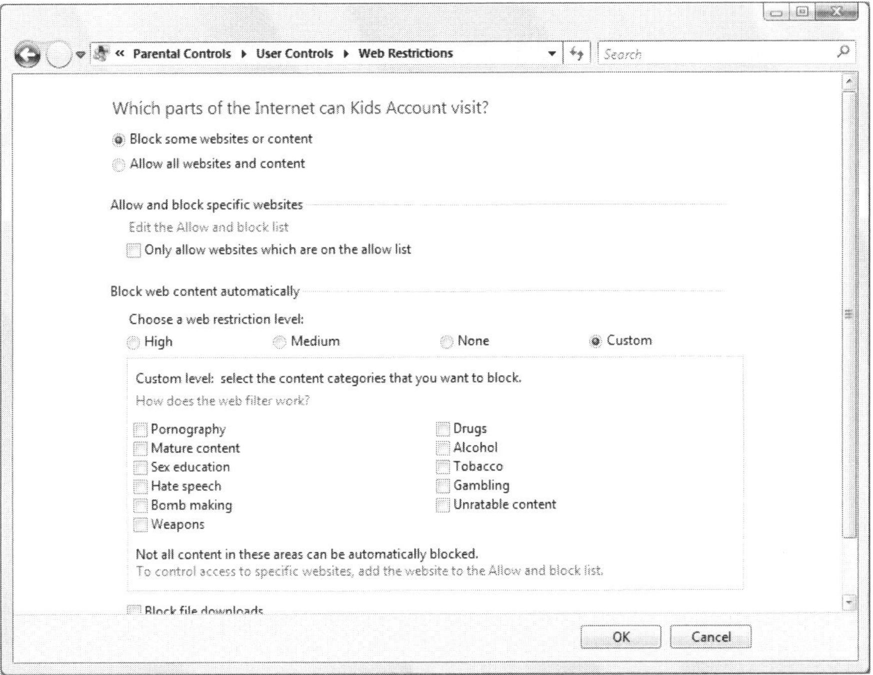

FIGURE 21.13

You can customize automated Web content filtering.

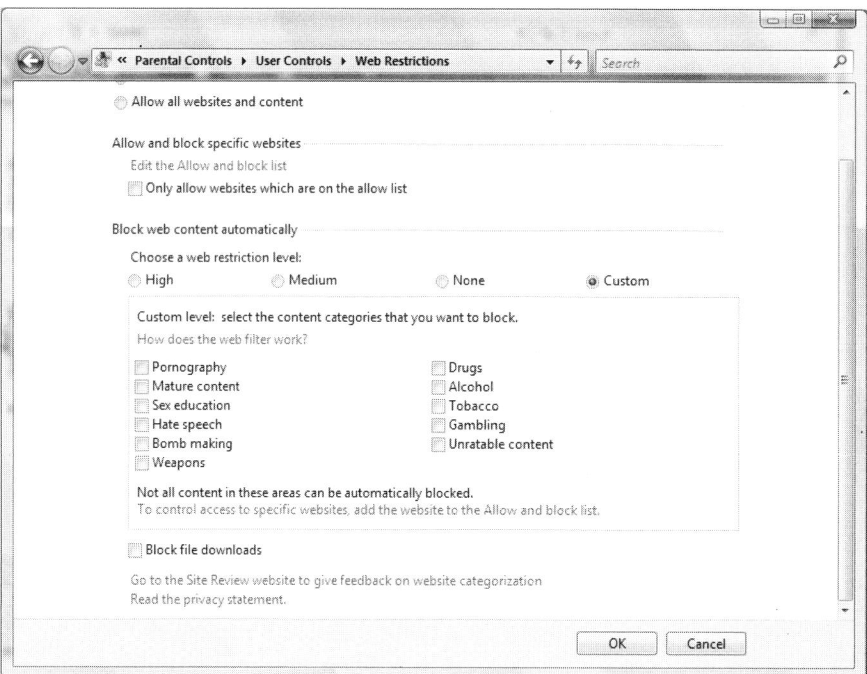

Time limits

I know I said that sleep is for the weak, but even the strong need to sleep sometimes. You can enforce time limits by clicking the Time limits link in the window shown earlier in Figure 21.11. This option enables you to allow or block access to the account by the time of day. The Time Limits interface is shown in Figure 21.14.

You can block access to the computer by the hour, each day of the week. The interface is simple: Each hour of each day is arranged in a grid of blocks. Click blocks to toggle them restricted or available. You can click and drag to toggle multiple blocks at the same time. Restricted hours are shaded, and allowed hours are blank.

FIGURE 21.14

You can control account access time limits via the Time Restrictions page.

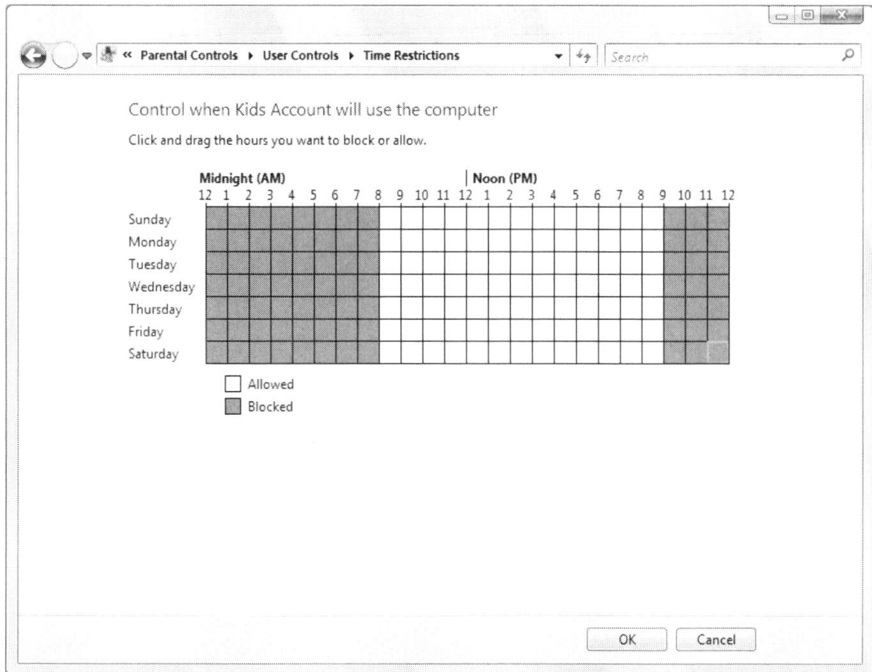

The configuration shown in Figure 21.14 will block access every day between 9:00 p.m. and 8:00 a.m..

TIP Time restrictions are perfect for preventing a child from wandering to the computer in the middle of the night and learning how to make bombs from household chemicals. Time restrictions do *not* replace the need to monitor young children while they use the computer.

Games

You can block access to games by clicking Games in the window shown back in Figure 21.11. You'll see an interface like that shown in Figure 21.15.

FIGURE 21.15

You can control access to games via the Game Controls page.

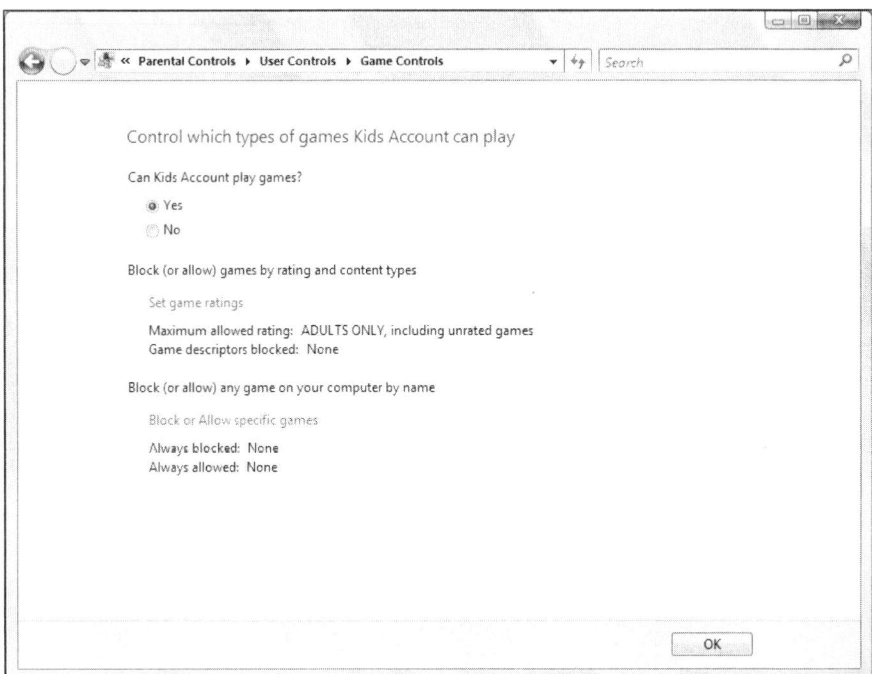

In the Game Controls page, you can dictate game access to an account in three ways: You can block all games by clicking the appropriate radio button at the top of the window; you can block games based on ESRB (Entertainment Software Ratings Board) ratings; or you can block specific games manually.

To block games based on ESRB ratings, click the Set Game Ratings link. The window changes to the one shown in Figure 21.16.

At the top of this window, you can elect whether to block games that aren't rated at all. Below that, you can choose a minimum rating: All games of that rating and above are restricted.

FIGURE 21.16

With the Game Overrides page, you can block games by ESRB rating.

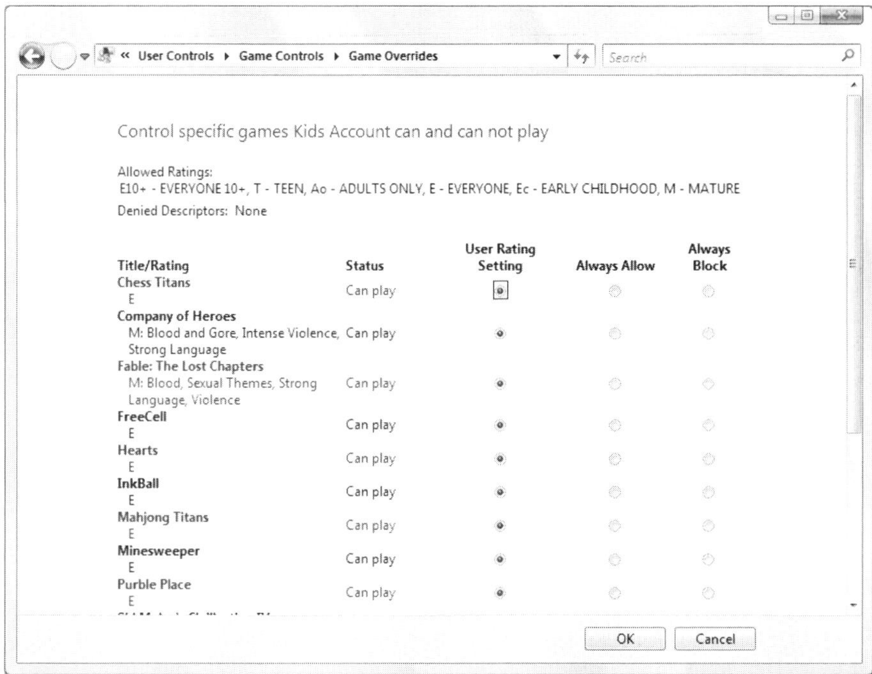

Ratings, in order from the child-friendliest to those whose games likely contain the most objectionable content, are:

- EC (Early Childhood; games for little kids)
- E (Everyone; games that generally lack objectionable content)
- E10+ (Suggested for any player age 10 or older)
- T (Teen; may contain content inappropriate for children under 13)
- M (Mature; intended for people aged 17 and up)
- AO (Adults Only; contains content intended only for grownups)

The level you dictate blocks everything at that level plus every level beyond it. For example, click E10+ to have Windows restricts games rated E10+, T, M, and AO.

If you scroll down in this window, you encounter a list of the types of content that you may find objectionable. Even if a game falls into a rating that isn't restricted, Windows will check for any of the types of content whose check boxes you select. This feature gives you greater control over content; you can restrict games with everything from comic mischief to graphic violence, and everything in between.

You can also block or allow games by title. If you return to the window shown in Figure 21.15 and click Block or Allow specific games, a window like the one shown in Figure 21.17 appears.

FIGURE 21.17

You can control access to games by title.

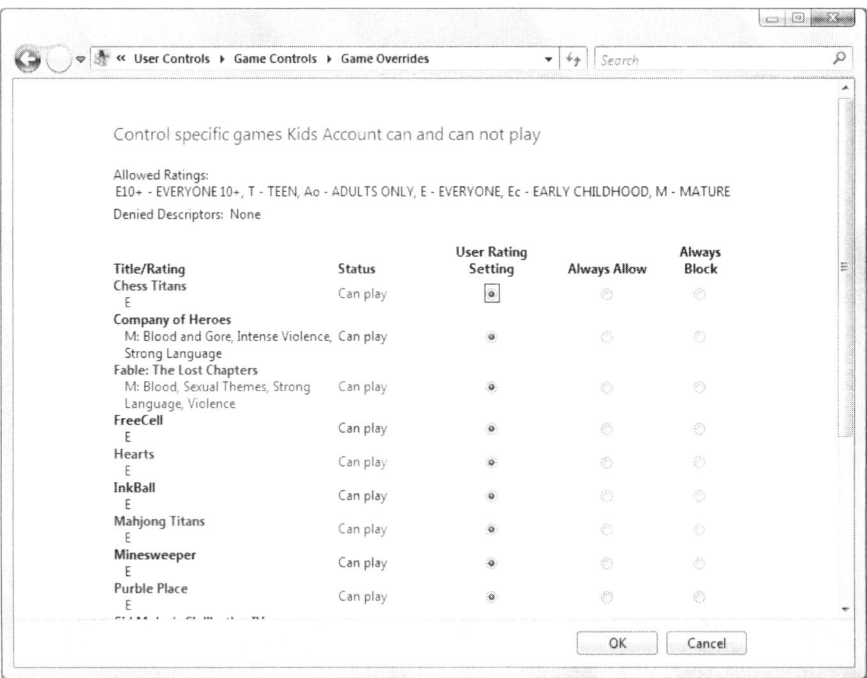

This window lists every program that Windows recognizes as a game, and each listing has three radio button options. The first option defers access to the ESRB rating controls. The second always allows access to the game, and the third always blocks access to the game.

Programs

Click Allow and Block specific programs in the window shown earlier in Figure 21.11 to set up access or restrictions to various programs installed on the computer. A window like the one in Figure 21.18 appears.

If you elect to block specific programs, a list of executable program files appears. Each item in the list is preceded by a check box. Select the check box of every program you want the user account to have access to.

This task can be daunting. The best way to tackle it is to click the Check All button, which fills in every check box, and then comb the list for stuff you *don't* want the account to be able to run. If you work it the other way around (checking boxes you want to allow), you might miss something important and elementary (for example, the Windows Contacts program, Acrobat Reader, or WordPad) and inconvenience a user, who will have to seek permission to access restricted programs.

FIGURE 21.18

You can control access to programs in the Application Restrictions dialog box.

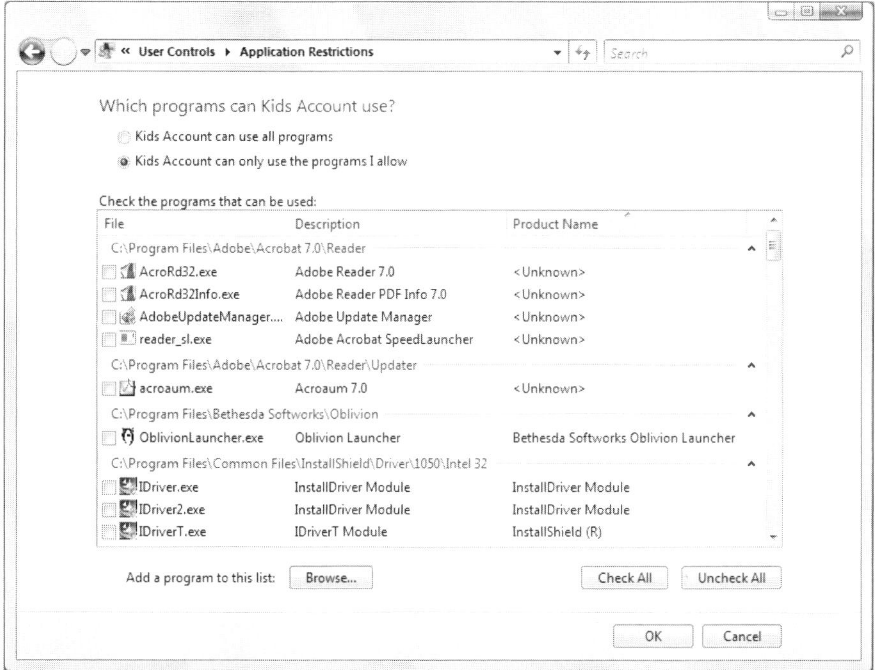

Parents, Be Informed

In the past decade or so, much has been said and published about how dangerous violent videogames might be to youngsters — or anyone, for that matter. The ESRB does its part to give parents the tools they need to know what kind of content that games contain, but parents need to be proactive and use this information if they wish to control what their children are getting into.

A few years ago, I did an investigative news piece about children's ability to purchase games rated M. I sent several children under age 13 to various stores with cash and had them buy copies of the latest version of a franchise known for its violence and sexual overtones. In virtually every case, the kids bought the games without question from the store clerks.

None of the store managers would comment on the record for the article.

Let's be realistic. If you're a parent, it's up to *you,* not the government or the stores, to determine what games your children play. The ESRB slaps a big rating on every game, along with content descriptors that indicate what kinds of possibly objectionable material the game might contain (violence, blood, gore, nudity, and so on).

There is no reason for a parent to buy a kid the game he wants, only to be startled when the parent sees that game on the six o'clock news being vilified by Joe Lieberman.

Parents: learn the ratings. Read the boxes. Do some research. And use the parental controls!

Summary

What's a computer without games? A boring, utilitarian appliance, if you ask me. Gaming is an essential part of the computer experience. Without games, a computer is no more fun than a refrigerator or a drill press. In fact, it's less fun than a drill press. Trust me.

Windows Vista Ultimate is ready to play games. It's loaded with the best version of DirectX to date; when games start to take advantage of it, the whole experience will change for the better. That's saying something, because gaming is already the ultimate way to waste time.

The Games folder is, basically, a repository for certain shortcuts. But it's more than that: It's a central location for launching, tweaking, and generally enjoying your games, and also for determining which games may run well on your PC thanks to the performance analysis score.

The Games folder is also one way to access Parental Controls. Some may view these controls as draconian censorship; I know that when I was 10 years old, I would' have been livid if my Commodore 64 had content locks that my parents put in place. As a parent of young children, however, I can appreciate the need for access restrictions. I can't always be sitting at their sides when they surf the Web or play games, so by enabling the Parental Controls I can rest assured that they won't find my copy of Quake 4 and scare themselves to death.

Chapter 22

Installing Games (and Other Programs)

IN THIS CHAPTER

- Installing Windows Vista games
- Installing older games
- Adding a game to the Games folder
- Installing other programs
- Adding and removing Windows Vista components

What's an operating system without software? Windows Vista Ultimate comes with a lot of stuff, to be sure. Without purchasing another software package you can edit video, track contacts and appointments, view and edit photos, listen to music, watch and create DVDs, and much more. In the end, however, it's an operating system, and the primary function of an OS is to act as an interface between you, your computer's parts, and the software you choose to install.

Vista being a Windows operating system, you can be sure that just about any software package made for the PC will come in a version that runs on your computer. That includes games, utilities, applications, and all manner of software; put simply, because the vast majority of the world's PCs run Windows, the vast majority of commercial software is designed for Windows.

Of course, Windows Vista is brand new. Because of that, it'll probably take a while before a whole ton of software comes out that takes full advantage of its features, or that requires Windows Vista to run. You'll still want to install games and other programs that were designed for earlier versions of Windows. Windows XP will still be in use — and supported by Microsoft — for years to come, and because it has a larger install base than Vista will have at first, expect a great deal of even brand-new software to support it as well as Vista.

With the exception of a percentage of hardware device drivers, most programs designed for Windows XP will work on Windows Vista. You may have to tweak the compatibility settings to get some "legacy" software to function properly (check out Chapter 25 for details). Most of the games and applications I've installed that have come out in the past year or so have worked fine without the need to tweak them, but there have been some stubborn titles that have needed a little help. Note also that really old, 16-bit software isn't supported under Windows Vista at all.

When you install games and other programs, the installation routines will suggest a location in the file system to which to install them. You can usually change the file location, and I tell you how in this chapter. They'll also install program folders into the Start Menu, and they may install desktop icons as well. Games designed for Windows Vista should install shortcuts to launch them right in the Games folder. Other games will use the traditional Start Menu, but you can add their shortcuts to the Games folder manually. You learn how to do that, too, in this chapter.

Installing a Game

Unless you waited for Windows Vista Ultimate to start your journey into the world of computer gaming, you probably have a few — if not stacks and stacks — of pre-Vista games that you would like to install. You might also have some newer games, released after Vista came along, that you'd also like to add to your hard drive. Doing either is a cinch.

Basically, installing a game follows the same routine that it did with Windows XP and earlier versions of Windows. In case it's a new procedure to you, I'll take you through the installation of a pre-Vista game: Human Head Studio's fantastic shooter, *Prey*.

Prey comes on three CD-ROMs or, if you happen to have a DVD-ROM version, on a single DVD. To start the installation, simply place the first CD-ROM or the sole DVD-ROM into the drive. Unless you've disabled it, the AutoPlay should fire up and show you the option window shown in Figure 22.1.

FIGURE 22.1

The option window, shown when AutoPlay detects new media

Note the check box option Always do this for software and games. Check it if you want AutoPlay to run the file associated with AutoPlay on any media you place in the optical drive. Then, click the option under Install or run program. The *Prey* AutoPlay launches, displaying the screen shown in Figure 22.2.

FIGURE 22.2

Choose a language here.

In this screen *Prey* prompts you to choose your language. The default is English. Click the drop-down menu and choose an alternative, if necessary, then click OK. The language selection box disappears, and you may then click Install on the *Prey* startup window. Next comes the ESRB advisory screen shown in Figure 22.3.

FIGURE 22.3

Are you old enough to play *Prey*?

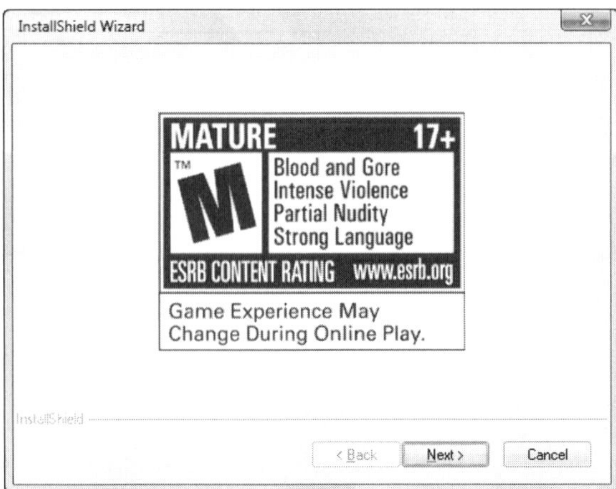

Click Next if you're at least 17 years old. If not, you should consider a more wholesome game like something in the *Reader Rabbit* series. What are you doing with a copy of *Prey* anyway?

CROSS-REF **For information about how to set Parental Controls in Vista, see Chapter 11.**

After you click Next, a screen like the one in Figure 22.4 welcomes you to the InstallShield Wizard. Click Next.

FIGURE 22.4

Welcome to this installation.

You then have to enter the CD key that came with the software (see Figure 22.5). It's located somewhere on the CD packaging or the documentation that came with the game. Enter it carefully; if you enter it incorrectly, the game will use your Internet connection to notify the FBI. Ha ha! Seriously, if you blow it the first time, you'll have to re-enter it correctly.

FIGURE 22.5

Enter your CD key in this screen.

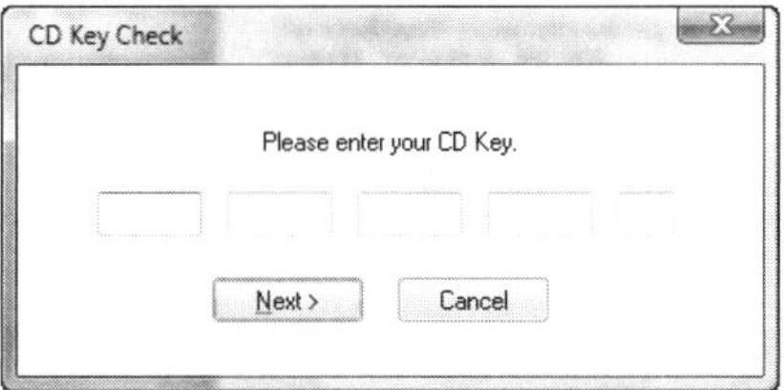

Click Next and then click OK on the notification that tells you not to share your CD key with anyone. Next up is the license agreement, which is shown in Figure 22.6.

Someone, somewhere, expects you to read this thing. It's a long document, written in legalese, which tells you how you're allowed to use the game. I've never read a license agreement in my life and I've never been arrested, but I don't pirate software. You shouldn't, either. When you're done with the license agreement, click the radio button signifying that you agree to its terms, and click Next.

FIGURE 22.6

Read the license agreement thoroughly....

The next couple of screens install an anti-cheating application called *PunkBuster* that's supposed to prevent people from being jerks during online play. Click Next on its intro page. A smaller dialog box then appears, asking whether you want to install it. It's up to you. I always do, because I hate cheaters. If you do install it, you'll have to accept another license agreement and click Next. The following window asks you where you want to install *Prey*, as shown in Figure 22.7.

FIGURE 22.7

Choose the folder in which you want to have *Prey* installed.

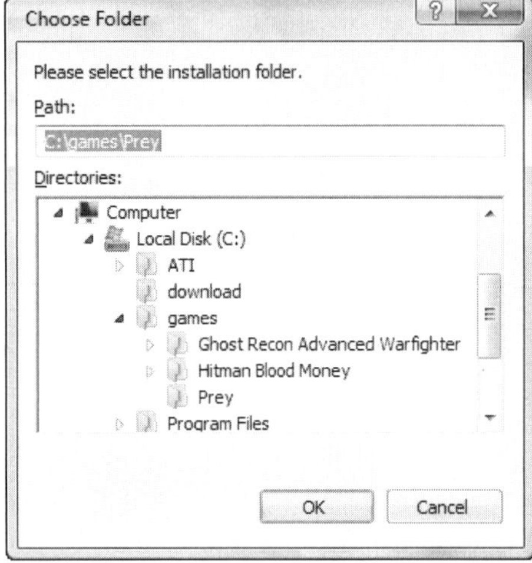

You can install *Prey* to the default installation folder shown (C:\Program Files\Prey), or choose a different folder. Click Next to accept the default, or Change to install it to a different folder. I like to create a folder called C:\Games and install my games in subfolders within. I click Change and navigate the file browser as shown in Figure 22.8.

I usually simply type in the path to which I want to install the game. For *Prey*, I'll use C:\Games\Prey. You either type in your chosen path or navigate with the mouse. When you've chosen a destination, click OK. The Choose Destination Window appears again, with the new path in place of the default (Figure 22.9).

NOTE *Prey* is a legacy game that would have installed to the C:\Program Files folder. Were I installing a Windows Vista specific game, I'd install to the default directory, as such games are designed specifically to take advantage of Windows Vista's organizational system.

FIGURE 22.8

Browse to a new destination.

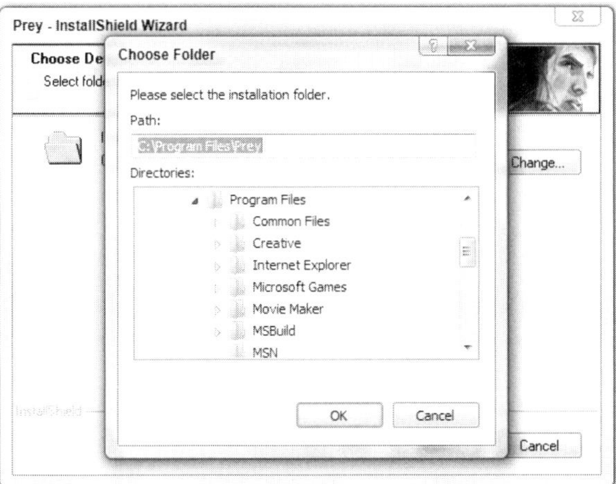

FIGURE 22.9

Prey's destination is set.

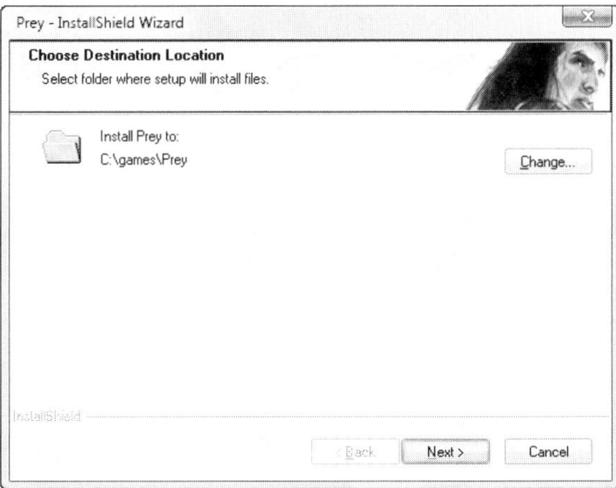

Click Next to view a useless page in the wizard that tells you it's ready to perform the installation. Note that, in Prey's case, it doesn't give you the chance to select a program folder, nor does it ask whether you want a desktop icon or not. It creates the program folder of its choice and a desktop icon, whether you want one or not. Click Install to proceed.

Filling Up the Hard Drive

One thing to watch out for when you're installing game after game is the amount of space remaining on your computer's hard drive. Today's games are massive. Microsoft Flight Simulator X is so big, it comes on two DVDs and takes up 15GB of hard drive space!

When you install a game, don't just go by the hard drive space requirement on the game box. Factor in the inevitable patches you'll have to download, which can run from a few to hundreds of megabytes; the extra space for game saves; mods for the game that you might wish to download and enjoy; and extra space. You should never let your hard drive get more than 80 to 90 percent full.

If you do, and the drive fragments (see the Appendix) you'll run into serious performance issues. A full and fragmented hard drive can cause everything to load more slowly, and if the computer doesn't have a ton of memory and uses its paging file often the slowdowns can even affect programs that are already open.

Here's another thought: never assume a hard drive is too big. When you're ready to upgrade a hard drive, get something downright cavernous. Get the highest capacity your wallet can muster. Games and other programs will continue to grow in size; what was yesterday's massive, unfillable hard drive is today's insufficient trifle of space.

The installation wizard then starts copying files while displaying a progress bar, as shown in Figure 22.10.

If your version came on multiple CD-ROMs, the installation will pause and ask you to insert the next CD. Do it, and click OK.

FIGURE 22.10

The installation progress bar

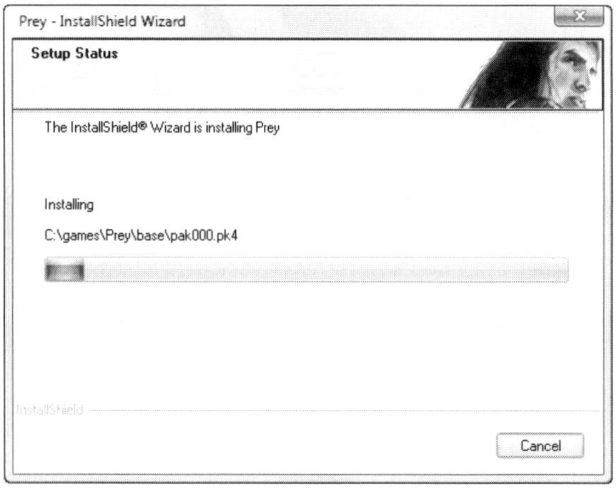

Finally, the wizard displays the dialog box shown in Figure 22.11. The installation is complete. *Prey* offers two check boxes: Display Game Notes and Launch Prey Now.

TIP I know what I said about the license agreement. In all seriousness, you should read the game notes (in other words, the readme file) that comes with *Prey* and any other game you install. It might contain anything from manual errata and known compatibility issues to hints on getting the game to play as smoothly as possible.

When you're done, click Finish. The installation is complete.

FIGURE 22.11

The installation of *Prey* is complete!

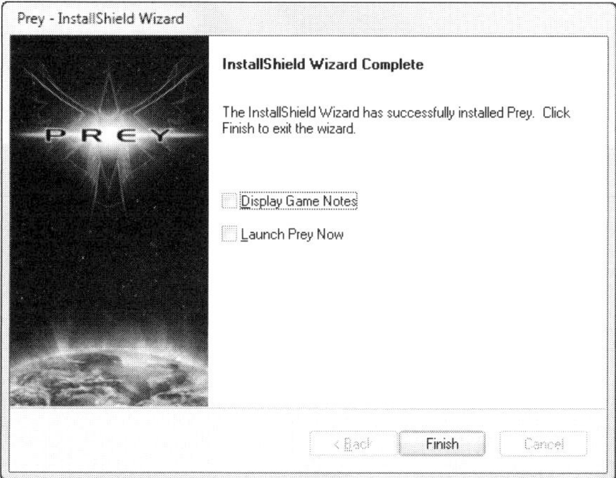

Adding a Game to the Games Folder

Games that weren't written specifically with Windows Vista in mind might not be aware of the Games folder. You might have to add their shortcuts to the Games folder manually. The process is simple; just follow this procedure:

1. **Click Start.**
2. **Click Games.** Your desktop should resemble the desktop shown in Figure 22.12.

FIGURE 22.12

The desktop with the Games folder open

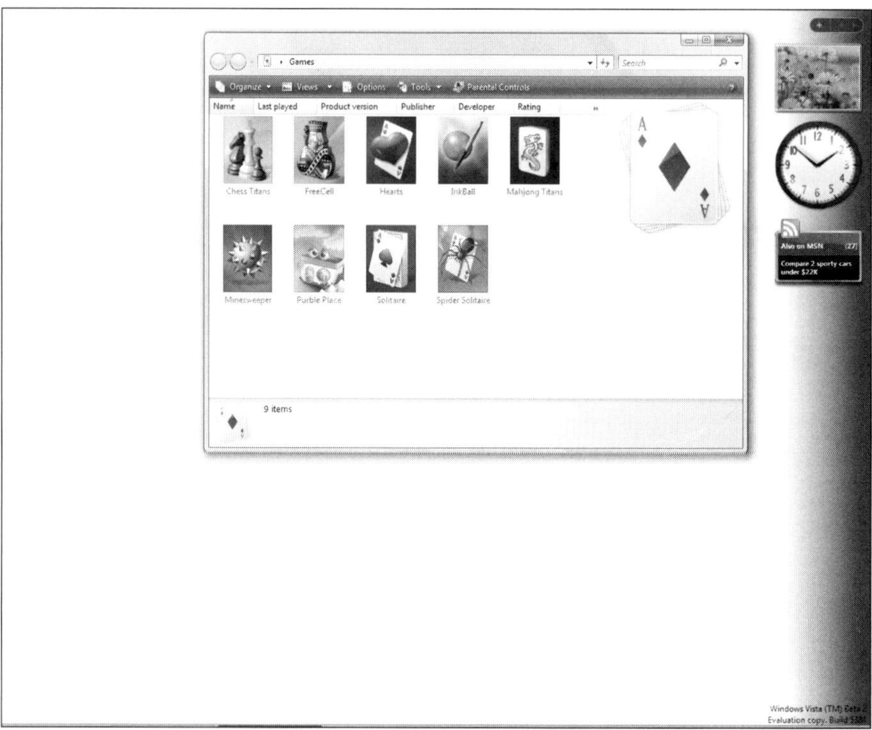

3. Click Start again.
4. Navigate to the program folder containing the game that you want to add to the Games folder; for example, **All Programs\Prey** (see Figure 22.13).

FIGURE 22.13

Navigate to the Start Menu.

5. **Drag the game launch icon from the Start Menu to the Games folder.** Windows copies the shortcut to the Games folder, as shown in Figure 22.14.

FIGURE 22.14

The game shortcut is now in the Games folder.

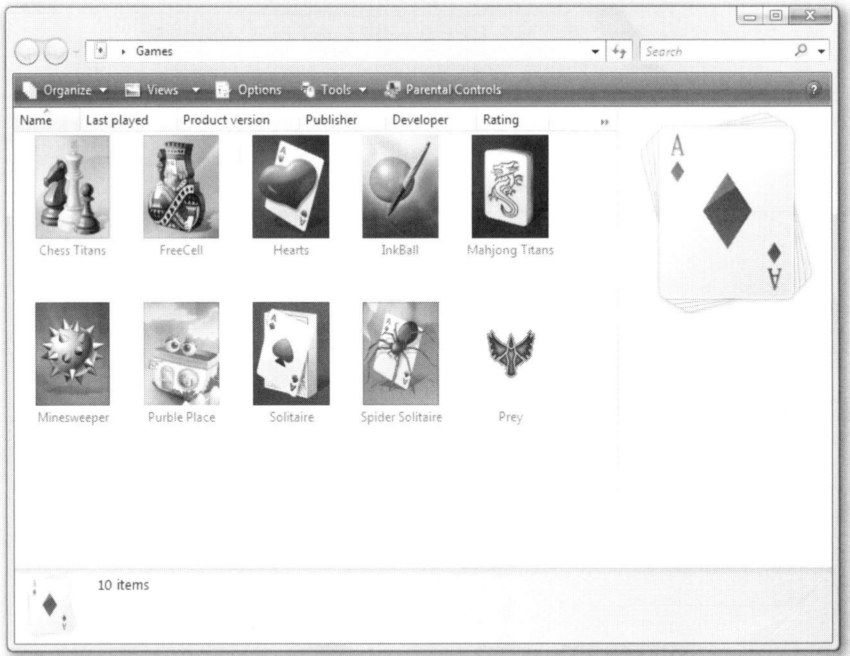

NOTE If the game doesn't report its Entertainment Software Rating Board (ESRB) rating and other information to Windows Vista, such data won't be available in the Games folder. You can use Parental Controls to block games individually and also to block any unrated games. See Chapter 11 for details. Note also that Microsoft plans to have over two thousand games fully rated so you won't have to worry about doing that.

Installing Other Programs

Installing other programs is very similar to installing games. You simply follow the steps in the installation wizard as it walks you through the process. Most programs, by default, prompt you to install them in a subfolder in the C:\Program Files folder, which is a good place for them. The installer might name the subfolder after the title of the program, the program's publisher, or the program's developer.

The installed programs will create program groups in the Start Menu, and they might create desktop icons.

If you don't want a program's icon on your desktop, simply right-click it and click Delete, or drag it into the recycle bin (if the recycle bin is on your desktop).

Turning Windows Features On or Off

Installing games and anything else from installation media is one thing; installing Windows Vista's native components is another. You never really install or uninstall Windows Vista components; you turn them on or off.

Windows Vista comes with a host of programs, applications, and features. You can selectively turn such features on or off as you please using Control Panel. Click Start ➪ Control Panel ➪ Programs, and finally, under Installed Programs, click Turn on or off Windows features. The dialog box shown in Figure 22.15 appears.

FIGURE 22.15

The Turn Windows features on or off dialog box

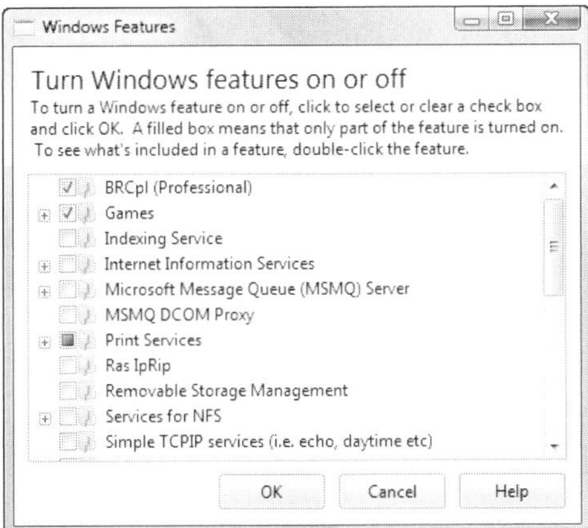

In older versions of Windows, this procedure was called Add/Remove Windows Components and was part of Control Panel's Add/Remove Programs applet.

You need administrative privileges to turn Windows features on or off.

To enable or disable features, simply scroll through this window. If you don't know what a feature does, you should probably leave it at its default. Features whose check marks are filled in are enabled; features without check marks are disabled.

For example, if you want to disable Windows Collaboration, scroll down until you see it listed (see Figure 22.16). Click to remove the check mark, and click OK.

A small window with a progress bar appears, as shown in Figure 22.17.

FIGURE 22.16

You can remove Windows Collaboration, if you want, by clearing its check box.

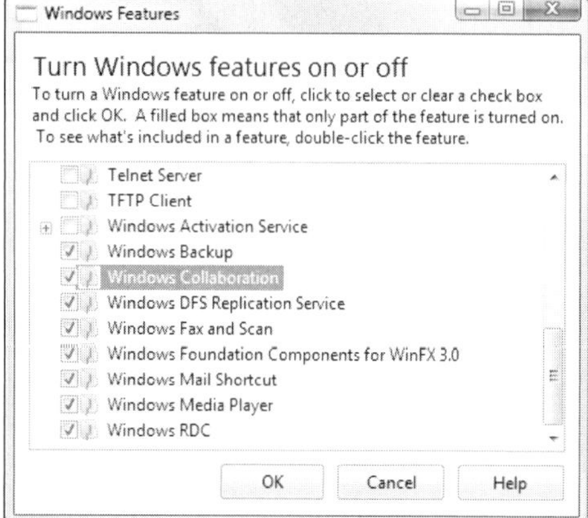

FIGURE 22.17

Windows has to think for a moment.

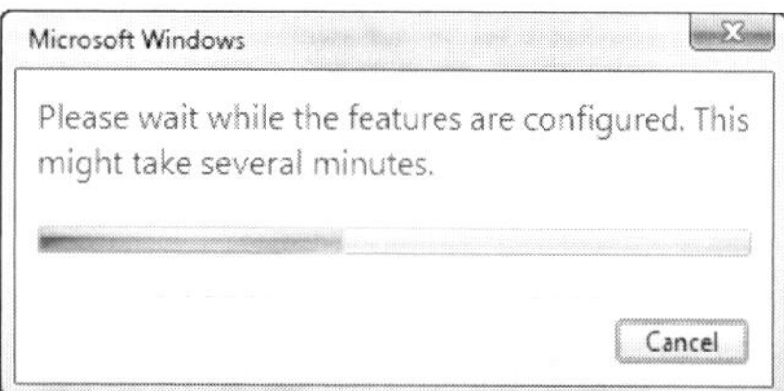

When the removal is done, the open dialog boxes disappear. You can now close Control Panel.

Summary

Installing games, or anything else for that matter, is really not a big deal. Even if you've never done it before, you'll find that all you basically do is pop in the installation media (a CD or DVD) and run through a wizard that prompts you every step of the way. The best wizards have the defaults all set for you so you can just keep clicking OK or Next or whatever and blast your way through.

Chapter 23

Optimizing Games for Performance and Visuals

IN THIS CHAPTER

Optimizing games

Understanding the need to optimize

Introducing game detail settings

Using the graphics card's control applet

Tips for optimizing games

I strongly prefer the gaming experience offered by a computer over a game console that you connect to a television. I live and die by my keyboard and mouse; those game pad things just don't pack the precision that I need. I can get user-created modules and play online without paying a premium for a special gaming network. I can do a million other things with my computer when I'm done playing. I'm a PC guy.

Console gaming does have one, distinct advantage over PC gaming, however. Console games are always optimized. They're built for a specific and never-changing set of hardware components. PC games are designed for a variable platform that could include any number of combinations of motherboard, CPU, graphics, audio, and networking hardware.

PC gamers have to take some extra time to make sure their games run as smoothly as possible, with the best-looking visuals the PC can handle. Computer gaming enthusiasts are always looking for balance between frame rates and beauty. That's especially true of gamers buying newer games with more feature-packed but demanding graphics engines and running them on older components. Not everyone has a system with a dual-core CPU and a pair of top-of-the-line ATI graphics cards in CrossFire mode.

Although optimizing Windows Vista itself is possible, you can also optimize individual games. Most of the settings you need are within the games' interfaces, but you can also make changes to the graphics card's own control applet.

CROSS-REF See Chapter 27 for more information on optimizing Windows Vista.

Optimizing games takes patience, time, and lots of experimentation. The good news is that it's a fantastic excuse to play a game for a long time. When I blow an afternoon playing Call of Duty 2, I can alleviate the guilt by convincing myself that I was *optimizing* it.

Why Optimize?

The trade-off between looks and performance is subjective. Some gamers want their games to run as quickly as possible, at the highest frame rates they can achieve. Others want realism; they'll happily sacrifice some performance for graphical splendor. Most of us, however, look for a healthy balance that includes some of both.

Modern games can look very pretty. Even the aging *Doom3* is a gorgeous game, and many current games are based upon its graphics engine. The most beautiful games use the latest graphical trickery, like intense programmable shaders for lighting, high-polygon models for realistic characters, massive textures for a crisp and realistic sheen, and so on.

Those nifty graphics come at a price. Unless a system is outfitted with the very latest and most powerful graphics hardware, games set at the peak of their visuals can bog down and run slowly. It's for that reason that graphics card control applets and games themselves offer options to tweak the visuals: Turn them up, and the game looks better but runs more slowly; turn them down and the game might not be as pretty but it will run smoothly.

Frame rates and playability

You might hear or read a lot of stuff about a game's frame rate. Console manufacturers boast that all of their games run at 60 fps (frames per second) or higher (although I've seen them slowed to a crawl in graphics-heavy sequences of certain titles, and that should *never* happen on a console).

So what's the big deal about 60 fps? The key concept here is *playability*. A game's frame rate determines not only how smoothly the animations take place, but also how responsive the game itself acts.

NOTE Like any animation, a game's motion is an illusion. Nothing on your screen really moves. That's true not only of gaming, but also of television and movies. One frame, or still picture, is shown, followed by another that's slightly different, then another, and on and on. When they're shown fast enough with small enough changes between one frame and the next, the viewer perceives fluid motion.

The graphics subsystem of your computer doesn't move stuff around. It draws frames. As it draws frames, it works with the CPU to interpret changes between one frame and the next based on the point of view of the player. In one frame, a rocket is coming toward you. It takes a few frames for you to react. You dodge. The rocket, getting larger as it gets closer, now moves off to the side as you scramble out of the way. It happens in two seconds; your computer may have animated 120 or more frames.

A game is considered playable at about 30 fps. Higher frame rates (more frames shown each second) are better, to a point. Higher frame rates cause you to perceive more fluidic, smoother motion, and the game seems to respond to your input more reliably. The sweet spot of frame rates is 60 fps. The differences between lower frame rates and 60 fps are easily perceptible, but seeing differences in animation above 60 fps becomes very difficult.

As the frame rate drops below 30 fps, the playability diminishes. The player starts to notice the lack of fluidity in the animation; the responsiveness seems to deteriorate. If the frame rate drops much below 20, you can start to see individual frames rather than motion.

Visuals and realism

Now let's turn to the other side of the equation. As you crank up a game's detail options, increasing things like texture detail, model detail, the display resolution, antialiasing, and so on, the game begins to look more realistic.

Realism can make a difference. The more realistic a game looks, the easier you can become immersed in its world as you play. When you can see details disappear in the distance or perceive individual polygons that make up a 3D structure, making yourself believe you're living in the game world is harder.

NOTE Not all games have to look realistic. Casual games, board games on the PC, and less graphical games like those included with Windows Vista don't necessarily need to look like real life. On the other hand, first-person games like *Oblivion* and *Call of Duty 2* should look as realistic as possible to make them more immersive.

Look at the difference. Figures 23.1 and 23.2 are screens from *The Elder Scrolls IV: Oblivion*. They show the same wooded scene. Figure 23.1 has its details set at "ultra-high quality." Figure 23.2 shows the game with its settings dialed down.

Which would you rather play? Details can make the difference between immersive gameplay and less enjoyable play. The goal of most gamers is to make the game as pretty as it can be while keeping the frame rate at a playable level.

FIGURE 23.1

Oblivion, with high detail levels

FIGURE 23.2

Oblivion, with much lower detail levels

In-Game Settings

The kind of games that punish your system's graphics equipment almost always have a host of options that let you optimize them in quite a number of ways. Every game is different, but a core set of options is available in almost every title.

NOTE In most cases, the performance options are contained within the game's actual interface. Sometimes, however, some or all of a game's options require you to set them before you launch the game. *Oblivion* is such a game; the options screen it offers before you actually launch the game is shown in Figure 23.3.

FIGURE 23.3

Some of *Oblivion's* options must be set before you launch the game proper.

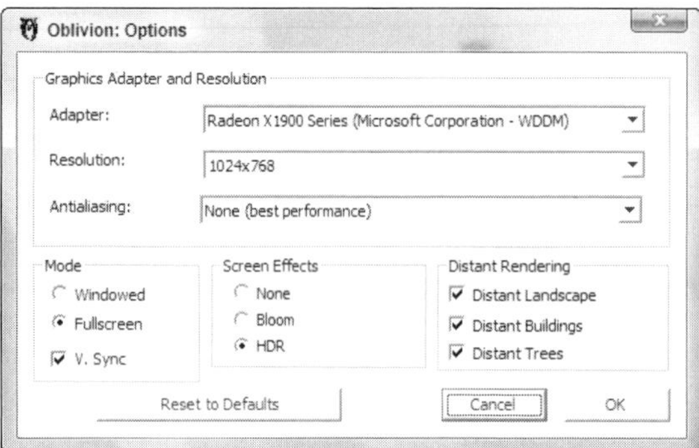

Now, let's take a trip through the options found in most games, using the phenomenal *Company of Heroes* (one of the first titles in the Microsoft's "Games for Windows" marketing campaign), published by THQ, as an example.

To tweak game options in most games, you first launch the game. Doing so is easy enough; just click Start ➪ Games, and then double-click the game's shortcut. Most games require the installation media (the CD or DVD that the game comes on) to be in the optical drive.

The game will probably display a bunch of developer and publisher logos, and possibly a cinematic sequence, before it gets to its main screen (Figure 23.4). Sometimes you can skip these screens by pressing Esc or Enter. When the game's main screen finally arrives, look around for an Options menu.

FIGURE 23.4

The *Company of Heroes* main screen

For some reason, games based on most Id Software game engines (the *Doom* and *Quake* series) hide their graphics options in a menu called "System."

The Options menu (Figure 23.5) in *Call of Duty 2* has a tab called Graphics. Click it to find the graphics options (Figure 23.6).

FIGURE 23.5

The *Company of Heroes'* Options menu

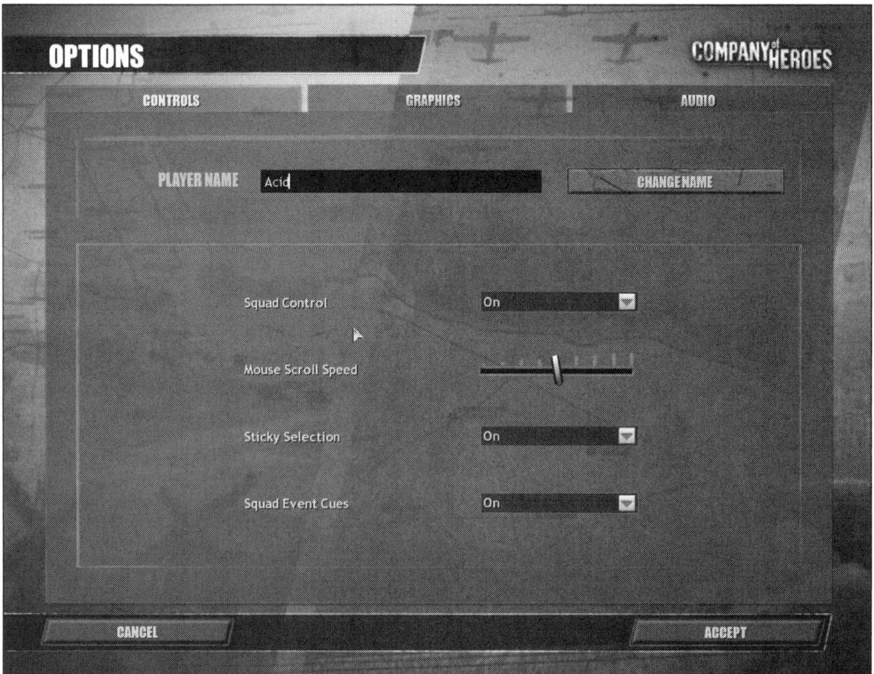

FIGURE 23.6

The *Company of Heroes* graphics options

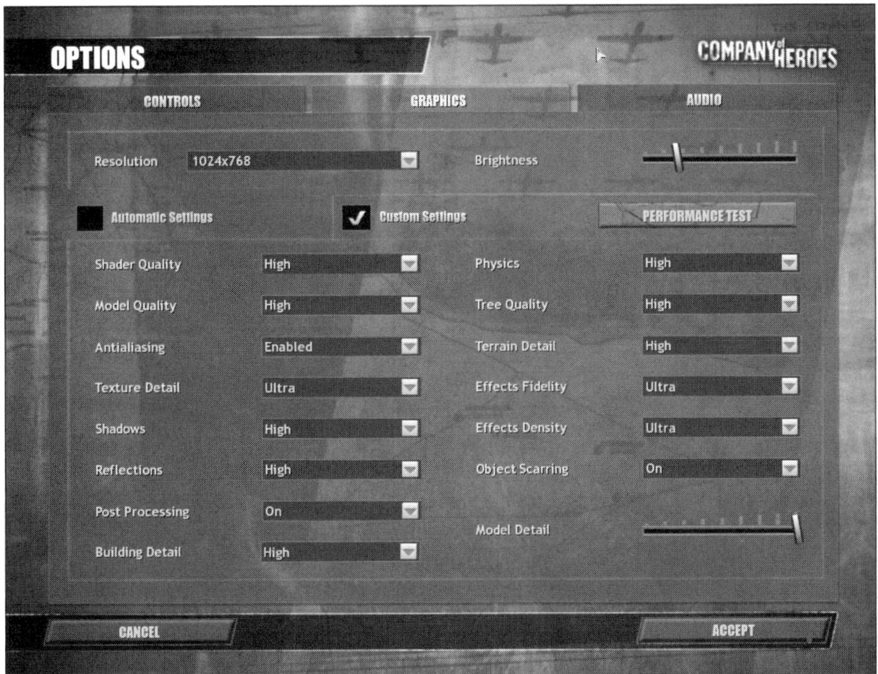

The graphics menu has more than 15 options. The following sections give you a rundown.

Resolution

The screen resolution determines how many pixels the game will cram onto the screen. Games look richer and more detailed at higher resolutions, but cranking up the pixel count degrades performance. I consider 1024x768 to be the minimum acceptable resolution, and depending on how powerful the graphics card is in the computer I'm playing on, I try to get it up to 1600x1200.

Shader Quality

Some games might ask which shader model you want to use (Shader Model 2, Shader Model 3, and so on). The shader model is part of Direct3D, and it indicates how sophisticated the lighting effects can be. The later the version, the more realistic the lighting. Be sure your graphics card can handle the shader model you choose.

In *Company of Heroes*, the Shader Quality option only includes Low and High. High results in better lighting effects, but hurts game performance.

Antialiasing

Antialiasing smoothes out jagged edges of textures and polygons, giving the game a more lifelike look. *Company of Heroes* only allows you to turn it on or off (and turning it on can hamper performance). Some games allow different levels of antialiasing, which indicate the number of samples the antialiasing engine takes to reduce "jaggies" while preserving image integrity.

Antialiasing levels are usually notated with an *x*. 2x antialiasing uses two samples; 8x uses eight. When you elect to force the system's GPU to crunch more samples, expect performance to drop proportionately.

Check out Figures 23.7 and 23.8 for the difference antialiasing makes in game visuals.

FIGURE 23.7

A *Company of Heroes* screen with antialiasing off...

FIGURE 23.8

...and with antialiasing on. Look at the flagpole and the ropes hanging from it.

Texture detail

Textures are the art applied to polygons to make them look solid and realistic. Detailed textures — those with higher resolutions — require lots of memory on your system's graphics card.

Company of Heroes has four detail settings, from Low to Ultra. If your graphics card has lots of memory, you won't notice a major performance hit by cranking it up.

Compare the image in Figure 23.9 to that in the last couple of figures. Figures 23.7 and 23.8 were taken at Ultra texture detail, and Figure 23.9 at Low. Look at the ground, and at the face of the building, for the most dramatic differences.

FIGURE 23.9

Company of Heroes with low texture detail.

Shadows and Reflections

The Shadows and Reflections effects affect the realism by a surprising amount. Realistic shadows and realistic reflections both require graphics muscle, but they also make the game look so much more believable.

Company of Heroes has both options, and each has multiple levels. You can set shadows to high, medium, low, or off, and reflections to high or low.

Building, model, and terrain detail

Most games contain detail-level options for a number of onscreen elements. *Company of Heroes* offers control over the detail bestowed upon buildings, character models, and terrain. You control building and terrain detail levels via multiple options in pull-down menus, and you control model detail with a slider.

Check out Figures 23.10 and 23.11. In the former, all three detail levels are set to their highest. In the latter, I've turned the model detail down all the way. Look at the soldier; he appears more blurry and less defined in Figure 23.11.

FIGURE 23.10

Models with maximum detail...

FIGURE 23.11

...versus those with minimum detail.

Visual effects quality

Two options control the quality of visual effects like explosions and other pyrotechnics. The Effects Fidelity control affects how much detail goes into each special effect, while the Effects Density controls the number of particles stuffed into each effect.

Both make the game look better at Ultra or High quality, but the game runs better if they're set to Medium or Low quality.

Texture filtering

Although you don't see it in *Company of Heroes'* graphics options screen, another option that many games offer is texture filtering. Texture filtering is intended to smooth textures, which otherwise might appear pixilated. Games typically offer options of bilinear, trilinear, and various levels of anisotropic filtering.

Bilinear filtering is the simplest and least GPU-demanding of the three types of filtering but it doesn't account for depth. *Trilinear* does to some extent, and it looks better than bilinear filtering, but anisotropic filtering is superior. *Anisotropic* filtering uses sample methodology similar to that of antialiasing, and it's more demanding of the PC's graphics subsystem than the other filtering methods.

You can often set the anisotropic filtering level from 2x (two samples, the lowest quality) to 16x (the highest quality). Higher-quality anisotropic filtering settings result in more realistic-looking textures, especially those on 3D objects that stretch off into the distance.

Examples of Game-Specific Tweaks

Most of the aforementioned options are common to a great deal of games. However some games, *Company of Heroes* being one, have visual quality options specific to their own graphics engines. You may have noticed in Figure 23.6 some such options. They include things like Physics, Tree Quality, Post Processing, and Object Scarring. Following are the effects of tweaking such options, which again are specific to *Company of Heroes*; don't expect to find them in every game you encounter!

Physics

It's hard to see the effects of changing physics options in screen shots. Suffice it to say, physics options affect how well physical mechanics are applied to various objects in the game world. For example, when something blows up next to, say, a stack of barrels, the Physics option will tweak how realistically the barrel stack collapses and how convincingly the barrels bounce and roll about. The higher settings require more power, not from the graphics card but from the system's CPU and the memory subsystems.

Tree Quality

This setting affects just what it says: the visual quality of the various trees rendered throughout the game world. More detailed trees require more powerful graphics cards.

Figure 23.12 shows a tree with the Tree Quality setting set to low. Meanwhile, Figure 23.13 shows the same tree with the quality set to high. Notice that the tree looks a bit more realistic in the second figure; the leaves, especially, are more lifelike. It's easier to see when the game is in motion than it is to see in black and white screen shots.

FIGURE 23.12

A tree with Tree Quality set to low

FIGURE 23.13

A tree with Tree Quality set to high

Post Processing

Post Processing deals with shader quality; in other words, how realistic the lighting looks in a given scene. Enabling post processing gives the lighting and shading of a 3D game like *Company of Heroes* a more realistic tilt, but it requires graphics hardware capable of high-end shading and also diminishes game performance.

Figure 23.14 shows a scene with Post Processing set to off. Figure 23.15 shows the same scene with Post Processing turned on. Again, it's easier to see in a game in motion, but the latter screen shows a more realistic-looking building with more convincing shading.

FIGURE 23.14

Post Processing is turned off in this screen.

FIGURE 23.15

In this screen, Post Processing is turned on.

Object Scarring

In some games, objects can show damage from explosions, gunfire, and other forms of abuse. *Company of Heroes* uses this to make war-torn France look that much more realistic. With Object Scarring turned on, the graphics engine can add damage textures to various 3D objects within the game. With it turned off, objects don't look damaged until they're completely destroyed.

Figure 23.16 and 23.17 show the same structure after it's been hit by an antitank weapon. In the former shot, Object Scarring is turned off and the building looks unscathed; in the latter, with Object Scarring on, it shows some signs of damage (notice the broken boards).

Minor differences like these add up in two ways. On the positive side, enabling higher-quality graphics makes the game world more lifelike and enveloping; on the negative side, higher quality taxes the graphics subsystem more and can negatively affect the game's performance.

FIGURE 23.16

This base structure has taken damage, but you can't tell.

FIGURE 23.17

Now that Object Scarring is turned on, the structure looks damaged.

Graphics Card Settings

Just as specific games have their own graphics settings, graphics cards have settings for their 3D acceleration capabilities that give you some global control of how they animate games.

NOTE My system is fitted with an ATI Radeon X1900 series graphics card, and I'm using beta drivers, so the things you see in this part of this chapter might look different on your system: Your system might not have an ATI card, or the control applet included with the final Vista drivers may look different.

Currently, the best way to invoke my graphics card's settings applet is to double-click the icon in the System Notification Area, if there is one. Otherwise, click Start ➪ All Programs ➪ Catalyst Control Center, and launch it from there.

Figure 23.18 shows the main page of ATI's graphics card control applet, CATALYST Control Center.

FIGURE 23.18

A graphics card control applet — ATI's CATALYST Control Center

This little application gives you big control over a graphics card. Notice the menu on the left of the window — it allows you to navigate to different areas of the control center.

For gaming options, zero in on the menu item called 3D. Clicking the + sign next to it reveals a submenu as shown in Figure 23.19.

FIGURE 23.19

Catalyst Control Center with the 3D submenu expanded

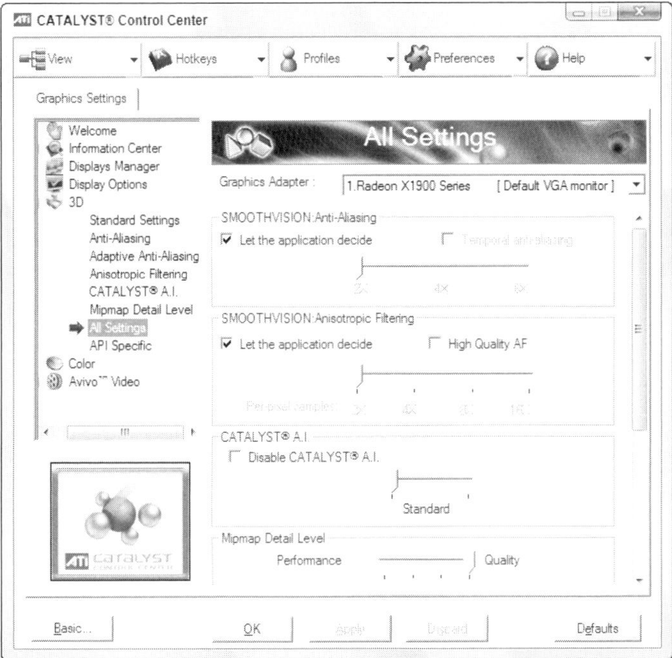

Clicking All Settings in the submenu fills the main window with all the options available for 3D performance and quality. Such a beast is shown in Figure 23.20.

FIGURE 23.20

Catalyst Control Center with all 3D options displayed

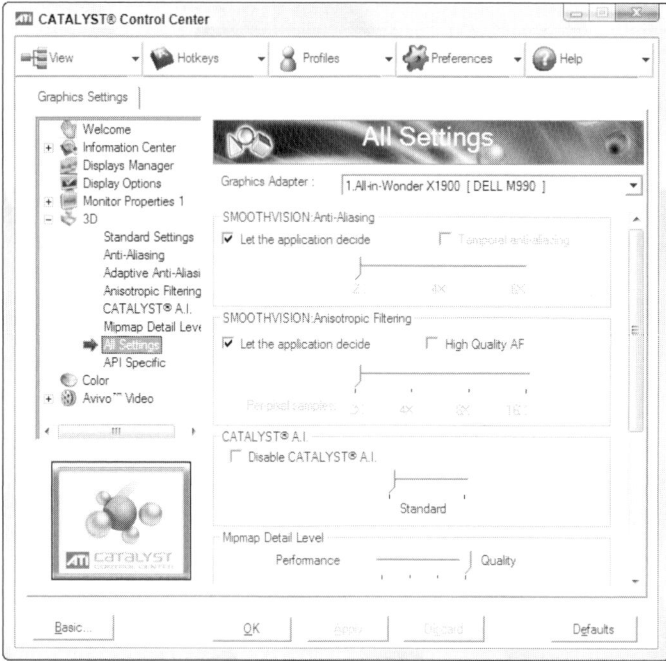

The first two menu items handle antialiasing and anisotropic filtering. Each of these two items has an option to allow 3D applications to control its feature. Although many games allow you to control these items within the games' own options menu, you can force them (in other words, override the game's settings) here.

Force the options by sliding the slider to the levels of antialiasing and anisotropic filtering you desire. Antialiasing can use two, four, or six samples; anisotropic filtering uses samples in increments from 2 to 16.

NOTE Note the other check box options. They are brand-specific options; other GPU makers' driver applets might not offer them. For example, if you have an Nvidia-based graphics, card, it'll have features specific to Nvidia and lack ATI-specific features.

Other antialiasing and anisotropic filtering options include Temporal antialiasing (which improves visual quality by changing sample patterns every other frame) and High Quality Anisotropic Filtering (which uses a better filtering method, but may impact performance).

Other items in the options menu that aren't brand-specific include the option to synchronize a game's frame rate with the monitor's vertical refresh rate (but only if the former would be faster than the latter). This option is often referred to as VSYNC. If game frame rates creep higher than the monitor's refresh rate, graphical glitches might appear. Many games offer control over VSYNC, but you can force it on or off here.

You can also adjust the amount of MIP mapping that a 3D engine uses. MIP maps are collections of textures for the same object; as the object moves farther from the player's point of view, a less-detailed texture is applied to it than if it were close. Tweaking this setting affects MIP mapping for quality or performance.

Getting Games to Look Good and Run Well

Optimizing a game takes patience. You're looking for the perfect mesh of good looks and great performance, and finding it can take a while.

The performance and visual quality you can achieve depends largely on the prowess of your computer's hardware. The guy whose PC has a dual-core CPU and a pair of graphics cards working in SLI mode will have a better time of it than someone using aging equipment. If your system meets the minimum or, preferably, the recommended system specifications of a game, however, you will find balance.

When you're trying to find the sweet spot between looks and frame rates, bear these hints in mind:

- **Close every program you don't absolutely need running.** Get rid of instant messaging clients, e-mail readers, and browsers. You might even shut down or disable antivirus software while the game is running (be sure to turn it back on when you're done gaming, or take advantage of your AV software's ability to shut down for a given amount of time if that option is available).
- **Experiment.** Start by setting the game's options to the graphics levels you desire, and if the game runs slowly or unresponsively back off one item at a time.
- **Prioritize.** Pick the options you really feel strongly about. I, for example, don't mind running a game at a lower resolution if I can eliminate jaggies through antialiasing. I hate jaggies; I'll turn down model and texture detail before I turn off antialiasing. On the other hand, I have yet to be impressed with shadows in consumer-level 3D computer graphics, so I don't mind turning them down. Experiment with various detail settings and decide which features you like the most.
- **Override.** If a game doesn't offer antialiasing but you feel the same way I do about jaggies, force antialiasing through the graphics card's control applet. On the other hand, if you could care less about smooth MIP mapping transitions, turn the anisotropic filtering down to save performance.
- **Upgrade.** Who would upgrade a computer just to play a new game with better detail levels? Me. You might consider it, too. A more powerful graphics card or a boost in system memory will enhance all of your games, not only new ones.

- **Read.** Check out game readme files for hints, go to game Web sites and forums, and research specific games to see what the developers suggest and what other gamers have done to achieve optimal looks and performance.
- **Compromise.** How I hate that word. I want *all* of my games to run at 60 fps at the highest detail setting, but that's just not going to happen unless I spend another thousand bucks on my computer. I have no choice but to compromise — but I would rather a game look good at 30 fps than look dull at 60 fps.

Summary

Those console kids have it made. They get to pop in a new game, grab a controller and play.

I would love to experience that, but the vast majority of console games fail to appeal to me, and those that do are usually better controlled with my computer equipment. I own a $90 mouse, and I know how to use it.

Therefore, I spend time optimizing my games. When I acquire a new game, after I install it I spend no less than ten minutes, and often a half hour or more, just getting the settings to where I feel I'm getting the best graphical experience at a playable frame rate.

I do that by delving into the game's options menu and sniffing out the graphics options screen. Then I experiment with resolution, filtering, model details, texture details, and a whole bunch of other stuff. I play for a while between each configuration change I make to see whether I've caused the game to drop to an unplayable frame rate or to become too ugly to bother with.

I've become an expert in wrenching the graphics card's 3D settings to my liking, and to tweaking everything in sight just to squeeze a few extra frames into each second of play. When I finally get a game to look its best and play with grace, I can proudly display my end result. Those console gamers have nothing on my games.

Chapter 24

Game Options, Conventions, Controllers, and Updates

IN THIS CHAPTER

Keeping your games up to date

Setting up game controllers

Launching games

Setting in-game options

Understanding game conventions

Something's gone horribly wrong.

Scientists are missing, and others are reporting nigh-impossible occurrences. Nightmare creatures are appearing out of thin air; humans are transforming into demonic beings right before the eyes of their colleagues; once-sterile walls are crawling with some sort of fleshy, organic material. As you approach the facility in the space-based troop transport, you check your pulse rifle and your plasma blaster: locked and loaded. Nothing's going on there that the Marines can't sort out — their own way....

The last time you saw the citadel, it was being racked by explosions. The resulting tremors were shaking it apart. Somehow, you wake up on the ground, terra firma, but you're not out of danger. The earth cracks and opens up below your feet as frightened soldiers, once your enemies but now barely noticing you, flee. You hear something about an antimatter buildup, and you realize what you must do. Grabbing your gravity gun, you rush *toward* the tower to stop the reaction before it destroys your world....

The Nazi soldiers have retreated across the two bridges that divide the town, but they haven't given up. Once their reinforcements arrive, they'll push back, and you have only precious moments to prepare to defend what's left of the church where you set up your forward command post. Your engineers scramble to set up sandbags, tank traps, mines, and other defenses that will slow, but not stop, the German counterattack. Calling in squads of riflemen, antitank gunners, and heavy weapons teams as quickly as you can, you try to fortify the ruins around you. Where are those Shermans that the colonel promised would be here an hour ago? You won't stand a chance without them....

Tense situations should be relegated to the games themselves, not to setting up and maintaining your computer so you can play them. Windows Vista Ultimate is designed to eliminate the frustrations that plague computer gamers, and drive some gamers to switch to consoles. Console games may pale in comparison to PC games in terms of depth and functionality, but they *just work*. You pop the disc in and it goes.

With Windows Vista, PC gaming is closer than ever to being as simple as it is on consoles. Setting up controllers is a breeze; keeping games up to date with the latest patches and enhancements is simple.

But even though the setup is simple, if you're new to computer gaming you might find yourself a little bit lost by the conventions that so many PC gamers have come to take for granted. Though you'll find similarities between consoles and PCs (even many of the same games are ported to both platforms), PC gaming is significantly different from TV gaming. Most of it is done without a gamepad; PC gamers prefer keyboards and mice. Some genres in PC gaming are rare in the console world, like real-time strategy games and adventure games. You can find a lack of some common console genres on the PC, too: Not nearly as many racing games or platform games are on the PC as are on consoles. Don't worry; getting used to playing with a keyboard and mouse, after being accustomed to twiddling your thumbs on dual-analog controllers, is easier than you may think.

This chapter introduces all kinds of game-related stuff: using game controllers, launching games in Windows Vista, keeping games up to date, and more!

PC Gaming 101

With the growing crossover between the PC and console gaming markets, most people, even casual and non-gamers, have at least heard of some of the major PC franchises. The *DOOM* games, for example, were made infamous by congressional witch hunts into game violence; later, the release of *DOOM 3*, shown in Figure 24.1, spawned a really bad movie starring "The Rock." *Half-Life* and *Half-Life 2* are massively popular among computer gamers, because it offers some of the most engaging, story-driven gameplay ever. *Call of Duty*, shown in Figure 24.2, originally a PC franchise, has crossed over into the console realm with amazing success.

FIGURE 24.1

DOOM 3

FIGURE 24.2

Call of Duty 2

Other games and franchises may not be as well known, but they are nevertheless shaping gaming even as we speak. The phenomenal *Company of Heroes*, shown in Figure 24.3, is garnering massive critical acclaim as I write this book. The *Battlefield* series, complete with the recent release of *Battlefield 2142* (Figure 24.4), is an excellent example of how multiplayer gaming can reach tremendous heights.

FIGURE 24.3

Company of Heroes

FIGURE 24.4

Battlefield 2142

Other games have smaller, cult followings, as happened with the recent rebirth of *Sam & Max*, shown in Figure 24.5. *Sam & Max* is an adventure game whose beloved characters haven't been seen in game form since the mid-1990s. *Psychonauts*, a platformer, despite disappointing sales, made huge fans out of PC and console gamers alike.

FIGURE 24.5

Sam & Max: Episode 1 "Culture Shock"

The prevailing genres

PC games come in a variety of genres, but most of them fall into two categories: first-person shooters (Figure 24.6) and subgenres like first-person stealth games or first-person role-playing games, and real-time strategy games (Figure 24.7). That's not to say that there aren't plenty of other game types; it's just that these two garner the most coverage and seem to spawn the largest number of games.

FIGURE 24.6

Half-Life 2 is an example of a first-person shooter.

A third, popular genre is the massively multiplayer online role-playing game (MMORPG), an example of which is shown in Figure 24.8. While local content is stored on your hard drive, you play the game on servers shared by hundreds if not thousands of other players. The servers represent persistent worlds, complete with cooperative multiplayer against computer-controlled bad guys and player-versus-player combat. Some such games are played from a first-person perspective, whereas others feature a top-down perspective in which you view the game world from above.

FIGURE 24.7

Dawn of War: Dark Crusade is a popular real-time strategy game.

NOTE Offline role-playing games are popular, too. Most currently take the form of first-person games, but you can still find a few top-down versions.

FIGURE 24.8

Guild Wars is a wildly successful MMORPG.

Whatever happened to...

Some genres that were once extremely prevalent have all but vanished. They're still represented by a handful of games that come out each year, but where they were dominant in gaming days gone by, they now cater to small groups of die-hard fans.

Flight sims

Simulations of airplanes, both civilian and military, were once among the most common games on the store shelves. Companies would actually fight over the rights to build games based on certain planes in use by the U.S. Air Force (Figure 24.9) and the U.S. Navy. Now, the release of a new flight sim is a rare and wonderful occurrence.

FIGURE 24.9

An oldie but goodie: *Jane's USAF*

The only franchise that consistently does well commercially, in terms of sales and popularity, is the *Flight Sim* series from Microsoft. Older flight sims, like *Falcon 4.0*, continue to maintain their popularity even as they age (in fact, an update of *Falcon 4.0* called *TK* was released in 2006), but no new flight sim franchises have cropped up in recent years.

Turn-based war games

There used to be a time when simulations of historical battles and campaigns, as well as sims of theoretical engagements and future-themed wars, were hugely popular. Games for 8-bit computers like *Gettysburg: The Turning Point* and *Battles of Napoleon* kept gamers riveted for hours on end. Those slow-paced titles didn't sit well with younger gamers, however, and real-time strategies have gradually edged them out.

Racing games

I remember when every company that made game controllers was tripping over itself to release driving wheel controllers. Racing games were popular on the PC back in the mid-1990s. These days, the release of a new title (Figure 24.10) is a rare occasion.

FIGURE 24.10

GTI Racing is a rare, modern racing game.

Platform games

Still popular with the consoles, platform games (Figure 24.11) don't happen very often on PCs. Seeing a popular character like Mario, Sonic, or some other console mainstay show up on a Windows machine is rare.

FIGURE 24.11

Psychonauts is a highly underrated platform game.

Adventure games

Adventure games, like *Sam & Max* (shown in Figure 24.12), used to be huge. Puzzle-based head scratchers like *Myst* revolutionized PC gaming back in the early 1990s. The premise was always simple: Visit a game area, click on things to find out more about them or to pick stuff up, and use the objects that you find to solve puzzles. LucasArts, especially, was known for some adventure gaming classics, such as *Grim Fandango* and *Full Throttle*.

FIGURE 24.12

Sam & Max is one of the few modern adventure games.

NOTE All those genres mentioned above still don't account for every single computer game on the market. Some games will always exist that defy classification, like *The Sims* (a virtual dollhouse or a god game?), *Civilization 4* (turn-based strategy, war game, or god game?) and *Grand Theft Auto* (a driving game, or simply a thug simulator?). The PC is an open-ended platform that creative developers can use to really build just about any game type you can think of, and some that nobody has imagined yet.

The necessity of patches and updates

Like Windows Vista itself, most commercial games are built of hundreds of thousands of lines of code. Although programmers do their very best to make sure your games run smoothly and efficiently, are compatible with your hardware, and are free of glitches, they're not always successful.

Most games are subject to several updates, or patches, throughout their lifetimes. Patches do anything from fixing bugs to updating compatibility and improving game performance. Some updates even contain new content for their games, including new levels or maps to play on and new character models or skins to enjoy.

Keep your games up to date. Check the developers' and publishers' sites often for news of patches and updates. Keeping your games current enhances your enjoyment of your titles and also ensures compatibility when you want to play online.

The mouse and keyboard as game controllers

Some console players can't believe it, but most PC gamers don't have gamepads. Instead, they use the controllers that God bestowed upon all worthy computers: mice and keyboards.

Just because office workers and other boring people slave over their mice and keyboards to crunch their never-ending spreadsheets doesn't mean that they're not ideal controllers for games. In fact, several makers of such input hardware cater to gamers with high-precision mice and specially designed keyboards especially for playing games.

TIP **You can play entire sessions of some games without even touching the keyboard! Real-time strategies, turn-based strategies, and some other genres lend themselves to mouse-only control schemes. For example, when I play *Company of Heroes,* I rarely if ever use the keyboard for anything. The same goes with oddball games like *DEFCON* and *Rag Doll Kung Fu,* and some MMORPGs like *Guild Wars.* Although you *can* use the keyboard to supplement your gameplay (for example, by using keyboard shortcuts for choosing units or casting spells) you don't always have to. In fact, the truly competitive players use keyboard shortcuts all the time, because they're much faster than using the mouse alone.**

In a typical first-person shooter (FPS) game, you look around and steer using the mouse. You fire your weapons with the mouse buttons, and you use the keyboard for everything else (choosing weapons, moving around, talking to your teammates, and so on).

In a typical real-time strategy (RTS) game, you use the mouse to select units, move around the map, give orders, and so on. The keyboard is handy for creating groups of units and using shortcuts to navigate to various areas like your headquarters or battle scenes.

When other controllers are needed

Sometimes, however, you will want to use a special controller. Some parts manufacturers cater to FPS players by creating special command pads that incorporate the keys most used in that genre.

Other genres demand special controllers. For example, getting your money's worth out of a flight sim without using a joystick is almost impossible. A gamepad is necessary for some action games, especially console ports. If you're into the rare driving game, you won't get more enjoyment out of it than by using a well-designed driving wheel.

The downside of joysticks and driving wheels is that they force you to make more room on your desk or displace your keyboard entirely. That's a small price to pay for the level of immersion and realism well-designed controllers bring to the gaming experience, though.

NOTE Some trends just aren't welcome at all. Case in point: the oddball controller. Throughout the 1990s, controller companies tried to capitalize on the popularity of certain genres, especially FPS games, by creating bizarre controllers that supposedly enhanced your game. These included the SpaceOrb and the dreadful FragMaster.

Unfortunately, such controllers usually came with incredibly difficult learning curves. They just weren't natural. You had to manipulate some sort of joystick bastardization, like a two-handed grip or a goofy ball attached to a gamepad-like device. Rather than enhance a gamer's experience and increase his precision, they tended to induce incredible amounts of frustration and weren't worth the plastic they were made of.

Until command pads started to arrive to market just a year or two ago, FPS controllers were junk. The best players used mice and keyboards (fittingly enough, command pads are simply extensions of keyboards anyway).

Keeping Games Up to Date

Updating games is essential. Most commercial games are massive works of programming, and the work is done by large teams of producers, developers, programmers, level designers, scripters, artists, and playtesters. Although they do their best to create stable and highly playable games, things do go wrong.

Why update?

Games almost always ship with a few imperfections, some more than others. Even though few games actually make it to store shelves completely broken (like the notorious *Battlecruiser 3000 A.D.*, which was so buggy that it, and its creator Derek Smart, gained an impressive amount of notoriety), few games actually make it to market with no bugs at all.

Games, like Windows Vista, are designed to run on a PC that may be comprised of literally thousands of different parts. Computers contain motherboards, CPUs, graphics cards, sound cards, networking equipment, storage, and more, and all that stuff is made by a whole bunch of different manufacturers. It would be virtually impossible for game testers to test their games on virtually every combination of hardware that can combine to make a PC. Throw in different versions of the hardware device drivers, different versions of Microsoft's DirectX multimedia library, and all the little programs that might be running in the background when someone plays a game, and you have a vast cauldron of hardware and code soup that can cause all kinds of unexpected problems.

For example, a graphics card from manufacturer A might contain a chipset from manufacturer B. Its drivers might work well with most games, but it might cause weird graphics corruption on a particular game. Maybe the problem only happens on a computer that also has a motherboard designed by manufacturer C, with a chipset from company D, and a CPU that came from chipmaker E — and all that when used with an antivirus utility from software company F running in the background.

Game developers try to track down all kinds of problems that crop up when their software is released into the wild, as well as errors that playtesters didn't catch, and they subsequently release patches to fix such maladies.

Furthermore, lots of game updates contain new features and even new content. After a game is released, players might clamor for some interface feature that the developers hadn't thought of. A subsequent patch might make it happen. Another update might contain eight new multiplayer maps along with code and feature fixes.

Patches and updates are freely released enhancements to your games. You have no reason not to download and install them as they come out. In some cases, you have no choice; for example, when a patch for a popular multiplayer game hits the Internet, you might not be able to play on patched servers with an unpatched client.

How to update

The key to knowing when to update is awareness. You should check gaming news sites such as Blue's News (`www.bluesnews.com`), 1UP (`www.1up.com`), and others, and also check the game publisher's Web site for news of upcoming or recently released patches.

NOTE Some games have their own built-in patch systems. For example, *Company of Heroes'* autorun screen, shown in Figure 24.13, has a button labeled Check for Updates. When you click it, your browser launches to a site that shows you the latest updates for the game (Figure 24.14). You can then download and install them.

FIGURE 24.13

Note the Check for Update button.

FIGURE 24.14

Company of Heroes needs a patch!

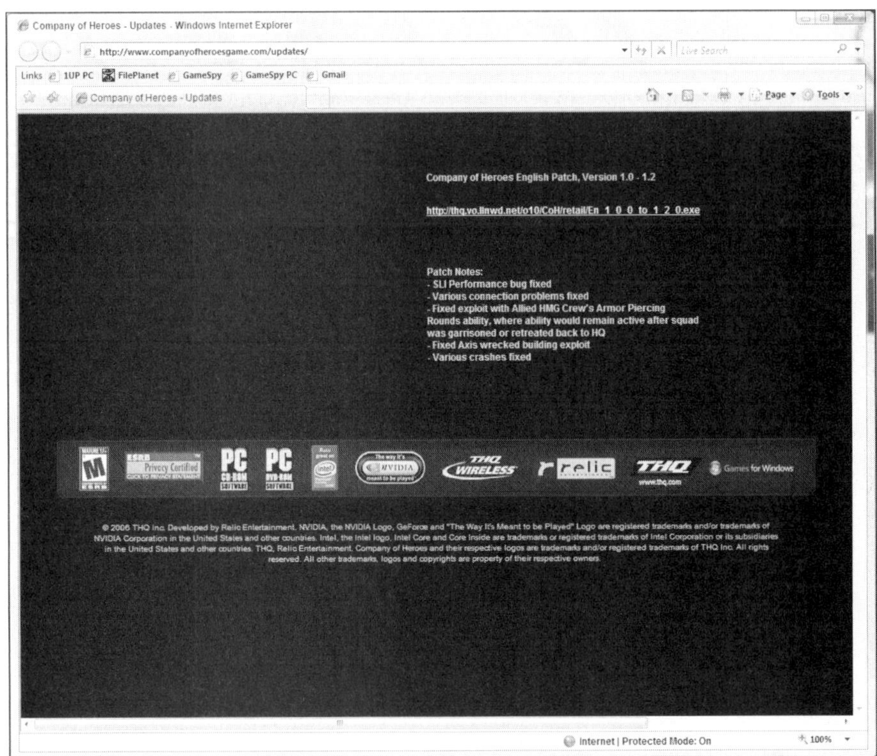

When you find a patch, download it. I like to create a \patches folder in my \downloads folder just for game patches (Figure 24.15).

FIGURE 24.15

Downloading the *Company of Heroes* patch

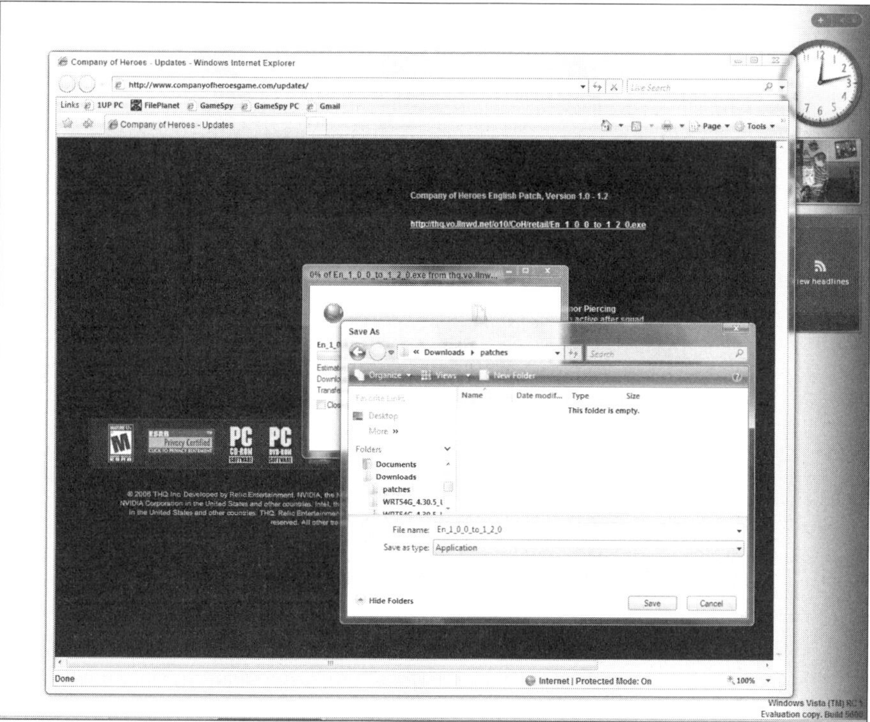

After the patch downloads, install it. The vast majority of patches are executable files that fully automate the patching process. When I run the *Company of Heroes* patch, it installs itself with just a single mouse click (Figure 24.16).

FIGURE 24.16

The *Company of Heroes* patch goes in smoothly.

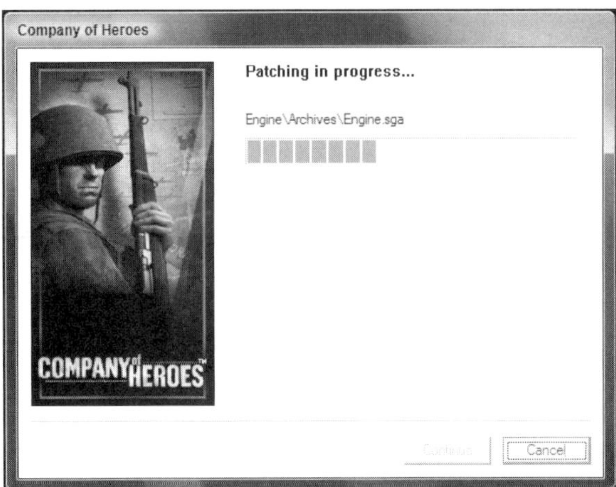

After the patch installs, you're ready to play the newly enhanced game.

TIP Be sure to keep your system's device drivers up to date as well! See Chapter 2 for details.

Installing and Configuring Game Controllers

Game controllers can include anything from an enhanced keyboard or mouse to a joystick or a gamepad. Gaming keyboards and mice install just like any keyboard or mouse; you simply plug in the USB peripheral, install the drivers, and you're off and running.

Joysticks, gamepads, and driving wheels are a bit different — but just a little bit. They often don't need drivers, although they *may* come with drivers and special programming software to boot. If your gaming peripheral came with drivers, you need to follow the instructions that came with it.

TIP Do indeed read the instructions that come with your controllers. Sometimes, they instruct you to install drivers before you even hook up the product; in other cases, you need to plug in the peripheral and then install the drivers. The drivers and other software contain their own interface and functionality that differs from Windows Vista's controller setup interface.

Installing, for example, a new USB gamepad is quite simple. Thanks to USB's plug-and-play technology, Windows can often detect and configure the device with little or no help from you. The DirectInput portion of the DirectX API library standardizes the various axes and buttons found on such controllers, so Windows can recognize just about any standard controller made for USB.

NOTE Legacy controllers used a sound card's game/MIDI port to communicate with the computer. Thus far, I have not been able to get Windows Vista to recognize such a controller. Whether that's by design or simply a lack of sufficient driver support for my sound card (the drivers are in pre-beta) remains to be seen.

In the remainder of this section, I take you through a typical gaming device installation and configuration using a Logitech RumblePad 2 gamepad. The steps are as follows:

1. **Plug the gamepad into a USB port.** Windows Vista displays a balloon by the system notification area informing you that it has detected new hardware. It then tells you it's installing the necessary HID (human interface device) drivers for it, as shown in Figure 24.17. Finally, it tells you your hardware is installed and ready to use.

FIGURE 24.17

Windows is installing drivers for my gamepad.

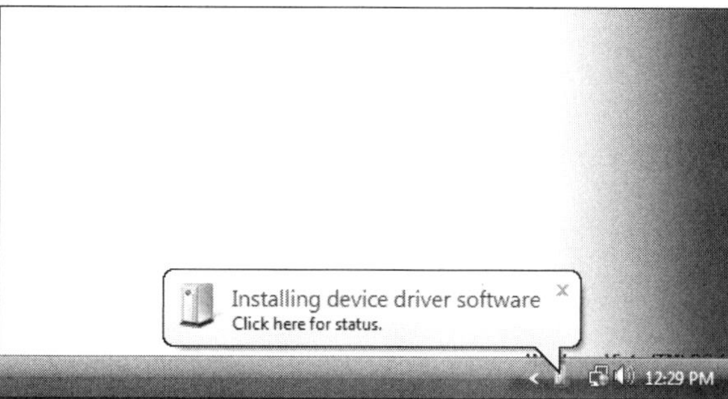

2. **Access the gamepad's properties in the Game Controllers applet by choosing Start ➪ Control Panel.**
3. **Click Hardware and Sound, scroll down until you see Game Controllers, and click it.** The Game Controllers window appears (Figure 24.18).

FIGURE 24.18

The Game Controllers window

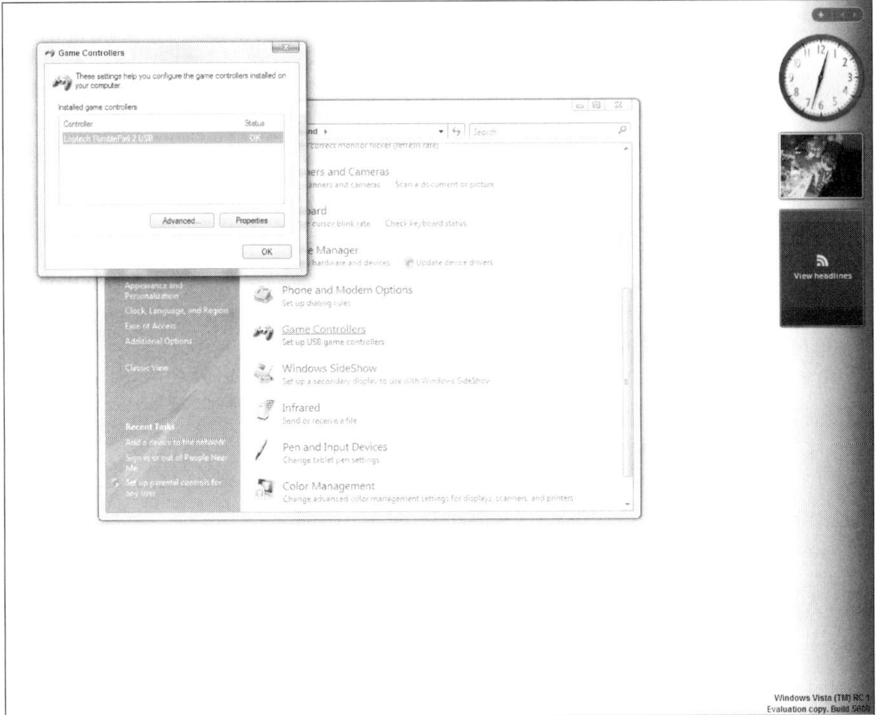

4. **Click the Properties button.** A properties window specific to your device appears, as shown in Figure 24.19. It shows the various axes and buttons and allows you to adjust them: If you move a control along an axis or press buttons, the applet responds with visual feedback.

FIGURE 24.19

Properties for my RumblePad 2

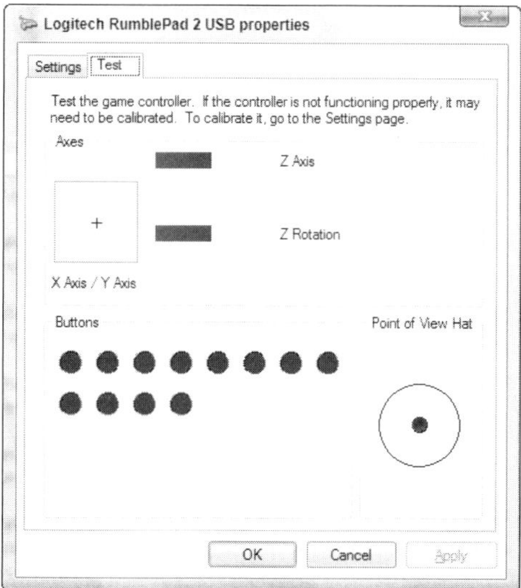

5. **To manually calibrate the device, click the Settings tab and then click the Calibrate button.** Windows runs through a routine in which you move various controls around. Simply follow the prompts to calibrate your controller.

NOTE Calibrating a digital controller is rarely necessary. Calibration tells the computer information about the range of motion of your controller and where the center and extremes of its axes are. The only reason to calibrate would be if you noticed your game controls "drifting" in one direction (that is, if your plane in a flight sim kept banking to the left when you weren't touching the joystick).

So you can see what a calibration routine is like, the following steps take you through a calibration routine for the RumblePad 2.

1. **After you click Calibrate (see the preceding steps), the Device Calibration Wizard starts** (Figure 24.20). Click Next.

FIGURE 24.20

The Device Calibration Wizard

2. Leave the handle centered and press a button on the controller, just as the screen that appears prompts you to (Figure 24.21).

FIGURE 24.21

Meandering through the Calibration Wizard

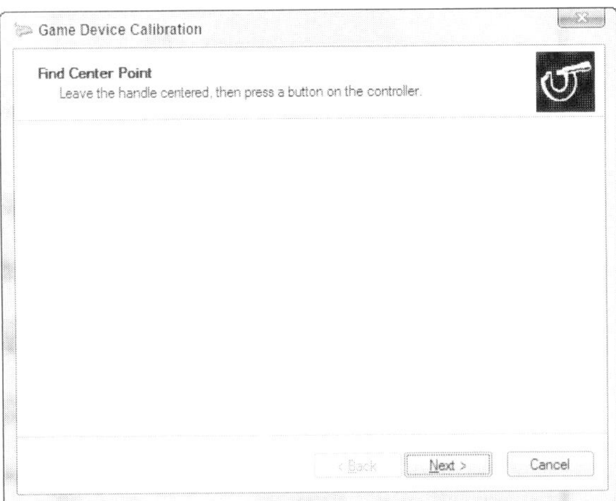

3. Move the stick that controls the X-Y axis (the main stick on a joystick, or the left analog stick on a gamepad) through its full range of motion, and then press a button (Figure 24.22).

FIGURE 24.22

Gauging the X-Y axis during calibration

4. **Leave the handle centered again and press a button, as prompted** (Figure 24.23). Now it's time to tackle the other axes.

FIGURE 24.23

Verifying the center point of the X-Y axis

5. **Move the Z axis all the way to its extremes (usually by twisting the joystick handle or moving the right thumb stick on a gamepad) and press a button, as indicated in Figure 24.24.**

FIGURE 24.24

Measuring the Z axis during calibration

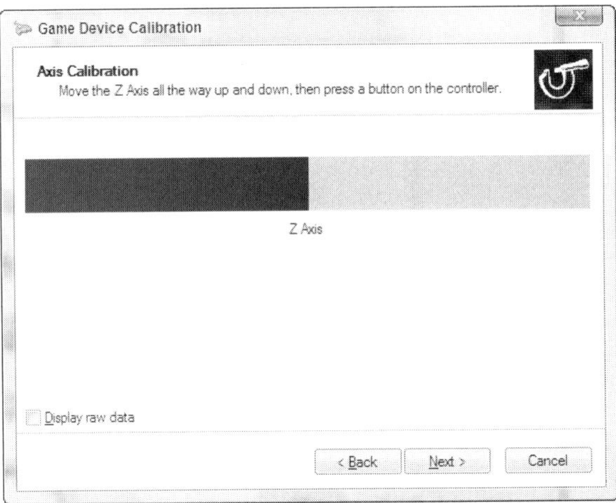

6. **Do the same thing with the N axis (usually the throttle on a joystick, and the other axis of the right thumb stick on a gamepad), as shown in Figure 24.25.**

FIGURE 24.25

The Z-rotation axis is also called the N axis.

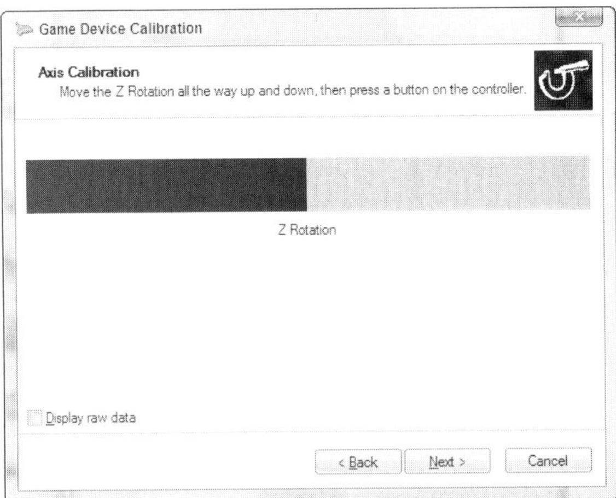

7. **Click Finish to save your calibration.** The Calibration Wizard closes. You can test the controls in the Game Controllers' Properties screen.

NOTE You never have to calibrate mice or keyboards. Calibration is strictly for controllers with analog inputs, such as joysticks, analog gamepads, and driving wheels.

Launching a Game

Now it's time to play. When you're ready to launch a game, you normally go about it in one of three ways.

Autorun

When you insert a CD or DVD, Windows detects it and sees whether it has an autorun routine. If it does, Windows offers to run it for you. When a game is allowed to autorun, it normally shows a screen with a bunch of buttons on it.

The first time you autorun a game, one of the buttons will offer to install it for you. After installation, that button usually changes to something like *Play* or *Launch [game]*. *DOOM 3* has a fairly standard autorun routine (Figure 24.26), complete with creepy music and sound effects.

FIGURE 24.26

DOOM 3's autorun screen

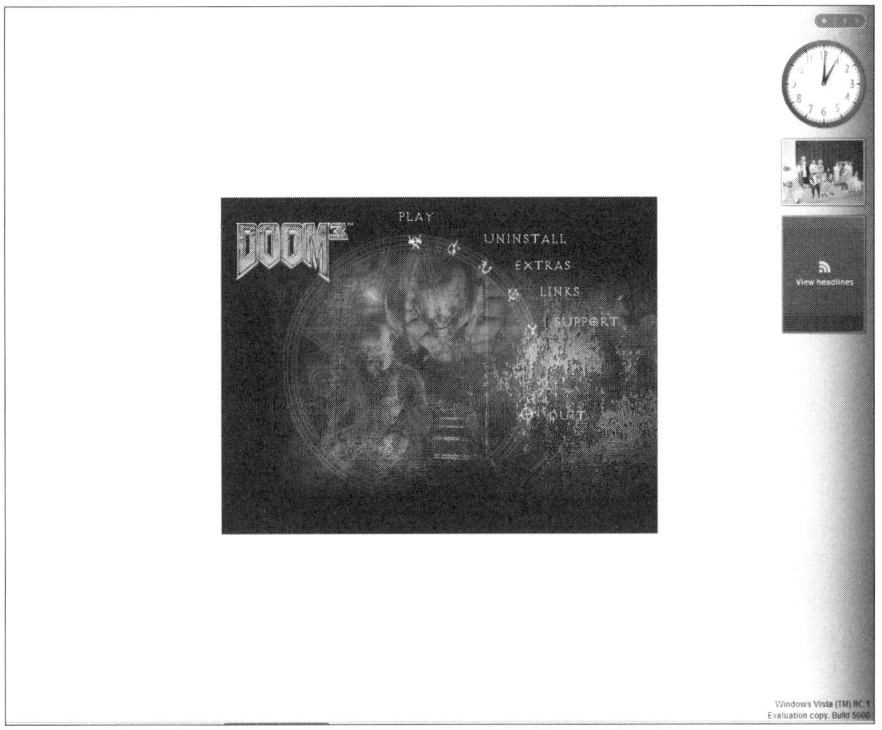

To play a game through its autorun routine, simply pop in the installation media (the CD or DVD that the game came on, which you probably must have in the drive when you run the game anyway), and then click the appropriate button to start the game.

The Games folder

Of course, you can also start a game via the good-old Games folder (Figure 24.27). Click Start ➪ Games to invoke this folder that lists all the games it recognizes on your system. To launch a game, make sure its installation media is in the optical drive (if necessary; some games don't require it) and then double-click its icon.

FIGURE 24.27

The Games folder contains most of the fun stuff on my PC.

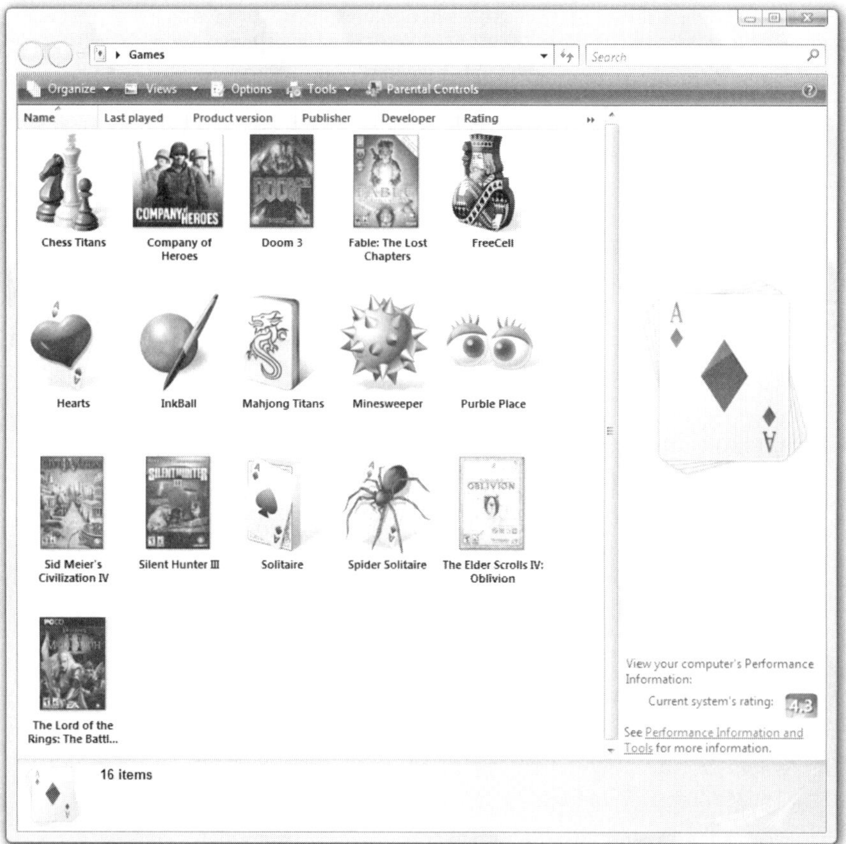

The Start Menu

You can also navigate the Start Menu for the most inconvenient way to launch a game. You need to click the Start button, go to All Programs, and find the folder the game was installed in. See Figure 24.28.

FIGURE 24.28

You can always dig through the Start Menu to launch games.

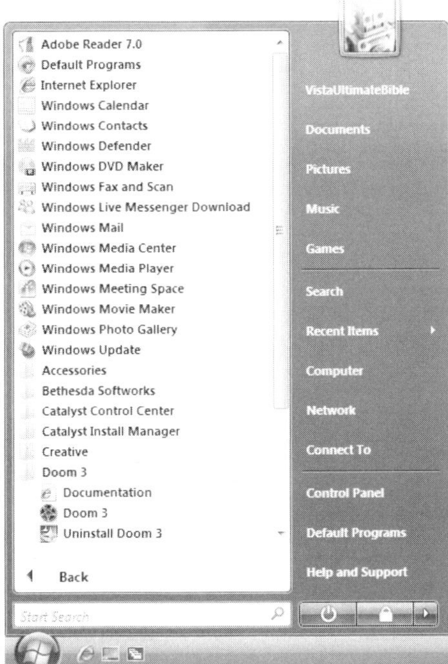

Setting Game Options

The vast majority of game titles feature a number of options screens for customizing the gaming experience. A standard interface for game options screens doesn't exist; most are unique to the game itself. Some games feature fun and interactive interfaces, like *Psychonauts'* brain-based interface (Figure 24.29), whereas others are relatively nondescript, like the one in *Company of Heroes* (Figure 24.30).

FIGURE 24.29

The *Psychonauts* options interface

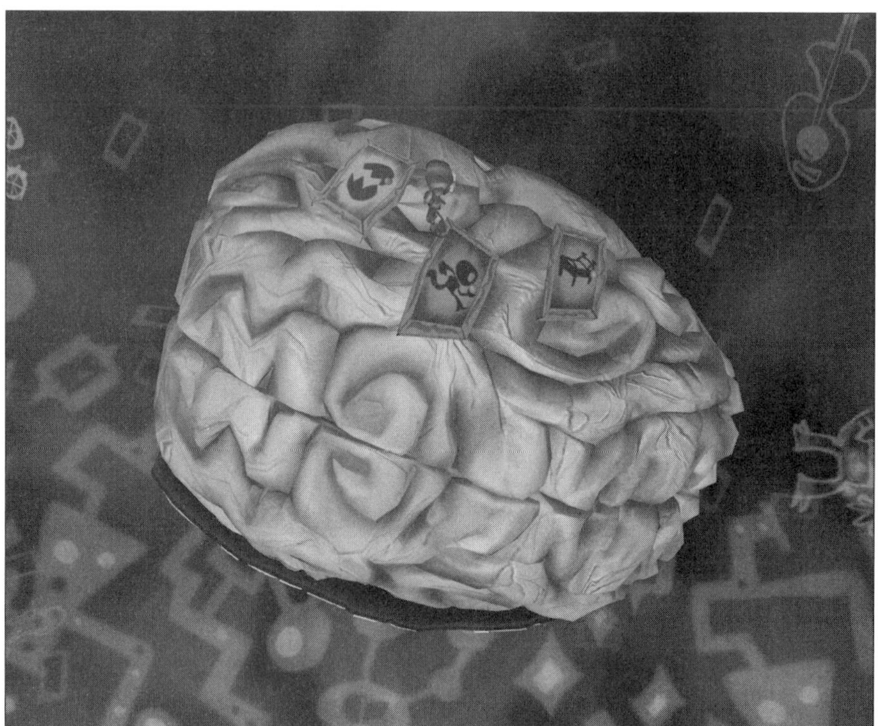

Although game options vary from title to title, you can find some consistency. (I cover graphics and performance options in Chapter 23.) The following sections detail some other options that appear in almost every game.

FIGURE 24.30

Call of Duty 2's options interface

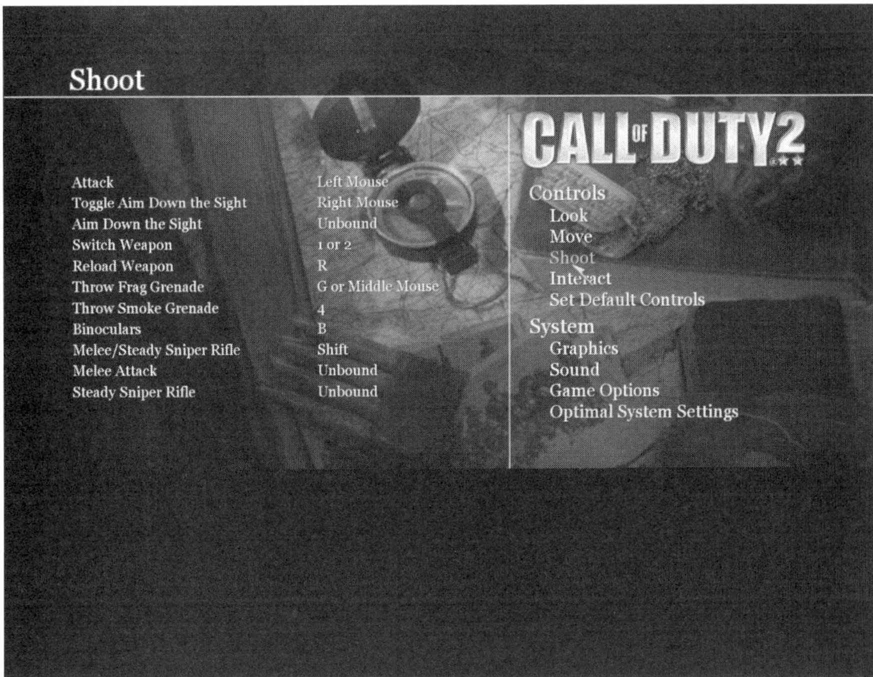

Controls

Many games offer to allow you to customize their controls in several ways. Some, like *Call of Duty 2* (shown in Figure 24.31), have the controls broken up into different subcategories, like movement, interaction, weapons, and so on.

FIGURE 24.31

Call of Duty 2's control options

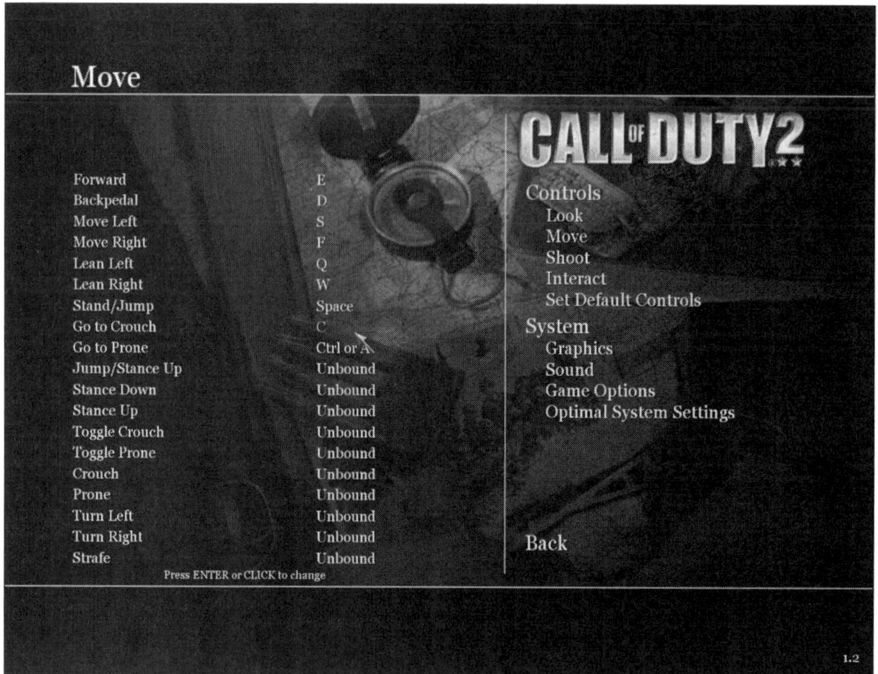

You can usually change the key controls as you see fit. For example, most first-person shooters use the W, A, S, and D keys to move the character around. I prefer E, S, D, and F, because it gives me more room for pinkie-activated keys. I change those controls on a screen like the one shown in Figure 24.32.

FIGURE 24.32

Call of Duty 2's movement controls

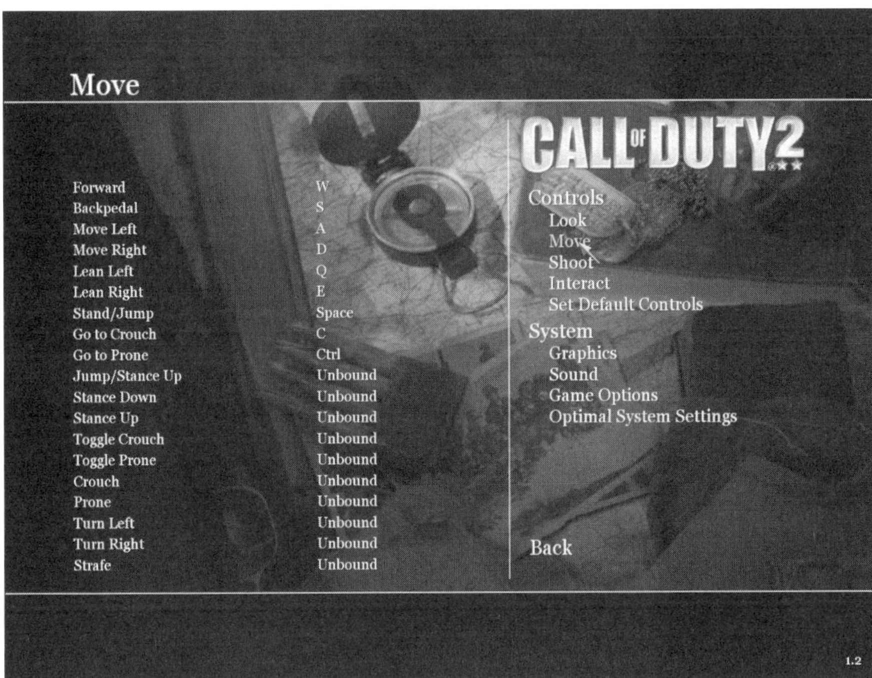

Another control option found in most games is mouse sensitivity. You can tweak it to affect how far the point of view moves with each twitch of the mouse. Low sensitivities offer more precision but require greater motion on your part; higher sensitivities reduce precision but also move your point of view more quickly. In RTS games, mouse sensitivity is often replaced by scroll speed, or how fast the viewpoint scrolls around the map when you move the mouse cursor to the edge of the screen. Typically, you make the adjustments with a slider like that shown in Figure 24.33.

FIGURE 24.33

The slider represents the mouse sensitivity in *Call of Duty 2*.

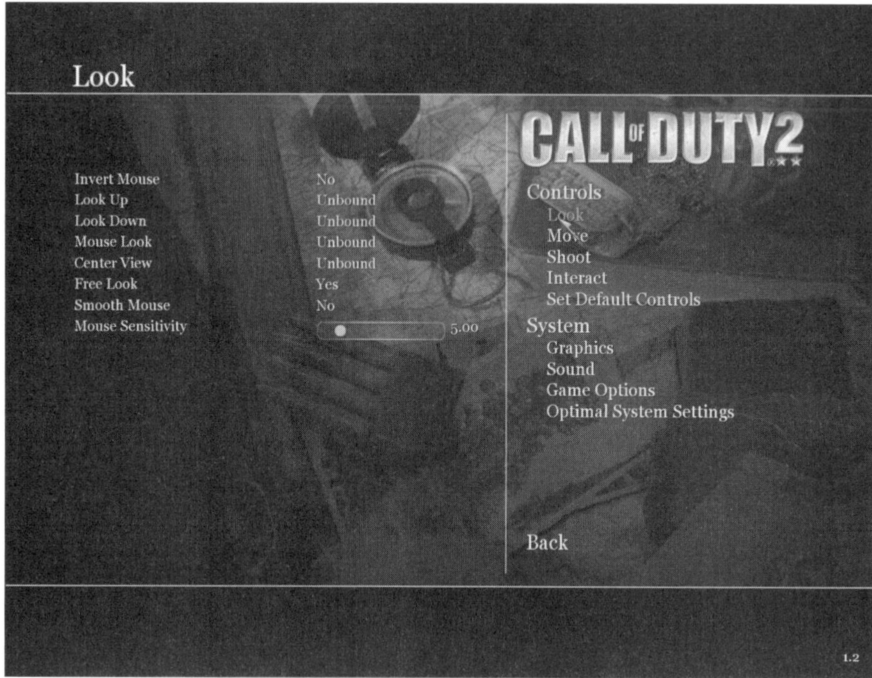

You often find options to toggle free look (the mouse always looks around) and mouse smoothing (averaging the mouse motions for smoother mouse movement).

Audio

Sound options (Figure 24.34) typically offer one or more volume sliders and sometimes control over the audio API and sound quality.

Sliders usually allow you to adjust the master volume and sometimes the music volume. In some cases, you can even tweak the sound of ambient, background noise and the volume of in-game voices.

Sound quality is usually measured in kilohertz (KHz), or thousands of cycles per second. Higher numbers are better, and they typically range from 8 KHz to 44 KHz, although some games go as high as 96 KHz on sound cards that support it.

FIGURE 24.34

Call of Duty 2's audio controls

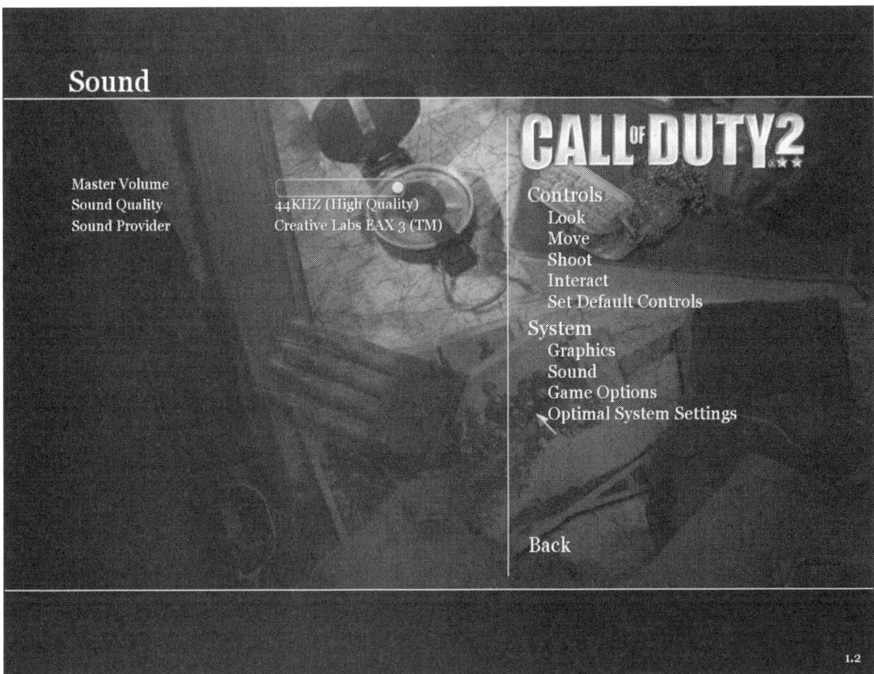

The audio API option tells the game which programming scheme to use to process game sounds. Typically, you can choose from a software API (which is lower quality than hardware accelerated APIs) and hardware APIs like OpenAL and various versions of EAX. Your sound card can support various APIs, and you should choose the best one that your sound supports.

Other game options

Other options are varied. Some games offer difficulty options, some give you the ability to turn off blood and gore, many ask whether you want to see subtitles when people speak, some wonder whether you would like to see a crosshair when you point your gun, and so on. *Call of Duty 2's* miscellaneous game options are shown in Figure 24.35.

FIGURE 24.35

Call of Duty 2's game options

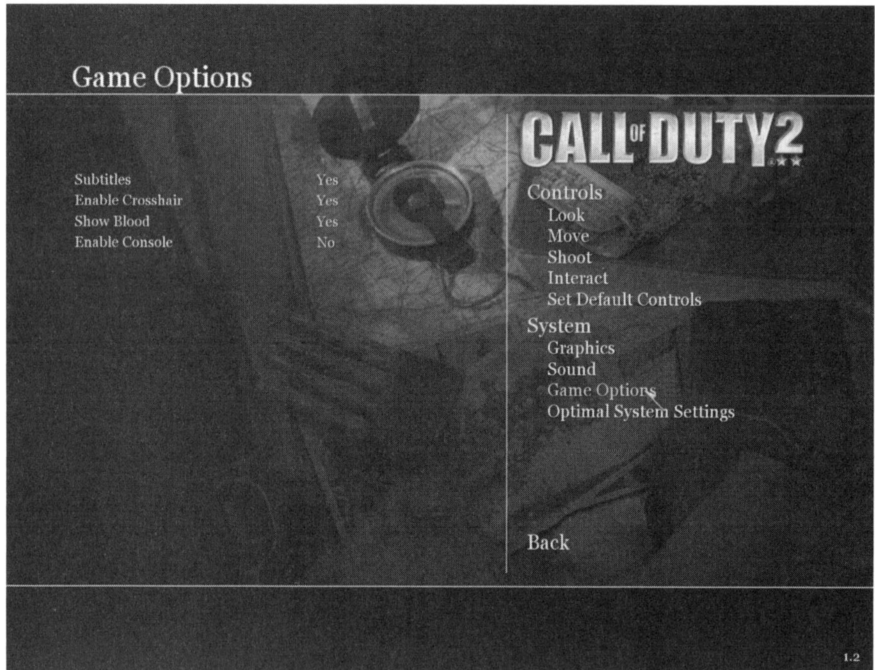

Mods: Expanding Your Games' Horizons

One option you'll see in some games references mods. What, exactly, is a mod? Good question.

A *mod* is a variation of a game, often created by individuals who are simply fans of the game. Mods can be very simple: Some involve only weapon balance, altering the damage that various weapons do, whereas others give you control over some basic function like the width of your point of view. Other mods are vast and sweeping, changing the look and feel of the game into something totally new. Mods that change every aspect of a game are called total conversions.

Mods are examples of community ingenuity. People create mods because they're easier to create than entire games; you already have a full game, so the engine, graphics, and so on are already built. Mods give armchair developers, artists, and script writers an outlet to introduce their own creations to the world of gamers.

To run a mod, you need a copy of the game upon which it's based. A mod usually uses the game's own code beneath its own scripts and art, so without the game itself no engine or platform exists on which the mod can run.

Downloading and installing mods is a great way to extend the life of your games. They're potluck — some are fantastic (like *Iron Grip: The Oppression for Half-Life 2,* shown in the following figure) and some are not so good. Check out community sites regarding your favorite games, and gaming sites in general, for news about mod development and availability.

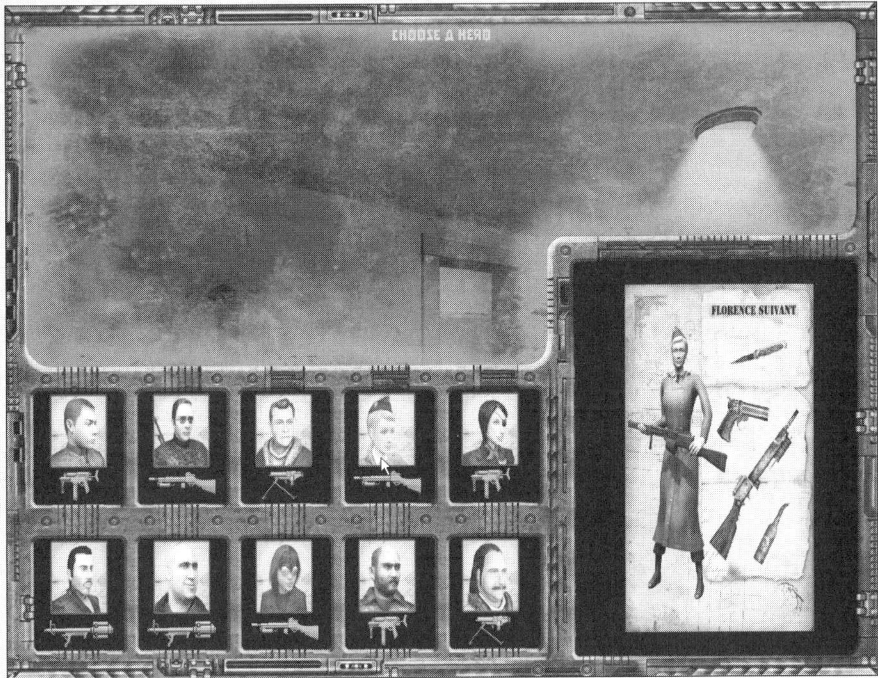

You can choose from several characters in Iron Grip: The Oppression.

Summary

The dropship enters the atmosphere and starts to vibrate violently. Marines like you, who've been through dozens of drops, are used to it. But this time, something isn't right. It's more than just turbulence. The ship rocks, twirls, and suddenly your stomach jolts into your throat as you feel yourself falling. "*We've been hit*" someone screams, and with a metallic roar the side of the ship disappears. Debris and blood are everywhere. You struggle out of your restraint and reach for one of the chutes on the wall. Through the tear in the hull, you see the ground, then the sky, swirling maddeningly. Marines are in free-fall. Someone's screaming. You catch hold of a chute as the ship jerks again, tossing you out into the open air — or whatever passes for air on this rock. As you fall, free of the doomed dropship, you're shocked at the sight of your vessel; it's twisted beyond recognition, falling like a stone to the ground. You're determined to strap the chute onto your back. You have 20 minutes of oxygen, two clips of ammo for your sidearm, and a mile of atmosphere between you and the planet below.

Games put you in situations you'll never encounter in your life, allowing you to live out adventures from your desk chair. Of course, reality is always just a fatal exception error away, so be sure to keep your games patched and updated to prevent crashes that would otherwise rip you from the total immersion of the game world.

You can control most PC games with only a mouse and a keyboard, and they're surprisingly intuitive controllers for gaming considering all the wacky game peripherals that have traditionally populated store shelves. It sometimes helps to have a specialized controller like a gamepad or a joystick, and Windows Vista makes installing, configuring, and calibrating them simple work.

After you've installed and launched a game, you should go into its options pages and set it up how you see fit, tweaking the controls, the mouse sensitivity, the audio options, and so on. Map the keys however you want; I always customize the key mappings before I play. Games have some conventions, but I've developed my own.

Chapter 25

Game Compatibility Issues

IN THIS CHAPTER

- Understanding compatibility modes
- Setting compatibility modes for games
- Getting Windows XP games to run on Windows Vista
- Getting older games to run on Windows Vista

I never get rid of old games. I don't know why, but I still have copies of games from the days of the Commodore 64 (and I don't even know where my C64 is).

There's no way I'll get those games to work on Windows Vista, but I can certainly try to get my PC games up and running. I still have games from pre-Windows 95/DOS days; I have dozens of games for Windows 95, 98, and Me; and I have piles of Windows XP games. Heck, XP games will probably still be arriving to store shelves for at least another year or so after Windows Vista comes out.

When Windows XP burst into our lives, it was substantially different from any consumer Windows operating system that preceded it. Windows 95, 98, and Me were all based on the Windows 95 kernel, which was basically a mesh of 16-bit and 32-bit code designed to bring 32-bit to the masses while maintaining 16-bit compatibility. Windows XP, however, was based on the purely 32-bit Windows NT kernel, and although it managed to run some legacy programs, it wasn't designed for compatibility with DOS and Windows 3.x programs.

Windows XP introduced compatibility modes, mainly for games but also for other legacy programs. If a game written for Windows 95 didn't run on XP, you could try to fool it into thinking it was running on 95. On rare occasions, that ploy actually worked and the game ran flawlessly.

Windows Vista continues the tradition, but with a more robust compatibility mode feature. It features the manual compatibility modes of Windows XP, but it also invokes itself at certain times. For example, when a program installer checks the Windows version and determines it's not, say, XP, the Windows Vista Program Compatibility Assistant, shown in Figure 25.1 may appear and ask whether you want to go ahead with the installation anyway. That doesn't guarantee the program you're installing will actually run, but at the very least it'll try to install.

FIGURE 25.1

The Program Compatibility Assistant can be helpful in getting programs to install.

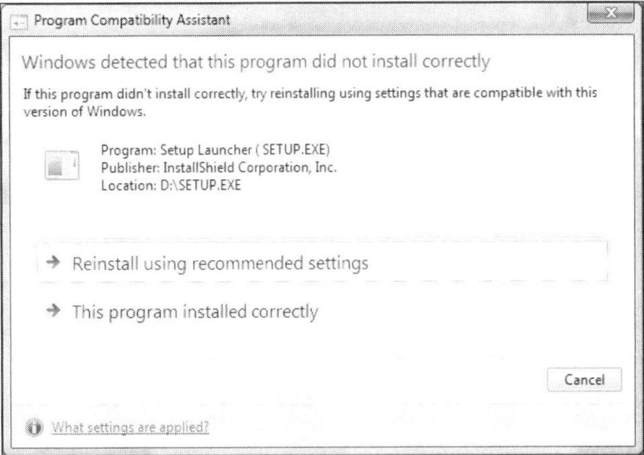

As discussed in Chapter 15, DirectX 10 (the preferred DirectX set of multimedia libraries) isn't backward compatible, as older versions of DirectX were. In lieu of backward compatibility, Microsoft included DirectX 9L, an update of DirectX 9.0c beefed up for the new Windows Display Driver Model (WDDM) in Windows Vista. This program can help get some older games to work.

Read on to find out how to deal with game compatibility issues. Getting old games to run on new operating systems can be tricky, and this chapter shows several examples of what to do when a game won't run on Windows Vista Ultimate.

Gaming and Compatibility

Windows Vista tries its very best to run whatever you want it to run. In testing a great deal of games from anywhere between 1996 and 2006, I've had mixed luck.

To put it more bluntly, I had terrible luck.

Games designed for Windows 95, 98, and Me were stubborn, to say the least. Games designed for DOS did not work at all, in any scenario. Failures ranged from hangs to messages looking for elements of DirectX that no longer exist, and access violations (probably programs trying to grab resources that Vista maintains tighter control over than in earlier operating systems).

Note that I was working with Beta 2, and that I tried a number of games but by no means every game in the world. As later builds, and eventually the release build, become available, legacy compatibility might improve.

The good news is that Windows XP — at least, DirectX 9 games — appear to be ready for the transition. Through the use of the compatibility mode options, I managed to get most of the games I tested to work, although gameplay was a bit less responsive than it was when they were running under Windows XP.

Working through installation issues

Sometimes, you won't even get an old game to install. It might try, the Program Compatibility Assistant might even give it a whirl, but sometimes the installation simply won't happen. I've had some games simply abort the installation silently, without offering up even a cryptic and mysterious error message. Others crash and cause Windows Vista to ask me whether I want to terminate the installer.

In the case of a failed installation, there's not much you can do. Manually unpacking the files isn't usually possible or practical, as most games require more than a simple file copy to function: They might need to create files during the installation, they might need registry values written, and so on.

TIP **You can manually set a compatibility mode for the Setup file on installation media. Simply explore the media and look for the Setup.exe file (not the autorun file), and follow the procedure for setting compatibility options for shortcuts in the next section to set its compatibility mode.**

If you do get a game to install, you should copy its shortcut into the Games folder for ease of access. If it's a DOS game that doesn't create a shortcut, you can create one:

1. **Click Start.**
2. **Click Games.**
3. **Click Start again.**
4. **Click Computer.**
5. **Navigate to where you installed the DOS game and look for the .EXE, .COM, or .BAT file that launches it.**
6. **Click that file and drag it into the Games window.** Windows Vista creates a shortcut to the file in the Games folder.

Setting compatibility options

If a game won't run, you might have to manually assign it a compatibility mode. Doing so is a simple procedure, but it's not guaranteed to work.

1. **Open the Games folder by choosing Start ➪ Games.** The Games folder, shown in Figure 25.2, appears.
2. **Right-click the game to which you want to assign a compatibility mode** (Figure 25.3).

FIGURE 25.2

The now-familiar Games folder

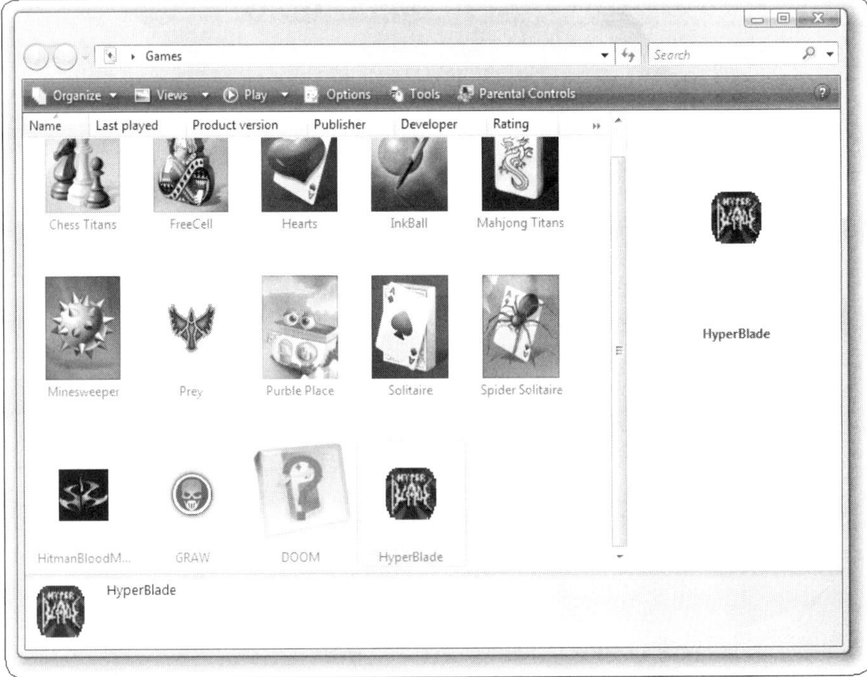

FIGURE 25.3

Right-click on the game to invoke the context menu.

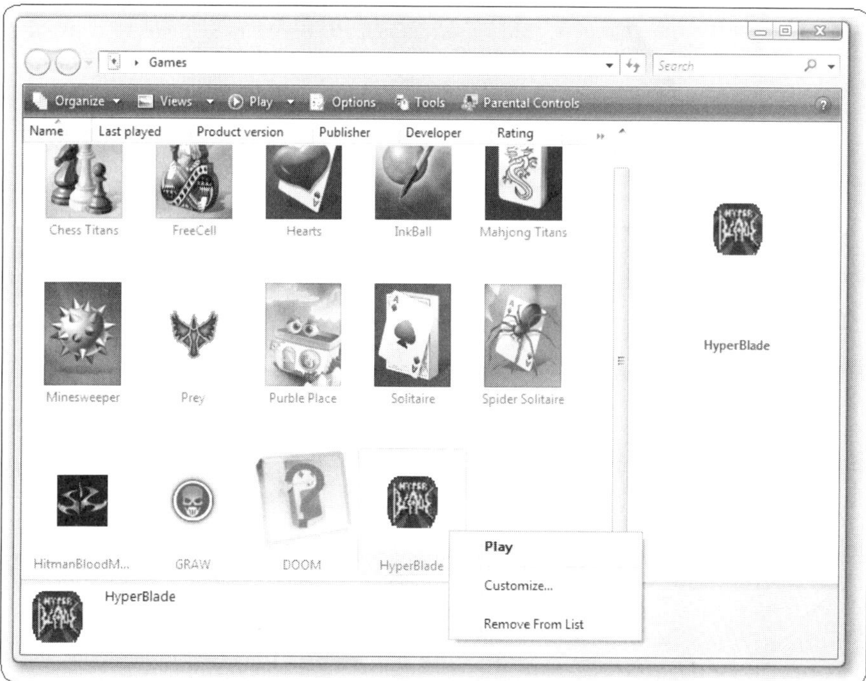

3. **Click Customize.** The dialog box shown in Figure 25.4 appears.

FIGURE 25.4

The Customize dialog box

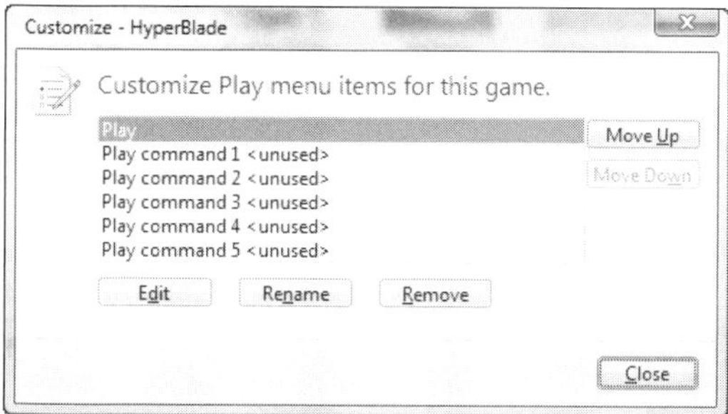

4. **Click Edit.** The game's Shortcut tab in the Play Properties dialog box appears, as shown in Figure 25.5.
5. **Click the Compatibility tab** (Figure 25.6).
6. **Under Compatibility mode, click the check box to select it, then click the drop-down menu and select the Windows version you want the game to think it's running under** (Figure 25.7).
7. **Click OK, and then close the Customize dialog box.**

FIGURE 25.5

The properties dialog box for the selected game

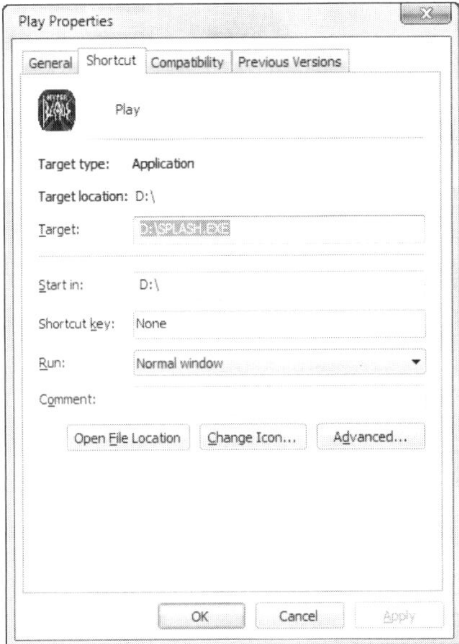

FIGURE 25.6

The Compatibility tab in the game's Play Properties dialog box

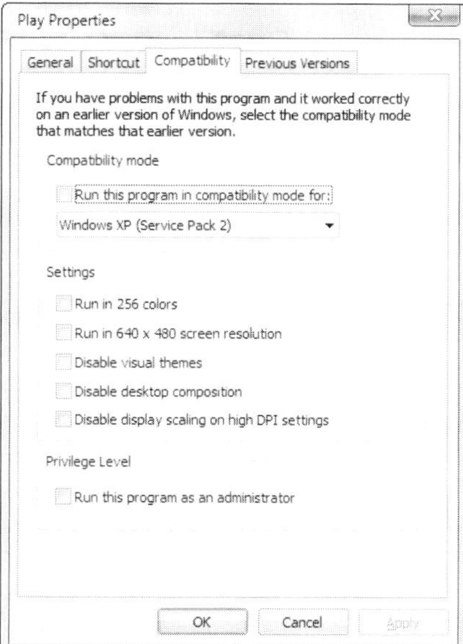

FIGURE 25.7

Choose a Windows version.

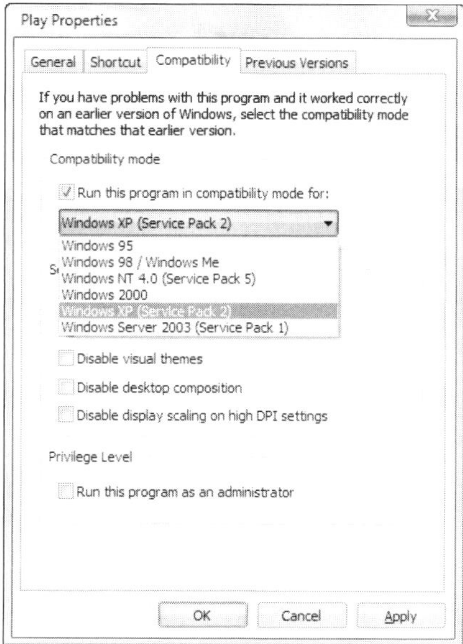

From this point on, when you launch the game you've just tweaked through the Games window, Windows Vista will try to convince the game that it's running on the Windows version you've selected.

The Compatibility tab shown in Figure 25.6 contains other options, each with its own check box:

- **Run in 256 colors:** Most modern games run in 16-bit or 32-bit color. This option forces the game to run in 8-bit color (256 colors). This option is great for games that won't run in higher color modes.
- **Run in 640 x 480 screen resolution:** As stated, this option runs the game in the relatively low-resolution, VGA-friendly, 640 x 480 pixels mode.
- **Disable visual themes:** Sometimes, visual themes interfere with older programs that were written before Windows XP. Disable them with this option.
- **Disable desktop composition:** This option disables the Windows Aero 3D effects for programs that can't deal with them.
- **Disable display scaling on high DPI settings:** Users of extremely high resolution monitors sometimes tweak font and icon scaling for the sake of readability; if they don't, the text often appears too small to read. This option disables such scaling to prevent anomalies in games that use Windows elements (such as fonts) so that it looks the way the game developer intended it to look.
- **Run this program as an administrator:** Some older programs don't have any idea what different types of user accounts do. They'll only run for administrators. Check this box to appease them.

Running Windows XP Games on Windows Vista

In this section I have three case studies of Windows XP games that I installed on Windows Vista Ultimate. In most cases, I eventually got the game to work. The games in question are *Hitman: Blood Money*, *F.E.A.R.*, and *Prey*.

All three games installed perfectly.

Hitman: Blood Money

Hitman: Blood Money, a tense, tactical third-person game from Eidos, wasn't happy with Windows Vista at first, but after a short bout of experimentation I got it working.

Hitman installed flawlessly, but it wasn't aware of the Games window. In fact, few games (other than, oddly enough, *Grand Theft Auto: San Andreas AO Version*) are. I manually dragged the Start Menu icon into the Games folder and launched the game.

It exited without any sign of an error. It failed to display a dialog box of any sort; Windows Vista's error reporting didn't even show up. It simply dumped to the desktop. I rebooted, just in case.

To get *Hitman* to work (see Figure 25.8), I simply set its compatibility mode to Windows XP using the steps outlined earlier in this chapter. The game ran fine after that, with a complete lack of any visual glitches. Performance was comparable to that of running it on Windows XP.

FIGURE 25.8

Hitman: Blood Money ran fine after a minor adjustment.

F.E.A.R.

Sierra's *F.E.A.R.* installed normally and predictably, but it insisted on installing the August 2005 version of DirectX 9.0c. However, because DirectX files are protected from being downgraded, it didn't affect DirectX 9L.

The game ran fine, but quite slowly, after installation. Mouse response was sluggish. I exited the game and opened the Games folder and experimented with some compatibility settings.

Setting it to run as if the OS was Windows XP had no effect.

I then disabled both themes and Windows desktop composition. Immediately, without the need to reboot, the game ran almost flawlessly. After re-enabling themes, the game still runs fine. Because disabling the desktop eye-candy rendering has an effect, the sluggishness I experienced could be due to a compatibility problem with WDDM and the current beta driver for my ATI Radeon X1900-based graphics card.

In any case, the system hog of a game that it is, *F.E.A.R.*, shown in Figure 25.9, works well under Windows Vista.

FIGURE 25.9

F.E.A.R. in all its glory

Prey

Prey, an action shooter from 2K Games, installed without a problem, but it wouldn't run under any circumstances.

It would crash, displaying a *Doom3* engine status screen, shown in Figure 25.10, that had halted upon unloading an OpenGL DLL. OpenGL is a 3D graphics standard. The top of the status window read "The current video card/driver combination does not support the necessary feat" and that's that.

This problem is likely due to a lack of sufficient OpenGL support in the current beta graphics card drivers for my system's X1900 card.

FIGURE 25.10

Crash!

Getting two out of three to work isn't bad. A number of other Windows XP games are known to work under Vista including *Grand Theft Auto: San Andreas*, *Call of Duty II*, *Half-Life 2*, *Guild Wars*, *World of Warcraft*, *Company of Heroes*, *Oblivion*, *Microsoft Flight Simulator X*, *LEGO Star Wars II: The Original Trilogy*, and many more.

Running Older Games on Windows Vista

Sadly, Windows XP games were the only legacy games I had any luck with getting to run on Windows Vista. I had planned this chapter to be much longer, exploring Windows 9x games and even DOS games, but none of the ones I experimented with — or even read about — would run whatsoever.

Say farewell to *Duke Nukem 3D*. Adios *MDK*. Hasta luega, *Rocket Jockey*.

The lack of compatibility is unfortunate, but not unexpected. Many legacy games were written specifically for older, outdated instances of DirectX. For example, I tried to install and run *HyperBlade,* a terrific Activision bloodsport that's sort of like a high-speed jai-alai on skates. It installed after some wrangling, but it refused to run, looking for a DLL from DirectX 2 (see Figure 25.11)! This game hails from the days of proprietary 3D cards and software, such as 3Dfx Voodoo Graphics and Rendition hardware and the associated APIs.

My suggestion for compatibility with games you still own and love is to hold on to copies of your older Windows operating systems, and possibly DOS boot disks for pre-Windows 95 games. With any luck, we'll see better compatibility when Windows Vista reaches its final version.

FIGURE 25.11

Sorry! Your game won't run.

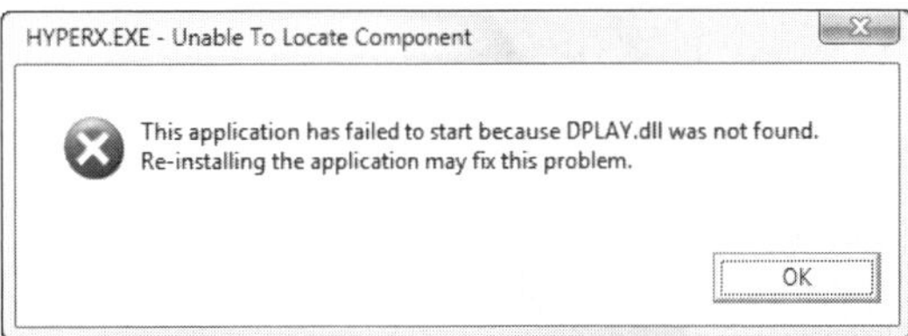

Summary

Sometimes, you can get old games to run on Windows Vista. Sometimes you can't. It's really nothing more than a crap shoot.

Windows Vista includes a number of compatibility tools that work to allow you to get pre-Vista games to run on the new operating system. They do the trick, most of the time, but they're not foolproof. In my experiments, I could get *most* Windows XP games to run on Windows Vista, but Windows 9x games were far less likely to make peace with the new OS.

All is not lost, however. As Windows Vista makes its way into the world, it's likely that some old games will receive patches from their makers to work with the new operating system, and Windows Vista itself might receive updates to smooth compatibility problems.

Chapter 26

Integrating Windows Vista with the Xbox 360

IN THIS CHAPTER

Looking at media extenders

Using the Xbox 360 as a media extender

Introducing Xbox Live Anywhere

Looking at the universal controller

Interestingly, not everyone prefers gaming on PCs. This fact baffles me, as I find PC games to have more depth, more flexibility, and more replay value in the form of user-created modifications than console games.

On the other hand, there's something to be said for relaxing on the family room couch, eating chips, and playing a game on a big television set. For hot-seat multiplayer games, nothing beats a console with multiple controllers. Some consoles even do online multiplayer gaming, although you often have to pay for the privilege.

Microsoft's current console, the Xbox 360, was the first "next-generation" console to hit the market. By next-generation, the industry means the one after the 2005-and-before crop that included the original Xbox as well as Sony's PlayStation 2 and Nintendo's GameCube.

Windows Vista is designed to interact with Xbox 360 in several ways. The two can share game controllers; the Xbox 360 can act as a media extender for the operating system; and, hopefully by the time you read this, the two can share the Xbox Live gaming service (called Live Anywhere on non-Xbox platforms).

Thus, with an Xbox 360 in your gaming arsenal, you're empowered to further blur the gap between the PC and the entertainment console. When you are able to log in to the same gaming service from the Xbox 360 and the Vista-equipped computer, you'll extend the already-thriving Live community to your PC (and possibly to other platforms in the future). When you can plug a USB dongle into your computer and use your Xbox 360 wireless controller to play games on the computer, you won't have to spend hard-earned cash on PC-specific game peripherals. And when you can blast your tunes, watch your digital movie files, and browse through your photographs, all of which are stored on your computer, through the entertainment system connected to your Xbox 360, your media won't be trapped in the computer room anymore.

Gamers and PC enthusiasts especially will appreciate the Xbox 360 integration, but there are limitations to the interaction between Xbox 360 and Windows Vista. The Xbox 360 is not and will not be a PC platform, and Vista won't be a console platform; you won't be able to install and play the same copies of your games on both systems. Even if you have copies of the same title for both platforms, you won't necessarily be able to play cross-platform multiplayer games.

Those aren't unexpected or unreasonable caveats, however, and the level of interaction between console and computer hasn't ever been as lofty as it is between the Xbox 360 and Windows Vista.

Keep reading to see how Windows Vista Ultimate and the Xbox 360 can work together to make gaming and multimedia a better experience in your house...and beyond!

The Xbox 360 as a Media Extender

The computer isn't always in a convenient location for users to enjoy its various photo, film, and music files. Even if your PC is equipped with a big LCD monitor and speakers that sound as good as reality, you might not want to be confined to a desk or table as you crank up some old Bowie.

That's where a media extender comes in.

What is a media extender?

A *media extender* is a device that allows access to a computer's or network storage device's media files in a different location from where the computer or storage device is located. For example, at home, this means the ability to access media files that are stored on your basement office computer from the family room's entertainment center.

Some media extenders have their own storage in the form of hard drives, whereas others do not. What they all have in common is that they're either wired or wireless network devices that let you play media, usually stored on a PC or some sort of network attached storage device, on a TV or stereo system.

With a media extender, you can sit back on the love seat, rather than the computer chair and watch, for example, home videos that you've captured to your computer. You can blast digital music from your PC's hard drive through your TV or entertainment center speakers. You can gaze at your collection of digital photos on a big screen. All these activities are quite simple to do.

Using the Xbox 360 as a media extender

If you already have an Xbox 360 connected to the same network as your Windows Vista computer, you're almost done with the installation. If your Xbox 360 isn't networked, you have to patch it in by connecting a drop cable from the Xbox 360's Ethernet port to a hub or router on your network. You may also need to update your Xbox 360 via Microsoft's Xbox Live service before it will work with Vista.

CROSS-REF For more information on Microsoft's Xbox Live and Live Anywhere feature, see the section, "Xbox Live and Live Anywhere," later in this chapter.

NOTE If you've used Windows XP with a media extender such as the Xbox 360, you probably had to install extra software, or run a Media Center Edition version of Windows XP. Windows Vista, however, is ready to cooperate with the Xbox 360 upon installation. You can enable media sharing through Windows Media Player 11, as described in the steps that follow.

When your Xbox 360 is connected to the network and turned on, go to your Windows Vista machine and perform these steps:

1. **Open Windows Media Player 11 through the Start Menu.**
2. **Right-click on an empty area of the toolbar, hover the cursor over Tools, and click Options.** The window shown in Figure 26.1 appears.

FIGURE 26.1

The Windows Media Player 11 options dialog box

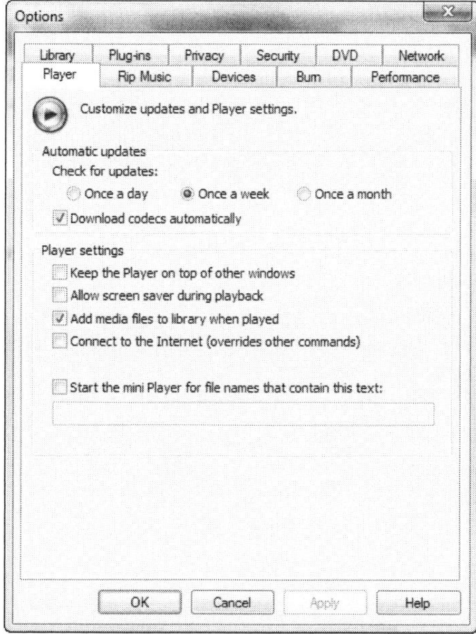

3. **Click the Library tab in the Options dialog box, as shown in Figure 26.2.**

FIGURE 26.2

The Library options page

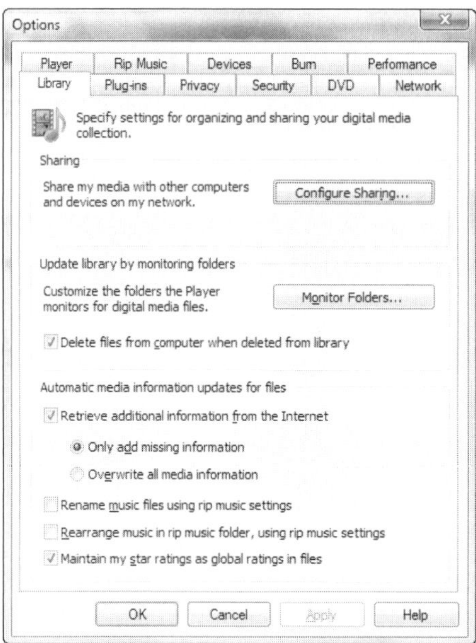

4. **Click the Configure Sharing button.** The Media Sharing dialog box appears, as shown in Figure 26.3.

FIGURE 26.3

Configuring your sharing preferences

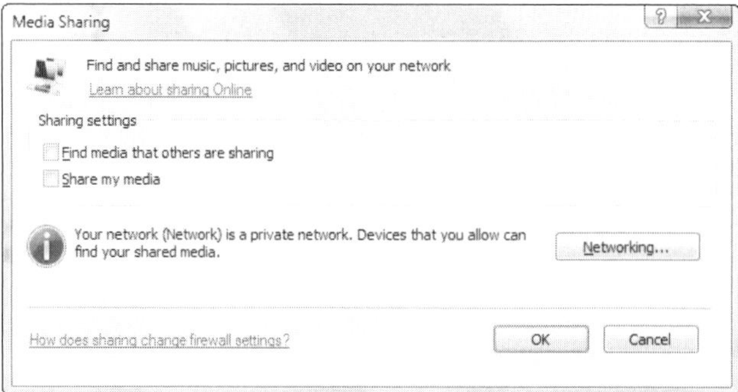

5. **Select the Share My Media check box, and click OK.** The screen shown in Figure 26.4 appears. It may show other items besides those shown here.

6. **Click the Xbox 360 icon and then click the Allow button.**

FIGURE 26.4

Now you must enable sharing for the Xbox 360.

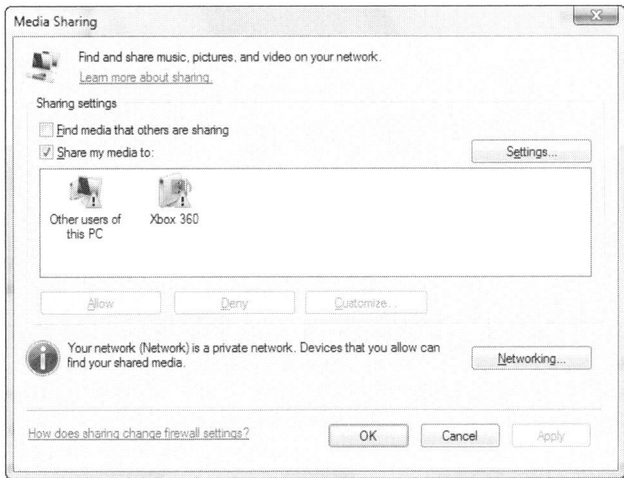

7. **If you want, click the Customize button to customize your media sharing.** The screen shown in Figure 26.5 appears. You can select which media types you want to share, and customize them by rating.

CROSS-REF For more information about customizing your media sharing settings, see Chapter 19.

8. **When you are done, click OK on all the open windows.**

FIGURE 26.5

Optional: Customize your media sharing.

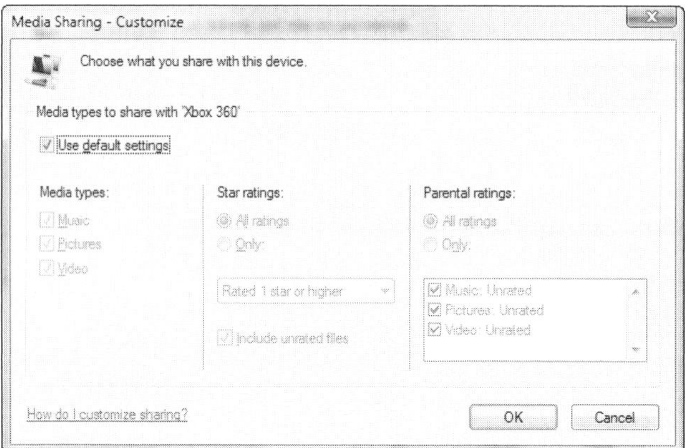

After you've performed those steps, you can head over to your Xbox 360 and surf through your media files and play them through the entertainment center it's connected to.

NOTE Your current network connection must be to a private network in order for Windows Vista to allow sharing of media files. You cannot share them on a public network in this fashion. To disable public sharing, choose Start ➪ Network ➪ Network and Sharing center, and make sure that Public Folder Sharing is set to *off.*

NOTE Neither Windows Media Player 11 nor Windows Media Center need to be open for you to enjoy your media files through your Xbox 360. The only requirement is that your Windows Vista computer must be on and logged in.

Xbox Live and Live Anywhere

Live Anywhere is a new feature stemming from the well-established Xbox Live. An online gaming service, the Live family allows you to share information about your gaming habits with your friends throughout the Live network. You can send and receive messages and share in online gaming. Xbox Live has been around for years, but Live Anywhere is brand new.

Xbox Live

Xbox Live is a subscription-based online gaming service that, among other things, allows Xbox and Xbox 360 gamers to form together into a vast online community. Depending on the level of the service, it allows users to perform a number of feats.

Users create nicknames (called Gamertags), and choose an online appearance, a motto, and more, all of which are linked to their accounts. The service offers all kinds of downloads, including demos, trailers, updates to the Xbox 360 firmware, and more.

Many games offer competitive or cooperative play via Xbox Live. People on Xboxes far away from each other can join in the same game server, and their performance can be tracked and linked to their Xbox Live profile. These performance stats are called their Gamerscores.

Microsoft has decided to extend the Xbox Live service to Windows Vista users. Gamers who use Windows Vista will be able to sign on to their Xbox Live accounts — or create new ones — and share in the fun of the online community.

Live Anywhere

Live Anywhere is a new service that extends the Xbox Live functionality to Windows Vista and possibly beyond. Through Live Anywhere, you can log in to the service with your Gamertag and experience the full functionality of the service as it's offered through Xbox. Figure 26.6 shows a *Halo 2* screen with Live Anywhere in the foreground.

FIGURE 26.6

Check out Live Anywhere via *Halo 2*.

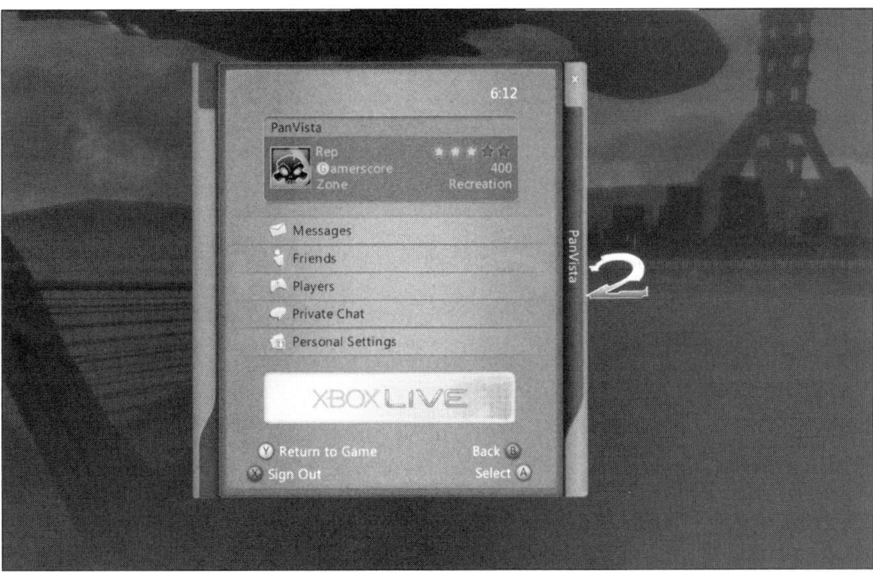

Photo courtesy of Microsoft.

This access means you can check up on your friends and their Gamerscores while keeping track of yours, download trailers and game demos, check out Live Arcade games, and communicate with your gamer friends across platforms.

Some games will even allow cross-platform multiplayer gaming: You'll be able to play via Windows Vista with gamers who are playing on their Xbox 360 consoles. That doesn't necessarily mean that *all* Live Anywhere–enabled games will offer such functionality. (See the sidebar, "Myths and Truths about Live Anywhere" later in this chapter.)

NOTE **Games must be Live-enabled to function with Live Anywhere. Two titles have been announced, both by Microsoft: *Halo 2* and *Shadowrun*. If the Live Anywhere service takes off and becomes possible, expect many more; service compatibility is open to every game developer.**

Live Anywhere has a bright future. Microsoft has stated that it's looking at options to make the Live Anywhere service compatible with mobile devices; users may one day be able to check into some of its services from cell phones and other pocket gadgets. Users will be able to potentially play some Live Arcade games on their PDAs and send text and voice messages to other Live members from the road.

Myths and Truths about Live Anywhere

Currently, rumors are flying around the Internet like angry gnats about what, exactly, Live Anywhere will allow players to do. Here are some of them, and the truths behind them.

Myth

All Xbox Live Anywhere–compatible games will allow people to play across platforms; for example, play *Halo 2* or *Shadowrun* from PCs and Xbox 360s on the same server.

Fact

Although this is one *option* for *some* games, not all games will allow cross-platform multiplayer. Xbox Live Anywhere–compatible games will simply allow player performance to be tracked in various games, and allow other community features.

Myth

You'll be able to play Xbox 360 games on your PC with Live Anywhere.

Fact

No, you won't. Both platforms are still discrete. If the same game is released for both platforms, you'll need one copy for your PC and one copy for your Xbox 360 to play it on both platforms.

Myth

Live Anywhere will only be for gaming.

Fact

Microsoft has indicated that it intends to extend the service to mobile and other devices, as well as the PC. Although you'll be able to play some games on some mobile devices, you can also simply log in to the service and check out what's going on with your friends, their current Gamerscores, and so on.

Myth

Live Anywhere is going to cost a fortune.

Fact

While pricing for Live Anywhere accounts hasn't been announced yet, Xbox Live has a free tier as well as a paid tier with more features. The paid tier, Xbox Live Gold, only costs around $50 for a full year of service at the time of this writing.

Life Through Live

Having spent most of my life as a PC gamer, I didn't discover Xbox Live until I got my Xbox 360, which I bought specifically for the purpose of writing this chapter. While similar services for PC gamers have been around for years (such as GameSpy Arcade), I'm surprised that one as robust as Live is only now emerging.

Xbox Live is pure genius. I've enjoyed games like Rockstar Games' *Table Tennis* and, more recently, the phenomenal *Gears of War* (see the following figure) against people far away simply by networking my Xbox 360 to my broadband router and subscribing to the Xbox Live Gold service.

continued

continued

Gears of War

Figure courtesy of Edelman.

You can talk via a headset over Xbox Live, just as you can through many PC games. In fact, the service is divided into four zones, so you can say what you wish when you want to. Some are family friendly and cursing is discouraged; others are purely for smack-talking punks.

Xbox Live even features an online marketplace where you can buy movie rentals, download game demos, and even buy classic arcade games. Simply transfer some real money into Microsoft Points via the Xbox Live interface, and spend the points on goodies you can download right to your Xbox 360.

A reformed, old school, anti-console, PC gamer, I'm now convinced that consoles and PCs can share the gaming market. Xbox Live on the Xbox 360 is what it took to change my ways.

The Universal Controller

Why buy a PC gamepad when you already have one? That's the question posed by the philosophy of the Universal Controller, a game controller scheme that will make it possible to use the same controller on both Xbox 360 *and* Windows Vista–enabled computers. Rather than purchase a special USB controller for your PC when you may already have an Xbox 360 and some controllers for it, you can use the Xbox 360 controllers right on your PC.

This feat is made possible through an interface called *Xinput*.

The Xinput API

Xinput is an application programming interface (API). An API exists for compatibility; if a game, an operating system, and some computer hardware all conform to the same API, they should (in theory) all work together.

Xinput is the input API for Xbox 360, and it's also compatible with Windows Vista. This compatibility makes using the same controllers on each platform possible, and that's exactly what Microsoft plans for you to be able to do.

Controllers designed for Xinput will be useable on both the Xbox 360 and Windows Vista computers. Such plug-and-play devices further bridge the functionality between the two platforms.

Xbox Wireless gamepad and Windows Vista

The gamepad that came with your Xbox 360 — that cool, wireless one, shown in Figure 26.7 — will work with your computer if all goes as planned. Microsoft plans to release a USB dongle that will accept input from the wireless controller and enable you to use it to control your PC games.

FIGURE 26.7

The Xbox 360 controller

Photo courtesy of Microsoft.

That's fantastic for games that conform to gamepad-like conventions. For the platformers and other games that make their way to PC, the Xbox 360 gamepad could be the ultimate controller. It's wireless, it has a long battery life, it's comfortable, and it's responsive.

Universal USB controllers

The Xbox 360 contains standard, physical USB ports for input from wired devices. As controllers are released that conform to its Xinput standard, they should also work flawlessly in Windows Vista. One such controller is the wired, USB version of the Xbox 360 controller, shown in Figure 26.8.

FIGURE 26.8

A wired, USB Xbox 360 controller

Photo courtesy of Microsoft.

Thus, if you love driving games enough to buy a driving wheel controller for Xbox 360, it could work with Windows Vista as well. The same goes for joysticks, rudders, gamepads, and any other controller you could think of. It's all up to controller manufacturers to conform to the Xinput standard; if they do, expect to use the same controllers on your Vista machine as you do with your Xbox 360.

Summary

I hate dot-com buzzwords like *synergy*, but if there ever was a time to use it, this is the moment. Microsoft has taken two diverse and competing platforms and broken down at least part of the wall between them.

The Xbox 360 as a media extender works flawlessly with Windows Vista. The operating system detects it on a network, allows quick and easy setup, and then you just leaf through your media files with the Xbox 360's wireless controller and enjoy them on your television through your good living room speakers.

Then, take that controller into the computer room and play a game of *Psychonauts* or *Shadowrun* with it. The Universal Controller system enables you to use the same gadgetry on your Xbox 360 and your Vista-loaded computer.

As you play Live Anywhere–compliant games, be sure to sign in to Live Anywhere and make some friends from around the world. Challenge them to games, brag about your Gamerscore, and customize your Gamertag. Let the world know about you: Live Anywhere is a gaming network with a sprinkle of MySpace stirred in.

Part VIII

Under the Hood: Tweaking Windows Vista Ultimate

Windows Vista is yours to do with as you please. Like any operating system, it's full of behind-the-scenes settings that you wouldn't normally have access to. Some of them can affect its performance, both overall (in its shell, so to speak), and in games and multimedia applications.

Part VIII takes you through those settings and tells you how to turn Windows Vista Ultimate into a lean and hungry prize fighter. As it stands, the operating system wants to be ready for virtually anything you might want to do with it; you can save lots of calculations by turning off everything you don't need. Learn how to do that by turning the page.

IN THIS PART

Chapter 27

Optimizing for Gaming and Multimedia

IN THIS CHAPTER

Looking at ways to optimize for gaming

Looking at ways to optimize for multimedia

Many users will be looking to Windows Vista for its enhanced gaming and multimedia experience. As I've discussed in earlier chapters, Microsoft has really improved its multimedia and gaming experience with the arrival of Vista Aero and Microsoft DirectX 10.

You can take a number of steps to maximize performance when using multimedia or playing games under Windows Vista.

This chapter discusses how to optimize your system for these specific purposes and how to implement these tweaks.

Optimizing for Gaming

Gamers will be very interested in finding out how to fine-tune Windows Vista for use with PC games. Because Windows Vista is designed for next-generation PC games, you can be sure that these games will require high-end hardware for your PC.

Unfortunately, Windows Vista has a reputation of being somewhat of a resource hog, so optimizing your system — and operating system — for maximum performance is really in your best interest.

Some of the easiest ways to improve your gaming experience in Windows Vista include the following:

- Increase your RAM to 2GB.
- Consider using a video card with at least 512MB of RAM.
- Use flash drive for flash memory to increase performance.

- Make sure that you are using Vista-compatible hardware drivers.
- Shut down unnecessary services.

Increasing RAM

Windows Vista doesn't have high RAM requirements — officially. However, I suggest having no less than 1GB of RAM on board, not counting any flash memory. If you want to do some serious gaming, you'll want at least 2GB of RAM on your computer, in addition to flash memory, and a high-end video card with plenty of memory on board.

This advice assumes that you are looking to play next-generation Windows Vista games. If you are playing less-demanding video games, for example, many of today's best sellers, you can get by with far less. However, if you're reading this chapter, you are most likely a more serious gamer, and you know that the suggested or minimum requirements simply won't do.

Using a souped-up video card

If you're going to game, or play any Vista-designed games, you need to make sure you have a decent video graphics card that will support many of the things that next-generation games require. For example, you'll want to make sure that you have Microsoft DirectX 10 support for your machine; by supporting the latest version of Windows DirectX, you can also be sure that your card will support other important technologies like Shader Model 4.0.

When upgrading hardware to run with Windows Vista, one of the authors used a mid-level video card with 512MB memory on board.

NOTE A few high-end gamer cards have 640MB or 768MB of RAM, but most max out at 512MB. What's important for best game performance are more robust, high-end GPUs that run at higher clock rates and faster video memory.

A limited number of video cards are Vista-capable at the moment; as Windows Vista becomes increasingly available, manufacturers will update their product lines to provide more Windows Vista video card options. These video cards will likely have more graphic capability as well, including DirectX 10 compatibility.

Most major video card manufacturers provide a list of Vista-compatible video cards; please visit individual manufacturers' Web sites for more details. Be sure that the video card indicates that it is Aero compatible and not simply Vista ready.

Using ReadyBoost

Windows Vista introduces a great new feature called ReadyBoost, which is like a triple-dose of caffeine for your computer.

If you have a USB drive lying around, you can put it to good use and get a performance boost. Like caffeine, ReadyBoost can provide a temporary jolt that increases performance. When you are logged into Windows Vista, you must simply plug in your USB drive and wait for the AutoPlay window to appear, as shown in Figure 27.1.

FIGURE 27.1

Windows ReadyBoost can greatly improve your computer's performance.

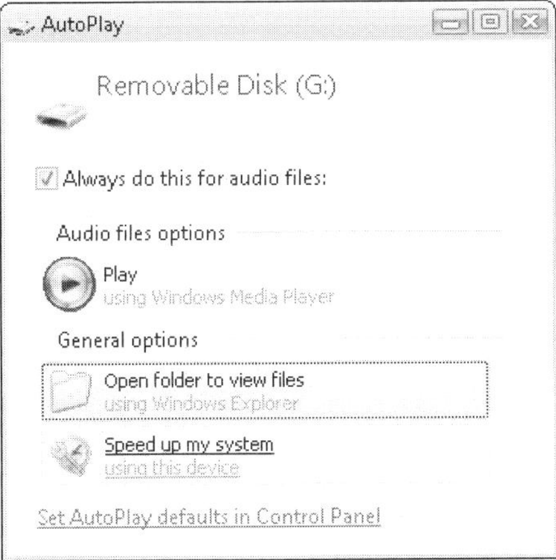

It's important to remember that ReadyBoost is nothing more than flash memory; it's not RAM. That's the beauty of this feature, though; it's virtual memory that can make a fast machine blazing fast. Above all, with the current prices of flash drivers, adding virtual memory to your machine as a temporary solution is cheaper than spending a lot of money on comparatively more expensive RAM for your computer.

You can tell Windows Vista how much of your flash drive to use with Windows Vista. One of the authors used a 2GB memory stick and set aside 1800MB and enjoyed a huge jump in performance.

NOTE Not all flash memory sticks are fast enough to work with ReadyBoost. When you attach a USB memory stick, Vista runs a speed check to make sure the flash drive is fast enough. If it's not, then it won't allow you to use the flash stick for ReadyBoost.

Checking your drivers

Not every hardware manufacturer has rushed to put Windows Vista drivers out on the market. In fact, in many cases, your Windows XP or Windows 2003 drivers are sufficient to run many applications. However, if you're looking to game, you will definitely want to make sure you have everything Windows Vista compatible.

Using Windows Update, you can often find the latest drivers available for your hardware. I recommend running frequent checks using Windows Update or scheduling checks in order to make sure that you have the most up-to-date drivers and updates available. This is especially true for audio and video cards, which are most susceptible to driver changes for use with Windows Vista, especially in conjunction with next-generation games.

Ending unnecessary services

I recommend, albeit with some reservation, shutting down any services that you are not using. Only users who are comfortable with their computers and Windows operating systems should perform this task. Shutting down the wrong services could affect your Windows session or cause things to stop working.

By going to the Services MMC (Microsoft Management Console), as shown in Figure 27.2, you can select which process you want to kill.

FIGURE 27.2

The Services MMC lets you end services that may be unnecessary.

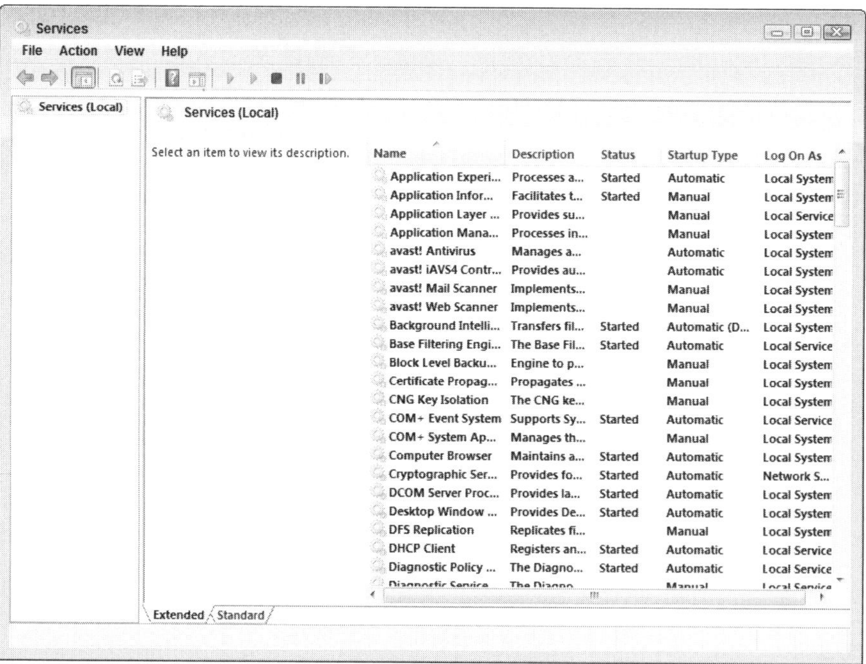

The easiest way to access the Services MMC is to type **services.msc** in the Start Menu's Search box. After you authorize the access of this window by typing in the administrator password when prompted, Vista displays the window.

The Services MMC lets you set how services should perform for Windows Vista and your applications. You can probably shut down or disable a number of services to free up system resources.

To change the status of a service, simply double-click it click the Stop button in the Input Services Properties dialog box, as shown in Figure 27.3.

FIGURE 27.3

You can change a service's status to Stopped.

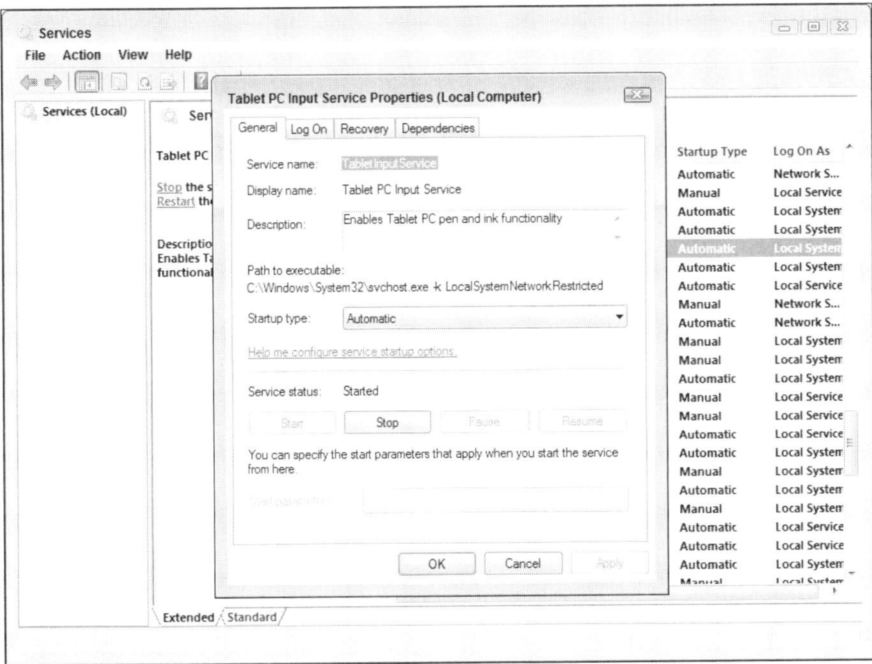

For example, you can probably disable or shut down:

- Tablet PC Input service (unless you are using Tablet PC)
- Windows time
- Secondary logon
- Fax

- Print spooler (if you're not planning on printing)
- Offline files
- Routing and remote access

Ultimately, the decision comes down to you! Look carefully through the list and if you determine that you won't be using that service based on applications that it affects, then you may want to consider stopping it.

Looking at a few other optimizations

You can do a few other things to make your Windows Vista experience even better for gaming. Before implementing these methods, take into consideration your current performance. Many of these techniques are very good for weaker machines, but might not make that much difference overall when you are working with a workhorse computer.

For example, the system restore feature is known to use more than its fair share of system resources. To disable system restore, follow these steps:

1. **Open the Control Panel.**
2. **Click System and Maintenance.**
3. **Click System.**
4. **Click Advanced System Settings.**
5. **Select the System Protection tab.**
6. **Select any available drives displayed in the Automatic restore points section of the System Protection tab, as shown in Figure 27.4.**
7. **Deselect any check boxes.**
8. **Click Apply.**
9. **Click OK.**

The downside to this is that Vista will no longer create restore points when you install new drivers or software, so you cannot "roll back" to previous restore points if you run into trouble. If you have a high-performance system, consider leaving System Restore enabled.

FIGURE 27.4

Disabling service restore points can improve performance.

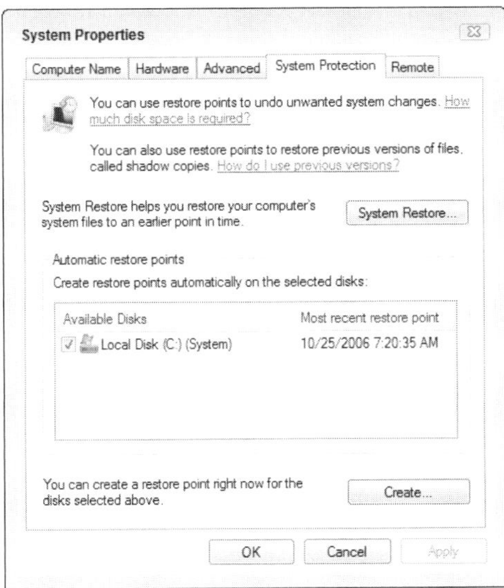

After you validate this window, you will no longer have automatic restore points, which means that you will start saving the system resources that had been consumed by the System Restore service.

One more trick you might consider is to limit the number of windows that appear in Flip 3D. Too many windows open can cause the system to slow down when you toggle among them.

You can change this setting through the Registry Editor. Of course, if you do this, I suggest that you do so carefully because the registry is always tricky business. To start, open the Registry Editor by typing **regedit.exe** in the Start Menu's Search box, then follow these steps:

1. **Open HKEY_CURRENT_USER.**
2. **Go to Software ➪ Microsoft ➪ Windows ➪ DWM.**
3. **Create a new DWORD (32-bit) value.**
4. **Name it** Max3DWindows.
5. **Double-click the new value and set it to no less than 5 and no more than 10.**

You need to reboot your computer in order for this change to take effect.

Optimizing for Multimedia

Optimizing for using multimedia with Windows Vista is very similar to optimizing for gaming. After all, both can have rather hearty resource appetites.

If you plan on using Vista's multimedia capabilities, first make sure your hard drive is properly defragmented in order to guarantee performance. For more information on defragmenting your drive, please refer to the Appendix in the back of this book.

Like with gaming, I recommend having as much RAM as possible in your machine. Make sure that your processor is sufficient for what you are planning to do in terms of multimedia. A graphic developer would probably have more stringent requirements than a user who wants to simply watch DVDs or listen to music. In fact, the optimization tips that are detailed earlier in this chapter also apply to users who are planning on taking advantage of Windows Vista's multimedia capabilities.

You can do several things to keep control of system resources. For example, if you are using the rip CD feature for your audio CDs, you can set the bit rate to a lower speed so that your audio files require less disk space. If you don't rip many CDs, you might not need to change this setting. However, if you plan on keeping a copy of your entire CD collection on your hard drive, you may want to consider slightly lowering the sound quality in return for less disk consumption.

Another time and resource saver is to disable to Autorun feature. Fortunately, Windows Vista has greatly simplified how to disable this feature, and in what capacity. To modify or disable Autorun, type **Autorun** in the Start Menu's Search box. As you can see in Figure 27.5, Windows Vista provides you with AutoPlay options for various types of media and situations.

You can disable everything in one click by deselecting the Use AutoPlay for all media and devices option. If you want to use AutoPlay for specific applications or to indicate which application should be used to open certain media, you can manually change these items, as displayed in Figure 27.6.

After making your choices, simply click Save.

FIGURE 27.5

The AutoPlay window is a wonderful enhancement in Windows Vista.

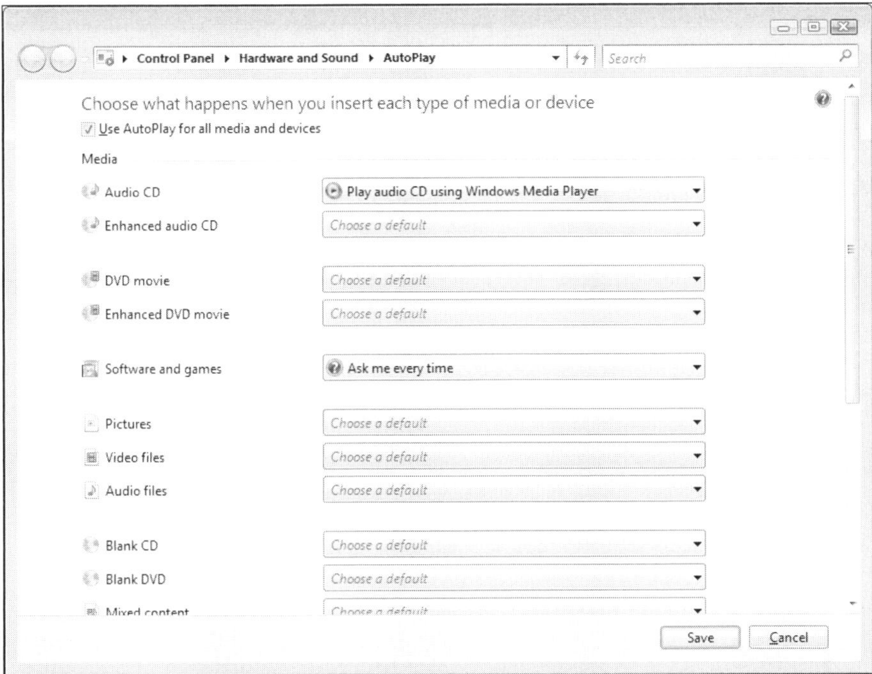

As you become more familiar with Windows Vista, you will determine what customizations can improve the performance of your system. In addition to the tips in this chapter, I suggest using third-party optimization applications that can help you make changes to your computer or Windows Vista through the use of a convivial user interface. These applications, which are discussed in Chapter 28, help to lessen the risk of your making a potential mistake that can't be undone.

FIGURE 27.6

You can decide which applications open certain media.

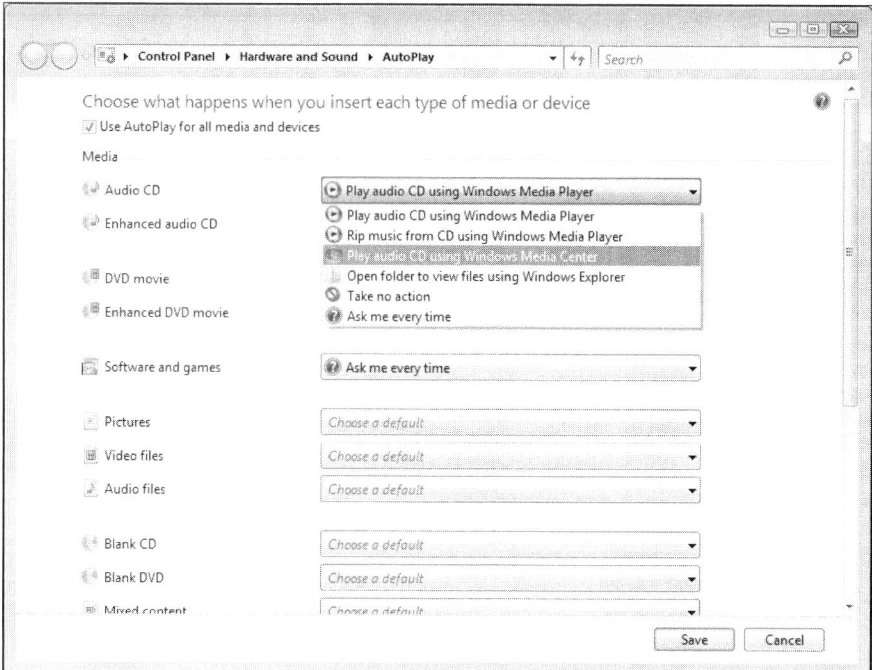

Summary

In order to take advantage of the many new multimedia features, not to mention the new graphic capabilities, offered in Windows Vista, you need to make sure that you have done all you can to maximize your computer's performance.

You can do a number of small things to decrease the number of system resources or services that are used. You can also do things to reduce the amount of hard drive or memory that is used when performing certain tasks.

Before you spend money on a third-party application that will customize, or tweak, your Windows Vista installation, take a good look around your computer and see whether you can find some things you can do yourself to increase performance.

Chapter 28

Tweaking Windows Vista Ultimate for Peak Performance

IN THIS CHAPTER

- Tweaking the registry
- Tweaking individual applications
- Making hardware tweaks

If you want to keep an object running smoothly for years to come regularly performing maintenance or caring for it is important, generally speaking. This is as true for cars, as it is a garden, and even your computer. Windows Vista, like its predecessor, needs occasional maintenance to perform optimally. You can perform a number of tweaks, or changes, in Windows Vista Ultimate Edition to make sure your operating system is in the right shape to deliver peak performance.

You can tweak a number of Windows Vista elements, including the user interface, Windows registry, individual applications, and even hardware. This chapter gives you a closer look at these items.

Tweaking the Vista Registry

One of the more obvious ways of maximizing Vista's performance is through its registry. Of course, it's important to note that only experienced Windows users should attempt to modify the registry. Any mistakes you make could prove to be costly and destabilize your system.

Also available are a number of third-party applications designed to tweak Windows Vista's registry through the use of a user interface, which reduces the risk of your deleting or modifying something you shouldn't.

Before you make any changes to the registry, you need to have a clear idea of what you hope to achieve and how to do it. Changing the registry is really the sort of operation where you should not just open up and start cutting!

If you've never had to use the Windows registry before, let's take a quick look at what it is and what it does . The *registry* is a database that stores information about your computer and operating system; for example, hardware, software, and users are all there. Every time you install a new piece of hardware or software, or make changes in the Control Panel, they are stored in the registry as *keys*. You can think of the registry as a very large keychain; however, just like with real keychains, sometimes keys become obsolete or unnecessary and you may need to tidy up things.

Using the Registry Editor

The "old school" method of modifying your registry is through the Registry Editor application in Windows. Registry Editor has been around for some time now, though very likely you haven't ever used it. As I've said before, editing your registry is some pretty serious business; if you're not comfortable with doing it, or assessing the potential risks, don't do it. The Windows Vista Registry Editor is exactly the same as the version shipped with Windows XP, as shown in Figure 28.1.

FIGURE 28.1

The Windows Vista Registry Editor is a familiar sight to Windows users.

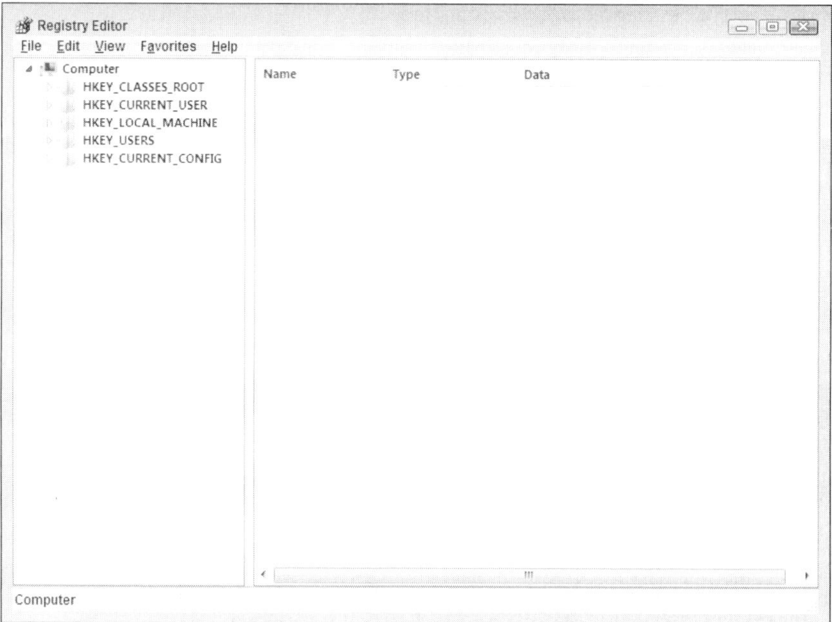

You can easily access the Registry Editor by typing **regedit** in the Start Menu search box. The User Account Control asks you to authorize access by clicking Continue. The Registry Editor appears with an expanded menu of the five registry key sections:

- HKEY_CLASSES_ROOT
- HKEY_CURRENT_USER
- HKEY_LOCAL_MACHINE
- HKEY_USERS
- HKEY_CURRENT_CONFIG

The HKEY_CLASSES_ROOT section stores information about registered applications. The HKEY_CURRENT_USER section stores information explicitly about the user currently logged on to the computer. The HKEY_LOCAL_MACHINE section stores PC settings and preferences. The HKEY_USERS section stores information about all users on the computer; after the user logs in, the HKEY_CURRENT_USER section takes over. The HKEY_CURRENT_CONFIG section stores run-time information; this information is generated when a computer boots and is not permanently stored.

You can expand one of the sections and drill down to the desired registry key. After you find the specific registry key to modify, you can both double-click the key name or right-click the key name and select Modify. An Edit String window appears that lets you modify the existing string value. When you finish, click OK. Your changes are immediately recording into the registry and appear in the Registry Editor as shown in Figure 28.2.

FIGURE 28.2

Editing registry key values is simple.

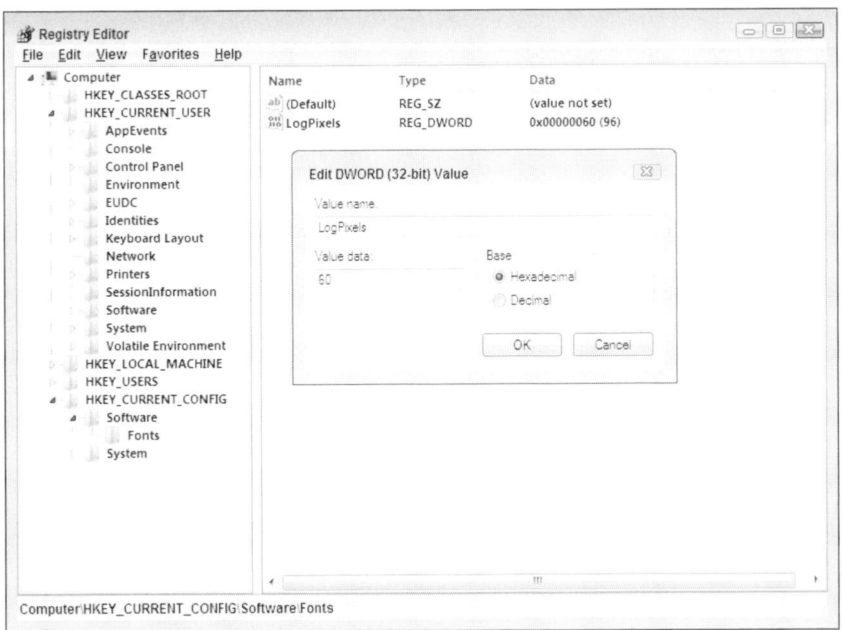

Advanced users may find that they need to actually add to the registry instead of simply modifying it. Once again, if you have the feeling that you shouldn't be performing this sort of procedure, you are probably right. If you need to add a key or string value to the registry, first go to its location in the Registry Editor. On the right side of the Registry Editor, right-click on an open area and select New and then select either a New Key or one of the values.

If you're creating a new registry key, it will appear in the hierarchical menu on the left side of the Registry Editor. It is called New Key #1 by default; you can either modify its default string value as detailed in an earlier paragraph or you can create a new string value as mentioned in the previous paragraph.

Windows lets you create one of six kinds of values:

- **String value:** A text string with a fixed-length
- **Binary value:** A string with raw binary data
- **DWORD (32-bit) value:** A string with a number containing 4 bytes; it must be 32-bit
- **Qword (64-bit) value:** A string with a 64-bit integer as a number
- **Multi-string value:** A multiple string; often used with lists or multiple form values
- **Expandable string value:** A data string with a variable length

You can also perform command-line registry operations, though I discourage it unless you are an expert Windows user. To do this, simply type **reg** at a command prompt. For information on performing specific actions, type **reg /?** at the command prompt and you can read the online help as shown in Figure 28.3.

Using tweaking applications

The most efficient way of tweaking your computer's registry is to use one of the many third-party applications currently available. I recommend taking this approach for a number of reasons:

- Tweaking applications don't let you do anything you're not supposed to do.
- You don't directly access the Windows registry.
- You can easily roll back any changes you have made.

CAUTION Remember that even though third-party tweak applications may be relatively safe, they're not fail proof. With that point in mind, performing a backup or a system restore point before using any applications to modify your Windows registry is a good idea.

FIGURE 28.3

You can access registry online help from the command line.

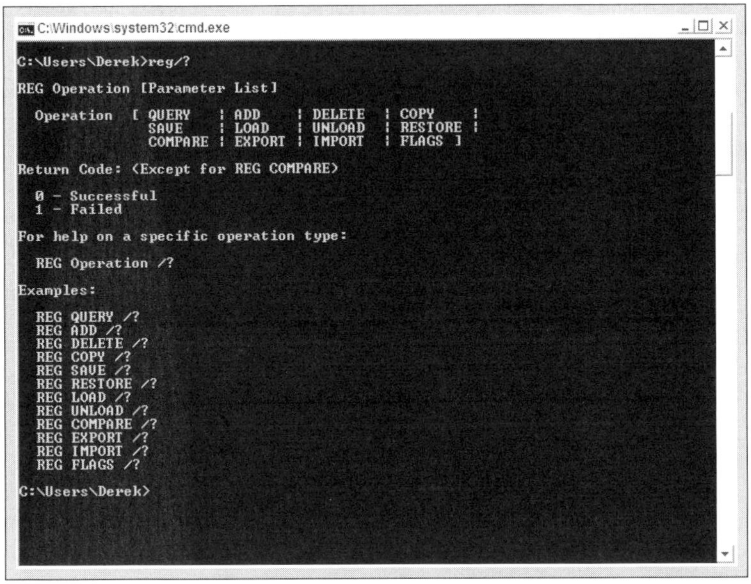

```
C:\Windows\system32\cmd.exe

C:\Users\Derek>reg/?

REG Operation [Parameter List]

  Operation  [ QUERY   | ADD    | DELETE  | COPY    |
               SAVE    | LOAD   | UNLOAD  | RESTORE |
               COMPARE | EXPORT | IMPORT  | FLAGS ]

Return Code: (Except for REG COMPARE)

  0 - Successful
  1 - Failed

For help on a specific operation type:

  REG Operation /?

Examples:

  REG QUERY /?
  REG ADD /?
  REG DELETE /?
  REG COPY /?
  REG SAVE /?
  REG RESTORE /?
  REG LOAD /?
  REG UNLOAD /?
  REG COMPARE /?
  REG EXPORT /?
  REG IMPORT /?
  REG FLAGS /?

C:\Users\Derek>
```

So, why would you want to tweak Windows Vista? After all, this chapter repeatedly mentions the potential dangers of doing it. Tweaking your Windows Vista experience can be a largely positive exercise that lets you further enjoy your Windows experience. Although it won't turn an average computer into a super-machine, it can be beneficial to enhancing the overall experience. For example, you may want to tweak the Windows Vista registry so that you can log into the Local Administrator account if you are already logged in as a standard user. You may also want to disable the ubiquitous security dialog boxes that always seem to appear.

However, tweaking isn't all about doing something clandestine or even something that "Microsoft doesn't want you to do." For example, you can use a tweak application to easily dictate how you want things to appear in Vista. These small modifications can make some difference in terms of aesthetics, saving time, or improving efficiency.

Most of the third-party applications let you manage basic tweaks, such as desktop optimization, the Start Menu, Web browsers, hardware, system information, the System folder, and so on.

Currently, only a few tweak applications are currently available for Windows Vista. As Vista rolls out and becomes more widely used, you can be certain that more will become available. I recommend three tweak applications for use with Windows Vista; please visit their respective Web sites for more information on their capabilities. These applications are:

- **TweakVI from Totalidea Software** (`www.totalidea.com`) shown in Figure 28.4, is designed to let you fine-tune and optimize your Windows Vista experience. A freeware version exists, as does a subscription-based application that features additional plug-ins . The freeware version enables you to perform most of the basic tasks mentioned earlier in this section; however, if you are looking to perform more advanced optimizations, such as those you can do with the UAC feature, you need to take a subscription.

FIGURE 28.4

TweakVI is a third-party interface tweak application.

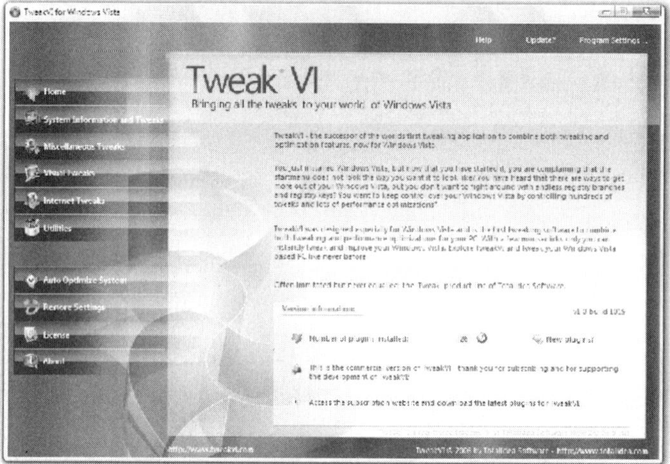

- **TweakVista** (`www.tweakvista.com/tweakvistautility`) shown in Figure 28.5, is a strong application that can help you make the most of Windows Vista. TweakVista is currently available as a freeware application.
- **VistaBootPRO** (`www.vistabootpro.org`) shown in Figure 28.6, includes a support forum, which may offer helpful ideas for tweaking Windows Vista. VistaBootPRO is currently available as a freeware application.

FIGURE 28.5

TweakVista is another option when considering Vista tweaking.

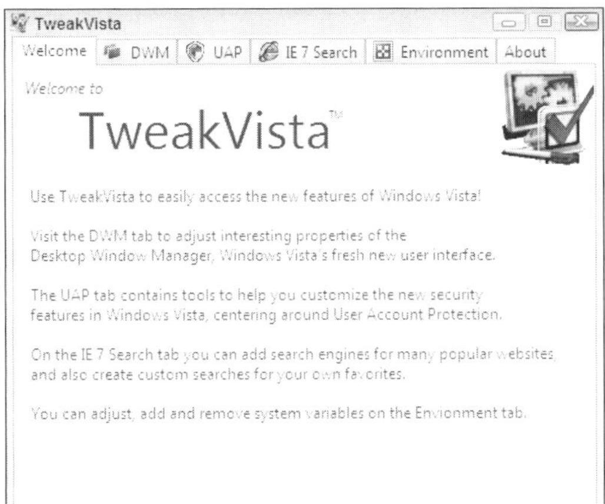

FIGURE 28.6

VistaBootPRO provides a support forum full of great ideas for Vista tweaking.

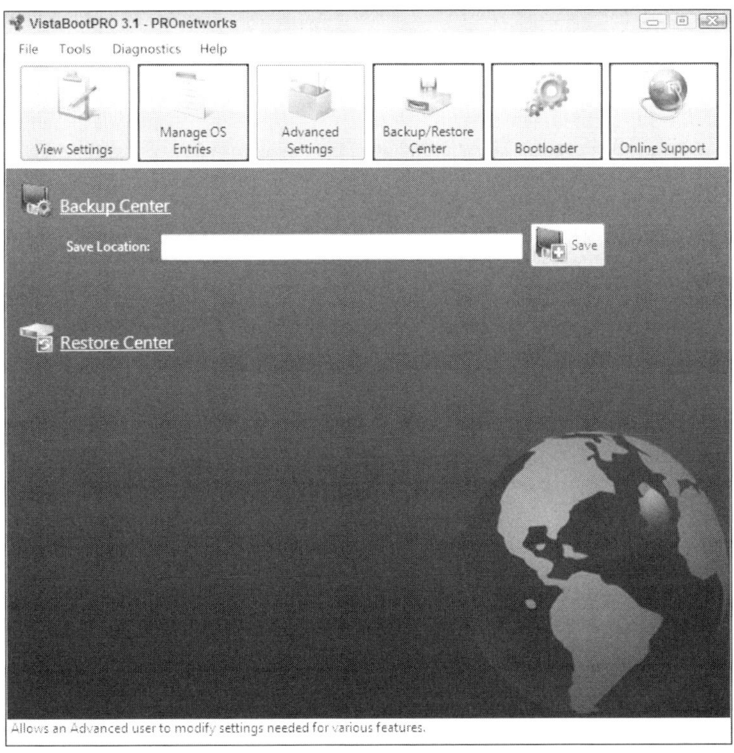

Tweaking Individual Program Properties

As you become increasingly accustomed to working with Windows Vista, you will eventually have an operating system that runs smoothly according to your dictates. That doesn't mean, however, that you can't improve performance of individual applications. Fine-tuning individual programs will not necessarily improve your back-end performance, but it can improve your front-end experience. For example, changing how Internet Explorer operates won't make a slow computer lightning-fast; however, it can decrease the amount of time needed to launch the application or before it becomes operational. Tweaking applications that appear in your startup menu can decrease the amount of system resources used when you boot your computer.

Fine-tuning applications

There's no hard-and-fast rule when it comes to fine-tuning individual applications to improve Windows Vista performance. As far as I know, no third-party applications are available that help you tweak applications like exist for operating systems. However, what I can offer you is some good advice on how to make your system and applications work a little better:

- Make applications launch with the minimum features
- Limit the number of startup applications
- Make Internet Explorer more efficient

Launching applications with minimum features

As with operating systems, an application can take a long time to open depending on how many of its components are scheduled to load at the application's startup. When an application starts up, it has to load a number of files, such as drivers, as well as preferences, and so on. This process can be time consuming, depending on how many system resources are currently available. If you are opening your tenth window, you can be sure that it will take longer to load than if it were your first or second window.

For example, certain application suites (especially when it comes to computer maintenance) actually load several applications at once. Suppose you are launching a security suite application; you may actually load antivirus software, system surveillance software, and a firewall all at the same time. Loading all of these applications at once increases the amount of time necessary to get the suite up and running.

Although I cannot advocate disabling a particular application, I do recommend analyzing your system needs to determine whether any applications may be superfluous. For example, if you are using the Windows Vista firewall, then you don't need to use a third-party firewall. By disabling one or the other, you can free system resources and improve the performance of your security suite in our example.

Other ways to launch applications with fewer features include disabling any demos or tips that load at startup, as shown in Figure 28.7. How you go about disabling tips or application startup features depends on the application. In some applications, a window may appear at startup and offer a check box that allows you to disable tips at startup. Other applications may have options in the Preferences or Options window that lets you enable or disable startup features. I recommend consulting the user documentation for your application to find specific information on disabling startup components.

FIGURE 28.7

Disabling tips can help reduce the launch time of your application.

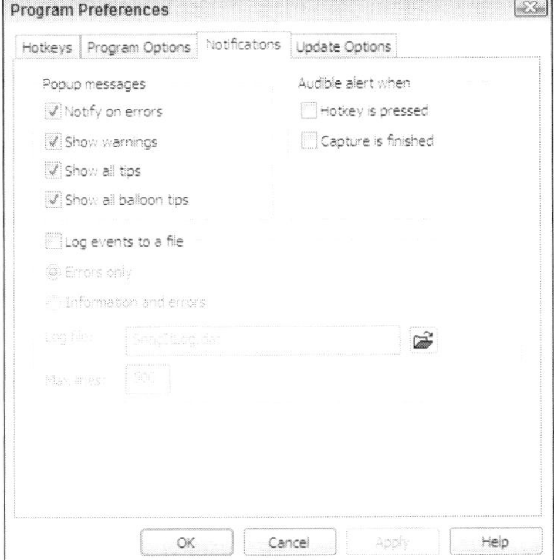

Limiting startup applications

Windows Vista has greatly improved the startup application load process. Compared to Windows XP, it's certainly much faster in terms of loading the various processes and applications that appear in the notification area of your Windows Vista desktop or in the Start Menu, as illustrated in Figure 28.8. However, there is always room for improvement.

Windows Vista greatly facilitates startup program management; you can now manage what applications appear at startup from Windows Defender using the Software Explorer. You can access the Software Explorer from the Windows Defender Tools menu.

FIGURE 28.8

Startup applications still appear in the Start Menu.

In the left window of the Software Explorer, the name of the startup program appears by manufacturer, as shown in Figure 28.9. It features the application name and its classification. After you click on the program name, information about the application appears in the right side of the window. This description contains file location information, publisher information, startup type, registry location, and so on.

Underneath the application information, you can remove or disable the application by clicking one of the buttons. If the application is currently disabled, you can also enable it from this window.

FIGURE 28.9

The Software Explorer feature in Windows Defender lets you disable Startup programs.

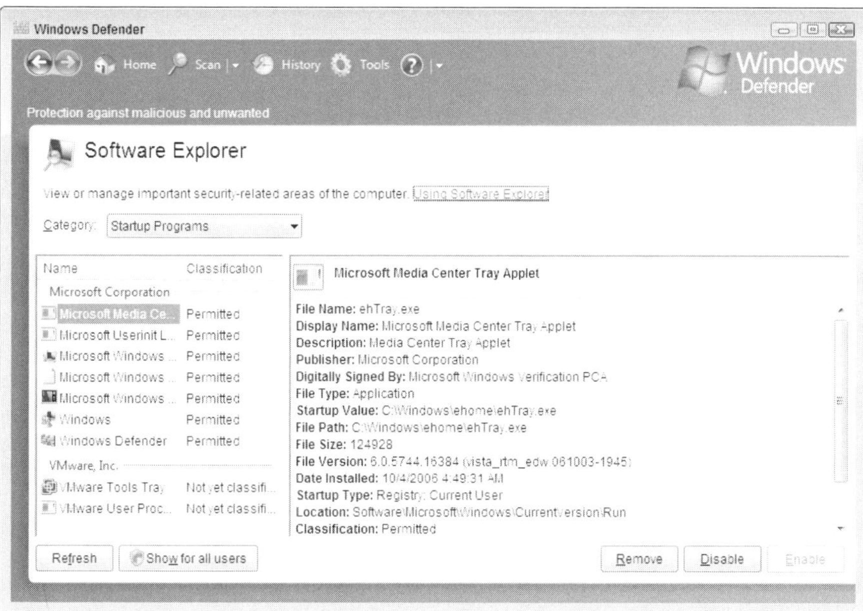

To improve performance, when installing software, you may want to disable any options for the application to appear at Startup (for example, the application appears in the notification area) or to launch when Windows starts, as shown in Figure 28.10. Some applications let you set whether to minimize the application to the taskbar. If this option exists in your application's preferences, make sure that it is disabled.

Though these settings may seem like they are random, inconsequential, and have no bearing on system or application performance, they actually do. When you perform these tweaks for multiple applications, you will notice a real difference in how your computer runs and how your applications load and respond.

FIGURE 28.10

Set application preferences so that they don't appear at Startup or minimize to taskbar.

Making Internet Explorer work for you

Internet Explorer, most likely one of the most-used applications on computers these days, is also one of the easiest to tweak for improved performance.

Striking the right balance between convenience and security is important. Be sure to assess your potential risk before disabling any Internet Explorer features.

One of the quickest ways to improve Internet Explorer's performance is by using the General tab of the Internet Options window. Set your home page to blank by clicking the Use blank button, as shown in Figure 28.11. By using a blank screen as your home page, the Web browser loads considerably faster, because it doesn't have to look up a Web address and then load any Java or ActiveX features.

FIGURE 28.11

You can configure Internet Explorer to load faster by using a blank page as your home page.

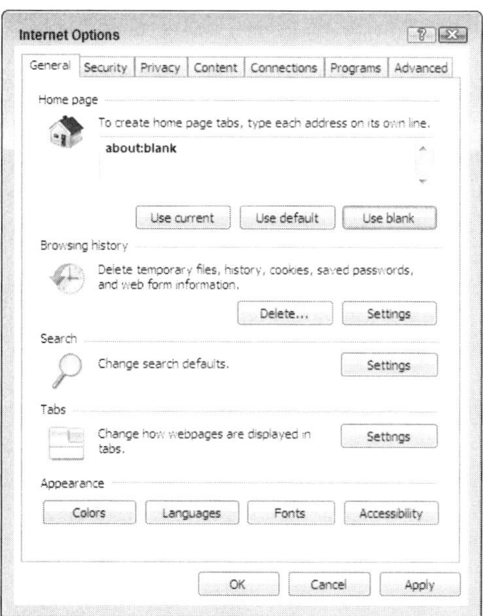

You can also increase performance by opting to block popups from your computer. Some of your usual Web sites may likely require the use of a popup; for example, Web sites that provide account information often display such information in another screen that appears as a popup. Internet Explorer allows you to either temporarily allow popups or, more conveniently, accept popups from a specific Web site or domain, as shown in Figure 28.12. I recommend that you use this latter option so that you only encounter popups from intended Web sites.

FIGURE 28.12

Blocking popups can enhance computer performance.

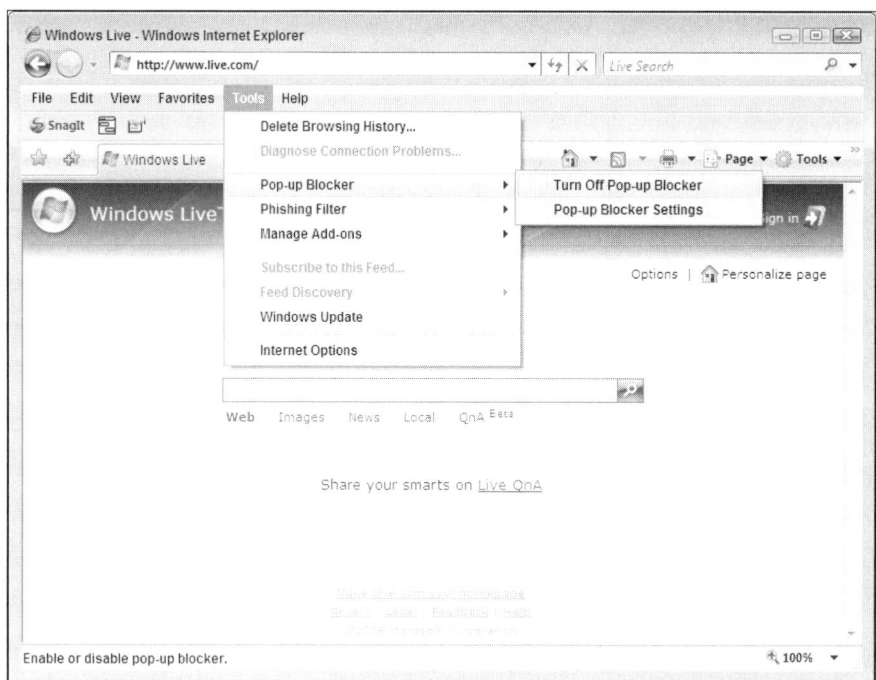

Using Security settings in the Internet Options page, you may want to set custom levels to allow certain actions. For example, you may want to allow the use of ActiveX scripts without the use of prompts, as shown in Figure 28.13. Doing so allows for a smoother, uninterrupted user experience. Of course, I once again caution users to balance their convenience concerns versus the need for security. I personally prefer the added inconvenience of having to validate certain actions on occasion — especially on computers with multiple users because your changes may affect others — as opposed to having an "anything goes" policy that might eventually do more harm than good.

FIGURE 28.13

Configure Internet Explorer security settings to improve performance.

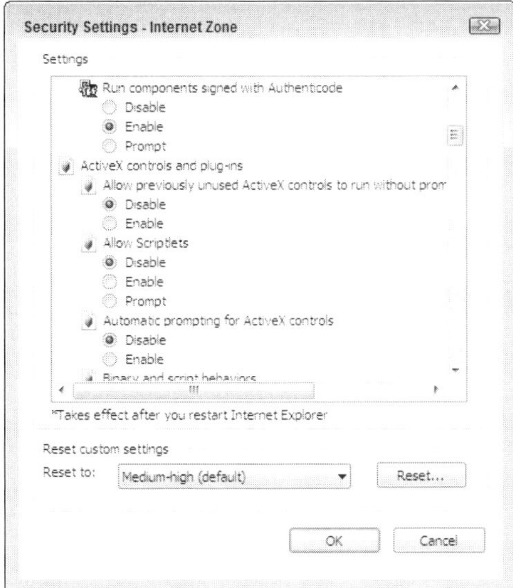

Tweaking Hardware

Tweaking hardware is as risky as tweaking the Windows registry; of course, you can define hardware tweaking in several ways. The best way to manage your hardware so that it provides optimal performance is to take care of your hardware.

I recommend regularly testing hardware performance; I discuss this topic in greater detail in the Appendix. Some of the things you may want to do include

- Performing regular hard disk fragmentation scans (and subsequent defragmentation)
- Performing regular system diagnostic tests
- Making sure that you buy hardware that is compatible with Windows Vista
- Making sure that your system doesn't have any hardware conflicts

If you decide to modify any hardware settings, such as hard drive configuration, be sure to first consult the manufacturer's documentation before performing any such procedure.

Your hard drive is the central hardware location in terms of performance tweaking. The easiest way to enhance performance is to keep your drive well maintained. This means frequently testing the fragmentation level. Fragmentation occurs when you write files to your hard drive; as you save and delete files, gaps are created on your hard drive. New files try to save to these gaps, but efficiency is decreased by as much as 200%. By using Windows Vista's defragmentation tool, shown in Figure 28.14, you can make sure that your hard drive operates at maximal performance and remains free of gaps.

FIGURE 28.14

The Windows Vista Disk Defragmenter helps you keep your drive running smoothly.

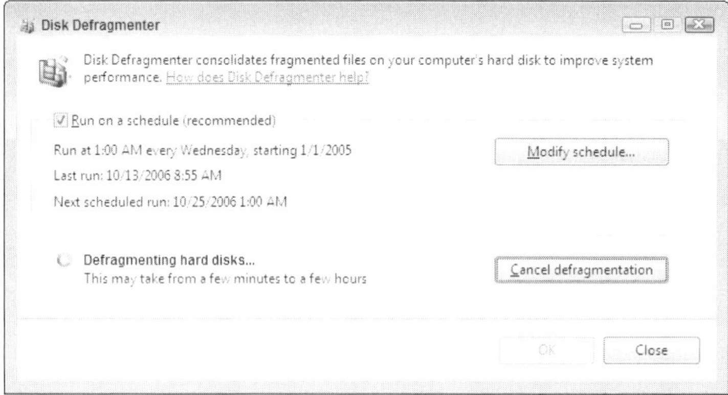

If you use a third-party application, you may be able to run disk tests to check for any other disk errors and repair them as necessary. You can also use one of a number of system tools available with Windows Vista Ultimate from the Performance Information and Tools section of the Control Panel, as shown in Figure 28.15.

FIGURE 28.15

The Control Panel helps you maintain performance via Performance Information and Tools.

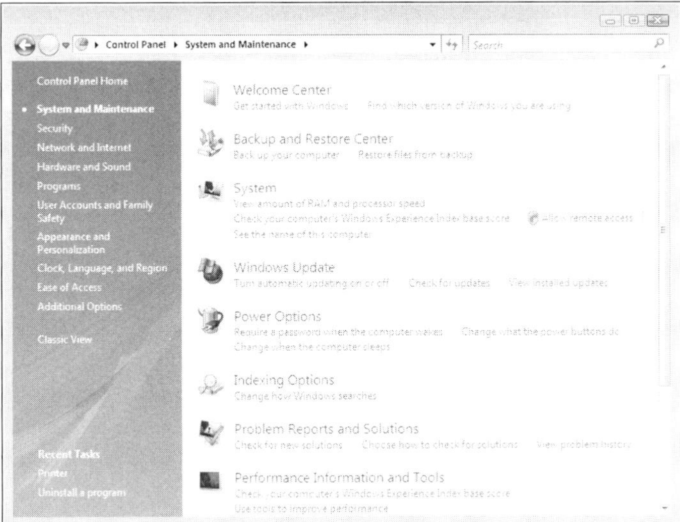

Once you open the Performance Information and Tools window from the Control Panel, you can access the aforementioned Windows Defender application to manage Startup applications on the left pane of the window. You can also use the Open Disk Cleanup tool to remove unnecessary files from your computer. If you opt to use this tool, it gives you the option of cleaning only your files or files for all users on your computer.

The Advanced Tools section, shown in Figure 28.16, provides a number of reports and performance enhancements that enable you to quickly and safely tweak your computer. They include system health reports, which determine how healthy your computer is. You can also access processor and memory usage from the Performance Options, which lets you dictate Windows performance for your computer. In addition to manually tweaking performance settings, you can tell Windows to adjust for either best performance or best appearance, whatever is best for your computer.

FIGURE 28.16

The Advanced Tools window provides additional enhancements.

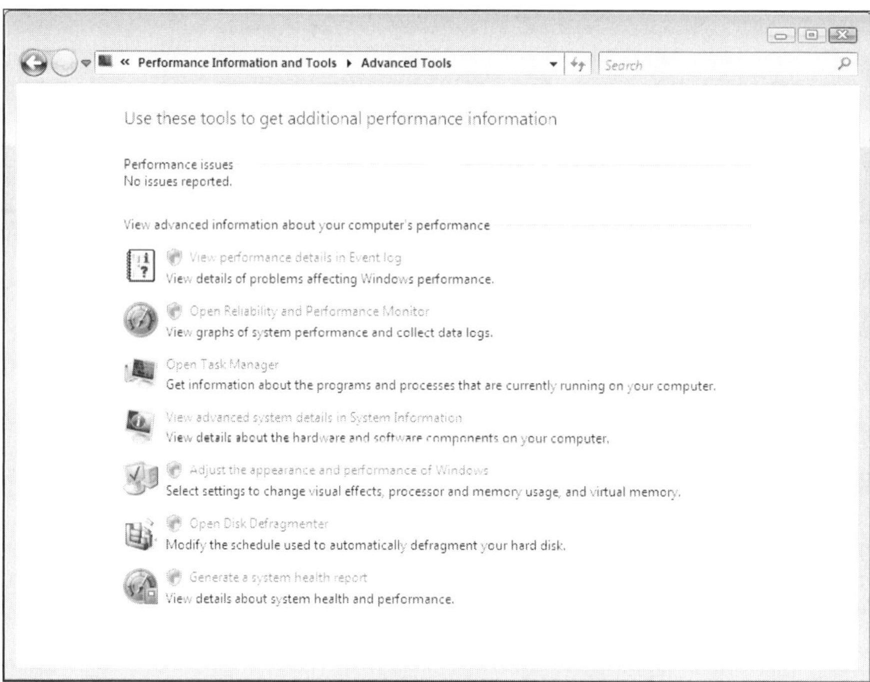

On a similar note to regular maintenance, I also recommend performing regular system diagnostic tests on your computer. Your computer's manufacturer can provide a diagnostic utility from their support Web site. System diagnostic tests run a complete battery of tests on your computer, from hard drives, to memory, to audio, to display, and everything in between. This comprehensive test lets you check on the status of your hardware.

NOTE **If you end up buying new hardware for your computer, make sure that it is compatible with Windows Vista. This recommendation might not apply to hardware such as hard drives or memory, but it will certainly make a difference for hardware such as video graphic cards. The newer your computer is, the less likely such issues will affect you. However, if you are using an older computer or a budget model, you are most likely going to spend more time thinking about your hardware.**

The Device Manager feature in Windows, which you access from the System menu of the Control Panel, is particularly helpful when dealing with your hardware. One way to make sure your hardware is working smoothly is to make sure that no hardware conflicts are occurring on your computer.

The Device Manager displays a list of devices and resources for your computer (you can sort these devices in the View menu by type or connection). If you expand each device or resource, the related piece of hardware appears. If a conflict exists, a yellow warning sign appears over the icon next to the hardware name. By right-clicking the hardware name, you can tell Windows to resolve the conflict.

Summary

A number of options are available to you for improving the Windows Vista experience. Don't feel that you have to use Windows Vista straight out of the box or that the default configuration is necessarily best tailored to your computer.

Using some of the features included with Windows Vista Ultimate, as well as some of the newly available third-party tweak applications, you can create a Vista experience that takes advantage of your computer specificities.

Riskier options are also available, such as modifying the Windows registry; however, this modification comes at a potentially great risk and should really only be performed by advanced Windows users. Remember, if you mistakenly change or delete a key or value, you could potentially cause irreparable damage to your computer.

I recommend using a combined approach: Use your preferred third-party tweaking tool in conjunction with the various tools provided by Windows Vista, such as the defragmentation tool or health reports.

Appendix

Maintaining Windows Vista Ultimate

Maintaining the health of your computer is an essential part of its enjoying a long and healthy life. Like your car, use takes its toll and wear and tear can decrease performance if you don't regularly maintain your computer. You can use a number of easy ways to keep up your computer that are both inexpensive and not too invasive.

Windows Vista Ultimate is the crown jewel of the Windows Vista family; it has more features that require more performance from the operating system, as well as your computer and its hardware. This also means that you may likely have to do more to keep it running smoothly.

This appendix discusses ways for you to keep your computer running smoothly, including taking care of your file system and managing hardware upgrades. This appendix also looks at utilities you can use to keep Windows Vista going strong.

IN THIS APPENDIX

Protecting your file system

Managing Windows Vista and hardware upgrades

Looking at helpful utilities

Working with the File System

Windows features several built-in tools to help you keep your computer running properly. Two of the most valuable on-board applications are Disk Defragmenter and Disk Cleanup.

Long-time Windows users are most likely no strangers to these tools; they both perform valuable services even though neither one enjoys the limelight unlike other Windows applications.

Disk Defragmenter

One of the easiest ways to maintain your computer and its file system is to regularly defragment your computer. As you use your computer, the files become fragmented. Your disk stores files in the same cluster; of course, files on your hard drive aren't for life! As you delete these files, gaps are left between files. When you install an application, it tries to use this space (gaps), which affects performance in the program and your system.

Few problems with your computer are more inconvenient than working with a heavily fragmented disk; it's almost like having a 1-ton weight put on your back. Your computer can literally slow to a crawl, to the point that getting anything done is almost impossible. Certain activities can cause your computer to fragment more quickly. For example, large installations, watching DVDs, or extensive Web surfing tends to impact performance. For these reasons, you should consider defragmenting your computer regularly. For example, I tend to defragment once every seven to ten days, depending on use.

Windows Vista, like its predecessors, offers a disk defragmentation tool called Disk Defragmenter, which is shown in Figure A.1. To access the Disk Defragmenter, go to Start ➪ Accessories ➪ System Tools.

FIGURE A.1

The Windows Vista defragmentation tool

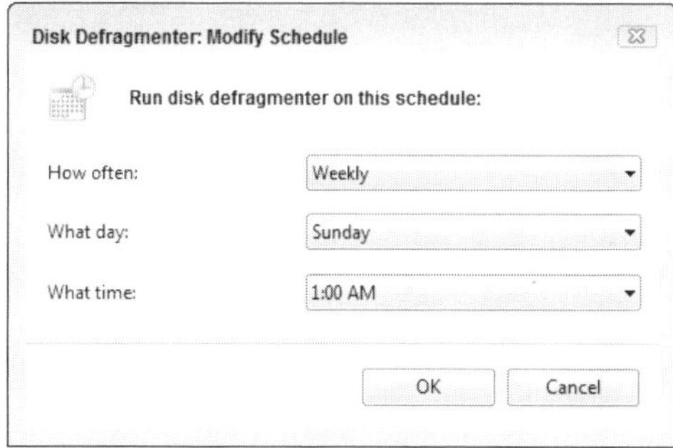

The User Account Control asks you to approve the use of this tool before you continue. Click Continue, and it appears. If you're used to working with Windows XP, you'll notice how much more compact and easy to follow the Windows Vista version is comparatively.

You can schedule defragmentation sessions for times that are convenient to your schedule. If you click Modify Schedule, another window appears that allows you to set frequency, as shown in Figure A.2.

FIGURE A.2

Set defragmentation times that are convenient for you.

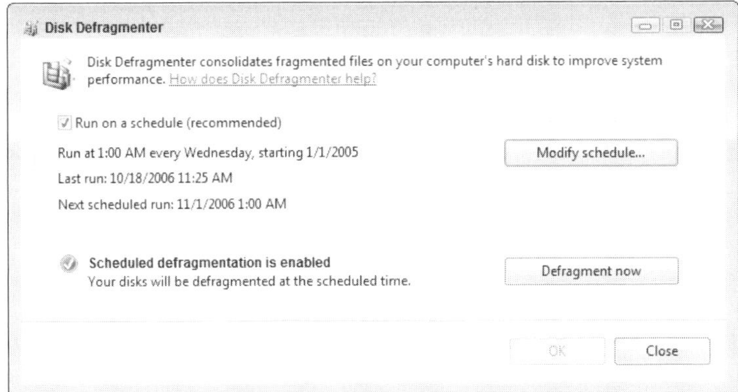

Once you set up a schedule, the Disk Defragmenter updates and displays the new next scheduled run. Of course, you can deselect this option by checking the radio box.

You can also manually defragment your drive; this isn't as hard as it sounds! Simply click Defragment Now and the procedure begins. The progress is measured across the bottom of the tool, as shown in Figure A.3.

FIGURE A.3

Disk Defragmenter lets you know what's going on.

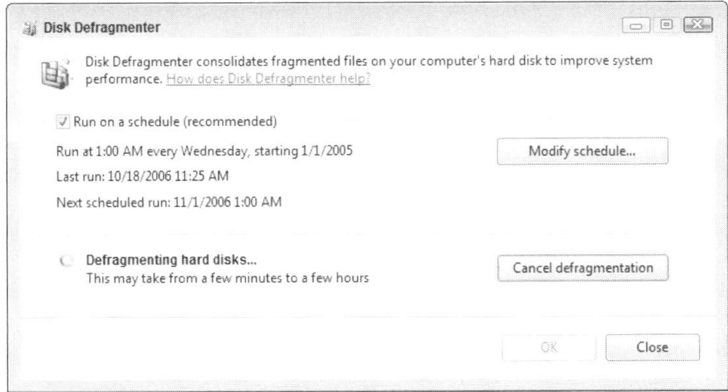

Once defragmentation is complete, you should notice a clear difference in performance. Applications should launch faster; folders should open faster, and so on.

Disk Cleanup

You may also want to use another important system tool found in the same location called the Disk Cleanup. This feature lets you clean house; in other words, rid your computer of temporary files or any other unnecessary files. You can select whether to only clean files related to your user account or for all user accounts, as shown in Figure A.4.

FIGURE A.4

Pick your or all user accounts to clean.

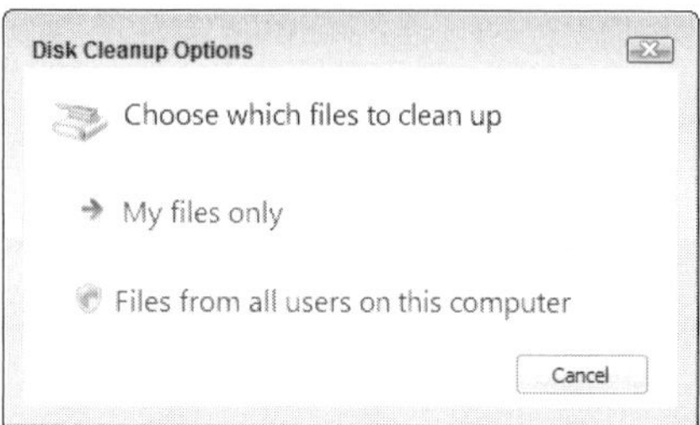

Once you make your choice, Disk Cleanup calculates the files that will be deleted. Disk Cleanup then displays the amount of disk space you can recover if you follow its suggestions, as shown in Figure A.5. You can also view the files that will be removed by clicking the View Files button.

FIGURE A.5

Win back disk space by removing unnecessary files.

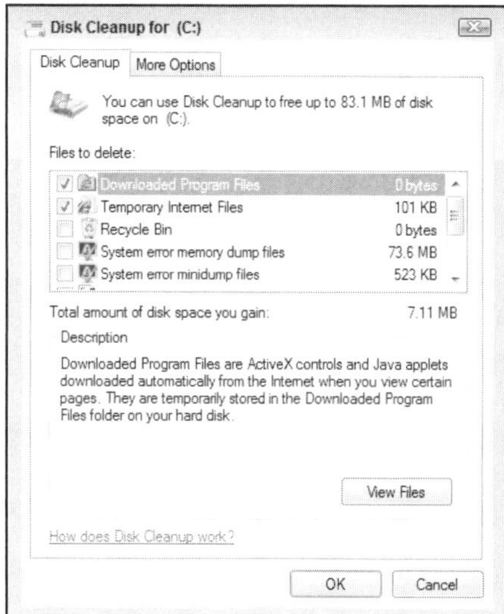

CAUTION You'll notice in Figure A.5 that not every box is checked. Be sure to verify what you are deleting before you go through with it. Once you decide what to delete, click OK and Disk Cleanup removes those files.

Performing Windows Vista and Hardware Upgrades

Windows Vista is a truly plug and play operating system, which reduces the amount of actual configuration you need to do when upgrading hardware. For example, if you've ever had to install Windows Vista on your computer, you may have noticed that you probably didn't have to find any installation CDs during the procedure.

When you upgrade your hardware and reboot Windows Vista, it will try and install the necessary driver on its own. Should a compatible driver not be found, you may have to provide a driver or access to one. If you buy any hardware that is designed for Windows Vista, you can generally expect it to be plug and play.

I also recommend using the Windows Vista Upgrade Advisor, currently available at `www.microsoft.com/windowsvista/getready/upgradeadvisor/default.mspx`. This will help you maintain the best computer environment possible by indicating any weak links in your current configuration. As mentioned above, the best way to guarantee smooth transition for use with Windows Vista, I recommend buying products that are supported by Windows Vista.

If you are preparing to switch to Windows Vista, you will most likely need to upgrade hardware, such as memory. If you want to take advantage of the Aero experience, you may need to replace video cards. In both cases, Windows Vista recognized both additions without any real work on our part.

Looking at Other Helpful Utilities

There are a number of additional utilities out there that can help you keep your system running smoothly. There are also some applications on-board that will help you run a tight ship as well.

For example, you should regularly check for spyware and other malware. Windows Vista offers Windows Defender, Microsoft's spyware scanning and removal tool, as shown in Figure A.6.

Windows Defender also is helpful in improving performance; the Software Explorer tool in Windows Defender lets you determine which applications appear at startup.

Microsoft is also releasing the Windows Live OneCare program for Windows Vista, since it's been available for Windows XP for some time. This subscription-based suite provides a number of utilities to keep your computer running smoothly, as well as antivirus protection.

FIGURE A.6

Windows Defender keeps your machine safe from spyware attack.

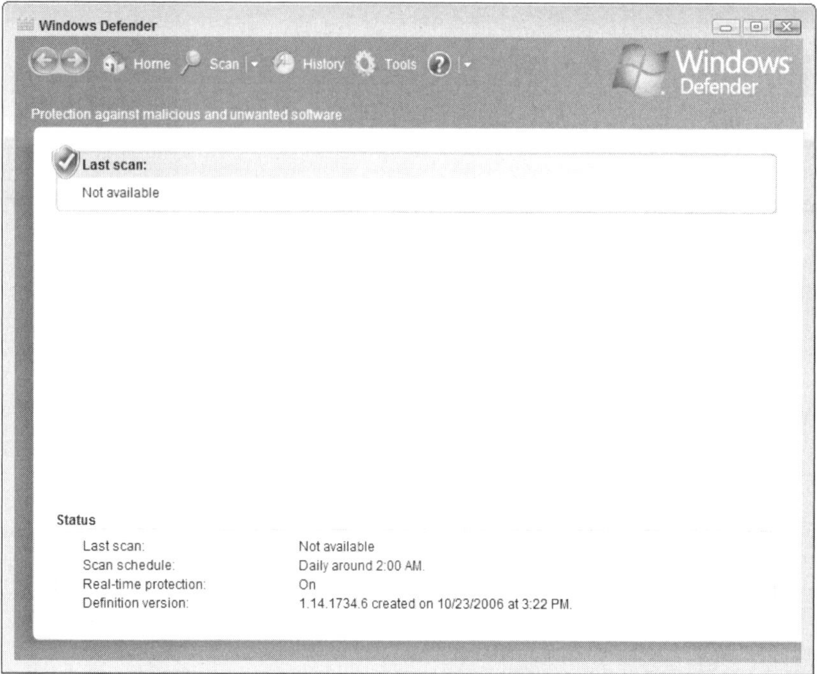

There are also a number of third-party options that are available for users:

- **General system health applications:** Suites such as Norton SystemWorks have a long history of protecting Windows machines. A robust application, you can have antivirus software, e-mail protection, disk health, Windows health, and maintenance. For more information on Norton SystemWorks, visit `www.symantec.com`.
- **Antivirus applications:** A number of new antivirus applications are now available for Windows Vista, including Avast, Grisoft, and PC-Cillin. As Windows Vista becomes the standard Windows operating system, more and more software developers will release compatible programs for Windows Vista. You can find more information on these applications at `www.avast.com`, `www.grisoft.com`, and `www.trendmicro.com`. The Avast Anti-Virus interface is shown in Figure A.7.

FIGURE A.7

Avast Anti-Virus is a very capable antivirus program available for Windows Vista.

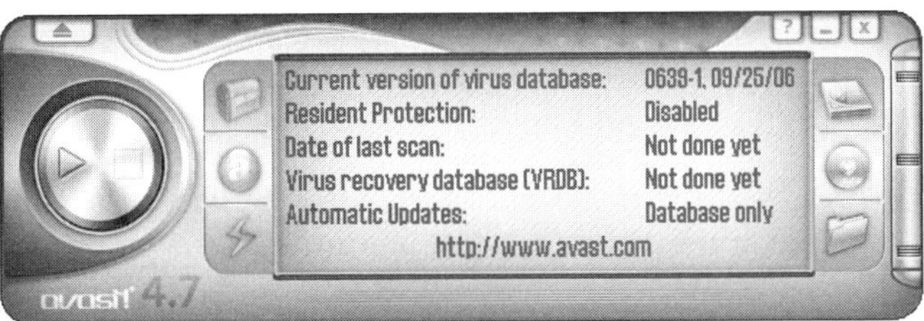

- **Spyware applications:** Third-party spyware applications can also help you; like antivirus software, not every spyware application finds the same thing. Applications such as LavaSoft or Spybot – Search and Destroy are two strong applications that can provide your computer with maximum protection. You can find more information at `www.lavasoftusa.com` or `www.safer-networking.org`. LavaSoft's Ad-Aware SE program interface is shown in Figure A.8.

FIGURE A.8

LavaSoft can provide additional protection against spyware.

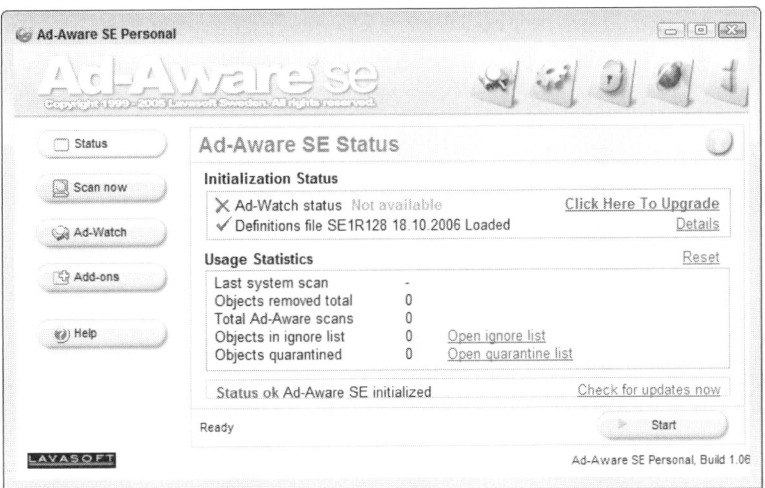

Whatever applications you use to protect your computer, keep in mind that there's nothing wrong with doubling up on protection. For example, I tend to use two different spyware applications. And not all disk cleaning applications do as thorough of a job as well. As a result, I have two different applications that respond to this need.

Summary

Maintaining your computer and Windows Vista is a relatively easy exercise. There are a number of applications that are bundled with Windows Vista Ultimate to facilitate this concern. There are also a number of third-party applications, many of which are free, that can help you cover all the bases so that your computer performs well.

One of the biggest things you can do for your computer is to regularly defragment your hard drive. Failure to do so can result in greatly decreased performance that can make productivity difficult at best, impossible at worst.

Regularly cleaning up your hard drive can also benefit your computer's performance. When you install applications, installers leave temporary files behind that gather like dust. Using Window's Disk Cleaner application, you can get rid of unnecessary temporary files, old logs, clean the Recycle Bin, etc.

There are other equally important tasks you can perform to keep your computer running well. For example, regularly performing virus scans, scanning incoming e-mail, performing spyware scans, and updated maintenance can all make your computer run better.

Fortunately, most of these tasks can be automated or scheduled so that you don't have to remember to do so manually. Most applications let you schedule scans on a daily, weekly, or monthly basis at a time of your choosing.

I cannot stress enough the importance of maintaining your computer. The earlier analogy to a car is very apropos; neglecting your computer can lead to undesired results and decrease the lifespan of your computer. Most of these things can be programmed in a matter of minutes, so be sure to take the proper precautions.

Index

NUMERICS

A

B

C

D

E

F

G

H

I

N

O

P

Q

R

S

T

W

X

Z